READING ROMANS WITH ST. THOMAS AQUINAS

Reading Romans

WITH ST. THOMAS AQUINAS

Edited by Matthew Levering & Michael Dauphinais

The Catholic University of America Press
Washington, D.C.

Design and typesetting by Kachergis Book Design

Frontispiece: from the *Acts of the Apostles* printed in
Tbilisi, Georgia, in 1709. The work of art itself is in the
public domain because its copyright has expired.

Library of Congress Cataloging-in-Publication Data
Reading Romans with St. Thomas Aquinas / edited by
Matthew Levering and Michael Dauphinais.
p. cm.
Includes bibliographical references (p.   ) and index.
ISBN 978-0-8132-1962-2 (cloth : alk. paper) —
ISBN 978-0-8132-1963-9 (pbk. : alk. paper)   1. Thomas,
Aquinas, Saint, 1225?–1274. In Epistolam ad Romanos
expositio.   2. Bible. N.T. Romans—Commentaries—
History and criticism.   I. Levering, Matthew, 1971–
II. Dauphinais, Michael, 1973–   III. Title: Reading
Romans with Saint Thomas Aquinas.
BS2665.53.T563R66 2012
227′.10609—dc23
2011039161

To Mercedes Cox

Contents

Introduction

The first great commentator on the letter to the Romans, Origen of Alexandria, remarks that "there are two reasons why the letter that was written to the Romans is considered to be harder to understand than the Apostle Paul's other letters."[1] The first reason is that Paul "makes use of expressions which sometimes are confused and insufficiently explicit."[2] Here Origen has in view not only issues related to predestination and free will, but also controversies "concerning the law of Moses, about the calling of the Gentiles, about Israel according to the flesh and about Israel which is not according to the flesh, about the circumcision of the flesh and of the heart, about the spiritual law and the law of the letter, about the law of the flesh and the law of the members, about the law of the mind and the law of sin, about the inner and the outer man."[3] The second reason for the letter's difficulty is that Paul "stirs up very many questions in the letter and the heretics, especially propping themselves on these, are accustomed to add that the cause of each person's actions is not to be attributed to one's own purpose."[4]

Although the letter to the Romans is difficult and open to heretical misappropriation, Origen considers it to be preeminent in its witness to Paul's maturation toward spiritual perfection. Appealing especially to Paul's exhortation in Romans 8:35, "Who shall separate us from the love of Christ?," Origen argues that "the Apostle seems to have been more perfect in this letter than in the others."[5] The difficulty of the letter is matched by its spiritual elevation. As a result, it requires more from readers than do the other letters.

In the prologue to his own commentary on Romans, Thomas Aquinas takes as his guiding text Acts 9:15 (Vulgate), where the Lord tells Ananias to go to Saul of Tarsus to heal Saul from the blindness he received in his encounter with the Lord Jesus on the Damascus Road: "This man is to me a chosen vessel [*vas electionis*] to carry my name before the Gentiles and kings and the

---

1. Origen, *Commentary on the Epistle to the Romans*, Books 1–5, trans. Thomas P. Scheck (Washington, D.C.: The Catholic University of America Press, 2001), preface of Origen, 53.

2. Ibid. 3. Ibid., 57.
4. Ibid., 53. 5. Ibid.

sons of Israel." Citing Jeremiah 18:4, Isaiah 45:9, Romans 9:20, and 2 Timothy 2:20, Aquinas reflects on how God's election arranges "the variety of construction among his vessels."[6] He finds that Paul was a vessel of the kind described in Sirach 50:9, "a vessel of solid gold adorned with all kinds of precious stones." He was golden "on account of his brilliant wisdom"; he was solid on account of his charity; and he was adorned with precious stones on account of his virtues.[7]

As a vessel, Paul poured forth "the mysteries of the most lofty divinity" and the truth about the life of virtue. He carried Christ's "name" in his body, configured to Christ's sufferings, and in his teaching of grace and mercy. According to Aquinas, Romans explores ecclesial grace "as it is in itself."[8] The letter to the Romans merits its foremost place among Paul's writings, Aquinas observes, not only because "the order of teaching requires that grace should first be considered in itself," but also because the message of evangelical grace constitutes a rebuke to all worldly pride, symbolized by the Roman Empire.[9]

Thus Aquinas, like Origen, affirms the preeminence of the letter to the Romans both with regard to its difficult content—the mystery of divine grace—and because of Paul's spiritual perfection as manifested in the letter.

Contemporary exegetes concur with the pride of place that Origen and Aquinas, among many others, associate with the letter to the Romans. For example, the distinguished Anglican exegete N. T. Wright introduces his commentary on Romans by affirming, "Romans is neither a systematic theology nor a summary of Paul's lifework, but it is by common consent his masterpiece. It dwarfs most of his other writings, an Alpine peak towering over hills and villages."[10] The Methodist exegete Ben Witherington III underscores the difficulty of the letter: "Embarking on a study of Romans is rather like beginning a long journey—it requires a certain amount of preparation, patience, and faith, as the goal of understanding this formidable discourse is not reached for a considerable period of time."[11] This warning echoes that of the Latin translator of

6. Thomas Aquinas, *Lectures on the Letter to the Romans*, trans. Fabian Larcher, O.P., ed. Jeremy Holmes (Ave Maria, Fla.: Aquinas Center for Theological Renewal), § 1, http://www.avemaria.edu/uploads/pagesfiles/4283.pdf.

7. Ibid.

8. Ibid., § 11.

9. Ibid., § 12. For discussion of the canonical order of Paul's letters, see Brevard S. Childs, *The Church's Guide for Reading Paul: The Canonical Shaping of the Pauline Corpus* (Grand Rapids, Mich.: Eerdmans, 2008).

10. N. T. Wright, *The Letter to the Romans: Introduction, Commentary, and Reflections*, in vol. 10 of *The New Interpreter's Bible*, ed. Leander E. Keck (Nashville, Tenn.: Abingdon Press, 2002), 395–770, at 395.

11. Ben Witherington III, *Paul's Letter to the Romans: A Socio-Rhetorical Commentary* (Grand Rapids, Mich.: Eerdmans, 2004), 1.

Origen's commentary, Rufinus, who observes that in interpreting the letter, Origen "is taken out into such a deep sea that anyone who follows him out there encounters enormous fear lest he be overwhelmed as much by the greatness of his thoughts as by the immensity of the waves."[12]

For various reasons, Aquinas's commentary on Romans has not received much attention.[13] Yet this situation has long been due to change, since interest in Aquinas's biblical commentaries—and more broadly, interest in reading Aquinas's theology in light of his sources (biblical, patristic, and philosophical)—is burgeoning.[14] As we suggested in *Reading John with St. Thomas Aquinas*, the interplay between theological exegesis and speculative theology that one finds in Aquinas's biblical commentaries constitutes an ecumenical resource for exegesis today, although this requires adjusting one's concept of history to include not only its linear dimension but also its participatory dimension (the unity and pattern that it possesses as created and redeemed by God), as Henri de Lubac understood so well.[15] Contemporary biblical scholars, too, have begun to take a strong interest in the history of exegesis and in an explicitly "theological" exegesis.[16]

12. Origen, *Commentary on the Epistle to the Romans*, preface of Rufinus, 51.

13. Although there are exceptions such as Thomas Dolmanyi's *Der Römerbriefkommentar des Thomas von Aquin: Ein Beitrag zur Untersuchung seiner Auslegungsmethoden* (Bern: Peter Lang, 1979), and Steven C. Boguslawski, O.P.'s *Thomas Aquinas on the Jews: Insights into His Commentary on Romans 9–11* (Mahwah, N.J.: Paulist Press, 2008).

14. See, for instance, Thomas G. Weinandy, O.F.M. Cap., Daniel A. Keating, and John P. Yocum, eds., *Aquinas on Scripture: An Introduction to His Biblical Commentaries* (London: T&T Clark International, 2005), and works cited therein.

15. See Michael Dauphinais and Matthew Levering, eds., *Reading John with St. Thomas Aquinas: Theological Exegesis and Speculative Theology* (Washington, D.C.: The Catholic University of America Press, 2005). See also Henri de Lubac, S.J., *Exégèse médiévale*, currently being translated into English as *Medieval Exegesis*, vol. 1, *The Four Senses of Scripture*, trans. Mark Sebanc (Grand Rapids, Mich.: Eerdmans, 1998); vol. 2, *The Four Senses of Scripture*, trans. E. M. Macierowski (Grand Rapids, Mich.: Eerdmans, 2000); and vol. 3, *The Four Senses of Scripture*, trans. E. M. Macierowski (Grand Rapids, Mich.: Eerdmans, 2009); as well as de Lubac, *History and Spirit: The Understanding of Scripture according to Origen*, trans. Anne Englund Nash and Juvenal Merriell (San Francisco: Ignatius Press, 2007). Matthew Levering develops this perspective in his *Participatory Biblical Exegesis: Toward a Theology of Biblical Interpretation* (Notre Dame, Ind.: University of Notre Dame Press, 2008). See also Hans Boersma, *Nouvelle Théologie and Sacramental Ontology: A Return to Mystery* (Oxford: Oxford University Press, 2009), chapter 5.

16. See, e.g., Brevard S. Childs, *The Struggle to Understand Isaiah as Christian Scripture* (Grand Rapids, Mich.: Eerdmans, 2004); Judith Kovacs and Christopher Rowland, *Revelation: The Apocalypse of Jesus Christ* (Oxford: Blackwell, 2004); Ellen F. Davis and Richard B. Hays, eds., *The Art of Reading Scripture* (Grand Rapids, Mich.: Eerdmans, 2003). See also Jeffrey P. Greenman and Timothy Larsen, eds., *Reading Romans through the Centuries: From the Early Church to Karl Barth* (Grand Rapids, Mich.: Brazos Press, 2005); William S. Campbell, Peter S. Hawkins, and Brenda Deen Schildgen, eds., *Medieval Readings of Romans* (New York: T&T Clark International, 2007).

Although the date and place of Aquinas's commentary on Romans cannot be known with certainty, Jean-Pierre Torrell suggests that Aquinas's commentary on Romans was prepared in the last period of his life, the years 1272–73 in Naples. Torrell states that "everything seems to indicate that Thomas indeed gave a course at Naples on Romans, of which he rapidly corrected the first eight chapters."[17] The remaining chapters of the commentary are a *reportatio*, notes from Aquinas's lecture formally written down by a scribe but not corrected by Aquinas.

In probing Aquinas's exegesis of Romans, the essays in this volume address such themes as "flesh" and "spirit," faith and circumcision, the Church, preaching, the Jewish people, the relationship of faith and the moral life, the Holy Spirit, worship, justification, predestination, and various dimensions of Aquinas's exegetical practice. The essays are by biblical scholars, medievalists, experts in patristics, and systematic theologians. As befits contemporary exploration of Romans, Catholic and Protestant scholars contribute essays in an ecumenical spirit. Given the importance of Aquinas's witness to biblical revelation as received in the Church (preeminently by the Fathers), this volume can only scratch the surface of the topic. It will have succeeded if it serves as an invitation to further research.

Because the essays address a wide array of overlapping themes, the remainder of this introduction offers a brief synopsis of each of the essays.

Bernhard Blankenhorn takes up St. Paul's flesh/spirit language in Romans 6–8. Drawing not only upon Thomas Aquinas's commentary on Romans but also upon contemporary biblical exegesis, St. Augustine's exegesis and theology, Aquinas's commentary on Galatians, and the *Summa theologiae*, Blankenhorn asks whether the tension between Paul's meaning and Aquinas's more Platonic understanding of Paul's use of "flesh," as well as Aquinas's interpretation of "spirit" as indicating the Holy Spirit, fatally undermines Aquinas's exegesis. Sensitive to the sources and development of Aquinas's thought, Blankenhorn shows how Aquinas's reading of Romans 7–8 apprehends Paul's key point regarding the healing of the whole person (not only the "flesh") by grace. With keen insight into the multifaceted interplay of Scripture, Greek philosophy, and the Fathers in Aquinas's theology, Blankenhorn also shows how the *Summa theologiae* deepens Aquinas's portrait of disordered self-love and of grace, thereby enriching our understanding of the path taken by Aquinas's commentary.

Markus Bockmuehl takes up Aquinas's discussion of Romans 4 on Abra-

---

17. Jean-Pierre Torrell, O.P., *Saint Thomas Aquinas*, vol. 1, *The Person and His Work*, trans. Robert Royal (Washington, D.C.: The Catholic University of America Press, 1996), 253.

ham's faith. The question is whether Aquinas finds any significance in the faith not only of the uncircumcised Abraham, but also of the circumcised Abraham. In answer, Bockmuehl shows that for Aquinas, as for Paul, Abraham's faith is not impeded by being circumcised: rather, circumcision provides a visible sign of faith. As a sign, circumcision assisted faith and thus led to the forgiveness of sins through implicit faith in Christ, although after the coming of Christ baptism accomplishes this more directly and efficaciously. Having shown that Aquinas grants significance to the faith of the circumcised, Bockmuehl suggests that this may have implications for contemporary Jewish believers in Jesus.

Beginning with the distinction asserted by Yves Congar and others between a sacramental ecclesiology and a juridical one, Hans Boersma probes the value of the ecclesiology of Aquinas's commentary on Romans for ecumenical dialogue between Protestants and Catholics. As Boersma points out, Aquinas links all of Paul's letters to the Gentiles under the rubric of the exposition of grace as it is found in the Church. Boersma thus highlights the ecclesiological significance of Aquinas's discussions not only of faith but also of the power of the Gospel and of the office of preaching. Likewise, he shows that Aquinas appreciates the identity of the people of God as formed in the history of salvation. For Aquinas, Christ is the center of all history, and "predestined" as such; others are predestined in Christ. The "mystical body" is not primarily a juridical reality for Aquinas, as if it merely were one among many political bodies. Instead, Aquinas emphasizes that believers are incorporated into the body of Christ, the Church, through the grace of the Holy Spirit that frees us from slavery to sin. Since this incorporation takes place through faith and the sacraments of faith, the "body of Christ" is not severed from the visible Church's sacramental structures. In all of these ways, Boersma finds that Aquinas's ecclesiological vision in the commentary on Romans provides a resource for all Christians who seek to apprehend and live out Paul's vision of Christian communion.

John F. Boyle relates Aquinas's commentary on Romans to his *Summa theologiae*. As he recognizes, many readers of the biblical commentaries look for insights that will enrich their study of the *Summa*. Boyle proposes that it might be better to read the *Summa* so as to enrich our understanding of the biblical commentaries. The *Summa theologiae* seeks to provide students with the tools necessary for reading Scripture. Aquinas recognizes that Scripture does not possess the speculative structure of a medieval *Summa*, but he nonetheless holds that Scripture teaches about divine realities in an intelligible fashion. With regard to Romans, Aquinas therefore emphasizes the causal connection between Paul's treatment of the saving power of grace and his treatment of the Christian moral life. In this way Aquinas avoids separating what belongs together—as for instance in his treatment of chapter 13, where he places Paul's discussion of the political order within Paul's broader emphasis on the life of grace. Likewise, Boyle notes that reading the *Summa* on justification helps the reader of the commentary not lose sight of the various dimensions of God's transformative work. In turn, Boyle concludes, reading the commentary helps the reader of the *Summa* see more clearly how such realities as the Holy Spirit, predestination, grace, faith, and Christ's redemptive work—realities discussed apart from each other in the *Summa*—relate to each other in the *Summa*'s dynamics as well. To understand the realities described by Paul in Romans, in short, we need both the *Summa* and the commentary.

Edgardo Colón-Emeric explores the appropriation of Aquinas's theology by the Spanish Dominican Bartolomé de las Casas, known for his protection of the Indians against Spanish exploitation. Colón-Emeric begins by surveying Aquinas's commentary on Romans 10:17, "Faith comes from what is heard, and what is heard comes from the word of Christ." In discussing this text, Aquinas treats human preaching, which receives its authority from divine commission, as well as God's interior teaching of the believer, God's movement of the will by the grace of the Holy Spirit, and predestination. Whereas Aquinas assumes that most people have heard the Gospel, Las Casas recognizes that this is not the case. Following Aquinas's commentary on Romans 10, Las Casas argues that God aids such people primarily by sending preachers—a sign of the unfolding of God's predestination—even though God can bring about faith solely through interior revelation. Against the view that the Indians should be baptized without preparation, therefore, Las Casas argues that just like all other humans, the Indians need preachers who speak to their intellect and attract their will. As Colón-Emeric shows, Aquinas and Las Casas, like Paul, affirm the power of preaching the Gospel in the life of grace.

Holly Taylor Coolman inquires into the contributions that Aquinas's theology may have to offer to overcoming anti-Jewish attitudes among Christians. She first surveys contemporary discussion of Aquinas's statement in the *Summa theologiae* that continued practice of the Torah's ceremonial laws constitutes a mortal sin. Michael Wyschogrod and Jeremy Cohen express grave concern about this position, while another Jewish theologian, David Novak, suggests that it may apply solely to Jewish Christians. John Hood and Steven Boguslawski point to the significance of Aquinas's positive statements about the Jewish people, especially his view in the commentary on Romans that the Jewish people retain an important role in the history of salvation. Accepting Wyschogrod's and Cohen's view that Aquinas in the *Summa* means to say that the ceremonial precepts are deadly not only for (Jewish) Christians but also for

Jews, Coolman argues that Aquinas's reasoning in the commentary on Romans challenges the *Summa*'s logic about the ceremonial precepts, especially in light of Aquinas's understanding of promulgation as a necessary component of law.

Adam Cooper reflects upon the relationship between moral and intellectual formation in Aquinas's commentary on Romans 1:18–25. Cooper first presents Origen's treatment of Paul's words, and on this basis shows how deeply influential patristic exegesis is upon Aquinas's interpretation. Central to Aquinas, as to patristic thinkers and to Paul, is the connection between moral failings and the clouding of one's intellectual vision. When knowledge of God does not manifest itself in worship of God, deficiencies in one's knowledge of God will appear. Cooper explores the consequences of this point for human apprehension of the natural law. The natural law in its fundamental precepts cannot be blotted out from our practical knowing, but the secondary dictates of the natural law can be—necessitating the cultivation of the virtue of prudence as the point of intersection not only of speculative and practical knowledge, but also of such knowledge and our passions. As Aquinas emphasizes in the commentary, the restoration of our moral organism begins with the assent to truth that is faith in Christ.

Gilles Emery examines Aquinas's teaching on the Holy Spirit in his commentary on Romans. While he finds that the doctrine is the same as in Aquinas's speculative works, he notes that the commentary shows the integration of realities that in the speculative works are treated separately and whose interrelatedness can therefore be missed. After commenting on the basic elements of Aquinas's exegesis (its "intertextual" use of Old and New Testament passages to interpret Romans, its dependence upon the councils of the Church and upon the Fathers, and its doctrinal and practical aim), Emery turns to Aquinas's presentation of Paul's letters as concerned with the grace of the New Law. In his commentary on Romans, as Emery documents, Aquinas includes speculative exposition of the Holy Spirit's procession from the Father and the Son, along with the Holy Spirit's names of "love" and "gift" and with divine attributes appropriated to the Holy Spirit. Emery emphasizes, however, that the commentary focuses upon the relationship of Christ and the Holy Spirit. Included in this relationship are the Apostles and indeed all members of the Church, who receive the grace of the Holy Spirit (adoptive filiation) through Christ the "Head" of the mystical body. The Holy Spirit not only establishes believers in virtue, preeminently faith, hope, and love, but also guides believers by means of his gifts, helps believers in prayer, and inspires Scripture and its ecclesial interpretation. In Emery's hands, the contemplative depths of Aquinas's insight into the Holy Spirit's activity, an activity to which Paul bears witness in Romans, are revealed in detail.

Scott W. Hahn and John Kincaid explore instances of a multiple literal sense in Aquinas's commentary on Romans and show the significance of this exegetical approach for the contemporary debate over the meaning of Romans stimulated by the "New Perspective" on Paul. For example, they treat Romans 3:3 and apply Aquinas's reasoning, including what might seem to be a metaphysical tangent, to the debate over whether the *pistis Christou* refers to Christ's faith or to faith in Christ. They argue that the distinction between history, etiology, and analogy provides the basis for Aquinas's understanding of the multiple literal sense. Another example that they take up is the interpretation of "the righteousness of God" (Rom 1:17): here they place Aquinas in fruitful dialogue with James Dunn. They conclude that the multiple literal sense exemplifies the kind of covenantal, participatory hermeneutic that befits the believer who recognizes the divine Author at work in Scripture.

Mary Healy examines how Aquinas engages the Old Testament in his commentary on Romans. She begins by noting the sheer volume of Old Testament citations in the commentary; forty-one of the forty-six books of the Old Testament appear in Aquinas's commentary on Romans, with the psalms, Isaiah, and the wisdom literature being most cited, while the books from Joshua through 2 Kings appear only twenty-eight times. As she points out, Aquinas understands authorial intention (human and divine) in terms of the realities pointed to rather than a subjective intention. Differentiating the spiritual and literal senses of Scripture, she notes that in his commentary on Romans, Aquinas rarely cites the Old Testament in the spiritual sense but nonetheless does cite Old Testament texts in a way that would seem to us to be a spiritual sense. Aquinas sometimes pays attention not to what the Old Testament verse means in its context, but rather to the associations with other biblical texts that the imagery of the Old Testament verse may suggest. Asking whether Aquinas's use of the Old Testament in the commentary on Romans represents exegesis or eisegesis, Healy identifies key principles of Aquinas's exegesis, among them the theological/doctrinal profundity of Scripture, the unity of the biblical canon, and a hermeneutic of faith that allows Aquinas to perceive the divine Author. These principles, she suggests, offer a path forward as regards the contemporary reintegration of exegesis and theology.

Matthew Levering focuses on Aquinas's discussion of Romans 8, with the goal of placing Aquinas's doctrine of predestination in the context of his doctrine of the grace of the Holy Spirit. Levering first describes Aquinas's account of predestination in the *Summa theologiae*, including his account in the *tertia pars* of the predestination of Christ. Since Romans 8:30 plays a significant role in the *Summa*, Levering turns to Aquinas's commentary on Romans and traces the panoply of realities that Aquinas explores in his commentary on Romans 8: the fulfillment of the Mosaic law through the grace of the Holy Spirit, the Incarnation and Paschal mystery of Christ, adoptive sonship, suffering and glorification, the transformation not only of humans but of the whole creation, the diverse degrees of charity among the saints, the unique mission of the Virgin Mary and the Apostles, the Holy Spirit's intercession on our behalf, God's drawing good out of evil, God's infinite mercy. These interrelated realities reflect the richness of the unfolding of God's eternal plan for elevating rational creatures to union with himself ("predestination"). In this context, Levering devotes special attention to Aquinas's interpretation of Paul's teaching that God "foreknew" and "predestined" humans. Aquinas understands predestination not to be about individual salvation but to be about the accomplishment of the unity of the mystical body in and through the missions of the Son and Spirit.

Bruce Marshall identifies two ways of looking at justification; one focuses on God's transformation of sinners, the other on God's merciful forgiveness of sinners. After surveying relevant texts from the Council of Trent, he asks which of these two ways informs Aquinas's commentary on Romans 4, traditionally a favorite chapter for those who emphasize justification's character as God's merciful forgiveness of sinners. Abraham's faith, Aquinas observes, constitutes his justice. God is right to consider Abraham to be just, because God has given Abraham faith. Yet Aquinas also gives a significant place, Marshall shows, to God's not imputing a sin to a sinner, God's willingness not to hold our sins against us. In order to show how this is so, Marshall discusses in some detail Aquinas's understanding of sin *(peccatum)* and fault or guilt *(culpa)*, as well as the consequences of sin: the degradation of the sinner's natural good, the "stain" *(macula)*, and the punishment *(poena)*. In not imputing sin to us, God prevents the consequences of sin from marring us, so that we do not have to undergo the punishment. Such forgiven sins become an occasion for us to rejoice in God's unfathomable mercy. Broadly speaking, justification's character as God's transformation of sinners underlies, for Aquinas, God's merciful non-imputation of sins. It is ultimately God's transforming grace, rooted in Christ's Paschal mystery, that frees us from sin's consequences. Even so, as Marshall points out, Aquinas holds that God also "covers" our sins in the sense that God treats them as though they had not happened. The forgiven sins of our past cannot be transformed, but they truly are past. Both aspects of justification, then, are necessary for understanding Aquinas's interpretation of Romans 4.

Charles Raith compares Aquinas and Calvin on Romans 7:14–25. Unlike many modern commentators, Aquinas and Calvin read the "I" of Romans 7:14–25 as referring to the Apostle Paul himself. Raith therefore explores the different understandings of Paul that Aquinas and Calvin develop in their commentaries on this passage. For Aquinas, in the state of grace Paul's bodily passions are still rebellious, but his rational powers are able to resist their rebellious promptings. By contrast, Calvin considers that grace regenerates part of the soul but not all, so that the "affections" that arise from the Holy Spirit contrast with the appetites of the flesh. For Aquinas Paul commits a venial sin of omission in not preventing the disordered desires that his mind resists, whereas for Calvin even Paul's best work is corrupted by sin and requires God's forgiveness. Aquinas's differentiation of venial sin from mortal sin is not accepted by Calvin, and their accounts of Christian "perfection" and of merit flow in large part from this difference. In addition, Aquinas finds in Romans 7:14–25 indications of the grace that Paul receives so as to fulfill his ministry as an apostle. Calvin sees Paul as exemplifying not apostolic grace but the struggles of the everyday believer. Raith concludes that the interpretation of this passage provides significantly different conceptions of the Christian life, even while Aquinas and Calvin are joined in a common concern to understand the movements of sin and grace.

Geoffrey Wainwright identifies passages in Aquinas's commentary that bear centrally upon worship. Treating Romans 1, he brings out Aquinas's emphasis on God's glory and on our rendering glory to God through worship that recognizes God's glory. Likewise we are called to honor, give thanks, and offer sacrifice to God as Creator and benefactor. Following Paul, Aquinas identifies false worship as rooted in self-idolatry. Wainwright notes that worship is put on the right footing again, for Aquinas and Paul, by Christ's bearing the penalty due to sin and thereby bestowing the grace that enables us to glorify God for his gracious action. Due to the indwelling and intercession of the Spirit, we are united to the Son and enabled to cry out to the Father in prayer and praise, in a manner that will lead to our glorification. As Wainwright points out, Aquinas comments on Romans 12:1 that we must offer up to God all our goods—soul, body, and possessions—in various expressions of sacrificial worship. Aquinas also attends to the unity of worship to which Christians are called (Rom 15), a unity that Paul's ministry aims to serve. The honor and glory due to the Trinity have the last word in Romans 16, which Wainwright rightly takes as evidence of the centrality of doxology for worship, doctrine, and life.

Michael Waldstein compares Luther and Aquinas on Romans 1:17. Luther depicts justification as a marriage between the sinless Christ and his sinful Bride, and he is aware of the ecclesial, rather than merely individual, dimension of this marriage. Yet Luther famously rejects the doctrine of "formed faith," faith formed by love, because he fears that this would introduce human works into the faith that justifies. Love is a "work" that has no place in the marital union itself, although Luther grants love a place among the household servants. After noting how Aquinas understands formed faith in his commentary on Romans, Waldstein shows that the commentary's portrait of "merit" is also marital, focused upon an enjoyment of God made possible by God. Similarly, in the commentary Aquinas argues that our love is primarily God's work of grace, while being at the same time, in a noncompetitive manner, the work of our free will. The marital or participatory understanding of human love of God is also found, Waldstein points out, in Aquinas's commentary on Romans 5:5, "God's love has been poured into our hearts through the Holy Spirit that has been given to us." Waldstein concludes that Luther would have benefited from deepening his "spousal logic of justification."

Robert Louis Wilken brings Aquinas's commentary on Romans into dialogue with those of Origen and Augustine. Praising Aquinas for writing a genuine commentary rather than trying to tie together all the loose ends of the letter to the Romans, Wilken emphasizes that Aquinas never has solely Romans in view: rather Aquinas approaches each verse with the whole of Scripture in mind, as Wilken shows by noting some of Aquinas's Old Testament citations. This means that, as with the Fathers, biblical language and resonances govern the commentary, although technical theological language is present as well. Giving examples of Aquinas's debt to the Fathers, Wilken notes that Aquinas's treatment of Romans 12:1 is drawn partly from Augustine, and he connects Aquinas's exegesis of Romans 2:13–17 with the approaches of Origen and Augustine. Origen reads the passage as being about natural law; Augustine argues that the Gentiles who follow the law do so by grace; Aquinas draws a distinction that enables him, as is his wont, to agree in a certain way with both. At the same time he follows Augustine's (rather than Origen's) understanding of the meaning of "law" in Romans, with consequences for his understanding of Israel. Above all, says Wilken, Aquinas is like the Fathers in that he focuses primarily not on understanding Paul's thought but on understanding the salvific realities to which Paul directs attention.

Bernhard Blankenhorn, O.P.

⟲

1   Aquinas on Paul's Flesh/
    Spirit Anthropology in Romans

I will primarily argue that, despite numerous exegetical limitations, the late
St. Thomas Aquinas achieved a broad and faithful appropriation of St. Paul's
flesh/spirit anthropology in the Epistle to the Romans. Second, I will show
that Aquinas's interpretation of key Romans passages on flesh/spirit does not
adequately manifest his reception of the Pauline doctrine. Only the *Summa
theologiae* allows a just evaluation of that reception. Third, I will show that a
study of Aquinas's Pauline exegesis must take into account the way in which
St. Augustine mediates and guides that reading of Scripture.

I will begin with a brief historical study of St. Paul's flesh/spirit language
in Romans 7–8. I will consider how this language functions within the main
theological and pastoral arguments of Romans, especially in light of 1 Corinthians and the cosmology that such language presumes. Only by recognizing
how and why Aquinas receives and develops Paul's teaching can we begin to
determine the ways in which Aquinas can participate in the theological and
ecclesial exegeses that are the necessary complements to historical exegesis.[1]
Second, I will offer a summary of St. Augustine's various interpretations of
flesh/spirit language, especially in light of the doctrinal stakes involved.
Third, I will analyze Aquinas's interpretation of the letter and the doctrine
of Pauline flesh/spirit in the *Romans Commentary* (chapters 6–8), in the *Galatians Commentary* (chapter 5), and in select articles on sin and grace in the
Summa theologiae.

1. On theological and ecclesial exegesis, see J. A. DiNoia, O.P. and Bernard Mulcahey, O.P.,
"The Authority of Scripture in Sacramental Theology: Some Methodological Observations," *Pro
Ecclesia* 10, no. 3 (2001): 329–45; Matthew Levering, *Participatory Biblical Exegesis* (Notre Dame,
Ind.: University of Notre Dame Press, 2008); Denis Farkasfalvy, O. Cist., "Inspiration and Inter-
pretation," in *Vatican II: Renewal within Tradition*, ed. Matthew L. Lamb and Matthew Levering
(New York: Oxford University Press, 2008), 77–100.

Flesh/Spirit in Romans

A proper understanding of Paul's flesh/spirit language demands a sufficient awareness of its cosmological background. In Paul's Hellenized Jewish
culture, *pneuma*, or spirit, is a higher reality that has its own power of movement and knowledge.[2] *Pneuma* is a vital element of any living person. There
are many types and qualities of *pneuma* at work in the world.[3] Paul usually
does not employ the term to refer to the Holy Spirit. The latter doctrine especially emerges in light of the Gospel of John, the Book of Acts, and the early
Christian tradition. For Paul, *pneuma* is not purely spiritual. Good *pneuma*
is divine stuff, a life force that joins us to God. Christians are one *pneuma*
with the Lord (1 Corinthians 6:17). Stanley Stowers has argued that the
basic model for this participation language is that of genetic descent, of rela-
tives sharing the "stuff" of their ancestors.[4] Paul argues in Galatians 3 that
through Christ, we have received God's *pneuma*, which in turn connects us
with the blessings promised to Abraham, as we now become his descendents
in sharing his "stuff."[5] Romans 8 employs a similar logic. The same *pneuma*
or life force that belongs to Christ now dwells in believers. Christians have a
portion of Christ's "stuff" and thus are alive, while their *sarx* is dead because
of sin (8:9).

Pneuma clearly does not refer to the individual soul or a spiritual substance. We might say that it is a metaphorical term, yet only with significant
qualifications. *Pneuma* is very real, an active force at work in the universe, but
it is not an individual thing. Similarly, Paul often employs the term *sarx* to refer to something other than an individual body, and in that sense is speaking
metaphorically, yet *sarx* or flesh is no less real than *pneuma*.

Part of the difficulty in interpreting Pauline *sarx* is rooted in the multiple
uses and meanings of the term. In 1 Corinthians 5, Paul addresses the problem
of the man who has sexual relations with his stepmother. He must be expelled
from the community, since his immorality is corrupting the communal body
of Christ. Dale Martin has pointed to the medical background of such pollu-
tion language. The incestuous man should be turned over to Satan, who will
destroy the *sarx*, so that the *pneuma* may be saved. But whose spirit does Paul

2. Stanley Stowers, "What Is 'Pauline Participation in Christ'?" in *Redefining First-Century Jewish and Christian Identities: Essays in Honor of Ed Parish Sanders*, ed. Fabian E. Udoh et al. (South Bend, Ind.: University of Notre Dame Press, 2008), 355.

3. Ibid., 363.

4. Ibid., 358.

5. Ibid., 359–60. The latter point about sharing in Abraham's "stuff" still seems open to debate, unlike the notion of receiving divine "stuff" through Christ.

have in mind? The text is not clear.[6] Yet Paul's main concern is for the health of the communal body, lest the presence of the divine spirit leave the temple (1 Corinthians 6:12–20).

The bulk of Paul's references to *sarx* are negative. The flesh is connected to this world and opposed to God's plan, which plan is represented by *pneuma* (Romans 8). Both *sarx* and *pneuma* seem to pervade the cosmos as active influences that can move in and out of bodies. They help constitute material reality, including the human being. *Sarx* and *pneuma* interact and wage war against one another, as is evident in 1 Corinthians and Galatians 5.[7]

Paul often employs flesh/spirit language in the context of moral exhortation, and this is certainly the case in Romans 7–8. Paul has at least two major tasks in these chapters. First, he seeks to demonstrate that, despite its radical limitations, the law is good and in no way a cause of sin. Second, Paul's polemic about the law's limits in Romans 2–3 and 6–7 has opened him to the charge of moral laxity: if the law is so inadequate, then what clear ethical boundaries exist for Christians? If there are no such boundaries, then Paul's argument about the law and the work of Christ falls apart, and he has failed to deal with the problem of the relation between Jews and Gentiles.

In Romans 6, Paul begins his response by comparing two states: slavery to sin and slavery to God. Through baptism, Christ has freed believers from the former, not to belong to themselves, but to belong to God. In this context, Paul employs the term "sin" to describe not so much certain human acts, but a power that is opposed to God and in whose sphere sinners dwell.

In Romans 7, Paul employs the language of flesh to refer to believers' previous existence in this sphere. "While we were living in the flesh, our sinful passions, aroused by the law, were at work in our members to bear fruit for death. But now we are discharged from the law, dead to that which held us captive, so that we serve not under the old written code but in the new life of the Spirit" (7:5–6).[8] Paul is clearly contrasting two states: the way of death and the way of life. The former binds a person to the law in a certain way, while the latter frees him or her from the law. Paul here describes pre- and post-baptismal states. The unbaptized are in the flesh while the baptized are in the spirit. He immediately anticipates an objection: is the law sin (7:7)? Not at all, but the force of personified sin, which is a power at work in the cosmos, used the law as a means to increase sinful desire (7:8). Paul constructs the cat-

---

6. Dale B. Martin, *The Corinthian Body* (New Haven: Yale University Press, 1995), 169.

7. Ibid., 172–73.

8. In the section on Paul, biblical citations come from the *Revised Standard Version*. In the section on Augustine and Aquinas, I have translated directly from the Latin biblical text employed by the respective theologians.

egory of personified sin in order to exonerate the law (7:12–13). *Sarx* refers to the platform for the sphere of sin. It is the slavery of sin taking root in the human being without life in Christ (7:14).

Paul then turns to his famous lament that concludes Romans 7. As Krister Stendahl and others have shown, only post-Augustinian moral psychologies enable us to interpret this passage autobiographically. Paul is not speaking about himself, for he had no difficulty fulfilling the law before his encounter with Christ, as he states in Philippians 3. The purpose of Romans 7 is to deal with the relation of Jews and Gentiles in light of the Christ event. It is an argument about the law.[9] Romans 8 will show how the transformation of the believer through Christ's spirit avoids the trap of libertinism.

The "I" of Romans 7 knows what is good, for he knows the law, which is good, and he wants to accomplish the good, that is, obey the law, but finds himself incapable of doing so (7:16–17). The "I" has been sold to sin (7:14), has sin dwelling within (7:17). No good dwells in the *sarx* of the "I." Personified sin has its own proper region within the "I," and this sin is the true agent of sinful action. Paul's defense of the law also turns into a defense of the "I." On the surface, Paul excuses the sins of Christians in their pre-baptismal existence, yet this is hardly his purpose. Rather, he aims to continue the contrast between life with and without Christ already described in chapter 5, and to show that this contrast does not contradict the law's goodness. Paul is hardly trying to describe the moral psychology of the non-Christian.

Romans 7 neatly parallels Romans 8. *Sarx*, the "place" in which the sphere of sin has taken root, is destroyed through the gift of Christ's life-giving stuff, his *pneuma* (8:2), which is why believers are no longer in the flesh at all (8:7). Having been transferred from one sphere to another, the Christian attains a new capacity to obey God's spirit instead of the flesh (8:4). Christ's *pneuma* is not just life-giving, but directive. Understood in its cosmological context, Paul's language of *pneuma* shows that his teaching on participation in Christ's life is pervaded by "realism." The believer has been truly transformed by the *pneuma* or stuff of Christ. Such infusion of "divine fluid" enables the Christian to obey God's law.[10] In other words, the roots of intrinsic justification are Pauline.

Romans 8:5–13 continues the contrast between flesh and spirit. Life in each sphere involves an opposing set of desires, works, and outcomes. Paul's dualism is moral and metaphysical. Each way of being is accompanied by a radically different way of living. Yet the contrast is also rhetorical. The two spheres are not always neatly separated. Hence, Rome's Christians still need

9. Krister Stendahl, "The Apostle Paul and the Introspective Conscience of the West," in *Paul among Jews and Gentiles* (Philadelphia: Fortress Press, 1976), 80–92.

10. Stowers, "What Is 'Pauline Participation in Christ'?" 365.

to hear moral exhortations to avoid the works of the flesh (8:13). Life in the spirit would seem to exclude all sin (meaning grave sin such as fornication and murder), yet sin remains a very real possibility for the believer. Paul's cosmology has demonstrated the law's goodness, yet it is also in danger of leading his hearers toward moral triumphalism. The tension within Paul's thought in Romans, between the dualistic cosmology and the moral exhortation, does not seem to bother him. The cosmology is a theological tool for Paul's argument about the law and the moral behavior of Christians, and not a complete theological anthropology worked out for its own sake. He is writing a pastoral letter, not a treatise of systematic theology.

I have purposely avoided a detailed examination of every mention of *sarx* in Romans. Rather, I have sought to focus on the overall aim of flesh/spirit language in Romans, especially in light of the presumed cosmology, one that seems to best manifest itself in 1 Corinthians. A focus on Paul's broader theological and rhetorical aims seems ideal for an evaluation of Aquinas's exegesis of flesh/spirit in Romans. The great value of reading Paul with the theological tradition, especially Augustine and Aquinas, is found not so much in the discernment of the meaning of particular phrases and verses, but rather in uncovering the broader vision of God, the human being, and the Christian life that the Scriptures seek to present to us.[11]

Flesh/Spirit in St. Augustine

Aquinas's interpretation of Pauline flesh/spirit is incomprehensible without Augustine. More than any other thinker, the Bishop of Hippo influenced Aquinas's reading in this area, and we can say the same for virtually all of Thomas's medieval contemporaries, not to mention Martin Luther and John Calvin. Augustine's interpretation of Pauline flesh/spirit is complex and nuanced. I can only offer a few highlights.

The reading I will propose is, like that of Paul, a historical reconstruction, and thus not identical with Aquinas's Augustine. However, Aquinas had a fairly strong awareness of the internal evolutions and complexities of Augustine's doctrine of sin and grace, as well as Augustine's diverse ways of reading Pauline flesh/spirit. The historical reading also allows us to recognize aspects in the thought of Augustine that Aquinas overlooked or ignored.

Augustine's understanding of flesh/spirit in Romans, as well as in Galatians 5, clearly evolved throughout his career. The early Augustine proposed that Paul's Romans 7 description of the human being divided between the law

11. I am indebted to my confrere and teacher Gregory Tatum, O.P., of the École biblique et archéologique française in Jerusalem for his invaluable guidance on flesh/spirit in St. Paul.

of the spirit and the law of the flesh refers to humanity under the law but before grace. The young Augustine is not dogmatic on this point. He expresses this view in his *Exposition on Galatians*, as well as in question 66 of the *Book on 83 Diverse Questions*. The latter text divides human history into four states or ways of being: (1) the state of innocence, (2) the state of the law before grace, (3) the state of grace in this life, and (4) the state of glory. Augustine interprets Romans 7:15–23 as pertaining to the second state, and Romans 7:24–25 as well as Romans 8 as a description of the third state. Paul's dualistic cosmology that served as an instrument to defend the goodness of the law and the need for Christ's saving work has now been transformed into stages in the salvation history of all of humanity, without exception.

The doctrinal context at this stage in Augustine's career is also important. As Paula Fredriksen has pointed out, Augustine had to reclaim Paul from the Manichees, for the flesh/spirit language of Romans had reinforced their dualism.[12] Yet the early polemic against the Manichees did not sufficiently move the young Augustine away from his own somewhat dualistic anthropology. In the early works, he still refers to the body as "a heavy chain" or "a cage."[13] One finds hints of this dualism in Augustine's commentary on Romans 7 in the same question 66. Pauline flesh refers to carnal desires, passions, and pleasures, which are opposed to eternal, spiritual goods.[14] Augustine's comments here are extremely brief, perhaps more a manifestation of anthropological assumptions than a developed systematic reflection. The disordered will or egotistical tendencies of the spirit are noticeably absent. Only the Pauline phrase "the prudence of the flesh" that is an enemy to God pushes Augustine to speak of the soul's desire for lower, temporal goods.[15] But that was before the Pelagian controversy began.

In his middle period, Augustine further nuanced his reading of flesh/spirit in the course of his work *The Literal Interpretation of Genesis*. Here, he insists that the subject or seat of concupiscence is both the body and the soul. The Galatians 5 passage, "the flesh lusts against the spirit and the spirit against

12. Paula Fredriksen, "Beyond the Body/Soul Dichotomy: Augustine on Paul against the Manichees and the Pelagians," *Recherches Augustiniennes* 23 (1988): 87–114. See Augustine's *De magistro*, Corpus Christianorum Series Latina (hereafter CCSL) 29 (Turnhout: Brepols, 1970), bk. 12, ch. 39; *De duabus animabus*, in *Six traités anti-manichéens*, Bibliothèque augustinienne 17 (Paris: Desclée de Brouwer, 1961), bk. 13, ch. 19.

13. Augustine, *De moribus ecclesiae catholicae et de moribus manichaeorum*, in *Problèmes moraux*, Bibliothèque augustinienne 2 (Paris: Desclée de Brouwer, 1948), bk. 1, ch. 22; idem, *Soliloquia*, in *Dialogues philosophiques*, vol. 1, Bibliothèque augustinienne 5 (Paris: Desclée de Brouwer, 1948), bk. 1, ch. 14.

14. Augustine, *Mélanges Doctrinaux*, Bibliothèque augustinienne 10 (Paris: Desclée de Brouwer, 1952), 246–52.

15. Ibid., 250.

the flesh," means that the spirit is concupiscent, together with the flesh. Here, Augustine identifies spirit with the soul and flesh with the mortal body, an interpretation already implicit in question 66. In other words, he offers a literalistic reading, when Paul was speaking of opposed metaphysical and moral spheres, not body and soul. Furthermore, for Paul, the "lust" of the spirit is not a negative or sinful reality, as it is for Augustine. This misreading of Galatians is clearly open to anthropological dualism, yet Augustine's aim moves in the very opposite direction. His main concern is to demonstrate that the biblical text does not exclude the soul as a seat of concupiscence. He thinks that the text obviously speaks of the body as a subject of concupiscence.[16] Augustine misunderstands the biblical verse in question, yet the overall outcome is not far from Paul's teaching: the problem is disordered desire in the whole fallen person. Just as Augustine begins to get Paul wrong in the details, he moves closer to Paul's broader vision of the human being in the sphere of the flesh.

The dispute with Pelagius led Augustine to further revise his reading of Paul. Concupiscence, meaning all of the effects of original sin, prevents the human being from attaining salvation without the gift of a purely gratuitous grace. Once graced through faith and baptism, the disordered, ungodly human desires that are the consequence of the Fall still continue to weigh us down, although grace now enables us to resist them. Thus, Paul's man delivered to sin in Romans 7:14–25 is *also* a reference to the Christian living in grace who continues to suffer from the fallen condition. The preferred interpretation of the young Augustine that restricted the divided man to those without grace is left behind. The shift is very clearly announced in Retraction 26.[17]

For the mature Augustine, the root cause of the fallen human condition is found in the will, for even when elevated by grace, the believer continues to suffer from a disordered inclination to self-love. As Stephen Duffy points out, it is disordered love (*cupiditas, amor sui*) that gives rise to "desires of the flesh," including unrestricted sensual passions, lust for power, jealousy, hatred, greed, and selfishness.[18] The late Augustine's stress is not so much on sin as a result of the soul's entanglement with the body but rather on sin as a result of the will's

16. Augustine, *De Genesi ad litteram*, vol. 2, Bibliothèque augustinienne 49 (Paris: Desclée de Brouwer, 1972), bk. 10, ch. 12; Peter Burnell, "Concupiscence," in *Augustine through the Ages: An Encyclopedia*, ed. Allan D. Fitzgerald, O.S.A. (Grand Rapids, Mich.: Eerdmans, 1999), 226.

17. Augustine, *Rectractationum*, CCSL 57 (Turnhout: Brepols, 1984), bk. I, ch. 26, p. 84: "Ubi illud quod ait apostolus: *Scimus autem quia lex spiritalis est, ego autem carnalis sum*, exponere uolens dixi: *Id est carni consentio nondum spiritali gratia liberatus.* Quod non sic accipiendum est, quasi spiritalis homo iam sub gratia constitutus etiam de se ipso non possit hoc dicere et cetera usque ad eum locum ubi dictum est: *Miser ego homo, quis me liberabit de corpore mortis huius?*, quod postea didici, sicut sum iam ante confessus."

18. Stephen J. Duffy, "Anthropology," in *Augustine through the Ages*, 28. Augustine is alluding to Galatians 5:19–21.

own decision. Thus, Augustine understands the biblical category "flesh" not merely as sensual indulgence, but as a fault within the soul itself.[19]

The increasing focus on the will and self-love as the root cause of the fallen human condition is necessarily accompanied by a developing and complex sense of the term "concupiscence," which is also the most important term for the Western theological tradition's interpretation of Pauline flesh/spirit. In Augustine's anti-Pelagian period, concupiscence seems to become a technical term for the disordered will inherited from Adam.[20] In book 14 of *The City of God*, we learn that concupiscence can refer to a disordered desire for wisdom or power.[21] In fact, the two cities are divided by those who live according to the flesh, meaning self-love, and those who live according to the Spirit, meaning the love of God.[22] Augustine wants to ensure that "living after the flesh" is not understood simply in reference to a life pursuing bodily pleasures, as promoted in Epicurean philosophy, and that "living after the spirit" is not understood simply in reference to a life pursuing spiritual goods, as promoted in Stoic philosophy. Rather Scripture "uses this word ['flesh'] in many other significations ... for man himself, the nature of man taking the part for the whole." Augustine then presents an interpretation of Galatians 5:19–21: "Among the works of the flesh ... we find ... pleasures of the flesh ... and vices of the soul ... idolatries ... heresies ... envyings."[23] Augustine's attentive reading of Galatians clearly moves away from dualism.

Yet in book 13 of *The City of God*, Augustine also presents a very literalistic reading of flesh, as he refers to Galatians 5:17. Adam and Eve take fig leaves to cover their shame. They had begun to experience a new movement of the flesh, for it had become disobedient to the spirit, that is, the soul, just as the spirit has rebelled against God. And so, because the soul deserted its divine superior, it could no longer govern its servant the body. "Then began the flesh to lust against the Spirit, in which strife we are born."[24]

The late Augustine is quite clear that Pauline flesh refers to many forms of rebellion, yet in the hierarchy of the wounds of sin or concupiscence, the disordered movements of the body continue to occupy a place that is second only to the disordered will. Augustine notes that Romans 7:24–25 describes the present experience of the body.[25] The "law in my members" (Romans 7:23) is the

19. Ibid., 29.

20. Burnell, "Concupiscence," 226.

21. *De civitate Dei*, CCSL 48, bk. 14. Cf. Duffy, "Anthropology," 29.

22. Ibid., bk. 14, ch. 1.

23. Ibid., bk. 14, ch. 2, using the Marcus Dods translation (New York: The Modern Library, 1994), 443.

24. Ibid., bk. 13, ch. 13, quoting Dods, 422.

25. Augustine, *De nuptiis et concupiscentia*, in *Premières polémiques contre Julien*, Bibliothèque

concupiscence of the flesh.[26] Retraction 15 identifies the "sin dwelling in me" of Romans 7:20 with carnal concupiscence, which is in direct opposition to the will, though Augustine's exposition is in the context of his emphasis on the voluntary nature of all sin, in opposition to the Manichean doctrine of the good and bad soul.[27] In book 14 of *The City of God*, Augustine laments sexual desire as "the great force" that refuses to be integrated harmoniously and continues to clash with reason and will.[28] In this context, he cites Wisdom 9:15: "Reason is pressed down by the corruptible body."[29] Only the resurrection of the flesh at the end of time will bring about complete healing from the wounds of sin. However, by grace, concupiscence can steadily diminish in the baptized who pursue spiritual progress.[30] The irony is that the late Augustine clearly leaves behind the anthropological dualism of his early period and simultaneously adopts an interpretation of the Pauline *sarx* as a reference to the ever-rebellious bodily passions of the Christian, though this meaning remains secondary to *sarx* as disordered self-love. On the surface, the Pauline exegesis of the late Augustine can often sound more dualistic, but once it is understood in the context of closely related mature doctrines, we can see that Augustine is often not far from Paul's intended meaning behind the flesh language. Still, the growing tendency toward a literalistic exegesis of particular Pauline verses sets the stage for interpretive missteps by Augustine's disciples through the centuries.

Paul's teaching on flesh/spirit undergoes obvious and significant transformations in the works of Augustine. The cosmological background of flesh/spirit seems to have become unintelligible to Augustine. The worldview dominant in fourth-century Latin culture was already so different that Augustine could no longer recognize the references to two metaphysical and moral spheres. He does not seem to hesitate to refer flesh/spirit to body and soul in various, qualified ways throughout his career.

augustinienne 23 (Paris: Desclée de Brouwer, 1974), bk. 1, cch. 31–36; bk. 2, ch. 2 & 6. See Thomas F. Martin, *'Miser ego homo': Augustine, Paul and the Rhetorical Moment* (Ann Arbor, Mich.: University Microfilms, 1995); Allan D. Fitzgerald, O.S.A., "Body," in *Augustine through the Ages*, 107.

26. Augustine, *Contra duas epistulas pelagianorum*, in *Premières polémiques contre Julien*, bk. 1, ch. 8. Cf. Paula Fredriksen, "Paul," in *Augustine through the Ages*, 624.

27. Augustine, *Rectractationum*, CCSL 57 (Turnhout: Brepols, 1984), bk. 1, ch. 15, p. 46: "in me habitat peccatum (Rom 7:20) ... hoc peccatum ... poena peccati est; quando quidem hoc de concupiscentia carnis dicitur, quod aperit in consequentibus dicens: 'Scio quia non habitat in me hoc est in carne mea bonum: uelle enim adiacet mihi, perficere autem bonum, non' (Rom 7:18) ... non perficit bonum, quia inest adhuc concupiscentia cui repugnat voluntas; cuius concupiscentiae reatus in baptismate soluitur, sed infirmitas manet."

28. *De civitate Dei*, bk. 14, ch. 16.

29. *De civitate Dei*, bk. 19, ch. 27.

30. Augustine, *De perfectione iustitiae hominis*, in *La crise pélagienne*, vol. 1, Bibliothèque augustinienne 21 (Paris: Desclée de Brouwer, 1966), bk. 13, ch. 31; Burnell, "Concupiscence," 225.

Augustine is also facing a new set of pastoral and doctrinal challenges that did not exist for Paul. The latter employed a particular cosmology as a source of arguments to solve certain pastoral challenges facing the Roman Christians. Augustine turns to Paul's cosmological language that had functioned as a tool in arguing about the law and moral behavior, abstracts it from Paul's pastoral concern, and transforms it into a systematic anthropology that tackles new theological challenges, such as Manichean dualism or Pelagius's excessive optimism. Romans 7 takes on a new meaning in Augustine because it has become a source of answers to a set of questions that Paul never posed.

A just evaluation of Augustine's exegesis should not focus so much on the details of his interpretation, which are often clearly problematic, if not simply erroneous. Rather, given that Paul's cosmological categories are tied to his culture and not by themselves inspired doctrine, we should ask: how well did Augustine retain Paul's fundamental and inspired doctrinal intentions that are expressed through the first-century Hellenistic cosmology? Does Augustine succeed in "translating" Paul's central theological intuitions into a late antique Christian metaphysics? Such a translation is always inevitably a development of doctrine as well, yet its faithfulness can be measured in relation to Paul's driving doctrinal intuitions.[31]

This last point is important as we evaluate Augustine's mature exegesis. He insists that the primary problem of the human condition is in the will, a precision not found in Paul. But I would argue that Augustine's answer in fact retains one of Paul's fundamental insights within the context of Augustine's metaphysics. The mature Augustine aims to show that disordered bodily desires are not the primary challenge in the moral life. Augustine's emphasis on the will partially moves away from a literalistic reading of *sarx* and toward a vision of the whole person being drawn toward or dwelling in an ungodly sphere. Augustine's vision of the ungraced human being as wholly and radically turned away from God appears as a faithful translation of Paul's flesh/spirit dualism, though the pre-Christian Paul now also dwells in that sphere. The mature Augustine successfully employs the disordered will to describe the sphere of flesh. Yet Augustine's "translation" of Pauline cosmology certainly also brought about a significant transformation, as two nebulous metaphysical and moral spheres that move in and out of human bodies now become more interiorized: the root of flesh is located in the desires of the will. Augustine

31. An evaluation of Augustine as exegete of Paul thus inevitably presupposes a speculative judgment concerning the purpose of Augustine's exegesis. Since the theologian's aim is never simply a faithful historical analysis of the biblical text according to the human author's original intention, the historical evaluation of theology is necessarily also a speculative or systematic enterprise, i.e., it presumes theological criteria to evaluate the success or failure of the theologian's project.

thus opens the path to what Krister Stendahl calls "the introspective conscience of the West."[32]

Augustine also detects the wounds of the disordered will and passions in the life of believers, beginning with himself. The unresolved tension in Paul between dualist cosmology and moral exhortation is resolved. Romans 7–8 has become a source for systematic theological anthropology, perhaps an inevitable evolution. Partly due to the pressure exerted by the Pelagian controversy, Augustine had to deal with a tension that Paul had left unresolved. The way out of the dilemma chosen by Augustine was the (erroneous) expansion of the "I" in Romans 7 to include every human being, with or without grace.

But overall, Augustine's mature doctrine of the disordered will enables him to offer a nuanced and historically more faithful (if imperfect) reading of Paul's flesh/spirit language in Romans. This central Augustinian doctrine will also be crucial for Aquinas's appropriation of Pauline flesh/spirit anthropology.

St. Thomas Aquinas's *Romans Commentary* on Flesh/Spirit

I will focus my study of flesh/spirit in Aquinas on his *Romans Commentary* and the *Summa theologiae*, along with a brief consideration of the same theme in the *Galatians Commentary*.[33] I do not see a single passage in Aquinas that offers an adequate synthesis of his appropriation of flesh/spirit anthropology. The doctrine has to be reassembled.

Aquinas begins to tackle Paul's flesh/spirit anthropology in the third *lectio* on Romans 6, in his exposition of verse 12. Paul states: "Do not let sin reign in your mortal body, so that you not obey its concupiscences." Here, Paul is speaking of *soma*, not *sarx*, but since it is a "body of death" that has deadly desires that befit an ungodly life, Aquinas treats the passage as the equivalent of flesh. Aquinas refers back to Romans 6:6. The "old man" or the "body of sin" has been destroyed through the Cross. He alludes to the transforming effect of baptism, which grants access to mystical union with the dying and resurrecting Christ.[34] Thomas notes that the "body of sin" refers to the power of

32. Stendahl, "The Apostle Paul and the Introspective Conscience of the West."

33. In the past forty years, Thomists and other scholars of Aquinas seem to have paid little attention to Thomas's teachings on concupiscence and the effects of original sin. I also do not know of any extensive study of Thomas's exegesis of Pauline flesh/spirit. However, for an introductory study of flesh/spirit in Aquinas and Martin Luther, see Gilles Berceville, O.P., and Eun-Sil Son, "Exégèse biblique, théologique et philosophique chez Thomas d'Aquin et Martin Luther commentateurs de Romains 7, 14–25," *Recherches de Science Religieuse* 91 (2003): 373–95.

34. "Dying and resurrecting" is Aquinas's technical terminology that focuses on the power of the very act or event of Christ's death and resurrection, not just the risen person of Christ. See

sin, which has been diminished, though not destroyed, in us. Thomas employs a metaphorical sense of "body" to describe Paul's cosmology.[35]

Aquinas immediately proceeds to explain why Paul does not say: "Let sin not *exist* in your mortal body." The body must die because of the Fall, and even after baptism, sin necessarily dwells in the body in the form of the sparks of sin, the *fomes peccati*. An inclination to sin always remains in the unglorified body. God has freed us from the power of the sparks of sin, and we must not let them regain dominion. To explain this doctrine, Thomas cites Wisdom 9:15: "the corruptible body weighs down the soul."[36]

Notice that Thomas has switched from the metaphorical sense of the term "body" at the beginning of the paragraph to a literal sense, from "body" as a symbol for the power of sin, to "body" as a physical reality in tension with the soul. What triggered this shift? The first cause is Paul himself, because he speaks of a mortal body, a body headed for death. But Paul seems to switch back and forth between the metaphorical and literal senses with great ease. When Paul speaks about not obeying the desires or concupiscences of the mortal body, he is not restricting the meaning of desires to what medievals and moderns call "sins of the flesh." The subsequent phrase, "Do not yield your members as arms of iniquity," refers to the whole human being as a moral agent. But Thomas takes the term "mortal body" as a clue that Paul has moved to the literal sense of "body." Thomas also seems to detect a further clue in the text, because verse 12 concludes with an exhortation not to obey the mortal body's desires, or, following Thomas's Vulgate translation, "concupiscences." For Thomas, the most natural association with concupiscence is the *fomes peccati*, the sparks of sin, which he primarily relates to disordered sensual inclinations.[37] It is precisely the term "sparks of sin" that emerges in the present

---

Jean–Pierre Torrell's note on *Summa Theologiae* III, q. 56, a. 1 in *Encyclopédie Jésus le Christ chez saint Thomas d'Aquin* (Paris: Cerf, 2008), 1224–26.

35. Thomas Aquinas, *Super epistolam ad Romanos Lectura* (henceforth *In ad Rom.*) in *Super Epistolas S. Pauli Lectura*, vol. 1, ed. Raphaelis Cai, 8th ed. (Rome: Marietti, 1953), 6, lect. 2, § 480: "Sic igitur vetus homo noster dicitur esse simul crucifixus cum Christo, inquantum praedicta vetustas virtute Christi sublata est. Vel quia totaliter est amota, sicut totaliter amovetur in Baptismo reatus et macula peccati. Vel quia diminuitur virtus eius, sicut virtus fomitis vel etiam consuetudinis peccandi."

36. *In ad Rom.* 6, lect. 3, § 493: "Non autem dicit: non sit peccatum in vestro mortali corpore, quia quamdiu corpus nostrum est mortale, id est necessitati mortis addictum, non potest esse quin in corpore nostro sit peccatum, id est fomes peccati. Sed ex quo a Deo liberati sumus a regno peccati debemus conari, quod peccatum in corpore nostro dominium iam amissum in nobis non recuperet. Et hoc est quod dicit *non regnet peccatum in vestro mortali corpore*. Et hoc quidem necessarium est cavere, dum corpus mortale gerimus, quia dicitur Sap. IX, 15: *Corpus quod corrumpitur aggravat animam*."

37. See *Summa theologiae (ST)* (Ottawa: Commissio Piana, 1953), I-II, q. 91, a. 6, co.

passage. The sin that is still in our mortal body and never lost in this life is the *fomes peccati*.[38]

Thomas thus begins to distance himself from the historical sense of the Pauline text. The primary explanation for this gap in this particular passage relates to the Augustinian tradition and its influence on Aquinas, which becomes clear as we ponder the rest of the paragraph. The *fomes peccati* are the inclination to sin that remains present in the mortal body. Yet that same inclination that Paul simply refers to as "sin" has lost its dominating power. But we need to remain aware of this enduring weakness. Wisdom 9:15 itself speaks of this reality: "The body corrupts and weighs down the soul." The whole human being is weighed down, but Thomas focuses on the cause of the problem, which he identifies as the body's enduring disordered inclinations. Suddenly, Thomas's anthropology sounds surprisingly Platonic. While there is certainly a great deal of Plato in Aquinas, anthropology is one part of Aquinas's thought that is usually very un-Platonic and much more Aristotelian.

The Augustinian influence on this passage can be clearly traced. In book 19 of *The City of God*, Augustine notes that in this life, reason never has full authority over vice. He is certainly alluding to the effect of concupiscence. Augustine confirms his teaching by citing Wisdom 9:15: "the body corrupts or weighs down the soul."[39] Thomas could also be referring to Augustine indirectly, via the *Summa halensis* discussion of concupiscence. Alexander notes that concupiscence in the flesh is a punishment for original sin, inclining the soul's tendency to its own (moral) corruption, a position he confirms by citing Wisdom 9:15.[40] Alexander is alluding to the same passage in *The City of God*. Like Augustine and Alexander, Thomas does not comment on Wisdom 9:15,

---

38. On concupiscence in Aquinas, see Conan Gallagher, "Concupiscence," *Thomist* 30, no. 3 (1966): 228–59. Commenting on Romans 6:12 and the phrase "do not let sin reign in your mortal body," Peter Lombard identifies this "sin" with concupiscence. But the latter is far more than the inclination to "sins of the flesh." Rather, it can refer (1) to innate vices, or (2) to the first, nonvoluntary movement toward sin that the human being cannot prevent completely, or (3) to delight in such movement, or (4) even to consent to the same inclination. Lombard therefore interprets flesh as referring to both any inclination to sin and the inclination to sins of the flesh. Lombard's reading of flesh/spirit in Romans 7–8 and Galatians 5 is frequently both metaphorical or holistic and literalistic. In this, he follows a pattern set by Augustine, if not before him, perhaps by St. Ambrose (*In Ep. Ad. Rom*, PL 191, col. 1407, 1434–5; *In Ep. Ad Galat.*, PL 192, col. 158).

39. Augustine, *De civitate Dei*, bk. 19, ch. 27, p. 697: "Quia enim Deo quidem subdita, in hac tamen condicione mortali et corpore corruptibili, quod agrauat animam, non perfecte uitiis imperat ratio."

40. Alexander of Hales, *Summa theologica seu sic ab origine dicta "Summa Fratris Alexandri,"* studio et cura Patres Collegii S. Bonaventurae. 5 vols. Quaracchi: Editiones Collegii S. Bonaventurae ad Claras Aquas, 1924–1948, II-II, inq. 2, tract. 3, q. 2, c. 3, a. 1, p. 253: "Concupiscentia aliquando accipitur pro lege carnis vel lege membrorum, et secundum modum dicitur esse in carne tamquam poena iuste inflicta … concupiscentia respeciat utrumque, est in anima tamquam

but simply uses it as a proof text for the enduring presence of concupiscence in the bodily appetites. I will return to Thomas's use of Wisdom 9:15 below.

Yet Thomas's exegesis is not restricted to a literalistic misreading of Paul. For Aquinas immediately switches back to a metaphorical sense of "body." Not allowing sin to reign in our mortal bodies means not letting it reign in the human being. Sin's domination in the whole person occurs through interior consent to concupiscence.[41] The term "mortal body" now refers to body and soul in the present, fallen condition (with or without grace). Thomas's philosophy of human action is the underlying motive for this interpretation: the reign of sin demands consent, for by definition, sin is a free act. Consent lies in the will, in the soul, which is why Thomas twice refers to "the consent of the mind." Within two paragraphs, Thomas has moved from a metaphorical sense of "body" to a literal meaning and then back to a metaphorical sense, yet without explicitly alerting the reader. Thomas moves between these realms with great ease, but not quite as quickly as Paul moves from the literal to the cosmological sense.

In Romans 6, *lectio* 4, Thomas comments on verse 19, where Paul explains: "I speak in human terms, because of the weakness of your flesh. For as you have yielded your members to serve uncleanness and iniquity, so now yield your members to serve justice, unto sanctification." Paul speaks to the Romans in simple terms, not as to the wise and strong, but rather offering milk to children, for they are still weak. Thomas explains that this weakness is not from the spirit, by which he means the soul, but from the flesh. He again quotes Wisdom 9:15 on the body weighing down the soul. He also cites Matthew 26:41: "The spirit is willing, but the flesh is weak."[42] For Aquinas, the term "flesh" here refers to the body insofar as it is a source of moral weakness. He then expounds on the middle of verse 19, where Paul says, "as you have yielded your members to serve uncleanness and iniquity." Thomas identifies uncleanness as carnal sins, such as fornication, and iniquity as spiritual sins,

---

in subiecto, in carne vero propter hoc quod inclinat aliquo modo ipsam animam per sui corruptionem et ita causaliter sumeretur: 'Corpus enim quod corrumpitur, aggravat animam,' Sap 9,15."

41. *In ad Rom.* 6, lect. 3, § 494: "Deinde, cum dicit *ut obediatis*, etc., exponit admonitionem praemissam. Circa quod considerandum est, quod dupliciter peccatum regnat in homine. Uno modo per interiorem consensum mentis. Et hoc removendo dicit *ut obediatis concupiscentiis eius*. Obedire enim per consensum mentis concupiscentiis peccati est peccatum regnare in nobis. Eccli. XVIII, 30: *Post concupiscentias tuas non eas.*"

42. Ibid., lect. 4, § 505: "Causam autem assignat, subdens *propter infirmitatem;* perfectis enim sunt perfectiora praecepta tradenda. I Cor. II, 6: *Sapientiam loquimur inter perfectos.* Hebr. V, 14: *Perfectorum est solidus cibus.* Infirmioribus sunt danda leviora praecepta. I Cor. III, 1 s.: *Tamquam parvulis in Christo, lac potum dedi vobis, non escam.* Hebr. V, 12: *Facti estis quibus lac opus est.* Haec autem infirmitas non ex spiritu sed ex carne venit, quia *corpus quod corrumpitur aggravat animam,* ut dicitur Sap. IX, 15. Et ideo subdit *carnis vestrae.* Matth. XXVI, v. 41: *Spiritus quidem promptus est, caro autem infirma.*"

especially offenses against one's neighbor.[43] In the previous *lectio*, the "members" were identified as the seat of the sparks of sin, suggesting that "members" refers to our fallen corporeal side.[44] But in the present passage, Thomas clearly reads the term *members* to include the fallen side of the whole person, as he connects it with sins of the flesh and sins of the spirit. The dualistic sounding interpretation of the phrase "infirmity of the flesh" is quickly nuanced and qualified with a holistic, metaphorical interpretation of the subsequent part of the same verse. Thomas misreads Paul's "infirmity of the flesh," but quickly moves back toward a reading that more faithfully translates Paul's sphere of the flesh into Aquinas's cosmology.

The heart of Thomas's exegesis of the *letter* of Paul's flesh/spirit anthropology is naturally found in chapter 7 of his *Romans Commentary*. A first key passage concerns verse 5: "when we were in the flesh." Thomas notes that Paul is referring to his readers' way of life before their conversion, when they were subjected to the concupiscence of the flesh. The reading is literalistic. Paul did not intend to exclude the meaning that Aquinas has identified, yet the apostle's use of "flesh" envisages a much broader category of sins and disorders.[45]

The third *lectio* of chapter 7 explicitly tackles Augustine's evolving interpretation of Paul's carnal self or carnal "I" in Romans 7. Thomas notes that in the *Book on 83 Diverse Questions*, the early Augustine interpreted the carnal self as a reference to any human being existing in sin, meaning the state of mortal sin. But in *Against Julian*, the late Augustine interpreted the carnal self as a reference to Paul's own person, with the implication that this self refers only to believers.[46] Ignoring the nuance of Retraction 26, which expanded the carnal self to include all human beings, Thomas favors what he holds to be Augustine's mature interpretation. Yet he decides to expound the text in reference to sinners and believers, thus unknowingly reflecting the complexity of the late Augustine. Thomas often employs such a generous approach in his biblical commentaries, offering multiple possible readings of the inspired text. He states that the late Augustine's interpretation is better, yet he does not exclude the earlier version as false.[47]

43. Ibid., lect. 4, § 506: "Et hoc est quod dicit *sicut enim exhibuistis membra vestra servire,* scilicet per executionem mali operis, *immunditiae et iniquitati* corde conceptae: ut immunditia referatur ad peccata carnalia, Eph. V, 3: *Omnis fornicatio, aut immunditia nec nominetur in vobis,* etc.; iniquitas autem refertur ad peccata spiritualia et praecipue quibus laeditur proximus."

44. Ibid., lect. 3, § 494: "Et ad hoc excludendum subdit *sed neque exhibeatis membra vestra peccato,* id est fomiti peccati, *arma iniquitatis,* id est instrumenta ad iniquitatem exequendam."

45. *In ad Rom.* 7, lect. 1, § 530.

46. Thomas makes an exception for the sinless Blessed Virgin Mary, fully sanctified in the womb after her conception. See *ST* III, q. 27, a. 3.

47. *In ad Rom.* 7, lect. 3, § 558: "Deinde cum dicit *ego autem carnalis sum,* etc. ostendit

Thomas then begins to ponder the details of Romans 7:14 ("I am carnal") with the early Augustine. The "I" stands for reason, since this is the most important part of the human being. Reason is carnal in two ways. First, reason is carnal in that it consents to what the flesh instigates. Reason or the soul being instigated to sin by the flesh sounds like a conflict between the soul and disordered bodily desires. But Thomas explains this doctrine by citing 1 Corinthians 3:3, which mentions jealousy and strife. The quote matches a curious phrase a few lines before, where Aquinas explains that "the human being is called carnal because his reason is carnal." Reason itself becomes fleshly, a clearly metaphorical use of the term "carnal." Those not in grace have consented to the instigations of the flesh. In other words, a major cause of carnal reason is found in its consent to disordered bodily desires. Metaphorical flesh (disordered reason) is caused by disordered flesh in the literalistic sense. Again, Thomas shifts between metaphorical and literal senses without alerting the reader.[48] Yet Thomas's approach to metaphor is quite different from Paul's. Aquinas's exegesis first distinguishes between reason or the immaterial soul on the one hand and the body with the sensitive appetites on the other. He then ponders the ways in which the term "carnal" can be predicated of each. By contrast, Paul's metaphorical use of flesh refers to a metaphysical/moral state that is radically opposed to God. Yet Thomas's overall reading is not necessarily in contradiction to Paul, since the outcome of Aquinas's analysis is a manifestation of the entire person immersed in an ungodly way of life. Like Augustine, Thomas is unable to recognize Paul's cosmological background. Hence, Thomas sometimes misinterprets Paul in the details, yet soon arrives at a very Pauline theological conclusion. However, Thomas's identification of the cause of carnal reason is probably the opposite of Paul's. The second half of Romans 1 identifies idolatry as the root cause of various perversities, including sexual sins. Paul roots the "sins of the flesh" in the "sins of the spirit." In fact, Thomas will propose a similar doctrine in the *Summa theologiae*, as we will see.

---

conditionem hominis. Et potest hoc verbum dupliciter exponi. Uno quidem modo, ut Apostolus loquatur in persona hominis in peccato existentis. Et ita hoc Augustinus exponit in libro LXXXIII quaestionum. Postea vero in libro contra Iulianum, exponit hoc ut Apostolus intelligatur loqui in persona sua, id est, hominis sub gratia constituti. Prosequamur ergo declarando qualiter haec verba et sequentia diversimode possunt utroque modo exponi, quamvis secunda expositio melior sit."

48. Ibid., lect. 3, § 560: "Dicitur autem homo carnalis, quia eius ratio carnalis est, quae dicitur carnalis dupliciter. Uno modo ex eo quod subditur carni, consentiens his, ad quae caro instigat, secundum illud I Cor. III, 3: *Cum sit inter vos zelus et contentio, nonne carnales estis*, etc. Et hoc modo intelligitur de homine nondum per gratiam reparato. Alio modo dicitur ratio esse carnalis, ex eo quod a carne impugnatur, secundum illud Gal. V, 17: *Caro concupiscit adversus spiritum*. Et hoc modo intelligitur esse carnalis ratio etiam hominis sub gratia constituti. Utraque enim carnalitas provenit ex peccato, unde subdit *venumdatus sub peccato*."

Thomas then turns to the late Augustine for an explanation of Romans 7:14 ("I am carnal"). Reason is said to be carnal because it is fought by the flesh, as Galatians 5:17 says: "the flesh lusts against the spirit." Under the influence of the late Augustine, Thomas proposes that Galatians 5 and Romans 7 refer to the same subject, namely, the graced human being. Even those in grace suffer from carnal reason, yet not in the same way as sinners, for the carnal reason of the human being in grace clearly does not give in to temptations toward mortal sins of the flesh. Each carnality, that is, the carnal reason of the graced and ungraced human being, comes from sin. Thomas alludes to original sin, for Romans 7:14 speaks of being "sold to sin."[49] Thomas again uses "carnal" in both metaphorical and literal ways. Reason or the human soul is fleshly because it is inclined to sin, yet the cause is found in the fallen sensitive appetites. But here too, Thomas's metaphorical interpretation is not metaphorical enough, since reason is carnal because of its inclinations to carnal or bodily sins. Thomas's metaphorical reading of flesh is partly rooted in a literalistic reading of the same term.

Thomas sees the need to explain the root of this carnality further. The rebellion of flesh against spirit comes from our first parents, because it pertains to the sparks of sin. Carnality involves some form of subjection to the flesh. Yet it is also caused by actual sins, meaning, human beings obeying their carnal concupiscences. Thomas assumes the doctrine that the sensual soul or the emotions are the subject of the *fomes*.[50] Interestingly, Thomas follows the late Augustine in citing Galatians 5:17 as a description of the graced human being's continuing struggles against disordered carnal desires, but he does not mention Augustine's original interpretation of spirit lusting against flesh as disordered self-love.[51]

Thomas consistently applies his two Augustinian readings to Romans 7.

---

49. Ibid.

50. Ibid., lect. 3, § 561: "Sed tamen notandum quod carnalitas quae importat rebellionem carnis ad spiritum, provenit ex peccato primi parentis, quia hoc pertinet ad fomitem, cuius corruptio ex illo peccato derivatur. Carnalitas autem quae importat subiectionem ad carnem, provenit non solum ex peccato originali, sed etiam actuali, per quod homo obediendo concupiscentiis carnis, servum se carnis constituit; unde subdit *venumdatus sub peccato*, scilicet vel primi parentis, vel proprio. Et dicit *venumdatus*, quia peccator seipsum vendit in servum peccati, pretio propriae voluntatis implendae. Is. l, 1: *Ecce in iniquitatibus vestris venditi estis.*"

51. Thomas consistently refuses to follow Augustine on spirit lusting against flesh as a negative reality. He was certainly aware of this Augustinian doctrine, since Peter Lombard discusses it in his Gloss on Galatians 5 (*In Ep. Ad Galat.*, col. 158). Thomas's *Galatians Commentary* explains spirit lusting or desiring (*concupiscit*) against flesh in consistently positive terms: the spirit lusts by delighting in virtuous acts and the contemplation of divine things (§ 311), lusts by seeking the spiritual goods above it (§ 312), lusts against the flesh by refusing not any carnal desire, but superfluous carnal desires (§ 313).

Concerning verse 15b ("I do not do what I want, but I do the very thing I hate"), Thomas explains with the early Augustine that for the human being in sin (i.e., not in grace), the will for the universal good exists, but his or her judgment and choice of particular goods is perverted by disordered habits or passions. Thomas does not go into detail, but he easily could have specified that such habits refer to unbelievers' pride or disordered self-love, along with the disordered passions. Elsewhere in the *Romans Commentary*, Thomas clearly follows the late Augustine in emphasizing that the mortal sinner is radically turned away from God and in need of a gratuitous operative grace of conversion for which no adequate natural preparation or disposition exists.[52] In other words, Aquinas maintains that the human being's natural inclination to the universal good is fully compatible with a Pauline-Augustinian doctrine of the ungraced human being's helplessness before God and utter need for the purely gratuitous gift of justification.

Thomas then turns to the late Augustine's interpretation in his exposition of Romans 7:15b. The graced human being wills both the universal and the particular good, but he or she seems unable to complete the good act because of disordered desires arising in the sensitive appetites, for which Aquinas references Galatians 5:17.[53] The late Augustine's application of the carnal self to believers pushes Aquinas toward a literalistic reading of Pauline flesh, especially since Aquinas here refuses to expand the metaphorical reading of flesh to include the graced human being's continuing weakness of will or disordered self-love, as Augustine did in book 14 of *The City of God*. This omission of a key Augustinian doctrine is highly significant. I will return to it below.

Romans 7:17 exclaims: "It is no longer I that do it, but sin which dwells within me." Thomas notes that the sinner (someone in a state of mortal sin) is

---

52. *In ad Rom.* 3, lect. 3, § 302; c. 4, lect. 1, §§ 325, 329–330. The classic Thomistic exposition is found in *ST* I-II, q. 109, aa. 6–7.

53. *In ad Rom.* 7, lect. 3, § 565: "Dicit ergo primo quantum ad omissionem boni *non enim ago hoc bonum, quod volo agere.* Quod quidem uno modo potest intelligi de homine sub peccato constituto: et sic hoc quod dicit *ago* est accipiendum secundum actionem completam, quae exterius opere exercetur per rationis consensum. Quod autem dicit *volo* est intelligendum non quidem de voluntate completa, quae est operis praeceptiva, sed de voluntate quadam incompleta, qua homines in universali bonum volunt, sicut et in universali habent rectum iudicium de bono, tamen per habitum vel passionem perversam pervertitur hoc iudicium et depravatur talis voluntas in particulari, ut non agat quod in universali intelligit agendum et agere vellet. Secundum autem quod intelligitur de homine per gratiam reparato, e converso oportet intelligere per hoc quod dicit *volo* voluntate completa perdurante in electione particularis operationis, ut per hoc quod dicit *ago* intelligatur actio incompleta, quae consistit tantum in appetitu sensitivo non perveniens usque ad rationis consensum. Homo enim sub gratia constitutus, vult quidem mentem suam a pravis concupiscentiis conservare, sed hoc bonum non agit propter motus inordinatos concupiscentiae insurgentes in appetitu sensitivo. Et simile est quod dicit Gal. V, 17: *Ut non quaecumque vultis, illa faciatis.*"

the servant of sin in that he is not so much acting as acted upon by sin. The one who is free acts "by himself" (*per seipsum*).[54] Aquinas here alludes to what Servais Pinckaers has described as freedom for excellence, a doctrine with deep Johannine, Pauline, and Augustinian roots.[55] The human being immersed in vice is not free because he or she is incapable of choosing the true good. Grace brings freedom, the capacity to act according to one's nature, *per seipsum*. This interpretation seems to be in complete harmony with Paul. The realm of true freedom is the realm of the Spirit, the realm of acting in a God-like way.

But, continues Thomas, the same passage (Romans 7:17) can "rightly and easily" be understood about the human being in grace. Such a person's reason does not seek sensual pleasures in a disordered way. Such excessive desires come from the spark of sin. Paul says: "It is no longer I that do it." The human being doing something refers to acting by reason. But the motions of concupiscence are not from reason, which is why the sparks of sin operate, but not the human being properly speaking: "it is no longer I that do it, but sin which dwells within me." Thomas here alludes to the inclination to grave sins of the flesh to which the believer refuses consent, thus avoiding the sin, in contrast to the mortal sinner, who does consent.[56]

Perhaps the most striking aspect of this passage is its apparent assumption about the graced human being. When Thomas speaks of the operation of reason, he clearly refers to both intellect and will, since the will is the immediate principle of operation in his anthropology. By itself, the intellect does nothing. Thomas seems to suggest that the graced immaterial soul, which he here calls "reason," is largely healed of the effects of the fall. Its main challenge comes from the lingering effects of the sparks of sin in the sensitive appetites. However, this implication cannot be taken as a definitive element of Thomas's anthropology. Later on, I will show that crucial aspects of Augustine's doctrine of the disordered will and self-love weighing down even the good Christian remain in Aquinas, especially the late Aquinas. Yet it is striking how little place is granted to the inherent weakness of the will in the *Romans Commen-*

---

54. Ibid., lect. 3, § 569: "Quod autem homo carnalis venumdatus sub peccato, quasi aliqualiter sit servus peccati, ex hoc apparet quod ipse non agit sed agitur a peccato. Ille enim qui est liber, ipse per seipsum agit et non ab alio agitur."

55. Servais Pinckaers, O.P., *The Sources of Christian Ethics*, trans. Mary Thomas Noble, O.P. (Washington, D.C.: The Catholic University of America Press, 1995), chapters 15–16.

56. *In ad Rom.* 7, lect. 3, § 570: "Et hoc quidem recte ac faciliter potest intelligi de homine sub gratia constituto, quod enim concupiscit malum secundum appetitum sensitivum ad carnem pertinentem, non procedit ex opere rationis, sed ex inclinatione fomitis. Illud autem homo dicitur operari quod ratio operatur, quia homo est id quod est secundum rationem: unde motus concupiscentiae, qui non sunt a ratione sed a fomite, non operatur homo sed fomes peccati, qui hic peccatum nominatur."

tary, whose composition followed shortly after that of the *Prima secundae*. Augustine's doctrine of continuing disordered self-love in the depth of the believer's partially healed heart enabled the Bishop of Hippo to offer a metaphorical reading of Pauline flesh, a crucial hermeneutical tool that seems to be missing in Aquinas's *Romans Commentary*.[57]

Romans 7:18 presents Paul's famous lament (though not about himself): "I know that nothing good dwells within me, that is, in my flesh." Thomas takes this passage as a reference to the seat of grace. The proper subject of the grace of Christ is the mind, meaning the immaterial soul, which includes intellect and will.[58] The phrase "no good" refers to "no good of grace," since a broader reference would appear to be Manichean.[59] Since grace is immaterial, it is properly found in the soul. Thomas also explains that "flesh" here refers to the sensitive appetites inasmuch as their inclinations are contrary to those of reason. Again, he cites Galatians 5:17.[60] Thomas notes that this Romans verse would probably be superfluous if it did not refer to the human being in grace, since no good of grace dwells in any part of the sinner, neither in his flesh nor in his spirit.[61] As with Thomas's comments on Romans 7:15, his appropriation of the late Augustine leads to a literalistic misreading of Pauline flesh. Such an interpretation would seem to make Aquinas's anthropology somewhat dualistic in comparison to Paul, yet Thomas's literalistic interpretation of flesh/spirit in this passage is driven by the need to reject Manicheanism,[62] a threat

---

57. In commenting on Romans 6–8, Thomas offers a single, summary treatment of pride as the beginning of all sin (7, § 538). But this doctrine is hardly integrated into his treatment of flesh/spirit. It emerges in the context of knowledge of the law leading to sin (Romans 7:7).

58. *In ad Rom.* 7, lect. 3, § 573: "Probat ergo primo quod peccatum habitans in homine operetur malum quod homo facit. Quae quidem probatio manifesta est secundum quod verba referuntur ad hominem sub gratia constitutum, qui est liberatus a peccato per gratiam Christi, ut supra VI, 22 habitum est. Quantum ergo ad eum in quo Christi gratia non habitat, nondum est liberatus a peccato. In carne autem gratia Christi non habitat sed habitat in mente, unde infra VIII, 10 dicitur, quod *si Christus in nobis est, corpus quidem mortuum est propter peccatum, spiritus autem vivit propter iustificationem.* Igitur adhuc in carne dominatur peccatum quod operatur concupiscentia carnis. Carnem enim hic accipit simul cum viribus sensitivis. Sic enim caro distinguitur contra spiritum et ei repugnat, in quantum appetitus sensitivus tendit in contrarium eius quod ratio appetit, secundum illud Gal. V, v. 17: *Caro concupiscit adversus spiritum.*" Cf. § 580.

59. Ibid., lect. 3, § 575: "Et per hoc patet, quod hoc verbum non patrocinatur Manichaeis, qui volunt carnem non esse bonam secundum naturam, et ita non esse creaturam Dei bonam, cum scriptum sit I Tim. IV, 4: *Omnis creatura Dei bona est.* Non enim hic Apostolus agit de bono naturae, sed de bono gratiae, quo a peccato liberamur."

60. Ibid., lect. 3, § 573, cited above.

61. Ibid., lect. 3, § 576: "Si vero hoc referatur ad hominem sub peccato existentem, superflue additur quod dicit *hoc est in carne mea.* Quia in homine peccatore bonum gratiae non habitat nec quantum ad carnem, nec quantum ad mentem; nisi forte quis extorte velit exponere hoc esse dictum quia peccatum, quod est privatio gratiae, quodammodo a carne derivatur ad mentem."

62. We find a similar exegetical motive in Augustine, as was noted above.

that remained current in Thomas's day in the form of Catharism, a heresy that sparked the founding of Aquinas's Order of Preachers in Southern France. "Good" must refer to grace, since the alternative meaning would appear to condemn the body as naturally evil. Yet grace by definition is properly found in the soul, since, for Aquinas, grace is a created immaterial reality. But the very need to interpret the term "good" in this way is made possible only by Aquinas's failure to remain on the metaphorical plane of *sarx*.

Romans 7:22–23 contrasts flesh and spirit in somewhat different terms: "For I delight in the law of God, according to the interior man, but I see in my members another law at war with the law of my mind." Thomas explains that the human being delights in the law with his or her reason, for the law is in harmony with reason.[63] The interior man refers to the soul. Thomas is careful to reject dualism, noting that the term "interior man" here refers to what is primary in us, so that the interior man is not the whole of what is essentially the human being. He explicitly contrasts his position with Plato, who defined the human being as a soul using a body. Thomas also notes that the exterior man refers to what is apparent, namely, the body.[64] He deliberately opposes Platonic dualism in the midst of a commentary that inserts a soul/body distinction into the biblical text.

A proper metaphorical reading of "flesh" would have enabled Thomas to avoid this difficulty. Perhaps one of the reasons that Thomas fails to see the consistently metaphorical sense of the Pauline text is found in Aquinas's assumption that Paul has a firm soul/body distinction. That distinction goes beyond what today's more Jewish reading of the historical Paul would acknowledge. For while Paul's eschatology seems to demand a certain soul/body distinction, his Jewish roots clearly distinguish his anthropology from various types of Greek soul/body distinctions. But Thomas was convinced that a Christianized Aristotelian soul/body distinction is true, and therefore, he would have looked for the presence of this doctrine in Scripture. Thomas also found a very clear soul/body distinction in the Bible, namely, in Wisdom 9:15, which presents a fascinating fusion of Greek philosophical, biblical, and Jew-

63. This reading could be influenced by Peter Lombard. He states that "the other law in my members" (Romans 7:23) refers to the cause of sin being in the flesh and not the soul, since through the transfer of flesh (or human procreation), the sin of Adam is passed on. "The law of the mind" refers to the law of reason (*In Ep. Ad. Rom*, col. 1425).

64. *In ad Rom*. 7, lect. 4, § 585: "Nullus enim delectatur nisi in eo quod est sibi conveniens. Homo autem secundum rationem delectatur in lege Dei; ergo lex Dei est conveniens rationi. Et hoc est quod dicit *condelector legi Dei secundum interiorem hominem*, id est secundum rationem et mentem, quae interior homo dicitur, non quod anima sit effigiata secundum formam hominis, ut Tertullianus posuit, vel quod ipsa sola sit homo, ut Plato posuit, quod homo est anima utens corpore; sed quia id quod est principalius in homine dicitur homo, ut supra dictum est."

ish anthropologies. Thomas cites Wisdom 9:15 several times in his comments on flesh/spirit, usually in the context of discussing the sparks of sin.[65] Thomas's exegesis harmonizes different biblical texts far more than we do with our modern methods. This helps to explain why he identifies a soul/body distinction in Paul's discussion of flesh/spirit. In part because of the Book of Wisdom, Thomas is convinced that Paul has a firm soul/body distinction, which helps to open the door to the more literalistic reading of flesh/spirit.

Another aspect of Thomas's use of Wisdom 9:15 is worth noting. Believing its author to be Solomon, Thomas did not recognize its Greek philosophical roots. It served as a convenient proof text for the effects of original sin on the body in relation to the soul, already beginning with Augustine. Yet one senses Thomas's unease with the passage. He seems to expound on it only once, as he comments on Galatians 5:19 (see below). Usually, he simply cites the verse and moves on. It is as if he can smell the Platonic influences behind Wisdom 9:15![66]

Two other brief passages on Romans 7 are worth considering. Romans 7:23 speaks of "the law of sin which dwells in my members." Thomas identifies this law as the sparks of sin. This spark or law is rooted in the sensitive appetite, whence it is diffused to the other parts of the person. It resists reason, which is Paul's "law of the mind," because for Aquinas, the law of Moses or the Ten Commandments largely overlap with the natural law.[67]

In Romans 7:24, Paul exclaims: "Wretched man that I am!" Thomas employs his usual Augustinian readings. For the human being in grace, his or her misery is found only in the flesh, a sure reference to the sparks of sin or disordered desire for sensual pleasure that are kept in check. But the (mortal) sinner is wretched in both mind and body.[68] Neither the law of sin in the members nor the wretchedness of the human being is explicitly connected to an abiding disorder in the will of the believer. Thomas even implies a partial exclusion of such a disorder: the justified man is miserable *only* in the flesh. Such is the impression left by the text, but Thomas will correct and nuance it elsewhere.

---

65. Cf. ibid., lect. 4, § 590; *ST* I, q. 94, a. 2, obj. 2.

66. Chrysostome Larcher speaks of undeniable Platonic echoes in Wisdom 9:15. See his *Etudes sur le Livre de la Sagesse* (Paris: Lecoffre, 1969), 269.

67. *In ad Rom.* 7, lect. 4, § 588: "Haec autem lex originaliter quidem consistit in appetitu sensitivo, sed diffusive invenitur in omnibus membris, quae deserviunt concupiscentiae ad peccandum. Supra VI, 19: *Sicut exhibuistis membra vestra servire immunditiae*, etc. Et ideo dicit *in membris meis*. Haec autem lex duos effectus in homine habet. Primo namque resistit rationi, et quantum ad hoc dicit *repugnantem legi mentis meae*, id est legi Moysi, quae dicitur lex mentis inquantum consonat menti, vel legi naturali, quae dicitur lex mentis quia naturaliter menti indita est. Supra II, 15: *Qui ostendunt opus legis scriptum in cordibus suis*. Et de hac repugnantia dicitur Gal. V, v. 17: *Caro concupiscit adversus spiritum*."

68. Ibid., lect. 4, § 590: "Unum quidem confitetur, scilicet suam miseriam, cum dicit *infelix*

I will briefly consider two key passages on flesh/spirit in chapter 8 of Thomas's *Romans Commentary*. First, he identifies the law of the Spirit in Romans 8:2 with the Spirit himself as well as his transforming interior effects. The Spirit dwells in the hearts of believers, teaching them to act in a way pleasing to God and redirecting their affect, that is, their will. The Spirit is the interior teacher who both illumines the mind and inclines the will through the gift of charity. The Spirit is the law written on the hearts of believers. The law of the spirit also includes the Spirit's created effects of faith working through love.[69] The justified man who suffers from carnal reason is healed from within. Aquinas transforms Paul's *pneuma* as divine stuff flowing through the bodies of Christians into a systematic exposition of the Holy Spirit's indwelling that brings about moral enlightenment and a new capacity for moral action. Aquinas thus retains Paul's intention to describe a moral/epistemological sphere pleasing to God, a sphere in which the Christian discovers a new moral capacity. Thomas's description of intrinsic grace parallels Paul's realistic vision of *pneuma*. His comments on Romans 8 successfully translate Paul's *pneuma* cosmology into his own original Augustinian-Dionysian-Aristotelian-biblical cosmology, even though he cannot understand Paul's cosmological language within its original cultural context.

Second, the sin that Christ has condemned in the flesh (Romans 8:3) refers to, among other things, the weakening of the sparks of sin in our flesh through the power of Christ's passion.[70] The healing of the disordered emo-

---

ego homo; quod quidem est per peccatum quod in homine habitat, sive quantum ad carnem tantum sicut in iusto, sive etiam quantum ad mentem sicut in peccatore. Prov. XIV, 34: *Miseros facit populos peccatum.* Ps. XXXVII, v. 7: *Miser factus sum et curvatus sum usque in finem.*"

69. *In ad Rom.* 8, lect. 1, §§ 602–3: "Quae quidem lex potest dici, uno modo, Spiritus Sanctus, ut sit sensus: *Lex spiritus,* id est lex quae est spiritus. Lex enim ad hoc datur, ut per eam homines inducantur ad bonum; unde et Philosophus in II Ethic. dicit quod intentio legislatoris est cives facere bonos. Quod quidem lex humana facit, solum notificando quid fieri debeat; sed Spiritus Sanctus, mentem inhabitans, non solum docet quid oporteat fieri, intellectum illuminando de agendis, sed etiam affectum inclinat ad recte agendum. Io. XIV, 26: *Paracletus autem Spiritus Sanctus, quem mittet Pater in nomine meo, ille vos docebit omnia,* quantum ad primum, *et suggeret vobis omnia,* quantum ad secundum, *quaecumque dixero vobis.* Alio modo *lex spiritus* potest dici proprius effectus Spiritus Sancti, scilicet fides per dilectionem operans. Quae quidem et docet interius de agendis, secundum illud infra: *Unctio docebit vos de omnibus,* et inclinat affectum ad agendum, secundum illud II Cor. V, 14: *Charitas Christi urget nos.* Et haec quidem lex spiritus dicitur lex nova, quae vel est ipse Spiritus Sanctus, vel eam in cordibus nostris Spiritus Sanctus facit. Ier. XXXI, 33: *Dabo legem meam in visceribus eorum, et in corde eorum superscribam eam.* De lege autem veteri supra dixit solum quod erat spiritualis, id est a Spiritu Sancto data."

70. Ibid., lect. 1, § 609: "Sed melius est ut dicatur *damnavit peccatum in carne,* id est debilitavit fomitem peccati in carne nostra, *de peccato,* id est ex virtute passionis suae et mortis, quae dicitur peccatum propter similitudinem peccati, ut dictum est, vel quia per hoc factus est hostia pro peccato, quae in sacra Scriptura dicitur peccatum. Os. IV, 8: *Peccata populi mei comedent.* Unde dicit II Cor. V, 21: *Eum qui non noverat peccatum pro nobis Deus fecit peccatum,* idest hostiam pro peccato."

tions begins in baptism through a real sharing in the supernatural power of the dying and resurrecting Christ now available in the sacraments, a doctrine Thomas beautifully expounds in his commentary on Romans 6:1–5. Thomas's conviction concerning the real intrinsic power of grace is rooted in his sacramental realism and the doctrine of Christ's instrumental causality, both of which have profound Pauline and Patristic roots.[71]

Thomas's discussion of the diminished sparks of sin balances the earlier comments on Romans 8:2, where he focused on the healing of intellect and will through the law of the Spirit. Aquinas now adds his Christological convictions concerning the transformation of the whole person through mystical, sacramental union with Christ. In his comments on Romans 8:2, Thomas's focus on the law of the Spirit moving intellect and will left out what Paul meant to include. For the Apostle was referring to the Spirit's transformation of the whole person, since the whole Christian dwells in the sphere of *pneuma*. Thomas's emphasis on Christ's death weakening the sparks of sin that reside in the flesh is also too narrow, for this time, Aquinas fails to add a metaphorical reading of flesh as a legitimate possibility. Thomas restricts Paul's meaning in each case ("the law of the Spirit," "sin in the flesh"), yet the overall outcome is surprisingly Pauline: the gift of the Spirit that is the fruit of Christ's passion, death, and resurrection brings about the intrinsic transformation of the whole person, mind, heart and body; that is, the whole person is transferred from the sphere of *sarx* to the sphere of *pneuma*. The details of Thomas's exegesis are problematic from a historical perspective, yet the doctrinal synthesis he constructs largely overcomes these difficulties. Aquinas's conviction about the intrinsic power of Christ's passion applied to us in baptism leads him to emphasize that conversion and the following of Christ bring about the gradual healing of the whole person, which seems to be one of Paul's main points in Romans 8 (even if Paul's assumption about his pre-Christian moral integrity would have struck Aquinas as strange). Aquinas distinguishes flesh and spirit where Paul did not (the law of the spirit, flesh as the sparks of sin), yet he also unites these themes to return to Paul's driving intention. It seems that one can explain this oddity only by recognizing that Aquinas's overall theological anthropology is very much in harmony with the anthropology that Paul describes in Romans 7–8. Aquinas's exegetical insights lead him astray here and there, yet his driving theological intuitions bring him back to the Pauline teaching.

In summary, there are five key characteristics of Aquinas's reading of flesh/

---

71. See my "The Place of Romans 6 in Aquinas's Doctrine of Sacramental Causality: A Balance of History and Metaphysics," in *Ressourcement Thomism: Sacred Doctrine, the Sacraments and the Moral Life*, ed. Reinhard Hütter and Matthew Levering (Washington, D.C.: The Catholic University of America Press, 2010), 136–49.

spirit in the *Romans Commentary*. First, influenced by Augustine, Thomas often combines metaphorical and literalistic readings of flesh. Second, Thomas favors the (narrowly interpreted) late Augustine's conclusions on the identity of the carnal self in Romans 7, which in turn pushes him toward a more literalistic exegesis of flesh. Third, even Thomas's metaphorical readings of flesh are problematic, as they focus on temptations rooted in the fallen sensitive appetites. Thomas's metaphorical flesh is not metaphorical enough. Fourth, the Augustinian explanation that roots the disorder of the passions in self-love is noticeably and completely missing in the *Romans Commentary* treatment of flesh/spirit. Fifth, Thomas sometimes misinterprets Paul on the details of flesh/spirit, yet then tends to proceed to broader theological conclusions that are surprisingly close to the historical Paul.

Aquinas received an already systematized Paul from Augustine and his disciples. The original cosmology had already become unintelligible in Augustine's time. Furthermore, Augustine had legitimized a partial equivalency between Pauline flesh and the body weighed down by sin. Yet Thomas's adherence to Augustine was not driven by blind obedience to theological authority. Aquinas's subtle yet radical transformation of key Augustinian doctrines, including the central anthropological doctrines of the *imago Dei* and illumination epistemology, manifests Thomas's willingness to break with the Latin Father who seems to dominate much of medieval theology. Such a break with the weaker aspects of Augustine's exegesis seems not to have been possible in this part of Aquinas's appropriation of Pauline anthropology, most likely due to an absence of adequate exegetical tools. Yet Augustine had also successfully translated key Pauline intuitions about sin and grace, which in turn helped Aquinas's exegesis. Augustine's positive influence on that exegesis becomes much more evident in Thomas's treatment of Pauline flesh/spirit in the *Galatians Commentary* and the *Summa theologiae*.

Thomas's *Galatians Commentary* on Flesh/Spirit

Thomas often cites Galatians 5:17 in his discussion of flesh/spirit in the *Romans Commentary*, partly because he follows Augustine in mistakenly identifying the human subject of Galatians 5, where Paul offers a moral exhortation to Christians, with the carnal self of Romans 7. A quick glance at Thomas's direct comments on this passage and the surrounding verses in Paul's letter promises to be enlightening.[72]

72. This commentary is difficult to date. Jean-Pierre Torrell proposes that it could have been taught between 1265 and 1268. See his *Saint Thomas Aquinas*, vol. 1, *The Person and His Work*, trans. Robert Royal (Washington, D.C.: The Catholic University of America Press, 1996), 255.

Galatians 5:16–17 begins a section in Paul's letter that offers an extensive list of vices, both spiritual and carnal: "Walk by the Spirit, and do not gratify the desires of the flesh. For the flesh lusts against the spirit, and the spirit against the flesh. The two are directly opposed. That is why you do not do what you want to do." Thomas's comments on these two verses offer a simple, literalistic reading of "flesh." The desires of the flesh are pleasures of the flesh. They are not any sensual desires, but superfluous wants that go beyond bodily necessity, beyond that which remains within the natural order. Flesh lusting against spirit refers to carnal concupiscence. The pleasures of the flesh seek the goods that are below us, drawing the spirit away from the spiritual goods that it naturally seeks, since spirit lusts against the flesh.[73] Thomas's exegesis in this fourth *lectio* on Galatians 5 is terribly unsatisfying.

But the beginning of the subsequent *lectio* presents a very different kind of reading. Galatians 5:19 speaks of the works of the flesh, but Thomas notices that the list includes idolatry and divisions among believers. He offers two

73. Thomas Aquinas, *Super epistolam ad Galatas Lectura* [henceforth *In ad Gal.*], in *Super Epistolas S. Pauli Lectura*, vol. 1, ed. Raphaelis Cai, 8th ed. (Rome: Marietti, 1953) 5, lect. 4, §§ 309–313: "Ideo autem spiritu ambulandum est quia liberat a corruptione carnis. Unde sequitur *et desideria carnis non perficietis*, id est delectationes carnis, quas caro suggerit. Hoc desiderabat Apostolus, dicens Rom. c. VII, 24: *Infelix ego homo, quis me liberabit de corpore mortis huius? gratia Dei*, etc. Et postea concludit in octavo capite (v. 1): *Nihil ergo damnationis est his, qui sunt in Christo Iesu, qui non secundum carnem ambulant.* Huius rationem, ibidem (v. 2), subiungit dicens: *Quia lex spiritus vitae in Christo Iesu liberavit me a lege*, etc. Et hoc est speciale desiderium sanctorum, ut non perficiant desideria ad quae caro instigat, ita tamen, quod in hoc non includantur desideria quae sunt ad necessitatem carnis, sed quae sunt ad superfluitatem. Consequenter cum dicit *Caro enim concupiscit*, etc., ponit necessitatem huius beneficii, quae est ex impugnatione carnis et spiritus. Et primo ponit ipsam impugnationem; secundo manifestat eam per evidens signum, ibi *Haec enim invicem adversantur*, etc. Dicit ergo: necessarium est quod per spiritum carnis desideria superetis. Nam *caro concupiscit adversus spiritum.* Sed hic videtur esse dubium, quia cum concupiscere sit actus animae tantum, non videtur quod competat carni. Ad hoc dicendum est, secundum Augustinum, quod caro dicitur concupiscere inquantum anima secundum ipsam carnem concupiscit, sicut oculus dicitur videre, cum potius anima per oculum videat. Sic ergo anima per carnem concupiscit, quando ea, quae delectabilia sunt, secundum carnem appetit. Per se vero anima concupiscit, quando delectatur in his quae sunt secundum spiritum, sicut sunt opera virtutum et contemplatio divinorum et meditatio sapientiae. Sap. VI, 21: *Concupiscentia itaque sapientiae deducet ad regnum perpetuum*, etc. Sed, si caro concupiscit per spiritum, quomodo concupiscit adversus eum? In hoc, scilicet quod concupiscentia carnis impedit concupiscentiam spiritus. Cum enim delectabilia carnis sint bona quae sunt infra nos, delectabilia vero spiritus bona quae sunt supra nos, contingit quod cum anima circa inferiora, quae sunt carnis, occupatur, retrahitur a superioribus, quae sunt spiritus. Sed videtur etiam dubium de hoc quod dicit, scilicet quod *spiritus concupiscit adversus carnem.* Si enim accipiamus hic spiritum pro Spiritu Sancto, concupiscentia autem Spiritus Sancti sit contra mala, consequens videtur quod caro, adversus quam concupiscit spiritus, sit mala, et sic sequitur error Manichaei. Respondeo. Dicendum est quod spiritus non concupiscit adversus naturam carnis, sed adversus eius desideria, quae scilicet sunt ad superfluitatem. Unde et supra dictum est: *Desideria carnis*, scilicet superflua, *non perficietis.* In necessariis enim spiritus non contradicit carni, quia, ut dicitur Ephes. c. V, 29, *Nemo carnem suam odio habuit.*"

possible interpretations. The first invokes book 14 of *The City of God*. "Flesh" is taken for the whole human being, referring to the person who lives for him- or herself, doing everything out of disordered self-love, which is called the work of the flesh. Thomas here describes a human being in the state of mortal sin. The second possibility concerns the root and end of sin. Idolatry and other "noncarnal" sins are ultimately carnal because they are consummated in car- nal pleasure, such as luxury and gluttony. Thomas could be alluding back to Romans 1, which roots the radical perversities and sins of the pagans in idola- try. Thomas argues that the root of sin matches its consummation, because the sparks of sin are the principle or beginning of all sins. Again, Thomas cites Wisdom 9:15, but now adds a brief (and rare) explanation on the body weigh- ing down the soul. Solomon describes how the body weakens the intellect's capabilities and hinders the soul's perfect or complete operation, an allusion to virtuous acts.[74]

Thomas does not tell us which interpretation is better, a move that is somewhat typical of his exegetical style. The present passage is significant because, for the first time in his biblical commentary on Paul's flesh/spirit, Thomas evokes Augustinian self-love to explain the metaphorical sense of flesh. Unlike the *Romans Commentary*, the disordered will makes an appear- ance in Thomas's *Galatians Commentary* exposition of flesh/spirit. We can al- ready see that Thomas's exposition of flesh/spirit in the *Romans Commentary* does not present his complete view on the subject. This will become even more evident as I consider a few key passages in the *Summa theologiae*.

Aquinas's *Summa Theologiae* on Flesh/Spirit

The treatise on sin and grace in the *Summa theologiae* (I-II, q. 81–114) oc- casionally cites a flesh/spirit passage from Romans 7. These Pauline quotations essentially serve as convenient proof texts in the *sed contra* of various articles,

---

74. *In ad Gal.* 5, lect. 5, § 320: "Dubitatur autem circa primum. Primo quidem de hoc quod Apostolus hic quaedam ponit, quae non pertinent ad carnem, quae tamen dicit esse opera carnis, sicut idolorum servitus, sectae, aemulationes, et huiusmodi. Respondeo. Dicendum est, secundum Augustinum Lib. XIV de Civ. Dei, c. II, quod secundum carnem vivit quicumque vivit secundum seipsum. Unde caro hic accipitur pro toto homine. Quidquid ergo provenit ex inordinato amore sui, dicitur opus carnis. Vel dicendum est, quod aliquod peccatum potest dici carnale dupliciter, scilicet quantum ad consummationem: et sic dicuntur carnalia illa tantum quae consummantur in delectatione carnis, scilicet luxuria et gula; et quantum ad radicem: et sic omnia peccata di- cuntur carnalia, inquantum ex corruptione carnis anima aggravatur, ut dicitur Sap. IX, 15; ex quo intellectus debilitatus facilius decipi potest, et impeditur a sua perfecta operatione. Unde et ex hoc sequuntur vitia, scilicet haereses, sectae, et alia huiusmodi. Et hoc modo dicitur quod fomes est principium omnium peccatorum." Thomas returns to the same Augustinian exegesis of Gala- tians 5 in *ST* I-II, q. 72, a. 2, ad 1.

usually confirmed by Augustine's interpretation. The sense is consistently literalistic, with a focus on "flesh" as signifying the sparks of sin. The metaphorical interpretation of flesh/spirit is noticeably absent.

Yet I will argue that Thomas's use of flesh/spirit passages in the *Summa* is misleading if we wish to evaluate how Thomas appropriates the teaching that stands behind the flesh/spirit language. Thomas is hardly original in his use of Romans 7 as a short authoritative response on the continuing burden of sensual concupiscence in the lives of Christians. Alexander of Hales, among others, preceded Aquinas on this point. Furthermore, Thomas's direct use of Romans 7 appears not to have a significant function in his overall *Summa* doctrine of sin and grace. The biblical quotations tend to remain isolated in the *sed contra*. The articles that employ Paul's flesh/spirit passages can easily reach their conclusions on the basis of other Scripture passages, established Catholic doctrine, Thomas's appropriation of Augustinian and Aristotelian anthropology, Christian experience, and other theological sources.[75] In other words, Thomas's use of Romans 7 has little of the nuance and complexity that we saw in his *Romans Commentary*. One could easily conclude that the *Summa* appropriation of these passages manifest Thomas's (unsuccessful) appropriation of Pauline flesh/spirit *doctrine*, but I will show that this is precisely not the case. Thomas's analysis of the root causes of sin and his mature doctrine of the relative fragility of the human being with or without grace tells us far more about the relation between Aquinas's thought and Paul's flesh/spirit doctrine in Romans. A brief look at some key articles will confirm this claim.

I noted above that a discussion of pride and disordered self-love was very

75. In *ST* I-II, q. 74, a. 3, s.c., Thomas uses Romans 7:15 to show that sin can be found in "sensuality." But the key to Thomas's conclusion in the corpus is found in the connection he posits between the emotions and the will. I-II, q. 74, a. 4, s.c. interprets Romans 7:14 with the late Augustine, referring it to graced human beings, leading to the conclusion that disordered motions of the sense appetites by themselves do not constitute mortal sins, since the man in grace is said to experience them. But the main point of the article is that mortal sin must involve the ultimate end, which is chosen or refused through reason, not the emotions alone. I-II q. 77, a. 2, s.c. speaks of the law in my members of Romans 7:23 as concupiscence repugnant to the law of the mind, which proves that reason can be conquered by passion. The corpus of the texts appeals to everyday experience and numerous other biblical passages to prove the same point. I-II q. 77, a. 8, s.c. refers Romans 7:5 to sins of passion that bring death, i.e. mortal sin. But the main point of the article is that mortal sin can be enacted only with the consent of reason (i.e., intellect and will), which the Romans passage hardly proves. I-II q. 83, a. 1, s.c. refers the flesh in which no good dwells (Romans 7:18) to the body in distinction from the whole soul, both immaterial and sensual. The soul alone is the subject of virtue (which obviously includes the emotions for Thomas). Thomas's Aristotelian virtue ethics and anthropology demand the same conclusion. I-II q. 91, a. 6, s.c. cites Romans 7:23 in reference to the sparks of sin, but the corpus discussion has little relation to Romans. There are also two very interesting uses of Romans 7 in I-II q. 109 (a. 8, co. and a. 10, ad 3), to which I will refer below.

much absent from the *Romans Commentary* treatment of flesh/spirit. This gap is significant, for the doctrine of disordered self-love is central to Augustine's appropriation of Paul's flesh/spirit cosmology that is faithful to the apostle while developing his thought. Ironically, Augustine is in some ways omnipresent in chapters 6 through 8 of Thomas's *Romans Commentary*, except for this part of the Bishop of Hippo's teaching. The great Latin Father is also a crucial influence on the *Summa* treatise on sin and grace, but in a new way.

Question 77 of the *Prima secundae* treats the sense appetite (in its disordered desires) as a cause of sin. The first two articles of question 75 already offered a systematic presentation of the will as the primary cause of sin. But in question 77, Thomas sees the need to return to the problem of the fallen will in a discussion of the disordered emotions as causes of sin. Article 4 asks whether the love of self is the principal cause of sin. We are clearly in Augustine's territory, as confirmed by the *City of God* citation in the *sed contra*, which refers to the source of the two cities' identities: love of God and love of self. The article's corpus recalls the disordered desire for temporal or mutable goods as the definition of the cause of sin. But where does this unnatural appetite come from? The answer is simply the disordered love of self.[76] Thomas then explicitly rejects sensual concupiscence as the root cause of sin. Responding to an objection that cites Romans 7:8 on "sin working all concupiscence in me," Aquinas simply roots all such disordered desire in the primary disorder of excessive self-love.[77] The ultimate problem of the human being is found not in the disordered passions but in the depths of his will, the faculty of love. Thomas's analysis of vice and the passions departs from Aristotle and the ancient Greeks on a crucial point and joins Augustine.[78] Thomas thus also moves toward the Pauline meaning of flesh.

76. *ST* I-II, q. 77, a. 4, co.: "Respondeo dicendum quod, sicut supra dictum est, propria et per se causa peccati accipienda est ex parte conversionis ad commutabile bonum; ex qua quidem parte omnis actus peccati procedit ex aliquo inordinato appetitu alicuius temporalis boni. Quod autem aliquis appetat inordinate aliquod temporale bonum, procedit ex hoc quod inordinate amat seipsum, hoc enim est amare aliquem, velle ei bonum. Unde manifestum est quod inordinatus amor sui est causa omnis peccati."

77. *ST* I-II, q. 77, a. 4, obj. 2: "Praeterea, Apostolus dicit, Rom. 7:8: *Occasione accepta, peccatum per mandatum operatum est in me omnem concupiscentiam*, ubi Glossa dicit quod *bona est lex, quae, dum concupiscentiam prohibet, omne malum prohibet*, quod dicitur propter hoc, quia concupiscentia est causa omnis peccati. Sed concupiscentia est alia passio ab amore, ut supra habitum est. Ergo amor sui non est causa omnis peccati." Ad 2: "Ad secundum dicendum quod concupiscentia, qua aliquis appetit sibi bonum, reducitur ad amorem sui sicut ad causam, ut iam dictum est."

78. The judgment of Alasdair MacIntyre and John Rist is therefore correct, namely, that because of his doctrine of grace (and sin), Aquinas breaks with the ethics of Aristotle on crucial points. See MacIntyre's *Whose Justice? Which Rationality* (London: Duckworth, 1988), 205; John M. Rist, "Augustine, Aristotelianism and Aquinas: Three Varieties of Philosophical Adaption," in

The very next *Summa* article (I-II, q. 77, a. 5) further develops this Augustinian response. In scholastic theology, 1 John 2:16 had become a quasi-definition for three types of sins: concupiscence of the flesh, concupiscence of the eyes, and concupiscence of life.[79] Thomas considers in what way these three disordered desires are causes of sin. All disordered desires of the emotions are covered by these categories. Aquinas's analysis treats each of them as a modality or expression of disordered self-love. Thomas thus moves toward Augustine's mature, relatively holistic theological anthropology that refuses to grant the soul/body tension primacy in the hierarchy of the perduring wounds of sin.[80]

Thomas is not piously repeating a central Augustinian doctrine, even though its absence in Aquinas's direct treatment of flesh/spirit language might leave that impression, given the oddity of omitting any discussion of the believer's disordered will during the extensive discussion of sin in chapters 6–8 of the *Romans Commentary*. The same impression can be gained from the relative absence or sparsity of the language of disordered self-love in the *Summa* treatise on sin and grace, which Thomas barely discusses outside of the two articles just mentioned. Yet that too can be explained. Aquinas prefers to speak of the disordered will or pride rather than disordered self-love, while the intended teaching behind all three terms is largely the same. Three key texts confirm this interpretation of Aquinas.

First, in I-II, q. 82, a. 3, Thomas adopts Augustine's teaching on the disobedience of the will as the cause of the loss of original justice. Once the human being was no longer subject to the will of God, the soul's passions became disordered and turned toward changing goods. The rebellious will of Adam and Eve is the root of all disordered desire. This loss of original justice is what is formal or most important in original sin. What is material or consequent upon this loss is the disorder of (sensual) concupiscence. The enduring wounds of sin mirror the root cause of Adam and Eve's rebellion.

Aquinas the Augustinian, ed. Michael Dauphinais, Barry David, and Matthew Levering (Washington, D.C.: The Catholic University of America Press, 2007), 89. However, Thomas does not break with Aristotle on our fundamental inclination toward the good. Rather, in a synthesis of Aristotelian ethics and the Augustinian doctrine of sin and grace, he maintains that sin weakens this inclination without destroying it (see *ST* I-II, q. 85, aa. 1–2).

79. E.g. *Summa halensis* III, inq. 3, tract 7, q. 1, prologue.

80. *ST* I-II, q. 77, a. 5, co.: "Respondeo dicendum quod, sicut iam dictum est, inordinatus amor sui est causa omnis peccati. In amore autem sui includitur inordinatus appetitus boni, unusquisque enim appetit bonum ei quem amat. Unde manifestum est quod inordinatus appetitus boni est causa omnis peccati. Bonum autem dupliciter est obiectum sensibilis appetitus, in quo sunt animae passiones, quae sunt causa peccati, uno modo absolute, secundum quod est obiectum concupiscibilis; alio modo, sub ratione ardui, prout est obiectum irascibilis, ut supra dictum est."

Second, in I-II, q. 83, a. 4, Thomas states that the actual inclination to sin that remains in us is chiefly a problem of the will. Thomas devotes most of the article to Augustine's *The City of God* teaching that the "infection" of original guilt *manifests* itself most of all in the motions of our sexual organs. Aquinas nuances the teaching by relating the term "infection" to the transfer of original sin, which occurs through procreation, since that is how fallen nature is passed from one human being to another.[81] Thomas's answer is a clear, implicit rejection of the notion that the chief inclination to sin is caused by disordered sensual desires. Original sin may be most *apparent* in such desires, and they are closely connected to the *transmission* of original sin, but in the order of moral action, these desires are hardly the primary difficulty.

Finally, I-II, q. 84, a. 2, ad 3, identifies pride with self-love. Since pride is the beginning of all sin, self-love is also the root of all sin. As noted above, Thomas prefers to describe the heart of our fallen condition not so much in terms of excessive self-love, but rather in terms of pride and the disordered will.[82]

The primacy of will in our continuing inclination toward sin, and self-love as the root of all disordered desire, are Thomas's two unspoken doctrines that underlie his entire study of flesh/spirit in the *Romans Commentary*. It is perplexing that Aquinas fails to mention the disordered will and self-love in his exegesis of flesh/spirit and his extensive discussions of concupiscence in chapters 6–8 of the same commentary. But once we recognize this strange oversight, we also find that Thomas's personal appropriation of Paul's flesh/spirit *doctrine* is far more nuanced than the *Romans Commentary* lets on. Thomas's flesh/spirit doctrine is also far more Augustinian than the commentary suggests (here I am thinking of the late Augustine). This, too, is strange, since Thomas's flesh/spirit exegesis in the commentary is already in some ways heavily marked by the late Augustine. That also means that Thomas's flesh/spirit doctrine is far more open to the proper metaphorical reading of the terms than the commentary suggests. In Romans, Paul uses the term "flesh" to describe a metaphysical and moral sphere radically opposed to God in which unbelievers dwell. Galatians 5 shows that the believer has been partially but not fully healed through grace, and thus continues to struggle against egocentric and ungodly desires, a doctrinal conviction that manifests itself in the moral exhortations found in Romans 6 and 8. Thomas expresses a similar doctrine by his conclusion that the believer is not yet fully ordered to God because of (1) continuing weakness of will, and (2) the disordered passions that have been

---

81. We might also keep in mind Thomas's subtle correction of Augustine on the possibility of sexual intercourse without lust in *ST* II-II, q. 153, a. 2.

82. In the *Summa theologiae*, Thomas uses the term *amor sui* thirty times, but *superbia* over two hundred times.

only partially healed through grace.[83] In other words, Thomas's exegetical failure to offer a properly metaphorical reading of Pauline flesh goes against his own Augustinian doctrinal convictions as expressed in the *Summa*. The primary problem with Thomas's exegetical mistake is not doctrinal but linguistic, a failure to recognize the genre of Paul's flesh/spirit language as excluding a literalist reading. The main inspiration for this exegetical mistake seems to have been none other than Augustine.

The focus of my study of Thomas's flesh/spirit doctrine in the *Summa* up to now has mostly concerned the continuing effects of the fall for all of humanity, including those in grace. Yet a proper study of Thomas's appropriation of Pauline flesh/spirit is not complete unless we return to Paul's cosmology, a background notion that served Paul's argument about the law in Romans 7, which Augustine transformed into a systematic anthropology. One might be tempted to conclude that Aquinas pays insufficient attention to this cosmology in his *Summa* teaching on sin. Here, too, a proper exegesis is tricky, because Aquinas's treatment of the state of sin is not complete in the *Prima secundae* questions on sin. Instead, we need to consider the treatise on grace at the end of the *Prima secundae* for a more adequate response. The same section of the *Summa* will also better manifest Thomas's appropriation of Paul's *pneuma* cosmology.

I will briefly mention three key aspects of Thomas's mature doctrine of grace that show his appropriation of Paul's flesh/spirit doctrine. Bernard Lonergan and Joseph Wawrykow have already offered thorough analyses of Aquinas's evolution in the areas of divine supernatural motion, the gratuity of grace, and justification.[84] My brief comments will build on the fruits of their labor insofar as it relates to the theme of Pauline flesh/spirit.

First, Aquinas's teaching on justification evolved significantly. The constant theme that runs through much of the young Thomas's *Sentences* treatise on grace (book II, distinctions 26–29) is that the human being prepares for justification by his or her own natural abilities: "The human subject is always susceptible to grace."[85] "Good ungraced works cause a certain ability for grace."[86] This notion of self-preparation for grace is so strong that Thomas

83. Therefore, Thomas's anthropology could well be as holistic as Paul's, though Thomas's understanding of the soul/body distinction is quite different from Paul's.

84. Bernard Lonergan, S.J., *Grace and Freedom: Operative Grace in the Thought of St. Thomas Aquinas*, vol. 1 of *Collected Works of Bernard Lonergan* (Toronto: University of Toronto Press, 1988); Joseph P. Wawrykow, *God's Grace and Human Action: "Merit" in the Theology of Thomas Aquinas* (Notre Dame, Ind.: University of Notre Dame Press, 1995).

85. Thomas Aquinas, *Scriptum super Sententiis* II (Paris: Sumptibus P. Lethielleux, 1929), d. 26, q. 1, a. 2, ad 2: "receptibilitas gratiae semper subjectum consequitur."

86. *Scriptum super Sententiis* II, d. 27, q. 1, a. 4: "Sed tamen opera bona ante donum gratiae facta ... causant enim quamdam habilitatem ad gratiam."

implies that the supernatural habit, including justification, is *almost* merited: "If the human being would prepare himself by doing what is within himself, without a doubt grace would follow."[87] "A human being, even if he would never have committed sin or sinned by omission … would have sinned in this, that he did not prepare himself for grace."[88] In other words, if the fallen creature would act virtuously, grace would almost naturally follow, and hence grace seems virtually merited. This *quasi* semi-Pelagian tendency in the young Thomas is amplified in his notion of ungraced works as the material cause of sanctification, with grace being the formal cause. The natural material cause limits the gratuity of grace, so that the formal cause of justification (grace) is virtually necessary once there is a due disposition of the matter. As Joseph Wawrykow has pointed out, Thomas posits the congruent merit of the first grace (i.e., justification) through the human being's ungraced good works.[89] All of this implies a fallen nature that is relatively intact. The early Thomas has no adequate medieval equivalent to Paul's *sarx* cosmology.

The *Summa* treatment of conversion is radically different. The human being before justification is radically incapable of preparing for grace without God's supernatural help. The natural virtues as a material cause of justification are absent. Without a gratuitous, presanctifying divine motion that turns us back toward God, we are not susceptible to grace. The preparation for grace demands God's unmerited motion in our free decision. This is abundantly clear in I-II, q. 109, a. 6. The same weakness pertains to the sinner who has fallen from the life of grace.[90] The egocentric existence of Pauline flesh is so radical that only gratuitous grace can turn us toward a God-centered life.[91] Lonergan and Wawrykow help us to recognize how crucial Aquinas's mature

87. Ibid., d. 28, q. 1, a. 3, ad 5: "Si autem praepararet se faciendo quod in se est, proculdubio gratiam consequeretur per quam vitam aeternam mereri posset."

88. Ibid.: "homo etsi numquam transgrederetur vel omitteret, nihilominus tamen peccato originali subjectus esset, a quo non nisi per gratiam liberari potest: pro quo merito subiret damnationem, et etiam ad legitimam aetatem deveniens in hoc ipso peccaret quod se ad gratiam non praepararet."

89. Ibid., d. 27, q. 1, a. 4, ad 4: " indignum potest sumi dupliciter. Vel negative tantum, et sic Deus dat gratiam indignis, quia his qui non sunt sufficienter ad hoc digni, sed tamen habent aliquam dispositionem ad recipiendum, ex quo dicuntur quodammodo ex congruo gratiam mereri." See Wawrykow, *God's Grace and Human Action*, 84–91.

90. *ST* I-II, q. 109, a. 7. One should also note Bernard Lonergan's masterful exposition of Aquinas's evolving understanding of divine action. A rich, original metaphysics of divine operation joined with a more biblical and Augustinian understanding of providence provide part of the essential foundation for Thomas's mature doctrine of grace. The late Aquinas's teaching on grace is much more Pauline partly because of metaphysical developments. Athens need not be opposed to Jerusalem.

91. The same mature doctrine is clearly reflected in *In ad Rom.* 3, lect. 3, § 302; 8, lect. 3 § 635, lect. 6, § 707.

metaphysics of divine motion was in his evolution toward a richly Pauline doctrine of the gratuity of grace. Paul's dualistic cosmology may have found its medieval equivalent.

Second, Thomas's convictions about the moral capacities of the ungraced human being follow a parallel development. The young Thomas insists that all mortal sin can be avoided even without grace.[92] All direct moral precepts can be fulfilled without the help of grace.[93] The ungraced person can love God above all things with a natural love.[94] The moral abilities of the sinner are astounding.

In I-II, q. 109, a. 8 of the *Summa*, Thomas insists that the ungraced human being is incapable of avoiding all further mortal sins. Such a moral triumph would essentially require a heart firmly set on the good, that is, on God. Yet the infinite good is precisely where the ungraced heart is not adequately ordered. Life is filled with potential pitfalls, many of which cannot be foreseen. Our natural practical reason often struggles to discern the good and the bad in concrete situations, a task that becomes impossible to fulfill perfectly without a heart already utterly inclined to God and guided by his Spirit. Interestingly, the two main challenges facing the sinner that Thomas mentions are the disordered heart and the limits of practical reason, not the sparks of sin in the sensitive appetites.[95]

Third, and here we return to the believer's struggle against "flesh" in Galatians 5 and Romans 6, the late Aquinas insists that the graced human being has a radical dependency on the interior workings of the Spirit to remain in grace because of a certain fragility, in contrast to his earlier, more optimistic anthropology.[96] In the *Romans Commentary*, Thomas tends to focus his expli-

92. *Scriptum super Sententiis* II, d. 28, q. 1, a. 2: "Sed peccatum mortale requirit consensum determinatum; unde si potest vitare hoc et illud, potest eadem ratione vitare omnia.... Peccatum autem committendum potest homo vitare etiam sine gratia, quantumcumque in peccato mortali existat."

93. Ibid., d. 28, q. 1, a. 3: "Dicendum est ergo quod praecepta legis, quantum ad id quod directe sub praecepto cadit, potest aliquis implere per liberum arbitrium sine gratia gratis data vel gratum faciente, si tamen gratia accipiatur pro aliquo habitu infuso."

94. Ibid., ad 2: "Potest enim aliquis, etiam caritatem non habens, diligere proximum et Deum, etiam super omnia."

95. On the other hand, the same *Summa* article (I-II, q. 109, a. 8, co.) refers to the corruption of the sensual appetite as the main reason for the believer's inability to avoid all venial sins, an explication of Romans 7:25: "In my mind, I serve the law of God, but in my flesh the law of sin." Yet the challenge here is venial sins, not mortal sins. Furthermore, I would argue that this too can be understood only in light of Thomas's previous discussion on self-love as the root of all sin and the weakness of the will as the primary challenge in the moral life. See also the study of q. 109, a. 9 below.

96. See *Scriptum super Sententiis* II, d. 29, expos. lit.; Thomas Aquinas, *Quaestiones disputatae de veritate* q. 24, a. 13.

cation of the moral challenge facing believers on the sparks of sin residing in the sensitive appetites. But the key article in the *Summa* treatise on grace (I-II, q. 109, a. 9) has a much more holistic approach to the ongoing struggle between flesh and spirit. Those who are in grace continue to suffer from the corruption of the flesh, which "serves the law of sin," quoting Romans 7:25. Yet there is also a certain obscurity of mind, for Romans 8:26 states that "we do not know how to pray as we ought." We cannot adequately foresee the challenges of life, and we do not know ourselves perfectly, for as Wisdom 9:14 says, "The thoughts of mortals are timid, and uncertain [is] our foresight." Therefore, it is necessary that we be directed and protected by God's continuing influence of grace. That is why we pray: "lead us not into temptation." Sanctifying grace has begun to transform our interior being, yet that process is hardly consummated in this life. In this article, Thomas mentions three continuing sources of fragility: the sparks of sin, the limits of the practical intellect, and a lack of self-knowledge. He sees no need to mention the obvious, namely, disordered self-love.[97]

Thomas thus develops an anthropology that can account for Paul's moral exhortations in Galatians 5 and Romans 6–8. Paul focused on pastoral aims in his letters and seemed unaware of a need to develop a systematic anthropology. Yet once the theological question emerges and a simple *sarx/pneuma* dualism becomes inadequate for dealing with the moral challenges of Christians, some type of doctrinal development seems necessary. Aquinas's systematic doctrine continues Augustine's project of filling gaps in Paul's anthropology.

I should mention a crucial difference between Aquinas and Augustine on

---

97. *ST* I-II, q. 109, a. 9, co.: "Respondeo dicendum quod, sicut supra dictum est, homo ad recte vivendum dupliciter auxilio Dei indiget. Uno quidem modo, quantum ad aliquod habituale donum, per quod natura humana corrupta sanetur; et etiam sanata elevetur ad operanda opera meritoria vitae aeternae, quae excedunt proportionem naturae. Alio modo indiget homo auxilio gratiae ut a Deo moveatur ad agendum. Quantum igitur ad primum auxilii modum, homo in gratia existens non indiget alio auxilio gratiae, quasi aliquo alio habitu infuso. Indiget tamen auxilio gratiae secundum alium modum, ut scilicet a Deo moveatur ad recte agendum. Et hoc propter duo. Primo quidem ratione generali, propter hoc quod, sicut supra dictum est, nulla res creata potest in quemcumque actum prodire nisi virtute motionis divinae. Secundo, ratione speciali, propter conditionem status humanae naturae. Quae quidem licet per gratiam sanetur quantum ad mentem, remanet tamen in ea corruptio et infectio quantum ad carnem, per quam *servit legi peccati*, ut dicitur ad Rom. 7:25. Remanet etiam quaedam ignorantiae obscuritas in intellectu, secundum quam, ut etiam dicitur ad Rom. 8:26: *Quid oremus sicut oportet, nescimus.* Propter varios enim rerum eventus, et quia etiam nosipsos non perfecte cognoscimus, non possumus ad plenum scire quid nobis expediat; secundum illud Sap. 9:14: *Cogitationes mortalium timidae, et incertae providentiae nostrae.* Et ideo necesse est nobis ut a Deo dirigamur et protegamur, qui omnia novit et omnia potest. Et propter hoc etiam renatis in filios Dei per gratiam, convenit dicere: *Et ne nos inducas in tentationem*, et, *Fiat voluntas tua sicut in caelo et in terra*, et caetera quae in oratione Dominica continentur ad hoc pertinentia."

the fragility of the will, the key doctrine that enables them to appropriate the properly holistic reading of Pauline flesh. The late Aquinas can make sense of the ungraced human being as radically turned away from God in his will without following the Augustinian implication that the will radically darkens or weakens the speculative intellect. It is striking how little the late Aquinas modifies his confidence in the pagan philosophers' capacity for truth, all the while turning toward an Augustinian analysis of justification and the weakness of the ungraced will. Aquinas insists on maintaining a kind of firewall between the will and the speculative intellect, though it is not impregnable.[98] Thus, the *Summa* treatise on grace focuses its analysis of human weakness on the will and the limits of the practical intellect while hardly mentioning the speculative intellect. Augustine and Aquinas hardly intend the same doctrine when they refer to "self-love." The same neat separation between the will and the speculative intellect continues in Aquinas's analysis of the graced person's moral challenges.[99] The late Aquinas's more Augustinian doctrine of sin and grace equips him with significant theological tools by which he can more fully appropriate some of Paul's doctrinal intuitions behind the flesh/spirit language and its properly metaphorical meaning, even as he never quite attains a metaphorical reading of the biblical letter. Yet Aquinas moves closer to Paul with Augustine while refusing to follow a common medieval Augustinian interpretation of self-love as it relates to the integrity of the speculative intellect, the innate human ability to grasp the truth. Thomas's mature flesh/spirit anthropology does not simply become more Pauline by becoming more Augustinian. Aquinas's thought is far more subtle and complex. Is that not the genius of Aquinas: a constant return to the biblical and patristic sources in an ever-original way?

Finally, Aquinas argues for a tight connection between metaphysics and our ethical capacities. The sphere of flesh that is the fruit of the Fall intrinsically restricts the ability of the sinner to choose and enact the good. Likewise, the sphere of the Spirit transforms believers from within. Only their new metaphysical status enables them to live the law of Christ. The inseparability of metaphysics and ethics is precisely what we find in Paul's flesh/spirit cosmology in Romans. Created grace thus appears as the adequate medieval translation of Paul's metaphysical/moral cosmology. Without intrinsic, created grace, Thomas's doctrine would be inadequately Pauline!

---

98. *ST* I-II, q. 85, a. 3.

99. See Alasdair MacIntyre, *Three Rival Versions of Moral Enquiry: Encyclopaedia, Genealogy and Tradition* (Notre Dame, Ind.: University of Notre Dame Press, 1990), 82–115.

Evaluation

A few characteristics of Aquinas's Pauline exegesis manifest themselves in his treatment of flesh/spirit. First, Thomas does not always recognize the literary genre that Paul employs. Yet such limitations need not be fatal for the project of understanding the teaching of Romans.

Second, Thomas sometimes limits the sense of Paul's letter too much, yet he also appropriates much of the fuller Pauline teaching in other exegetical passages or in broad theological conclusions, often in ways that can easily escape our awareness.

Third, Augustine's exegesis both helps and hinders Thomas. Thus, the late Aquinas's more Augustinian notions of self-love and the ungraced will being turned away from God involve a doctrinal reception and development of Pauline flesh/spirit, leading to a faithful transformation of the dualist cosmology of Romans into a new metaphysics of grace and human action. However, the incorrect Augustinian identification of the carnal self in Romans 7 leads Aquinas to various misinterpretations.

Fourth, Aquinas's doctrinal exegesis receives a just evaluation only when we consider not only his explicit treatment of particular biblical themes but also the way Thomas's theology integrates the central notions of those themes. Thus, a proper recognition of Aquinas's reception and development of flesh/spirit demands a study of numerous passages that do not contain any explicit discussion of Romans 6–8, Galatians 5, or terms such as "flesh," "spirit," and "concupiscence." We can understand Aquinas the exegete only through a synthetic and historically rigorous reading. Too many unsaid yet crucial doctrines operate in the background of the biblical commentaries, at least when it comes to the theme of flesh/spirit, though I suspect that there are many other examples. This should not surprise us. Thomas's commentaries originated as classroom lectures to students who would also hear the systematic lecture on the themes raised in the biblical text. There was no need to explain everything in the biblical lecture.

Two further elements shared by Aquinas and Augustine are worth noting. First, a striking commonality runs through their exegesis of flesh/spirit. On the surface, both theologians sometimes favor a literalistic reading of the text, which in turn gives some of their comments on Paul a (non-Pauline) dualistic flavor. Here, persisting stereotypical views of Augustine seem to find confirmation, while our stereotype of Aquinas's anthropology as Christian Aristotelianism seems to be contradicted by what appears to be a good dose of biblical Platonism: "the body weighs down the soul." In reality, both thinkers ultimately root their analysis of the notion behind flesh/spirit language in the

fragility of will, enabling them to avoid anthropological dualism and to inte-
grate properly the flesh/spirit doctrine of Romans. Aquinas's anthropology is
much more Augustinian than many realize, but precisely not in going beyond
Aristotle and toward dualism. Rather, original and distinct reflections on the
goodness and weakness of the human will lead Augustine and Aquinas beyond the limitations of their contemporaries, whether Manichean, Pelagian,
or quasi semi-Pelagian, and toward a richly Pauline anthropology.

Second, neither exegete worked in the ideal conditions that a culture of
rigorous historical interpretation can provide. Augustine's exegesis was often driven and perhaps distracted by the intense theological controversies
of his day. Without the Pelagian controversy, would he have changed his mind
about the carnal self in Romans 7? Aquinas's exegesis was driven by the goal of
a theological synthesis that manifests the truth of the faith and refutes error,
one that discerns the rationality of the Catholic tradition (with a small *t*) while
also recognizing its limitations and false turns. He, too, was thus "distracted"
in ways that probably hindered him from attaining an accurate historical interpretation of numerous Pauline passages. Yet ultimately, Augustine's polem-
ics seem to have taken the Bishop of Hippo on a detour toward a much richer
appropriation of Pauline flesh/spirit. Ultimately, a new metaphysics of divine
motion, Augustinian anthropology, and a closer attentiveness to the Pauline
text led Aquinas in the same direction.

Conclusion

Evaluating Aquinas's exegesis is a laborious, complex task, moving from
the historical sense of Scripture, to the patristic and early medieval traditions, to Aquinas's biblical commentary, then to his systematic works and
back again. But precisely by reading Aquinas in light of the historical meaning of the biblical text, and precisely in tracking Aquinas's false turns, successful detours, subtle nuances, unspoken assumptions, doctrinal evolutions, and
interaction with the interpretive tradition, we discover a medieval exegetical
project of striking breadth and depth that still has much to teach contemporary theology and biblical studies. Thomists have only begun to pursue this
Ressourcement reading of Aquinas.[100] Should we be surprised that modern exegetes have hardly paid attention to the Angelic Doctor?

100. A noteworthy example is Matthew Levering's "Biblical Thomism" that he develops in
virtually all of his books.

Markus Bockmuehl

2   Aquinas on Abraham's Faith in Romans 4

One of the more tantalizing and yet surprisingly neglected exegetical puzzles in Romans is this: does Paul depict the covenantal, circumcised, Jewish observant life of faithfulness as overtaken and replaced by an entirely law-free faith in Christ, or does he instead envisage such Jewish Torah praxis as in some sense tolerated or even affirmed and taken up within the Messianic faith? Two millennia of Gentile Paulinism may understandably have left little incentive to press for an answer; but the question as such does seem exegetically relevant to the figure of Abraham in chapter 4, as also to chapters 9–11. In other words, is only the *uncircumcised* Abraham the forefather of Christ-faith, or is there a sense in which the *circumcised* Abraham too serves as the type of what an observant Jewish faith in the Messiah might mean?

Needless to say, the answer to this question does matter enormously for a reading of Romans. If it is true, as N. T. Wright likes to say, that circumcised faithfulness is merely the boat we once needed to get to shore but that we have now left behind as surplus to requirements,[1] then Christ evidently does supplant and replace the circumcised faithfulness of Abraham. That is, to be sure, a view with extensive patristic and Reformational pedigree. Nevertheless, and quite apart from its unfortunate anti-Jewish potential, it would seem to generate a number of exegetical difficulties for the reader of Romans 4. Most egregious of these difficulties, one might argue, is that Abraham himself appears on that reading to *regress* from the life of "Christic" faith to the life of "nomi-

---

1. N. T. Wright, *The Last Word: Beyond the Bible Wars to a New Understanding of the Authority of Scripture* (San Francisco: HarperSanFrancisco, 2005), 57, writes, "It is not hard to imagine illustrations of how this continuity and discontinuity function. When travelers sail across a vast ocean and finally arrive on the distant shore, they leave the ship behind and continue over land, not because the ship was no good, or because their voyage had been misguided, but precisely because both ship and voyage had accomplished their purpose." He cites Gal 3:22–29 as illustrating this perspective, which he regards as exemplifying the right balance between continuity and discontinuity.

stic" works. He would suddenly appear rather hamstrung, indeed counterproductive, as an exemplar of the point Paul wishes to illustrate.

Here I shall not be able to offer an analysis either of Paul's letter to the Romans, the making of books about which knows no end,[2] or of Aquinas as theologian or exegete, a topic of immense importance about which I know very little. Aquinas's view of Abraham, more generally, is a matter of considerable interest that would also merit more extensive analysis than we can undertake here. This is not least because of his controversial handling in the *Summa* of divine command ethics in relation to the story of the binding of Isaac in Genesis 22, a passage of vital importance to Jewish and patristic thought that, on most modern accounts, Paul largely ignores.[3]

For present purposes, I wish to offer a few observations about Aquinas's handling of Abraham's faith in his exposition of Romans 4, focusing especially on the relationship of Jewish to Gentile faith. Once biblical scholars look past the unfamiliar Aristotelian form of highly structured presentation, it is not difficult to see here a careful exegete at work who repeatedly allows his critical questions to be both generated and addressed by a close reading of the biblical text.

Romans 4

Just as the end of Romans 3 brought proof from Scripture that all are sinful, so chapter 4 is Paul's quite ingenious proof that righteousness comes by faith. Paul here argues that the Torah *itself* shows God's free gift of righteousness to be based not on a Jewish ancestral privilege but on sheer grace and election. Unless Paul can prove this from the Torah itself, he will have lost the sympathies of his Jewish Christian readers in Rome. In brief, the argument is that Abraham himself, the father of the covenant, is the chief example of faith-based righteousness because in Genesis 15:6, significantly *before* he is ever circumcised in chapter 17, we read that he believed in God, and God counted this as his righteousness. This point is of course familiar to modern commentators but well captured by Aquinas too, who comments explicitly that Paul's argument rides on the narrative *sequence* of Genesis (§ 339).

2. In addition to the ever-burgeoning commentary literature, a recent starting point for exegetical and tradition-historical study of Abraham's faith in Romans 4 is Benjamin Schliesser, *Abraham's Faith in Romans 4: Paul's Concept of Faith in Light of the History of Reception of Genesis 15:6*, Wissenschaftliche Untersuchungen zum Neuen Testament 2:224 (Tübingen: Mohr Siebeck, 2007).

3. See discussion and references in Brian Stiltner, "Who Can Understand Abraham? The Relation of God and Morality in Kierkegaard and Aquinas, " *Journal of Religious Ethics* 21 (1993): 221–45, 233–36. Romans is sometimes said to touch on the Aqedah at 3.25 and 8.32; cf. elsewhere Heb 11.17–19.

We do well to remind ourselves that Paul is here walking an exegetical tightrope. In ancient Judaism, Abraham is indeed a paragon of faith in the promises of God, a faith that can be described in terms remarkably reminiscent of Paul. Thus an early rabbinic commentary on Exodus 14:31 comments that according to Genesis 15:6 "our father Abraham inherited this world and the world to come only by virtue of his faith in the Lord."[4] At the same time, however, the patriarchs were believed to have practiced the Torah even before it was revealed, since in fact on the Jewish reading of Proverbs 8 the Torah existed since before creation. At the sharp end of that conviction was a belief, explicit in the *Psalms of Solomon* (9.8–9) but perhaps implicit here (cf. Luke 3:8; John 8:39, 53), that all Jews enjoy an unassailable superiority before God, purely by virtue of their biological desent from Abraham. This is a kind of popular racial chauvinism that is also occasionally echoed in Old Testament passages such as Ezra 9:2.[5]

That opposing Jewish view may or may not be at the forefront of the Apostle's concern here. Taken at face value, however, Paul's argument does certainly run dangerously close to denying what most Jews in the first century would have believed about Abraham—and what, we may presume, most of the Jerusalem church may well have believed. At least in that sense Protestant commentators are perhaps not far from the mark when they see Paul agitated by the Jewish Christian suggestion that full incorporation into the promise of Abraham required emulating his Torah observance as well as his faith. As Aquinas too repeatedly reminds us (§ 327, 377), in 1 Maccabees 2:52 as in Sirach 44:20 Abraham's faith was demonstrated precisely when it was tested— above all in the binding of Isaac. Hebrews (11:17–19)[6] and the Letter of James, too, show an Abraham who is saved by a faith demonstrated in his trusting praxis; to that extent ancient Christian and Jewish readings are remarkably cognate. And it is perhaps only the polemical context of Romans 4 that causes Paul conveniently to sidestep Scripture's own statement in Genesis 26:5 that "Abraham obeyed my voice and kept my charge, my commandments, my statutes, and my laws" (using both of the resonant Hebrew words *mitzvah* and

---

4. *Mekhilta de-Rabbi Ishmael:* וכן אתה מוצא שלא ירש אברהם אבינו העולם הזה והעולם הבא אלא בזכות אמנה שהאמין בה' (*Mek. Beshallaḥ* 6, ed. Horovitz/Rabin p. 114, l. 15).

5. Commentators sometimes like to cite the late rabbinic view that on the Day of Atonement God forgives the sins of Israel and not the Gentiles (e.g. Robert Jewett, *Romans: A Commentary*, Hermeneia (Minneapolis: Fortress Press, 2006), 317, citing C. E. B. Cranfield, *A Critical and Exegetical Commentary on the Epistle to the Romans*, 2 vols. (Edinburgh: T&T Clark, 1975–79), 1:234, and others), though whether that is either logically or chronologically apposite here seems doubtful.

6. On Abraham's faith in Hebrews 11 cf. my remarks in Markus Bockmuehl, "Abraham's Faith in Hebrews 11," in *The Epistle to the Hebrews and Christian Theology*, ed. Richard J. Bauckham et al. (Grand Rapids: Eerdmans, 2009).

torah).[7] That reading of Abraham is perhaps also in the mind of the Qumran author who commends to rival priestly authorities in Jerusalem that they observe his interpretation of "a few of the works of Torah" so that this may be "reckoned to you as righteousness"[8]—a position that would appear to run pretty clearly counter to what Paul has in mind here.

In fact, of course, Paul nowhere in chapter 4 *denies* that Abraham kept the Torah, or claims that he was a scoundrel. This may be an awkward observation for a certain kind of hyper-Protestant reading that likes to absolutize the force of the "justification of the impious" in 4:5.[9] Paul's argument about Abraham rides not on the patriarch's prior godlessness but on the narrative fact that circumcision, which is one of the "works of the law," was instituted long *after* God had already declared Abraham righteous because of his faith. Abraham, in other words, was *uncircumcised* when he was justified. That is all Paul is trying to say: not that circumcision brought Abraham no moral benefit, merely that the chronological priority of Abraham's justifying faith is what makes him the father of the covenant for *both* Jews and Gentiles. Not in his *circumcised* but in his *uncircumcised* state did Abraham's faith make him righteous and the father of many nations. That is indeed a radically new statement for a first-century Jewish audience.[10]

Aquinas here suggests an interesting Aristotelian correlation of the faith-versus-works tension, which takes seriously both aspects of the dilemma and assigns them a logical and causal relationship of which even Calvin might have approved (§ 325): "A man's works are not proportioned to *causing* the habit of this righteousness; rather, a man's heart needs first to be justified inwardly *by God*, so that he can perform works proportioned to divine glory."[11]

7. This view is expanded in Second Temple and rabbinic Judaism: see, e.g., Sir 44.19; *Pr. Man.* 8; 1 Macc 2.52; *Jub* 23.10; *2 Bar.* 57.2; Philo, *Migr.* 130–31; *Her.* 8–9; *Abr.* 275–76 and *passim; m. Qidd.* 4.14; *Targ. Neof.* Gen 26.5. Douglas J. Moo, *The Epistle to the Romans,* New International Commentary on the New Testament (Grand Rapids: Eerdmans, 1996), 256, is characteristic of Protestant commentators' impatience and incredulity at the "nomistic" Jewish notion that Abraham observed *Torah* and commandments even before Sinai. But that is precisely what is asserted in Gen 26:5, a passage to which Jewish writings frequently refer.

8. 4QMMT C 27, 31.

9. So e.g. Ernst Käsemann, *Commentary on Romans* (London: SCM Press, 1980), 111–12; Jewett, *Romans: A Commentary,* 314.

10. Cf. the contrasting links with Rom 1 noted by Edward Adams, "Abraham's Faith and Gentile Disobedience: Textual Links between Romans 1 and 4," *Journal for the Study of the New Testament* 65 (1997): 47–66.

11. 4, lect. 1: "Et ideo opera hominis non sunt proportionata ad huius iustitiae habitum causandum, sed oportet prius iustificari interius cor hominis a Deo, ut opera faciat proportionata divinae gloriae." Emphasis added. All translations are from *Lectures on the Letter to the Romans,* trans. Fabian Larcher, O.P., ed. Jeremy Holmes (Ave Maria, Fla.: Aquinas Center for Theological Renewal), http://www.avemaria.edu/uploads/pagesfiles/4283.pdf.

Lutheran exegesis by contrast has frequently regarded verse 2 as Paul's attack on self-righteousness, the idea that one can accumulate meritorious brownie points before God. But Paul's point in this whole chapter is not so much that Abraham was a scoundrel before he was justified, but that he was *not circumcised*. That is to say, the reference to "works" here is not good works in general but specifically works of the law, understood in the sense of specific Jewish observances. Circumcision and other Jewish legal observances may well command respect, but they do not confer any special status before God. The Reformers' application of this principle to the idea of earning God's favor with good works may well be true *by extension*, but it is not what is intended here in the first place.

In verses 4–5, Aquinas shows a good awareness of the Pauline argument about grace and works. "Faith alone," he writes, is accounted as righteousness "without outward works … so that in virtue of it [Abraham] is called righteous and receives the reward of righteousness, just as if he had done the works of righteousness" (§ 330 with reference to 4:5 and 10:10).[12]

If we may be permitted an insight drawn from the last generation's "New Perspective" scholarship on Paul (E. P. Sanders, James D. G. Dunn, and others), this also makes good sense in the covenantal context of righteousness in ancient Judaism. Jewish works of the law were not the way *into* the covenant of election and grace, but they were indeed required to *maintain* the covenant—to the point where the Torah was the key to life. Such works received a reward, but that reward was itself the fruit of prevenient grace—even if, as critics of the New Perspective have shown, that distinction between entering and maintaining the covenant is in some Jewish sources difficult to verify.[13]

Faith, on the other hand, does count as righteousness, by way of a free gift. The notion that God justifies the *ungodly* (τὸν ἀσεβῆ, v. 5) is indeed a radical and jarring idea, and might well be unwelcome in a Jewish context.[14] Aquinas does not address this point, perhaps because Abraham was not in any obvious sense ungodly; nor of course, despite scholarly claims to the contrary, does this passage make Paul say so.[15] Paul's expansion of the principle here perhaps

---

12. 1, lect. 4: "sola sine operibus exterioribus, ad iustitiam, id est, ut per eam iustus dicatur, et iustitiae praemium accipiat, sicut si opera iustitiae fecisset."

13. So, e.g., Friedrich Avemarie, *Tora und Leben: Untersuchungen zur Heilsbedeutung der Tora in der frühen rabbinischen Literatur*, Texte und Studien zum antiken Judentum 55 (Tübingen: Mohr Siebeck, 1996).

14. Cf. James D. G. Dunn, *Romans*, 2 vols., Word Biblical Commentary 38 (Dallas: Word Books, 1988), 1:204ff.

15. Contra Hans Hübner, *Law in Paul's Thought: A Contribution to the Development of Pauline Theology*, Studies of the New Testament and Its World (Edinburgh: T&T Clark, 1984), 121, also cited in Francis Watson, *Paul, Judaism, and the Gentiles: Beyond the New Perspective*, rev. ed. (Grand Rapids, Mich.: Eerdmans, 2007), 40, and (more critically) 262n11.

reflects Jesus's attitude that he came not for the righteous but for sinners (Mt 9:13). God justifies even the ungodly: that paradox shows how powerfully and exclusively it is grace that is at work.

Turning to the nature of faith in the following verses, Aquinas at first introduces a somewhat circuitous and exegetically fanciful distinction between three different kinds of believing: believing that God is *(Deum)*, believing God *(Deo)*, and believing "in" or "unto" God *(in Deum)*, which for Thomas exemplify respectively the subject matter of faith as a theological virtue, the act of faith, and the ordering of faith to God as its object by means of charity. Paul's Greek usage differs too, but does not obviously lend itself to this semantic distinction.

More interesting for our purposes is the way Aquinas negotiates the conceptual tension between the human act of faith and the divine act of justification. In their resistance to medieval notions of infused grace the Reformers sometimes struggled to present an account of that tension which on the one hand safeguards divine sovereignty in salvation and on the other hand makes that salvation in some sense contingent upon its human reception and appropriation. At times this tended to make faith into a virtual equivalent of the sort of human work that was meant to be rejected. Aquinas, by contrast, interestingly sidesteps this problem by letting the divine gift of righteousness begin with faith *as its first manifestation* in the believer (§ 331): "Not that he merits justice through faith, but because the believing itself is the first act of the justice God works in him." In other words, Aquinas takes the free gift of justification by faith to be a seamless whole of which human faith and works are equally the divinely occasioned fruits.

In this respect it is worth briefly retracing our steps to the beginning of the chapter and noting Aquinas's interesting rhetorical linkage of what Abraham "found" (4:1) with the previous chapter's question of whether a Jewish observance like circumcision can have any *benefit* (3:1). This is a point not often exploited in contemporary commentaries, but for Aquinas the flow of Paul's argument requires that this question cannot be dismissed. He suggests (§ 322) that God's character according to Isaiah 48:17 ensures that God always "teaches useful things." This conviction should not simply be subsumed under a kind of theological rationalism, but rather sets the stage for the Israel-focused theodicy question of Romans 9–11, a section expressly addressed to the problem of whether God can be said to have changed his mind in relation to his promises to the Jews.[16]

16. For discussion of Aquinas's commentary on Romans 9–11 see now Steven C. Boguslawski, *Thomas Aquinas on the Jews: Insights into His Commentary on Romans 9–11* (Mahwah, N.J.: Paulist Press, 2008).

In verses 6–8 Paul links the assurance about Abraham's faith-based righteousness in Genesis 15:6 explicitly to a quotation from Psalm 32:1–2 about the forgiveness of sins. That link up till now was in Romans perhaps implied rather than stated, most clearly in 3:24–26. Aquinas sees here an occasion (§ 335) to discourse about the threefold distinction of original, mortal, and venial sin, which has of course a venerable and in some ways attractive pedigree in Catholic doctrine, but for which, like most Protestant exegetes, I struggle to find support in this or any other passage of Paul's letters. Let him who is free from inculturated doctrinal shibboleths cast the first stone; yet it seems to me that although he is fully committed to the necessary dialogue of Christian doctrine and exegesis, Aquinas here (as also, e.g., in 5:12, following Augustine on original sin) firmly lowers the dogmatic portcullis on the task of patient exegesis.

In Romans 4:9–12, Paul draws important links between Christian faith and the faith of Abraham. Abraham is not just the forefather of those who are circumcised, but the ancestor of *all* those who are justified by faith. In this sense Abraham is "our" father to both Jews and Christians. It is also this perspective that introduces potentially important links with chapters 9–11: Abraham is the father of all those who believe with the same faith of Abraham (note again v. 12); Israel, therefore, consists of all those who exercise Abrahamic faith in Abraham's God.

As Aquinas brings his first lecture on Romans 4 to a close at verses 9–10, he concludes with an important statement about the validity of justification by faith for both Jew and Gentile. In fact Aquinas offers a reading that looks beyond the Lutheran-sounding starkness of Paul's not-this-but-that language in verse 10 to conclude that the righteousness of faith by which sins are freely forgiven occurs "*not only* in circumcision *but also* in uncircumcision" (§ 340). That same idea is repeatedly rehearsed in lecture 2 ("the blessing of forgiveness of sins is obtained *not only* in circumcision *but also* in uncircumcision," § 341, 344).[17] In keeping with verse 11 and the context of Genesis 17:10, circumcision is recognized quite rightly as the sign and seal of the covenant, and indeed of the righteousness of faith. This recognizes the force of the Genesis account (and indeed of the Jewish understanding of circumcision) with a perspicacity that is often lacking in contemporary commentators on this text: Abraham's circumcision, in other words, is neither an irrelevance nor an obstacle to his justification by faith. It did not secure his justification, but it did sign and seal it; Paul says in verse 11, "He received the sign of circumcision as a seal of the righteousness that he had by faith."

---

17. 4, lect. 2: "beatitudo remissionis peccatorum non solum est in circumcisione, sed etiam in praeputio."

In other words, it is not the case for Paul, as hyper-Protestant commentators sometimes imply, that Abraham's faith somehow ceased or diminished when he was circumcised. As Adolf Schlatter rightly stresses, "Becoming the father of believing Gentiles does not mean that Abraham ceases to be the father of Israel. Circumcision does not oppose faith but confirms it."[18] But neither does Paul here engage in the sort of *legerdemain* attributed to him by Ernst Käsemann, for whom the only circumcision in view here is that which belongs *not* to Jews but to Christians—the circumcision of the heart—so that "only the Christian is the true Jew."[19]

Aquinas rather daringly suggests *au contraire* that circumcision had a "visible likeness" to Abraham's faith, in that it hinted at both the multiplication of descendants and the removal of fault: even "the secret of the incarnation of Christ from the seed of Abraham," Thomas thinks, "was enclosed under the seal of circumcision" (§ 343).[20] All this of course goes well beyond what Paul says, but it does arise from taking seriously the Apostle's frequently underinterpreted claim that in addition to Abraham's being the Father in faith to the uncircumcised, circumcision had the purpose of making Abraham also the father of the *circumcised* who walk in that same justifying faith (v. 12). Verse 12 provides a precedent of *Jews who share the faith of Abraham*, as being Abraham's true spiritual heirs along with Gentile Christians. This is important for understanding chapters 9–11. For Paul, those who share in the righteousness reckoned to Abraham are not just Gentile believers in Christ but also Jews who share the faith that Abraham already had before he was circumcised.[21] Cutting the Gordian knot in which much twentieth-century exegesis tied itself because of Paul's slightly awkward repetition of the article,[22] it

18. Adolf Schlatter, *Gottes Gerechtigkeit: Ein Kommentar zum Römerbrief*, 5th ed. (Stuttgart: Calwer Verlag, 1975), 165 (my translation). Cf. very similarly Joseph A. Fitzmyer, *Romans: A New Translation with Introduction and Commentary*, Anchor Bible 33 (New York: Doubleday, 1993), 381.

19. "Only the Christian is the true Jew.... [Circumcision] appertains only to believers." Käsemann, *Commentary on Romans*, 116, rightly criticized by Jewett, *Romans: A Commentary*, 320n167; cf. Dunn, *Romans*, 2:211 ("faith rather than the outward ritual... The true Jew is ἐν κρυπτῷ and circumcision is of the heart ἐν πνεύματι (2:29)").

20. 4, lect. 2: "Claudebatur ergo sub signaculo circumcisionis secretum incarnationis Christi ex semine Abrahae."

21. So e.g. Cranfield, *A Critical and Exegetical Commentary on the Epistle to the Romans*, 1.238, "But, while recognizing that Paul is here concerned with a kinship with Abraham which depends on the sharing of his faith, we must be careful to avoid the mistake of concluding from what is said here that Paul intended to deny the reality of the kinship κατὰ σάρκα (cf. v. 1) with Abraham of those Jews who did not share his faith or that he believed that such Jews were altogether excluded from the promises." Contrast Watson, *Paul, Judaism, and the Gentiles: Beyond the New Perspective*, 261, who denies that Abraham in any way connects Christians with non-Christian Jews.

22. καὶ πατέρα περιτομῆς τοῖς οὐκ ἐκ περιτομῆς μόνον ἀλλὰ καὶ τοῖς στοιχοῦσιν τοῖς ἴχνεσιν τῆς ἐν τῇ ἀκροβυστίᾳ πίστεως τοῦ πατρὸς ἡμῶν Ἀβραάμ.

seems right at any rate to conclude with Aquinas that the Apostle has not two distinct modes of salvation in view, but an all-inclusive one applied to Jewish and Gentile believers.[23]

In other words, what Paul appears to envisage here is that Abraham is a pioneer of saving Christ-faith, which already justifies him fully in his Gentile uncircumcised state, but which also receives its sign and seal in circumcision.[24] Aquinas likewise wishes to ensure that this ancestry of Abrahamic faith is reaffirmed for Jewish believers too, for whom in a striking *relecture* of one of the Fourth Gospel's darkest pieces of polemic he positively reappropriates the statement "Abraham is our father" (Jn 8:39; § 344).

Aquinas then offers an important excursus on the significance of circumcision, which he appears to regard as quasi-sacramental in function—expressing "in a bodily sign something that was to occur spiritually."[25] Circumcision was instituted for divine worship, but also as a sign of Abraham's obedience of faith, as a bodily sign of a spiritual reality, and to distinguish the elect from all other nations (§ 346–47). At the same time, Thomas sees it as a figure for the true circumcision to be accomplished in Christ, not just spiritually in the removal of concupiscence and the effects of sin from the soul (citing Col 2:11), but also physically in the bodily resurrection to come in the eighth millennium, corresponding to the eighth day of circumcision (§ 348).[26] Citing the

---

23. Pasquale Basta, *Abramo in Romani 4: L'analogia dell'agire divino nella ricerca esegetica di Paolo*, Analecta Biblica 168 (Rome: Pontificio Istituto Biblico, 2007), who generally argues for Paul's employment in this chapter of a *gezerah shawah* interpretation using Ps 32:1–2 and Gen 15:6, discusses this question at length (214–18), and concludes that clearly the argument is inclusive of all who believe: there are two ways of faith, united in the nucleus of faith and different only in the sign of faith. Cf. further 256, citing J.-N. Aletti.

24. Francis Watson, *Paul, Judaism, and the Gentiles: Beyond the New Perspective*, 267 (who regards Paul, less plausibly in my view, as intending a new "Christian" polity separate from the synagogue), also rightly recognizes in verses 10–12 evidence that "since Abraham enjoyed righteousness by faith both before and after he was circumcised, he aptly symbolizes the union of Gentile and Jewish Christians."

25. 4, lect. 2: "ad exprimendum in signo corporali id quod spiritualiter erat faciendum." Unlike most modern commentators Karl Barth, *Der Römerbrief*, 2nd ed. (Munich: Kaiser, 1922), 107–8, likewise speaks of circumcision as a *sacramental sign of the covenant*, though based on Abraham's faith *as a Gentile*; in that sense it is precisely Abraham's *circumcision* that seals "the faith of the uncircumcised" (109, my translation; contrast, e.g., Dunn, *Romans*, 1:209, and others cited there). On a more discordant note, Barth goes on to insist that genuine faith is "faith without circumcision" (109–10); indeed in the first edition of 1919 he affirms that "Abraham's path of faith is *not* the way of the Jew *but* the way of the Gentile, of Abraham as a human being" (ibid., 89, my italics and translation).

26. Thomas Domanyi, *Der Römerbriefkommentar des Thomas von Aquin: Ein Beitrag zur Untersuchung seiner Auslegungsmethoden*, Basler und Berner Studien zur historischen und systematischen Theologie 39 (Bern: Peter Lang, 1979), 159–61, regards this passage as one of the few clear applications of the "tropological" and "anagogical" method in the Romans commentary.

Venerable Bede with approval (from Peter Lombard's Gloss), Aquinas explicitly correlates the function of circumcision under the Law with that of baptism in the era of grace (a point that seems less obvious in Romans than in Col
2:11). What this means for him is the surprising recognition that "the power of
circumcision extended to the removal of original sin" (§ 349).[27] That removal,
however, is not *ex opere operato* but "through faith in Christ, of which circumcision was a sign, it removed original sin and conferred the help of grace to act
righteously" (§ 349).[28] That, then, is the significance of Abraham's circumcised
faith. By contrast "Baptism, as the sign of present grace, produces a more copi-
ous and more beneficial effect of grace" (§ 350).[29]

Returning to Paul's argument, Aquinas notes that in verse 13 Abraham
becomes an inheritor of "the world." This is a line similarly taken in Sirach
44:21 and other Jewish texts, as commentators amply document.[30] The reference is sometimes assumed to be to the world to come, although Aquinas
not unreasonably links it to the blessing that through Abraham's seed is in
Genesis 12:3 said to extend to all the families of the world. In keeping with
Galatians 3:16, however, Thomas finds that seed more specifically identified
with *Christ* as the one in whom Abraham inherits the world, and with Christians, who through Christ are the spiritual seed of Abraham (§ 351).[31] This is
a point subsequently expanded in the discussion of verse 16, where the promise to Abraham's descendant is said to encompass *everyone* who would be "in
any way descended from Abraham" (§ 361, citing Sir 44:11).[32] In the *Summa*,
Aquinas singles out Abraham together with David as the two most important ancestors to whom God makes a special promise that is fulfilled in Jesus:
Christ is the seed through whom the world will be blessed, and he it is who
will establish the kingdom of David.[33]

Significantly for our understanding of Romans 4, this universality of
Abraham's descendants relates *both* to those of his children who observe the
Law and to those who do not, since faith is common to both sorts of descen-
dants (§ 362–63). Lest one be tempted to conclude that the set of believing

27. 4, lect. 2: "virtus circumcisionis se extendebat ad deletionem originalis peccati."
28. 4, lect. 2: "per fidem Christi, cuius circumcisio signum erat, auferebatur peccatum origi-
nale et conferebatur auxilium gratiae ad recte agendum."
29. 4, lect. 2: "Baptismus est signum praesentis gratiae qui copiosiorem et utiliorem effectum
habet gratiae."
30. For references, see, e.g., Fitzmyer, *Romans*, 385; Dunn, *Romans*, 1.213; somewhat differently Jewett, *Romans: A Commentary*, 327.
31. Similarly *Summa theologiae (ST)* III, q. 31, a. 2, also cited by Matthew Levering, *Christ's
Fulfillment of Torah and Temple: Salvation according to Thomas Aquinas* (Notre Dame, Ind.: University of Notre Dame Press, 2002), 68 and n68.
32. 4, lect. 3: "omni homini qui fuerit qualitercumque semen Abrahae."
33. Cf. Levering, *Christ's Fulfillment of Torah and Temple*, 68, citing *ST* III, q. 31, a. 2.

observers of the Law is empty, Aquinas follows up with the assurance that God's life-giving power means "Jews, who were dead in sin for acting against the Law, he vivifies with faith and grace to enable them to realize the promise to Abraham" (§ 364).[34]

Turning to the subject of Abraham's hope against hope in verse 18, Aquinas affirms that this means that, contrary to the aspect of hope in natural and human causes, Abraham believed solely in hope of the divine promise (§ 368). Abraham exercised this hope and faith with firmness, thereby demonstrating that faith is a virtue not of weakness but of great strength: "For as temperance is shown not to be weak, because it is not overcome by strong temptations, so faith is shown not to be weak but strong, because it is not overcome by great difficulties."[35] That strength is doxologically derived in keeping with verse 20: Abraham's faith grew strong in proportion as he gave glory to God, just as "whoever is not firm in faith detracts from God's glory either in regard to his veracity or his power" (§ 376).

On an unexpectedly wry and humorous note, Aquinas offers an aside on the curious problem that Paul sees Abraham in Genesis 15 to be in his physical and reproductive capacity as good as dead, and yet reading on in Genesis we find him after Sarah's death merrily taking another wife called Keturah, with whom he goes on to have another six children. How can this be? Aquinas's Viagra-like solution is to see Isaac's birth as a miracle with excess benefit to spare: "Abraham's reproductive power was miraculously restored both in regard to Sarah and to all women" (§ 372).[36]

Finally, picking up on Paul's argument about the relevance of the Old Testament in 4:23–24 and reiterated in 15.4 (cf. 2 Cor 1:20, etc.), Aquinas finds the example of Abraham's faith powerfully relevant to the present day: just as faith was reckoned to Abraham as righteousness, so also it will be reckoned to us. The Old Testament promise was written in relation to Abraham so that he

---

34. 4, lect. 3: *Iudaeos, qui erant mortui in peccatis, contra legem agentes, vivificat per fidem et gratiam, ut promissionem Abrahae consequantur.* Contrast, for example, the anti-"New Perspective" discussion of Francis Watson, who is on the one hand struck by the surprising emphasis on Christian Jews as compared with Galatians (Francis Watson, *Paul, Judaism and the Gentiles,* Society for New Testament Studies Monograph Series 56 [Cambridge: Cambridge University Press, 1986], 259–60), although he also follows a widespread Protestant conviction that "the fact that Paul regards the church as the seed of Abraham does not mean that he regards it as existing in a salvation-historical continuum with Israel" (Watson, *Paul, Judaism and the Gentiles,* 222n81, interestingly omitted from the 2007 edition).

35. 4; lect. 3: "Sicut enim temperantia ostenditur non esse infirma, quae magnis concupiscibilibus non vincitur, ita fides ostenditur non esse infirma, sed fortis quae a magnis difficultatibus non superatur."

36. 4; lect. 3: "Abrahae miraculose restituta erat vis generandi et quantum ad Saram et quantum ad omnes mulieres."

might become an example for us, but it was written for us that he might raise our hope for righteousness (§ 378). The Old Testament is no mere ornament, but speaks in its own voice of the coming Christ.[37]

In this way Christ as the hermeneutical key to the Old Testament underscores the relevance of this whole Abraham story. The uncircumcised Abraham believed and thus became the father of all who believe, but unlike some interpreters Thomas goes out of his way to apply this not only to Gentile believers but to Jewish ones too. Just as Abraham's faith received its sign and seal in circumcision, so circumcised faith receives its empowerment in the grace that comes in Christ. The simplest and most radical implication from this reading of Romans 4 might be that all truly Abrahamic faith, whether Gentile or Jewish, is Christ-faith. The same faith is reckoned as righteousness to all who believe in Abraham's God, who has also brought the dead to life, namely by raising Jesus. This is not perhaps all that might need to be said about *present-day* circumcised faith, but one important implication is strikingly phrased by St Thomas in relation to 2 Corinthians 4:13:

> This justice [of God] is revealed in the gospel inasmuch as men are justified by faith in the gospel in every age. Hence he adds, *from faith to faith*, i.e., proceeding from faith in the Old Testament to faith in the New, because in both cases men are made just and are saved by faith in Christ, since they believed in his coming with the same faith as we believe that he has come. Therefore, it is stated in 2 Cor 4(:13), "We have the same type of faith as he had who wrote, 'I believed, and so I spoke.'"[38]

Conclusion

For the New Testament scholar, Aquinas as a guide to these matters takes some getting used to, in his ponderously Aristotelian presentation as much as in flighty excursuses and occasional dogmatic heavy-handedness. It is, however, clear that he stands in a centuries-old tradition of gloss and exposition that is unfamiliar not only to many contemporary exegetes but also, as Domanyi notes, to an image of Aquinas that was for too long constructed almost exclusively on the basis of the *Summa*.[39] The other thing that seems noticeable in an age of supposedly more ecumenically minded exegesis is that Aquinas's exegetical take on Romans is at odds with some of today's more stridently Protestant approaches, whether of liberal or of conservative persuasion. For purposes of the present volume, however, it seems most important to note the

---

37. Cf. Domanyi, *Der Römerbriefkommentar des Thomas von Aquin*, 176.

38. On Romans 1:17 (§ 102; a passage also rightly noted by *Der Römerbriefkommentar des Thomas von Aquin*, 171) and again on Romans 5:15 (§ 442). Emphasis in original.

39. *Der Römerbriefkommentar des Thomas von Aquin*, 18.

fact that Aquinas's exegesis manages to highlight Abraham's importance for Jewish-Gentile and Christian-Jewish relations in sometimes nimble and unencumbered ways. It may be that on these topics the Angelic Doctor's intellectual world, shared with fellow Abrahamic Aristotelians such as Maimonides, Saadya, and Averroes,[40] may yet have a contribution to make today to the exploration of a common conversation about Paul's Abraham—a conversation that could benefit considerably if it included Messianic and other Jews.

40. On the link with Saadya see, e.g., Eleonore Stump, "The God of Abraham, Saadia and Aquinas," in *Referring to God: Jewish and Christian Philosophical and Theological Perspectives*, ed. Paul Helm (New York: St. Martin's Press, 2000), 95–119.

Hans Boersma

∽

3 *Ressourcement* of Mystery
The Ecclesiology of Thomas Aquinas and the Letter to the Romans

Ressourcement of a Sacramental Ecclesiology

Yves Congar (1904–95), in a 1974 Aquinas Lecture at Blackfriars, Oxford, on the topic of "St. Thomas Aquinas and the Spirit of Ecumenism," held out the Angelic Doctor as a source of inspiration for discussion between Catholics and Protestants.[1] While recognizing the tension between "the ontological and sapiential point of view of Thomas and the existential-dramatic approach of Luther," Congar pointed out that nonetheless not just Catholics but also Protestants were looking to Thomas Aquinas (1224/25–74) as a source of inspiration.[2] With some degree of relish, it seems, Congar quoted Karl Barth (1886–1968):

An attentive reading of the works of the *Doctor Angelicus* permits one to verify in him certain lines of force which, even if they do not lead directly to the Reformation, do not tend, any the more, towards Jesuitical Romanism. Thus when one knows how to use intelligently this immense compendium of the previous tradition which constitutes the Summa, one remarks that its author is, on many issues, an evangelical theologian useful to know.[3]

I wish to thank Darrell W. Johnson and Matthew Levering for their helpful comments on an earlier draft of this paper.

1. Yves M.-J. Congar, "St Thomas Aquinas and the Spirit of Ecumenism," *New Blackfriars* 55, no. 648 (1974): 196–209. Cf. Fergus Kerr, "Yves Congar: From Suspicion to Acclamation," *Louvain Studies* 29, nos. 3–4 (2004): 273–87, at 280–87.

2. Congar, "St Thomas Aquinas and the Spirit of Ecumenism," 200.

3. Ibid. The quotation is from Karl Barth, *Die kirchliche Dogmatik*, vol. 1, bk. 2, *Die Lehre vom Wort Gottes: Prolegomena zur kirchlichen Dogmatik* (Zollikon: Evangelischer Verlag, 1938), 686. I have retained Congar's own translation. Cf. idem, *Church Dogmatics*, vol.1, bk. 2, *The Doctrine of the Word of God*, ed. G. W. Bromiley and T. F. Torrance, trans. G. T. Thomson and Harold Knight (London: T&T Clark, 2004), 614.

Congar, along with other *ressourcement* theologians in the decades leading up to the Second Vatican Council (1962–65), engaged in just the kind of "attentive reading" to which Barth alluded. What is more, Congar came to conclusions rather similar to those of the Protestant Swiss theologian.

Particularly Thomas's ecclesiology—one of Congar's key areas of interest—came out looking remarkably evangelical in the writings of the Dominican scholar from Le Saulchoir. This is not to say that Congar painted St. Thomas as an evangelical Protestant. Congar was genuinely Catholic in his convictions, and his strong ecumenical inclinations did not cause him to ignore the differences between Catholicism and Protestantism. Protestant ecclesiology, Congar was convinced, did not take the structures of the Church sufficiently seriously—the result, he believed, of the Protestant lack of focus on the sacramental means of salvation in the economy of redemption. But Congar was equally convinced, along with Barth, that Thomas did not tend toward what Barth termed "Jesuitical Romanism." One of the main reasons for Congar's interest in Thomas was that he saw in him an ally in his own opposition to the juridicizing that he believed had increasingly put its stamp on the Church's structures since the eleventh-century Gregorian Reform.[4] These juridicizing tendencies had resulted, argued Congar, in the manuals *De ecclesia*, which had originated in the early fourteenth century and had set off an approach to ecclesiology that, according to Congar, suffered from juridicizing and intellectualizing tendencies. The result had been a loss of the Church as mystery of faith. In order to recover a sense of mystery, Congar believed it was necessary to work out a doctrine of the Church that would focus on the communion of the Church as the fellowship of believers, the assembly of the faithful *(congregatio fidelium)*, and so on the unity and peace of the Church. He maintained that the neo-Thomist establishment had focused on the Church as sacramental means *(sacramentum)*, whereas Thomas's own primary interest was the sacramental reality *(res)*. Put differently, Congar argued that a *ressourcement* of St. Thomas's ecclesiology required a shift from a one-sidedly juridical to a more spiritual view of the Church.[5]

As I already indicated, Congar realized that his reading of Thomas Aqui-

4. Yves M.-J. Congar, *Tradition and Traditions: The Biblical, Historical, and Theological Evidence for Catholic Teaching on Tradition*, trans. Michael Naseby and Thomas Rainborough (London: Burns and Oates, 1966), 135; idem, *L'Église: De saint Augustin à l'époque moderne*, Histoire des dogmes 3 (Paris: Cerf, 1970), 112; idem, *Power and Poverty in the Church*, trans. Jennifer Nicholson (London: Chapman, 1965), 104–6; idem, *Fifty Years of Catholic Theology: Conversation with Yves Congar*, ed. Bernard Lauret (Philadelphia: Fortress, 1988), 40–44.

5. See Hans Boersma, *Nouvelle Théologie and Sacramental Ontology: A Return to Mystery* (Oxford: Oxford University Press, 2009), Chapter 7.

nas through the lens of a sacramental ecclesiology by no means turned the thirteenth-century theologian into a Protestant. A sacramental ecclesiology, such as proposed by Congar's reading of St. Thomas and officially propounded in *Lumen gentium*, still presents challenges to Protestantism, since this renewed focus on the life of the Church as its sacramental purpose *(res)* does not negate the significance of the Church's structures as the sacramental means *(sacramentum)*. Particularly those evangelical groups that regard sacraments as extraneous signs that *point* merely toward internal realities, without having a real, inherent connection to them, would take little solace from Congar's *ressourcement* of St. Thomas or from *Lumen gentium's* understanding of the Church as sacrament. But also more sacramentally inclined Protestants from the Lutheran and Reformed traditions will continue to struggle with the way in which Congar's version of Thomas relates sacrament and reality—particularly when it comes to questions of papal authority and infallibility.

That said, it seems to me, for two reasons, that Congar's Thomas—who I believe was largely endorsed by Vatican II—holds ecumenical significance. The first reason is that Congar pointed out that the neo-scholastic juridicizing and intellectualizing of ecclesiology endangered an authentically Thomist sacramental view of the Church, since for Thomas, the Church had primarily been a mystery to be entered into and explored by faith. This accentuation of the reality of the spiritual unity of the Church had also been one of the Reformation's main concerns, and Congar's reading of Thomas thus opens up possibilities of genuine ecumenical convergence. The second reason is that Congar presents a necessary challenge to Protestant (and, especially, evangelical) ecclesiologies. Congar purposely set forth what he called a "sacramental ontology" *(ontologie sacramentelle)*, which he framed by interpreting time in a sacramental fashion.[6] Past, present, and future were not simply chronologically distinct moments in time; rather, in faith and through the sacraments, they converged as the eschatological future entered into time. Cosmic time and the time of human history coincided sacramentally in the Church. Thus, Congar explained, "the time of the Church" *(le temps de l'Église)* was sacramental in character.[7] I do not have the time to explore all the implications of what I believe to be a profound insight.[8] Suffice it to say that for Congar, and

6. Congar, *Tradition and Traditions*, 259. Cf. Johannes Bunnenberg, *Lebendige Treue zum Ursprung: Das Traditionsverständnis Yves Congars*, Walberger Studien 14 (Mainz: Grünewald, 1989), 211–12.

7. Congar, *Tradition and Traditions*, 259–60.

8. One of the more immediate implications, as Matthew Levering rightly pointed out to me in personal conversation, is the fact that the joining together of cosmic time and human history—implying that all chronological moments of time are sacramentally present in each other—takes up and elevates the basic creaturely reality of time as created participation in divine eternity.

also for others associated with *nouvelle théologie*, this sacramental ontology affected the approach to the nature-supernatural relationship, to the historical and spiritual meanings of Scripture, to the continuing development of the Christological deposit of faith, and to the relationship between the structure and the life of the Church.[9] As a Protestant in the Reformed tradition, I must regretfully acknowledge that the decline of a sacramental ontology has seriously affected our ecclesiology; the charge that, all too often, Protestants do not have an ecclesiology carries some degree of validity. In short, a *ressourcement* of the ecclesiology of St. Thomas along the lines of Congar presents challenges to Catholics and Protestants alike, and in both directions I believe these challenges to be generally on target.

In this chapter, therefore, I will follow Congar's lead by engaging in a discussion of the ecclesiology found in Thomas Aquinas's commentary on Romans.[10] The focus on the Epistle to the Romans means that I will make no attempt to present Thomas's overall understanding of the Church. Not only would that be beyond my abilities as a nonexpert in Thomas Aquinas, but also it would require a discussion of numerous ecclesiological issues that Thomas's Romans commentary barely touches on, such as the role of the magisterium and of the pope, the relationship between Eucharist and Church, and the place of the angels within the Church. Even the description of the Church as the gathering of believers *(congregatio fidelium)* falls outside the scope of this paper, despite the fact that it was Thomas's second most favorite description of the Church and highly significant for a retrieval of a sacramental ecclesiology focusing on the unity of the believers.[11] Instead, I will take St. Thomas's commentary as my guide, and I will argue that it offers support for a sacramental ecclesiology along the lines advocated by *nouvelle théologie*, notably Henri de Lubac (1896–1991) and Yves Congar. That is to say, the sacramental ecclesiology of Thomas's Romans commentary demands from us a *ressourcement* of the Church as mystery and as such provides a suitable context for further ecumenical discussion between Catholics and Protestants. In the process of arguing for the sacramental

9. Cf. Boersma, *Nouvelle Théologie and Sacramental Ontology*, passim.

10. I use the Latin text of Aquinas's *Super epistolam B. Pauli ad Romanos lectura* from *Corpus Thomisticum*, ed. E. Alarcón (Pamplona: Universidad de Navarra: 2000–), http://www.corpustho misticum.org/cr000.html. For English translation, see Thomas Aquinas, *Lectures on the Letter to the Romans*, trans. Fabian Larcher, ed. Jeremy Holmes (Ave Maria, Fla.: Aquinas Center for Theological Renewal), http://www.nvjournal.net/index.php?option=com_content&view=article&id=53& Itemid=62.

11. Cf. Joseph P. Wawrykow, "Church," in *The Westminster Handbook to Thomas Aquinas* (Louisville, Ky.: Westminster/John Knox, 2005), 25–28, at 25: "Aquinas's favorite designation is church as 'mystical body of Christ' *(corpus mysticum Christi)*, followed in terms of frequency by another cherished designation, namely, church as 'congregation of the faithful.'"

character of Thomas's ecclesiology, I will highlight five elements of his Romans commentary: (1) its ecclesial focus, (2) its kerygmatic focus, (3) its historical focus, (4) its Christological focus, and (5) its sacramental focus.

The Church as Mystery

Before moving to these five characteristics, I want to sketch what I mean by Thomas's approach to the Church as mystery. For this purpose, I will turn briefly to a second *ressourcement* scholar, the Jesuit patrologist from Fourvière, Henri de Lubac. His historical study of Eucharist and Church in the Middle Ages, *Corpus mysticum* (1944), discussed the developments surrounding the approach to the threefold body *(corpus triforme)* of Christ: his historical body (born of the Virgin), his sacramental body (in the Eucharist), and his ecclesial body (the Church).[12] For the present discussion, I will highlight two results of de Lubac's impressive scholarly research: (1) the medieval view of the body of Christ as "mystical body" and hence of the Church as mystery; and (2) the shift in terminology used for the Church from "true body" to "mystical body," which took place in the High Middle Ages.

First, de Lubac explained that in the Middle Ages, the threefold body of Christ was regarded as one body, despite the fact that different aspects could be distinguished. The three aspects—the historical, the sacramental, and the ecclesial—were not seen as three separate bodies, but as three aspects of the one body of Christ. Within this one body, the sacramental or Eucharistic aspect was designated as the "mystical body" *(corpus mysticum)*.[13] The fact that it was the sacramental body—not the ecclesial body—that was referred to as "mystical body" is important in the light of later linguistic and theological developments. De Lubac then explained that the adjective "mystical" depended on the noun "mystery" (μυστήριον), "to which both the Latin *mysterium* and *sacramentum* correspond."[14] Medieval theologians talked about the "mystical body" of the Eucharist and about the "mystery" of the Eucharist both to indicate that the Eucharist was a sign of something else and to refer to the obscure depths hidden in the Eucharist.[15] The ecclesial body was the sacramental reality to which the Eucharist pointed and which the Eucharist made present.

---

12. Henri de Lubac, *Corpus mysticum: L'Eucharistie et l'Église au Moyen Âge: Étude historique*, Théologie 3 (Paris: Aubier, 1944), trans. Gemma Simmonds with Richard Price and Christopher Stephens as *Corpus Mysticum: The Eucharist and the Church in the Middle Ages: Historical Survey*, ed. Laurence Paul Hemming and Susan Frank Parsons (London: SCM, 2006).

13. De Lubac, *Corpus mysticum*, 28–36, 41–45.

14. Ibid., 45.

15. Ibid., 46–48.

Thus, there was a dynamic movement from the sacrament to its mysterious reality, from the sacramental to the ecclesial body. As de Lubac put it: "[A] mystery, in the old sense of the word, is more of an action than a thing."[16] The medieval use of the term "mystery" obviously did not have the modern connotation of a secret that further rational, discursive thought would gradually be able to uncover. Instead, the term had a sacramental connotation. The historical, sacramental, and ecclesial aspects of the body of Christ were sacramentally connected. Thus, to say that the Eucharistic body was a "mystical body" was to say that it represented and contained a deeper, spiritual reality.[17]

Second, the Eucharistic controversies surrounding Berengar of Tours (†1088) made it increasingly difficult to sustain the sacramental link between the sacramental and the ecclesial body.[18] Over against Berengar's "spiritualist" view of the Eucharist, the Church increasingly emphasized Christ's real presence in the Eucharist and began to separate this sacramental body from its dynamic purpose, namely the sacramental reality of the unity of the Church. The emphasis on transubstantiation, insisted de Lubac, led to a disintegration of the threefold body. A linguistic change accompanied these theological developments. Starting in the twelfth century, the term "mystical body" *(corpus mysticum)* came to refer to the Church rather than to the Eucharist. At the same time, the expression "true body" *(corpus verum)* no longer referred to the unity of the Church as the reality *(res tantum)* of the sacrament; instead, it was now the Eucharist that became the "true body." Thus, the twelfth century witnessed a "slow inversion,"[19] with *corpus mysticum* moving from Eucharist to Church and *corpus verum* moving from Church to Eucharist.[20] The widening gap between Eucharist and Church had made it possible, by the fourteenth century, to interpret the "body of the Church" *(ecclesiae corpus)* by means of analogies with juridical, social, and political bodies.[21] These comparisons, de Lubac maintained, would in turn radically alter the meaning of the Church

16. Ibid., 49.

17. For further discussion of the meaning of the term "mystery," see Henri de Lubac, *Medieval Exegesis: The Four Senses of Scripture*, vol. 2, trans. E. M. Macierowski (Grand Rapids, Mich.: Eerdmans, 2000), 19–27; Yves Congar, *Un Peuple messianique: L'Église, sacrement du salut; Salut et libération* (Paris: Cerf, 1975), 47–55

18. For what follows, see de Lubac, *Corpus mysticum*, 143–67.

19. Henri de Lubac, *Catholicism: Christ and the Common Destiny of Man*, trans. Lancelot C. Sheppard and Elizabeth Englund (San Francisco, Calif.: Ignatius, 1988), 100n68.

20. Cf. Susan K. Wood, *Spiritual Exegesis and the Church in the Theology of Henri de Lubac* (Grand Rapids, Mich.: Eerdmans, 1998), 63–68.

21. De Lubac, *Corpus mysticum*, 114–16. Cf. the analysis of the linguistic developments of *corpus mysticum* in Ernst H. Kantorowicz, *The King's Two Bodies: A Study in Mediaeval Political Theology*, 2nd ed. (Princeton, N.J.: Princeton University Press, 1997), 193–232.

as *corpus mysticum:* it would become simply one social body among many.[22] Thus, when the Reformation dissociated the mystical body of Christ from the visible Church, the Catholic Church was without adequate response: the common premise on both sides of the Reformation divide was a separation between sacramental body and ecclesial body.[23] De Lubac was convinced that both Catholicism and Protestantism needed to restore the sacramental cast of the doctrine of the Church.

When we move to St. Thomas's commentary on Romans, we find that he designates the Church as "mystical body." Aquinas refers to the Apostle's admonition not to think too highly of oneself (Rom 12:3), and he explains that the Pauline admonition is

based on the mystical body's likeness to a natural body. First, he touches on three things in a natural body; first, its unity when he says: *For as in one body;* secondly, the multiplicity of members when he says: *we have many members;* for the human body is an organism consisting of various members; thirdly, the variety of functions when he says: *all the members do not have the same function.* For the variety of members would serve no purpose unless they were ordered to different functions. Then he likens these three aspects to the mystical body of Christ, which is the Church: "He made him the head over all things for the church, which is his body" (Eph 1:22).[24]

St. Thomas goes beyond the Pauline metaphor of the Church as the body of Christ to refer to it as the *mystical* body. His language thus fits in with the later development sketched by de Lubac, according to which *corpus mysticum* no longer denoted the sacramental body but instead referred to the ecclesial body.

Thomas's use of *corpus mysticum* to describe the Church (rather than the body of Christ in the sacrament) raises the question whether the concomitant theological changes described by de Lubac have also found their way into Thomas's theology: the separation between the sacramental and the ecclesial body; the heightened emphasis on real presence and transubstantiation over against a spiritual eating in faith; and the understanding of the ecclesial body

---

22. De Lubac reiterated his displeasure with this understanding of the Church as simply one body among many in *The Splendor of the Church,* trans. Michael Mason (1956; repr., San Francisco, Calif.: Ignatius, 1999), 128–30.

23. De Lubac, *Corpus mysticum,* 114–17.

24. *In ad Rom.* 12, lect. 2 (§§ 972–73). "Praemissa admonitione, hic apostolus rationem assignat sumptam ex similitudine corporis mystici ad corpus naturale. Et primo in corpore naturali tangit tria. Primo quidem corporis unitatem, cum dicit *sicut enim in uno corpore;* secundo, membrorum pluralitatem, cum dicit *multa membra habemus:* est enim corpus humanum organicum ex diversitate membrorum constitutum; tertio officiorum diversitatem, cum dicit *omnia autem membra non eumdem actum habent.* Frustra enim esset membrorum diversitas, nisi ad diversos actus ordinarentur. Deinde aptat haec tria ad corpus Christi mysticum, quod est Ecclesia. Eph. I, v. 22: *ipsum dedit caput super omnem Ecclesiam, quae est corpus eius.*"

as just one of many social and political bodies. Mostly, these specific questions fall beyond the scope of Thomas's Romans commentary. The underlying, general question, however, is pertinent for our present purpose: does St. Thomas already reflect a move away from the unity and life of the Church as the sacramental reality *(res)* to questions of juridical structures *(sacramentum)*? In short, the question we need to address is the following: is Thomas's description of the Church as *corpus mysticum* indicative of a decline in sacramental ontology?

Characteristics of Thomas's Ecclesiology

Ecclesial Focus

This question brings us to the five elements that struck me as important in my reading of St. Thomas's Romans commentary. First, the very fact that the commentary is distinctly ecclesial in character is worthy of notice. This ecclesial character may not be immediately obvious considering the absence of any extended discussion of the Church. And, of course, ecclesiology is notable for its absence not only from this commentary, but also from Thomas's work in general. Discussions of Thomas's ecclesiology regularly mention this absence of anything resembling an explicit exposition *De ecclesia*.[25] The explanation may partially be historical, seeing that the first ecclesiological treatise was not written until the early fourteenth century, by James of Viterbo (ca. 1255–1308).[26] Thomas Aquinas was not alone in his omission of a treatise *De ecclesia*. It seems likely, however, that this historical factor is interwoven with theological factors. In a 1939 essay on "The Idea of the Church in St. Thomas Aquinas," Congar argued that the reason for the absence of an explicit ecclesiology was that the entire *secunda pars* of Thomas's *Summa theologiae*, dealing with Christian faith and morals as the movement of human beings toward God, constituted his ecclesiology: "To define the Church as a body having community of life with God is to conceive of it as humanity vitalized

---

25. See, for example, George Sabra, *Thomas Aquinas' Vision of the Church: Fundamentals of an Ecumenical Ecclesiology*, Tübinger theologische Studien 27 (Mainz: Matthias-Grünewald, 1987), 19–33; Thomas F. O'Meara, *Thomas Aquinas: Theologian* (Notre Dame, Ind.: University of Notre Dame Press, 1997), 137; Aidan Nichols, *Discovering Aquinas: An Introduction to His Life, Work, and Influence* (Grand Rapids, Mich.: Eerdmans, 2002), 120; Herwi Rikhof, "Thomas on the Church: Reflections on a Sermon," in *Aquinas on Doctrine: A Critical Introduction*, ed. Thomas G. Weinandy, Daniel A. Keating, and John P. Yocum (London: T&T Clark, 2004), 199–223, at 199.

26. Cf. Congar's expressions of displeasure with the treatises of *De ecclesia* as originating with James of Viterbo's *De regimine Christiano* in "The Idea of the Church in St. Thomas Aquinas," *Thomist* 1, no. 3 (1939): 331–59, at 331, 358; idem, *Lay People in the Church: A Study for a Theology of the Laity*, rev. ed., trans. Donald Attwater (1965; repr., Westminster, Md.: Christian Classics, 1985), 43.

Godwards by the theological virtues, which have God for their object, and organized in the likeness of God by the moral virtues."[27] If the entire dynamic process of the deifying return to God constitutes the Church, a separate ecclesiology hardly seems necessary. According to Congar, then, the absence of an explicit ecclesiology was the result of Thomas's sacramental vision. He argued that Thomas's focus was less on the external and juridical sacramental means than on the internal and spiritual reality of grace.[28]

This explanation is in keeping with St. Thomas's approach in the Romans commentary. It is true that the commentary as a whole contains precious little discussion that is explicitly ecclesiological in character. But this observation needs to be qualified in two ways. First, Thomas's expositions on circumcision and baptism, on the role of faith, on the Jew-Gentile relationship, on predestination, and especially, of course, on the body of Christ, are all ecclesiological in character. Although Thomas does not use any of these themes to construct a theology of the Church, he does present numerous issues that would have to find a place within a treatise on the Church, if one were to write one. Second, when he explains the purpose of the various Pauline letters, he categorizes the fourteen letters, which he argues are all about Christ's grace (*gratia Christi*), in an explicitly ecclesiological fashion. The grace of Christ may be considered in three ways:

In one way, as it is in the Head, namely, Christ, and in this regard it is explained in the letter to the Hebrews. In another way, as it is found in the chief members of the Mystical Body, and this is explained in the letters to the prelates. In a third way, as it is found in the Mystical Body itself, that is, the Church, and this is explained in the letters sent to the Gentiles.[29]

---

27. Congar, "Idea of the Church," 337. Cf. ibid., 339: "For St. Thomas, the Church is the whole economy of the return towards God, *motus rationalis creaturae in Deum* [the movement of the rational creature into God], in short, the *Secunda Pars* of his *Summa Theologica*." Sabra expresses his disagreement with this explanation, arguing that although it is true that everything is ecclesiological in Thomas's theology, one could say the same thing about the doctrine of God or of Christ (*Thomas Aquinas' Vision of the Church*, 27). Thus, he maintains that the deeper explanation is that "in contrast to those later authors, he [i.e., Thomas] did not view the church in predominantly juridical, political and sociological terms" (ibid., 29). So, for Sabra the absence of ecclesiological treatise supports his overall thesis that Thomas's ecclesiology is more theological than juridical in character. Sabra may well be right in this explanation, but it seems to me identical to what Congar was arguing. For Congar, since the entire *secunda pars* was ecclesiology, Thomas regarded the Church primarily as the dynamic movement of the deifying return to God. In other words, according to Congar, too, Thomas's ecclesiology was more theological than juridical in character.

28. Congar later presented an additional (but similar) rationale ("Traditio thomistica in materia ecclesiologica," *Angelicum* 43, nos. 3–4 [1966]: 405–28; reprinted in idem, *Thomas d'Aquin: Sa vision de théologie et de l'Eglise* [London: Variorum, 1984]). Cf. Sabra, *Thomas Aquinas' Vision of the Church*, 21–22.

29. *In ad Rom.*, prol. (§ 11). "Est enim haec doctrina tota de gratia Christi, quae quidem

Thus, St. Paul's letters to the Gentiles are, in Thomas's view, ecclesiological in nature. They deal with the grace of Christ as it is found *in the Church*, the mystical body. Thomas then goes on to explain that the letter to the Romans discusses the grace of Christ "as it is in itself" *(secundum se)*, while the letters to the Corinthians and the Galatians discuss the sacraments, and Ephesians, Colossians, and Thessalonians deal with the unity that Christ's grace produces in the Church.[30] Romans, in other words, while its immediate focus is on *gratia Christi* "as it is in itself," is part and parcel of an overall ecclesiological exposition: the grace of Christ exists in the Church, comes to believers in the sacraments, and thus produces the unity of the Church. Thomas's larger picture of the way in which St. Paul's letters cohere thus obviates the need for an explicit ecclesiological discussion in his commentary on Romans. This larger picture itself is very much ecclesiological in nature. It focuses on the grace of Christ, which, in the Church and through the sacraments, produces the unity of the Church. This seems rather like the sacramental ecclesiology advocated by de Lubac and Congar, according to which the structures of the Church, and especially, of course, the sacraments themselves, function as the *sacramentum* that produces the reality *(res)* of the Church's unity.

Kerygmatic Focus

The second item I want to highlight is the kerygmatic focus of those ecclesiological elements that we do find in this commentary. Although I have just emphasized the role of the sacraments in producing the unity of the Church, for St. Thomas they do not function in isolation. The preaching of the Gospel and the faith that results from this preaching are crucially important to the Angelic Doctor. Commenting on Paul's eagerness to preach the Gospel, which the Apostle describes as "the power of God" (Rom 1:16),[31] St. Thomas explains: "This can be understood in two ways. In one way, that the power of God is manifested in the Gospel: 'He has shown the people the power of his works' (Ps 111:6); in another way, that the Gospel itself contains in itself God's power, in the sense of Ps 68 (v. 33): 'He will give to his voice a voice of power.'"[32] Thomas then goes on to explain how faith leads to salvation: "This

---

potest tripliciter considerari. Uno modo secundum quod est in ipso capite, scilicet Christo, et sic commendatur in epistola ad Hebraeos. Alio modo secundum quod est in membris principalibus corporis mystici, et sic commendatur in epistolis quae sunt ad praelatos. Tertio modo secundum quod in ipso corpore mystico, quod est Ecclesia, et sic commendatur in epistolis quae mittuntur ad gentiles."

30. Ibid.

31. "For I am not ashamed of the gospel: it is the power of God for salvation to every one who has faith, to the Jew first and also to the Greek."

32. *In ad Rom.* 1, lect. 6 (§ 98): "Quod potest intelligi dupliciter: uno modo, quia virtus Dei

happens in three ways. First, through preaching: 'Preach the gospel to every creature. He who believes and is baptized will be saved' (Mk 16:15). Secondly, by confessing the faith: *with the mouth confession is made unto salvation* (Rom 10:10). Thirdly, by the Scripture; hence even the written words of the Gospel have a saving power, as Barnabas cured the sick by placing the Gospel upon them."[33] Salvation is the result of the Gospel as it is written down in the Scriptures, as it is preached, and as it is confessed in faith.

When in Romans 10:15, the Apostle quotes Isaiah's exclamation about the beauty of the feet of those who preach good news (Isa 52:7), Thomas presents two interpretations to his readers for their consideration:

This can be interpreted in two ways: in one way, so that by feet is understood their procedure, namely, because they [i.e., the preachers] proceed according to due order, not usurping the office of preachers: "How graceful are your feet in sandals, O queenly maiden!" (Song 7:1). In another way, by feet are understood their affections which are right, as long as they announce God's word not with the intention of praise or gain but for the salvation of men and the glory of God: "Their feet were straight" (Ez 1:7)."[34]

The task of preaching properly proceeds only on the basis of a divine mandate, and it needs to take place with the appropriate subjective intentions on the part of the preacher. Only in this way can the feet of the preacher be said to be beautiful.

When two verses down, in Romans 10:17, the Apostle again connects faith to hearing and preaching,[35] Thomas raises the question of how this can be squared with the idea of faith as a divinely infused virtue *(virtus infusa divinitus)*. He deals with this dilemma by making a distinction between the subjective disposition and the objective contents of the faith: the inclination of the heart is indeed a gift of grace and does not come from hearing, but the decision

---

in Evangelio manifestatur secundum illud Ps. CX, 6: *virtutem operum suorum adnuntiavit populo suo;* alio modo, quia ipsum Evangelium in se Dei virtutem continet, secundum illud Ps. LXVIII, v. 34: *dabit voci suae vocem virtutis.*"

33. *Ibid.* 1, lect. 6 (§ 100): "Secundo, per quem modum Evangelium salutem conferat, quia per fidem, quod designatur cum dicitur *omni credenti.* Quod fit tripliciter: primo per praedicationem; Mc. ultim.: *praedicate Evangelium omni creaturae; qui crediderit et baptizatus fuerit salvus erit.* Secundo per confessionem; infra X, 10: *oris confessio fit ad salutem.* Tertio per Scripturam, unde etiam verba Evangelii scripta virtutem salutiferam habent, sicut beatus Barnabas infirmos curabat, Evangelium superponendo."

34. *In ad Rom.* 10, lect. 2 (§ 840): "In his autem verbis, primo, commendatur processus praedicatorum, cum dicit *quam speciosi pedes,* quod dupliciter potest intelligi. Uno modo ut per pedes intelligantur eorum processus, quia scilicet ordinate procedunt, non usurpantes sibi praedicationis officium. Cant. VII, 1: *quam pulchri sunt gressus tui in calceamentis, filia principis.* Alio modo possunt intelligi per pedes affectus qui rectitudinem habent, dum non intentione laudis aut lucri verbum Dei annuntiant, sed propter hominum salutem et Dei gloriam. Ez. I, 7: *pedes eorum, pedes recti.*"

35. "So faith comes from what is heard, and what is heard comes by the preaching of Christ."

about *what* to believe does come from hearing.[36] Ever concerned with the primacy of grace, Thomas safeguards its infused character. In no way, however, does this minimize for him the importance of the office of preaching: the preacher proclaims Christ and is thus responsible for the contents of the faith that is to be passed on. The Reformed scholar George Sabra rightly comments:

> When one reflects on what Thomas says about the word of God, one is struck by the immense power attributed to it. To affirm that it effects forgiveness and sanctification, leads to eternal life, nourishes the soul, cleanses the heart, etc., is to ascribe mighty effects to it. If one compares these effects to what Thomas writes about the effects of the sacraments, one finds a great similarity. Preaching and teaching the word of God seem to function also as means of grace, so when the church "administers" the word it appears to be doing something quite similar to the administering of the sacraments, as far as the results are concerned.[37]

Indeed, Sabra goes so far as to insist that for Thomas "the office of preaching and teaching was superior to that of administering the sacraments."[38] Be that as it may, it is clear that the task of preaching is hugely significant to Thomas, not in the least because it is a prerequisite to people's acceptance of the Gospel in faith.

Redemptive Historical Focus

The redemptive historical focus of Thomas's Romans commentary is the third aspect that I would like to bring to the fore. One of the main interests of the pre-conciliar *ressourcement* movement was its desire to take history more seriously as a theological category than had been the case in the neo-scholastic commentatorial tradition. Marie-Dominique Chenu's (1895–1990) retrieval of Thomas Aquinas positioned the Angelic Doctor squarely within the context of the twelfth- and thirteenth-century rediscovery of nature and against the backdrop of the changeover from monastic schools (tied in with the feudal system) to the university system (connected to the rising merchant class).[39] Congar, as Chenu's student, was similarly interested in history. His interpretation of Thomas's ecclesiology highlighted its redemptive historical character. One of the results of Congar's interest in the progression of redemptive

---

36. *In ad Rom.* 10, lect. 2 (§ 844). "Dicendum est ergo, quod ad fidem duo requiruntur: quorum unum est cordis inclinatio ad credendum et hoc non est ex auditu, sed ex dono gratiae; aliud autem est determinatio de credibili et istud est ex auditu. Et ideo Cornelius qui habebat cor inclinatum ad credendum, necesse habuit ut ad eum mitteretur Petrus, qui sibi determinaret quid esset credendum."

37. Sabra, *Thomas Aquinas' Vision of the Church*, 147–48.

38. Ibid., 152.

39. See especially Marie-Dominique Chenu, *Aquinas and His Role in Theology*, trans. Paul Philibert (Collegeville, Minn.: Liturgical Press, 2002).

history was his strong appreciation of the Church as the "people of God" *(populus Dei)*. Congar believed that the centrality of this notion in *Lumen gentium* was definite theological gain. "The idea of the People of God," Congar wrote at the time of the Second Vatican Council,

in the first place, enables us to express the continuity of the Church with Israel. It at once invites us to consider the Church inserted in a history dominated and defined by God's Plan for man. This plan is one of covenant and salvation: People of God connotes Plan of God, therefore sacred history. We know that this Plan and this history are translated into a positive and gracious historical intervention.[40]

Congar was encouraged by the rediscovery of the notion of the "people of God" between 1937 and 1942 through the work of theologians such as Mannus Dominikus Koster (1901–81), Lucien Cerfaux (1883–1968), and others:[41] "One of the greatest recoveries of contemporary Catholic theology has been that of the eschatological sense, which implies a sense of history and of God's plan as leading everything to a consummation."[42] Congar believed the image of the "people of God," with its background in the narratives of Israel's desert journey—highlighting the many shortcomings and failings of the Old Testament people of God—was helpful particularly because it accentuated the historical situation in which the Church found herself in the "in-between" period. He also drew attention to the fact that the renewed focus on divine election and on historicity was of ecumenical value in the dialogue with Protestants, particularly since the notion of the "people of God" suggested "less sharply defined frontiers."[43]

In his discussion of the various metaphors that the Angelic Doctor used to describe the Church, Sabra points out that the Church as "people of God" is the one metaphor that for Thomas has a more political and juridical connotation, since, according to Thomas, the notion of *populus* implies the common consent of law as well as an ordered community.[44] Thus, Sabra comments:

40. Yves M.-J. Congar, "The Church: The People of God," in *The Church and Mankind*, vol. 1 of *Concilium: Theology in the Age of Renewal* (Glen Rock, N.J.: Paulist, 1965), 11–37, at 19.

41. Ibid., 14–18. Cf. Yves M.-J. Congar, *This Church That I Love*, trans. Lucien Delafuente (Denville, N.J.: Dimension, 1969), 12–16. Congar referred, among others, to Mannes Dominikus Koster, *Ekklesiologie im Werden* (Paderborn: Bonifacius, 1940); Lucien Cerfaux, *La Théologie de l'Église suivant saint Paul*, Unam Sanctam 10 (Paris: Cerf, 1942).

42. Congar, *This Church*, 18. See further Cornelis Th. M. van Vliet, *Communio sacramentalis: Das Kirchenverständis von Yves Congar—genetisch und systematisch betrachtet* (Mainz: Matthias-Grünewald, 1995), 201–8, 219–24.

43. Congar, "Church: The People of God," 28. At the same time, Congar added that "Protestant thought fails to see what the incarnation of the Son of God has introduced that is new and definitive. No doubt it is on the Christological level that this inadequacy begins. As a result the idea of the Body of Christ is not given its full value" (29).

44. Sabra, *Thomas Aquinas' Vision of the Church*, 48.

The designation *populus*, as used by *Lumen Gentium*, is also meant to emphasize the pilgrim-status of the church and to bring to the fore an eschatological dimension of the church (e.g., "messianic people"). It is also quite clear that the New People of God embraces the *whole* church. The same cannot be said of Thomas's notion of *populus*. The gulf that separates Thomas's use of this designation from that intended by Vatican II is perhaps as vast as the centuries that lie between them.[45]

Sabra maintains that for St. Thomas, the notion of *populus Dei* lacks historical and eschatological dimensions, while it refers mostly to the "people"—as distinct from the hierarchy—ruled by the political order of law.

This political and juridical connotation of the notion of the "people of God" might seem to undermine Congar's *ressourcement* of the Angelic Doctor, at least on this point.[46] But it seems to me that Thomas's Romans commentary asks for a somewhat more nuanced picture. It is true that Thomas does not negate the juridical connotation (with its elements of law and order) of the notion of *populus Dei*. And the *populus* are sometimes indeed those who are in a position of obedience toward their hierarchical leadership.[47] These aspects, however, do not take center stage in Thomas's commentary. Instead, the passages in which he works with the notion of *populus* in an ecclesial context often arise directly from the issue of the Jew-Gentile relationship. The Jews are the people of God to whom God gave his promise of descendents.[48] They are the people who were circumcised so they could be distinguished from other peoples.[49] They are the people whom God has adopted as his own.[50] With the

45. Ibid., 48–49.

46. Indeed, Sabra directly takes issue with Congar's interpretation of Thomas's use of *populus* as being identical with the *ecclesia* (ibid., 49). Cf. Yves M.-J. Congar, "'Ecclesia' et 'populus (fidelis)' dans l'ecclésiologie de S. Thomas," in *St. Thomas Aquinas 1274–1974: Commemorative Studies*, vol. 1, ed. Armand A. Maurer et al. (Toronto, Ont.: Pontifical Institute of Mediaeval Studies, 1974), 159–73. Reprinted in idem, *Thomas d'Aquin: Sa vision de théologie et de l'Eglise* (London: Variorum, 1984).

47. E.g., *In ad Rom.*, prol. (§ 4): "And just as in the Old Testament after the law of Moses the prophets were read to instruct the people in the teachings of the law—'Remember the law of my servant, Moses' (Mal 4:4)—so also, in the New Testament, after the gospels are read the teachings of the apostles, who handed down to the faithful the words they had heard from the Lord: 'For I received from the Lord what I also delivered to you" (1 Cor 11:23).'" ("Et sicut in veteri testamento post legem Moysi leguntur prophetae, qui legis doctrinam populo tradebant secundum illud Mal. IV, 4: *mementote Moysi servi mei* ita etiam in novo testamento, post Evangelium, legitur apostolorum doctrina, qui, ea quae a domino audierunt, tradiderunt fidelibus, secundum illud I Cor. XI, 23: *accepi a domino quod et tradidi vobis*.") See also *In ad Rom.* 12, lect. 3 (§ 997); 13, lect. 1 (§ 1039).

48. *In ad Rom.* 3, lect. 1 (§ 253): "For God promised to multiply that people and make it great: 'I will multiply your descendants' (Gen 22:16)." ("Promisit enim Deus populum illum multiplicare et magnificare, ut patet Gen. XXII 16: *multiplicabo semen tuum*.")

49. *In ad Rom.* 4, lect. 2 (§ 347): "The third reason was to distinguish the people worshiping God from all other peoples." ("Tertia est ut per hoc signum populus ille Deum colens, ab omnibus aliis populis distingueretur.") For similar references to the "people" as the Jewish nation

coming of Christ, Thomas maintains, circumcision (the Old Testament sacrament of initiation) was replaced by baptism.[51] As a result, Thomas maintains that both divine election and the adoption as sons has been extended to the Gentiles. Gentile believers, too, are now the "people of God."

Aquinas reflects on this inclusion of the Gentiles in the "people of God" particularly in connection with St. Paul's discussion of Hosea 2:23 and 1:10 in Romans 9:25–26.[52] The Gentiles, explains Thomas, used to be cut off from three blessings that the Jews enjoyed: divine worship, divine love, and deliverance from original sin through circumcision.[53] The first of these, divine worship *(divinus cultus)* constituted the reason why the Jews were called the "people of God."[54] Thomas argues, however, that thanks to the reconciliation effected by Christ, the Gentiles, too, have now become the "people of God":

> But the Gentiles were alienated from the society of this people, as it says in Eph (2:12): "Alienated from the commonwealth of Israel and strangers to the covenants of promise." However, through Christ they have become God's people: "He gave himself for us to purify for himself a people of his own" (Tit 2:14). And that is what he says: *Those who were not my people,* i.e., the Gentiles, *I will call my people,* i.e., that they be my people.[55]

This inclusion of the Gentiles means that they are now referred to as "sons of God" *(filii Dei)* and are reckoned as the people of God.[56] Their inclusion in

---

distinguished from other nations, see *In ad Rom.* 5, lect. 6 (§ 463); 9, lect. 1 (§ 744); 9, lect. 2 (§§ 750, 761); 9, lect. 5 (§ 809); 9, lect. 3 (§ 850); 11, lect. 1 (§§ 861, 862, 872); 11, lect. 4 (§§ 918, 923). In addition to these references, St. Thomas quotes numerous Old Testament passages that refer to the Jewish covenant "people" of God. I should also note that Thomas often uses the word *gens* (and sometimes *plebs*) rather than *populus* as referring to the Jewish covenant people. It does not seem to me that Thomas has particular reasons for choosing one term rather than another. I have restricted my analysis mainly to his use of the term *populus*.

50. *In ad Rom.*, 9, lect. 2 (§ 749): "First, therefore, he says: It has been stated that the promises, the adoption of sons, and glory referred to people whose fall is to me a source of great sadness and unceasing sorrow." ("Dicit ergo primo: ita dictum est quod eorum sunt promissa et adoptio filiorum et gloria, pro quorum casu est mihi magna tristitia et continuus dolor.") Cf. *In ad Rom.*, 9, lect. 2 (§ 761).

51. *In ad Rom.* 4, lect. 2 (§ 349).

52. "As indeed he says in Hosea, 'Those who were not my people I will call "my people," and her who was not beloved I will call "my beloved."' And in the very place where it was said to them, 'You are not my people,' they will be called 'sons of the living God.'"

53. *In ad Rom.* 9, lect. 5 (§ 799).

54. Ibid.: "divinus cultus, ratione cuius dicebantur populus Dei, quasi ei servientes et eius praeceptis obedientes."

55. Ibid.: "Sed ab huius populi societate gentiles erant alieni, secundum illud Ephes. II, 12: *alienati a conversatione Israel et hospites testamentorum. Sed per Christum facti sunt populus Dei. Tit. II, 14: dedit semetipsum pro nobis, ut emundaret sibi populum acceptabilem.* Et hoc est quod dicit *vocabo non plebem meam,* id est, gentilitatem quae non erat plebs mea, *plebem meam,* id est, ad hoc ut sit plebs mea."

56. Cf. ibid. 15, lect. 1 (§ 1160): "The third authority contains the devotion of the Gentiles to

this people of God is due to faith in Jesus Christ. Whereas proselytes to Judaism had to leave their native land and journey to Judea, this is not necessary for those converted to Christ: "Therefore, to each one living in his own place, *where it was said to them* in former times, 'You are not my people,' *there will be called sons of God* by divine adoption: 'To all who believed in his name, he gave them power to become children of God' (Jn 1:12)."[57] The result of this Gentile inclusion is that Thomas can speak in a rather loose way about the customs of the "people of God," simply referring to them as customs of the faithful.[58] In short, it seems that Thomas is content to follow the biblical usage of the expression *populus Dei*, and as a result he retains its redemptive historical use as found in Paul's letter to the Romans. If the Jewish nation are called the "people of God," then the Church, those adopted as sons of God through faith and baptism, can also be called the "people of God."

Christological Focus

Thomas's ecclesiology is characterized, fourthly, by a Christological focus. Although Congar genuinely recommended the term "people of God" as a suitable designation for the Church, he was apprehensive about the fact that it did not appear to have a Christological referent. The absence of such a Christological element meant that the expression "people of God" was unable to highlight the Christological newness of the Church. As a result, Congar cautioned against absolutizing the expression. Taken on its own, it focused too much on the "wilderness wanderings" of the people and thus on the "not yet" of the eschaton. Congar was convinced that Protestant ecclesiology, with its historical focus on the "people of God," did insufficient justice to the radical newness given with the Incarnation.[59] Therefore, the term *populus Dei* had to be supplemented with the notion of the Church as *corpus Christi*.[60] Commented Congar: "Under the new Dispensation, that of the promises realized through the incarnation of the Son and the gift of the Spirit (the 'Promised

---

God. Hence he adds: *And again* it is written in Ps 117 (v. 4): *Praise the Lord, all Gentiles,* i.e., confess His goodness: 'From the rising of the sun to its setting the name of the Lord is to be praised' (Ps 113:3); *and let all the peoples,* not only the Jewish people, *praise him.*" ("Tertia autem auctoritas continet devotionem gentium ad Deum. Unde subdit *et iterum* scriptum est in Psalmis *laudate, omnes gentes, dominum,* scilicet eius bonitatem confitentes, Ps.: *a solis ortu usque ad occasum laudabile nomen domini; et omnes populi,* non solum populus Iudaeorum, *magnificate eum.*")

57. *In ad Rom.* 9, lect. 5 (§ 800): "Unicuique ergo in loco suo habitanti, *ubi dictum est eis,* olim ex divina sententia, *non plebs mea vos, ibi vocabuntur filii Dei* per divinam adoptionem. Io. I, 12: *dedit eis potestatem filios Dei fieri his qui credunt in nomine eius.*"

58. Ibid., 14, lect. 1 (§§ 1098, 1100).

59. Congar, *This Church,* 29.

60. Ibid., 29–38; Congar, "The Church: The People of God," 29–37.

One'), the People of God was given a status that can be expressed only in the categories and in the theology of the Body of Christ."[61] Ecclesiology needed to be framed in Christological categories.

Also, here, I believe, Congar showed himself a true disciple of Thomas Aquinas. We have already seen that Aquinas uses the expression "mystical body" as designation for the Church and that, in fact, for the Angelic Doctor, the Pauline corpus is centered on the grace of Christ as found in the Church, with the letter to the Romans itself focusing on this grace of Christ "as it is in itself" *(secundum se)*. Accordingly, the Christological aspect shows up throughout the Romans commentary. It occurs, first of all, in connection with the doctrine of predestination. Rational creatures, Thomas avers, are united to God by grace.[62] This can refer either to the various graces that God freely gives to people *(gratia gratis data)*, such as the gift of prophecy, or to the sanctifying grace of adoption *(gratia gratum faciens)*.[63] Christ, too, can be said to be predestined, as Romans 1:4 makes clear. In his case, the union is a "union in personal being [*esse personali*]; and this is called the grace of union."[64] St. Thomas then adds, "Therefore, just as a man's union with God through grace of adoption falls under predestination, so also the union with God in person through the grace of union falls under predestination. And as regards this he [i.e., Paul] says, *who was predestined son of God.*"[65] Thomas then connects the "grace of adoption" (in the case of human beings) to the "grace of union" (in the case of Christ):

Now it is obvious that anything which exists of itself is the measure and rule of things which exist in virtue of something else and through participation. Hence, the predestination of Christ, who was predestinated to be the Son of God by nature, is the measure and rule of our life and therefore of our predestination, because we are predestined to adoptive sonship, which is a participation and image of natural sonship: "Those whom he foreknew he also predestined to be conformed to the image of his Son" (Rom 8:29).[66]

---

61. Congar, "The Church: The People of God," 35.

62. *In ad Rom.* 1, lect. 3 (§ 46).   63. Ibid.

64. Ibid.

65. Ibid.: "Sicut ergo hominem esse unitum Deo, per gratiam adoptionis, cadit sub praedestinatione, ita etiam esse unitum Deo, per gratiam unionis in persona, sub praedestinatione cadit. Et quantum ad hoc dicit *qui praedestinatus est filius Dei.*"

66. Ibid. 1, lect. 3 (§ 48): "Manifestum est autem quod id quod est per se est mensura et regula eorum quae dicuntur per aliud et per participationem. Unde praedestinatio Christi, qui est praedestinatus ut sit filius Dei per naturam, est mensura et regula vitae et ita praedestinationis nostrae, quia praedestinamur in filiationem adoptivam, quae est quaedam participatio et imago naturalis filiationis, secundum illud Rom. VIII, 30: *quos praescivit et praedestinavit conformes fieri imagini filii sui.*"

Predestination of human beings is patterned on the predestination of the Son of God; or, we could even say, predestination of human beings is a sharing in or a participation in the predestination of Christ *(participatio et imago naturalis filiationis)*. In his commentary on Romans 8:29–30,[67] Thomas again connects our sonship to that of Christ: "For just as God willed to communicate His natural goodness to others by imparting to them a likeness of his goodness, so that he is not only good but the author of good things, so the Son of God willed to communicate to others conformity to his sonship, so that he would not only be the Son but the first-born among sons."[68] Our sonship is tied in with that of Christ. All of this, according to Thomas, clearly excludes the idea that grace is given because of our merits.[69]

When Thomas speaks of the actual, temporal inclusion of human beings in Christ through faith, it does not take long before he has recourse to "body of Christ" language. Understandably, this language occurs most emphatically in connection with Romans 12:1–2, where St. Paul himself uses the analogy of the human body.[70] Here, Thomas reflects on the unity of the natural body, on the multiplicity of its members, and on the variety of its functions. He then moves from the natural body to the body of Christ. In Thomas's own words: "Then he [i.e., Paul] likens these three aspects to the mystical body of Christ, which is the Church: 'He made him the head over all things for the church, which is his body (Eph 1:22).'"[71] Thomas explains that the Apostle touches first on the number of the members, then on the unity of the mystical body, and finally on the variety of functions that the members have with regard to the common good of the body.[72] The discussion is limited to the Pauline anlogy between the natural body and the body of Christ, and in no way does Thomas attempt to interpret the "body of Christ" by using the analogies of political or social bodies, which, as we have seen, was de Lubac's concern about

67. "For those whom he foreknew he also predestined to be conformed to the image of his Son, in order that he might be the first-born among many brethren. And those whom he predestined he also called; and those whom he called he also justified; and those whom he justified he also glorified."

68. *In ad Rom.* 8, lect. 6 (§ 706): "Sicut enim Deus suam naturalem bonitatem voluit aliis communicare, participando eis similitudinem suae bonitatis, ut non solum sit bonus, sed etiam auctor bonorum, ita filius Dei voluit conformitatem suae filiationis aliis communicare, ut non solum sit ipse filius, sed etiam primogenitus filiorum."

69. Ibid. 8, lect. 6 (§ 703).

70. Romans 12:4–5: "For as in one body we have many members, and all the members do not have the same function, so we, though many, are one body in Christ, and individually members one of another."

71. *In ad Rom.* 12, lect. 2 (§ 973): "Deinde aptat haec tria ad corpus Christi mysticum, quod est Ecclesia. Eph. I, v. 22: *ipsum dedit caput super omnem Ecclesiam, quae est corpus eius.*"

72. Ibid. 12, lect. 2 (§§ 973–75).

the later medieval use of "body of Christ" language. The Church, for Thomas Aquinas, is not simply one body among many.[73] With regard to the unity of the body—which, as we have seen, de Lubac and Congar regarded as the sacramental reality or the dynamic aim of the Eucharistic celebration—Thomas comments:

> This mystical body has a spiritual unity through [which] we are united to one another and to God by faith and love: "There is one body and one spirit" (Eph 4:4). And because the Spirit of unity flows into us from Christ—"Anyone who does not have the Spirit of Christ does not belong to him" (Rom 8:9)—he adds *in Christ*, who unites us to one another and to God by his Spirit whom he gives us: "That they may be one even as we are one" (Jn 17:22).[74]

The Spirit of Christ unites us to Christ as the head of the mystical body. The result of this incorporation into Christ is the renewal of one's life. In his commentary on Romans 6, Thomas reflects on our dying with Christ and on our being made alive with him. Our being crucified with Christ results in "the removal of past sins," and it also "makes us beware of future sins."[75] The fact that we now live with the risen Christ means that we have "the faculty of never returning to sin."[76] By being incorporated into Christ *(incorporati Christo Jesu)* we die to sin and live for God.[77] This does not mean a sinless life; the inclination to sin remains.[78] But it does mean that we have been freed from the kingdom of sin and that sin has lost its dominion over us.[79] As a result of this incorporation into Christ, believers now observe the Law "not as existing under the Law but as free."[80]

The incorporation into Christ is, according to Thomas, the result of faith and of the sacraments of faith. We have already seen the importance that he assigns to faith in connection with the preaching of the Word. Throughout his

---

73. Cf. Sabra, *Thomas Aquinas' Vision of the Church*, 65–66; Jean-Pierre Torrell, "Yves Congar et l'ecclésiologie de Saint Thomas d'Aquin," *Revue des sciences philosophiques et théologiques* 82, no. 2 (1998): 201–42, at 212.

74. *In ad Rom.* 12, lect. 2 (§ 974): "Huius autem corporis mystici est unitas spiritualis, per quam fide et affectu charitatis invicem unimur Deo, secundum illud Eph. IV, 4: *unum corpus, et unus spiritus.* Et quia spiritus unitatis a Christo in nos derivatur, supra VIII, 9: *si quis spiritum Christi non habet, hic non est eius ideo subdit in Christo,* qui per spiritum suum, quem dat nobis, nos invicem unit et Deo. Io. XVII, 2 s.: *ut sint unum in nobis, sicut et nos unum sumus.*"

75. Ibid. 6, lect. 2 (§ 481): "Deinde cum dicit *ut destruatur,* etc., ponit effectum praedicti beneficii duplicem; quorum primus est remotio praecedentium delictorum. Et hoc est quod dicit *ut destruatur corpus peccati....* autem effectus est ut caveamus a peccatis in futurum: et hoc est quod subdit dicens ut *ultra non serviamus peccato.*"

76. Ibid. 6, lect. 2 (§ 484): "facultatem numquam de caetero ad peccatum redeundi."

77. Ibid. 6, lect. 2 (§ 491).   78. Ibid. 6, lect. 2 (§ 493).

79. Ibid.

80. Ibid. 6, lect. 3 (§ 497): "non quasi sub lege existens, sed sicut liber."

Romans commentary, he highlights the indispensable character of faith for salvation. Faith is the result of predestination.[81] Faith leads to justification and adoption as sons.[82] Faith is what characterizes us as the seed of Abraham.[83] And faith unites us to Christ as the head of the mystical body. This last point needs to be emphasized, because the more scholastic discussion of Christ's headship in the *Summa* may give the impression that *all* people belong to the body of Christ, since also unbelievers have Christ as their head; they have him as their head *potentialiter*.[84] While this (potential) inclusion of unbelievers in the body of Christ is certainly an aspect of Thomas's thought, in his biblical commentary on Romans 8:9,[85] he restricts the headship of Christ in a rather unencumbered fashion to the believers: "For just as that is not a bodily member which is not enlivened by the body's spirit, so he is not Christ's member who does not have the Spirit of Christ: 'By this we know that we abide in him, because he has given us of his own Spirit' (1 Jn 4:13)."[86] The body of Christ is thus, for Thomas, simply a way of speaking about those who by faith have been incorporated into Christ—the Church, in other words.[87]

Sacramental Focus

The centrality of faith is not something that Thomas would in any way oppose to the efficacy of the sacraments. The final focus of Thomas's ecclesiology that I want to mention, therefore, is its sacramental character. God incorporates people into Christ and into his mystical body by the combined means of faith *and* the sacrament of baptism. It would be unthinkable for Thomas to separate the two. The mystical body can thus not be played out over against the structures of the visible Church. In fact, it is precisely a characteristic of the new covenant that the sacraments are more than merely external signs. In his discussion on the freedom from sin (Rom 6:14),[88] Thomas comments that God's

81. Ibid. 4, lect. 1 (§ 330).   82. Ibid. 8, lect. 6 (§§ 703, 708).
83. Ibid. 4, lect. 2 (§§ 352–53). Cf. ibid. 9, lect. 2 (§ 753).
84. *Summa theologiae* III, q. 8, a. 3. Cf. Rikhof, "Thomas on the Church," 215; Sabra, *Thomas Aquinas' Vision of the Church*, 174, 178.
85. "Any one who does not have the Spirit of Christ does not belong to him."
86. *In ad Rom.* 8, lect. 2 (§ 627): "Sicut non est membrum corporis quod per spiritum corporis non vivificatur, ita non est membrum Christi, qui spiritum Christi non habet. I Io. IV, 13: *in hoc scimus quoniam manet in nobis, quoniam de spiritu suo dedit nobis.*" Cf. also ibid. 5, lect. 5 (§ 443); ibid. 8, lect. 1 (§ 605).
87. Nicholas M. Healy argues, wrongly it seems to me, that for St. Thomas, since all people are members of Christ's body but not of the Church, "body of Christ" is not synonymous with "Church" ("Ecclesiology and Communion," *Perspectives in Religious Studies* 31, no. 3 [2004]: 273–90, at 282). Potential inclusion in the body does not, however, amount to actual inclusion. Nonbelievers are potentially members not just of the body of Christ but also of the Church.
88. "For sin will have no dominion over you, since you are not under law but under grace."

grace, making men freely obey the Law, was not conferred by the sacraments of the Old Law, but Christ's sacraments conferred it. Consequently, those who submitted themselves to the ceremonies of the Law were not, so far as the power of those sacraments were concerned, under grace but under the Law, unless they happened to obtain grace through faith. But one who submits to Christ's sacraments obtains grace from his power, so as not to be under the Law but under grace, unless they enslaved themselves to sin through their own fault.[89]

The idea that the Old Testament sacraments did not confer grace is something that St. Thomas repeatedly mentions. Circumcision, he comments in his commentary on Romans 4:11,[90] "was not the cause but the sign of justice."[91] Unlike circumcision, "the burial of baptism causes the death of sin, because the sacraments of the New Law bring about what they signify."[92] The sacraments, under the new covenant, cause what they signify, unless people enslave themselves to sin through their own fault. Faith and love and the sacrament of faith (i.e., baptism) combine to incorporate a person into Christ and so to deliver him from damnation.[93] Because for Aquinas, the sacraments truly contain the grace toward which they point, they have an indispensable instrumental role in the realization of the reality of the unity of the Church. Although Aquinas's attention may be more on the sacramental reality of the actual grace of Christ, he does not ignore the instrumental means that lead to a participation in this grace. Congar, it seems to me, followed his thirteenth-century teacher when he tried to hold together the sacramental structures of the Church and the reality of its life.

Conclusion: Ecclesiology in Ecumenical Discussion

The Romans commentary does not discuss the Eucharist in any detail. As a result, Aquinas does not address the issue that occupied de Lubac: the

---

89. *In ad Rom.* 6, lect. 3 (§ 498): "Hanc autem gratiam facientem homines libere legem implere, non conferebant legalia sacramenta, sed conferunt eam sacramenta Christi; et ideo illi qui se caeremoniis legis subiiciebant, quantum pertinet ad virtutem ipsorum sacramentorum legalium, non erant sub gratia, sed sub lege, nisi forte per fidem Christi gratiam adipiscerentur. Illi vero qui se sacramentis Christi subiiciunt, ex eorum virtute gratiam consequuntur, ut non sint sub lege, sed sub gratia, nisi forte per suam culpam se subiiciant servituti peccati."

90. "He received circumcision as a sign or seal of the righteousness which he had by faith while he was still uncircumcised."

91. *In ad Rom.* 4, lect. 2 (§ 341): "circumcisio non erat causa iustitiae, sed signum." Cf. also ibid. 4, lect. 2 (§ 349); ibid. 11, lect. 4 (§ 920).

92. Ibid. 6, lect. 1 (§ 475): "Baptismi causat mortem peccati, quia sacramentum novae legis efficit quod signat."

93. Ibid. 8, lect. 1 (§ 596): "Quarum primam ponit dicens *iis qui sunt in Christo Iesu*, id est qui sunt ei incorporati per fidem, et dilectionem, et fidei sacramentum." For the link between baptism and incorporation into Christ, see also ibid. 13, lect. 3 (§ 1079).

relationship between the sacramental and the ecclesial body of Christ. It is nonetheless clear that St. Thomas's ecclesiology is sacramental in character. Together, faith and baptism incorporate people into Christ and thus cause the unity of the body of Christ. The resulting unity of this mystical body is a central concern to the Angelic Doctor. There is little or no indication in his commentary on Romans that Thomas is particularly interested in the juridical structures of the Church. This is not to say that he does not have any such interests. We are dealing here with the commentary on a letter in which, as Thomas sees it, the character of Christ's grace is central. It is nonetheless striking that throughout our discussion of the various aspects of Thomas's ecclesiology, we have found support for the manner in which *nouvelle théologie*—de Lubac and Congar, in particular—engaged in a *ressourcement* of Thomas's ecclesiology. Each of the five foci that I have highlighted—the ecclesial, the kerygmatic, the historical, the Christological, and the sacramental aspects— point to an ecclesiology that has the mystery of the Church's sacramental reality *(res tantum)* as its central concern.

Thomas's entire theology (as well as his commentary on Romans) is a description of the creature's deifying return to God. In this return, the preaching of the Gospel, along with the faith that should result, is crucially important. The redemptive history of the people of God—first Jews and then also Gentiles—has led to the new covenant in which through faith and baptism, people are included in the Church. The combination of the expressions "people of God" and "mystical body of Christ" serves in St. Thomas to combine the historical continuity and the Christological newness of the Church. The sacramental reality of the Church is the very grace of Christ *(gratia Christi)*, which Thomas believes is the topic of St. Paul's letter to the Romans. As a result, the Church, for Thomas, is primarily a mystery to be entered into and explored by faith. Whatever juridical or structural elements may be necessary, even indispensable, to an understanding of the Church, they are not Thomas's ultimate focus. We may well refer to his theology as a dynamic communion ecclesiology, whose various foci provide a great deal of ecumenical convergence between Catholics and Protestants.

To be sure, the *ressourcement* of a sacramental ecclesiology like that of Thomas Aquinas presents a challenge to Protestants. Thomas's discussion of the causal character of the sacrament of baptism is part and parcel of a genuinely sacramental understanding of the Church, and this may well cause discomfort for some Protestants. Indeed, the issue of whether the reality of grace is already present in the sacramental sign is perhaps the underlying issue that to a large extent keeps the ecclesiologies of the Catholic Church and of Protestantism apart. I am afraid that I simply do not know of a way to overcome these differences. Overall, however, the ecclesiology of Thomas's commentary is surprisingly hospitable to Protestants. As a Protestant, I believe we would do well to consider the biblical expositor, St. Thomas, as a source who has shaped and who should continue to shape the Protestant tradition of biblical interpretation. And, I would suggest, a reading of Thomas's commentary on Romans with an eye to his ecclesiological concerns may perhaps allow Catholics to understand even better some of the concerns that motivate their Protestant interlocutors.

John F. Boyle

4   On the Relation of St. Thomas's
Commentary on Romans to the
Summa theologiae

In this essay, I would like to reflect on the relationship between St. Thomas's
commentary on Romans and his *Summa theologiae*. The commentary and the
Summa are obviously different kinds of works and yet both products of the
same theological mind. There is clearly some overlap. The *Summa* is far from
devoid of scriptural content. The commentary is far from devoid of speculative distinction and definition. Nevertheless, many readers of St. Thomas desire, I think, to find more speculative matter in the commentary. If Scripture
is the foundation of theology, then more of the speculative science ought to be
spelled out in the commentary. There should be full and rich expositions of
grace, along the lines of questions 109–14 of the *Prima secundae* of the *Summa theologiae*. What such readers of St. Thomas want is for the commentaries
on Scripture to illuminate the *Summa*. But what if it is rather more the other
way around? Might we not ask the *Summa* to illuminate Scripture? Might
not the *Summa* give its reader the foundational conceptual tools to be better
able to undertake the serious study of sacred Scripture? The *Summa* after all
is for beginners in theology, that is, for those preparing for the careful and
sustained exposition of sacred Scripture.

Let us consider, as an example, the final verses of chapter 13—the verses
that were the occasion of St. Augustine's conversion: "Let us walk honestly,
as in the day: not in revelries and drunkenness, not in chambering and im-
purities, not in contention and envy: but put ye on the Lord Jesus Christ, and
make not provision for the flesh in its desires." In commenting on the list of
six sins, St. Thomas distinguishes between the first four, which pertain to the
corruption of the concupiscible appetite, and the last two, which pertain to
the corruption of the irascible appetite. The corruption of the concupiscible

appetite is intemperance, which, St. Thomas reminds his reader, concerns the delights of touch. He then considers the first four sins precisely as instances of intemperance in food, drink, sleep, and sex.[1] The analysis, term by term, is careful and precise. Readers of the *Summa* will recognize the essential division of the sense appetites and with that division the division of the moral virtues (and their opposing vices). The particulars of temperance with regard to touch are essential to the analysis of temperance in the *Summa*.[2]

St. Thomas's quick and tidy analysis of Romans here is insightful; the six sins are not random, but reflective of ordered reality. His command of the speculative analysis of the sensitive appetites in general and of temperance in particular permits him to see what is at work in St. Paul. For the student of St. Thomas as a commentator on St. Paul, the *Summa* is thus a valuable tool. St. Thomas does not repeat the analyses of the *Summa;* he presumes them.

So do we have simply discrete passages of Scripture interpreted in the light of *Summa* articles? We might if St. Thomas thought of the Epistle to the Romans as consisting of discrete passages, but he does not. For St. Thomas, the epistle is a coherent intellectual whole. It is not a *Summa* or work of systematic scholastic theology; but that makes it no less speculatively and intellectually coherent and unified. That St. Thomas thinks so is manifest in his use of the *divisio textus.*

I have argued elsewhere that the division of the text is a theologically significant tool in the scholastic theologian's tool kit.[3] It is, in principle, exquisitely simple. The commentator articulates the theme of the work being commented on and then undertakes the division of the whole according to the theme. The division continues apace down to each verse and sometimes even beyond. The division provides a frame for thinking about the book being commented upon as a whole. Each part (of whatever size) stands in relation to all the other parts.

In the case of the Epistle to the Romans, St. Thomas understands St.

---

1. Thomas Aquinas, *Super epistolam ad Romanos lectura*, in vol. 1 of Thomas Aquinas, *Super epistolas s. Pauli lectura*, edited by R. Cai., 8th ed. (Turin: Marietti, 1953), on 13:13, lect. 3, §§ 1074–1078. Subsequent citations to chapter and verse being commented on (where appropriate), followed by St. Thomas's internal division (prologus or lectio) and the paragraph number of the Marietti edition.

2. Cf. *Summa theologiae (ST)* II-II, q. 141, aa. 3–5.

3. John F. Boyle, "The Theological Character of the Scholastic 'Division of the Text' with Particular Reference to the Commentaries of St. Thomas Aquinas," in *With Reverence for the Word: Medieval Scriptural Exegesis in Judaism, Christianity and Islam*, ed. Jane McAuliffe, Barry Walfish, and Joseph Goering (Oxford: Oxford University Press, 2003), 276–83, and John F. Boyle, "Authorial Intention and the *divisio textus*," in *Reading John with St. Thomas Aquinas: Theological Exegesis and Speculative Theology*, ed. Michael Dauphinais and Matthew Levering (Washington, D.C.: The Catholic University of America Press, 2005), 3–8.

Paul's principal teaching to be grace considered in itself.[4] The division of the text then situates the elements of the epistle within a frame structured by the signal theme of grace.

Let us return to the two verses at the end of chapter 13 and see the immediate context from the division of the text.[5] These verses are, according to the division, within a section embracing both chapters 12 and 13 in which St. Thomas says St. Paul addresses the use of grace by which man might be perfect, first with regard to the holiness that man maintains for God (c. 12), second with regard to the justice that he shows his neighbor (c. 13:1–10), and finally with regard to the purity that he preserves in himself (c. 13:11–14).[6]

This consideration of the perfection of man, however, is set within a still larger frame in which chapters 12–15:13 set out moral teaching in general, which is part of a division covering the final five chapters on the exhortation to the use of grace. The exhortation to the use of grace, however, stands as part of a yet larger division, which ultimately brings us to the whole. The principal division of the letter covers 1:16 through to the end and is articulated by St. Thomas as St. Paul's instructing of the Romans concerning the truth of the grace of Christ. Of this, there are two parts: the power of grace (chapters 1–11) and the exhortation to the use of that grace (chapters 12–16).[7]

Grace is thus the defining theme of the whole, and we can see it in the division of the letter. This does not mean that every single comment on every single verse or set of verses must make mention of grace. That would be silly. It does mean that the commentary on each and every verse is to be understood in the context of grace. And what is this grace? When St. Thomas introduces the power of the grace of Christ, St. Thomas speaks of evangelical grace.[8] It is this that is being divided throughout the rest of the commentary. "Evangelical grace" is St. Thomas's turn of phrase, not St. Paul's, and it is not a common turn of phrase in St. Thomas, appearing uniquely here in the commentary on the Epistle to the Romans. What does St. Thomas mean by this term "evangelical grace"? He discussed the Gospel *(evangelium)* when explaining what it means that St. Paul has been separated unto the Gospel of God (1:1). He notes the threefold union of man to God proclaimed in the Gospel: the union through the grace of union in the incarnation, through the grace of adoption, and through the glory that is the life to come.[9] The Gospel for which St. Paul

---

4. Prol., § 11.
5. The broad division of the Epistle to the Romans is provided as an appendix to this essay.
6. On 12:1, lect. 1, § 953.
7. On 1:16, lect. 6, § 97.
8. Ibid.: "Et primo ostendit virtutem evangelicae gratiae."
9. On 1:1, lect. 1, §§ 23–24.

has been separated is a Gospel of grace by which man is united to God. These three aspects of union are themselves intimately related: the grace of adoption by which the Christian is a child of God in this life is caused by the incarnation and is ordered to the final state of eternal glory in the life to come. St. Thomas explicitly links St. Paul separated unto the Gospel and the grace that is the subject of the epistle in the division that begins the whole instruction on grace at 1.16: "here he [the Apostle] begins to instruct them [the Romans] concerning those things which pertain to the evangelical teaching unto which he had said he was separated. And first he shows the power of evangelical grace [cc. 1:16–11:36] and second he exhorts them to perform works of this grace [cc. 12–16]."[10] What the division gives us is not simply two parts, but the relation of the two parts. The truth of grace is twofold: its power and its use by the Christian. The chapters on the use of grace make sense only if one knows what one is using. It is easy enough to see the latter chapters as simply chapters of moral exhortation; St. Thomas wants to be clear that this exhortation is understood precisely in the context of grace. The moral life flows directly from the power of the grace of Christ.

This relationship of the two parts of the principal division on grace suggests something further about the division of the text. In St. Thomas's hands, the division often articulates the very causality of things. It is noteworthy how often St. Thomas renders the thought of St. Paul into an argument; frequently he says St. Paul "proves" or "concludes." A true and valid argument is such precisely in that it articulates a true causality. Theological argument—for which St. Paul provides the example in *Summa theologiae* I, q. 1, a. 8—articulates the truths of the faith precisely by articulating the causal unity in what has been revealed. At their best, a commentary and its division articulate the causal relations of the truths of the faith. Such is the case in this division: it is the very power of grace in the first part that makes possible the moral and spiritual life to which St. Paul exhorts his readers in the second. In the division at chapter 12, this evangelical grace, whose power has been articulated in the previous eleven chapters, is to be used such that the twofold causality of God and human cooperation effect the perfection of man in holiness, justice, and purity. Thus it is that the consideration of temperance is to be understood in the context of the spiritual perfection of man that arises from his cooperation with the threefold evangelical grace that unites him to God.

At the same time, the division of the text imposes its own constraints on the interpretation of the text, as can be seen in St. Thomas's interpretation of

10. On 1:16, lect. 6, § 97: "hic incipit [Apostolus] instruere eos [Romanos] de his quae pertinent ad evangelicam doctrinam in quam se segregatum praedixerat. Et primo ostendit virtutem evangelicae gratiae, secundo exhortatur ad executionem operum huius gratiae."

the first ten verses of chapter 13, which have been the subject of much deliberation on the relation of the Christian to the political order. While that relation
is part of St. Thomas's consideration, it is not at the heart of it. The issue is
the virtue of justice lived in relation both to superiors and to fellow men. The
unity of the division stipulates the higher context of this justice, namely, the
perfection of man, a perfection here horizontally situated in relation to man's
holiness and purity. The relation to the political order is thus rendered secondary, or perhaps better, reconfigured in relation to the spiritual perfection of
man in grace.

The power of the division to articulate a whole of which each element is
an integral part thus suggests a way of thinking about the relationship of the
commentary to the *Summa*. The division means that one should not think
simply of discrete passages and their own particular exposition, but rather
should see them in their conceptual relation one to another, each illuminating
different aspects of the reality of grace, the life of grace, as presented in the
epistle. The danger, to quote the old proverb, is to lose the forest for the trees.
The *Summa* is especially helpful for looking at the trees; the division is helpful
for seeing the situation of the trees within the forest.

There is yet another way in which to look at the consideration of grace in
the commentary with reference to the *Summa*, and here we might look more
immediately to the systematic character of the *Summa*. Let us take the case of
justification, or justifying grace, found in question 113 of the *Prima secundae*.
Although justification is fundamentally one grace considered an act of God,
it is made up of four instantaneous elements: the infusion of grace, the movement of the free choice to God through faith, the movement of the free choice
away from sin, and the forgiveness of guilt *(remissio culpae)*. As St. Thomas
explains so beautifully in the *Summa*, the justification of the impious is a
movement and accordingly follows the *ratio* of a movement: the motion of the
mover (the infusion of grace), the motion of the mobile as a motion to a terminus (the motion of the free choice to God through faith), the motion of the
mobile as a motion from a terminus (the motion of free choice from sin), and
finally the completion of the motion in its coming to its end (the forgiveness
of guilt).[11] The unity of motion is such that this is indeed a singular movement
of the soul. The four components are found, implicitly and explicitly, throughout the commentary on the Epistle to the Romans. The movement toward
God through faith is famously significant in the commentary. In all such passages, one could bring to bear the analysis of the *Summa*. Such would serve to
remind the reader that each element is part of a singular movement of grace.

11. *ST* I–II, q. 113, a.8 co.

The reader of St. Thomas ought not forget that a discussion of that first movement of grace through faith is necessarily and systematically bound with the full movement of the justification of the impious as articulated in the *Summa*. Here again, the *Summa* serves the commentary. It prevents the reader of the commentary from becoming too narrow or limited in his reading of justification with regard to a single aspect in the comments on an individual verse. This, in conjunction with the division's constant reminder of the integrity of the text, helps the reader maintain a view of the systematic whole.

I have so far focused on how the *Summa* may help one read St. Thomas's commentary. But one might well ask if the commentary can help one read the *Summa*? There is little, if any, strictly systematic exposition in the commentary that would serve to elucidate the systematic analysis of a given article of the *Summa*. But that is the wrong thing to look for. What the commentary offers is a breadth of scope in the interrelationships of the material that is very difficult to maintain in the reading of the *Summa*. For example, according to St. Thomas's division, the first of the evils that grace frees man from in 5:12–6:23 is slavery to sin. We find here some discussion of the *remissio culpae* that is part of the movement of the grace of justification. In chapter 5, St. Paul compares Adam and Christ, and as such it is only fitting that the consideration of grace here is intimately tied to the saving action of Christ. Indeed, the Christological detail is splendid, and it is detail one simply does not find in I–II, q. 113. One does find it in the *tertia pars* of course, and the *divisio textus* of the *Summa* ultimately links them. But here in the commentary we find an immediate linking brought out in the fine details of both division and commentary.[12] Or with regard to the movement toward God through faith, St. Thomas, as commentator on St. Paul, must consider the relation of faith to hope and especially to charity, to the saving work of Christ and to the action of the Holy Spirit in the human soul. What is remarkable is the wealth of interconnected systematic material throughout the commentary in relation to the foundational consideration of grace: the operations of the Holy Spirit, the sacraments, the theological virtues of faith, hope, and charity, predestination and divine love. What the commentary brings out is precisely the rich dynamics of the systematic material, not simply further systematic analyses.

How then might we articulate the relationship of commentary to *Summa*? The genius of scholastic thought is, in part, its ability to distinguish, to take things apart. No one can take something apart, can dissect it, quite like St. Thomas. But our knowledge of something is not simply a matter of knowing its components, however well articulated. They stand in relation one to

---

12. See especially on 5:13–21, lect. 5–6, §§ 430–467.

another, and here too we see in St. Thomas's speculative works the effort to
see the parts in relation one to another and to the whole. But if we may continue the analogy from biology, there is dissection; but there is a still further
aspect to be considered: how these pieces all work in the living organism when
they are operative in relation one to another. Let me propose, only partially in
jest, that the *Summa* is like lab work and the biblical commentary is like field
work. The *Summa* gives us the categories and distinctions we need to understand more clearly and fully the reality described in its living form by St. Paul
in the Epistle to the Romans. Commentary and *Summa* stand in dynamic
complementarity one to another so as to provide together a fuller picture of
the reality of grace.[13] Here we see a consummate achievement of St. Thomas's
scholasticism.

Appendix: Aquinas's Division of the Epistle to the Romans

    I. Salutation 1.1–1.7
    II. The business of the letter 1.8–16.27
        A. indicates his affection for the Romans 1.8–1.15
        B. instructs them concerning the truth of the grace of Christ 1.16–16.27
            1. the power of evangelical grace 1.16–11.36
            a. sets forth the power of grace 1.16–1.17
            b. explains it 1.17–11.36
                (1) grace is necessary for salvation 1.17–4.25
                    (a) necessary to Gentiles for salvation because their wisdom
                        could not save them 1.17–1.32
                    (b) necessary to Jews for salvation because circumcision and the
                        law are insufficient for salvation cc. 2–4
                        i) not justified by the law c. 2
                        ii) not justified as a people c. 3
                        iii) not justified by circumcision c. 4
                (2) grace is efficacious and sufficient for salvation 5.1–11.36
                    (a) what goods follow from grace 5.1–5.11
                    (b) from what evils grace frees us 5.12–8.39
                        i) freed from slavery to sin 5.12–6.23
                        ii) freed from slavery to the law c. 7
                        iii) freed from damnation 8.1–8.39

13. In the articulation of grace, the Epistle to the Romans is itself just a part. St. Thomas provides a division of the whole of the Pauline corpus with regard to grace (prol., § 11). It is in the
fourteen epistles considered in their unity that Thomas maintains we see yet more fully the lived
reality of grace in the mystical body.

(3) the origin of grace: whether from election of God alone or from the merits of preceding works 9.1–11.36

    (a) election of the gentiles c. 9

        i) dignity of the Jews 9.1–9.3

        ii) how the gentiles are lifted to that dignity 9.6–9.33

    (b) the fall of the Jews 10.1–11.36

        i) the fall to be lamented c. 10

        ii) the fall not universal 11.1–11.10

        iii) the fall not irreparable 11.11–11.36

2. exhorts to performing works of grace; teaches the use of grace 12.1–15.13

  a. sets out moral teaching in general 12.1–15.13

    (1) the use of grace that man might be perfect 12.1–13.14

      (a) with regard to sanctity c. 12

      (b) with regard to justice 13.1–13.10

      (c) with regard to purity 13.11–13.14

    (2) that the perfect might support the imperfect 14.1–15.13

  b. treats specific issues 15.14–16.27

    (1) pertaining to himself 15.14–15.33

    (2) pertaining to others c. 16

Edgardo Antonio Colón-Emeric

❧

5 Thomas's Theology of Preaching in Romans
A Lascasian Application

Throughout history, Thomas Aquinas has been called many things—a Christian philosopher, a scholastic theologian, the *doctor angelicus*, the *doctor communis*, the dumb ox—but "preacher" is not one of them. Few outside the Dominican Order are likely to rank him as worthy of admission to the pantheon reserved for princes of preaching such as Augustine or Chrysostom. I would venture to guess that despite their undisputed theological worth, the writings of Thomas are not considered standard texts for courses in homiletics.[1] And yet, as a member of the *Ordo Praedicatorum*, Thomas was both an accomplished preacher and a teacher of preachers.[2] Indeed, in the sixteenth century, the theology of the Angelic Doctor inspired and disciplined the sermons of the boldest defenders of the Indians.[3] The most famous of these protectors,

---

1. Despite their excellent worth, there is no entry for Aquinas in either William H. Willimon and Richard Lischer, eds., *Concise Encyclopedia of Preaching* (Louisville, Ky.: Westminster/John Knox Press, 1995) or Richard Lischer, ed., *The Company of Preachers: Wisdom on Preaching: Augustine to the Present* (Grand Rapids, Mich.: Eerdmans, 2002).

2. A more thorough inquiry into Thomas's theology of preaching than the one that I am engaging in here should consider the Angelic Doctor's practice of preaching. Unfortunately, not many of his sermons were preserved. However, an examination of those sermons that are extant reveals that Thomas's preaching was thoroughly doctrinal and pastoral. On Thomas Aquinas as a preacher see Jean-Pierre Torrell, *Saint Thomas Aquinas*, vol. 1, *The Person and his Work*, trans. Robert Royal (Washington, D.C.: The Catholic University Press of America, 1996), 69–74. See also Clyde E. Fant Jr. and William M. Pinson, Jr. eds., *20 Centuries of Great Preaching: An Encyclopedia of Preaching* (Waco, Tex.: Word Books, 1971), 1:183–202; Hughes Oliphant Old, *The Reading and Preaching of the Scriptures in the Worship of the Christian Church: The Medieval Church* (Grand Rapids, Mich.: Eerdmans, 1999), 408–36.

3. Throughout this essay, I will use the term "Indians" to name the native inhabitants of the lands encountered by the Spaniards in their search for a route to India. Of course, the term is problematic on many grounds, but the alternatives (Amerindian, Native American, indigenous) fare no better. In any case, "indios," or Indians, was what Las Casas called the peoples to whose defense he dedicated his life, and it is in that spirit that I use the term.

Fray Bartolomé de las Casas, learned how to preach "prophetically" from reading Thomas.[4] It is my hope and contention that by considering the manner
of Las Casas's application of the theology of Aquinas to the context of the
Indies, we will grow in appreciation for the richness of resources present in
Thomas Aquinas's theology for engaging the great social crises of our day.

To begin with: Who was Bartolomé de las Casas? He was one of the Spanish *conquistadores* who sailed to the "new world" in search of adventure and
fortune. After a few years in the island of La Hispaniola, he traveled to Cuba
in 1513 to serve as a missionary to the Indians and chaplain to the Spanish
troops. In return for his services, Las Casas received an *encomienda*. That is
to say, he became a prosperous landowner and slaveholder. Unfortunately for
Bartolomé, he was a priest and he had to preach from the Bible. While preparing his Sunday sermon he ran across the following text from Ecclesiasticus
34:21–27:

If one sacrifices ill-gotten goods, the offering is blemished; the gifts of the lawless are
not acceptable. The Most High is not pleased with the offerings of the ungodly, nor
for a multitude of sacrifices does he forgive sin. Like one who kills a son before his
father's eyes is the person who offers a sacrifice from the property of the poor. The
bread of the needy is the life of the poor; whoever deprives them of it is a murderer. To
take away a neighbor's living is to commit murder; to deprive an employee of wages is
to shed blood.

Las Casas heard this text as a direct condemnation of the way in which he
and his fellow Spaniards had exploited the Indians. His treatment of his Indian slaves had been enlightened and gentle by Spanish standards. Yet, in depriving the Indians from their liberty he had committed murder. Confronted with
such a prophetic text, Las Casas faced the same set of choices faced by preachers
throughout history: change texts, accommodate the text, or preach the text.
He chose the last of these; he preached the text and then did something that
few preachers dare to do: he accommodated his life to the text. In brief, Las Casas freed his slaves and became the indefatigable defender of the Indians until
his death in 1566. In his theological advocacy of the Indians Las Casas drew on
Scripture, of course, and also on the theology of Thomas Aquinas.[5]

Las Casas was not the first person to look to Thomas for answers to the
difficult questions raised by the context of the Americas, but he was in all

4. Cf. Isacio Pérez Fernández, "El protector de los indios y profeta de los españoles," *Studium*
14, no. 3 (1974): 543–65, and "El perfil profético del padre Las Casas," *Studium* 15, no. 2 (1975):
281–359.

5. In 1522, after the failure of his attempt at melding evangelism and colonialism in Cumaná,
Venezuela, the previous year, Las Casas entered the order of Saint Dominic and spent the next four
years in Santo Domingo studying the writings of Thomas Aquinas.

likelihood the first Dominican to apply Cajetan's reading of Thomas to these questions.[6] Fray Bartolomé's engagement of Cajetan is an interesting though insufficiently appreciated chapter in the history of Thomistic theology.[7] However, that is not the chapter that I am writing at present. Instead, I intend us

6. Isacio Pérez Fernández, "La doctrina de Santo Tomás en la mente y en la acción del Padre Las Casas," *Studium* 27, no. 2 (1987): 270–95. Pérez convincingly shows that the influence of Cajetan's thought on Las Casas's interpretation of Thomas is profound. Cajetan's commentaries on the *Secunda secundae* arrived in Santo Domingo sometime between 1519 and 1520, just prior to Las Casas's entrance into the Dominican order. For a somewhat different and more critical note on the influence of Thomas Aquinas's theology in Las Casas's thought see Enrique Ruiz Maldonado, "Tomás de Aquino, Bartolomé de las Casas y la controversia en las indias," *Studium* 14, no. 3 (1974): 519–42. In Ruiz's judgment, Las Casas is a selective and not very original reader of his theological authorities, including Thomas Aquinas. He cites traditional texts when they support his argument and omits them when they could be used otherwise. As evidence Ruiz singles out the fact that in his dispute against Sepúlveda, Fray Bartolomé did not cite the key text on unbelief in the *Summa theologiae* II-II, q. 10, a. 10. The alleged reason for the bishop of Chiapas's reticence is that he does not wish to arm his opponent with arguments based on authority (534). In contrast, Ruiz admires Francisco Vitoria for his scholastic rigor and liberality of spirit, and it is a mark against Las Casas that he does not draw more richly on the Salamancan's work *De indis* (540). Ruiz excuses Las Casas from the need to attain Vitoria's level of theological coherence since the endeavor of advocating for the Indians did not require it, but then again, he describes Fray Bartolomé's passion for the dignity of the Indians as "casi neurótica" (527n23). I think that Ruiz's assessment though correct in part errs on the whole. Las Casas does not write with the precision of Vitoria, but Fray Bartolomé is not writing from Salamanca. Moreover, if by theological coherence Ruiz has in mind Vitoria's presentation of seven legitimate titles for the conquest of the Indies, then Las Casas's alleged lack of liberality of spirit and scholastic rigor seems virtuous. For as Las Casas pointed out (and Ruiz knows; see the quote on page 534) those hypothetically legitimate titles are based on an entirely fictitious situation: gentle Spaniards arriving peacefully on the shores of the Americas to be met with fierce resistance by the Indians. Cf. Marcel Bataillon, *Estudios sobre Bartolomé de las Casas* (Barcelona: Ediciones Península, 1976), 22–26.

7. Throughout his writings, Las Casas shows proves himself a grateful pupil of Cajetan and never misses the opportunity to heap praises on him for addressing the situation of the Indies in his commentary on the *Secunda secundae* of the *Summa theologiae*. Las Casas tells the story of how word of the abuses of the Indians reached Cajetan in Rome by way of Jerónimo de Peñafiel on behalf of Pedro de Córdoba, vicar of the Dominicans in Spain. Cajetan's expression of disbelief at the behavior of the Spanish crown is lovingly preserved by Las Casas: "Et tu dubitas regem tuum esse in inferno?" ("And you doubt that your king is in hell?") (cited by Isacio Pérez Fernández in "La doctrina de Santo Tomás en la mente y en la acción del Padre Las Casas," 274). Cajetan promised to address himself against the despotism of Spain in his commentary on q. 66, a. 8 of the *Secunda secundae*. Cajetan's intervention consisted in introducing a threefold distinction into the category of unbelievers in their relation to Christian jurisdiction. First, some unbelievers, like the Jews living in Spain, are subject to Christian rule *de jure et de facto*. Second, some unbelievers, like the Muslims occupying the Holy Land, are subject to Christians *de jure non de facto*. Third, some unbelievers, like the Indians living in the Americas, are subject to Christians *nec de jure nec de facto*. Las Casas considers this threefold distinction crucial for understanding the true status of the indigenous inhabitants of the Indies. For this reason, he appeals to this distinctions numerous times in his apologetic writings. See Jesús Ángel Barreda, "Primera anunciación y bautismo en la obra de Bartolomé de Las Casas," *Ciencia Tomista* 116 (1989): 291–316.

to consider Las Casas's application of Thomas's commentary of Paul's Epistle to the Romans for the context of the conquest. In particular, I want us to draw our attention to Las Casas's appropriation and use of Thomas's theology of preaching as found in the Angelic Doctor's commentary on Romans 10. Our inquiry will be divided into two parts. First, we will consider Thomas's homiletical reflections in Romans, paying particular attention to the nature and necessity of preaching. Second, we will consider Las Casas's application of Thomas's theology to the defense of the Indians. I will conclude the paper with a brief historical postscript.

Aquinas's Theology of Preaching in Romans

Thomas does not provide us with a single, unified study on the subject of preaching. Nevertheless, the Angelic Doctor makes important contributions to a theological understanding of preaching throughout his theological corpus and in particular in his commentary on Paul's Letter to the Romans. The biblical center of gravity for his reflections lies in Romans 10:17, "Faith comes from what is heard, and what is heard comes from the word of Christ." This statement gives rise to two important questions. First, how is faith dependent on hearing? Second, have all heard?

First, how is faith dependent on hearing? Faith is the supernatural gift that renders the *credibilia* of Christianity intelligible. By the light of faith the intellect is elevated and the will is inclined to adhere to God. As such, faith is the foundation of the spiritual life. Now, faith requires hearing. Aquinas comments that "two things are required for faith: one is the inclining of the heart to believe; and this does not come from hearing, but from the gift of grace; the other is a decision about what to believe and this comes from hearing. Thus, Cornelius whose heart was inclined toward belief, needed Peter to be sent to him to point out what he should believe."[8]

Faith is not the result of a fortuitous encounter between an exterior word and an interior movement. The graced movement of the will is precisely oriented to dispose the listener to believe the word of the preacher. The inclination of the heart toward belief is caused by an interior movement of God's grace. The specific things to be believed come from what is heard. This hearing can come about in two ways. First, God can make himself known by means of an interior word alone, as in the case of those who receive the gift of prophecy. The chief exemplars of this gift are the authors of Scriptures, the prophets, and

---

8. Thomas Aquinas, *Lectures on the Letter to the Romans*, trans. Fabian Larcher, O.P., ed. Jeremy Holmes (Ave Maria, Fla.: Aquinas Center for Theological Renewal), cap. 10, lect. 2, http://www.avemaria.edu/uploads/pagesfiles/4283.pdf.

the apostles. The second and more common way that the good news can be heard is through the exterior word of a preacher of the Gospel.

For Thomas, the preacher is an instrument of the Holy Spirit.[9] Through the words of the preacher the graced intellect is led by the Holy Spirit from the principles that can be derived from nature to those that can be attained only by faith. What renders the sermon a suitable vehicle of the work of the Spirit is not chiefly the quality of the delivery or the holiness of the deliverer, desirable as both of these are, but the validity of the mission and the orthodoxy of the delivered content. As Benoît-Dominique de La Soujeole illustrates, the main requirement for a piano to be a fit instrument for performing a Chopin sonata is not the aesthetic value of the piano but its fine tuning.[10] An out-of-tune concert grand will be outperformed by a well-tuned humble upright any day of the week. In the same way, what makes a sermon the word of God is the fundamental harmony of the message of the preacher with the faith of the Church.

The sermon is the word of Christ, Thomas explains, "either because it is about Christ: 'We preach Christ' (1 Cor 1:23), or because they have been sent by Christ: 'For I received from the Lord what I also delivered to you' (1 Cor 11:23)."[11] The preacher of the Gospel is one who is sent by God. Either directly as in the case of John the Baptist or mediately by the authority of a bishop who, according to Thomas, "takes God's place" *(qui gerunt vicem Dei)*. The authority of the preacher comes from a divine commission. It is not a role that one can claim for oneself. The one who is not sent is not authorized. Such a person is not only unworthy of preaching *(non digne)*, he is actually incapable of doing so *(non capax)*.[12] Winsome, truthful speech is not enough, nor is the belief in an inward call a sufficient qualification. Qualification for the office of preacher requires the conferring of a special character—a canonical mission. Augustine Rock observes that for Aquinas authorization by a bishop is integral to the possibility of preaching.

As the Scriptures provide for no further preachers except those who are the successors of the apostles, the only sure sign of a true interior mission has been exhausted. The other two signs of such a mission, as St. Thomas points out, are inadequate, for the truth can be preached *per accidens*, and miracles can be simulated. There remains, then, in our times only the mission communicated through the Church as certainly acceptable.[13]

9. Cf. Benoît-Dominique de La Soujeole, "Le mystère de la prédication," *Revue Thomiste* 107, no. 3 (2007): 355–74. Cf. *Summa theologiae (ST)* II-II, q. 177, a. 1.

10. Cf. La Soujeole, "Le mystère de la prédication," 368.

11. *Lectures on Romans*, cap. 10, lect. 2.

12. Cf. Augustine Rock, *The Theological Concept of Preaching according to St. Thomas Aquinas* (Dubuque, Iowa: Wm. C. Brown, 1958), 108.

13. Ibid., 118.

The divine sending mediated through the Church is the most distinctive and defining characteristic of preaching, which distinguishes it from other types of discourse even of a theological kind. For Thomas, the canonical mission can be considered the formal cause of preaching. "Thus," as Rock remarks, "without due mission, there is no preaching. Only the word proposed by one duly sent is indeed the word of the Lord, or preaching."[14]

The apostolic commission and the apostolic tradition are the principal conditions of possibility for preaching; these two constitute the material and formal causes of preaching.[15] Hence, where these two are lacking there is no preaching. However, there is more to preaching than transmitting an authorized word. Preaching is rendered credible by the deeds of the preacher. In Romans 15:14 Paul "boasts" about how Christ had worked through him to "win obedience from the Gentiles, by word and deed."[16] What Paul means to say, according to Thomas, is that he brought people to faith through right deeds. In other words, there is a connection between "the faith preached" and "the good life of the preachers."[17] In fact, to preach in a state of sin is a sin. The instrumental efficacy of the apostolic message is facilitated by the authenticity of an apostolic life. "But," Thomas warns, "all this would be insufficient, unless the Holy Spirit stirred the hearts of their hearers to believe."[18] The words of the preacher are not in themselves the cause of faith. As Thomas observes "although one cannot believe, unless he hears the word of the preacher, nevertheless, not everyone who hears believes."[19]

Not all have believed. But have all heard? What about a child abandoned in the jungle? Or what about someone who grew up far away from any contact with Christianity? Is such a person guilty of rejecting a Gospel they never heard? In scholastic theology, the problem of the boy raised in the wilderness usually arose in the context of discussing the necessity of explicit faith. According to Hebrews 11:6 "without faith it is impossible to please God" (sine fide impossibile est placere Deo). But how much must one believe explicitly in order to approach God? What faith is required, for example, of a Christian boy kidnapped by the Saracens and raised among Muslims? Alexander of Hales answers this question in the following way: "If the boy does what is within him then the Lord will illumine him either by an interior inspiration (per occultam inspirationem) or by an angel or by a person."[20] Thomas considers the problem of a person growing up outside the Christian sphere in his

---

14. Ibid., 106.

15. Cf. ibid., 60, 102.

16. *Lectures on Romans* 15, lect. 2.

17. Ibid.

18. Ibid.

19. *Lectures on Romans* 10, lect. 2.

20. Cite in Louis Capéran, *Le problème du salut des infidèles* (Toulouse: Grand Séminaire, 1934), 185.

Commentary on the Sentences (*Sent.* 3, d. 25, a. 2, a. 1 ad 1 and *Sent* 2, d. 28, q. 1, a. 4, qla. 4), in the *Disputed Questions on Truth* (*De veritate* 14, a. 11 ad 1), and here in his Commentary on Romans 10:18.

The answer is that according to the Lord's statement (Jn 15:22) those who have not heard the Lord speaking either in person or through his disciples are excused from the sin of unbelief. However, they will not obtain God's blessing, namely, removal of original sin or any sin added by leading an evil life; for these, they are deservedly condemned. But if any of them did what was in his power, the Lord would provide for him according to his mercy by sending a preacher of the faith as he sent Peter to Cornelius and Paul into Macedonia. Nevertheless, the fact that they do what is in their power, namely, by turning to God, proceeds from God's moving their hearts to the good: "Turn us to thee, O Lord, that we may be turned" (Lam 5:19).[21]

Interestingly, the Angelic Doctor does not consider this problem in his discussion of the necessity of explicit faith in the *Summa theologiae* (*ST* II-II, q. 2, a. 5). This omission has led some of Thomas's interpreters to consider the solution proposed in Romans to be an intermediate stage of development between the youthful and not sufficiently Augustinian answer to this question in the *Commentary on the Sentences* and the mature treatment of the *Summa*.[22] Henri Bouillard argues that Thomas's silence on this matter is evidence that by the time of the *Secunda secundae*, Thomas implicitly admits that the number of people who have not heard the Gospel is far from small. Allegedly, the reason why Thomas neglects to raise the objection of the *puer in silvis* among the objections to the question of "whether one is to believe anything explicitly" is because the Angelic Doctor no longer considers this an exceptional case.[23] However, the scholarly consensus regarding the dating of the *Secunda secundae pars* of the *Summa theologiae* (1271–72) vis à vis the *Commentary on Romans* (1272–73) makes it difficult to sustain Bouillard's argument from silence.[24] Hence, I believe that we can say with a good degree of confidence that the teaching of Thomas in Romans on the question of the child *nutriti in sylvis* is his mature reflection on this topic.[25] Let us now turn to the interpretation of this teaching.

First (pace Bouillard), Thomas considers this an exceptional case. Thomas took it for granted that echoes of the Gospel (*fama praedicationis apostolicae*)

21. *Lectures on Romans* 10, lect. 2.
22. Cf. Henri Bouillard, *Conversion et Grâce chez S. Thomas d'Aquin* (Paris: Aubier, 1941), 235.
23. Ibid., 234.
24. For the dates of composition of these two works see Jean-Pierre Torrell, *Saint Thomas Aquinas*, vol. 2, *Spiritual Master* (Washington, D.C.: The Catholic University of America Press, 2003), 333 and 340.
25. Cf. Capéran, *Le problème du salut*, 198–99.

had reached every nation on the planet.[26] After all, as Thomas observes in his exposition of Romans 10:18, "Matthew preached in Ethiopia, Thomas in India, Peter and Paul in the west."[27] However, Thomas knows that not every single individual on the planet has heard the preaching of the Gospel. For instance, Thomas believes that the Gospel had not made as much of an inroad in northern Europe as in other parts of the world.[28] The spread of the Gospel is not uniform. Some hear first, some later. There are two possible reasons for this delay. On the one hand, the delay can be attributed to the devil. Like the "north wind that drives away the rain" (Prv 25:23), the devil constantly (if futilely) attempts to frustrate God's saving work among humans by chasing away the preachers of Christian doctrine, whom Thomas likens to rain-laden clouds. On the other hand, the delay can be attributed to God, who commands these clouds to go hither and thither, pouring their teachings where he would like to reap a harvest. At times, God commands these clouds not to rain. Thomas reminds us that in the book of Acts God delayed the preaching of the Gospel in Asia and instead directed Paul to travel to Phrygia and Galatia (Acts 16:6). The reason for the uneven distribution of preachers can be the result of sin. In this connection Aquinas cites Isaiah 5:6, "I will command the cloud to rain no rain upon it." But this draught of the word needs to be understood as not simply punitive but also pedagogical. Paul's delay in reaching Rome was part of God's disciplines so that "recognizing their own conduct as the obstacle hitherto preventing [Paul's] visit, they might amend their lives."[29] The times and places of the spread of the Gospel are governed by divine providence.[30] Not all hear at the same time. In any case, if they have not heard they are not condemned for the sin of unbelief, but for other sins that they will not be able to avoid unless God heals the wound caused by original sin.

Second, people who have not heard the preaching of the Gospel are not simply floating in a soteriological vacuum. God's grace is present and active in such a way that if they do what lies within them, God will provide for them the aids needed to attain the forgiveness of sins. This "doing what lies within" *(facienti quod in se est)* was famously misunderstood both in Europe and, as we shall see, in the Americas. Suffice it to say that Thomas is not semi-Pelagian. When he says that God gives grace to those who do what lies within their power, he is referring to the power that lies only within those who are

---

26. Cf. *ST* I-II,q. 106, a. 4, ad 4.

27. *Lectures on Romans* 10. lect. 3.

28. Cf. Jean Pierre Torrell, "Saint Thomas et les non-chrétiens," *Revue Thomiste* 106, no. 1 (2006): 17–49.

29. *Lectures on Romans* 10, lect. 5.

30. *Lectures on Romans* 15, lect. 3, § 1178.

already moved by God's grace.[31] Aquinas underscores the necessity of grace by citing the passage from Lamentations 5:19, "Turn us to thee, O Lord, that we may be turned." Thomas's teaching on preaching in Romans cannot be understood apart from his reflections of predestination. Paul himself warrants this connection: "Those whom he predestined, he also called" (Rom 8:30). This Augustinian note marks a definite improvement, or at least a clarification, of the Angelic Doctor's teaching when compared to that of the *Commentary on the Sentences* or even the *Disputed Questions on Truth*. The Angelic Doctor comments that "predestination begins to be carried out with the person's being called."[32] The call is twofold. There is the exterior call that comes by way of preaching. There is also the internal call, which consists in an *instictus mentis*, a spiritual instinct, by which God moves the heart to assent to the gift of faith. This interior call is absolutely essential for the salvation of the sinner. As Thomas explains, "our heart would not turn itself to God, unless God himself drew us to him."[33] Thus, ultimately, preaching is efficacious only among the predestined.[34]

Third, even in exceptional cases where people who have not heard the Gospel cooperate with God's overtures of grace, and such a thing is rare, the ordinary way in which God provides for these persons is by sending them a preacher. This is faith from what is heard. As we saw, hearing is twofold: internal and external. One can hear God speaking directly to the soul by means of an internal audition. But as Thomas explains, this first kind of hearing "pertains to the gift of prophecy, which is given to certain definite persons but not to all."[35] Moreover, when this gift is given, it is given not for the salvation of the individual but for the strengthening of the Christian community. It is a *gratia gratis data*, not a *gratia gratum faciens*. Hence, the interior hearing cannot be the common way in which God comes to the help of the honest pagan. The faith is heard because it is preached, and it is preached because preachers are sent. In his mercy, God provides preachers to those who are predestined to be conformed to the image of his Son. For this reason, God sent Peter to Cornelius, Paul to the Macedonians, and Bartolomé de las Casas to the Indians. Unlike Alexander of Hales, Thomas makes no mention of angelic preachers.

---

31. Ángel Santos Hernández, *Salvación y Paganismo: El problema teológico de la salvación de los infieles* (Santander, Spain: Editorial Sal Terrae, 1960), 169.

32. *Lectures on Romans* 8, lect. 6.

33. Ibid.

34. For further reflections on Aquinas's teaching on predestination in the Romans commentary see Michal Paluch, *La profondeur de l'amour divin: Evolution de la doctrine de la prédestination dans l'oeuvre de saint Thomas d'Aquin* (Paris: Libraire Philosophique J. Vrin, 2004), 249–72.

35. *Lectures on Romans* 10, lect. 2, § 837.

Las Casas's Reading of Thomas

Thomas's theology of preaching was deeply formational for Las Casas. Fray Bartolomé's most significant piece of scholastic theology, *De unico*, is in effect an extensive meditation and application of Thomas Aquinas's theology of preaching for the context of the Americas. The major thesis of this treatise is the following: "The one and only way to instruct human beings in the true religion was instituted by divine providence for all the world and for all times, namely, that way which is persuasive of the intellect with reasons and is gently alluring and encouraging of the will."[36]

In any chain of events, God is the first one to act. In order to preserve the excellence of the order that his wisdom has disposed and in order to defend the dignity of human nature, God moves humans to their supernatural end in a way that is similar to the way in which he moves other creatures to their natural end. However, God does not merely move creatures to act, but grants them forms, virtues, operative principles so that creatures might incline themselves toward their action in a manner that is connatural, easy, and smooth. In other words, the creature not only is moved but moves itself to its proper end. If God provides all creatures with the abilities that they need in order to attain their natural end, then how much more will God grant humans the graces that they need in order to attain their supernatural end?

All humanity is one.[37] There is only one human species, one human nature, one human race. There is only one perfect fulfillment, one final goal, one end, one Gospel for this species: a graced union with God by knowledge and by love. Hence, there is only one way to proclaim this Gospel, one way to at-

---

36. Bartolomé de las Casas, *Obras Completas*, vol. 2, *De unico vocationis modo* (Madrid: Alianza Editorial, 1990), 16. Henceforth referred to as *De unico*. All translations are my own. This work was in all likelihood the fruit of Las Casas's Dominican studies in Santo Domingo. It was composed sometime between 1522 and 1526. For centuries, Lascasian scholars knew of this work (Las Casas himself alludes to it numerous times throughout his latter writings), but it was presumed lost until a manuscript was discovered in 1889 in Oaxaca. Sadly, this work, which lay unedited and unpublished until 1942, is not extant in a complete version. The Oaxaca codex contains only chapters 5, 6, and 7 of the first book. For more information on the dates of composition and the textual problems in *De unico* see Jesús Ángel Barreda, "Ideología y pastoral misionera en el 'De unico vocationis modo,'" *Studium* 21 (1981): 186–354, and also his introduction to *Obras Completas*, vol. 2, *De unico vocationis modo*, I–XVI.

37. The unity of humanity is a central Lascasian theme. See Bartolomé de las Casas, *Apologética Historia Sumaria*, vols. 1 and 2, ed. Edmundo O'Gorman (México City: Instituto de Investigaciones Históricas de la Universidad Nacional Autónoma de México, 1967), 257–58. See also Lewis Hanke's excellent study of Las Casas's debate with Sepúlveda on this very issue, *All Mankind Is One: A Study of the Disputation between Bartolomé de Las Casas and Juan Ginés de Sepúlveda in 1550 on the Intellectual and Religious Capacity of the American Indians* (DeKalb: Northern Illinois University Press, 1974).

tain this goal, one way to perfect this nature: by persuading the intellect with reasons and by gently alluring the will. This is the theological premise and refrain of this treatise. Las Casas offers an extensive defense of this premise by means of a variety of arguments drawn from philosophy, theology, Scripture, church history, and even canon law. In the context of this defense, Las Casas considers the case of the person raised in the jungle from Thomas's commentary on Romans 10.

Surprisingly, Las Casas refrains from immediately applying this case to the Indians. Certainly Las Casas does not think that any rumor of the Gospel had reached the peoples of the Americas prior to the arrival of the Spaniards. The situation that Thomas had considered exceptional is now found to be very common. Here were lands that were apparently disconnected from God's works of salvation in Israel and the Church. The obvious and frequently asked question was: how could whole groups of peoples find themselves cut off for so long from any possibility of hearing the Gospel of salvation? This was not Las Casas's question. The animating concern in Las Casas's work is not the soteriological status of non-Christians but their salvation through preaching. Las Casas resists a facile identification of the Indians with the jungle men, because such an identification was being utilized by his opponents in ways that actually hindered the preaching of the Gospel. Because of the limited focus of the present study I mention only one, the Franciscan Toribio Motolinía.

Toribio de Benavente, also known by the indigenous name Motolinía ("the poor one") was one of the twelve Franciscans who arrived in Mexico in 1524 to evangelize the indigenous people.[38] Motolinía had imbibed deeply the spirit of Joachim of Fiore. The discovery of the Americas was considered by many Franciscans as an apocalyptic event whose significance was comparable to that of the creation of the world and the incarnation of the Word. The religious conquest of the Indies was the prelude to the advent of the kingdom.[39] For this reason, Motolinía and many of his confreres proposed and practiced a quick baptism with minimal preparation. According to an eyewitness account, two Franciscan priests baptized 15,000 people in one day. In other words, each priest baptized 313 people per hour, 5.2 per minute![40] Such actions might seem extreme, but they were warranted by the extraordinary circumstances of the discovery. In a letter to Charles V, Motolinía explains himself: "Since it falls to Your Majesty's office to makes haste that the holy gospel be

38. See Gustavo Gutiérrez, *Las Casas: In Search of the Poor of Jesus Christ* (Maryknoll, N.Y.: Orbis Books, 1993), 136–37; Luis N. Rivera, *A Violent Evangelism: The Political and Religious Conquest of the Americas* (Louisville, Ky.: Westminster/John Knox Press, 1992), 57.

39. See Alain Milhou, "Las Casas: Prophétisme et millénarisme," *Études*, March 1992, 398–99.

40. Barreda, "Primera anunciación y bautismo," 309.

preached throughout these lands, and since they who do not wish to hear the holy gospel of Christ of their own will should be forced, here the proverb applies, 'Better forced to be good than free to be bad.'"[41]

Motolinía's conflict with Las Casas arose over the latter's refusal to baptize an Indian man whom the bishop of Chiapas considered ill-prepared for the sacrament.[42] As a Dominican, Las Casas consistently emphasized the practice of preaching before and after baptism.[43] By all accounts, the Dominicans of his diocese in Chiapas had the custom of sending the catechumens back to their villages at the end of their instruction in the faith, hoping that they would return to ask for baptism at later time.[44] Las Casas's application of Thomas's commentary on Romans in his fight against the likes of Motolinía boils down to this: whether one grows up in the wilderness, among Saracens, or among Spanish wolves, God aids the one who does what is within him (*facienti quod in se est*) by sending preachers. Baptizers come second.

Is baptism necessary for salvation? Fray Bartolome's answer to this question is unequivocally affirmative. Indeed one of the great evils of the wars in the Indies is that the Spaniards are with no regard for age, sex, or dignity, "killing all sorts of people without distinction, who then depart this life without faith or sacraments and, in this way, fall into certain condemnation, which is the supreme evil."[45] Of course, Las Casas goes on to say that the condemnation of those culpable for these crimes is even greater. In any case, baptism is necessary because it is by means of this sacrament that the supernatural virtues, first among them faith, are infused.[46] However, as a rule, faith is not enough: "It is true that the habit of faith by itself could suffice, if God willed, but the common law, at least for adults, necessarily requires exterior teaching, instruction, narration, exposition, explication or explanation of what is to be believed."[47]

The act of faith is a complex interaction of intellect and will. Not every-

---

41. Cited by Gutiérrez in *Las Casas*, 137.

42. See Rivera, *A Violent Evangelism*, 232.

43. Barreda tells us that in 1532 Cardinal Cajetan, as superior general of the Dominican Order, addressed the question of the relation between preaching and baptism facing the Dominicans in the new continent (*in novo continente*). Cajetan states: "Ad hoc dicitur quod proculdubio perfectus ordo baptismi est ut baptizandi instruantur in fide priusquam baptizentur et post baptismum instruantur in observatione mandatorum Christi: nam salvator hunc instituit matth. ult. dicens discipulis docete omnes gentes batpizantes eos docents eos servare quaecumque mandavi vobis" (cited by Barreda, 313).

44. Barreda, "Primera anunciación y bautismo," 314.

45. *De unico*, 507. For other texts on the necessity of baptism for salvation in *De unico*, see Barreda, "Ideología y pastoral misionera," 327–30.

46. Ibid., 73.

47. Ibid.

one who thinks believes, but all who believe think. Furthermore, only the one who wants to believes, and in order to believe it is necessary to think, inquire, and reason. As an infused light, the virtue of faith strengthens the agent intellect so that it can extract intelligible forms from the arguments proposed by the preacher. These forms are then stored in the possible intellect so that the person can consider them and believe. The intellect is moved to understand by the will. Faith requires an act of deliberation because the intellect does not have a clear vision of its object. In the act of faith, the seeker is not trying to demonstrate the truth of what is to be believed but rather is investigating the reasons why it is to be believed. Faith says believe that God is Triune; it is God himself who has declared this through his Son and confirmed it with miracles in the Church, and God's testimony is most believable. The will assents to the things proposed by faith, mainly, for the sake of the promised reward—eternal life. It is this promised good that induces the will to command the intellect to assent and adhere to the things proposed by the faith as worthy of belief. The intellect does not attain the perfect knowledge that comes from seeing its object. Even in its assent to the truths proposed by faith, the firmness of its adhesion comes from a foreign agent, as it were, from the will. For this reason, the intellect does not attain rest in the act of faith; its investigation and reflection continues. By its very nature, faith is always in search of greater understanding.

Without preaching, the infused habit of faith remains in some way bound and dormant *(quodam modo sopiti et ligati)*.[48] According to Fray Bartolomé, "the infused habit [*habitus infusi*] is stimulated and actualized, so to speak [*ut sic dicerim*], by the acquired ones [*per acquisitos*] from the instruction of parents and teachers, or by the study of Christian doctrine."[49] In other words, listening to preaching is ordinarily necessary for salvation. In support of this claim, Las Casas appeals to Thomas's comments on Romans 10:

48. Ibid., 74.

49. Ibid., 76. Las Casas's use of language is somewhat hard to follow at this point. Throughout this section of his argument he talks about infused habits and acquired habits in a manner that seems inconsistent with Thomas's usage. Fray Bartolomé applies the term *habitus adquisitus* to the acts of the *habitus infusus*. It is unlikely that Las Casas is the originator of this turn of phrase, given his perceived need for accompanying the term *habitus adquisitus* with clarifying remarks such as "so-called" *(dicuntur)* and "so to speak" *(ut sic dicerim)*. Las Casas's usage is unusual enough that the editors of the Spanish translation in *Obras Completas 3* feel the need for their own parenthetical comments, inserting *"ejercicio de las virtudes"* after every occurrence of *adquisitus*. Even allowing for the somewhat idiosyncratic (though not original) use of scholastic terminology, it is not clear that Las Casas's understanding of how the infused virtues grow is in agreement with Aquinas's. For Thomas, the infused habits differ from the acquired in profound ways (Cf. *ST* I-II, q. 63; II-II, q. 24, a. 12). At the very least, Las Casas's argument would benefit from drawing more directly on Thomas at this point.

According to the saints, especially Saint Thomas, it must be held as most certain that if someone grows up in the jungle or among wild animals, and follows the dictates of natural reason in desiring good and avoiding evil, which is to say that he does not place any obstacles but does what is within him, God will reveal to him through an interior inspiration all the things that must be believed, or he would send him a preacher of the faith, as he sent Peter to Cornelius and Paul to the Macedonians.[50]

Las Casas rightly observes that the issues addressed in Romans 10 are also treated in 2 *Sententiarium* d. 28, q. 4 ad 4, and 3 *Sententiarium* d. 25, q. 2, a. 1, q1a. 1 ad 2. But the same teaching is more clearly articulated *(expressius)* in *De veritate* 14, a. 11 ad 1, and *In ad Romanos* 10, lect. 3, which he conflates in *De unico*. Las Casas does not offer a reason for favoring these latter texts over the former. One explanation that we can probably discard is that Las Casas is drawn to the more mature teaching of Romans' commentary. There is no evidence that the bishop of Chiapas perceives any theological development from the early to the late Thomas. More likely, Fray Bartolomé is drawn to the way that these latter texts underscore the role of the preacher as an instrumental cause of salvation. Only in the *De veritate* and *In ad Romanos* does Thomas unite the hypothetical case of the person raised in the wilderness to the historical examples of Peter being sent to Cornelius and Paul to the Macedonians. In short, in Thomas's reflections on Romans (and *De veritate*), Las Casas finds support for his thesis that the ordinary way in which God draws people to faith is not through the gift of prophecy but through the office of preaching. Those who preach are to follow in the footsteps of the apostles; they are to be imitators of Peter and Paul.[51]

Las Casas draws two practical implications from the connection between preaching and salvation. First, it is most desirable that adult candidates for baptism receive instruction on the articles of faith *before* they are baptized, so that afterward they can grow in holiness by exercising the infused habits of faith, hope, and love in accordance with the catechetical instruction that they received. Second, it is almost certain that an adult who is baptized without prior instruction or a child who is baptized but grows up outside the Christian community will not be able to grow in grace until he is brought into the church, where he can hear the faith proclaimed. In either case, preaching is indispensable for progress in Christian life. Las Casas comments that

50. *De unico*, 74.

51. Las Casas devotes a substantial portion of *De unico* to considering the significance of the example of the apostles, especially Paul, for the practice of preaching. Interestingly, Las Casas's portrayal of Paul is much more indebted to his reading of Chrysostom than of Aquinas. However, in his affection for the "golden mouthed," Las Casas is a faithful disciple of Aquinas. According to some stories, Thomas is supposed to have said that he would prefer a good translation of Chrysostom's homilies on Matthew to all the treasures of Paris (cf. *De unico*, note 78).

preachers are those who dispose exteriorly to faith and remove obstacles. The same could be said regarding grace, charity, and other gifts. By motivating, instructing, exhorting, correcting or by utilizing any other kind of ministry, preachers move others toward the reception of faith and grace, and in this way preachers cooperate so that grace is given to someone, or if given, so that it is not lost. Nevertheless, only God can confer grace or faith effectively without the assistance of any creature.[52]

Only God is the principal and proper cause of faith. Indeed, God can bring about faith without any preaching whatsoever by directly infusing the habit into the person, but this is not his usual way of operating in the world. Ordinarily, the act of faith requires a human agent, a guide or preacher who proposes credible truths with examples and reasonable arguments.[53]

In his apocalyptically induced haste, Motolinía had treated the Indians as lost children incapable of reaching the age of discretion. Las Casas insisted that the Indians were not children lost in the wilderness, living without society and without law. All humanity is one, and the only way to draw the Indians to faith is by persuading their intellect with reasons and gently alluring the will. Las Casas reminds his readers that, according to Augustine, "to believe is to think with assent" (credere est cum assensu cogitare).[54] What will people whose land has been stolen think about? Will they give assent to the teachings of their destructors? Will people's hearts be encouraged by the slaughter of their families? Faith cannot be forced. The one and only way to lead people to communion with God takes time. No one come to the fullness of the knowledge of God all at once. If one is to understand and accept the message of the Gospel, one needs time: time to listen, time to meditate, time to deliberate, time to ask questions. If there are things that force or cut short this time, if there are things that disturb the senses, and trouble the imagination, then the intellect is darkened, the will repelled, and the way to faith hindered.[55]

Can one wait for informed consent when someone's eternal destiny, so to speak, hangs in the balance? Might not a Christian out of genuine concern and love for their neighbor force them to take the Gospel medicine before it is too late? Is not Motolinía's prescription more prudent than Las Casas's? "Better forced to be good than free to be bad"?[56]

Las Casas addresses these concerns by telling an apocryphal story from the life of Clement. One day, Clement's father became ill, so ill that it seemed that he might not survive. The problem, however, was not the illness itself but the fact that unlike his children, Clement's father was not a Christian. Clement and his brothers greatly desired the conversion of their father, so they set

52. De unico, 72.
53. Ibid.
54. Ibid., 28.
55. Ibid., 48.
56. Cited by Gutiérrez in Las Casas, 137.

out to bring the saintly Peter to their father's house so that he could preach the Gospel and hopefully convert him. Peter gladly accompanied them but gently refused their invitation to preach.

> I know that you have great affection for your father; therefore I am afraid that you will urge him to take upon himself the yoke of religion, while he is not yet prepared for it; and to this he may perhaps assent, through his affection for you. But this is not to be depended on; for what is done for the sake of men is not worthy of approbation, and soon falls to pieces.[57]

Instead of preaching, Peter suggests that they wait a year. During this year, Peter and Clement's brothers should discuss Scripture together within earshot of their father, so that he will ask for the yoke of Christianity himself. One of Clement's brothers, Nicetas, immediately protests that during that year their father may well die and be consigned to the eternal torment of hell. To which Peter replies, "Salvation is not attained by force, but by liberty; and not through the favor of men, but by faith in God. Then, besides, you ought to consider that God is prescient, and knows whether this man is one of his. But if he knows that he is not, what shall we do with respect to those things which have been determined by him from the beginning?"[58]

Las Casas draws two lessons from this anecdote. First, preachers of the Gospel need to be gentle. The teaching of the faith needs to be conducted with the utmost respect for human dignity and freedom. Second, preachers of the Gospel need to be patient. A significant amount of time might elapse between the rain and the harvest, between preaching and conversion. On the one hand, preachers can never lose sight of the particularities of human nature. The human is a rational (as distinct from intellectual) creature. Barreda states, "Faith does not normally come *ex abrupto;* it is not explained as a rupture against the laws of pedagogy."[59] As such, the human who is led to faith needs time: time to do what lies within him *(facienti quod in se est),* time to consider the things proposed by preachers; time to prepare himself for receiving the gift of faith, the sacrament of baptism, and true penitence.[60] On the other hand, preachers must never forget that only God can save and that his ways are mysterious. God will enlighten whomever he will, whenever he will. The connection between someone doing what lies within him and the reception of grace is not automatic. The fruitfulness of preaching cannot be understood apart from

57. *De unico*, 48–50. For the English translation of "Recognitions of Clement" I am using the version found in Alexander Roberts and James Donaldson, eds., *Ante-Nicene Fathers*, vol. 8 (Peabody, Mass.: Hendrickson, 1999), 192.

58. "Recognitions of Clement," 193.

59. Barreda, "Ideología y pastoral misionera," 251.

60. Cf. *De unico*, 509.

the doctrine of divine providence and the mystery of predestination. God foreknows those whom he predestined. Unshakeable confidence in God's salvific, albeit inscrutable, will is the ultimate ground for Las Casas's patience and hope. In Clement's story, after a long time, his father converted and asked for baptism. In Las Casas's history, many Indians are predestined to be conformed to the image of Christ.[61] The fact that God has sent them preachers is evidence that some have cooperated with God's overtures of grace, for preaching is the necessary means *(necessarium medium)* for leading to salvation those whom God predestined.[62] If the Indians are given the opportunity to hear the Gospel in "the only way," that way which persuades the intellect with reasons and gently alluring the will, God will not deny them his grace but turn them to himself. In sum, God's word will not return to him empty; many will believe, because God infallibly desires that there be Indians in heaven.

Postscript

To the end of his days, Fray Bartolomé insisted that his defense of the Indians was not a Lascasian innovation but a derivation from what the Angelic Doctor had taught. As Las Casas explained to his Dominican brothers, "I affirm no proposition on this subject, regardless of how difficult or harsh it may be, that I do not prove by principles obtained from his doctrine."[63] Las Casas never claimed to be an original thinker or a speculatively brilliant theologian,

61. Bartolomé de las Casas, *Obras Completas*, vol. 3, *Historia de las Indias* (Madrid: Editorial Alianza, 1994), 339–40.

62. Bartolomé de las Casas, *Obras Completas*, vol. 9, *Apología* (Madrid: Editorial Alianza, 1988), 188. The significance of the doctrine of predestination in the theology of Las Casas has not been adequately explored. The doctrine became a point of dispute in the controversy between Las Casas and Sepúlveda. The Spanish humanist appealed to Thomas's doctrine of the man raised in the wilderness as an argument for the military conquest of the Indians. After all, if the Indians had done what lay within their power, God would not have denied them his grace, and they would have steered away from such abominable practices as human sacrifice and anthropophagy. The fact that these people are idolaters is evidence that they have refused God's overtures of grace. For Sepúlveda, the doctrine of the *facienti quod in se est* has a clear application in the context of the Americas—war! See Juan Ginés de Sepúlveda, *Obras Completas*, vol. 3, *Democrates Secundus*, ed. A. Moreno Hernández, trans. Ángel Losada (Salamanca: Exmo. Ayuntamiento de Pozoblanco, 1997), 83. In his dispute against Sepúlveda, Las Casas appeals to Thomas's commentary on Romans 10 to argue that God grants grace to those who do what lies within them in accordance with the divine purpose of predestination. The doctrine of predestination is vital for understanding Las Casas's theology of history, and I intend to pursue this subject in a future study. For some tentative (albeit problematic) forays into this subject see Carlos Castillo Mattasoglio, *Libres para creer: La conversión según Bartolomé de las Casas en la Historia de las Indias* (Lima: Fondo Editorial de las Pontificia Universidad Católica del Perú, 1993), 349–54; Gutiérrez, *Las Casas*, 252–54.

63. Bartolomé de las Casas, "Carta a los dominicos de Chiapa y Guatemala," in *Obras Completas*, vol. 13, *Cartas y Memoriales* (Madrid: Alianza Editorial, 1995), 355.

yet therein lay his virtue. Las Casas recognized the richness of the theology of Aquinas for a new situation. In spite of the differences between the Middle Ages, the time of the conquest, and our contemporary situation, the teaching of the *doctor communis* on humanity's nature and destiny is indeed a *philosophia perennis*, because all humanity is one. Las Casas helps us see that it is precisely the universal character of Thomas's teaching that allows it to be contextual without a contrived *aggiornamento*. Those who would preach good news to the poor and deliverance to the captives would do well to attend to the teachings of the Angelic Doctor. One does not have to be a Marxist to be prophetic or socially relevant. The example of Las Casas suggests that being a theologian and preacher of liberation lies at the heart of what it means to be a Thomist.[64]

By way of conclusion, I offer a historical postscript to Las Casas's application of Thomas's theology of preaching. After his publication of *De unico*, many complained that its plan for preaching the Gospel was impractical.[65] It made for wonderful rhetoric but it was not realistic, and they dared Las Casas to show them otherwise. Las Casas accepted the challenge and set out to start a church in the province of Tuzutlán in Guatemala. This area had thrice repelled the Spanish conquistadors, who called it *Tierra de Guerra*, Land of War. In August 1537, Luis Cáncer, a Dominican trained by Las Casas in the only way and learned in the native languages, arrived to those lands. He bore no arms; he carried no gold. All he had were some verses that he had composed in the indigenous tongue narrating the history of Christianity. He taught these verses to some Indian traders he befriended, who in turn recited them for the local people. Soon these verses became a hit. The native inhabitants memorized them. They repeated them to each other. They even requested new ones. By October of that same year, the tribe had built a church; they abolished sacrifices and began to bear the Gospel to other tribes. Ten years later the territory was officially renamed *Tierra de la Vera Paz*, Land of True Peace. *Fides ex auditu.*

64. Cf. Isacio Pérez Fernández, "De Las Casas a Marx," *Studium* 17, no. 2 (1977): 345–64.
65. I am indebted to Lewis Hanke's masterful telling of this account in his introduction to Bartolomé de las Casas, *Del único modo de traer a todos los pueblos a la verdadera religion*, ed. Agustín Millares Castro (Pánuco, México: Fondo de Cultura Económica, 1942), xxxiii–xxxviii.

Holly Taylor Coolman

6 Romans 9–11

Rereading Aquinas on the Jews

Given the events of the twentieth century—including both atrocities committed against the Jews and new openness and dialogue between Jews and Christians—it is not surprising that the question of Aquinas's understanding of the Jews has received regular treatment.

Aquinas stands as a profoundly influential voice within the Christian tradition, a thinker who is receiving renewed attention from both Catholics and Protestants. Any attempt to reassess the major strands of traditional Christian thinking on Judaism must take account of his thought. Furthermore, as is discussed further below, Aquinas's own historic situation was marked by important shifts in Christian responses to Judaism. There is much to be learned in attending closely to his claims.

In fact, over the last three decades, important work has been done on this question. In light of the painful reality of the persecution Jews have suffered, this research has tended to occur against a backdrop of very practical questions: Does the work of Aquinas contribute to pernicious anti-Jewish tendencies in Christian thought? Does it offer resources for positive constructive work? According to the scholarship to date, certain elements of Aquinas's thought fall into the first category, while others fall into the second.

In this chapter, I give a brief summary of that scholarship, noting in particular the element in Aquinas's thought that is most clearly negative with regard to present-day Judaism—his condemnation of the practice of the ceremonial law—and the element in Aquinas's thought that has been most consistently recognized as positive—his assertion that, ultimately, "all Israel will be saved." Not incidentally, given the focus of this volume, the more positive element is seen most clearly in Aquinas's *Commentary on Romans*. The Romans commentary has only quite recently been available from the Latin into English translation, and it seems likely that this lack of a translation has led to a much greater emphasis upon Aquinas's thought as it appears in the *Summa*, much widely available in translation, but also the source of Aquinas's more negative claim.[1]

I then go on to argue that there is, in fact, a profound connection between these two elements. Aquinas's negative claim regarding the ceremonial law, especially when seen in the context of his larger argument, is actually called into question by his more positive claim concerning the eventual salvation of the Jews.

The Ambivalence of Recent Scholarship

Serious questions have been raised regarding certain elements of Aquinas's thought that seem to disparage Judaism and exacerbate Jewish-Christian tensions. The renowned Jewish thinker Michael Wyschogrod raises what is perhaps the most troubling aspect of Aquinas's teaching regarding the Jews: his claim that after Christ, the practice of the ceremonial law constitutes mortal sin.[2] For Wyschogrod, it is a teaching that "strains contemporary Christianity's relationship with Judaism."[3] To make sense of Aquinas's claim regarding the ceremonial law, however, requires a bit of explanation.

Following earlier Christian interpreters, Aquinas divides the Mosaic law into three parts: the moral, the judicial, and the ceremonial. The "moral" and the "judicial" continue to have import for Christian practice. The "ceremonial," however, refers to commandments that are, by their very nature, anticipatory of the work of Christ, and these commandments, including, for example, the commandment to circumcise one's sons, are ones that Christians therefore may no longer observe. The "ceremonial law," thus, is a marker by which Christians distinguish Jewish obedience of God's Law from their own.

Specifically, Aquinas writes that observance of the ceremonial law is now both "dead" and "deadly." It is not difficult to see why such a claim might garner attention. Aquinas is insisting that the observance of the ceremonial law after Christ's appearing not only accomplishes nothing, but harms those who engage in it. Observant Jews, in other words, deal death to themselves in an ongoing way, as they observe the very rites that were commanded by God himself.

1. Torrell notes that between 1869 and 1874, a multi-volume French translation of all the commentaries on Paul's writings did appear: *Commentaires de saint Thomas d'Aquin sur tout les épitres de S. Paul*, trans. abbé Bralé, 6 vols. (Paris: Vivès). See Jean-Pierre Torrell, *Saint Thomas Aquinas*, vol. 1, *The Person and His Work*, trans. Robert Royal (Washington, D.C.: The Catholic University of America Press, 1996), 340.

2. Michael Wyschogrod, "A Jewish Reading of Thomas Aquinas on the Old Law," in *Understanding the Scriptures*, ed. Clemens Thoma and Michael Wyschogrod (Mahwah, N.J.: Paulist Press, 1987).

3. Wyschogrod, "A Jewish Reading of Thomas Aquinas," 138.

It is worthwhile here to note a possibility suggested by a second Jewish commentator, David Novak, who suggests that Aquinas's statement here is meant only for Jewish Christians, that he is reprimanding those who are baptized into Christ and yet continue to observe the ceremonial law. Novak indicates uncertainty as to whether Aquinas is thinking at all of other Jews.[4] Such an interpretation is, however, difficult to hold in light of the whole sequence of Aquinas's thought on the Law. As is discussed below, Aquinas discusses the Mosaic Law as a part of a larger reality of "Law," ordered toward its culmination in Christ. This larger reality seems to treat Jews and Christians together within the reality of this unfolding of God's revelation.[5] If Christ has come, in other words, then he has come.

Central in the research on Aquinas and the Jews, the work of Jeremy Cohen focuses upon situating Aquinas's thought firmly in the context of his own historical situation. In his first work on the matter, the *Friars and the Jews*, Cohen argues that a shift in the thirteenth century toward increasingly anti-Jewish policies on the part of Christian authorities was tied directly to the actions of certain members of the newly founded Dominican order, of which Aquinas was a member (as well as to actions of members of the Franciscan order, founded a few years earlier).[6] Among the Dominicans, Cohen describes the work of Raymond de Peñafort and Paul Christian (the latter a convert to Christianity from Judaism), who were eager to bring more fully into public view the "errors" of the Jews. In Cohen's later work, *Living Letters of the Law*,[7] Cohen treats Aquinas more directly, claiming that while Aquinas did not conform to the tactics of Peñafort and Christian, his ideas nevertheless offered them a form of intellectual support. Here, Cohen notes, among other factors, Aquinas's condemnation of the practice of the ceremonial law.

The work of John Y. B. Hood strikes a more ambivalent note.[8] Hood, too, takes note of Aquinas's claim concerning the ceremonial law, and yet Hood argues that Aquinas's overall position concerning the Jews is above all a conventional view, reflecting both the positive and the negative trajectories of thought that made up the standard teaching of the medieval Church.

Thus, although he acknowledges Aquinas's claim regarding the ceremonial

4. David Novak, *Talking with Christians: Musings of a Jewish Theologian* (Grand Rapids, Mich.: Eerdmans, 2005), 83.

5. "He seems to think that either the ceremonial law, after Christ, is obligatory for all or it is mortal sin for all, Jew or Gentile." Wyschogrod, "A Jewish Reading of Thomas Aquinas," 137.

6. Jeremy Cohen, *The Friars and the Jews: The Evolution of Medieval Anti-Judaism* (Ithaca, N.Y.: Cornell University Press, 1984).

7. Jeremy Cohen, *Living Letters of the Law: Ideas of the Jew in Medieval Christianity* (Berkeley: University of California Press, 1999).

8. John Y.B. Hood, *Aquinas and the Jews* (Philadelphia: University of Pennsylvania Press, 1995).

law, Hood notes that Aquinas also has much more hopeful statements. Drawing especially from Aquinas's *Commentary on Romans*, for example, Hood notes Aquinas's assertion that the Jews are destined for eventual salvation.

It is this point that becomes the primary focus of the more recent work of Fr. Steven Boguslawski. Centering his study upon the insights of the *Commentary on Romans*, Boguslawski offers a much more positive account of Aquinas on the Jews. He helpfully emphasizes some of the most important positive aspects of Aquinas's account: the dignity and privileges, for example, that the Jews continue to possess.[9] Following St. Paul, Aquinas asserts that "to them belong the adoption as children, the glory, the covenant, the giving of the law, the worship, and the promises; to them belong the patriarchs, and of their race, according to the flesh, is the Christ, who is over all things." Each of these prerogatives shows, according to Boguslawski, something about the "dignity" and "greatness" of the Jews.[10]

Not only does Aquinas want to praise the Jews. More importantly, Boguslawski notes, Aquinas insists that they will, eventually, be saved. Boguslawski helpfully notes that when the notion of election, which is central for Aquinas, is taken as an interpretive key to his thought, it becomes clear that the ultimate salvation of the Jews is *in no way* undermined. The salvation of the Gentiles in fact depends upon their being grafted into this covenant that is already made with the Jewish people. Thus, one of Boguslawski's most important claims is his even stronger emphasis on the element of Aquinas's thought noted by Hood: following the claims of Romans 11, Aquinas expects the future redemption of the Jews.

Although Aquinas does see the practice of the ceremonial law as deadly, Boguslawski's work makes clear that Aquinas does not think of the Jews, who continue this practice, as simply cast off by God. Aquinas does believe that the Jews have "fallen," that their hearts have been hardened, shown above all in the fact that they have not recognized Jesus as Christ and as God. However, as Boguslawski puts it succinctly: "For Thomas, the fall of the Jews is not universal; it is not irreparable, and it does not revoke Israel's prerogatives or dignity."[11] Or, to put it in a positive way: the Jews, *as a people*, have "ongoing rights and a role" in God's ongoing work.[12]

9. In particular, Boguslawski demonstrates the way in which Aquinas departs from Augustine in this regard.

10. Thomas Aquinas, *Lectures on the Letter to the Romans*, trans. Fabian Larcher, ed. Jeremy Holmes (Ave Maria, Fla.: Aquinas Center for Theological Renewal), cap. 9, lect. 1, http://www.avemaria.edu/uploads/pagesfiles/4283.pdf.

11. Steven C. Boguslawski, *Thomas Aquinas on the Jews: Insights into His Commentary on Romans 9–11* (Mahwah, N.J.: Paulist Press, 2008), 107.

12. Ibid., 67.

These more hopeful claims are clearly seen in Aquinas's *Commentary on the Romans*. One of the most crucial passages is Aquinas's commentary on Romans 11:11–12: "11 And so I ask, 'They have not stumbled so as to fall, have they?' Of course not! On the contrary, because of their stumbling, salvation has come to the gentiles to make the Jews jealous. 12 Now if their stumbling means riches for the world, and if their fall means riches for the gentiles, how much more will their full participation mean!"[13]

Aquinas notes that Paul's question can be interpreted as asking two different things: first, whether the fall of the Jews is without any benefit. This is clearly not so, says Aquinas. Paul himself says that God permits them to fall in order that their fall may be an occasion of salvation for others. Second, however, Paul might be asking, "Have they stumbled so as to remain fallen forever?" and to this, Aquinas quotes Psalm 41:8: "will he not rise again from where he lies?" In other words, *will the Jews not be brought again to full participation in God's plan of salvation?*

In his commentary on Romans 11:25, Aquinas is even more explicit. The verse on which he comments reads, "For I would not have you ignorant, brethren, of this mystery, lest you be wise in your own conceits: a blindness in part has come upon Israel, until the fullness of the Gentiles come in." Among other things, Aquinas says this:

It should be noted that the word, *until*, can signify the cause of the blindness of the Jews. For God permitted them to be blinded, in order that the full number of the Gentiles come in. It can also designate the termination, i.e., that the blindness of the Jews will last up to the time when the full number of the Gentiles will come to the faith. With this agrees his next statement, namely, *and then*, i.e., when the full number of the Gentiles has come in, *all Israel will be saved*, not some, as now, but universally all: "I will save them by the Lord their God" (Hos 1:7); "He will again have compassion upon us (Mi 7:19)."[14]

What, then, are we to say about St. Thomas Aquinas and the Jews? How are we to understand his claim that the ceremonial law is "deadly" together with his insistence that the Jews will eventually "rise again"? It is certainly possible to reconcile these two statements. Aquinas could hold that this current death-dealing practice of ceremonial Law is temporary. He could still, then, claim that the Jewish people are moving toward eventual redemption and, we might even say, resurrection. Indeed, both Hood and Boguslawski read Aquinas this way, with Hood describing the position as involving ambiguity and tension, and Boguslawski seeing it as reasonable within the framework of election.

13. Thomas Aquinas, *Lectures on the Letter to the Romans* 11, lect. 2.
14. Ibid., lect. 4.

Rereading Aquinas

In this chapter, however, I will move forward to ask how the claim regarding the eventual salvation of the Jews, drawn from the *Commentary on Romans*, might mitigate the more negative claim regarding the practice of the ceremonial law in the *Summa theologiae*. In reading the two texts together, we see some truly startling possibilities emerge. This is true in particular when we look at the logic that *stands behind* the claim that the ceremonial Law is now deadly. In the end, the recognition that Aquinas expects the future salvation of the Jews raises interesting questions about that logic, and, in turn, about the claim itself.

It is helpful first to consider Aquinas's thought on the matter more thoroughly. Aquinas's discussion of the Mosaic Law is framed within a larger discussion of law in general, the section of his *Summa* commonly known as the "treatise on the Law" and found in his *Summa theologiae* I-II, qq. 90–108. In fact, under this category of "Law," or *lex*, Aquinas actually discusses a great many things; in its account of eternal good and the means by which human beings come to participate in it, the treatise on the Law can function as a sort of microcosm of Aquinas's whole theological system.

Aquinas says that Law appears in four forms: (1) eternal, (2) natural, (3) human, and (4) Divine, with the divine divided further into (4a) Old and (4b) New. First and most foundational is the eternal law. The eternal law is that timeless form of law from which all other laws derive. The eternal law exists in God, and is so closely related to God that, Aquinas says, it "is not distinct from Himself."[15] We might think of the eternal law as God's own wisdom, providing the basis for every other form of wisdom that is.

Second, in a section much studied and debated,[16] Aquinas describes the natural law. The natural law is, above all, the participation of rational creatures in the eternal law and, more precisely, the participation of humanity's practical reason in the good. Common to all human beings, the natural law constitutes the way in which human beings qua human beings embody the

---

15. "[N]ec eius lex est aliud ab ipso." *Summa theologiae (ST)* I–II, q. 91, a. 1, ad 3. All English quotations from the *Summa theologiae* come from the translation of the Fathers of the English Dominican Province (New York: Benziger Brothers, 1947), reprinted by Christian Classics, 1981.

16. Although it is relatively quite brief, the section on natural law has certainly been the most studied section of the treatise on the Law. Unfortunately, the natural law is often treated as relevant strictly for questions of moral theology and is often abstracted from the treatise as a whole. Pamela Hall's excellent work in *Narrative and the Natural Law* is a welcome counterexample; her focus is the natural law, but her study is conducted within the context of the whole treatise (Notre Dame, Ind.: University of Notre Dame Press, 1994). See also Matthew Levering, *Biblical Natural Law: A Theocentric and Teleological Approach* (Oxford: Oxford University Press, 2008).

wisdom of law. Closely related to the natural law is the third form of law, human law, in which particular precepts governing a particular community are derived from natural law.

Fourth are the two most closely related forms of law, the Old Law and the New Law. Indeed, these two are described by Aquinas under a single term, Divine Law, so-called because it is a law given directly by God. This single entity, says Aquinas, is the form of law by which humanity is moved beyond natural faculties—expressed in the natural and human laws—and directed toward its final end, the vision of God, or "friendship with God."[17]

Especially at stake in understanding Aquinas's position on the Jews are his account of the Old Law and his explanation of the difference between the Old and the New. It is worth noting that Aquinas gives a great deal of space to the Old Law; indeed, within the treatise on the law, the questions dealing with the Old Law take up roughly fifteen times as much space as the single question devoted to the natural law and roughly twenty times as much space as the single question devoted to the New Law. In a large sense, Aquinas's exposition of the Old Law establishes his description of the Divine Law, and he insists that the New Law is "in" the Old Law "as the [full-grown] corn is in the ear."[18] Yet, the two are not identical.

In explaining the difference between the Old and New, Aquinas relies especially upon the notion of translation, turning to a quotation from the Epistle to the Hebrews: "The priesthood being translated, it is necessary that a translation also be made of the Law."[19] This "translation," for Aquinas, is not a change in substance, but rather a teleological progression from a less perfect to a more perfect form. Thus, he makes use of the analogy of the full-grown plant and the seed. They are, in essence, the same thing; one, however, exists at a later stage of maturity.

Seeing the shift from the Old Law to the New Law in the context of a teleologically governed process is crucial to understanding Aquinas's thought on the matter. And yet, for our purposes here, it is crucial to understand the relationship between the various forms of law within Aquinas's larger discussion of Law itself. Three interrelated points emerge as particularly important.

The first of these three points appears explicitly within a list that Aquinas offers of four fundamental characteristics that define "Law": It is (1) an ordinance of reason (2) made for the common good, (3) made by one who has care of the community, and one that (4) is promulgated.[20] Especially important for

17. "amicitiam hominis ad Deum." *ST* I–II, q. 99, a. 2, co.
18. "Sic igitur est lex nova in veteri sicut fructus in spica." *ST* I–II, q. 107, a. 3, co.
19. "Translato sacerdotio, necesse est ut legis translatio fiat." Cf. Heb 7:12.
20. "Et sic ex quatuor praedictis potest colligi definitio legis, quae nihil est aliud quam

our purposes are the claims Aquinas makes regarding promulgation, or the formal, public announcement of a law. Promulgation, Aquinas makes a point of insisting, is essential to the character of Law itself.[21]

This way in which Law is essentially linked to those receiving it points to a second defining way in which Aquinas described Law, relevant for our purposes here. It is clear throughout Aquinas's account, and it is already suggested by the four characteristics above. A law is given *to a people;* it never simply exists in a vacuum, as a conceptual reality; it always exists *in relation to a community.*

Finally, Aquinas describes a sense in which enforcement of the Law is necessary. This is apparent in a qualifying statement that Aquinas makes with reference to the lawgiver: he must be one who can provide enforcement. We might note in this regard Aquinas's insistence on the impossibility of a private person making Law: "A private person cannot lead another to virtue efficaciously; for he can only advise, and if his advise be not taken, it has no coercive power, such as law should have, in order to prove an efficacious inducement to virtue."[22] Law, then, is not fully Law without some coercive power to enforce it.

This claim about the lawgiver, furthermore, has a corollary for those under the Law: those under the Law must not only be made aware of the Law; they must be required to obey it. And yet Aquinas goes further, suggesting that when a Law functions most perfectly, those under the Law obey it not grudgingly, not strictly by coercion, but by choice.

We see hints of this in the way that Aquinas describes "participation" in a law by those who are ruled: a law is "in" a person "by participation as in one that is ruled. In the latter way each one is a law to himself, in so far as he shares the direction that he receives from one who rules him." Or we could turn to Aquinas's broader discussion of virtue, which ultimately requires not only certain action of obedience, but also "rectitude of will." When a people is simply forced to obey it, a law is not functioning in a perfect way.

So, this third element in Aquinas's thought could be put this way: while it is the case in human law that promulgation of law and enforcement of law are two distinct things,[23] nevertheless, in the most perfect embodiment of Law, these two would be inextricably joined. Law would not only advise, but "in-

quaedam rationis ordinatio ad bonum commune, ab eo qui curam communitatis habet, promulgata." *ST* I–II, q. 90, a. 4, co.

21. Here, he is echoing a previous claim by Gratian (commonly considered the father of the systematic study of canon law): "Leges instituuntur quum promulgantur." *Decretum Gratiani*, pt. I, c. 3, dist. VII.

22. "persona privata non potest inducere efficaciter ad virtutem. Potest enim solum monere, sed si sua monitio non recipiatur, non habet vim coactivam; quam debet habere lex, ad hoc quod efficaciter inducat ad virtutem." *ST* I–II, q. 90, a. 3, ad 2.

23. "lex est in aliquo non solum sicut in regulante, sed etiam participative sicut in regulato. Et

duce efficaciously," that people to whom it is given. And this will somehow happen in perfect accord with, rather than in opposition to, the will of the ones ruled.

This, as a matter of fact, is precisely the case with the New Law. In the New Law, Aquinas notes, the Spirit writes the Law on the hearts of human beings in such a way that promulgation and enforcement become intertwined. The New Law, Aquinas says, is "instilled into man, not only by indicating to him what he should do, but also by helping him to accomplish it."[24] This help, of course, consists in bringing those under the Law to obey the law *in compliance with their own will;* and because their hearts have been changed. Obedience is not only the Law's demand, but also their own choice.

Can this "instilling" of the New Law really be understood as its "promulgation"? The possibility seems much more reasonable if we consider Aquinas's argument regarding the natural law and promulgation. Aquinas poses the question of whether promulgation really is essential to law, after all, and cites the example of natural law. Natural law isn't really *promulgated*, is it?[25] It is, says Aquinas: "The natural law is promulgated by the very fact that God instilled it into man's mind so as to be known by him naturally."[26] It is clear the promulgation can indeed be a process that is as thoroughly "internal" as it is "external." For Aquinas, then, we might say that the New Law involves a process by which, in those united to Christ, the Divine Law comes to be promulgated in a way similar to that of the natural law. As the natural law is "instilled into the mind," so, analogously, in the context of this transformative work of the New Law, the Divine Law is "written on the heart."

With this in mind, then, we can come back to our original focus: Aquinas's discussion of the ceremonial law. In I-II, q. 103, a. 4, Aquinas asks the question of whether, after Christ's passion, the ceremonial law can be observed without committing mortal sin. As we have noted, Aquinas argues that observance of the ceremonial precepts in the present does constitute mortal sin, for "if they were observed, this would mean that something is still to be accomplished and is not yet fulfilled."[27]

Taking the example of circumcision, Aquinas quotes Galatians 5:2: "If you

---

hoc modo unusquisque sibi est lex, inquantum participat ordinem alicuius regulantis." *ST* I–II, q. 90, a. 3, ad 1.

24. "Et hoc modo lex nova est indita homini, non solum indicans quid sit faciendum, sed etiam adiuvans ad implendum." *ST* I–II, q. 106, a. 1, ad 2.

25. *ST* I–II, q. 90, a. 4, obj.1.

26. "promulgatio legis naturae est ex hoc ipso quod Deus eam mentibus hominum inseruit naturaliter cognoscendam." *ST* I–II, q. 90, a. 4, ad 1.

27. "quia si observarentur, adhuc significaretur aliquid ut futurum et non impletum." *ST* I–II, q. 107, a. 2, ad 1.

be circumcised, Christ shall profit you nothing."[28] He contrasts the present age with the past: "though our faith in Christ is the same as that of the fathers of old; yet, since they came before Christ, whereas we come after Him, the same faith is expressed in different words, by us and by them. The ceremonies of the Old Law betokened Christ as having yet to be born and suffer: whereas our sacraments signify Him as already born and having suffered."[29]

Aquinas further specifies his position in a contrast he draws between Jerome and Augustine. Jerome, he says, distinguishes two periods of time; before Christ's Passion, when the ceremonial law was neither dead nor deadly; and after Christ's Passion, during which the ceremonial law is both dead and deadly. The apostles, according to Jerome, therefore observed the ceremonial law after Christ's Passion only as a "pious pretense." Aquinas disagrees with Jerome's sharp distinction, arguing that it would hardly be fitting that the apostles "should have hidden things pertaining to the truth of life and doctrine."[30] Aquinas instead affirms the position of Augustine, who added to Jerome's two periods of time a third era, an in-between period lasting from Christ's Passion until the publication of the Gospel, during which the ceremonial law was dead, having been fulfilled in Christ, but was *not* deadly. It is now that Christ's work has been done *and* that the Gospel has been published *(divulgati)*, says Aquinas, we find ourselves in the era when the ceremonial law is both "dead and deadly." Aquinas, in other words, affirms along with Augustine, and against Jerome, that Christ's passion is not the only crucial moment in this unfolding economy. The publication of the Gospel is, in fact, crucial for a final move in which the Old Law is left behind and the New Law takes effect.

Recall that Aquinas's assessment of the law as both "dead" and "deadly" hangs upon his claim that not only is Christ's work fully accomplished, but the work of publication of the Gospel is now complete, as well. Although Aquinas does not say so explicitly, it seems reasonable to assume that publication of the Gospel—and the accompanying shift in practice of the Divine Law—is at least effectively synonymous with the promulgation of the New Law. If this is so, then the question that must be asked, in light of the *Commentary on Romans*, is whether the New Law has indeed been promulgated and the Gospel has indeed been fully published, even on Aquinas's own terms.

28. "Si circumcidimini, Christus nihil vobis proderit." *ST* I–II, q. 103, a. 4, s.c.

29. "Quamvis autem sit eadem fides quam habemus de Christo, et quam antiqui Patres habuerunt; tamen quia ipsi praecesserunt Christum, nos autem sequimur, eadem fides diversis verbis significatur a nobis et ab eis.... Et similiter caeremoniae veteris legis significabant Christum ut nasciturum et passurum: nostra autem sacramenta significant ipsum ut natum et passum." *ST* I–II, q. 103, a. 4, co.

30. "Sed quia indecens videtur quod Apostoli ea occultarent propter scandalum quae pertinent ad veritatem vitae et doctrinae." *ST* I–II, q. 103, a. 4, ad 1.

An Israel-Shaped Gap

Aquinas's *Commentary on Romans* anticipates a future salvation for the Jewish people, and in so doing, indicates that the New Law is a law intended not only for the Church, not even a Church containing some Jewish individuals, but for the Jewish people *as a people*. If the New Law is a law given to the Jewish people, however, its promulgation will be completed only when the New Law will be fully in effect among the Jewish people, when those who have stumbled *will rise*.

Recall that the New Law, by its very nature, is "written on the heart," is "instilled into man, not only by indicating to him what he should do, but also by helping him to accomplish it."[31] Wouldn't this mean that, at least with respect to the Jewish people, promulgation of the New Law is not yet complete? Wouldn't this mean that although Aquinas writes after the Passion of Christ, he writes before full completion of the promulgation of the New Law? Wouldn't it mean the same for our own age?

The implications of Aquinas's *Commentary on Romans* look as though they may be far-reaching, indeed. If the Jewish people are destined for eventual inclusion in the Gospel, if they will in fact come to live under the New Law, we must say, first of all, that there is a promise waiting for its fulfillment. Given Aquinas's logic, however, this yields a larger structural claim: the promulgation of the Gospel, although begun, is not completed. And this, in turn, leads to a crucial practical implication: we have not, in fact, entered an era when the ceremonial law is rendered deadly.

If this is so, then Aquinas's view as expressed in the Romans commentary offers much for consideration. Aquinas's hope for the future salvation of the Jewish people, expressed there, creates a very particular sense in which the narrative of God's work in history offered in the *Summa theologiae* must be reread. There is, in fact, in the publication of the New Law an Israel-shaped gap that almost imperceptibly changes everything.

These are issues that must be considered in understanding Aquinas's work. It is difficult to date Aquinas's lectures on Romans, but it seems likely that they occurred quite late in Aquinas's life.[32] Even given his powerful, synthetic intellect, could it be the case the Aquinas himself lacked time and opportunity to consider fully the implications of the Romans commentary for the story of unfolding revelation as it is laid out in the *Summa*?

---

31. "Et hoc modo lex nova est indita homini, non solum indicans quid sit faciendum, sed etiam adiuvans ad implendum." *ST* I–II, q. 106, a. 1 ad 2.

32. Cf. Torrell, *The Person and His Work*, 340.

The implications for a Thomistic contribution to contemporary Christian understandings of the people Israel, furthermore, are important and complex. What would it mean to affirm Aquinas's larger account of the unfolding history of God's salvific work, and yet to claim that we stand at a different moment in that unfolding history than Aquinas believed we did? Is it profitable to do so? These are the sorts of questions that are inevitably raised by the hopeful and far-reaching claims of the *Commentary on Romans* with regard to the Jews.

Adam G. Cooper

7 Degrading the Body, Suppressing the Truth
Aquinas on Romans 1:18–25

From at least the days of Socrates, a prominent tradition in both pagan and Christian thought has affirmed a curious reciprocal relationship between a person's moral condition and his or her grasp of reality. Over the centuries, this mutually influencing relation between knowledge and virtue has found expression in a variety of ways. On the one hand, there are statements asserting the relativity of moral goodness to intellectual clarity. Iris Murdoch has become famous for her doctrine that only "true vision occasions right conduct."[1] Simone Weil located the primary "*sine qua non* of goodness" in "the ability to see things as they are."[2] Josef Pieper, representing the great tradition of classical realism, said much the same thing in the opening lines of his masterpiece *Reality and the Good:* "All obligation is based on being. Reality is the foundation of ethics. The good is that which is in accord with reality."[3] Pieper extended this dependence to the social and political sphere as well, in such a way that "nations thrive in proportion to the depth of reality opened up to them."[4] Going back to the Middle Ages, we find Dante, in his *Divine Comedy,* likewise discerning that moral corruption is at root a failure in spiritual vision, a loss of "the good of intellect." Aquinas, both summing up and anticipating all these convictions, gives us the pithy axiom: "the good presupposes the true."[5]

1. Iris Murdoch, *Reality and the Good* (London: Routledge, 1970), 66.
2. As cited by Alasdair MacIntyre, "Moral Philosophy: What Next?" in *Revisions: Changing Perspectives in Moral Philosophy*, ed. Stanley Hauerwas and Alasdair MacIntyre (Notre Dame, Ind.: University of Notre Dame Press, 1983), 1–15, at 13.
3. Josef Pieper, *Living the Truth: The Truth of All Things and Reality and the Good*, trans. Lothar Krauth and Stella Lange (San Francisco: Ignatius Press, 1989), 111.
4. Josef Pieper, *Four Cardinal Virtues*, trans. Richard Winston et al. (Notre Dame, Ind.: University of Notre Dame Press, 1966), 98.
5. *Quaestiones disputatae de veritate* 21, a. 3.

On the other hand, there is the sense that intellectual perspicacity is influenced by, and even relative to, moral disposition. Just as moral goodness presupposes right vision, so too does right vision require moral goodness. There are some realities that can be known in their fullness only by a person in possession of a congruent moral quality. Henri de Lubac, commenting on the thought of Blondel, famously extended this dependence to the realm of ontological affirmation. In asserting "it is," the atheist philosopher or "bad man" opens up a contradiction within himself, for he denies the very Being upon whom every assertion of "it is" depends. In short, any clear and fully integral vision of the truth requires and presupposes a corresponding equilibrium of the will.[6]

Inasmuch as the good and the true are interrelated in this way, it follows that knowledge is indissolubly connected to the subjective dispositions and practical engagement of the knowing subject. Truth and error, conditions of the intellect, possess a moral dimension. Luigi Giussani has spoken of this phenomenon in terms of "the impact of morality on the dynamic of knowing."[7] Yet it is an old truth, once eloquently expressed by Plotinus: "To any vision must be brought an eye adapted to what is seen, and having some likeness to it. Never did eye see the sun unless it had first become sunlike, and never can the soul have vision of the First Beauty unless itself is beautiful."[8] It is the Aristotelian principle of *adequatio* applied to the moral sphere: the knowing subject must possess a real affinity or connaturality with the object of moral knowledge. You can know the truth only from the inside, as it were, by living it, being assimilated to it, giving yourself over to it, so that your life actually becomes a living measure and witness of it. This dynamic obtains all the more in the case of moral, practical truth. Only the good person can see clearly the good to be done. When faced with a moral decision, says Aristotle, "it is the good man's view of the truth that corresponds to the truth, and so he forms a correct judgement.... The good man shows his superiority above all in his power of seeing the truth in every department of conduct. He is, so to speak, the standard and yardstick of what is fine and pleasant."[9] Such a person has attained what Aquinas calls *veritas vitae*, truth of life. "Truth of life is the kind of truth by which something exists as true, not by which someone speaks what

6. Henri de Lubac, "The Conditions of Ontological Affirmation," in *Theological Fragments*, trans. Rebecca Howell Balinski (San Francisco: Ignatius Press, 1989), 377–92.

7. See *The Religious Sense*, trans. John Zucchi (San Francisco: Ignatius Press, 1990), 33.

8. Plotinus, *Enneads*, trans. A. H. Armstrong, Loeb Classical Library (Cambridge, Mass.: Harvard University Press, 1966) I, 6, 9.

9. *Nicomachean Ethics* 3, 4; translated as *The Ethics of Aristotle*, by J. A. K. Thomson, Penguin Classics (London: Penguin, 1953).

is true. Like everything else, one's life is called true on the basis of its reaching its rule and norm, namely divine law; by conforming to this, a life has upright-ness."[10]

Now it seems to me that this whole business of the relation between virtue and knowledge is not without some bearing on the topic of this essay, namely, Aquinas's exegesis of Romans 1:18–25. In that passage we read St. Paul's fa-mous charge to the effect that, despite the universal accessibility of divine knowledge, there are human beings who have suppressed the truth about their relation to God and their obligations to him; they have become darkened in their hearts and consciences; and they have subsequently been handed over by God to their sinful desires and the degradation of their bodies in sexual vice. Of these verses, patristic and medieval commentators were especially fascinat-ed by verses 19–20, with their background in Second-Temple Jewish sapiential tradition: even though God is invisible and transcendent, material creation, which is his own handiwork, clearly manifests his power and divinity for all to see. Throughout Christian history, theologians engaging in natural contem-plation *(physike theoria)*, or what is today called "natural theology," have re-turned again and again to these verses to inspire reflection on the cosmos as a vast book in which the author of creation is disclosed, as well as to defend the limited yet nonetheless effective power of human reason to infer the existence of God from the intelligent design evident in the universe.

One of the earliest systematic commentaries on this passage came from the pen of Origen of Alexandria, whose profound hermeneutical insights and exegetical method came providentially to exercise abiding influence on later generations.[11] Earlier Philonic exegesis had ascribed the evils of polytheism to ignorance *(agnoia)* and a certain blindness to reality.[12] Origen is certainly well aware of this connection. But his ire is particularly directed toward all those would-be sophisticrats who should know better. If it is true that by means of our natural reasoning all people have been granted enough wisdom to perceive God's invisible qualities by means of the visible cosmos, how much more should the "wise men of this world and those who are called philoso-phers, whose job it is in particular to discuss the created things of the world"

10. *Summa theologiae (ST)* II-II, q. 109, a. 2 ad 3.

11. Origen's *Commentary on the Epistle to the Romans* has come down to us in abridged form, via Rufinus, in Latin translation. See the English translation in two volumes by Thomas P. Scheck in *The Fathers of the Church*, vols. 103–4 (Washington, D.C.: The Catholic University of America Press, 2001–2).

12. See Kathy L. Gaca, "Paul's Uncommon Declaration in Romans 1:18–32 and Its Problemat-ic Legacy for Pagan and Christian Relations," in *Early Patristic Readings of Romans*, ed. Kathy L. Gaca and L. L. Welborn, Romans through History and Cultures Series (New York: T&T Clark, 2005), 1–33.

in order "to draw conclusions about the things which are not seen," abandon the worship of idols and effigies, and turn to the living God.[13] Such people certainly manifest a spiritual blindness, but it is a culpable blindness. By suppressing the evident truth of God's self-revelation, by failing to render due worship and thanks, Origen believes, "they have destroyed the image of God within themselves."[14] These comments recall Origen's response to the accusation of the learned pagan Celsus that Christianity is mere materialism for simpletons. Origen acknowledges that even if there are those simple Christians who have not delved into the deep questions of philosophy or theology, we nevertheless find that "they believe in the Most High God, in his only-begotten Son, the Logos of God, and that they often exhibit in their character a high degree of gravity, purity, and integrity; while those who call themselves wise have despised such virtues," and have instead wallowed in lawless lusts.[15] Origen pointedly targets even the great Socrates, who, on one occasion, having given utterance "to philosophical remarks of such profundity regarding the soul, and describing its passage (to a happier world) after a virtuous life," passed from those profound topics that God himself had revealed to him, and sent his friend Crito to the local shrine to sacrifice a chicken for Asclepius.[16] Such a contradiction rules out any progress in spiritual vision, for the privilege of seeing God is granted only to a pure, undivided heart.[17]

Other patristic commentators similarly traced this fall from knowledge and the true worship of God into ignorance and idolatry, a fall more manifest in the cultured Greeks than in the unlearned barbarians, in terms of a process of culpable self-destruction, an abandonment of wisdom with an inevitable descent into deeper and deeper moral darkness. Assuming the created congruity of human beings with God, the possession of an innate and providential capacity to know him in proportion to his self-disclosure, the Fathers found in this pericope an explanation of the moral depravity encountered in their contemporary milieu. As always, the pursuit of purely carnal interests on the part of rational beings had led to a smothering of the divine image, a darkening of the light within, without which the innate congruity with the divine light, so necessary for human judgment and action, was lost.[18]

---

13. Origen, *Comm. on Romans* 1.16.5–1.17.2 (Scheck, 90–92).

14. Ibid., 1.17.2 (Scheck, 92).   15. Origen, *Contra Celsum* 7.49.

16. Ibid., 6.3, with reference to *Phaedo* 66.

17. Ibid., 7.45. "The knowledge of God cannot enter into a heart that is not pure, or a soul given to sin and subservient to the desires of the flesh." Henri Crouzel, "Origène, précurseur du monachisme," in *Théologie de la vie monastique: Études sur la tradition patristique* (Paris: Aubier, 1961), 36.

18. John Chrysostom, *Homilies on Romans*, in *A Select Library of Nicene and Post-Nicene Fathers of the Christian Church*, first series, vol. 11, *Chrysostom: Homilies on the Acts of the Apostles*

How does Aquinas treat the same passage? In many respects, Aquinas adds nothing substantial to traditional patristic commentary. As it did for Origen and the other Fathers, this passage functions for the Angelic Doctor as one of the chief proof texts for natural theology and for the reasonableness of Christian belief in God. Like Origen and the other Fathers, Aquinas also discovers complex category distinctions where many modern commentators might see only repeated appositional expressions of the same idea. So, for example, the fluid sequence in Romans 1:20 of "invisible things of God" *(ta aorata autou)*, soon followed by "his eternal power and divinity" *(he te aidios autou dynamis kai theotes)*, becomes for Aquinas three distinct categories indicating what can be known about God, the first by negation, the second by causality, the third by participation. Moreover, these three categories are said to indicate "things about God," but fall short of saying precisely "what" God is in essence, which is unknowable to mortal human beings. Aquinas even cites a gloss speculating whether the same three categories might not possess Trinitarian significance, despite such knowledge being inaccessible without special revelation. And at another point, once again following patristic commentators right back to Origen, Aquinas distinguishes between two words that contemporary scholars might again consider virtual synonyms, namely, "ungodliness" *(asebeia / impietas)* and "injustice" *(adikia / injustitia)*, the first of which traditional exegesis reads as a sin against God and the second of which as a sin against fellow human beings.

But what may all too easily be overlooked by the contemporary reader lost in the complex details of these multilevel distinctions are numerous more subtle insights whose full understanding can be realized only by broader reference to the vast and profoundly interconnected world of Aquinas's moral psychology, his exposition of natural law, and his doctrine of virtue. In particular, Aquinas's comments on this passage invite reflection on the connection he sees between wrong moral choices and a consequent decline in intellectual acuity. By supplementing his comments on this text with material from his other more systematic writings, I hope to show that, on Aquinas's view, unless the knowledge of God naturally available through the reflection of reason on the external world is embodied in wholesome and congruent moral action, it cannot lead to its proper goal, which is supernatural union with God in divine worship.

Adopting this approach as our *modus operandi*, let us take as our point of departure Aquinas's comments on Romans 1:18. The verse reads: "The wrath of God is being revealed from heaven against all the ungodliness and wick-

---

and the Epistle to the Romans, ed. Philip Schaff and Henry Wace (Grand Rapids, Mich.: Eerdmans, 1978), 352.

edness [*impietatem et injustitiam*] of men, who suppress the truth by their wickedness." As just mentioned, Aquinas follows the tradition in distinguishing *impietas* and *injustitia* as two different sorts of sin. *Impietas* is a sin against God, but in particular, says St. Thomas, it is a sin against divine worship.[19] By his very existence, the human being owes a debt whose nature it is that it cannot be paid. Due recognition of this unpayable debt issues in thanks, devotion, and honor—first to one's parents, then to one's country, but above all to God. While toward our superiors this *pietas* takes the form of reverence, toward God it takes the exclusive form of *latria*, "the worship of a pious love," "which consists chiefly in sacrifices and oblations, through which man professes God to be the author of all good things."[20] Elsewhere Aquinas relates this interior summons to worship God to the obligation enjoined by natural law:

Natural law tells man that he is subject to a higher being, on account of the defects he finds in himself, and in which he needs help and direction from someone above him: and whatever this superior being may be, it is known to all under the name of God. Now just as in natural things the lower are naturally subject to the higher, so too it is a dictate of natural reason in accordance with man's natural inclination that he should tender submission and honour, according to his mode, to that which is above man.... [The] offering of sacrifice is therefore of the natural law.[21]

The specifically cultic meaning of the word *pietas* in turn sheds light for Aquinas on the function of the knowledge that people have suppressed by their *injustitia*, that is, their sins committed against one another. "True knowledge of God, by its very nature, leads people to the good," specifically, to the good of divine worship. But through the love of *injustitia*, this knowledge of God is "bound" *(ligatur)*, "held captive" *(captivitate detente)*, and so rendered inoperable, frustrated in its purpose, which is to lead its subjects to the act of adoring surrender to God.[22] As he repeats a little further on, "Although they possessed knowledge of God, they failed to use it unto good."[23] It's as though Thomas is saying that a person can start out with metaphysically accurate speculative knowledge of God. But if this knowledge doesn't translate into the practical sphere, into the sphere of moral action and the *pietas* of worship, it is somehow short-circuited and fails to reach its goal. Drawing on Psalm 11: 1, he goes on

---

19. Aquinas, *Lectures on Romans*, § 111; for the Latin, I have used the text *In Epistolam ad Romanos* in *Opera Omnia*, vol. 20, ed. S. E. Fretté (Paris, 1876). On the relation between *pietas* and justice, see further Josef Pieper, "The Rights of Others," in *Problems of Modern Faith: Essays and Addresses*, trans. Jan van Heurck (Chicago: Franciscan Herald Press, 1985), 203–18.

20. Aquinas, *Lectures on Romans*, §§ 142–43.

21. *ST* II-II, q. 85, a. 1; see also II-II, q. 121, a. 1.

22. Aquinas, *Lectures on Romans*, § 112.

23. Ibid., § 127.

to describe the final state of this decline in terms of the suppression and eventual disappearance of truth: "Truths have vanished from among the sons of men."[24]

The precise source or mode of this speculative knowledge of God that properly culminates in worship is further elucidated in the commentary where Aquinas refers to an "inner light" *(lumen interius).*[25] Repeated references to this inner light here and elsewhere suggest it refers to a kind of immanent moral sense, something like conscience or a sense of moral accountability. God manifests himself to human beings by a twofold mode: exteriorly and interiorly. On the outside there are external, sensible signs. On the inside there is this light peculiar to rational beings. Interacting with the exterior signs, it gives rise to intelligent recognition of the undivided divine essence and corresponding judgments in the moral sphere.[26] But even though that interior light is essentially a function of reason or intellect, it can be darkened or extinguished through the disordering of the will. Aquinas teaches clearly that the will can have a "deleterious effect" on cognitive capacity, even if only indirectly.[27] Through the substitution of finite goods for God, through the debasing pursuit of tactile pleasures as ultimate ends, the vital conditions for the knowledge of God are undermined and eventually destroyed. Aquinas says it is like a person turning his eyes away from the sun: everything is suddenly swathed in darkness. In the same way, anyone "who turns from God, trusting in himself and not in God, is plunged into spiritual darkness."[28] At the root of this decline toward spiritual instability is pride and self-trust, a failure in humility, the ascription of wisdom to one's own intellectual prowess, rather than to God.[29]

Once again these thoughts, expressed without much elaboration in the Romans lectures, can be supplemented with reference to Aquinas's moral psychology and his doctrine of natural law. First, let us draw on St. Thomas's moral psychology. These days we are used to thinking of intellectual excellence as an essentially genetic property. You get it from your mother or grandfather. But for Aquinas, intellectual excellence is a property of wisdom, and wisdom "is linked together with certain actions and dispositions in the will and also with states of emotion."[30] Thus, on Aquinas's account, as Eleonore Stump has explained,

---

24. Ibid., § 112.   25. Ibid., §§ 114, 116.

26. Ibid., §§ 114–17.

27. Eleonore Stump, *Aquinas* (London: Routledge, 2005), 349. Stump's analysis in chapter 11 of the dynamic interaction between intellect and will is especially lucid.

28. Aquinas, *Lectures on Romans*, §§ 129–30.

29. Ibid., §§ 130–31.   30. Stump, *Aquinas*, 353.

a person's moral wrongdoing will produce deficiencies in both her speculative and her practical intellect. In its effects on her speculative intellect, it will make her less capable of understanding God and goodness, theology and ethics. It will also undermine her practical intellect, leaving her prone not only to wrong moral judgements in general but also to wrong moral judgements about herself and particular actions of hers, and so it will lead to self-deception.[31]

The picture is further filled out by Aquinas's understanding of natural law. The human being's intuitive or connatural grasp of natural law, which is nothing less than his rational participation in the rule of divine wisdom, is "to a certain extent destroyed [*corruptus*] in the wicked; because in them the natural inclination to virtue is corrupted by vicious habits, and, moreover, the natural knowledge of good is darkened by passions and habits of sin."[32] Clearly then, in the case of Romans 1, we are not talking about a case of involuntary ignorance of God. For Aquinas, the ignorance referred to by St. Paul is the result of sin, for "although they possessed knowledge of God," that is, although they were endowed with the interior light of moral conscience, "they failed to use it for good," that is, they failed to follow its promptings to render God due *pietas*.[33]

These few comments help us see the extent to which Aquinas's understanding of the relation between knowledge and virtue differs from the Socratic identification of the two, the almost deterministic doctrine that every one who sins does so through ignorance, and that as long as a person is in possession of knowledge, he cannot sin.[34] Aristotle had long ago corrected the Socratics on this issue, pointing out that it is one thing to possess knowledge, but quite another to collaborate with it.[35] St. Thomas likewise, drawing St. Augustine into the conversation, argues that the interaction between reason and will is a complex business. Far too often it happens that we know perfectly well what is right, but some other urge or desire in us misdirects or "misprograms" the intellect, inducing it to propose some other thing as good.[36] The urge or desire responsible can arise from either our lower- or higher-order appetites, from sense or emotion. Either way, we are drawn away from what we know to

---

31. Ibid., 353–54.

32. *ST* I-II, q. 93, a. 6.

33. Aquinas, *Lectures on Romans*, § 127. Also ibid., § 851: "True wisdom … consists in the knowledge and worship of God."

34. See *ST* I-II, q. 58, a. 2.

35. *Nicomachean Ethics* 6, lect. 13.

36. I have borrowed the word "misprogram" from Stump, *Aquinas*, 357: "The misprogrammed intellect allows the will to want as good what it might have rejected before the misprogramming of the intellect; and the warped will, in turn, misprograms the intellect further. So the will and intellect are in a dynamic interaction which allows each of them to corrupt the other, one step at a time."

be right. For this reason, says Aquinas, "for a person to do a good deed, it is requisite not only that his reason be well disposed by means of a habit of intellectual virtue; but also that his appetite be well disposed by means of a habit of moral virtue."[37]

Is all this to suggest that the natural law can be abolished from the human heart?[38] Perhaps the strongest argument that it can be comes from the very obvious fact of human evil. "With every wrong action ... there is a misprogramming of the intellect; and the misprogrammed intellect twists the will, which in turn misprograms the intellect further."[39] In an ever-descending spiral, it seems that moral evil only begets more moral evil, both in the lives of individuals and in societies. Nor is it just a matter of reversing the cycle, for without the will or desire to do otherwise, the intellect remains blind to the truth, the knowledge of which alone unmasks evil as evil. Surely these symptoms, for which contemporary examples could no doubt be multiplied, indicate that the light of natural law can indeed be completely blotted out from our awareness.

Yet Aquinas quotes the authority of Augustine to the contrary: "Thy law is written in the hearts of men, which iniquity itself effaces not."[40] How then do we account for the fact that people don't seem to know it, or if they do, don't follow it? Aquinas answers by distinguishing between the primary and most general precepts of the natural law on the one hand, and the secondary and more detailed precepts on the other. The primary precepts are those very general moral impulses that set human beings apart as moral beings: the impulse to do good and avoid evil; the impulse to pursue the truth and shun deception. These precepts do not specify the objective content of good or evil. They simply compel us toward what we rightly or wrongly perceive to be good and away from what we rightly or wrongly perceive to be evil. In every act, the object of the will is always a good or an apparent good. The will cannot "will" evil, unless what is evil in some way appears good to reason.[41] It is this fundamental, self-evident orientation toward the universal good and away from evil that can in no way be effaced from the human heart.

The secondary precepts of the natural law are different. Proceeding from the primary precepts as conclusions or more specific applications to concrete objects and circumstances, these can be effaced. This helps explain why people act contrary to knowledge, for there can be a defect in particular knowledge, even though universal knowledge is correct. But even when particular knowledge is correct, reason can still be hindered by passion. Aquinas suggests at

---

37. *ST* I-II, q. 58, a. 2; see also *ST* I-II, q. 74, a. 5.
38. *ST* I-II, q. 94, a. 6.
39. Stump, *Aquinas*, 358.
40. Augustine, *Confessions* 2.
41. See *ST* I-II, q. 77, a. 2.

least three ways: through distraction, as when our desires for good things distract us from desires for better things; through opposition, as when our desires lead us toward things opposed to our good; and through psycho-physical suppression, as in times of sleep or illness.[42] Aquinas accepted Aristotle's theory about "the syllogism of the incontinent man," with its four propositions, not three.[43] Here Aristotle has us imagine a man who holds to two contradictory universal premises at the same time. The first is "All fornication is unlawful," while the second is "Pleasure is to be pursued." The result is conflict. As soon as a minor particular premise comes along, such as "this act of fornication is pleasurable," then in spite of the fact that the first universal premise requires you to conclude one way, the second universal premise requires you to conclude the other. With reason locked in this confused and divided state, it is left to passion to lead the day. All of which is in keeping with Aquinas's view that, as Stump observes, "moral evil will always result in internal divisions in the self, in disharmony in the will and corresponding double-mindedness in the intellect; and so moral evil is incompatible with inner peace."[44]

Much of what we have been saying is drawn from Aquinas's doctrine of natural law, compressed within a few questions in the *Summa theologiae*, but it also has deep connections with his expansive doctrine of virtue, and especially the virtue of prudence. Indeed, one could say that the human malady unfolded by St. Paul in Romans 1:18–25, with the suppression of the truth through disordered sensual attachments and the resulting degradation of the body, amounts to the loss of prudence from the human heart.

Prudence of course has nothing to do with either prudery or tactical cleverness. Recalling our opening remarks on the relation between moral goodness and intellectual vision, ancient definitions of prudence consistently link it metaphorically to the sense of sight. St. Augustine spoke of prudence as "love discerning aright" *(amor bene discernens);* Isidore of Seville defined a prudent man as "one who sees as it were from afar, for his sight is keen, and he foresees the event of uncertainties."[45] These definitions allow us to speak of prudence as a certain moral insight that involves the faithful recognition of reality as it is, the reverent openness of the human spirit to the truth in a particular situation, where "truth" means "nothing other than the unveiling and revelation of reality."[46] Prudence is a humble acceptance of the objective value of things, and a determination to respond accordingly. In other words, prudence is the practical side of wisdom. It is right knowledge geared toward concrete action.

42. *ST* I-II, q. 77, a. 2.
44. Stump, *Aquinas*, 359.
46. Pieper, *Four Cardinal Virtues*, 9.

43. *Nicomachean Ethics* 7, lect. 3.
45. See *ST* II-II, q. 47, a. 1.

If this is so, then it is clear that the kind of knowing that is prudence is not simply an isolated act of intellect, but a pervasion of the whole organism—mind, emotions, senses—with a stable habitude for doing good. In the words of that master of affective intellectualism, Pierre Rousselot, prudence "presupposes necessarily the presence of moral virtues in the sensitive faculties, and is not without implying also a certain virtuous disposition on the part of the body."[47] Accordingly, it should not surprise us to find that the vice that most effectively falsifies and corrupts prudence, and thus most damages the culminating of knowledge in divine worship, is unchastity. "Unchastity begets a blindness of spirit which practically excludes all understanding of the goods of the spirit.... This blindness is of the essence of unchastity itself, which is by its very nature destructive. It is not its outward effect and consequence, but its immanent essential property."[48]

These telling comments from Josef Pieper lead us to consider from yet another angle the mutually causal interaction, described in Romans 1, between the degradation of the body and the suppression of the truth. It is easy to stumble over the punitive action of God, who three times in a few verses is said to have handed the wicked over to the sinful desire of their hearts, leaving them prey to shameful lusts and depravity of mind (verses 24, 26, and 28). But according to Aquinas, this is a simple case of the punishment corresponding to the sin. "Just as man exchanged that which was of God for what is bestial, so God subjected the divine in man, namely, reason, to what is of the beast in him, his sensual desire."[49] But Aquinas is careful to note that God exercises this judgment not directly, as though God himself were responsible for man's affection for evil, but indirectly, "in as much as he justly withdraws the grace through which people are kept from sinning.... In this way, one's first sin is a cause of the next, which is at the same time a punishment for the first one."[50]

So it is that through the failure of a person's actions and choices to conform to the truth of things, through the unchaste "abandon and self-surrender of the soul to the world of sensuality,"[51] the entire cognitive process of coming to know the truth connaturally, a dynamic process embedded in the activity of a person's whole sensual-affective-intellectual complex and fulfilled in divine

47. Pierre Rousselot, S.J., *The Intellectualism of Saint Thomas*, trans. James E. O'Mahony (London: Sheed and Ward, 1935), 207.

48. Pieper, *Four Cardinal Virtues*, 159–60.

49. Aquinas, *Lectures on Romans*, § 137.

50. Ibid., 139. The same question arises later in his comments on Romans 9:14–33 (§ 793): "But God's action toward them is not that he disposes them to evil, since they themselves have a disposition to evil from the corruption of the first sin.... The only thing God does concerning them is that he lets them do what they want."

51. Pieper, *Four Cardinal Virtues*, 160.

worship, is corrupted at its foundations.[52] Moreover, since this process is the key to the perfection of moral conscience, and since in some way our actions actually determine our very being, its destruction implies the eventual abolition of man as such. We are left with a being for whom the lie has become the truth, for whom vice has become second nature, whose mind, in the judgment of Rousellot, "engages all its energies in the pursuit of bodily pleasures, and the minimum of speculative enquiry that is left is tinged with a metaphysic that is materialistic."[53] It hardly needs to be said that the alternative path of chastity and prudence by no means excludes sensual pleasure. It is disordered desire, concupiscence, that subverts the judgment of reason, not desire itself.[54] People are often surprised to learn that of all the vices opposed to temperance, Aquinas names first not lust, but insensibility.[55] Moral goodness is impossible without strong feeling and even a certain pleasurable delight. Intellect does not operate in a vacuum, but "resides in the entire unity of our self."[56] So too in this knowledge through connaturality, as Jacques Maritain remarked, "the intellect is at play not alone, but together with affective inclinations and the dispositions of the will, and is guided and directed by them."[57] The mind has access to reality only via feeling and desire, inclination and action, and thus can know the truth only through a kind of *passio*, what Dionysius the Areopagite famously called a "suffering" or direct experience of divine things. On this score, chastity has nothing in common with the Stoic or Kantian self-assertion of the will over against one's natural desires, but involves instead an affirmative and freely accepted participation of the whole person in all that makes for human happiness. "To the pure, all things are pure" (Ti 1:15).

And therewith lies the solution to the human malady. "Blessed are the pure in heart, for they shall see God" (Mt 5:8). Once again, purity and sight are conjoined. But here again St. Thomas surprises us. For in associating each

52. See John C. Cahalan, "Natural Obligation: How Rationally Known Truth Determines Ethical Good and Evil," *Thomist* 66, no. 1 (2002): 101–32.

53. Rousselot, *The Intellectualism of St. Thomas*, 210.

54. Aquinas, *Lectures on Romans*, § 298.

55. *ST* II-II, q. 142, a. 1.

56. Giussani, *The Religious Sense*, 34. See further Paul J. Wadell, C.P., *The Primacy of Love: An Introduction to the Ethics of Thomas Aquinas* (New York: Paulist Press, 1992).

57. Jacques Maritain, "On Knowledge through Connaturality," in *Natural Law: Reflections on Theory and Practice*, ed. William Sweet (South Bend, Ind.: Saint Augustine's Press, 2001), 15. On the relation between knowledge and affective love in Thomas's theology, see further Victor White, "Thomism and Affective Knowledge," *New Blackfriars* 25, no. 294 (1944): 321–28; Thomas Merton, *The Ascent to Truth* (London: Hollis and Carter, 1951), 204–13; Anthony Moreno, "The Nature of St. Thomas's Knowledge *per Connaturalitatem*," *Angelicum* 47, no. 1 (1970): 44–62; Walter Principe, "Affectivity and the Heart in Thomas Aquinas's Spirituality," in *Spiritualities of the Heart*, ed. Annice Callahan (New York: Paulist Press, 1990), 45–63.

of the beatitudes with its own particular virtue, he assigns purity of heart not first of all to chastity, but to the supernatural virtue of faith.[58] It is faith, says Aquinas, that takes hold of the purifying forgiveness of sins as it is concretely delivered in the performative word of the Gospel.[59] It is faith that receives the cleansing and sanctifying grace of the Holy Spirit in the heart and conscience.[60] It is faith that constitutes the "first motions" of the heart and mind toward God.[61] Thus it is faith that restores that "inner light" by which a person knows God and discerns what is good with a certain connatural affinity, so that, like seeing like, the person of faith does not simply know the truth from afar, but increasingly becomes in the concrete conditions of his physical and social existence a living measure of the truth, because for him the apparent good is also the real and ultimate good, a good that he cannot help but spontaneously desire.[62] Faith in Christ, which is nothing else than the operative grace of the Holy Spirit, the indwelling Christ himself, becomes a qualifying, transfiguring energy, "an interior habit ... inclining us to act aright, making us do those things that are becoming to grace, and shun what is opposed to it."[63] If pride and self-trust, the very opposites of prudence, lead away from divine wisdom and worship into spiritual darkness, then humility and trust in Christ, the very hallmarks of prudence, lead one to the splendid light of the truth, the wisdom by which a person genuinely knows and loves and worships God as God.[64] Faith in Christ, the assent to the truth through the will, whose mode is hope and whose inner form is love, brings about a real affinity between the human subject and God, a real assimilation to the divine nature, a real theandric union. Yet since a human person is a substantial unity of body and soul, and since the whole person is involved in moral choices in such a way that they are self-determining, this union can never be just a mat-

---

58. *ST* II-II, q. 8, a. 7; see Pieper, *Four Cardinal Virtues*, 171. On Romans 10: 9–10, Aquinas comments (*Lectures on Romans*, § 831): "Notice that he [St. Paul] says man believes with his heart, i.e., his will, because man cannot believe, unless he wills. For the intellect of the believer, unlike that of the philosopher, does not assent to the truth as though compelled by force of reason; rather, he is moved to assent by the will."

59. Aquinas, *Lectures on Romans*, §§ 98–99 (where Aquinas defines the "Gospel" as both a manifestation and a performative enactment of God's saving power). See also ibid., § 828: "For our heart is cleansed by the word of God: 'Now you are clean because of the word which I have spoken to you' (John 15:3)."

60. Ibid., § 108.

61. Ibid., §§ 302, 316.

62. See Livio Melina, *Sharing in Christ's Virtues: For a Renewal of Moral Theology in Light of Veritatis Splendor*, trans. William E. May (Washington, D. C.: The Catholic University of America Press, 2001), 41–47.

63. *ST* I-II, q. 108, a. 1 ad 2.

64. Aquinas, *Lectures on Romans*, §§ 129–31.

ter of heightened spiritual awareness, a faith of the intellect separated from inclination and outward activity, but will always involve real existential renewal, effected and marked by specific acts with definite objective content. It is true: Christ is the Christian's virtue, righteousness, and wisdom. But participation in Christ is an unfolding, dynamic trajectory whose goal is reached when the believer no longer possesses Christ's virtues only nominally, by imputation, or even by desire, but really, bodily, and in fact. Neither Christ nor the believer is an idea; their union is an actual, "one flesh" nuptial union. As Livio Melina puts it, "Our relationship with him cannot be exhausted in a merely intellectual assent to conceptual truths regarding him....The witness of faith demands that it be expressed in the "flesh," that is, in existence according to its concrete historical connotations."[65]

All this is to say that the wisdom that leads to the accurate recognition and affective enjoyment of God's good, pleasing, and perfect will is not a matter of objective calculation or mechanical obedience, but can be realized prudentially only in the living sacrifice of one's whole body-person in connatural union with Christ (Rom 12:1–3).[66] As Aquinas remarks, only the person whose affections are upright and sound and whose mind or spiritual "sense" has been renewed by grace can judge the good correctly.[67] Grace returns us not to a bare speculative knowledge of God, devoid of moral affectivity, but to the living wisdom of *pietas*, whose enfleshed contours culminate in *latria*. Indeed, "True wisdom ... consists in the knowledge and worship of God."[68]

So there we have some of St. Thomas's reflections, elucidated with reference to his systematic works, on a Pauline passage more usually treated by exegetes and theologians within the bounds of natural theology or the philosophy of religion. Perhaps, more broadly, they can serve to illuminate Aquinas's conviction that the unifying vision of God, which we can receive only as a supernatural gift, corresponds to, and, despite ourselves, does not contradict, the deepest yearning of our being for happiness, goodness, and truth. Perhaps also they will strengthen the constant claim of catholic Christianity, that God is not one among so many "facts" that can be known and proved mathematically, from a distance, in a state of moral debauchery, detachment, or indifference. Rather, to know God, something more than an act of reason is required, something more in the order of moral surrender. For God is a person, and a person "can only be reached by love."[69]

65. Melina, *Sharing in Christ's Virtues*, 109.

66. Aquinas, *Lectures on Romans*, §§ 957–67.

67. Ibid., § 967.   68. Ibid., § 851.

69. Jean Daniélou S.J., *God and the Ways of Knowing*, trans. Walter Roberts (Cleveland, Ohio: Meridian Books, 1957), 64.

Gilles Emery, O.P.

℘

8 The Holy Spirit in Aquinas's Commentary on Romans

In his *Summa theologiae*, St. Thomas offers an exposition of great breadth on the Holy Spirit in the inner mystery of God and in the divine economy. However, due to the specialized method and complex structure of this work, readers of the *Summa* do not always perceive there the significance of the teaching on the Holy Spirit. Indeed, this teaching is not limited to the questions that are specially devoted to the Holy Spirit in the Trinitarian life (*prima pars*, questions 36–38). Neither is this teaching limited to the treatise on the divine persons (questions 27–43), nor even to the treatise on God in himself (questions 2–43), because this fundamental teaching is then completed in a detailed fashion in all the other treatises where St. Thomas makes the most of the doctrine of the Holy Spirit as regards the subject under consideration (creation and providence, anthropology, moral theology, Christology, sacraments).[1] In order to apprehend the full significance of the doctrine of the *Summa* on the Holy Spirit, it is necessary then to know the different treatises, and it is also necessary to know the doctrinal structure of this work in order to perceive the internal connections. If one adds that this vast work consists of questions in which the theological content can be very difficult, one understands that the teaching of St. Thomas on the Holy Spirit sometimes discourages even the best intentions.

To accompany the reading of the *Summa theologiae* and of other synthetic works of St. Thomas, his biblical commentaries provide a very useful adjunct. These commentaries do not offer a different doctrine from his synthetic works. Rather, their genre is different. By means of direct contact with the biblical text whose words they explain and whose profound meaning they seek

1. I have tried to present this in an article (entitled "The Holy Spirit") to appear in the *Cambridge Companion to the Summa Theologiae*, ed. Philip McCosker and Denys Turner (Cambridge: Cambridge University Press, forthcoming).

to expose, these commentaries offer another access to the thought of St. Thomas. Aquinas's *lectura* on the Epistle to the Romans is a good example of such biblical exegesis. Despites its limits and its particular purpose (exegesis of a single epistle of St. Paul), this work presents a substantial theological doctrine. And since St. Paul here treats grace and the Christian life enabled by the gift of faith, one can expect to find here an important teaching on the Holy Spirit. The commentary on the Epistle to the Romans reflects the mature theological thought of St. Thomas. It appears that St. Thomas himself rapidly corrected the text of the first chapters of his commentary.[2] Perhaps this commentary dates from the last years of Aquinas's teaching, in Paris (1271–72) or in Naples (1272–73). One can fix with certitude neither the place nor the exact date of St. Thomas's course on the letter to the Romans, nor the date of its *reportatio*.[3] Although this work has been, even today, little used by studies devoted to Aquinas's Trinitarian theology, I will show that it deserves far greater attention for a better understanding of St. Thomas's doctrine on the Holy Spirit.[4]

Among the many aspects of biblical exegesis practiced by St. Thomas, it is necessary at least to note the three following characteristics in view of the present study. First, St. Thomas's biblical exegesis is "intertextual." In his commentary on the Epistle to the Romans, St. Thomas constantly has recourse to the Old Testament in order to show its fulfillment in the New. Likewise he appeals to other writings of the New Testament, because he considers the Bible in its unity in virtue of the same Spirit who has inspired it. Secondly, St. Thomas's exegesis is "traditional." His reading of the biblical texts is guided by the tradition of interpretation at the heart of the Church, in particular by the teaching of the councils (St. Thomas comments on St. Paul by referring

2. According to Father Torrell, this revision concerns the first eight chapters of the commentary on Romans: Jean-Pierre Torrell, *Saint Thomas Aquinas*, vol. 1, *The Person and His Work*, rev. ed., trans. Robert Royal (Washington, D.C.: The Catholic University of America Press, 2005), 252–54.

3. The date(s) of his commentary on St. Paul remain(s) very uncertain. The only certain thing is that the publication started from Naples. For a critical discussion based on the manuscript tradition, see Robert Wielockx, "Au sujet du commentaire de saint Thomas sur le *'Corpus paulinum'*: Critique littéraire," *Doctor Communis*, n.s., 13, nos. 1–2 (2009): 150–84. Wielockx also specifies that the revision by St. Thomas himself does not extend beyond the third *lectio* of chapter 13 (177).

4. I follow the Latin text of the Marietti edition: *Super epistolam ad Romanos lectura*, vol. 1 of *S. Thomae Aquinatis Super Epistolas S. Pauli*, ed. Raphaelis Cai, 8th ed. (Rome: Marietti, 1953), 5–230. My references to the commentary *(In ad Rom.)* indicate the chapter of the epistle followed by the "lecture" (lect.), as well as the numbers of the text according to the Marietti edition. A "lecture" *(lectio)* corresponds to a course of St. Thomas on a portion of the biblical text. On this meaning of "lectio," see Adriano Oliva, *Les débuts de l'enseignement de Thomas d'Aquin et sa conception de la sacra doctrina* (Paris: J. Vrin, 2006), 226–32. The commentary on the Epistle to the Romans comprises 67 lectures. For the English text, I made use of the translation of Fabian Larcher, O.P., as well as the translation prepared by Father Steven Boguslawski, O.P.: I thank him fraternally.

to the Councils of Nicaea, Constantinople, Ephesus, and Chalcedon!) and by the teaching of the Fathers of the Church (who are present even when they are not named). Thirdly, this biblical exegesis is "doctrinal." By this I mean, as an extension of the two preceding aspects, that this exegesis seeks understanding of the *truth* of Revelation in all its speculative and practical dimensions: it intends to nourish the contemplation of the truth, to avoid the contrary errors, and to clarify moral action.[5]

My exposition principally sets forth the words of St. Thomas himself. All the texts presented are drawn from the commentary on the Epistle to the Romans,[6] my intention being to make known the teaching of the commentary itself. I have assembled these texts, without pretending to be exhaustive, according to the main themes that St. Thomas develops on the subject of the Holy Spirit or that he presents in explicit relation to the Holy Spirit: the divine personality of the Holy Spirit; his sending in Christ and in the Church; the gifts of the Spirit, which are adoptive filiation, faith, hope, and charity; the New Law and liberty; prayer; and the inspiration of the Scriptures and their interpretation. A first section will be devoted to the subject matter of the Epistle to the Romans and to its plan. Without exhausting the richness of this commentary, I hope to succeed in giving some idea of the significance and the profundity of its teaching, capable of nourishing theological reflection as well as stimulating spiritual meditation.

The "Matter" of the Epistle and Its Plan according to St. Thomas

At the beginning of his epistle to the Romans, St. Paul designates himself as a servant of Christ, having received the apostolic vocation of announcing the Gospel of God (Rom 1:1). Commenting on this first verse of the epistle, St. Thomas explains that the word *Gospel* means the same thing as "good news" ("good annunciation").[7] And this is why the Gospel is good news: "For in it is announced the union of man to God, which is the good of man."[8] St. Thomas thus interprets the content of the Gospel in accord with "the union of man to God" *(coniunctio hominis ad Deum)* that happens in three different ways:

5. See St. Thomas, *Scriptum super Sententiis* I, prologus, a. 5. Marc Aillet, *Lire la Bible avec saint Thomas* (Fribourg: Editions Universitaires, 1993); Thomas Domanyi, *Der Römerbriefkommentar des Thomas von Aquin: Ein Beitrag zur Untersuchung seiner Auslegungsmethoden* (Bern: Peter Lang, 1979).

6. Only some indirect references in the notes indicate other works of St. Thomas.

7. *In ad Rom.* 1, lect. 1 (§ 23): "Evangelium autem idem est quod bona annuntiatio."

8. Ibid.: "Annuntiatur enim in ipso coniunctio hominis ad Deum, quae est bonum hominis."

A three-fold union of man to God is announced in the gospel. Indeed, the first is through the grace of union, accordingly Jn 1 [v. 14]: *The Word became flesh*. The second is through the grace of adoption, as is introduced in Ps 81 [v. 6]: *I said: You are gods and all sons of the Most High*. The third is through the glory of fruition, Jn 17 [v. 3]: *This is eternal life that they may know Thee [the only true God, and Jesus Christ, whom Thou hast sent]*.[9]

These explanations deserve the greatest attention because they shed light on the unity of the Epistle to the Romans. The Gospel concerns, in the first place, the union of God and man in the divine person of the Son, that is to say, the Incarnation, which St. Thomas here designates as "the grace of union" *(gratia unionis)*. In speaking of the hypostatic union as a "grace," St. Thomas emphasizes that the Incarnation of the Word is a pure gift of God that has no other origin than divine love, without any preceding merit: nothing has merited the Incarnation, so that the union of God and man in Christ appears as the supereminent model of all grace.[10] However, we should not confuse Christ, who is an incarnated divine person, with the saints who are simply human beings. This is why, in his commentary on Romans 1:4, St. Thomas specifies with the greatest care that Christ is not "adopted" as a child of God, because he is the Son of God by nature in his personal being. In Christ, man is not "united to God through the grace of adoption" as is the case in human beings who receive filial adoption. The union that one observes in Christ is a "union in personal being, and this is said [to be] the 'grace of union.'"[11] In the remainder of his commentary, St. Thomas observes many times that the conception of the humanity of Christ in the womb of the Virgin Mary is the work of the Holy Spirit.

The second mode of union of man with God is filial adoption, designated here by the expression "grace of adoption" *(gratia adoptionis)*. What Christ is by nature (he is the Son of God), he gives to believers to become "through grace." In his commentary on Romans 1:4, St. Thomas specifies that it is "sanctifying grace" *(gratia gratum faciens)* that is the "grace of adoption." This sanctifying grace is distinguished from charisms *(gratiae gratis datae)*. Whereas a charism, for example prophecy, unites a person to God "as regards an act of God" (God inspires the prophet, God gives to the prophet knowledge of events to come), the gift of sanctifying grace unites "to *God himself*."[12]

9. Ibid. (§ 24).

10. This theme is drawn from St. Augustine. See, for instance, St. Augustine, *Enchiridion* XI, 36.

11. *In ad Rom.* 1, lect. 3 (§ 46): "[…] Per unionem in esse personali: et haec dicitur gratia unionis." The commentary offers many detailed expositions of the Incarnation: see notably *In ad Rom.* 1, lect. 2 (§§ 34–41); *In ad Rom.* 1, lect. 3 (§§ 46–56); *In ad Rom.* 8, lect. 1 (§§ 606–11).

12. *In ad Rom.* 1, lect. 3 (§ 46): "[…] Deus solus, cui unitur rationalis creatura per gratiam. Uno modo quantum ad actum ipsius Dei […]; alio modo quantum ad ipsum Deum." Formally,

The remainder of the commentary of St. Thomas will show that this "grace of adoption" comes from Christ, who gives it by the Holy Spirit. As I have already noted, St. Thomas firmly excludes the idea that this grace of adoption is applied to Christ himself. It is applied only to the human beings to whom Christ communicates a *participation* of his filial divinity. The prologue of the commentary suggests this clearly enough: in making explicit the theme of adoptive filiation by means of Psalm 81:6 (or 82:6 according to the numeration of the Hebrew Bible: *You are gods and all sons of the Most High*), St. Thomas signifies that this filiation by grace constitutes a *divinization*.

Lastly, the third mode of union with God is accomplished by the "glory of fruition." This involves the completion of the second mode: in glory, God completes what he has prepared by his grace. This third mode is made explicit by the Johannine theme of eternal life arising from the vision of God: the vision is the source of fruition, that is to say, of perfect "enjoyment" of God in the charity of heaven. The remainder of the commentary will show that this glory, supreme union of human beings with God, is given by the Holy Spirit to those whom he prepares here below by his grace. Saint Thomas concludes his exegesis of Romans 1:1 by noting that this "good annunciation" is not of human origin, but divine: it was "done by God." This is why St. Paul speaks of "the Gospel *of God*":[13] this Gospel has been revealed to him by the Holy Spirit.[14]

This description of the Gospel in terms of "union with God" and of "grace" echoes the general prologue of St. Thomas's commentary on the epistles of St. Paul. According to St. Thomas, in fact, all the epistles of St. Paul treat of grace in relation to Christ: "This entire teaching is about Christ's grace."[15] Among the writings of the New Testament, these epistles receive an attention comparable to that which belongs to the Psalms in the Old Testament: "In each of these writings is contained almost the whole teaching of theology."[16] St. Thomas holds that the Pauline corpus consists of three kinds of letters that correspond to three ways of envisioning grace. (1) The Epistle to the Hebrews treats grace in Christ himself, insofar as Christ is the Head of the Church. This has to do with the "capital grace" of Christ. (2) The epistles to Timothy, to Titus, and to Philemon consider grace "in the chief members of the Mystical Body," that is to say, in the "princes" or "prelates" of the Church. (3) The

---

the union with God himself is procured by charity, which is a gift of sanctifying grace (cf. ibid.: "secundum effectum dilectionis").

13. *In ad Rom.* 1, lect. 1 (§ 24).

14. *In ad Rom.* 16, lect. 2 (§ 1224).

15. *Super Epistolas S. Pauli lectura*, prologus (§ 11): "Est enim haec doctrina tota de gratia Christi."

16. Ibid. (§ 6): "In utraque scriptura fere tota theologiae continetur doctrina."

epistles addressed to the "Gentiles" (to the Christians of the Nations) consider grace "in the Mystical Body itself, that is, the Church." Among these epistles addressed to "the Church of the Gentiles," some ponder the grace of Christ "as it exists in the sacraments of the Church" (the Epistles to the Corinthians and to the Galatians). Others consider grace more particularly insofar as it brings about the unity of the Church (Epistles to the Ephesians, Philippians, Colossians, and Thessalonians). As regards the Epistle to the Romans, which St. Thomas mentions in the first place of the third group, it concerns the grace of Christ "as it is in itself."[17] It is therefore fitting that, even if the Epistle to the Romans is not first according to chronology, it is placed at the head of the epistles of St. Paul.[18]

Before presenting the teaching of the commentary on the subject of the Holy Spirit, it is necessary to describe the plan of the Epistle to the Romans according to St. Thomas. The "epistolary tractate," which is entirely devoted to "the *truth of the grace of Christ*,"[19] comprises two principal parts. The first part teaches "the power of the evangelical grace" that is the means of universal salvation (Rom 1:16b–11:36). This part shows above all that *the evangelical grace is necessary for the salvation* of the Gentiles (Rom 1:18–32) and of the Jews (Rom 2:1–4:25), the latter not having been justified by the Law, or by the prerogatives of Judaism, or by circumcision. It then teaches that *the evangelical grace is efficacious and sufficient* (Rom 5:1–8:39), by manifesting the goods we attain through Christ's grace (Rom 5:1–11), and by manifesting the evils we are freed from by Christ's grace (Rom 5:12–8:39). These evils are the servitude of sin (grace offers liberation from original sin and the capacity to resist future sins), the servitude of the law, the "evil of fault" that separates one from God, and the "evil of punishment" (punishment for sin). The exposition of the liberation from punishment (Rom 8:10–39) comprises, in turn, two sections: that we are freed through the Holy Spirit in the future from bodily death and that in this life we are aided by the Holy Spirit against the weaknesses of the present life. This first part of the epistolary tractate is completed by the exposition of *the origin of evangelical grace* (Rom 9:1–11:36: the election of the Gentiles, and the "fall of the Jews"). The second part of the epistolary tractate

17. Ibid. (§ 11): "Nam ipsa gratia Christi tripliciter potest considerari. Uno modo secundum se, et sic commendatur in epistola ad Romanos."

18. Ibid. (§ 12). Saint Thomas indicates a twofold reason: "Both because of the dignity of the Romans, who ruled the other nations, since in this letter pride is rebuked, which is the source of all sin (Sir 10:14); and because the order of teaching requires that grace should first be considered in itself before being considered as it is found in the Sacraments."

19. Cf. *In ad Rom.* 1, lect. 5 (§ 74): "De veritate gratiae Christi." I present here the plan of the epistle according to the "divisions of the text" supplied by St. Thomas at the beginning of the main sections of his commentary.

(Rom 12:1–16:27) presents a moral instruction. Saint Paul here teaches "the usefulness of grace, so that man may be perfect" (Rom 12:1–13:14: the holiness of man before God, justice toward neighbor, and purity of man in himself), and then "the usefulness of grace, so that the perfect may sustain the imperfect" (Rom 14:1–15:13). This second part concludes with some "special and familiar admonitions" and a thanksgiving (Rom 15:14–16:27).

According to this plan, the central section of the epistle (Rom 5:1–8:39) shows the efficacy and the fully sufficient character of evangelical grace. It is in his commentary on this section, in particular on chapter 5 and on chapter 8 of the epistle, that the developments of St. Thomas concerning the Holy Spirit will be the most numerous and the most important. This central section considers two aspects of the grace of Christ: first, it sets forth *the goods that Christ procures for us* (we will find here the heart of the teaching of St. Thomas on charity as related to the Holy Spirit), and then *the evils from which the grace of Christ frees us* (we will find here, among others, a detailed exposition of the work of the Holy Spirit as well as a profound vision of the relationships that the Holy Spirit has with Christ).

The Divine Identity of the Holy Spirit

The commentary of St. Thomas does not dwell at length on the Holy Spirit in the immanent life of God the Trinity ("theology"), but rather explores the work of the Holy Spirit in the gift of salvation ("economy").[20] It is necessary to observe, however, that the references to what one today calls the "immanent Trinity" are not absent from the commentary, and that one finds a number of teachings concerning the person of the Holy Spirit and his distinctive property in the eternal Trinity.

First of all, St. Thomas explains that the Holy Spirit is *true God*. The apostolic faith avoids the errors of Arius, who held that the Holy Spirit is a creature, and it also avoids the position of Macedonius, according to which the Holy Spirit is inferior to the Father and the Son.[21] Following St. Augustine, St. Thomas demonstrates the divinity of the Holy Spirit by explaining that only three "things" (in Latin: *res*) are the object of the fruition of the human being, that is to say, the end pure and simple, properly divine, in which

---

20. On the distinction between "theology" *(theologia)* and "economy" *(dispensatio)*, see, for example, *Summa theologiae (ST)* III, q. 2, a. 6, ad 1. For more details, see Gilles Emery, "*Theologia* and *Dispensatio:* The Centrality of the Divine Missions in St. Thomas's Trinitarian Theology," *Thomist* 74 (2010): 515–61.

21. *In ad Rom.* 8, lect. 5 (§ 692). These are, for Aquinas, the two major heresies regarding the divinity of the Holy Spirit: see *Summa contra Gentiles*, bk. 4, ch. 16 (§ 3525).

humans find their happiness. These three *res* are the Father, the Son, and the Holy Spirit,[22] because only the "divine person" can procure the fullest happiness.[23] Although the commentary often describes the Holy Spirit as a "person,"[24] this personal dignity of the Holy Spirit appears as a given of faith that, in this context, seems not to require more detailed explication. Nonetheless, if one looks more closely, the commentary will demonstrate that, by his action, the Holy Spirit is revealed as a *person*, because he accomplishes the actions that are properly the actions of a person—even as the Holy Spirit reveals himself as *God* by accomplishing actions that belong exclusively to God.

Concerning the personal property of the Holy Spirit, the commentary testifies soberly to the constant teaching of St. Thomas. The Holy Spirit "proceeds as Love";[25] he proceeds from the Father and the Son in such a way that he is, in virtue of his unique procession, "the Love of the Father and the Son,"[26] the common Spirit of the Father and the Son: "The same is the Spirit of Christ and of God the Father; yet he is said *of God the Father* insofar as he proceeds from the Father; and he is said to be the Spirit *of Christ*, insofar as he proceeds from the Son."[27] According to a rule already well established by St. Augustine, St. Thomas adds that, because the Holy Spirit is the Communion and the Bond of love of the Father and the Son *(unio et nexus)*, it is necessary to recognize him each time that the Father and the Son are named, as one observes in particular in the salutations of St. Paul (here in Rom 1:7: *Grace and peace to you from God our Father, and the Lord Jesus Christ).*[28] The commentary thus specifies the eternal origin and hypostatic property of the Holy Spirit, but we will see that St. Thomas is concerned above all to emphasize the economic repercussions of this teaching: being Love in person, the Holy Spirit diffuses charity; because he proceeds from the Father and the Son, he unites

22. *In ad Rom.* 15, lect. 3 (§ 1182).

23. *In ad Rom.* 8, lect. 6 (§ 714). The divine person is given *ad fruendum* (in order that one might enjoy him), whereas rational creatures are given to us *ad convivendum* (in order to live with us, and us with them); as regards creatures inferior to human beings, they are there *ad utendum* (in order to use them, as means to serve God).

24. *In ad Rom.* 1, lect. 4 (§ 73): "Persona autem Spiritus Sancti"; *In ad Rom.* 1, lect. 6 (§ 122): "Persona Spiritus Sancti"; etc.

25. *In ad Rom.* 11, lect. 5 (§ 949): "Qui procedit ut amor." On Aquinas's doctrine of the Holy Spirit as Love, see Gilles Emery, *The Trinitarian Theology of Saint Thomas Aquinas* (Oxford: Oxford University Press, 2007), 225–45; Yves Congar, *I Believe in the Holy Spirit*, vol. 3, *The River of the Water of Life (Rev. 22:1) Flows in the East and in the West*, trans. David Smith (New York: Seabury Press, 1983), 116–27.

26. *In ad Rom.* 5, lect. 1 (§ 392): "Qui est amor Patris et Filii." See Anthony Keaty, "The Holy Spirit Proceeding as Mutual Love," *Angelicum* 77, no. 4 (2000): 533–57.

27. *In ad Rom.* 8, lect. 2 (§ 627), with reference to Jn 14:26 and Jn 15:26 (emphasis mine).

28. *In ad Rom.* 1, lect. 4 (§ 73).

the faithful to God the Father and he conforms them to Christ from whom he comes (this is the "economic" stake of the doctrine of the procession *a Patre et a Filio*). The accent placed on the Catholic doctrine of the procession *a Filio* does not lead St. Thomas to neglect the origin of the Holy Spirit *a Patre* by the same and unique spiration. The Holy Spirit receives, for example, the beautiful name of "the spiritual Seed proceeding from the Father."[29] This expression signifies the Holy Spirit according to the action that he exercises in our favor, in accordance with his eternal origin. At the same time, St. Thomas does not limit himself to explaining that the gift of the Holy Spirit manifests the identity and work of Christ; he emphasizes, with St. Paul, that the gift of the Holy Spirit supremely reveals the love of God the Father: "Just as the charity of God the Father is exhibited toward us through this [fact], that he gave his Spirit to us, . . . in this way also it is exhibited by the [fact] that he gave his Son to us."[30] The sending of the Son and the gift of the Holy Spirit are the revelation of the love of the Father.

This knowledge of the Holy Spirit is reserved to faith: philosophical reason is not capable of attaining it. Saint Thomas notes that the pagan sages, who were not able to discover the Father and the Son, found themselves in even greater difficulty as regards glimpsing anything that could evoke the Holy Spirit. He observes that some Platonic philosophers posed a "first principle" that one can distantly associate (by appropriation) with the person of the Father, as well as a "paternal intellect" that corresponds obscurely (by appropriation again) to the person of the Son; but these philosophers have not affirmed a third reality that, for the believer, could have presented any correspondence with the Holy Spirit.[31] By natural reason, philosophers could know only the essential attributes that belong to God insofar as God is the transcendent principle of the world: they have not been able to recognize the divine persons, because the properties that constitute and distinguish these persons are not accessible to us by way of causality.[32] These explanations find a place in the commentary on Romans 1:20, which constitutes a major locus of

29. *In ad Rom.* 8, lect. 3 (§ 636): "Semen autem spirituale a Patre procedens, est Spiritus Sanctus."
30. *In ad Rom.* 5, lect. 2 (§ 399).
31. *In ad Rom.* 1, lect. 6 (§ 122). On this theme transmitted notably by Peter Abelard, in reference to St. Augustine and Macrobius, see also *ST* I, q. 32, a. 1, ad 1.
32. Personal properties concern the relations of divine person to divine person, and not relations between the divine persons and the world (the divine persons are constituted in their distinct identity not by their relationship to the world, but by their eternal interpersonal relationships). That which natural reason can know of God is taken exclusively from effects created by God, in the measure to which these effects permit one to know what belongs necessarily to God as principle of the world. Our reason therefore cannot, by its natural light, establish the properties of divine persons. See Emery, *The Trinitarian Theology*, 22–26.

the Thomist doctrine of the knowledge of God by the natural light of human reason.

Many attributes appropriated to the Holy Spirit are founded directly on his eternal property. This is especially the case with goodness *(bonitas)*, which is appropriated to him because he proceeds as Love *(procedit ut Amor)* and because goodness is the very object of love.[33] At the same time, according to the Gloss to which St. Thomas refers, the divinity *(divinitas)* mentioned in Romans 1:20 designates the Holy Spirit "to whom goodness is appropriated."[34] The name "divinity" should probably be understood here under the aspect whereby, according to its origin, this word evokes the divine action of governing the world (the exercise of providence),[35] this action being itself appropriated to the divine goodness. Moreover, the designation of the Holy Spirit by the name "divinity" constitutes a beautiful confession of the Holy Spirit as God. The Latin text of the doxology of Romans 11:36 ("from Him, and through Him, and in Him") furnishes also the occasion of an appropriation to the Holy Spirit: the expression "in Him" *(in ipso)* is attributed to the Holy Spirit because it signifies the goodness by which God conserves creatures.[36] These appropriations are precious because they manifest indirectly the property of the Holy Spirit, who is Love. One should equally observe that the Trinitarian interpretation of the doxology of Romans 11:36 finds a beautiful echo in the exegesis of the final doxology of the epistle (Rom 16:25–27: "To him who is able to confirm you according to my Gospel and preaching of Jesus Christ, . . . the only wise God, through Jesus Christ, to whom be honor and glory unto the ages of ages"). According to St. Thomas, this final doxology is addressed not only to the person of the Father but "to God who is the Trinity."[37]

Christ, the Holy Spirit, and the Church

The relationships of Christ and the Holy Spirit are at the heart of the commentary of St. Thomas. Before we consider these relationships in the particular gifts of the Holy Spirit (filiation, justification, faith, charity, liberty, etc.),

33. *In ad Rom.* 11, lect. 5 (§ 949); cf. *In ad Rom.* 2, lect. 1 (§ 187).

34. *In ad Rom.* 1, lect. 6 (§ 122). Cf. Peter Lombard, *Collectanea in Rom.* 1:20 *(PL* 191, col. 1328).

35. Cf. *ST* I, q. 13, a. 8. This interpretation could also refer to the identification of the Holy Spirit with the "deity" as "communion" of the Father and the Son (mutual love); see St. Augustine, *De fide et symbolo* 9.

36. *In ad Rom.* 11, lect. 5 (§ 949). This conservation in the good is linked to final causality (§ 947). I recall in this regard that the action of the Holy Spirit is not limited to the supernatural order but concerns also (and first) the order of nature.

37. *In ad Rom.* 16, lect. 2 (§ 1223): "Deo qui est Trinitas"; cf. ibid., § 1227.

it is necessary to note the presence of the Holy Spirit in Christ himself, and
it is equally necessary to observe the giving of the Holy Spirit by Christ. This
will permit us to better understand the intrinsic connection of Christ and the
Holy Spirit in the constitution of the Church.

Christ was conceived of the Virgin Mary by the Holy Spirit: St. Thomas
sees here the sign of the divine power of Christ, attesting that he is the "Son
of God" (cf. Lk 1:35).[38] In connection with the conception of Christ, Aquinas emphasizes the fullness of grace in Christ, that is to say, the fullness of
the Holy Spirit that suffused the humanity of Christ. On the one hand, the
action of the Holy Spirit accounts for the sinlessness of Christ. Because "his
flesh was conceived through the Holy Spirit who takes away sin,"[39] Christ did
not receive sin from Adam.[40] He did not have a flesh of sin, but he has freely
assumed a flesh "in the likeness of the flesh of sin" (Rom 8:3), that is to say, a
flesh "capable of suffering."[41] On the other hand, the soul of Christ is full of
grace and truth (cf. Jn 1:14),[42] that is to say, filled with the fullness of the Holy
Spirit in person. This prerogative belongs exclusively to Christ: "To Christ
alone was the Spirit given without measure."[43]

The supreme fullness of grace in Christ is due to his divine personality:
"To each one God gives the grace proportionate to him according to that for
which he is chosen. Thus, Christ as man was given the most excellent grace
[excellentissima gratia], because for this he was chosen, so that his nature
would be assumed in the unity of the divine person."[44] Because of the hypostatic union, from the first instant of his conception, the humanity of Christ
was filled by the Holy Spirit with a grace without measure, unlimited, whose
abundance is completely unique to him. Immediately after Christ, St. Thomas
mentions his mother: "After him the blessed Mary had greatest fullness of
grace (post eum habuit maximam plenitudinem gratiae), who was chosen for
this that she would be the Mother of Christ."[45] And, after the Virgin Mary,
St. Thomas underscores the eminent place of the apostles among all the other
saints: "Among the rest, the Apostles were chosen for the greater dignity, so,

38. *In ad Rom.* 1, lect. 3 (§ 59).   39. *In ad Rom.* 8, lect. 1 (§ 608).

40. *In ad Rom.* 5, lect. 3 (§ 419).

41. *In ad Rom.* 8, lect. 1 (§ 608): "Non enim habuit carnem peccati, id est, cum peccato con-
ceptam, quia caro eius fuit concepta per Spiritum Sanctum qui tollit peccatum. [...] Sed habuit
similitudinem carnis peccati, id est, similem carni peccatrici in hoc quod erat passibilis."

42. *In ad Rom.* 8, lect. 2 (§ 629).

43. *In ad Rom.* 12, lect. 1 (§ 971). On the divine "missions," see Gilles Emery, *The Trinity: An
Introduction to Catholic Doctrine on the Triune God*, trans. Matthew Levering (Washington, D.C.:
The Catholic University of America Press, 2011), 178–94.

44. *In ad Rom.* 8, lect. 5 (§ 678).

45. Ibid.

namely, immediately receiving from Christ himself they would give over to others the things which pertain to salvation, and thus the Church by a certain mode would be founded on them."[46] This teaching, which St. Thomas repeats many times in his commentary, reflects the doctrine of the "visible missions" of the Holy Spirit to the apostles: the Holy Spirit was sent to them visibly (with the sign of the breath according to John 20:22 and that of the "tongues as of fire" in Acts 2:1–4) in order to signify the abundance of interior grace that he would confer upon them, so that they would transmit the grace of Christ by preaching and by the sacraments, in view of establishing the Church.

Because of their direct relationship to Christ, and in order to plant the Church in faith and love, God gave to the apostles a more abundant grace in comparison with the other saints.[47] "The Apostles possessed the abundance of the grace of the Holy Spirit more than all the others."[48] "The Apostles possessed the first fruits of the Holy Spirit [*primitias Spiritus Sancti*], because namely, the Apostles possessed the Holy Spirit earlier and more abundantly than the rest [*tempore prius, et caeteris abundantius*], just as with the fruits of the land that which first arrives at maturity is taken to be richer and greater."[49] "It is clear that the Apostles have precedence over all the other saints, by whatever prerogatives they may shine, whether of virginity, or doctrine or martyrdom, because they possess more abundantly the Holy Spirit."[50] This teaching is ecclesiological, Christological, and pneumatological in nature: in virtue of the superabundant sending of the Holy Spirit, the apostles transmit the grace of Christ in order to plant the Church in faith and in love. The exegesis of Romans 11:26 ("He who delivers shall come from Sion, that he may banish impiety from Jacob") furnishes a beautiful illustration of this teaching: according to St. Thomas, these words can designate either the coming of Christ the Savior, who came from the Jewish people, or the diffusion of the doctrine of Christ "through this, that the Apostles in the upper room in Zion received the Holy Spirit," so that "From Zion shall go forth the law" (Is 2:3).[51]

By the mysteries of his life in the flesh, Christ spreads the Holy Spirit by

46. Ibid.
47. Ibid.: "Et ideo Deus eis abundantiorem gratiam prae caeteris tribuit."
48. *In ad Rom.* 11, lect. 3 (§ 896). Saint Thomas refers here to the Gloss on Romans 8. Cf. Peter Lombard, *Collectanea in Rom.* 8:24 (*PL* 191, col. 1488). See also St. Thomas, *In ad Rom.* 15, lect. 3 (§ 1189): it is precisely the gift of the Holy Spirit that is transmitted by the ministry of St. Paul.
49. *In ad Rom.* 8, lect. 5 (§ 676). This beautiful explanation of the biblical theme of the "first fruits" is completed by a reference to Jeremiah 2:3: "Israel is sacred to the Lord, the first of his produce [*primitiae frugum eius*]."
50. Ibid.
51. *In ad Rom.* 11, lect. 4 (§ 918).

whom his humanity is filled. On the one hand, St. Thomas here emphasizes the principal role that belongs to the divinity of Christ: the gift of the Holy Spirit by Christ shows the filial divinity of Christ, because God alone can give the sanctifying Holy Spirit.[52] On the other hand, the humanity of Christ collaborates actively in the gift of the Holy Spirit. In order to account for the salvific value of the death and resurrection of Christ, St. Thomas has recourse to his doctrine of the instrumentality of the humanity of Christ. "It must be said that the death of Christ was salutary for us, not only by way of merit, but also by way of effecting it [*per modum cuiusdam efficientiae*]. For since the humanity of Christ was, by a certain mode, the instrument of his divinity, as the Damascene says, all the passions and actions of the humanity of Christ were salvific for us, namely, coming out of the power of his deity."[53] As instrument of his divinity, the human act of Christ collaborates with the act of his divine nature, under the motion of this divine nature. Thus, the human act of Christ concurs to procure this properly divine gift that is the sending of the Holy Spirit. Saint Thomas emphasizes that *all* the actions and the passions of Christ procure salvation for us. The commentary shows, however, the special place that belongs to the passion, the death, and the resurrection of Christ. Commenting on Romans 1:4, St. Thomas explains:

The Apostle says: it appears that Christ is the Son of God in power *according to the Spirit of sanctification*, that is, because he gives the sanctifying Spirit, indeed which sanctification began *from the resurrection of the dead, of Jesus Christ our Lord* (Rm 1:4), that is, from death, accordingly Jn 7:39: *The Spirit was not given as yet because Jesus was not yet glorified:* that is, it not thus to be understood that no one before the resurrection of Christ would have received the sanctifying Spirit, but because from that time, in which Christ rose, the Spirit of sanctification began to be given more copiously and more commonly.[54]

Saint Thomas here interprets St. Paul in the light of St. John and St. Luke, by indicating the role of Christ as *giver of the Holy Spirit:* it is by giving the sanctifying Spirit *(Spiritus sanctificans)* that Christ sanctifies. This work of sanctification manifests the divinity of Christ. Christ's resurrection appears as the pivot in the economy of the Holy Spirit, inasmuch as it inaugurates the

---

52. *In ad Rom.* 1, lect. 3 (§ 58): "Est enim proprium virtutis divinae per collationem Spiritus Sancti sanctificare homines. [...] Ex hoc igitur apparet Christum habere virtutem divinam, quia ipse dat Spiritum Sanctum."

53. *In ad Rom.* 4, lect. 3 (§ 380). Saint Thomas continues this explanation by the mention of the exemplary causality of the mysteries of Christ: while Christ's passion causes the extinction of sins, his resurrection justifies us by procuring the new life. In this way, under the aspect of exemplarity, St. Thomas shows the proper role that distinguishes the passion and the resurrection in the accomplishment of our salvation.

54. *In ad Rom.* 1, lect. 3 (§ 58).

age of the universal outpouring of the Holy Spirit. The qualification of abundance and universality *(copiosius et communius)* evokes the doctrine of the "visible mission" of the Holy Spirit to the Apostles.[55]

On these foundations, St. Thomas emphasizes that the grace spread by the Holy Spirit *is the grace of Christ*, that is to say, the fullness of grace that had been imparted to the humanity of Christ in order that Christ would make it overflow onto others ("capital grace"). On the one hand, the Holy Spirit communicates to believers a participation of the grace with which Christ himself was filled without measure. If we are renewed in the Holy Spirit, St. Thomas explains, it is "through the grace of Christ."[56] On the other hand, it is in giving the Holy Spirit that Christ communicates to us his own grace. "The charity of God is *in Christ Jesus our Lord* (Rom 8:39), because namely, it was given to us through him, insofar as he gives it to us through the Holy Spirit."[57] This is why St. Thomas identifies in some way the "grace of Christ" and the Holy Spirit.[58] We can understand that these are two aspects of the same reality: one of the aspects is created (sanctifying grace and the gifts of this grace), the other is uncreated (the Holy Spirit, who is the source and end of grace).

This teaching finds its summit in the explanation of the relationship that believers hold jointly with Christ and with the Holy Spirit. In his commentary on the eighth chapter of the epistle, St. Thomas explains that the Spirit of life, in Christ Jesus, frees us from sin and death, as much from spiritual death (the privation of grace by sin) as from corporeal death:

The Apostle adds: the Spirit *of life* (Rm 8:2); because just as the natural spirit produces the life of nature, in this manner the divine Spirit produces the life of grace: "The Spirit is the one who causes life" (Jn 6:64); "The Spirit of life was in the wheels" (Ez 1:20). However, he adds *in Christ Jesus* (Rm 8:2), because this Spirit is not given except to those who are in Christ Jesus [*iste Spiritus non datur nisi his qui sunt in Christo Iesu*]. For just as the natural spirit does not come to the member that does not have a connection to the head, thus the Holy Spirit does not come to the man who is not conjoined to Christ the head [*Spiritus Sanctus non pervenit ad hominem qui non est capiti Christo coniunctus*]. "This we know, that he remains in us, by the Spirit whom he gave to us" (1 Jn 3:24).[59]

55. See St. Thomas's commentary on the Gospel according to St. John: *Super Evangelium S. Ioannis lectura*, ed. Raphaelis Cai (Rome: Marietti, 1952), cap. 7, lect. 5 (§ 1093).

56. *In ad Rom.* 7, lect. 1 (§ 531): "In Spiritu renovati per gratiam Christi;" cf. *In ad Rom.* 5, lect. 1 (§ 385).

57. *In ad Rom.* 8, lect. 7 (§ 733).

58. Cf. for example *In ad Rom.* 8, lect. 2 (§ 628): "Per gratiam Christi sive per Spiritum Sanctum."

59. *In ad Rom.* 8, lect. 1 (§ 605).

These explications are limpid. In the life of grace, the Holy Spirit exercises a role analogous to that of the natural spirit in the natural life of the human being. The Holy Spirit is a principle of divine life who animates today the soul of the saints and who will in the future vivify their bodies. However, in order that the Holy Spirit might accomplish this work, it is necessary that he reach the human person. Here again, St. Thomas applies the analogy of natural life. The spirit (the breath) reaches only the members that are in communication with the head; this contact is an indispensable precondition for a member to benefit from the spirit that animates the body. The same holds for the Holy Spirit: he vivifies only the members who are united to Christ the Head; it is from Christ that the Spirit is spread in believers. A little further on, St. Thomas continues this teaching through a complementary aspect that specifies the relationship of the saints to Christ and to the Spirit:

If one does not have the Spirit of Christ, he does not belong to him (Rm 8:9). For just as there is no member of the body which through the spirit of the body is not vivified, so anyone who does not have the Spirit of Christ is not a member of Christ [*non est membrum Christi qui Spiritum Christi non habet*]. "By this we know that he remains in us, because he gave to us of his own Spirit" (1 Jn 4:13).[60]

Saint Thomas showed above that, in order to be vivified by the Holy Spirit, it is necessary to be united to Christ the Head. He shows here that in order to be a member of Christ, it is necessary to have the Spirit of Christ. These two aspects are complementary: the one is implied in the other. The use of the same analogy of the natural spirit shows the homogeneity of these two aspects: *our relation to Christ is in proportion to our relation to the Spirit, and conversely.* There is no living relationship with Christ outside the Holy Spirit. But neither is there a vivifying reception of the Holy Spirit outside of Christ. At this level, we discover that, in designating the Church as "Body of Christ" and as "Temple of the Spirit," one signifies the *same reality* under two indissociable aspects. These explanations shed a profound light on the reality of salvation and on the mystery of the Church. *Where there is the Holy Spirit (without whom there is no salvation), there is the Church, the Body of Christ; and where there is the Body of Christ, there is the Holy Spirit.*

Other passages present the joint work of Christ and the Holy Spirit in the Church. Among many texts, the commentary on Romans 12:5 is particularly illuminating. Here, St. Thomas shows that the unity of the Church is "spiritual." This means that ecclesial unity comes from *the Spirit who derives from*

---

60. *In ad Rom.* 8, lect. 2 (§ 627). On the analogy of natural life and the life of grace, see also *In ad Rom.* 1, lect. 6 (§ 108): "Just as the body lives through the soul in natural life, thus the soul lives through God in the life of grace."

Christ. The joint role of the Spirit and of Christ is found also at the heart of the unity of the Church as the Body of Christ:

The Apostle touches upon the unity of the mystical body, when he says: *We are one body* (Rm 12:5). "So that he may reconcile both in one body" (Eph 2:16). This mystical body has a spiritual unity, through which, by faith and the affection of charity we are united to one another in God, accordingly Eph 4:4: *One body, and one Spirit.* And because the Spirit of unity is derived in us from Christ; above (Rm 8:9): *If one does not have the Spirit of Christ, he does not belong to him.* For that reason he appends *in Christ* (Rm 12:5), who through his Spirit, whom he gives to us, unites us to one another and to God: *So that they may be one in us, just as we are one* (Jn 17:22).[61]

In this context (the relationship of believers with Christ and with the Holy Spirit), a significant place belongs to the theme of *conformation to Christ.* In a passage that comes just after the commentary on Romans 8:9 cited above, St. Thomas shows the work of the Holy Spirit in light of his eternal origin: he proceeds from the Father and the Son. The Holy Spirit proceeds from the Father and the Son as from one single Principle, by one and the same spiration.[62] However, St. Thomas distinguishes between the Holy Spirit's relation to the Son and his relation to the Father, in order to clarify the action of the Holy Spirit. Here is the first aspect:

The Apostle first shows what we receive from the Holy Spirit inasmuch as he is the Spirit *of Christ.* ... Therefore he says: It was said that *if one does not have the Spirit of Christ, he does not belong to him* (Rm 8:9), wherefore, since you are of Christ, you have the Spirit of Christ, and Christ himself dwells within you through faith, according to Eph 3:17: "Let Christ dwell in your hearts through faith." *But if Christ is* thus *in you* (Rm 8:10), then you are to be conformed to Christ. Now Christ came into the world in this way, so that in his spirit he would be full of grace and truth (Jn 1:14), but as concerns the body, he has a likeness of the flesh of sin, as was said above (cf. Rm 8:3). Wherefore this also must be in you, that your *body indeed on account of sin*, which until now abides in your flesh, *is dead*, that is, destined to the necessity of death ... ; *but the spirit lives*, who already is summoned back from sin ... : it lives by the life of grace, *on account of justification* (Rm 8:10), through which one is justified by God. "However, what I now live in the flesh, I live by faith in the Son of God" (Gal 2:20); above (Rm 1:17): The just one lives by faith."[63]

In this passage, St. Thomas describes two dimensions of the kenotic condition of Christ: in his soul, Christ enjoys the fullness without measure of the Holy Spirit that procures for him a supreme union with God by knowledge

---

61. *In ad Rom.* 12, lect. 2 (§ 974). Saint Thomas earlier specified (§ 973): "The mystical body of Christ, which is the Church."
62. *ST* I, q. 36, a. 4.
63. *In ad Rom.* 8, lect. 2 (§§ 628–29).

and charity; but Christ freely assumed a flesh subject to suffering and death. Now, the Holy Spirit procures precisely the indwelling of Christ for the just, and in such a way that the Holy Spirit renders the just *conformed to Christ in his condition of humility:* their flesh remains subject to suffering and to the necessity of death, but their spirit lives through grace. By the Holy Spirit, human beings are justified by being made conformed to Christ. This is accomplished by knowledge and love of God, as well as by association with the sufferings of Christ, that is to say, by participation in the *holy* but *passible* condition that Christ lived during his time on earth. Furthermore, in the context of the "conformation to the death of Christ" by baptism, St. Thomas offers a liturgical explanation in noting: "On Holy Saturday solemn baptism is celebrated in the Church when the burial of Christ is commemorated, just as in the vigil of Pentecost when the Holy Spirit is solemnized, from whose power the water of baptism receives the power of cleansing."[64] In his commentary on the eighth chapter, St. Thomas develops these explanations by setting forth the second aspect of the work of the Holy Spirit, insofar as the Holy Spirit proceeds from the Father:

Then the Apostle shows what we attain in the Holy Spirit, insofar as he is the Spirit of the Father, saying: *Because if his Spirit dwells in you,* namely of God the Father, *who raised Jesus Christ from the dead* (Rm 8:11). . . . Nevertheless Christ himself rose by his own power, because the power of the Father and of the Son is the same; it follows that the thing which God the Father did in Christ, he may also do in us. . . . After the resurrection, our bodies shall be wholly immortal. . . . And this *on account of his Spirit dwelling* in us, that is by the power of the Holy Spirit dwelling in us. Ez 37:5: "These things the Lord God says to these bones: Behold I shall send into you the Spirit, and you shall live." And this on account of *the indwelling Spirit,* that is on account of the dignity which your bodies have from him because they were receptacles of the Holy Spirit. 1 Cor 6:19: "Do you not know that your members are the temple of the Holy Spirit?" Certainly those, whose members were not a temple of the Spirit, rise, but shall have a body capable of suffering.[65]

Under this second aspect, which considers the Holy Spirit as he proceeds *from the Father,* he procures for the saints the *glorious* resurrection, that is to say, liberation from the mortal condition *and liberation from the passible condition.* The Holy Spirit thus gives a participation in the resurrection of Christ: by his Spirit, the Father does in the saints what he did in Christ, because the bodies of the saints are the temple of the Spirit. This eschatological action possesses an important Christological dimension (participation in the impassible

---

64. *In ad Rom.* 6, lect. 1 (§ 474).
65. *In ad Rom.* 8, lect. 2 (§ 630).

and glorious condition of the risen Christ) but St. Thomas refers it specially to the person of the Father, who is the Principle of the Son and of the Holy Spirit.

Adoptive Filiation

The commentary on Romans 8:14–17 contains a profound teaching on filial adoption. With St. Paul, St. Thomas explains that those who are led by the Holy Spirit receive the inheritance of eternal life, because the Holy Spirit makes them children of God. This adoptive filiation is manifested by the gifts of the Holy Spirit, by the confession of the Father, and by the testimony of the Holy Spirit himself.[66] The eschatological dimension of the action of the Holy Spirit is likewise found at the center of this section: "The life of glory shall be given to us through the Holy Spirit."[67] I will briefly present the principal traits of this teaching.

By procuring justification through living faith ("faith that works through charity": Gal 5:6), the Holy Spirit makes his beneficiaries children of God, because he is "the Spirit of adoption of sons" (Rom 8:15), that is to say, the Spirit "by whom we are adopted as sons of God."[68] The designation of the Holy Spirit as "the spiritual Seed proceeding from the Father" finds its explanation here: "Through this Seed certain people are generated into children of God."[69] The adoption brought about by the Holy Spirit gives a share in "the inheritance of God." "Now, the principle good by which God is rich, is himself. For he is rich through himself, and not through any other thing, because he does not need extrinsic goods.... Wherefore the children of God obtain God himself for an inheritance."[70] Believers receive today a foretaste of this inheritance insofar as God himself dwells in them by faith; this inheritance will be fully received when God will be contemplated and possessed in the clear vision. Saint Thomas constantly underscores the tension toward the eschatological accomplishment of adoptive filiation. "For this adoption begins through the Holy Spirit justifying the soul, ... but it shall be consummated through the glorification of one's body."[71] The Holy Spirit gives the life of grace here below, and the glory of the future life:[72] it is by the Holy Spirit that we will be given

---

66. *In ad Rom.* 8, lect. 3 (§§ 634–51).   67. Ibid. (§ 634).
68. Ibid. (§ 643).   69. Ibid. (§ 636).

70. Ibid. (§ 647): "Bonum autem principale quo Deus dives est, est ipsemet. Est enim dives per seipsum, et non per aliquid aliud. [...] Unde ipsum Deum adipiscuntur filii Dei pro haereditate." See also ibid., § 646.

71. *In ad Rom.* 8, lect. 5 (§ 680).

72. *In ad Rom.* 8, lect. 2 (§ 633).

the glorious life that will exclude all mortality.[73] "Through the Holy Spirit our mortal bodies shall be made to live, when our every weakness shall be taken away from us."[74]

To participate in the inheritance who is God himself, is to be "co-heirs with Christ" (Rom 8:17): such is the way in which God gives himself. The Holy Spirit associates his beneficiaries with Christ by making them share in the filiation of Christ; indeed, "if some are children, through the Spirit namely, it follows also that they are heirs, because the inheritance is owed not only to the natural Son, but also to the adopted son."[75] This is divinization. "For the adoption of children is nothing other than that conformity [*conformitas*]: he who is adopted as a son of God, is conformed to his true Son."[76] Divinization is a participation in the splendor of Christ: when Christ illumines the saints by the light of wisdom and grace, he makes them to become *conformed to himself*.[77] Thus, by his grace, the Holy Spirit restores to souls their beauty (*forma* and *decor*).[78]

This conformation to Christ possesses first of all an *ontological* dimension that concerns the renewal of the very being of humans adopted as children of God: it is a matter of a conformation to the *eternal filiation* of Christ, that is to say, his personal property insofar as he is begotten by his Father from all eternity. Through the gift of his grace, the Son of God ("the principle Son,"[79] who is Son "through eternal generation") communicates a conformity of his filiation to others.[80] Adoptive filiation is "a certain participation and image of the natural filiation" of Christ, the Son of God.[81] It enables the saints to bear in themselves the very image of the Son.[82] This conformation next possesses a *moral* dimension: it is the imitation of Christ in his human condition. Saint Thomas explains that, just as Christ ("the chief Heir") attained to the inheritance of glory by his sufferings, "for that reason it is necessary even for us to arrive at that inheritance through suffering.... For we do not immediately receive an immortal and impassible body, in order that we might suffer with Christ."[83] Such is the condition of the saints in their status as children of God: they remain subject to "the tribulations of this world" in order to be associated with the passion of the suffering Christ, in view of participating in the glorious life of the risen Christ.

---

73. *In ad Rom.* 8, lect. 3 (§ 634).
74. *In ad Rom.* 8, lect. 5 (§ 687).
75. *In ad Rom.* 8, lect. 3 (§ 646).
76. *In ad Rom.* 8, lect. 6 (§ 704).
77. Ibid.
78. *In ad Rom.* 12, lect. 1 (§ 966).
79. *In ad Rom.* 8, lect. 3 (§ 649): "Principalis Filius a quo nos filiationem participamus."
80. *In ad Rom.* 8, lect. 6 (§ 706).
81. *In ad Rom.* 1, lect. 2 (§ 48): "Quaedam participatio et imago naturalis filiationis."
82. *In ad Rom.* 8, lect. 6 (§ 705).
83. *In ad Rom.* 8, lect. 3 (§ 651).

In this context, St. Thomas presents a small treatise on the "fear of God." This appears in his commentary on Romans 8:15, showing that "those who receive the Holy Spirit are children of God."[84] With St. Paul, St. Thomas explores this filiation "from the distinction of the gifts of the Holy Spirit."[85] These gifts are fear and charity, but it is necessary to distinguish diverse forms of "fear" *(timor)*. (1) The first form is "worldly fear": this kind of fear flees an evil that is contrary to some corporeal or temporal good that is loved inordinately; such fear does not come from the Holy Spirit. (2) The second form is "servile fear," which is completely motivated by the concern to avoid the chastisement of God: the principal evil that it flees is punishment. Saint Thomas observes that to flee an evil through fear of God's chastisement is certainly laudable insofar as this fear regards God; however, to regard only punishment, without fleeing the spiritual evil that is opposed to God, does not come from the Holy Spirit. (3) To fear an evil because it is opposed to a spiritual good (to fear sins and separation from God) while keeping an eye on punishment is what St. Thomas names "initial fear" because "it is accustomed to be in people in the beginning of their conversion: For they fear punishment on account of former sins and they fear being separated from God through sin because of the grace infused by charity." (4) Lastly, "holy fear" or "chaste fear" is caused by perfect charity: such fear keeps both eyes fixed on the spiritual reality; it only fears separation from God; and it is thus that the love of charity produces the freedom of the children of God: the love of charity "makes men freely seek the honor of God, which is proper to children."[86]

With St. Paul, St. Thomas emphasizes that it is by the Spirit of adoption that the children of God address God as "Father." In the mouth of the children of God, this name "Father" is not only a sound of the voice, but it expresses "the intention of the heart" *(intentio cordis)*: "This greatness of intention proceeds from the affection of filial love, which the Holy Spirit effects in us. And therefore the Apostle says *in whom*, namely, in the Holy Spirit, *we cry out: Abba, Father* (Rom 8:15)."[87] To this passage from St. Paul, St. Thomas associates the adoration of God by the Seraphim in Isaiah 6:3 ("Holy, Holy, Holy is the Lord"), because "the name *seraphim* is interpreted 'fiery ones,' as if burning with the fire of the Holy Spirit."[88] Lastly, after having explored filial

---

84. Ibid. (§ 637).
85. Ibid.
86. Ibid. (§§ 638–42). On the second form of fear, see also *In ad Rom.* 9, lect. 5 (§ 809), where St. Thomas explains, with regard to the "law of justice": "It is called the law of justice, because it does not make people truly righteous, but only exteriorly, as long as they avoid sins not from love but from fear of punishment which the law inflicted."
87. *In ad Rom.* 8, lect. 3 (§ 644).
88. Ibid.

adoption by the gift of charity and by the confession of the Father, St. Thomas notes the testimony of the Holy Spirit himself in favor of the filiation of the children of God: this interior testimony is that of "filial love, which the Spirit produces in us."[89]

The theme of the "instinct of the Holy Spirit" is found directly linked to filiation, according to this passage of St. Paul that St. Thomas loves to cite: "For they who are led by the Spirit of God, these are sons of God" (Rom 8:14). What does it mean "to be led [*agi*] by the Holy Spirit"? According to a first element of interpretation, it involves the action of the Holy Spirit, who directs in the manner of a guide, "insofar as the Holy Spirit illumines us interiorly about what we ought to do."[90] This fundamental aspect concerns the *knowledge* that the Holy Spirit gives us. Saint Thomas does not stop with this first aspect, because the Spirit's action is not limited to illumining our mind as regards what we ought to do: he also *moves* our heart. In this case, the "spiritual" man does not act solely by himself, but under the motion of the Holy Spirit:

For those things are said to be led [*agi*], which are moved by a certain superior instinct [*superiori instinctu*]. Whence concerning brute animals we say that they do not lead but are led [*non agunt sed aguntur*], because they are moved by nature and not from their own motion for the purpose of doing their actions. However, similarly, the spiritual man [*homo spiritualis*] is inclined to do a certain thing, not as though from his own will principally but from the instinct of the Holy Spirit [*ex instinctu Spiritus Sancti*]. . . . And so it is said in Lk 4,1, that "Christ was led by the Spirit into the desert" [*Christus agebatur a Spiritu in desertum*]. Nevertheless, it is not excluded through this that spiritual men operate through the will and free choice, because the Holy Spirit causes the very movement of the will and of the free choice in them, accordingly, Phil 2:13: "God is the one who works in us to will and to perfect."[91]

This teaching illumines the profundity of the work of the Holy Spirit. Although, in the simple human performance of virtues, man inclines himself to action as a sovereign master who disposes of his faculties of action as he wishes (which he puts to work when it seems good to him), the gifts of the Holy Spirit produce a superior mode of action. In this case, the human being (the "spiritual" man, that is to say, one moved by the Holy Spirit) acts in virtue of a superior principle of action that is the "instinct" of the Spirit. Saint Thomas takes care to note that this motive instinct does not diminish human freedom, because the Spirit acts at the depth of our free will: the Holy Spirit

---

89. Ibid. (§ 645). This interior testimony of the Holy Spirit in the children of God is compared to the voice of the Father declaring of Christ: "This is my beloved Son, in whom I am well pleased" (Mt 3:17).

90. Ibid. (§ 635).

91. Ibid.

gives us the free mode of our acts and the very movement of the free will. In this manner, the action accomplished under the motive instinct of the Holy Spirit remains a fully free action. In a similar context, a little further on, St. Thomas explains that the motion of God and the human free will are not of the same order: God acts "as the one moving chiefly," so that human acts are exercised by man "as by one acting freely."[92] Mentioning again the motion of the Holy Spirit (cf. Rom 8:14), St. Thomas offers this precision: "The interior (or the exterior) operation of man is not to be attributed chiefly to man, but to God: 'God is the one who works in us to will and to accomplish for his good pleasure' (Phil 2:13)."[93] The concurrence of grace and of free will is characterized by the primacy *(principalitas)* of grace.[94] It is God who gives grace, and it is again God who gives the use of grace, by illumining the intelligence and by moving the human will. Here, St. Thomas shows that the full recognition of human freedom does not undermine the absolute priority of God (the Holy Spirit) who acts as first and transcendent cause, and who is precisely the cause of the free mode of the holy actions accomplished by the children of God.

Fully free in its ontological dimension of voluntary action, the action of the spiritual man is also fully good, because it accomplishes the good in accordance with the will of God: for those in whom the Holy Spirit is at work, all works together for the good. Saint Thomas summarizes this by explaining that the Spirit who directs the saints "in the right way" (Ps 26:11 [27:11]) is the Spirit who, dwelling in the saints, diffuses charity in them.[95] The "instinct" of the Holy Spirit, like the "prudence of the Spirit" that he will discuss further on, is inseparable from charity. In itself, this "instinct of the Holy Spirit" is not reserved to some rare elite souls: in his commentary on the eighth chapter of the epistle, St. Thomas attaches it directly to filiation, as a constitutive aspect of all Christian life. Further on, with regard to the dignity of the sons of God, he explains: "To be 'sons' applies to those who serve God out of love and are led by the Spirit of God [*Spiritu Dei aguntur*]."[96]

Elsewhere in his commentary, St. Thomas contrasts the "concupiscence of the flesh" that leads to death with the "instinct of the Holy Spirit" that procures life and peace. The "instinct of the Spirit" is then associated with the "prudence of the Spirit," which illumines and guides action (prudence is the right reason about things to be done): the Holy Spirit procures "an upright sense in spiritual matters"; he enables one to judge spiritual things by a kind of conformity arising from charity. "There is prudence of the Spirit [*prudentia Spiritus*] when someone, with the presupposed end of a spiritual good, takes

92. *In ad Rom.* 9, lect. 3 (§ 778).   93. Ibid. (§ 777).
94. Ibid.   95. *In ad Rom.* 8, lect. 6 (§ 699).
96. *In ad Rom.* 9, lect. 5 (§ 800).

counsel and judges and enjoins which things are ordered fittingly to this end. Whence such a prudence is *life*, that is, the cause of the life of grace and of glory: 'The one who sows in the Spirit, shall also reap life eternal from the Spirit' (Gal 6:8)."[97]

Faith, Hope, and Charity

Saint Thomas places the three theological virtues under the sign of the Holy Spirit. Faith, hope, and charity, which enable one to attain God himself, are procured by the Holy Spirit. Saint Thomas observes that, in the theologal organism, faith is the first effect of the action of the Holy Spirit. When he comments on the words of St. Paul teaching that we attain to grace through faith that justifies (Rom 5:1–2), St. Thomas specifies that this does not mean that faith precedes grace. It is necessary rather to understand that "the first effect of grace in us is faith."[98] Concerning the assent of faith, he adds that neither the human word of preachers nor miracles fully account for adherence to God: "All this would not suffice unless the Holy Spirit inwardly would move the hearts of those hearing to faith. Wherefore it is said in Acts 10:44 that, while Peter was speaking the words of faith, the Holy Spirit came upon all who were listening."[99] In this context, St. Thomas constantly insists on the interior action of the Holy Spirit, who illumines the intelligence and who moves the will for the adherence of faith. He emphasizes also that when faith is received with charity, the Holy Spirit himself dwells in the soul of believers. One can confess that "Jesus is Lord" (cf. 1 Cor 12:3) without having charity, but in this case the Holy Spirit does not dwell in one's heart. The full confession of faith in the risen Christ is accomplished by "formed faith" *(fides formata)*, that is to say, by "faith which works through love" (cf. Gal 5:6).[100] St. Thomas presents the faith that works through charity as the proper effect of the Holy Spirit.[101] Thus, the faith that procures justification is faith animated by charity. Commenting on the statement of St. Paul, "The just one shall live by faith" (Rom 1:17, citing Hab 2:4), St. Thomas explains, "The phrase, *lives by faith*, must be understood of formed faith."[102] The new life is procured

97. *In ad Rom.* 8, lect. 1 (§ 618, cf. §§ 610–17). This passage is completed by a statement of the "fruits of the Spirit." The concupiscence of the flesh designates the disordered inclination of the sensible appetite that results from the loss of original justice; cf. *In ad Rom.* 7, lect. 3 (§ 570).

98. *In ad Rom.* 5, lect. 1 (§ 383).   99. *In ad Rom.* 15, lect. 2 (§ 1171).

100. *In ad Rom.* 10, lect. 1 (§ 829).

101. *In ad Rom.* 8, lect. 1 (§ 603). The theme of "faith working through charity," whose formulation is drawn from the Epistle to the Galatians (Gal 5:6), appears in numerous occasions in the commentary: it is a veritable doctrinal keystone.

102. *In ad Rom.* 1, lect. 6 (§ 108).

by the indwelling of Christ and of the Holy Spirit in souls; and Christ and the Holy Spirit dwell in souls by "faith formed through charity."[103] Moreover, concerning the indwelling of the Holy Spirit in the soul of the saints, Thomas firmly excludes all "kenosis" *(exinanitio)* of the Holy Spirit. To affirm a kenosis of the Holy Spirit (or of the Father) would be "absurd" *(absurdum).*[104]

Among the many passages of the commentary devoted to charity, it is necessary to cite the exegesis of Romans 5:5 ("The love of God was poured into our hearts through the Holy Spirit, who was given to us"), which summarizes admirably the thought of St. Thomas and which constitutes, on the theological level as well as on the spiritual level, a veritable jewel. Before reading the following passage, it is necessary to observe the context: *hope.* Saint Thomas has shown that faith engenders the hope of having access to the inheritance of the children of God in glory, that is to say, the hope of receiving God himself. Here, he shows that the *certitude of hope* is sustained by the gift of the Holy Spirit that is charity:

The *charity of God* can be understood in a twofold way. In one way, as the charity by which *God loves us.* "I have loved you with an everlasting love" (Jer 31:3). In another way, the charity of God can be said to be that by which *we ourselves love God,* below 8:38f.: "For I am certain that neither death nor life will separate us from the love of God." Nevertheless, in both cases the charity of God is poured into our hearts through the Holy Spirit who was given to us. For the Holy Spirit, who is the Love of the Father and the Son, to be given to us, is to lead us to the participation of Love, which is the Holy Spirit, from which participation we are made lovers of God [*efficimur Dei amatores*]. And the fact that we love him is a sign that he loves us. Prov 8:17: "I love the ones loving me." "Not as if we have loved God first, but because he loved us first," as it is said in 1 Jn 4:10. Now the charity by which he loves us, is said to be *poured into* our hearts, because it is shown clearly in our hearts through the gift of the Holy Spirit impressed in us. 1 Jn 3:24: "By this we know, that he remains in us, from the Spirit which he gave to us." On the other hand, the charity by which we love God is said to be poured into our hearts because it extends itself to the perfecting of all habits and acts of the soul; for, as it is said in 1 Cor 13:4: "Love is patient, love is kind, etc."[105]

This passage concerns the *gift* of charity (charity *spread in our hearts*). This gift is assigned to the Holy Spirit because of his personal property in the eternal Trinity: he is the Love of the Father and of the Son. First, the Holy Spirit himself is given. In him, it is therefore *Love in person* that is given. Second,

103. Ibid.; see also *In ad Rom.* 8, lect. 2 (§ 626): "If the Spirit of God dwells in you, namely through charity"; cf. *In ad Rom.* 8, lect. 6 (§ 699), etc. The theme of the indwelling of Christ and the Holy Spirit is omnipresent.
104. *In ad Rom.* 1, lect. 2 (§ 35).
105. *In ad Rom.* 5, lect. 1 (§ 392).

this reception of the Holy Spirit by human beings occurs in the very mode of love. The fact that the Holy Spirit is given to us, explains St. Thomas, implies that "we are lead to the participation of Love, which is the Holy Spirit." The uncreated Gift (the Holy Spirit himself) comes into hearts by producing there a created gift (charity as a participation in Love). The transforming power of this created gift disposes us to receive the uncreated Gift in person. This is divinization. The Holy Spirit assimilates to himself the human beings to whom he is given. To receive the charity by which God loves us is thus to participate in the personal property of the Holy Spirit, that is to say, to participate in the *person* of the Holy Spirit (just as becoming "sons of God" is to participate in the personal property of the Son). By such participation in the Holy Spirit, human beings "are made lovers of God." The charity by which we love God comes from the charity by which God loves us, and it is its "sign." Saint Thomas underscores the perfective role of charity by which the children of God love God: this charity is the soul of morals and of all the interior actions of the saints. In conclusion to his exegesis of Romans 5:5, St. Thomas notes that both kinds of charity nourish the certitude of the virtue of hope. The charity by which God loves us assures us that he will not reject those whom he loves. And the charity by which we love God likewise supports hope, because God has prepared eternal goods for those who love him (cf. 1 Cor 2:9 and Jn 14:21).[106] Other passages describe the role of Christ in this gift of divine love: charity is procured for us by Christ, who has given us his Spirit; the charity of God is given us by Christ, "insofar as Christ gives it to us through the Holy Spirit."[107]

Charity procures a "right sense" of spiritual realities. It is the source of peace and of spiritual joy, because by it the Holy Spirit enables the children of God to rejoice in the goods of God and of neighbor.[108] Without reprising here the theme of "the instinct of the Holy Spirit," we should note the "knowledge by experience" that the Holy Spirit procures by the charity that he spreads. By uniting his beneficiaries to God who is the sovereign Good, the Holy Spirit gives them a right judgment as regards the spiritual good, and he enables them to know this good by experience, that is to say, to know the will of God by a kind of conformity. Saint Thomas has recourse to the example of the sense of "taste." When the sense of taste is corrupted (this infection is compared to the work of sin), it does not provide a right judgment concerning flavors; but

---

106. Ibid. (§ 393). Saint Thomas likewise explains that the "power [*virtus*] of the Holy Spirit" of which Romans 15:13 speaks must be understood of the charity that the Holy Spirit pours out into our hearts: *In ad Rom.* 15, lect. 1 (§ 1162). He also attaches fervor (*fervor*) to the Spirit, because it proceeds from charity: *In ad Rom.* 12, lect. 2 (§ 988).

107. *In ad Rom.* 8, lect. 7 (§ 733).

108. *In ad Rom.* 14, lect. 2 (§ 1128); cf. *In ad Rom.* 15, lect. 1 (§ 1162); etc.

when it is healthy (such health is compared with the work of grace), it allows one to have a right judgment about flavors. Thus, by a kind of conformity with God, the just person whose affection is healthy, and whose sense is renewed by grace, "experiences the will of God."[109]

Lastly, St. Thomas explains that the charity diffused by the Holy Spirit is the root of *merit*. He holds this doctrine in a sure and non-polemical manner, by showing that it nourishes hope and by emphasizing the priority that belongs to the action of the Holy Spirit. No one can have eternal life except through the grace of the Holy Spirit. Insofar as human acts are considered in their nature and as they proceed from the free will of man, they merit life eternal not "by condignity" *(ex condigno)*—because the inequality between God and human free will is too great—but only "in so far as they proceed from the grace of the Holy Spirit."[110] Insofar as the acts of the saints come from their free will, these acts merit eternal life only by some "congruity": eternal life is a good without proportion to the power of our created nature. However, insofar as these same actions of the saints come from the Holy Spirit, that is to say, insofar as the grace of the Holy Spirit heals and elevates the human act in order to lift it to the height of the divine Good and in order to move the human act toward God, these actions merit eternal life "condignly," in virtue of the providential disposition of God, because under this aspect holy actions have for their principle the grace of the Holy Spirit himself. The formula *ex condigno* indicates that there is a "similar dignity" ("condignity") between, on the one hand, the Holy Spirit who is the principle of the holy action, and, on the other hand, the eternal life that is its fruit. In the one who receives him, the Holy Spirit thus becomes "a font of water welling up unto eternal life" (cf. Jn 4:14).[111] When St. Thomas explains that "the sufferings of this present time are not worth comparing with the glory that is to be revealed to us" (Rom 8:18), he offers a similar teaching that, once again, underscores the central role of charity:

The sufferings of this time, if they are considered in themselves, fall far short in comparison to the abundance of glory.... But if the sufferings of this sort are considered as those which someone endures voluntarily on account of God out of charity, which the Holy Spirit produces in us [*propter Deum ex charitate quam in nobis Spiritus facit*], thus through the sufferings of this sort, by proportionate dignity [*ex condigno*], man

109. *In ad Rom.* 12, lect. 1 (§ 967).
110. *In ad Rom.* 6, lect. 4 (§ 517).
111. Ibid. Elsewhere, St. Thomas refers "good works" to the presence of Christ: these good works are accomplished by humans who have become "members of Christ" and who "remain in Christ": *In ad Rom.* 7, lect. 1 (§ 529). We have already noted that the presence of the Holy Spirit is inseparably and necessarily connected to belonging to Christ.

merits life eternal. For the Holy Spirit is the fount whose waters, that is their effect, well up into life eternal, as it is said in Jn 4:14.[112]

The extent of merit in relation to eternal life is measured by charity, "for the essential reward consists in the joy which is had from God; now it is manifest that, regarding God, they will rejoice more who love more [de Deo plus gaudebunt qui plus amant]." This charity does not come to the human being except through the grace of the Holy Spirit that is given to each "according to the measure of the gift of Christ" (cf. Eph 4:7).[113] The Holy Spirit is thus the soul of merit as he is the soul of charity: he enables the saints to participate in his personal property, which is Love.

The "Law of the Spirit" and Freedom

The commentary on the eighth chapter of the epistle presents an important teaching on the "law of the Spirit," according to Romans 8:2 in particular: "The law of the Spirit of life in Christ Jesus freed me from the law of sin and death." Saint Thomas explains that those who are "in Christ Jesus" are the human beings who are incorporated in Christ through faith, and love, and the "sacrament of faith."[114] He then notes that, because the law of the Spirit frees from sin and death, and since this law of the Spirit is "in Christ Jesus," "therefore, by the fact that someone is in Christ Jesus, he is freed from sin and death."[115] The "law of the Spirit" is the cause of a life that excludes sin (sin is "the spiritual death of the soul") and that excludes the corporeal death that is the effect of sin. This is why, in Christ Jesus, there is no longer any condemnation.[116] St. Thomas takes care to specify that "through the Holy Spirit sins are remitted."[117] Examining more closely the expression "law of the Spirit" (lex Spiritus), he discerns two senses of this expression:

112. In ad Rom. 8, lect. 4 (§ 655).

113. In ad Rom. 8, lect. 5 (§§ 677–78). Saint Thomas distinguishes here the "essential reward" (the joy to see God) and the "accidental reward" (the joy concerning good works done by man).

114. In ad Rom. 8, lect. 1 (§ 596).   115. Ibid. (§ 601).

116. Ibid.

117. Ibid. (§ 605), in reference to John 20:22: "Receive the Holy Spirit, whose sins you shall have remitted, they are remitted them." It is necessary to note on this subject the theme of the "sin against the Holy Spirit, which is unpardonable," which St. Thomas discusses at length with regard to Romans 2:5 ("in accordance with your hard and impenitent heart, you are storing up wrath for yourself"). Saint Thomas offers here a teaching whose essential elements he also formulates elsewhere: (1) for the doctors preceding St. Augustine, this "blasphemy against the Holy Spirit" (cf. Mt 12:31) consists in attributing the works of the Holy Spirit to an impure or demonic spirit; (2) for St. Augustine, this blasphemy is opposed to the Spirit insofar as it is the Spirit who remits sins: it is a matter then of "perseverance in sin" until the end ("final impenitence"); (3) and according to certain theologians more recent, this sin is called "against the Spirit" because it is opposed to the

In one way, this law can be said to be the Holy Spirit, so that the sense may be: *the law of the Spirit*, that is, *the law which is the Spirit*. For the law is given for this purpose, so that through it people may be led to the good; whence also the Philosopher in *Ethics* II says that the intention of the legislator is to make citizens good. However human law does that only by informing what one ought to do; but the Holy Spirit, indwelling the mind [*mentem inhabitans*], not only teaches what ought to be done by illumining the intellect about what to do [*intellectum illuminando de agendis*], but also inclines the affect toward acting rightly [*affectum inclinat ad recte agendum*].[118]

Let us note first that the role of the law is to lead humans to good. On this basis, here is the point of this first interpretation: *the law is the Holy Spirit in person*, insofar as the Holy Spirit himself dwells in the soul of the saints (with his gifts that are faith and charity, as we have seen above). Saint Thomas then remarks that the action of the Holy Spirit is exercised not only on the intelligence, but also (as we have likewise noted above) on the affectivity and in particular on the will. The Holy Spirit moves or inclines the will to act rightly.[119] In this manner, the Holy Spirit himself exercises, in a supereminent way, the role that belongs to the law: to lead men to the good. Saint Thomas then offers a second interpretation:

In another way *the law of the Spirit* can be said to be the proper effect of the Holy Spirit [*proprius effectus Spiritus Sancti*], namely, faith working through love. Such faith indeed teaches inwardly concerning the things to be done, according to what is said in 1 Jn 2:27: "His anointing will teach you everything," and it inclines the affect for acting, accordingly in 2 Cor 5,14: "The charity of Christ urges us."[120]

Here we find again the central role of "faith working through love." Saint Thomas sees this as a gift that comes specially from the Holy Spirit ("proper effect"). He likewise mentions the double aspect of the action of the Holy Spirit: *to illumine* the intelligence and *to incline* the voluntary affection. This second interpretation ought not to be opposed to the first. While the first exegesis considers principally the Holy Spirit as the uncreated Gift, the second exegesis concerns the created gift of charity animating faith. Insofar as the Holy Spirit is given and "dwells in the mind," he cannot be dissociated from his gifts of grace, no more than the gifts of this grace can be separated from the Holy Spirit who is their transcendent source and their end. The expression

goodness that is appropriated to the Holy Spirit: it is a matter then of sin committed with deliberate malice. See *In ad Rom.* 2, lect. 1 (§§ 187–188).

118. *In ad Rom.* 8, lect. 1 (§ 602).

119. In the same place (§ 602), St. Thomas proposes an interpretation of John 14:26 ("The Paraclete, the Holy Spirit, whom the Father will send in my name, he shall teach you all things") in the light of these two aspects of the "mission" of the Holy Spirit: the Holy Spirit *illumines* the soul, and he *moves* the soul to act rightly.

120. *In ad Rom.* 8, lect. 1 (§ 603).

"the new law" *(lex nova)* receives a similar interpretation: this formula can signify either the Holy Spirit himself or the law that the Holy Spirit imprints in our hearts.[121] The passage cited above on the subject of the Holy Spirit given solely to members of Christ ("this Spirit is not given except to those who are in Christ Jesus") appears precisely after these explanations.[122]

It is again the Holy Spirit and his work that St. Thomas invites us to consider when he sets forth the difference between the Old Law *(lex vetus)* and the New Law *(lex nova)*. The Old Law is certainly "spiritual" (cf. Rom 7:14), in the sense that it comes from the Holy Spirit "who is called the *finger of God"* (cf. Lk 11:20 and Ex 31:18). However, "the new law is not only called a *spiritual* law, but the law *of the Spirit* (Rom 8:2), because it is not only from the Holy Spirit, but the Holy Spirit imprints it in the heart that he inhabits [*eam imprimit cordi quod inhabitat*]."[123] Although the context is not identical, some similar explanations are offered in the commentary on Romans 2:28–29 with regard to the "true Jew" and to the "true circumcision of the heart in the Spirit." True circumcision is done *"in the Spirit*, that is, through the Holy Spirit, by whom superfluous thoughts and affections are cut away from the heart; or *in the Spirit*, that is, through a spiritual understanding of the law, not through a literal one," so that "interior Judaism and circumcision prevail over the exterior."[124]

The explanations given on the common action of Christ and the Holy Spirit, as well as on adoptive filiation, have already shed light on the theme of the "freedom which was conceded through Christ," which is "the freedom of the Spirit" *(libertas Spiritus)*: this freedom consists in the grace of Christ, spread by the Holy Spirit, by which believers are freed from sin (the spiritual death of the soul) in this life, and in virtue of which they will be freed from death (not only from the "state of death," but from the mortal and passible condition) in the future life, when the Holy Spirit will give the life of glory.[125] The plan of the

121. Ibid.: "Et haec quidem lex Spiritus dicitur lex nova, quae vel est ipse Spiritus Sanctus, vel eam in cordibus nostris Spiritus Sanctus facit."

122. See above, the passage corresponding to note 59.

123. *In ad Rom.* 7, lect. 3 (§ 557).

124. *In ad Rom.* 2, lect. 4 (§§ 244–45). See also *In ad Rom.* 9, lect. 5 (§ 809), where St. Thomas sets forth many interpretations of the expression "law of justice" *(lex iustitiae)*, of which the first is: "The law of justice is called the law of the Spirit of life, through which people are justified, to which the people of the Jews did not arrive, although they pursued it by observing the shadow [*umbra*] of this spiritual law, which consists in legal observances."

125. *In ad Rom.* 13, lect. 1 (§ 1017); *In ad Rom.* 8, lect. 1 (§§ 601 and 605, with respect to the "law of the Spirit of life"); *In ad Rom.* 8, lect. 2 (§§ 628–30); *In ad Rom.* 8, lect. 3 (§ 634). Saint Thomas presents the work of grace as an anticipation of the life of glory: inasmuch as the gift of grace confers the forgiveness of sins, it procures the "spiritual resurrection of the dead"; *In ad Rom.* 1, lect. 3 (§ 59).

epistle that St. Thomas describes in his "divisions of the text" concerning chapters 5 to 8 indicates the multiple aspects of this liberation "through the grace of Christ," that is, "through the Holy Spirit."[126] This work of liberation includes: the liberation from the servitude of sin (from original sin as well as from the sins that have abounded since original sin); the capacity to resist future sins (strengthening in the good); the liberation from the servitude of the Law; the liberation from damnation, which comprises in its turn two aspects: liberation from "fault," that is to say, from the fault and the state of fault that follows from sin, as well as the liberation from "punishment" (the punishment that sin incurs). According to St. Thomas, chapter 8 concludes with an exposition of the help of the Holy Spirit in the present life, which I will briefly set forth by showing the role that the Holy Spirit exercises in prayer.

The Help of the Spirit: Our Desires and Prayer

According to St. Thomas's commentary, verses 26–39 of the eighth chapter of the epistle are devoted to the help that the Holy Spirit gives us in the weaknesses *(defectus, infirmitates)* of the present life.[127] Earlier, St. Paul showed that on the day of our resurrection, our mortal bodies will be vivified by the Spirit, who will deliver us from our weakness. However, in this present life, we remain subject to weakness. This is why "the Spirit aids our weakness" (Rom 8:26), although he does not totally suppress this weakness *(infirmitas)*.[128] This section contains two parts. The first part concerns "the completion of the things desired" (Rom 8:26–27), while the second concerns "the direction of the exterior events," that is to say, the action of the Holy Spirit, who leads events by directing them for the good of the children of God (Rom 8:28–39). This fresco concludes the vast exposition of the liberation that the Spirit procures. Saint Thomas shows here that, supported by the Holy Spirit, the elect are not able to suffer detriment through the "evil of punishment" ("If God is for us, who is against us?"), and that neither may they suffer detriment through the "evil of fault" ("nothing can separate us from the charity of God").

The first part consists in a short treatise on the prayer of petition.[129] Saint Thomas here explains that the prayer of petition is the expression or "the explication of desires" *(desideriorum explicatio):* to pray to God, is to express to

---

126. Cf. *In ad Rom.* 8, lect. 2 (§ 628).

127. Cf. *In ad Rom.* 8, lect. 5 (§ 686); cf. *In ad Rom.* 8, lect. 2 (§ 628).

128. *In ad Rom.* 8, lect. 5 (§ 687).

129. Unless otherwise mentioned, all the following explanations concerning prayer refer to *In ad Rom.* 8, lect. 5 (§§ 686–94).

him our desires. To know what it is necessary to ask, is to know what it is necessary to desire. We can know "in general" what is fitting to desire and to request in prayer (the prayer of the Our Father teaches us), but by ourselves we can scarcely know what is fitting "in particular." Saint Thomas explains this difficulty in three ways. First, it can happen that a thing that is good for a person would not be so for another. When we want to perform an act of virtue (in order to accomplish the will of God, in accordance with the petition of the Our Father), it can be that this act is not fitting for us. Saint Thomas gives the following example that is inspired by St. Gregory the Great: "The rest of contemplation is not expedient for a person who can press onward usefully in action, and also the converse." Second, one can desire a temporal good in order to sustain one's life (following again the prayer of the Our Father: give us this day our daily bread), but temporal goods can become a danger: "For many perished on account of riches." Third, one can desire to be delivered from a temptation (as we also request in the Our Father), at a time when this temptation can be useful in order to guard our humility. As an example, St. Thomas mentions the "thorn in the flesh" that was given to St. Paul in order to preserve him from pride (2 Cor 12:7). And there are many more. Not only do we not know *what* to desire and to request "in particular," but also we do not know *how* to request it.[130] We can certainly know "in general" how to pray, but at times, because of the particular movements of our heart, we do not know how to pray "in particular": we cannot always discern "whether we ask for something out of anger, or out of a zeal for justice." Saint Thomas gives the example of the prayer of the sons of Zebedee (cf. Mt 20:20–21) who requested a good thing (participation in the divine glory) but in whom the request proceeded from vainglory or from pride.

This is why the help of the Holy Spirit is *necessary* for us. In his exegesis of Romans 8:26 ("the Spirit himself prays for us with inutterable groans"), St. Thomas first remarks that the Holy Spirit is God and that he cannot thereby pray in the sense in which an inferior addresses a superior. He then explains that "the Spirit asks for us" in the sense that "he makes us ask." "The Holy Spirit makes us pray, insofar as *he causes right desires in us*" (the prayer of petition is precisely the expression of a desire).[131] We then find once again the central role of charity that St. Thomas constantly highlights when explaining the action of the Holy Spirit. "Right desires originate from the love of charity,

---

130. Saint Thomas reads these two aspects (what to ask, and how to ask) in the Latin text of the epistle, on which he comments: "Nam quid oremus, sicut oportet, nescimus" (Rom 8:26).

131. The rectification of the heart by the Holy Spirit is a constant theme. See, for example, *In ad Rom.* 9, lect. 1 (§ 736): "Sometimes the conscience errs, unless it be rectified through the Holy Spirit."

which namely the Holy Spirit produces in us: 'The charity of God was poured into our hearts through the Holy Spirit, who was given to us' (Rm 5:5). But with the Holy Spirit directing and instigating our heart, our desires can not but be profitable to us." This action of the Holy Spirit is above our comprehension, to such a degree that "the movements of our heart cannot be sufficiently described, inasmuch as they proceed from the Holy Spirit." The divine charity spread by the Holy Spirit is the deep motive and reason of prayer.[132]

The Christian who prays nonetheless experiences the sorrow of the *delay* of that which he eagerly desires and ardently requests. "Therefore the Apostle adds *with groans*, namely which the Holy Spirit causes in our heart insofar as namely he makes us to desire heavenly things, which are delayed. These are the sighs or moanings of the dove, which the Holy Spirit makes in us." We find here again the movement toward the eschatological fulfillment of hope,[133] that is to say, toward "celestial glory," which St. Thomas refers anew to the Holy Spirit.

Saint Thomas concludes his exegesis of Romans 8:26–27 by showing "the efficacy of the help with which the Holy Spirit aids us": "The desires which the Holy Spirit causes in the saints are accepted by God, *because the Spirit intercedes for the saints*, i.e., makes them ask *according to the will of God*, i.e., for things pleasing to God.... As an example of this the Lord said to the Father: 'Not as I will, but as you will' (Mt 26:39)." Prayer animated by the Holy Spirit enables one to imitate Christ in his relationship to the Father.

Prophetic Inspiration, Holy Scripture, and Its Interpretation

At many places in his commentary, St. Thomas underscores the role of the Holy Spirit in the constitution, transmission, and interpretation of Scripture. First of all, he describes the action of the Holy Spirit in prophetic inspiration: the "prophets of God" speak neither by a human spirit, nor by unclean spirits (demons), but "they are inspired by the divine Spirit."[134] Now, prophecy is "a kind of apparition, arising from divine revelation, of things far remote." This is properly and specially applied to future realities that the human spirit cannot

---

132. See also *In ad Rom.* 15, lect. 3 (§ 1189).

133. Cf. *In ad Rom.* 8, lect. 5 (§ 681): "Hope is concerning those things which are not seen presently, but are expected in the future. But we have been saved in hope: therefore we expect the completeness [*complementum*] of salvation in the future."

134. *In ad Rom.* 1, lect. 2 (§ 26). The prophets speak that which God communicates to them. This does not mean that all is revealed to them, even when they are filled with the prophetic Spirit. Saint Thomas explains this with regard to St. Paul himself: *In ad Rom.* 15, lect. 3 (§ 1186).

see in advance *(futura contingentia)*, but also in a general way to "divine reali-ties" *(res divinae)* that are beyond our understanding because of the weakness of our intelligence. Certainly, God is not obscure—he is Light (1 Jn 1:5)!—"but divine things are far from our knowledge ... on account of the defect of our intellect, which is related to matters that are most evident in themselves as the eye of an owl to the light of the sun."[135] Understood in its standard mean-ing, prophecy thus concerns "the revelation of hidden things."[136] St. Thomas specifies that the gift (charism) of prophecy "existed not only in the Old Tes-tament but in the New as well: 'I will pour out my Spirit on all flesh: your sons and daughters shall prophesy' (Acts 2:17 citing Jl 2:28)."[137] Aquinas adds: "In the New Testament, those who explain the prophetic sayings are also called *prophets*, because Sacred Scripture is interpreted by the same Spirit from whom it was derived."[138]

The commentary shows the continuity of the action of the Holy Spirit in the diverse stages of the ecclesial process of Revelation. First, the Holy Spirit inspires the prophets. The divine action is not limited to the inspiration of the word proclaimed orally; it extends also to its being put into writing, that is to say, to the consignment of the prophetic words in the form of "scriptures" *(litteris scripta)*, so that these words might be *transmitted.*[139] The richness of the Scriptures is well expressed by the following remark on Romans 1:2. The Scriptures are *holy* (1) because they are inspired by the Holy Spirit, (2) because they contain holy things *(sancta continent)*, (3) and because they sanctify.[140] As we have noted above, the Holy Spirit intervenes equally in the explanation of the Scriptures, whose interpretation he guides: it is by the Spirit who inspired the Scriptures that they are also faithfully interpreted. Among the criteria of interpretation, St. Thomas specially mentions faith. Like the other charisms *(gratiae gratis datae)* given by the Holy Spirit, prophecy is ordained to "the building up of faith" *(ad fidei aedificationem)* in the Church. And therefore prophecy is to be used "according to the rule of faith" *(secundum rationem fidei)*, "so that faith may be confirmed" *(ut per hoc fides confirmetur).*[141] In the same way, it is to the Holy Spirit that one must attribute the spiritual under-

135. *In ad Rom.* 12, lect. 2 (§ 978).   136. Ibid..
137. Ibid.
138. Ibid.: "Sacra Scriptura eodem Spiritu interpretatur quo est condita."
139. *In ad Rom.* 1, lect. 2 (§ 26).
140. *In ad Rom.* 1, lect. 2 (§ 27). The third motif (the Scriptures "sanctify") is set forth in refer-ence to the words of Christ: "Sanctify them in the truth. Your word is truth" (Jn 17:17). The com-mentary of St. Thomas on the Gospel of St. John (cf. note 55 above) shows that the truth sanctifies in as far as Christ himself is the Word and the Truth, and in as far as Christ *sends the Holy Spirit.* See *In Ioannem* 17, lect. 4 (§ 2229).
141. *In ad Rom.* 12, lect. 2 (§ 979); cf. *In ad Rom.* 12, lect. 1 (§ 971).

standing of the Law[142] that concerns faith in Christ.[143] In addition, the interpretation of Scripture must take into account the sanctifying action of the Holy Spirit in the Church, that is to say, the *practice of the saints:*

As Augustine says in his book *Against Falsehood*, the meaning of Sacred Scripture is gathered from the acts of the saints [*ex actibus sanctorum*]. Indeed, the same Spirit by which the sacred Scriptures were edited, accordingly 2 Pt 1:21: "inspired by the Holy Spirit, the holy men of God spoke," moves holy men to act; below, 8:14: "those who are led by the Spirit of God are the children of God."[144]

Lastly, the interior action of the Holy Spirit is indispensable in order that the preached word might lead to faith, as we observed above: "The Holy Spirit inwardly moves the hearts of those hearing to faith."[145] And, as we also noted, the Holy Spirit is the source of the exterior confession of faith, just as he is the source of the interior act of faith, and the source of the action of the children of God whom he instructs and leads.[146] Thus, the Holy Spirit guides and animates, from one end to the other, the whole process of revelation and its fruitful reception in a holy life.

Conclusion

The commentary on the Epistle to the Romans shows the central role that St. Thomas recognizes for the Holy Spirit in the accomplishment of the divine economy. In reading this work, one is surprised that authors may judge that Aquinas's Trinitarian doctrine neglects the divine action, the Paschal mystery of Christ, or the gift of salvation.[147] Indeed, in the commentary on the Epistle to the Romans, the teaching on the Holy Spirit gives the premier place to his salvific action and to his relationship to the mystery of Christ. This evidence leads us to formulate three conclusions concerning the pneumatology of St. Thomas.

142. *In ad Rom.* 2, lect. 4 (§ 244).   143. *In ad Rom.* 10, lect. 1 (§ 822).

144. *In ad Rom.* 1, lect. 5 (§ 80). Cf. Saint Augustine, *De mendacio* XV, 26: "The reason why the Divine Scriptures contain not only God's commands, but the life and character of the just [*vitam moresque iustorum*], is this: that, if haply it be hidden in what way we are to take that which is enjoined, it may be understood by the actions of the just [*si forte occultum est, quemadmodum accipiendum sit quod praecipitur, in factis justorum intelligatur*]." *Corpus Scriptorum Ecclesiasticorum Latinorum*, vol. 41 (Vienna: F. Tempsky, 1900), 446.

145. *In ad Rom.* 15, lect. 2 (§ 1171); see above the passage whose reference is indicated in note 99.

146. *In ad Rom.* 10, lect. 1 (§ 829); *In ad Rom.* 8, lect. 3 (§ 635).

147. This reproach, often addressed to the Trinitarian theology of St. Thomas, is summarized well by Anne Hunt: "Elegant and sophisticated though it is, the Thomistic synthesis is found wanting, criticized for being remote from biblical witness and the events of salvation history wherein the mystery of the Trinity was revealed, remote from our experience, and so utterly abstract as to be practically meaningless." Anne Hunt, *What Are They Saying about the Trinity?* (New York: Paulist Press, 1998), 3.

First, the commentary on the Epistle to the Romans shows that the Holy Spirit is not found only here or there in the exposition of St. Thomas, but rather that he is present everywhere, particularly in the explanations that concern revelation, the reception of the gifts of God, the work of Christ, the union of the faithful to Christ, the life of charity, and its fulfillment in resurrection and eternal life. The commentary on the Epistle to the Romans does not develop at length the role of the Holy Spirit in creation (the first institution of creatures), but it constantly describes the eschatological dimension of the work of the Holy Spirit. This eschatological aspect is at the heart of the action of the Holy Spirit, and it sheds a significant light on the doctrine of salvation.

Second, the extent of the action of the Holy Spirit shows that if one follows St. Thomas, it is hardly possible to constitute a pneumatology aside from the doctrine of God and from Christology. In fact, the person and the action of the Holy Spirit are intrinsically connected to the Father and to Christ. To speak of the Holy Spirit is to speak of the Father and the Son, of their mutual love and their love for us, that is to say, to set forth the Christian teaching (the *sacra doctrina*) in its full amplitude. In other words, the doctrine of the Holy Spirit does not constitute a "chapter" in the exposition of the Christian mystery, but rather it is an integral part of Christian teaching about the plan of the Father and its accomplishment in Christ. On the one hand, having prepared human beings in view of Christ, the Spirit fills the holy humanity of Christ, in such a way that the human life of Christ reveals God and cooperates actively in the gift of salvation. On the other hand, Christ saves humankind by sending the Holy Spirit, thus leading human beings to the Father. We discover here the profound truth of the Augustinian tradition, which considers the Holy Spirit as the "Gift of the Father and of the Son."

Third, if one looks carefully at St. Thomas's commentary, one discovers that it accounts for the activity of the Holy Spirit by means of *two major themes:* (1) the Holy Spirit proceeds from the Father and the Son; (2) the Holy Spirit is personally Love. The second theme is attached directly to the teaching of St. Paul: the Holy Spirit is revealed by his action and by his gifts, the principal gift being the divine charity that he diffuses in our hearts. Now these are, precisely, the two themes that St. Thomas places at the center of his exposition on the person of the Holy Spirit in the Trinitarian treatise of the *Summa theologiae:* the Spirit proceeds from the Father and the Son (*prima pars*, question 36), and he is personally Love and Gift (questions 37 and 38).[148] This invites us

148. The Holy Spirit is personally the Gift (*ST* I, q. 38) because he is Love in person (q. 37). "The notion of *Gift* unfolds from that of *Love*" (*Scriptum super Sententiis* I, dist. 18, q. 1, a. 2, ad 4). The Holy Spirit is given by the Father and the Son in as far as he is *Love proceeding from the Father and the Son.*

to rediscover the Trinitarian treatise of the *Summa theologiae* and the questions that are specially devoted to the Holy Spirit. By exploring the personal properties of the divine persons and their eternal relations, St. Thomas also furnishes the *key* that permits one to understand in depth the work of these divine persons in the economy of creation and grace, that is to say, *to account for the teaching of Scripture* concerning the action of the Father, Son, and Holy Spirit. Indeed, St. Thomas does not content himself with "describing" the work of the Holy Spirit, but rather he proposes a doctrinal contemplation that shows the reasons of the action of the Holy Spirit. This is why, if it is necessary to recommend the reading of St. Thomas's biblical commentaries for understanding the breadth of his teaching on the Holy Spirit, it is also necessary to counsel reading the *Summa theologiae* in order to understand the speculative doctrinal principles (the "reasons of the truth") that permit one to account for the work of the Holy Spirit.

Scott W. Hahn and John A. Kincaid

⟋⟍

9 The Multiple Literal Sense in Thomas Aquinas's Commentary on Romans and Modern Pauline Hermeneutics

In the world of modern Pauline scholarship, one past interpreter of the Apostle who is often overlooked is Thomas Aquinas.[1] While we recognize this may be due to Thomas's pre-modern hermeneutic and scholastic terminology, we are convinced that modern interpreters of the Apostle have an invaluable resource in the *Doctor Communis*. In particular, in this chapter we suggest that Thomas's hermeneutic of the multiple literal sense could be an important tool that could help bridge some of the exegetical divides that currently plague modern Pauline hermeneutics.

In order to demonstrate this, we begin by elucidating Thomas's idea of Scripture's multiple literal sense. Next, we examine two instances of Thomas's use of the multiple literal sense in his commentary on Romans, beginning with Romans 3:3 and moving to an analysis of Romans 1:16–17 by bringing Thomas into conversation with James D. G. Dunn. We end the paper with some concluding suggestions concerning Paul's teaching in 1 Corinthians 2:6–16 and Thomas's teaching on the gift of wisdom in order to highlight how Thomas's hermeneutic of the multiple literal sense can enable us to read Scripture as *Dei Verbum*

We thank our colleagues who graciously agreed to read various drafts of this paper: Bryan Cross, Nathan Eubank, Taylor Marshall, Mark Reasoner, John Sehorn, Paul Shields, Barrett Turner, and Michael Waldstein. Their responses made it a stronger work.

1. Among the various exceptions to this assertion that could be mentioned, we would like to highlight the work of Christopher T. Baglow, *"Modus et Forma": A New Approach to the Exegesis of Saint Thomas Aquinas with an Application to the Lectura super Epistolam ad Ephesios*, Analecta Biblica 149 (Rome: Editrice Pontificio Instituto Biblico, 2002) and Mark Reasoner, *Romans in Full Circle: A History of Interpretation* (Louisville, Ky.: Westminster/John Knox, 2005).

mandates "in the light of the same Spirit by whom it was written."[2] Overall, we have two goals: first, to demonstrate that Thomas's use of the multiple literal sense does not lead to exegetical equivocation or confusion. Our second goal is the one we alluded to above, that is, to highlight how Thomas's hermeneutic of the multiple literal sense can offer a way forward beyond some of the exegetical impasses that currently exist among Pauline scholars. In order to reach these goals we must first begin by explaining what constitutes the hermeneutic of the multiple literal sense for Thomas Aquinas.

Thomas and the Multiple Literal Sense of Scripture

It should go without saying that we are not the first to discover Thomas's understanding of Scripture's multiple literal sense. Indeed, he affirms the multiple literal sense in six different texts, which his interpreters have studied and debated for centuries.[3] Nor does Thomas claim to have invented the idea, which, like so many of his other fundamental notions, he inherited from Augustine. In question four of *De potentia*, Thomas identifies two interpretive errors that must be avoided, and proceeds to explain both:

The first is for someone to say that something manifestly false must be understood in the words of Scripture ... for there cannot be anything false under divine Scripture passed on by the Holy Spirit, just as there cannot be anything false under the faith that is taught by it. The other is that someone wants to force Scripture to one sense in such a way that other senses that contain truth in themselves and that can, with due regard for the circumstances of the letter, be fitted to the letter are entirely excluded. For this belongs to the dignity of divine Scripture, that under one letter it contains many senses.[4]

2. *Dei Verbum 12*, as cited in *Catechism of the Catholic Church (CCC)* 111. For an attempt at drawing out the hermeneutical implications of this phrase, see Ignace de la Potterie, S.J., "Interpretation of Holy Scripture in the Spirit in Which It Was Written (Dei Verbum 12c)," in *Vatican II: Assessment and Perspectives I*, ed. René Latourelle (New York: Paulist Press, 1988), 220–66.

3. On the debate, see John F. Boyle, "Authorial Intention and the *Divisio Textus*," in *Reading John with St. Thomas Aquinas: Theological Exegesis and Speculative Theology*, ed. Michael Dauphinais and Matthew Levering (Washington, D.C.: The Catholic University of America Press, 2005), 3–8; Franziscus Cueppens, "Quid S. Thomas de multiplici sensu litterali in s. Scriptura senserit?" *Divus Thomas* 33 (1930): 164–175; Mark F. Johnson, "Another Look at the Plurality of the Literal Sense," *Medieval Philosophy and Theology* 2 (1992): 117–41; Robert G. Kennedy, "Thomas Aquinas and the Literal Sense of Scripture" (Ph.D. diss., University of Notre Dame, 1985); On the six texts and their dating, see Johnson, "Another Look at the Plurality of the Literal Sense," 120.

4. *Quaestiones Disputatae de Potentia Dei* q. 4, a. 1, translation ours. Thomas continues: "For this belongs to the dignity of divine Scripture, that under one letter it contains many senses in such a way that it is suited to different human minds, so that everyone is amazed that he can find in Scripture the truth he has conceived in the mind. By this it can also be defended more easily against unbelievers in that when anyone finds his own interpretation of Scripture to be false he can fall back on another one. Thus it is not unworthy of belief that Moses and the other authors of

In rejecting the first, Thomas simply affirms the divine inspiration of Scripture, and shows how it excludes the possibility of error for the divine and human authors. In rejecting the second, Thomas clearly asserts the possibility of multiple meanings in the literal sense, which then leads him to conclude, with St. Augustine, that "every truth that can be fitted to the divine Scripture with due regard for the circumstances of the letter, is its sense."[5]

It is possible that Thomas intends to state nothing more than a general pastoral norm, as opposed to an absolute rule for exegesis. That Thomas recognizes the spiritual value of plural meanings of the letter is evident when he further states: "For this belongs to the dignity of divine Scripture, that under one letter it contains many senses in such a way that it is suited to different human minds, so that everyone is amazed that he can find in Scripture the truth he has conceived in the mind."[6] Since, however, Thomas was never one to separate spirituality from scholarship, any more than Augustine, it seems more likely that he intends to affirm what is both solid pastoral advice and a sound rule of biblical interpretation.[7] We suggest that Thomas's view of the multiple literal sense is confirmed by his application of the principle in his many biblical commentaries, especially his commentary on the book of Romans. Here again, we are not the first readers of Thomas's commentaries to have noticed this pattern of multiple meanings of the letter. For example, John Boyle observes:

If a given passage of Scripture admits of two different interpretations, two different meanings such that they satisfy Thomas's modest criteria of legitimate interpretation—not contrary to truth and fitting the circumstance of the letter—what is one then to do? Which interpretation is the right one? The opportunities for this question abound in Thomas's commentary (on the Gospel according to St. John). Time and time again, Thomas provides two or more patristic interpretations for a single scriptural passage. He does not judge one to be correct, the other not; by his own crite-

---

the Holy Books were given to know various truths that men would be able to understand, and that they expressed them under one sequence of the letter, so that each of these senses is the sense of the author. Thus, even if other truths, which the author did not understand, are fitted to the letter by the interpreters of Sacred Scripture, without any doubt the Holy Spirit, who is the principal author of divine Scripture understood them. Consequently every truth that can be fitted to the divine Scripture with due regard for the circumstances of the letter, is its sense."

5. *De potentia* q. 4, a. 1: "Unde omnis veritas quae, salva litterae circumstantia, potest divinae Scripturae aptari, est eius sensus." Latin taken from *Corpus Thomisticum*, ed. E. Alarcón (Pamplona: Universidad de Navarra: 2000–), http://www.corpusthomisticum.org/qdp4.html, translation ours.

6. *De potentia* q. 4, a. 1, translation ours.

7. Thus, we can distinguish between objective and subjective grounds for a multiple literal sense: the objective ground is based primarily on the divine authorship of Scripture, and secondarily on the basis of refined styles of human communication (e.g., double entendre). The subjective ground is primarily based on a pastoral view of God's purpose in communicating truth to many people of varied capacities, and secondarily on the need to apply the rule of faith and charity to competing interpretations.

ria no such judgment can be made. So in answer to the question, "Which is the true meaning of the letter?" the answer is simply, all of the above. What Thomas does in practice by presenting multiple interpretations of the letter, he affirms in principle: the literal sense admits of many meanings.[8]

In this short but luminous essay on Thomas's treatment of "Authorial Intention and the *Divisio Textus*," Boyle notes this recurring tendency in the Doctor's commentaries without examining any specific instances. For purposes of illustration, we will now consider two examples from his Romans commentary where Thomas affirms a multiple literal sense.[9]

Thomas on Romans 3:3 and the *Pistis Christou* Debate

We begin our analysis of Thomas's use of the multiple literal sense by examining the virtue of "faith" as Paul introduces it in the rhetorical question in Romans 3:3: "Does their faithlessness nullify the faithfulness of God?" Here again, Thomas explains the literal sense by positing two views of faith:

253. [...] This can be understood in two ways: in one way, as referring to the faith by which one believes in God. For the faith of believers is not nullified by those who have not believed, because the evil in some members of society does not nullify the good in other members. [...] In another way, it can be understood as referring to the faith with which God is faithful in keeping his promises: "He who promised is faithful" (Heb 10:23). This faithfulness would be nullified, if it happened that the Jews had no advantage, just because some have not believed. For God promised to multiply that people and make it great: "I will multiply your descendants" (Gn 22:16).

According to Thomas and his use of the multiple literal sense in this passage, the first sense of faith is objective, that is, God as the object of our belief; while the second sense is subjective, since God is the subject who is faithful to fulfill his covenant promise to bless the seed of Abraham, as he swore on the occasion of the *Aqedah* (Gn 22:16). It is possible that modern Pauline scholars

8. Boyle, "Authorial Intention and the *Divisio Textus*," 5. He concludes: "Recall the principle from *De potentia*: one not ought to insist upon one's own interpretation to the exclusion of other interpretations which in their content are true and in which the circumstance of the letter is preserved. If Thomas is, at least to us, surprisingly uninterested in pursuing what is the meaning of the author as such, he is also uninterested in determining a single meaning of the letter. If the former is a dead end, the latter is simply the wrong question: There is not necessarily one single meaning for each passage of Scripture. Some admit of more."

9. Beyond our two extended examples, as was noted above Thomas employs the multiple literal sense frequently in his commentary on Romans, and as Boyle noted in regard to Thomas's commentary on John, often Thomas simply lays out the various options without adjudicating between them. For more examples of this in his Romans commentary, see numbers 98, 277, 424–27, 563, 565, 602–3, 658–74, 705, 728, 825, 828, 848, 856–58, 879, 881–82, among others.

might hear the familiar echoes of the contemporary *pistis Christou* (πίστις Χριστοῦ) debate in the interpretative options laid out by Thomas.

Ever since Richard Hays published his dissertation entitled *The Faith of Jesus Christ*, in defense of the subjective genitive reading, many interpreters have felt constrained to decide between the two apparent rival senses of "faith" in Paul: is it subjective genitive ("the faithfulness of Christ"), as advocated by Hays, along with Douglas Campbell and Luke Timothy Johnson among others,[10] or rather is it an objective genitive ("our faith in Christ"), as advocated for by Dunn and others? [11] While Romans 3:3 is not a perfect example, for in this instance it is clearly not the "faith of Christ" but the "faithfulness of God," and furthermore this is a case where the subjective genitive (God's faithfulness) certainly appears to be the primary meaning, we would suggest that it is possible to gain some valuable hermeneutical insights for approaching the *pistis Christou* debate from how Thomas handles this passage. While it is somewhat surprising to see how clearly Thomas sets forth the interpretive options, it is also a little disconcerting to see how Thomas apparently overlooks the apparent contradiction between the two different views. Or does he?

A closer reading of Thomas suggests that he proposes an integral reading of Paul's notion of faith, which affirms the first meaning, the faith of believers, and then subordinates it to the second, the faithfulness of God. Thus, Thomas shows how they are not only logically compatible, but mutually related. As his analysis demonstrates, he does this in three steps. First, Thomas traces Paul's point about God's faithfulness back to the historical setting of the original promise, when God first swore a covenant to bless the seed of Abraham on the occasion of the *Aqedah* (Gn 22:16). Thomas thereby establishes the historical grounds for the priority of God's faithfulness to his sworn promise. Thomas continues to track the Apostle's reasoning in the verses that immediately follow, and finds additional proof for the priority of divine faithfulness, especially in the face of human unbelief: "Then when he says, *Let it not be!*, he shows that it is unfitting for God's faithfulness to be nullified on account of men's unbelief. [...] Hence, it is plain that man's mendacity or unbelief in not adhering to the truth does not nullify God's truth or faithfulness."[12]

Second, Thomas advances a very different kind of proof, one that appears

---

10. See Richard B. Hays, *The Faith of Jesus Christ: The Narrative Substructure of Galatians 3:1–4:11*, 2nd ed. (Grand Rapids, Mich.: Eerdmans, 2002); Douglas A. Campbell, "Romans 1:17: A Crux Interpretum for the *Pistis Christou* Debate," *Journal of Biblical Literature* 113, no. 2 (1994): 265–85; Luke Timothy Johnson, "Romans 3:21–26 and the Faith of Jesus," *Catholic Biblical Quarterly* 44, no. 1 (1982): 77–90.

11. See James D. G. Dunn, "Once More, PISTIS CHRISTOU" in *Pauline Theology*, vol. 4, *Looking Back, Pressing On*, ed. E. E. Johnson and D. M. Hay (Atlanta: Scholars, 1997), 61–81.

12. § 254.

to be something of a metaphysical tangent. He immediately shifts the discussion away from the two aspects of faith, divine and human, over to a seemingly abstract analysis of the twofold nature of truth. Readers may ask, why the tangent? We would suggest that Thomas wants to demonstrate the priority of divine faithfulness in relation to human belief by building an argument on metaphysical grounds for the ontological primacy of God in the order of knowing and how this necessarily precedes and enables intellectual knowledge for humans, by way of a derivative participation in divine truth:

255. […] This is easier to understand, if we consider that truth implies agreement between thing and understanding. But things are in agreement with our understanding in one way and with God's in another way. For our intellect derives its knowledge from things; consequently, the cause and measure of our truth stems from the thing's being. For an opinion is called true or false depending on whether the thing is as stated or is not. Hence, our understanding can be true or it can be false, for it can be in agreement or disagreement. But whatever is open to being or not being needs someone acting to make it be; otherwise, it continues not to be. For as air without something illuminating it remains dark, so our intellect by itself, unless it is enlightened by the first truth, continues in falseness. Hence, of himself every man is false in his intellect and is true only in virtue of participating in the divine truth: "Send out thy light and thy truth" (Ps 43:3). The divine intellect, on the other hand, is the cause and measure of things. For this reason it is of itself unfailingly true, and everything else is true inasmuch as it conforms to that intellect. Similarly, considering truth on the part of the thing, man of himself does not have truth, because his nature is convertible into nothing. Only the divine nature, which is not produced from nothing or convertible into nothing, has of itself truth.

Thomas thinks his readers will grasp Paul's teaching about faith more easily once they step back and consider the human intellect's dependence on God as the First Truth. As divine truth is "the cause and measure of our truth," so divine faithfulness is the cause and measure of our faithfulness. In sum, it isn't one or the other; it's one (the divine), therefore the other (the human). Modern readers may be tempted to consider this line of reasoning as completely beside the point, or write it off as an unfortunate specimen of medieval eisegesis, in this case reading Aristotle's understanding of causality back into Paul. We would propose, alternatively, that Thomas's argument makes a great deal of interpretive sense, especially if we recognize that this second line of argument, on etiological grounds, demonstrates the subordination of human faith to divine faithfulness on the basis of metaphysical causality.

Third, Thomas completes his analysis of the twofold literal sense of faith in Paul by comparing our situation as believers to a similar situation in which a sinful David found himself trusting in God's faithfulness. In the next line of his commentary, Thomas notes how the next phase of Paul's argument involves a citation from the most famous of David's penitential psalms:

256. Then when he says, *As it is written*, he proves his statement on the authority of a text in Ps 51 (v.4): That *thou mayest be justified in thy words and prevail when thou art judged*. How this is to the point can be gathered from considering what the Psalmist had said just ahead of it. For he says just before this, "Against thee, thee only, have I sinned," and then: "So that thou art justified in thy sentence and blameless in thy judgment." For God through the prophet Nathan had promised David that God would establish David's kingdom forever in his seed, as is gathered from 2 Samuel (7:16). But later, when David fell into serious sin, namely, adultery and murder (2 Sm 11:2 ff), some said that on account of these sins God would not keep the promises made to him.

257. Hence, the Psalmist's intention bears on two things. First, that God's justice, which involves keeping His promises, is not changed on account of sin. Touching on this he says, *that thou mayest be justified in thy words*, i.e., that You may be shown just in your words, since You do not disregard them because of my sins: "All the words of my mouth are righteous" (Pr 8:8); "The Lord is faithful in all his words" (Ps 145:13). Secondly, that God's promise imitates men's judgment. And this is what he says, *and prevail*, namely, by keeping Your promise, *when thou art judged*, namely, by men, that on account of my sins You did not keep Your promises: "Do not be overcome by evil, but overcome evil with good" (Rom 12:21), which is said to men. Accordingly, it is truer of God.

On the basis of this argument from analogy, Thomas shows how Paul's citation of David's psalm reinforces the proper understanding of "faith" here in Romans 3; so God's faithfulness is clearly elevated over ours and made the source and measure of our own faith. Before moving on to consider our other text in Romans, two observations are in order.

First, Thomas's extended discussion of the proper understanding of the twofold meaning of faith consists of three distinct lines of argument. The first is advanced along the lines of *history*, as Thomas argues from Paul's use of the example of Abraham, who received the promise from God. The second is advanced along the lines of *etiology*, as Thomas argues for the priority of divine causality to human knowledge and belief. The third is advanced along the lines of *analogy*, as Thomas argues from Paul's comparative use of David to showcase God's faithfulness and mercy in the face of human sin. At this point it is worth noting these three lines of argument correspond to three functions of the literal sense mentioned by Thomas in article ten of the *Summa theologiae*, where Thomas builds on the teaching of Augustine and affirms that history, etiology, and analogy all belong to the literal sense.[13]

13. *Summa theologiae (ST)* I, q. 1, a. 10, ad 2: "Ad secundum dicendum quod illa tria, historia, aetiologia, analogia, ad unum litteralem sensum pertinent. Nam historia est, ut ipse Augustinus exponit, cum simpliciter aliquid proponitur, aetiologia vero, cum causa dicti assignatur, [...]"

As a second observation, we would point to the convergence of Thomas's view of the dual meaning of faith for Paul with the covenantal understanding of God's faithfulness and justice, pointing to an inseparable connection for Paul between God's faithfulness and justice and our own. Thus, God's justice is more than divine rewards for the good and divine punishment for the bad; God's justice consists rather of his faithfulness in keeping his sworn covenants to bless Israel and the Gentiles, even when they are unjust and unfaithful, through the promised seed of Abraham and David, that is, Christ. As Thomas notes:

258. It should be noted that God's promise to David was to be fulfilled in Christ's incarnation. Hence it was a predestinative prophecy, in which something is promised as destined to be fulfilled in every way; whereas something promised or foretold by a prophecy of warning is not predicted as destined to be fulfilled in every way but according to men's merits, which can change. Therefore, if the promise made to David had not been fulfilled, it would have been prejudicial to God's justice; whereas the non-fulfillment of a promise made through a prophecy of warning is not prejudicial to God's justice, but indicates a change in deserts. [...] Therefore, it is plain, according to this sense, that man's sin does not exclude God's faithfulness.

Thomas's comments are similar to Dunn's analysis when the latter states: "The covenant God counts the covenant partner as still in partnership, despite the latter's continued failure."[14] While this statement from Dunn clearly sounds like Thomas's analysis of Romans 3:3, he actually made it in the context of discussing the "righteousness of God" in Romans 1:16–17, the passage to which we now turn.

"analogia vero est, cum veritas unius Scripturae ostenditur veritati alterius non repugnare." Latin text taken from *Corpus Thomisticum*. Here Thomas is responding to Augustine's theory: "The writing which is called the Old Testament lends itself to a fourfold division; namely, according to history, according to etiology, according to analogy, and according to allegory" *(De utilitate credendi)*. Augustine distinguishes four senses of Scripture, but not the traditional four (literal, allegorical, moral, anagogical), which he and Thomas affirm elsewhere. Thomas clarifies Augustine's meaning by showing how these three elements (history, etiology, analogy) all pertain to the literal sense, while the allegorical is identified with the spiritual sense. It is also worth noting that in his *respondeo* Thomas follows Augustine in affirming the possibility of a text having multiple literal meanings: "Quia vero sensus litteralis est, quem auctor intendit, auctor autem sacrae Scripturae Deus est, qui omnia simul suo intellectu comprehendit, non est inconveniens, ut dicit Augustinus XII confessionum, si etiam secundum litteralem sensum in una littera Scripturae plures sint sensus" *(ST* I, q. 1, a. 10).

14. James D. G. Dunn, *The Theology of Paul the Apostle* (Grand Rapids, Mich.: Eerdmans, 1998), 344.

Thomas and James Dunn on Romans 1:16–17

We turn our attention to one of the most important and controversial passages in the entire Pauline corpus, Romans 1:16–17, by bringing Thomas into conversation with James Dunn. Before turning to a more extended analysis of Dunn's interpretation of this text, we will turn to Thomas's analysis of "the justice (righteousness) of God." Thomas states:

102. [. . .] This (the justice of God) can be understood in two ways. In one way it can refer to the justice by which God is just: "The Lord is just and has loved justice" (Ps 11:7). Taken this way, the sense is that the *justice of God*, by which he is just in keeping his promises, *is revealed in it* [*in eo*], namely, in the man who believes the Gospel, because he believes that God has fulfilled what he promised about sending the Christ. And this is *from faith*, namely, [the faithfulness] of God who promised: "The Lord is faithful in all his words (Ps 145:13); *to faith*, namely of the man who believes. Or it can refer to the justice of God by which God makes men just. For the justice of men is that by which men presume to make themselves just by their own efforts: *Not knowing the justice of God and seeking to establish their own justice, they did not submit to the justice of God* (Rom 10:3). This justice [of God] is revealed in the gospel inasmuch as men are justified by faith in the gospel in every age.

Pauline scholars will immediately recognize these two interpretative options as the two opposing sides of the contemporary debate on how to interpret Paul's phrase *dikaiosynē Theou* (δικαιοσύνη θεοῦ) that exists between many of the advocates of the New Perspective on Paul, who maintain that it refers to God's covenantal righteousness (subjective genitive), and the older Protestant and Catholic perspectives respectively, who maintain that it refers to the righteousness that God gives to those who believe (genitive of origin or objective genitive).[15] While it would be understandable to turn to Thomas in hopes that

15. For an overview of the history of interpretation of Rom 1:16-17, see Reasoner, *Romans in Full Circle*, 1–9. Although there is common ground between Catholics and Protestants in regard to recognizing that the righteousness of God is a gift that is given to us by grace through the redemption accomplished by Jesus Christ, the kind of common ground that allowed for the signing of the 1999 *Joint Declaration on the Doctrine on Justification*, there are still some important differences with respect to how one is given the righteousness of God. Many Protestant exegetes and theologians still hold to the Reformation's understanding of the "Great Exchange," which claims that we are justified because our sins are imputed to Christ, while his righteousness is imputed to us in an extrinsic and exclusively forensic manner through faith alone. For a summary of this position see Alister McGrath, *Iustitia Dei: A History of the Christian Doctrine of Justification* (Cambridge: Cambridge University Press, 1986; 2nd ed., 1998), 189. The Catholic understanding follows the patristic and Scholastic doctors by claiming that the Church's salvation is what Daniel Keating has called the "Graced Exchange," which can be neatly summarized in the axiom of "the Eternal Son of God became what we are so that we could become what he is." See Daniel A. Keating, *Deification and Grace* (Naples, Fla.: Sapientia, 2007), 11ff. For a popular, yet masterful account of the Catholic perspective on Pauline justification, see Pope Benedict XVI, *Saint Paul,*

he would be able to help adjudicate between these rival positions, what is fruitful about Thomas's analysis of this text is precisely that he does not adjudicate, but employs the hermeneutic of the multiple literal sense. Far from actually avoiding the issue, Thomas appears to offer both interpretative options as not only compatible, but valid. It even appears that Thomas presents the first view in such a way as to lead directly to the second, which accords with history and etiology, both of which belong to the literal sense. In other words, it is God's faithfulness to his historically situated covenant promises that leads him to make both Jew and Gentile righteous members of his covenant community. At this point it is conceivable that some modern interpreters of Paul will find this solution untenable, for this not only could lead to confusion and equivocation, but would mean that the human author meant to communicate more than one literal meaning, a conclusion that many an exegete would be hesitant to draw. However, perhaps to the surprise of some, James Dunn is not one of them.

Romans 1:16–17 has been one of the most important texts in Dunn's rather prolific engagement with the Apostle Paul, and while coming to some rather different conclusions than Luther, Dunn notes that "I could empathize with Luther's experience."[16] While the importance of Romans 1:16–17 can be seen in the various places where Dunn offers an extended analysis of the passage,[17] what is even more important for our purposes is how he interprets two key parts of the passage itself. The first part is Dunn's handling of *dikaiosynē Theou* in Romans 1:17 and the conclusions he is able to draw from that exegesis in his *The Theology of Paul the Apostle*. In his massive two-volume commentary on the book of Romans (1988), Dunn says this about the phrase *dikaiosynē Theou* (Rom1:17a):

---

trans. *L'Osservatore Romano* (San Francisco: Ignatius Press, 2009), 78–88 in particular. However, an increasing number of Pauline scholars maintain on exegetical grounds that the participatory aspects of justification must be affirmed if one is to interpret Paul rightly. See, e.g., Douglas A. Campbell, *The Deliverance of God: An Apocalyptic Rereading of Justification in Paul* (Grand Rapids, Mich.: Eerdmans, 2009); Tom (N. T.) Wright, *Justification: God's Plan and Paul's Vision* (London: SPCK, 2009); Michael J. Gorman, *Cruciformity: Paul's Narrative Spirituality of the Cross* (Grand Rapids, Mich.: Eerdmans, 2001); idem, *Inhabiting the Cruciform God: Kenosis, Justification, and Theosis in Paul's Narrative Soteriology* (Grand Rapids, Mich.: Eerdmans, 2009). For an account of the covenantal and participatory nature of biblical soteriology through adoptive sonship, see Scott W. Hahn, *Kinship by Covenant: A Canonical Approach to the Fulfillment of God's Saving Promises*, Anchor Yale Bible Reference Library (New Haven, Conn.: Yale University Press, 2009).

16. James D. G. Dunn, *The New Perspective on Paul*, rev. ed. (Grand Rapids, Mich.: Eerdmans, 2008), 3n8.

17. See James D. G. Dunn, *Romans 1–8*, Word Biblical Commentary 38a (Dallas: Word Books, 1988), 40–49 in particular, and *The Theology of Paul the Apostle*, 340–45. See also *The New Perspective on Paul*, "The Justice of God: A Renewed Perspective on Justification by Faith," 193–212.

Righteousness is not something which an individual has on his or her own, independently of anyone else; it is something which one has precisely in one's relationships as a social being. People are righteous when they meet the claims which others have on them by virtue of their relationship. [...] So too when it is predicated of God— in this case the relationship being the covenant which God has entered into with his people. [...] This understanding of Paul's language largely removes two issues which have troubled Christian theology for centuries. (1) Is "the righteousness of God" subjective or objective genitive; is it an attitude of God or something he does? Seen as God's meeting of the claims of his covenant relationship, the answer is not a strict either-or, but both-and, with the emphasis on the latter. [...] (2) δικαιοῦν, "to justify" does it mean "to *make* righteous" or "to *count* righteous?" This is the classic dispute between Catholic and Protestant exegesis. [...] Since the basic idea is of a *relationship* in which God acts even for the defective partner, an action whereby God sustains the weaker partner of his covenant relationship within the relationship, the answer is really *both*.[18]

Far from attempting to minimize his claim that both *dikaiosynē Theou* and *dikaioun* have multiple aspects to their literal meaning, Dunn reaffirms it ten years later in *The Theology of Paul the Apostle* (1998):

The recognition of the essentially relational character of Paul's understanding of justification also speaks with some immediacy to the traditional debates of post-Reformation theology. In fact, it largely undercuts them and leaves much of the dispute pointless. The debate on whether "the righteousness of God" was subjective or objective genitive, "an activity of God" or "a gift bestowed by God," can easily become another piece of either-or exegesis. For the dynamic of relationship simply refuses to conform to such analysis. In contrast, Paul took it for granted that God's righteousness was to be understood as God's activity in drawing individuals into relationship as "the power of God unto salvation." The other dispute, as already noted, was whether the verb *dikaioō* means "*make* righteous" or "*reckon as* righteous." But once again the basic idea assumed by Paul was of a relationship in which God acts on behalf of his human partner, first in calling Israel into and then in sustaining Israel in its covenant with him. So once again the answer is not one or the other but both. The covenant God counts the covenant partner still in partnership, despite the latter's continued failure. But the covenant partner could hardly fail to be transformed by a living relationship with the life-giving God.[19]

It is clear from these passages that Dunn is uncomfortable forcing the interpretation of *dikaiosynē Theou* and *dikaioō (dikaioun)*[20] into what he calls "an-

18. Dunn, *Romans 1–8*, 40–42 (italics his).

19. Dunn, *The Theology of Paul the Apostle*, 344 (italics his).

20. To mention a few on both sides of the *dikaioō* translation debate, for a defense of taking it to mean "to declare righteous" in an exclusively forensic manner, see Douglas J. Moo, *Romans 1–8*, Wycliffe Exegetical Commentary (Chicago: Moody Press, 1991), and *The Epistle to the Romans*,

other piece of either-or exegesis." Due to the relational and participatory nature of covenantal soteriology, Dunn claims these terms have multiple aspects to their literal meaning, and, much like Thomas, claims these aspects harmoniously work together to allow for a "both-and" interpretation. To be sure, Dunn is making his case on the basis of his definition of the words while Thomas's interpretation is primarily rooted in the belief that the text is divinely inspired.[21] Nonetheless, Dunn appears to be seeking to move from the sign to the signified in order to claim that the "righteousness of God" must entail both the subjective and objective meanings. Therefore, while operating from different sets of hermeneutical presuppositions, Dunn's reading of Romans 1:17 leads him to affirm something like a multiple literal sense, or at the least a complex and hierarchically structured literal sense, for the text appears to lead him to move from the sign to the signified in order to fully account for its meaning.

Turning now to the second aspect of Dunn's interpretation of Romans 1:16–17 relevant to our purposes, in his analysis of Paul's use of Habakkuk 2:4

The New International Commentary on the New Testament (Grand Rapids, Mich.: Eerdmans, 1996), and Thomas Schreiner's discussion of "God's Saving Righteousness," in Thomas J. Schreiner, *Paul: Apostle of God's Glory in Christ: A Pauline Theology* (Downers Grove, Ill.: InterVarsity Press, 2001), 189-217. For a defense of taking *dikaioō* to mean "to make righteous," see M. J. Lagrange, *Saint Paul: Epitre aux Romains* (Paris: J. Gabalda, 1950), and Edgar J. Goodspeed, "Some Greek Notes," *Journal of Biblical Literature* 73, no. 2 (1954): 86–91, and Chris VanLandingham, *Judgment and Justification in Early Judaism and the Apostle Paul* (Peabody, Mass.: Hendrickson, 2006), 242–332. While it is beyond the scope of this paper to comment on this debate at any great length, we are in significant agreement with the position of Michael Gorman in his recent work *Inhabiting the Cruciform God*, where he affirms that *dikaioō* is both juridical and participatory, noting that Paul is a soteriological realist who teaches that the saving righteousness of God is not imputed but cruciform and deiform. As Gorman affirms:"Does a participatory understanding of justification rule out its juridical dimension? By no means! Rather, it says that in Pauline theological forensics God's declaration of 'justified' now is a 'performative utterance,' an effective word that does not return void but effects transformation. Thus God's declaration now of 'justified!' accompanies the divine crucifixion and resurrection of the believer and effects, by the Spirit, a real, existential process of transformation, which is nothing like a legal fiction." Gorman, *Inhabiting the Cruciform God*, 101.

21. In other words, even on syntactical grounds alone it is possible to affirm a modified multiple literal sense. Due to both of our primary examples being genitive phrases, it is worth mentioning the "general" genitive of Max Zerwick, the "plenary" genitive of Daniel Wallace, and the "mystical" genitive of Adolf Deissmann as three examples of those who argue for the possibility of something like a syntactical multiple literal sense for certain genitives. See Maximilian Zerwick, S.J., *Biblical Greek*, English ed. adapted from the 4th Latin ed. by Joseph Smith, S.J. (Rome: Editrice Pontificio Instituto Biblico, 2005), 12–14; Daniel B. Wallace, *Greek Grammar Beyond the Basics: An Exegetical Syntax of the New Testament* (Grand Rapids, Mich: Zondervan, 1996), 119–21; Adolf Deissmann, *Paul: A Study in Social and Religious History*, trans. William E. Wilson (New York: Harper Torchbooks, 1957), 162ff. With that being said, analogous to how grace builds on nature in his theology in general, Thomas's account of the multiple literal sense builds on and surpasses these syntactical accounts by more directly rooting the multiple literal sense in the divine authorship of sacred Scripture.

in Romans 1:17b, he notices something very curious about how Paul chooses to cite the passage. Instead of deciding between the Septuagint's (LXX) rendering that "the righteous out of my faith (fullness) shall live" and the Masoretic Text's (MT) rendering that "the righteous (man) by his faith (fullness) shall live," Paul actually appears to choose neither rendering and instead opts for "the righteous out of faith/faithfulness shall live" (Rom 1:17b).[22] Beyond the interesting debate concerning which of the two versions Paul was more likely dependent on, Dunn finds Paul's choice to be of great significance, for he claims that it sheds light on Paul's hermeneutical method regarding the Old Testament. As Dunn notes:

> In the tradition of Jewish exegesis Paul would not necessarily want to narrow the meaning to *exclude* other meanings self-evident in the text forms used elsewhere, so much as to *extend* and broaden the meaning to include the sense he was most concerned to bring out. The various rules of interpretation already current in Pharisaic circles at the time of Paul (the seven "middoth of Hillel") were designed to draw out as much meaning as possible from the text.[23]

In other words, according to Dunn, Paul intentionally decided not to choose between the LXX and the MT, but in modifying the text by removing the possessive pronoun, Paul intended to draw out of the text an interpretation that includes both God's righteousness and human righteousness through faith. Dunn comments:

> It is unlikely that Paul in dictating these words was unaware of the two alternative renderings of the text—"by *his* faith(fulness) and "by *my* (= God's) faith (fulness)." Nor is it likely that he removed or ignored the possessive pronouns ("his," "my") with a view to persuading his addressees to take the verse in a wholly new and unexpected way. Had he entertained such an intention we would have expected a clearer formu-

---

22. The Dead Sea Scrolls (DSS), which sometimes preserve a text form antedating and different from the MT, in this case sides with the MT, based on the interpretation *(pesher)* offered in Column VIII of the Habakkuk *Pesher* (1QpHab). See *The Dead Sea Scrolls Study Edition*, vol. 1, 1Q1–4Q273, ed. Florentino García Martínez and Eibert J. C. Tigchelaar (Leiden: Brill, 1997), 17. The scribe exegetes the "just" as living "on account of their toil and of their loyalty to the Teacher of Righteousness."

23. Dunn, *Romans 1–8*, 45 (italics his). In fact, drawing on this notion of Rabbinic exegesis, Dunn claims in his *Unity and Diversity in the New Testament: An Inquiry into the Character of Earliest Christianity*, 2nd ed. (Philadelphia: Trinity Press International, 1990), that Paul is here using a "Pesher Quotation" (92). On page 91, Dunn defines a "Pesher Quotation" in the following manner: "In the case of midrash, pesher (and allegory) the OT text is usually quoted and then the interpretation added. But in this other type of exegesis the actual quotation of the text embodies its interpretation within the quotation itself—what is perhaps best described as a targumic interpretation or (as I prefer) a pesher quotation. The incorporation of the interpretation within the text itself sometimes leaves the text verbally unaltered, but usually it involves modifying the actual text form."

lation of the Habakkuk quotation, whereas in fact his quotation is so ambiguous that commentators have never been able to agree on how it should be read. The point which has usually been missed is that Paul's citation is *deliberately* ambiguous. That is to say, Paul does not want to give Hab. 2:4 a new sense and to do so by *excluding* the alternative understandings; if so, he made a bad job of it. Rather he wants to read *as much meaning* into the verse as possible—just what we would expect a Jewish exegete, especially a Pharisee, to do with a text of Scripture.[24]

While Dunn's claim depends in part on the rather conjectural hypothesis that Paul had access to both the LXX and the MT as we now have them,[25] Paul's citation of Habakkuk 2:4 does not specify whose faithfulness the righteous man will live by, so regardless of whether this ambiguity was intentional or not, Paul's citation lends itself nicely to a multiple literal sense reading. Due to the aforementioned ambiguity concerning whose faithfulness the righteous man will live by, it appears best to allow for both God's faithfulness and the believer's faithfulness to be valid interpretations of the text, for to necessarily limit the meaning of the text to an "either-or" is to force the text to be more specific than it is.[26] While Thomas does not employ the multiple literal sense for this verse, in light of our analysis above we would suggest that a multiple

24. Ibid., 48 (italics his). Fortunately, Dunn's previous statement on page 45 was much better than this one in regard to how Paul handled the texts of the Old Testament. In this passage on 48, Dunn says that Paul "wants to read as much meaning *into* the texts as possible," while on 45 he says that the Pharisees looked to "draw *out* as much meaning as possible from the text." While the difference might only be one of wording, we would suggest that Dunn's assertion that Paul looked to "draw out as much meaning as possible" from the text accords well with Paul's exegesis of the Old Testament, while any notion of Paul reading meaning into the text would be problematic. We would also suggest that Paul was an astute exegete of the Old Testament who was able to bring out the full meaning of Old Testament texts in light of Christ's eschatological redemption. For more in this regard, see G. K. Beale and D. A. Carson, eds., *Commentary on the New Testament Use of the Old Testament* (Grand Rapids, Mich.: Baker Academic, 2007).

25. In fact, while we find Dunn's explanation of Paul's use of Habakkuk 2:4 both interesting and possible, we are not entirely persuaded, for it is conjectural that Paul had before him both the MT and LXX as we now have them. Interestingly, in number 104 of his commentary, Thomas states that Paul is drawing on the LXX for Habakkuk 2:4, which does appear to be the more likely of the two sources, but even that is not demonstrable. So why do we make use of Dunn's analysis here? We draw on his analysis in order to highlight the importance of Thomas's multiple literal sense, for regardless of whether Dunn's hypothesis is valid, Paul's citation of Habakkuk 2:4 is precisely the kind of passage for which the multiple literal sense is able to draw out of the text the fullness of meaning intended by both the human and divine authors.

26. In light of our previous discussion concerning the meaning of the phrase *pistis Christou*, it is worth noting here that Reasoner follows Dunn in his interpretation of 1:17b, and allows this hermeneutical move to help clarify the *pistis Christou* debate. As Reasoner notes, "Since Paul drops the *mou* from the Septuagint of Habakkuk 2:4, choosing instead to say that the righteousness that comes *ek pisteōs eis pistin* in Romans 1:17, it seems best to follow Morna Hooker and Sam Williams in seeing Christ's faithfulness that calls for a human response of faithfulness within the *pistis Christou* phrase." See Reasoner, *Romans in Full Circle*, 39.

literal sense reading for 1:17b is consistent with Thomas's hermeneutical principle outlined in *De potentia*, namely, that it is a hermeneutical error "to force Scripture to one sense in such a way that other senses that contain truth in themselves and that can, with due regard for the circumstances of the letter, be fitted to the letter are entirely excluded."[27]

At this point we can begin to see more clearly both the benefit and the challenge that a critical reappropriation of Thomas's multiple literal sense offers to modern Pauline studies, for while such an approach allows for a richer and more comprehensive reading of texts such as Romans 1:17, it goes beyond simply a grammatical multiple literal sense by affirming that it "belongs to the dignity of divine Scripture, that under one letter it contains many senses."[28]As was noted above, for Thomas this is due to Scripture's dual authorship, for since God is the principal author of the sacred page the interpretative options cannot be limited simply to what was in the mind of the human author, but must include the divine author as well. For many modern exegetes, this is inherently problematic, for a clear and distinct idea of the divine mind is necessarily impossible, while ancients such as Thomas were not interested in a clear and distinct account of the divine mind in the modern sense, but a truthful account that is in accord with the limitations and capacities of human knowledge. In regard to the witness of Scripture, the words on the page reveal the mind of both the human and divine authors, and since the latter is perfect in knowledge and the creator of all that exists, his divine knowledge of words and things allow for the words of Scripture to signify more than what the human author could understand. While this could certainly lead to equivocation and confusion, Thomas is clear that as long as a given interpretation is in accord with the words and their context, as well as the realities of the deposit of faith, it can be reasonably asserted that such an interpretation is in accord with the mind of the divine author and the order of things as created by him. However, with this being said, at this point it could be reasonably asked: is the multiple literal sense of Thomas really necessary when modern exegetes like Dunn allow for a grammatically driven multiple literal sense and do so in a manner that does not open the door to uncritical pious conjecture?

We would propose that the answer to this question is yes, and that a careful appropriation of Saint Thomas's multiple literal sense can provide a path forward for modern Pauline scholars, a path beyond "either-or" exegesis and the gulfs that currently exist between those who hold to seemingly opposite positions on the *pistis Christou* and the *dikaiosynē Theou* debates. For while

---

27. *De potentia* q.4, a.1, translation ours.
28. Ibid., translation ours.

Dunn is clear that those who insist on the righteousness of God being either a subjective or objective genitive fall into "another" case of "either-or" exegesis, what often remains unclear is how today's readers of the Apostle Paul are able to move beyond this fallacy of the "exegetical false choice." We would like to suggest that Thomas's multiple literal sense offers such a hermeneutical way forward, an option that is not simply a grammatical one, although it includes that as well, but an ontological one.

While this hermeneutic may make some exegetes uncomfortable, we also hope we have accomplished our other goal, which was to show that Thomas's affirmation of multiple literal meanings for a given text does not necessarily lead to equivocation or confusion.[29] In fact, for Thomas the multiple literal meanings of a given text are distinct but not separate, or as Jacques Maritain has made famous, Thomas "distinguishes to unite."[30] This we also saw Dunn attempt to do in his handling of the righteousness of God, for while he noted

29. On the coordination of different meanings of the literal sense, in his work entitled *The One God*, Reginald Garrigou-Lagrange, O.P. asserts: "In reply to this we say if the names used were equivocal, as in the case of dog used to denote the terrestrial animal and the heavenly constellation, then I concede the assertion; but if the names are analogous, then I deny it. Thus heaven denotes both the starry firmament and the angels, and [daily] bread is understood in the ordinary sense of the term and it also means the Holy Eucharist. But if it is a case of two subordinated analogates, or of two that are co-ordinated under a higher, and if no false sense arises from this, then there is no equivocation." Garrigou-Lagrange, *The One God: A Commentary on the First Part of St. Thomas' Theological Summa*, trans. Dom Bede Rose, O.S.B., S.T.D. (St. Louis, Mo.: Herder, 1954), 91. Moreover, it is not as though exegetes who reject the multiple literal sense in favor of a simple solitary meaning can claim to have dispelled equivocation and confusion by arriving at a consensus regarding the literal sense of even a single verse or phrase in the New Testament. This is not to deny the indispensable role of the historical-critical method; however, it only serves as a reminder that the divine inspiration of Scripture is no less indispensable for proper exegesis. Cf. Scott W. Hahn, *Covenant and Communion: The Biblical Theology of Pope Benedict XVI* (Grand Rapids, Mich.: Brazos, 2009), 25–62 in particular.

30. Maritain's maxim may be applied to other areas of Thomas's exegesis. For example, by distinguishing between the literal and spiritual senses, we discover how they are united (as words and deeds) in the human testimony to God's saving acts. Care should be taken, then, not to treat the literal and spiritual senses as though they are hermetically sealed or separated from each other. For example, Paul describes Adam as a "figure" *(tupos)* of Christ in Rom 5:14; the literal sense of the text is inseparable from the Apostle's spiritual (allegorical) exegesis of Genesis 3, in view of the Christ event. Likewise, in 1 Corinthians 10:1–4 Paul compares ancient Israel's "baptism into Moses," along with the manna and water from the rock, with the New Covenant gifts of baptism and the Eucharist respectively. The literal sense of that text is Paul's spiritual exegesis of various Old Testament texts; or to be more precise, Paul's teaching about Christ and the sacraments is literally an allegorical and tropological reading of ancient Israel's Exodus traditions. Noting the convergence of the literal and spiritual sense in Paul may serve to correct a common misunderstanding, which assigns the literal and spiritual senses to the human and divine authors, respectively, as though they are divisible, like oil and water. Cf. Henri de Lubac, S.J., *Scripture in the Tradition*, trans. Luke O'Neill (New York: Herder and Herder, 2000); Richard Davidson, *Typology in Scripture* (Berrien Springs, Mich.: Andrews University Press, 1981).

two distinct aspects to the phrase, he was able to keep them united as a result of the relational nature of covenant soteriology. What makes Dunn advocate for multiple meanings for the righteousness of God is remarkably close to what serves as the basis for Thomas's use of the multiple literal sense, and that is the irreducible fullness of the covenant God. In other words, what Dunn is driving at is what Thomas lived by, for as an exegete of Scripture, the Angelic Doctor sought out not only a word or concept that allowed him to make the most sense of the text, but rather the reality that the texts revealed. In his engagement with the exegetical method of Thomas, Brevard Childs defined this as the "ontological interpretation" that was "an essential feature of Thomas's theological approach to the substance of scripture."[31] In fact, we would suggest that it was in this very pursuit of the ontological realities revealed by Scripture that Thomas was able to recognize that certain texts have multiple literal meanings, for the same God who created the world also authored the pages of Scripture, and by intimate knowledge of the divine author Thomas was unwilling to arbitrarily limit divine semiotics, for Thomas knew that God chose his words carefully and doesn't need human exegetes to make his revelation more precise.

Likewise, we would suggest that Thomas's subject, Paul, was able to expound the divine mysteries he received only through the grace of union with Christ. For Paul's Damascus Road encounter was far more than a religious experience, for in seeing the Risen Christ Paul saw the righteousness of God in a way that transcended his previous notions of what covenantal righteousness constituted, so that he could tell the Philippians, "whatever gain I had, I counted as loss for the sake of Christ. Indeed I count everything as loss because of the surpassing worth of knowing Christ Jesus my Lord" (Phil 3:7–8, RSV/CE).[32] Furthermore, as Dunn rightly notes, the righteousness of God is relational because it is personal and covenantal. We would further suggest that exegesis is relational because it is also covenantal, and therefore personal and participatory.[33] Indeed, in order to interpret most adequately the meaning

31. Brevard S. Childs, *The Struggle to Understand Isaiah as Christian Scripture* (Grand Rapids, Mich.: Eerdmans, 2004), 160. Cited in Matthew Levering, *Participatory Biblical Exegesis: A Theology of Biblical Interpretation* (Notre Dame, Ind.: University of Notre Dame Press, 2008), 11.

32. For some attempts at delineating the definitive nature of the Damascus Road encounter in the life and teaching of Paul, see James D. G. Dunn, "'A Light to the Gentiles' or 'The End of the Law'? The Significance of the Damascus Road Christophany for Paul," chap. 4 in *Jesus, Paul, and the Law: Studies in Mark and Galatians* (Louisville, Ky.: Westminster/John Knox, 1990), 89–107, and "Paul's Conversion: A Light to Twentieth Century Disputes," chap. 15 in *The New Perspective on Paul*, 347–365; Seyoon Kim, *The Origin of Paul's Gospel* (Eugene, Or.: Wipf and Stock, 2007).

33. For two recent attempts to expand on the claim that exegesis is a covenantal and participatory enterprise, see Levering, *Participatory Biblical Exegesis* and Scott W. Hahn, "Worship in the Word: Toward a Liturgical Hermeneutic," *Letter and Spirit: A Journal of Catholic Biblical Theology* 1 (2005): 101–36.

of the righteousness of God and justification for Paul of the Damascus Road revelation, one must know these realities by experience, for they are inherently relational. The multiple literal sense of Thomas Aquinas is one kind of hermeneutical method that results from a covenantal and participatory relationship with the Triune God and his divine mysteries, which have historical, etiological, and analogical aspects.[34] For those who know the Triune God through the Person of the Holy Spirit also know the principal Author of the text who inspired the human author to write words that are able to contain multiple true meanings.[35]

We can anticipate the kind of objections that this suggestion could raise from the current world of Pauline scholars, such as claiming that this hermeneutic is historically irresponsible or even neo-gnostic. Yet far from being gnostic and ahistorical, this is a pneumatic hermeneutic for everyone who is united to the trans-historical body of Christ by the Spirit, also known as the historically situated covenant people of God.[36] As Hays rightly notes in regard to Paul's reading of the Old Testament: "The story that Paul finds in Scripture is an account of God's dealing with a people. Consequently, *if we learned from Paul how to read Scripture, we would read it ecclesiocentrically*, as a word for and about the community of faith. Scripture discloses its sense only as the text is brought into correlation with living communities where the Holy Spirit is at work."[37] Furthermore, the basis for this kind of hermeneutic also comes from Paul himself. In contrasting the wisdom of "this age" with the wisdom of God, Paul tells the Corinthians:

Yet among the mature we do impart wisdom, although it is not a wisdom of this age or of the rulers of this age, who are doomed to pass away. But we impart a secret and hidden wisdom of God, which God decreed before the ages for our glorification. None of

34. This is not to imply that the multiple literal sense is the only hermeneutical method that can result from a covenantal and personal participation in the divine mysteries, but a rather important one, particularly for modern Pauline hermeneutics.

35. This is true whether or not the human author was aware of all of the possible meanings. As Thomas teaches in *De potentia* 4, a. 1: "Thus, even if other truths, which the author did not understand, are fitted to the letter by the interpreters of Sacred Scripture, without any doubt the Holy Spirit, who is the principal author of divine Scripture understood them. Consequently every truth that can be fitted to the divine Scripture with due regard for the circumstances of the letter, is its sense."

36. Levering relates this line of thinking to the biblical texts and their authors when he notes: "The texts and their human authors are already historically caught up in a participatory relationship, however obscure, with the trans-temporal realities of faith (Israel as God's covenantal people, Jesus Christ, the Mystical Body, the sacraments, and so forth)." See Levering, *Participatory Biblical Exegesis*, 5.

37. Richard B. Hays, *Echoes of Scripture in the Letters of Paul* (New Haven, Conn.: Yale University Press, 1989), 184 (italics his).

the rulers of this age understood this; for if they had, they would not have crucified the Lord of glory. But, as it is written, "What no eye has seen, nor ear heard, nor the heart of man conceived, what God has prepared for those who love him," God has revealed to us through the Spirit. For the Spirit searches everything, even the depths of God. For what person knows a man's thoughts except the spirit of the man which is in him? So also no one comprehends the thoughts of God except the Spirit of God. Now we have received not the spirit of the world, but the Spirit which is from God, that we might understand the gifts bestowed on us by God. And we impart this in words not taught by human wisdom but taught by the Spirit, interpreting spiritual truths to those who possess the Spirit. The unspiritual man does not receive the gifts of the Spirit of God, for they are folly to him, and he is not able to understand them for they are spiritually discerned. The spiritual man judges all things, but is himself judged by no one. "For who has known the mind of the Lord so as to instruct him?" But we have the mind of Christ. (1 Cor 2:6–16)

It is worth emphasizing that Paul is telling the Corinthians that only those who are taught by the Spirit of God are able to fully understand what he teaches, for they have the mind of Christ. Furthermore, in light of Paul speaking of the role that the Holy Spirit plays in relationship to understanding the wisdom of God, it is also worth connecting what Thomas teaches concerning the Holy Spirit's gift of wisdom to the enterprise of hermeneutics. According to Thomas, all those who are united to Christ through the Holy Spirit have the gift of wisdom, which enables them to know the truths of revelation by experience, or "to suffer divine things."[38] In fact, in teaching that the gift of wisdom corresponds to the seventh beatitude, Thomas teaches that all those who are indwelt by the Holy Spirit participate in the Sonship of Wisdom Begotten, Jesus Christ. In commenting on the reward promised in the seventh beatitude, Thomas teaches:

The reward is expressed in the words, *they shall be called the children of God.* Now men are called children of God in so far as they participate in the likeness of the only-begotten and natural Son of God, according to Rom. viii. 29, *Whom he foreknew . . . to be made conformable to the Image of His Son,* Who is Wisdom Begotten. Hence by participating in the gift of wisdom, man attains to the sonship of God.[39]

In light of our previous discussion concerning Dunn's appropriate emphasis on the relational nature of covenant soteriology, it would be hard to find a soteriology more relational and covenantal than Thomas's teaching that those who participate in the Spirit's gift of wisdom are "sons in the Son."[40] This

38. See *ST* II–II, q. 45, a. 2.

39. *ST* II–II. q. 45, a. 6, trans. the Fathers of the English Dominican Province (Notre Dame, Ind.: Christian Classics, 1981).

40. For two excellent works on the participatory nature of Thomas's soteriology, see Romanus

adoptive sonship allows for the children of God to know the truth by experience through the pneumatic gift of wisdom, a gift that can enable Pauline exegetes to move beyond simple talk about verbal signs, to actual participation in supernatural realities "from the inside."[41] For those who are open to such an ontological hermeneutic,[42] we have suggested that the multiple literal sense of Thomas Aquinas is an option worthy of careful reconsideration and critical reappropriation. For it is participatory, relational, and covenantal, as are two of the central realities Pauline exegetes attempt to interpret, *pistis Christou* and *dikaiosynē Theou*. For the multiple literal sense of Thomas Aquinas is unitary, but not solitary, for it seeks to interpret Scripture "in the light of the same Spirit by whom it was written."

Cessario, O.P., *The Godly Image: Christ and Salvation from Anselm to Aquinas* (Petersham, Mass.: St. Bede's Publishing, 1990), and Matthew Levering, *Christ's Fulfillment of Torah and Temple: Salvation according to Thomas Aquinas* (Notre Dame, Ind.: University of Notre Dame Press, 2002).

41. We are indebted to Father Brian Shanley for this wonderful phrase, "from the inside," to describe the knowing that results from the Holy Spirit's gift of wisdom. See his commentary on question one of the *Summa theologiae* in *The Treatise on the Divine Nature: Summa Theologiae I, 1–13*, trans., with commentary, by Brian J. Shanley, O.P. (Indianapolis: Hackett Publishing Group, 2006), 164.

42. According to Thomas, this pursuit of the realities revealed by God through human language is at the very heart of the virtue of faith. As he teaches, "The believer's act (of faith) does not terminate in the propositions, but in the realities (which they express)." *ST* II–II. q. 1, a. 2, ad 2, as cited in *CCC* 170.

Mary Healy

❧

10   Aquinas's Use of the Old Testament in
      His Commentary on Romans

Recent decades have witnessed a rediscovery of St. Thomas as biblical exegete. His biblical commentaries are attracting greater attention than ever before, and his theories of biblical interpretation, particularly his view of the literal and spiritual senses of Scripture, have been assiduously analyzed. Yet Aquinas's actual practice of exegesis, and particularly his use of Scripture to comment on Scripture, remains largely unexplored.[1] This state of affairs is partly due to the enormous gap between Thomas's pre-critical interpretive style and the methods and assumptions of modern historical-critical exegesis. In the face of the undeniable progress in determining the original meaning of biblical texts, what does medieval exegesis have to offer? How does one evaluate insights derived from interpretive approaches that are obscure, naïve, or illegitimate by today's standards? Ongoing efforts to bridge this gap are an essential part of reappropriating the Church's treasury of patristic and medieval reflection on Scripture, one of the most important tasks of theology today.

This chapter considers Thomas's use of the Old Testament in his commentary on Romans. But a caution is in order regarding this description of the task: although "use" is the standard expression for the various ways in which an author quotes, refers to, or alludes to an earlier text, it is a potentially misleading term. It could seem to suggest a certain instrumentalization of Scripture, as if one has a prior agenda toward the accomplishment of which one puts biblical texts to work. As Michael Waldstein and others have shown, this way of conceiving the commentator's task would be foreign to St. Thomas.[2]

1. This point is made and supported in detail by Christopher Baglow, *"Modus et Forma": A New Approach to the Exegesis of Saint Thomas Aquinas with an Application to the Lectura super Epistolam ad Ephesios*, Analecta Biblica 149 (Rome: Editrice Pontifio Istituto Biblico, 2002), 1–23.

2. Michael Waldstein, "On Scripture in the Summa Theologiae," *Aquinas Review* 1, no. 1 (1994): 73–94; Wilhelmus Valkenberg, *Words of the Living God: Place and Function of Holy*

Rather, in his view, Scripture itself sets the agenda, which it is the theologian's task to serve—just as a musician does not "use" the notes on the score but plays them and makes their melody sound forth. Such a utilitarian misconception illustrates the kinds of missteps that need to be avoided to arrive at a fair and balanced appraisal of Thomas's exegesis.

To this end, and seeking to understand Thomas's exegesis on its own terms, I will first offer some general observations on his Old Testament citations in the Romans commentary. I will then compare his reading of biblical texts with his own theoretical account of the distinctively Christian manner of interpreting the Old Testament as described in the *Summa*. Finally, I will seek to uncover some of the hermeneutical assumptions that are implicit in his method, and inquire as to what relevance or even fruitfulness they might have for biblical exegesis in the Church today.

Observations on Aquinas's Use of the Old Testament

Perhaps the most salient characteristic of Thomas's Old Testament citations is their sheer abundance. Thomas's writing rivals that of Paul himself in its profusion of biblical references woven into the text. The Romans commentary is a virtual tapestry of phrases drawn from nearly every part of the Bible, including some 1,200 explicit Old Testament citations. Of the forty-six books of the Old Testament canon, only five fail to appear (Judges, Ruth, Tobit, Jonah, and Haggai). Thomas's mind is evidently saturated with Scripture, and his mastery of the text is almost mind-boggling to twenty-first-century scholars more accustomed to finding our biblical citations via computerized search engines.

Aquinas shows a marked preference for the Psalms and wisdom literature, quoting from the Psalms far more frequently than from any other Old Testament book (280 times). The next most frequent is Isaiah (161 times), followed by four of the wisdom books: Sirach (85 times), Job (79 times), Proverbs (78 times), and Wisdom (67 times). The historical books, in contrast, appear relatively infrequently; the Deuteronomistic history (Joshua through 2 Kings), for instance, is cited only 28 times in all. Thomas's predilection for the wisdom writings is undoubtedly related to his well-known conviction that the literal sense alone provides a legitimate basis for theological argumenta-

---

Scripture in the Theology of St. Thomas Aquinas (Leuven, Belgium: Peeters, 2000); Baglow, '*Modus et Forma.*' See also the various essays in Thomas G. Weinandy, Daniel A. Keating, and John P. Yocum, eds., *Aquinas on Scripture: An Introduction to His Biblical Commentaries* (London: T&T Clark International, 2005); and in Michael Dauphinais and Matthew Levering, eds., *Reading John with St. Thomas Aquinas: Theological Exegesis and Speculative Theology* (Washington, D.C.: The Catholic University of America Press, 2005).

tion.[3] The wisdom literature is, for the most part, discursive rather than narrative, and its statements can be applied directly to the subject matter of Romans without the need to probe for hidden meanings beneath the surface. A few examples serve to illustrate this point. To corroborate Paul's assertion that all earthly power is from God, Thomas quotes Proverbs 8:15: "by me [divine wisdom] kings reign" (1022).[4] To reinforce the point that the truths of faith may be above reason but cannot contradict reason, he draws on Sirach 3:25, "Many things are shown to thee above the understanding of men," and Psalm 93:5, "Thy decrees are very sure" (828). Job 38:7 serves to refute Origen's error of the preexistence of human souls: "Where were you when the morning stars praised me together and all the sons of God made joyful melody?" (758). Even where the text uses poetic imagery, as in the latter case, its meaning contributes directly to the argument at hand.

Thomas's citations are almost always in the form of single, self-contained statements. He uses Old Testament citations like small spotlights, each shining from a different angle to illuminate another facet of the theological realities that he is expounding.[5] He rarely discusses an Old Testament passage or narrative episode as a whole, even where Paul is offering a sustained reflection on a biblical text. Moreover, unlike Paul, the other New Testament authors, and most of the Fathers, Thomas does not make use of allusions, echoes, or verbal resonances that can hint at allegorical linkages or create a subtle "meaning effect." Rather, he cites texts in a straightforward manner insofar as they serve to confirm, illustrate, or develop a point he is making in his exposition of Romans. His biblical references are invariably in the foreground rather than the background of the discussion. Likewise, the vast majority of Old Testament citations are read according to their literal sense; relatively few are interpreted spiritually (at least, according to Thomas's definition, as will be explained below).

The Senses of Scripture in Theory and Practice

What hermeneutical principles were operative in Thomas's use of the Old Testament? This question is best answered by comparing his actual practice in the commentary with the systematic treatment of the senses of Scripture

---

3. *Summa theologiae (ST)* I, q.1, a. 10; *Quodlibetum* VII, q. 6, a. 1–2. Cf. Augustine, *Epistle* 48.

4. All translations are taken from St. Thomas Aquinas, *Lectures on the Letter to the Romans by Saint Thomas Aquinas*, trans. Fabian Larcher, ed. Jeremy Holmes (Ave Maria, Fla.: Aquinas Center for Theological Renewal), http://www.avemaria.edu/uploads/pagesfiles/4283.pdf. Numbers in parentheses refer to paragraphs in the Marietti edition: *Super Epistolas S. Pauli Lectura* (Rome, 1953).

5. I owe this analogy to my colleague Daniel Keating.

found in his theological works. Aquinas's most thorough accounts of the senses of Scripture are in the *Summa* I.1.10 and the *Quodlibetum* VII.6.[6] His treatment both synthesized and developed insights germinating in the tradition prior to him. According to the medieval formula, Scripture has a fourfold meaning, consisting of the literal sense and the spiritual sense subdivided into the allegorical, the tropological, and the anagogical.[7]

The Literal Sense

The literal sense was traditionally defined as the *gesta*, the events recounted in Scripture. But Aquinas defines it as "that which the author intends" *(quem auctor intendit)*. This significant move allows him to include in the literal sense the whole range of devices by which an author can communicate meaning, including figurative modes of speech such as poetic imagery, parable, and metaphor.[8] In such cases, the literal sense is not the surface meaning of the words but *that which is signified by the literary figure*. As an example, Aquinas notes that the literal sense of "the arm of God" is not a physical limb but "God's operative power."[9]

It is crucial, however, not to confuse Thomas's view with the modern notion of authorial intention. In using the verb *intendere* he was not referring to the psychological intent of the author—the ascertainment of which, as modern literary critics have pointed out, is a dubious and highly speculative enterprise.[10] Rather, he was using *intendere* in its philosophical sense of "point to" or "refer to." The literal sense is not the subjective intention of the author but the *objective realities referred to by the text*, whether historical facts or atemporal truths. Thus Thomas also describes the literal sense as "the meaning whereby the words signify things [*res*]"[11] and uses "literal sense" and "his-

6. See also *Quaestiones disputatae de potentia Dei* 4, a. 1. According to the chronology of Jean-Pierre Torrell, the first series of *Quodlibeta* was written in 1256–59; part I of the *Summa* in 1265–67; and the lectures on Romans were delivered in 1271–72. See Torrell, *Saint Thomas Aquinas*, vol. 1, *The Person and His Work*, rev. ed., trans. R. Royal (Washington, D.C.: The Catholic University Press, 2005), 327–29.

7. The classic formulation is the couplet attributed to Augustine of Dacia: "Littera gesta docet, quid credas allegoria, Moralis quid agas, quo tendas anagogia."

8. This move was partly anticipated by Alexander of Hales and Albert the Great. See George Montague, *Understanding the Bible: A Basic Introduction to Biblical Interpretation*, rev. ed. (Mahwah, N.J.: Paulist Press, 2007), 57–59; Miguel Ángel Tábet, "Il senso litterale e il senso spirituale della Sacra Scrittura: Un tentative di chiarimento terminologico e concettuale," *Annales theologici* 9, no. 1 (1995): 3–5.

9. *ST* I, q .1, a. 10, ad 3.

10. See, e.g., Nigel M. Watson, "Authorial Intention: Suspect Concept for Biblical Scholarship," *Australian Biblical Review* 35 (1987): 6–13; Joseph A. Fitzmyer, "Problems of the Literal and Spiritual Senses of Scripture," *Louvain Studies* 20, nos. 2–3 (1995): 134–46.

11. *ST* I, q. 1, a. 10. Here he is closely following Augustine, *De Doctrina Christiana*.

torical sense" synonymously. Thomas also differs from modern interpreters in that he does not distinguish between the intention of the human author and that of God; because God is the primary author of Scripture, the literal sense is ultimately to be attributed to him. Thus the literal sense apparently can include meanings of which the human author was unaware.[12]

Aquinas emphasized the primacy of the literal sense as the indispensable foundation for every other possible sense. In this he exemplified the new approach to Scripture that had been gaining ground among the schoolmen of the Middle Ages.[13] For the patristic commentators, following Origen, exegesis had been largely characterized by the search for the spiritual sense, the deeper meaning in which every line of Scripture points in a veiled way to Christ. A quote from Cyril of Alexandria exemplifies the conviction animating this approach: in Scripture "the mystery of Christ [is] signified to us through a myriad of different kinds of things. Someone might liken it to a glittering and magnificent city, having not one image of the king but many, and publicly displayed in every corner of the city."[14] The patristic exegetical tradition was kept alive in the monasteries, where the spiritual life centered on the practice of *lectio divina*, through which the monks sought to contemplate and spiritually assimilate the inexhaustible mysteries hidden in the text. The scholastic theologians, in contrast, were motivated by more distinctly pastoral concerns: they studied Scripture in order to combat heresy, to develop formal theological arguments, and to meet the needs of the faithful by preaching and teaching in a manner that could be easily understood—aims for which literal interpretation is most suited. This trend, however, represented a shift in emphasis, not a decisive break with the past. While giving greater attention to the literal sense, the scholastics by no means denied that the Old Testament points in a veiled way to Christ.

Some examples from the Romans commentary serve to illustrate Thomas's use of the literal sense as he broadly construes it. Commenting on Paul's statement "Those whom he predestined he also called" (Rom 8:30), Thomas ex-

12. Aquinas asserts that "even if commentators adapt certain truths to the sacred text that were not understood by the author, without doubt the Holy Spirit understood them, since he is the principal author of Holy Scripture" (*De potentia* IV.1 resp.). Cf. also *ST* I, q. 1, a. 10: "Since the author of Holy Writ is God, who by one act comprehends all things by his intellect, it is not unfitting . . . if, even according to the literal sense, one word in Holy Writ should have several senses."

13. For a brief but insightful description of this shift and the historical and cultural factors underlying it, see Nicholas M. Healy, "Introduction," in *Aquinas on Scripture: An Introduction to His Biblical Commentaries*, ed. Thomas G. Weinandy, Daniel A. Keating, and John P. Yocum, 1–20 (London: T&T Clark International, 2005). For a more detailed account see Beryl Smalley, *The Study of the Bible in the Middle Ages* (Notre Dame, Ind.: University of Notre Dame Press, 1965).

14. Quoted in Robert L. Wilken, "How to Read the Bible," *First Things* 181 (2008): 24–27. Ironically, however, Cyril operates mainly within what Aquinas would call the literal sense.

plains that one of the ways God "calls" is through the mouth of preachers; he then quotes Proverbs 9:3 in support: "[Wisdom] has sent out her maids to call from the highest places" (707). The *literal* sense of this proverb, in Thomas's view, is that God addresses his people through human emissaries, prophets and teachers whom he sends to speak in his name. This is certainly a plausible explanation of what the sacred author intended to signify by the image of Lady Wisdom sending out her invitations. Thomas goes on to explain that the other way God "calls" is interiorly, by an "impulse of the mind whereby a man's heart is moved by God to assent to the things of faith or of virtue." To illustrate this point he draws on Isaiah 41:2: "Who stirred up one from the east and called him to follow?" This text refers to King Cyrus of Persia and asserts that it was God himself who inspired Cyrus to undertake the military conquests that eventually led to the return of the Jews from exile. Without any reference to its historical setting, Thomas draws on the text because of its indirect but literal affirmation of a truth of faith, namely, that to accomplish his purposes God prompts human beings—including even pagans—from within. He regards the text as having a theological as well as a historical referent, and in this case it is the latter that interests him.

The Spiritual Sense

If the literal sense encompasses all that is signified by the text by means of whatever literary forms and genres it employs, the spiritual sense, in contrast, is what is in turn signified by the *things or events* conveyed by the text. Underlying this principle is Thomas's crucial insight regarding the spiritual sense: whereas human beings write with words, God writes with history. That is to say, God acts in history according to a pattern such that the persons, objects, institutions, and events of the old covenant, interpreted properly, point forward to and illuminate the culmination of his plan in Christ. They may do so by signifying either the mystery of Christ himself (the allegorical or Christological sense), or how we ought to live life in Christ (the tropological or moral sense), or what lies ahead in eternal glory (the anagogical or eschatological sense). It follows that having a spiritual sense is a property unique to sacred Scripture as having a divine Author; no other text has this inner dynamic.[15] Only God could so order everything in salvation history that it would prefigure, foreshadow, and prepare for the greater things that lie ahead. It also follows that to grasp the mystery hidden in history requires a supernatural grace, which Thomas identifies as the gift of prophecy (978). But Thomas also seeks to correct the excesses of figural interpretation by insisting that the spiritual

---

15. See *Quodlibetum* VII, q. 6, a. 3.

sense is not open-ended. Because the realities that signify Christ are themselves communicated by means of the word, the spiritual sense "is based on and presupposes the literal."[16]

In the Romans commentary, on those few occasions where Aquinas makes use of a clearly allegorical (Christological) reading, his interpretation tends to be closely dependent on that of Paul, as for instance in his extended treatment of circumcision in commenting on Romans 4:11–15. In this case, as elsewhere, the focus of his interpretation is not the text (the narrative recounting the institution of the rite of circumcision in Gn 17) but its referent, the actual practice of circumcision as the outward sign of the old covenant.[17] For Thomas, the spiritual sense is a matter not of literary correspondences, or what is today called intertexuality, but of ontological participation.[18] It is the rites and institutions of the old covenant themselves that bear a "relation to Christ, to whom they are compared as the figure to the reality and as the members to the body" (348). Aquinas's attention to the referent allows a richer and more profound exploration of theological themes than is typical in exegesis that looks only for intertextual linkages. For instance, he notes an inner connection between circumcision and Abraham's act of faith: "Abraham believed that his seed would be multiplied; hence, it was fitting to receive its sign in the organ of reproduction" (343). Thomas also observes how circumcision expresses "something that was to occur spiritually, namely, just as superfluous skin was removed from the organ of reproduction, which is the chief servant of concupiscence, so every superfluous desire should be removed from man's heart, as Jer (4:4) says: 'Circumcise yourself to the Lord, remove the foreskin of your hearts.'" Finally he makes the interesting remark that "the secret of the incarnation of Christ from the seed of Abraham was enclosed under the seal of circumcision" (343).

There are cases where it is unclear whether Aquinas would consider his own reading of a particular text as literal or spiritual. For example, he draws on the Song of Songs (5:3) to support Paul's exhortation not to continue in sin because we have died to it: "I had bathed my feet; how could I soil them?" (471). It is clear that Thomas does not have the surface meaning of the text in mind. But it is hard to know whether he viewed this verse (with its baptismal overtones) as alluding to purification from sin in a general sense or to the old covenant rituals as prefigurations of baptism. In another place, to expound

16. *ST* I, q. 1, a. 10.

17. Cf. *ST* II-II, q. 1, a. 2, ad 2: "The believer's act [of faith] does not terminate in the propositions, but in the realities [which they express]."

18. See Francis Martin, *Sacred Scripture: The Disclosure of the Word* (Naples, Fla.: Sapientia Press, 2006), 262–75.

on Paul's description of disordered sexual lust in Romans 1, Thomas turns to Psalm 118:12: "They blazed like a fire of thorns" (150). In context the psalmist is clearly referring to enemy nations, thanking God for deliverance from their grasp: "All nations surrounded me... They surrounded me like bees, they blazed like a fire of thorns; in the name of the LORD I cut them off!" Thus Thomas would probably say that the literal sense of the blazing thorns (the *res* signified by the words) is enemy nations; the spiritual sense (that which is in turn signified by the *res*) is uncontrolled passions of the soul. On what grounds does Aquinas read hostile nations as a figure for carnal desires gone out of control?[19] Probably on the grounds that "burning" was a common figure for sexual desire in the Bible (Sir 9:8; Prv 6:27–29; 1 Cor 7:9) as in Greek literature, and that wicked behavior is associated with both fire and thorns.[20]

Aquinas's spiritual reading of the Old Testament is more restrained and disciplined than that of many earlier commentators. But there are occasions where the modern reader may wonder: is Thomas adhering to his own principle, that the spiritual sense is based on the literal, or is he not rather imposing an interpretation alien to the original meaning of the text?[21] In these cases it can be illuminating to consider the broader context of the passage cited as well as use of motifs appearing elsewhere in the Old Testament. What at first glance appears to be strong-arming a text to express something wholly unrelated to its original meaning may on closer inspection turn out to have a logical basis. For example, commenting on Paul's remark that he had wished to visit Rome but had been prevented, Thomas notes that it is God who arranges the travels of preachers. In support he quotes a text of Job: "The clouds scatter his lightning. They turn round and round by his guidance to accomplish all that he commands them" (Job 37:11–12), adding that "clouds" signify preachers (91). In the same context he cites Proverbs to describe the way Satan seeks to prevent the preaching that leads to salvation: "'the north wind drives away rain' (Prv 25:23), i.e., the doctrines of the preachers" (91).[22] The reader might object that there is nothing in the text of either Job or Proverbs to remotely suggest a reference to preaching, much less to the proclamation of the Gospel. The Job text is part of an encomium to the inscrutable wisdom and power of God manifested in creation; the proverb compares the rain that predictably

19. Note that it is not the *res* in itself but the *res* as conveyed by the words of Scripture that is significant; not enemy nations per se but enemy nations understood figuratively as bees and a fire attacking God's faithful servant signify the passions of the soul.

20. Cf. 2 Sam 23:6; Mt 7:16; Heb 6:8.

21. A complaint not unlike that often made against St. Paul!

22. The Vulgate translation, *ventus aquilo dissipat pluvias*, apparently misinterprets the Hebrew as "drives away rain" rather than "brings forth rain." The LXX has *exegeirei nephē* ("raises clouds").

follows the north wind to the anger aroused by a backbiting tongue. However, Thomas is undoubtedly aware that clouds, and rainclouds in particular, frequently function as a biblical image for the life-giving effect of sacred teaching, as in the Song of Moses: "May my teaching drop as the rain, my speech distil as the dew, as the gentle rain upon the tender grass, and as the showers upon the herb" (Dt 32:2; cf. Isa 55:10–11; Hos 10:12). Moreover, wind often appears in the prophetic tradition as an image for forces hostile to God's people.[23] Aquinas's use of these texts, then, is not arbitrary but is rooted in an interlocking network of associations found in Scripture itself. Moreover, in holding that the spiritual sense must be based on the literal *(quem auctor intendit)*, he apparently does not mean that it must be tied to that meaning with which the author endowed a text in its immediate context. Rather, it must be grounded in a proper interpretation of the Old Testament as a whole in its communication of revelation through both earthly realities and the events of salvation history. Aquinas's claim that the spiritual sense is based on the literal must be evaluated on the basis of his own understanding of what the literal sense is and how it functions.

In another passage, to explain how God can be said to search hearts (Rom 8:27) Thomas quotes the prophet Zephaniah: "I will search Jerusalem with lamps" (Zep 1:12), explaining that it is "not as though [God] investigates the secrets of the heart, but that he knows clearly the hidden things of the heart" (694). On what basis does Thomas identify Jerusalem with the heart? The quotation is from an oracle in which Zephaniah warns in figurative language that although God will punish Israel's enemies, he also will not spare those of his own people whom he finds guilty of idolatry. Thomas's interpretation, taking Jerusalem as a figure for the human heart, simply applies the same idea at a more interior level. Indeed, in the very same verse, as Thomas was doubtless aware, Zephaniah goes on to say, "I will punish the men ... who say *in their hearts*, 'The LORD will not do good, nor will he do ill.'"

Similarly, Aquinas comments on Paul's description of the progressive moral degeneration of those who reject the truth (Rom 1:18–32), noting that God "releases men to the desires of the heart as to cruel masters" (137). In support he cites a text from Isaiah: "I will give over the Egyptians into the hand of a hard master" (Is 19:4). He thereby makes the Egyptians a figure for the morally depraved, and the hard taskmaster a figure for their own corrupt and insatiable passions. In its original context, the text occurs in an oracle against Egypt, in which the prophet threatens that because of Egypt's hostilities against God's people, it will be subject to internal strife and subjugated to a

23. Cf. Isa 49:10; 64:6; Jer 4:11; Ezek 13:13; Mt 7:25.

foreign king, probably referring to the ruler of Assyria. Is there any discernable continuity between this literal sense and Thomas's tropological reinterpretation? Yes, if one considers the pervasive Old Testament motif—stemming from the golden calf apostasy with its overtones of sexual revelry (Ex 32:6, 25)—in which Egypt represents the perennial temptation of Israel to return to idolatry for the sake of pleasure, wealth, and power.[24] From there it requires only a small step to associate God's punishment of the Egyptians with his allowing the tyranny of sinful desires to become sin's own punishment, the dynamic described by Paul in Romans.

It must be admitted that there are also instances where, even granting Thomas's own definition of the literal sense, his reasoning for bringing a particular Old Testament text to bear on the subject matter of Romans is obscure or even forced. To explain that the saints on earth do not yet have the liberty of glory, which is release from the trials we endure on earth, he quotes Job: "who has let the wild ass go free?" (Job 39:5) (666). Where he expounds on how the Holy Spirit "intercedes for us with sighs too deep for words," he cites a simile from Nahum, "moaning like doves" (Na 2:7) (693). The phrase occurs in an oracle against Nineveh and describes the moaning of the palace maidens as the city is ravaged by plunderers. Thomas's justification for citing it at Romans 8:26 is the biblical association of the Spirit with a dove,[25] but here it results in an interpretation at odds with the original meaning.[26]

The examples given above demonstrate the futility of trying to draw a bright line between literal and spiritual interpretation of Scripture as practiced by Aquinas. The boundary between the two is fluid. As Hans Frei once pointed out, for pre-critical scholars "figuration or typology was a natural extension of literal interpretation. It was literalism at the level of the whole biblical story and thus of the depiction of the whole of historical reality."[27]

Thomas's Hermeneutical Premises

What are the hermeneutical premises that undergird Thomas's Old Testament interpretation, and is there anything they might contribute to biblical exegesis today? It has been observed with increasing frequency that what we

24. Cf. Dt 17:16; Neh 9:17; Jer 44:12–14; Hos 8:13, 11:5.

25. In such cases Thomas's approach is similar to, and may be influenced by, that of the ancient rabbis, who delighted in linking texts through word association.

26. In this case Thomas relies on a verbal parallel in the Vulgate, *gementibus/gementes*, which does not exist in the Greek: Rom 8:26 has *stenagmois;* Na 2:7 LXX has *phthengomenai.*

27. *The Eclipse of Biblical Narrative: A Study in Eighteenth and Nineteenth Century Hermeneutics* (New Haven, Conn.: Yale University Press, 1974), 2.

call pre-critical exegesis is often more satisfying, more theologically sugges-tive, and more spiritually nourishing than modern critical interpretation. But the question remains as to whether it is legitimate *as exegesis*—as "drawing out" the meaning of the text—as opposed to eisegesis, reading into the text. Is Thomas's use of the Old Testament as exemplified in his Romans commentary merely a quaint, imaginative, and perhaps edifying exploitation of verbal as-sociations, or does it have any objective exegetical basis? Perhaps the fact that it *is* so spiritually enriching should be taken as at least a partial clue to the answer. I would like to suggest several hermeneutical principles implicit in Thomas's work that could contribute to a renewal of both biblical exegesis and theology today.

One of the most striking premises of Thomas's use of the Old Testament is his assumption that Scripture is theologically robust. That is, it makes theo-logical truth claims that are internally consistent and rationally defensible, and that can be incorporated into a formal theological argument without fear that they will dissolve into a mass of inconsistencies or ambiguities. It might be objected that this assumption leads Thomas to proof-text—to mine the Old Testament for statements that support his argument, regardless of their original context and meaning. But even if he is not sensitive to critical ques-tions of philology, genre, literary context, sociocultural background, and so on, which today are recognized as essential to determining the literal sense, it does not follow that Thomas arbitrarily imposes a meaning. He conceived his task as that of faithfully interpreting Scripture by organizing its teaching into a coherent synthesis, not that of hunting for and bending texts to support a predetermined theological scheme. The texts determine the synthesis, not the other way around.[28] A retrieval of this confidence in Scripture (interpreted within the Church) as the genuine source of theology—not merely a quarry for theological vocabulary, themes, and images—could lead to a more consci-entious effort to *begin* from the word of God in addressing contemporary doc-trinal and disciplinary questions, and a confidence that therein we will most surely discover the truth and the will of God.[29]

Second, Thomas assumes the fundamental unity of the canon. For him, as for the ancient and medieval tradition as a whole, the sacred books are not merely the record of a multiplicity of ancient theologies attributable to vari-ous authors addressing various concerns in various historical contexts, but a single source of revelation bearing witness to a single economy of salvation.

28. It should also be pointed out, however, that the scholastic fondness for system degenerated in time to the distortion of proof-texting, where the system begins to take priority over the text.

29. See Raniero Cantalamessa, Lenten Sermon to the Pontifical Household, February 29, 2008.

For Thomas it is self-evident, for instance, that the words of Isaiah, "What I have heard from the LORD of hosts, the God of Israel, I announce to you" (Is 21:10), apply to Paul announcing the Gospel (24). Amos too speaks of Christ, as Thomas shows by adding a gloss to Amos 3:7: "'The Lord will not make a word,' *namely, make it be incarnate,* 'without revealing his secret to his servants the prophets'" (26).[30] So luminous is the Christological significance of the Old Testament that in response to the question, "Did the Jewish people not know the things which pertain to the mystery of Christ and to the calling of the Gentiles and the fall of the Jews?" Thomas can answer, "They knew fully" because they were "instructed by the law" (Rom 2:18) (850). For Thomas, the unity of the canon is ultimately grounded in a theology of history that recognizes all history as a divine plan at the center of which is the Lord Christ. As Paul put it, all things are "summed up" in Christ (*anakephalaiōsasthai*, Eph 1:10); that is, all history finds its intelligibility and ultimate meaning in him. The Old Testament truly announces the good news of Christ, not only via our "retrospective re-readings,"[31] but by a Spirit-conferred participation in the wisdom of God on the part of the sacred authors. If all Scripture is a unified witness to a single providential plan, the continuity between old and new is far greater than is usually regarded by exegetes today.

It follows that if a passage in one part of the canon appears to contradict another, part of the commentator's task is to show how they can be reconciled. Aquinas sees a need, for instance, to address the apparent inconsistency between Paul's sorrow over the unbelief of his fellow Jews in Romans 9:2 and the admonition in Sirach: "Give not up your soul to sadness" (Sir 30:22). He does so by arguing that since "charity requires that a person love his neighbor as himself, it is laudable for a wise man to grieve over a son of his neighbor as over his own" (738). Such an approach is markedly different from that of modern exegetes, who are generally content to let discrepancies and even contradictions stand as simply indicating different theologies among the various biblical authors, or even among layers of redaction within a single work. Reclaiming a faith that all Scripture is inspired by God and thus theologically reliable—on its own terms, not ours—could lead to a renewed effort to show how the different perspectives among the biblical authors are complementary rather than contradictory.

Finally, the above exegetical premises are ultimately dependent on a *hermeneutic of faith*—a profound awareness on Thomas's part that he is dealing

---

30. Italics added. Aquinas here relies on a parallel in the Vulgate between Amos 3:7, "non **faciet** Dominus Deus **verbum** nisi revelaverit" and John 1:14, "(Joh 1:14) **Verbum** caro **factum** est."

31. The phrase is from the Pontifical Biblical Commission document, *The Jewish People and Their Sacred Scriptures in the Christian Bible* (2002), 21.

with not merely a human document from the ancient past but a living, breathing Word in which God continues to speak. The recovery of such a faith perspective is crucial to overcoming the crisis of a truncated, reductive exegesis that attends only to the human dimension of the word and that has no power to edify, challenge, convict, or guide the faithful. Already a renewed attention to faith as the properly Christian hermeneutic is bringing streams of fresh water into what sometimes looks like the dry desert of contemporary academic biblical scholarship.

At the international Synod of Bishops on "The Word of God in the Life and Mission of the Church" in 2008, Benedict XVI made an intervention in which he stated:

> Where exegesis is not theology, Scripture cannot be the soul of theology and, vice versa, when theology is not essentially the interpretation of the Scripture in the Church, this theology has no foundation anymore. Therefore for the life and the mission of the Church, for the future of faith, this dualism between exegesis and theology must be overcome. Biblical theology and systematic theology are two dimensions of the one reality that we call Theology.[32]

A closer attention to Aquinas's use of the Old Testament in interpreting the New helps point the way toward a reintegration of Scripture and theology.

---

32. See Benedict XVI's post-synodal apostolic exhortation *Verbum Domini*, 35.

Matthew Levering

૦~

II   Aquinas on Romans 8
Predestination in Context

How can Thomas Aquinas's *Lectures on the Letter to the Romans* enrich our understanding of his theology of predestination? After a brief overview of Aquinas's theology of predestination in the *Summa theologiae*, I explore his exposition of Romans 8 in his commentary.[1] Although biblical commentators differ among each other about the precise meaning of *proorizein*, Romans 8 has long been crucial for the doctrine of predestination, especially Paul's statement that "those whom he foreknew he also predestined to be conformed to the image of his Son, in order that he might be the first-born among many brethren. And those whom he predestined he also called; and those whom he called he also justified; and those whom he justified he also glorified" (Rom 8:29–30). Aquinas quotes Romans 8:30 in the first two articles of his question on predestination in the *Summa theologiae*. In the *Summa theologiae*, however, he does not have space to examine how the earlier verses of Romans 8 build toward Paul's discussion of "those whom he predestined." By contrast, Aquinas's commentary on Romans 8 enables him to preface his discussion of predestination with a detailed exposition of law and grace, adoptive sonship, suffering and glorification, diversity and mission, and the Holy Spirit's work of building up the charitable unity of those who are in Christ Jesus. By emphasizing the historical unfolding of God's eternal plan for the temporal missions of Son and the Holy Spirit, Aquinas's commentary on Romans thus makes especially clear how the doctrine of predestination, in the *Summa theologiae*, takes on its true shape in the *secunda* and *tertia pars*.

---

1. See also Steven C. Boguslawski's summary of Aquinas on predestination and election in the *Summa theologiae* and the *Commentary on Romans* (focusing on Romans 8:29–33): Boguslawski, *Thomas Aquinas on the Jews: Insights into His Commentary on Romans 9–11* (New York: Paulist Press, 2008), 55–66, cf. 87–122.

Romans and Predestination in the *Summa theologiae*

In the question that Aquinas devotes in the *Summa theologiae* to Jesus Christ's predestination, he states that "predestination, in its proper sense, is a certain divine preordination from eternity of those things which are to be done in time by the grace of God."[2] Since God is not temporal, whereas God's effects in time are temporal, "predestination" describes how the eternal God efficaciously wills to unite his fallen creatures to supernatural friendship with him, a union that takes place in time through grace. Predestination has to do with human beings attaining an end that would not be possible for us by our natural powers alone.

As such, predestination is the highest part of divine providence. Providence describes God's plan for guiding all things to the goal for which he creates them. Human beings and angels possess an end "which exceeds all proportion and faculty of created nature; and this end is life eternal, that consists in seeing God."[3] From eternity, God in his wisdom has a plan for how rational creatures will attain this end that exceeds the abilities of created nature. This divine "idea of the order of some towards salvation"[4] is what is meant by "predestination." To come to share in the very life of the Trinity requires the gracious help of the Trinity. Those who attain salvation do so because God specially draws them, and enables them freely to attain to union with him beyond "all proportion and faculty of created nature."

In explaining this view of predestination, Aquinas repeatedly quotes Paul. He notes that Romans 8:30 describes the working out of predestination in time: "predestination is a kind of type of the ordering of some persons towards eternal salvation, existing in the divine mind.... The execution of predestination is the calling and magnification; according to the Apostle (Rom. viii. 30): *Whom He predestined, them He also called and whom He called, them He also magnified.*"[5] On this view predestination, or "preordination from eternity,"[6] cannot be separated from communal election.

How does predestination relate to Christ? Citing Ephesians 1:5, Aquinas holds that "Christ's predestination is the cause of ours: for God, by predestin-

2. Thomas Aquinas, *Summa theologiae (ST)* III, q. 24, a. 1.

3. *ST* I, q. 23, a. 1. For discussion see Jean-Pierre Torrell, O.P., "'Dieu conduit toutes choses vers leur fin.' Providence et gouvernement divin chez Thomas d'Aquin," in *Ende und Vollendung. Eschatologische Perspektiven im Mittelalter*, ed. J. A. Aertsen and M. Pickavé (Berlin: Walter de Gruyter, 2002), 561–94, at 581–85. See also Torrell's "Nature and Grace in Thomas Aquinas," in *Surnaturel: A Controversy at the Heart of Twentieth-Century Thomistic Thought*, ed. Serge-Thomas Bonino, O.P., trans. Robert Williams (Ave Maria, Fla.: Sapientia Press, 2009).

4. *ST* I, q. 23, a. 2, ad 3.   5. *ST* I, q. 23, a. 2.

6. *ST* III, q. 24, a. 1.

ing from eternity, so decreed our salvation, that it should be achieved through Jesus Christ."[7] God's election of Israel is fulfilled by the Paschal mystery of Christ Jesus. Aquinas states that "Christ is the Head of all men, but diversely."[8] The mystical body includes every human being, at least in potentiality during life on earth. Christ died for all human beings, and in this sense no human being is unrelated to Christ. Aquinas grants, however, that "some are in potentiality who will never be reduced to act."[9] To be a member of Christ's body in act rather than in potentiality means to have faith and charity, which are infused in human beings by the grace of the Holy Spirit according to the "preordination from eternity of those things which are to be done in time by the grace of God."[10]

Why does God make some, and not others, to be his "elect" (Rom 8:33)? Quoting Paul, Aquinas affirms that the answer must be found in God's eternal plan: "It is written (Rom. viii. 30): *Whom He predestined, them He also called.*"[11] How does this relate to the mysterious passage from Malachi 1:2–3 that Paul quotes in Romans 9:13, "Jacob I loved, but Esau I hated"?[12] With Paul, Aquinas insists that election does not introduce "injustice on God's part" (Rom 9:14). Even if some are not "elect," not "predestined" or "preordained," God does not cause their failure to attain salvation. In all cases, "guilt proceeds from the free-will of the person," even if that person is mysteriously not raised up, at the critical moment, by the grace of the Holy Spirit.[13]

God's election of human beings, Aquinas observes, flows from "His will, by which in loving He wishes good to someone," and this divine will "is the cause of that good possessed by some in preference to others."[14] Aquinas explains that God gives a share in his goodness to every creature, but the special sharing in God's goodness unto salvation belongs to "election":

> If the communication of the divine goodness in general be considered, God communicates His goodness without election; inasmuch as there is nothing which does not in some way share in His goodness.... But if we consider the communication of this or that particular good, He does not allot it without election; since He gives certain goods to some men, which He does not give to others. Thus in the conferring of grace and glory election is implied.[15]

---

7. *ST* III, q. 24, a. 4.   8. *ST* III, q. 8, a. 3.
9. Ibid.   10. *ST* III, q. 24, a. 1.
11. *ST* I, q. 23, a. 1, *sed contra*.

12. For Aquinas's exegesis of this section of Romans 9, see Michał Paluch, O.P., *La profondeur de l'amour divin: évolution de la doctrine de la prédestination dans l'oeuvre de saint Thomas d'Aquin* (Paris: J. Vrin, 2004), 255–62; Boguslawski, *Thomas Aquinas on the Jews*, 89–91.

13. *ST* I, q. 23, a. 3, ad 2.   14. *ST* I, q. 23, a. 4.
15. *ST* I, q. 23, a. 4, ad 1.

God chooses those whom he chooses not because they are good, but because he is good. Underscoring that election depends solely on God's will to have mercy, Paul describes how "when Rebecca had conceived children by one man, our forefather Isaac, though they were not yet born and had done nothing either good or bad, in order that God's purpose of election might continue, not because of works but because of his call, she was told, 'The elder will serve the younger'" (Rom 9:10–12).[16] As Aquinas comments, this emphasis on God's will as the sole reason for election requires a negative answer as regards "whether God pre-ordained that He would give the effect of predestination to anyone on account of any merits."[17] Election does not proceed from anything that humans do, but rather proceeds from God's choice, a choice grounded "in the goodness of God."[18]

How could God's goodness, however, be consistent with the election only of some? Would not perfect goodness be displayed much more clearly by the election of all, so that all come to share in the Trinitarian life? Although Aquinas repeats Augustine's observation that the spectrum of degrees of goodness in the final perfection of the universe manifests the diversity of the ways in which God's infinite goodness can be participated, Aquinas insists that why God chooses some rational creatures cannot be comprehended, although the goodness, justice, and mercy of God's plan can be affirmed. Predestination arises from the infinite depths of God's free volition: "why He chooses some for glory, and reprobates [i.e., does not choose] others, has no reason, except the divine will."[19]

16. In light of these verses, Paul W. Gooch argues that Romans 9–11, as a whole, "allows us to take God's sovereignty seriously by recognizing that he has the power to override all human freedoms. Nevertheless it also takes God's promise seriously: he will abide by his commitments, he will not be destructive but will show mercy. This preserves scope for human freedom and accountability" (Gooch, "Sovereignty and Freedom: Some Pauline Compatibilisms," *Scottish Journal of Theology* 40, no. 4 [1987]: 531–42, at 541). In Gooch's interpretation, unfortunately, God's power appears as competitive with human power.

17. *ST* I, q. 23, a. 5.

18. *ST* I, q. 23, a. 5, ad 2 and 3. On the role of free response to the grace of the Holy Spirit in the justification of the elect (with Paul's Letter to the Romans in view), see Joseph P. Wawrykow, *God's Grace and Human Action: "Merit" in the Theology of Thomas Aquinas* (Notre Dame, Ind.: University of Notre Dame Press, 1995), 284; Daniel A. Keating, "Justification, Sanctification, and Divinization in Thomas Aquinas," in *Aquinas on Doctrine: A Critical Introduction*, ed. Thomas G. Weinandy, O.F.M. Cap., Daniel A. Keating, and John P. Yocum (New York: T&T Clark International, 2004), 139–58, especially 146–47.

19. *ST* I, q. 23, a. 5, ad 3. For discussion see Paluch, *La profondeur de l'amour divin*, 264–66; Torrell, "'Dieu conduit toutes choses vers leur fin,'" 585; cf. Cornelius Fabro, "Le *Liber de bona fortuna* de l'*Éthique à Eudème* d'Aristote et la dialectique de la divine Providence chez saint Thomas," *Revue Thomiste* 88, no. 4 (1988): 556–72. On the basis of Jesus' words in Matthew 7:13–14, "Enter by the narrow gate; for the gate is wide and the way is easy, that leads to destruction, and those who

Aquinas on Romans 8:1–27

I now wish to examine this theology of predestination in light of Aquinas's commentary on Romans 8. By focusing first on Romans 8:1–27 before turning to the explicit appeal to predestination in verses 28–30, I inquire into what this context might add to our appreciation of Aquinas's citations of Romans 8:30 in *Summa theologiae* I, question 23, articles 1–2.

Law and Grace

Romans 8 begins with the affirmation, "There is therefore now no condemnation for those who are in Christ Jesus" (Rom 8:1).[20] There is no condemnation because Christ's Spirit gives those who are united in Christ's Body a new "law." Paul states that "the law of the Spirit of life in Christ Jesus has set me free from the law of sin and death" (Rom 8:2). Is the Mosaic law, then, a God-given "law of sin and death"? Paul continues in Romans 8:3–4: "God has done what the law, weakened by the flesh, could not do: sending his own Son in the likeness of sinful flesh and for sin, he condemned sin in the flesh, in order that the just requirement of the law might be fulfilled in us, who walk not according to the flesh but according to the Spirit." How does Aquinas interpret this passage?

Aquinas suggests that by "the law of sin and death," Paul means the fomes of sin, that is, "the law of evil inclinations which inclines to sin."[21] According

---

enter by it are many. For the gate is narrow and the way is hard, that leads to life, and those who find it are few," Aquinas supposes that "those who are saved are in the minority" (*ST* I, q. 23, a. 7, ad 3). However, citing a prayer from his missal, he states that "'to God alone is known the number for whom is reserved eternal happiness'" (*ST* I, q. 23, a. 7). For critical commentary, see Anselm K. Min, *Paths to the Triune God: An Encounter between Aquinas and Recent Theologies* (Notre Dame, Ind.: University of Notre Dame Press, 2005), 125–26, drawing upon Otto Hermann Pesch, *Thomas von Aquin: Grenze und Grösse mittelalterlicher Theologie* (Mainz: Matthias-Grünewald-Verlag, 1988), 153–55. On "sufficient" but inefficacious grace, see Réginald Garrigou-Lagrange, O.P., *Predestination*, trans. Dom Bede Rose, O.S.B. (Rockford, Ill.: Tan Books, 1998), 234–39; for concerns see Jean-Hervé Nicolas, O.P., "La volonté salvifique de Dieu contrariée par le péché," *Revue Thomiste* 92, no. 2 (1992): 177–96. See also Pierre Grelot, "Le retribution individuelle. Dossier biblique," *Revue Thomiste* 107, no. 2 (2007): 179–220.

20. For discussion see Bertrand de Margerie, S.J., "Mort sacrificielle du Christ et peine de mort chez saint Thomas d'Aquin, commentateur de saint Paul," *Revue Thomiste* 83, no. 3 (1983): 394–417.

21. St. Thomas Aquinas, *Super epistolam B. Pauli ad Romanos*, ch. 8, lect. 1, § 605. In quoting this work I employ *Lectures on the Letter to the Romans*, trans. Fabian Larcher, O.P., ed. Jeremy Holmes (Ave Maria, Fla.: Aquinas Center for Theological Renewal), http://www.avemaria.edu/uploads/pagesfiles/4283.pdf. For examination of Aquinas's exegetical method, using his commentary on Romans 5:12 as an exemplar, see Thomas Domanyi, *Der Römerbriefkommentar des Thomas von Aquin. Ein Beitrag zur Untersuchung seiner Auslegungsmethoden* (Bern: Peter Lang, 1979).

to Aquinas, Paul describes this "law" in Romans 7:23, which reads, "I see in my members another law at war with the law of my mind and making me captive to the law of sin which dwells in my members." In the *Summa theologiae* Aquinas explains why the fomes of sin, that is to say the impulse of sensuality, can be described as a "law" even though it deviates from reason.[22] In his commentary he simply points out that the grace of the Holy Spirit rescues human beings from this disordered "law" and from the damnation to which it leads.

Keeping in view that "the law of sin and death" (Rom 8:2) is not the Mosaic law, Aquinas inquires into why Paul teaches that the Mosaic law could not do what God accomplishes through the incarnate Son and the Holy Spirit. Recalling Hebrews 7:19, "For the law made nothing perfect," Aquinas comments on Romans 8:3, "Now the reason why the Law could not do this was not due to a shortcoming in the Law, but because it was weakened by the flesh, i.e., it was due to a weakness of the flesh in man with the result that in spite of the Law man was overcome by sinful desire: 'The spirit is willing, but the flesh is weak' (Mt 26:41)."[23] On this view, Christ Jesus does not negate the Mosaic law, because the Mosaic law's weakness "was not due to a shortcoming in the Law." The Mosaic law, while good in itself, could not rectify the disordered weakness of our will and passions. Aquinas quotes the prophet Jeremiah, who reveals God's promise to "make a new covenant with the house of Israel," by which God "will put my law within them" and "will forgive their iniquity" (Jer 31:31, 33–34).

How then does God's "own Son" (Rom 8:3) fulfill the Mosaic law so as to accomplish its goal of holiness in human beings? Rather than first speaking of the work of Christ, Aquinas points to the Holy Spirit received by "those who are in Christ Jesus" (Rom 8:1). The fulfillment of the Mosaic law consists in the holiness of God's people, and holiness comes about through the grace of the Holy Spirit. The "law of the Spirit of life" (Rom 8:2) is the "new law" prophesied in Jeremiah 31:33.[24] But why should the grace of the Holy Spirit be called a "law"? Drawing upon Aristotle's *Ethics*, Aquinas remarks that law has a pedagogical purpose; a good law instructs citizens about "what ought to be done."[25] By enlightening the mind and renewing and elevating the will, the

---

22. See *ST* I-II, q. 91, a. 6.

23. Aquinas, *Super epistolam B. Pauli ad Romanos*, ch. 8, lect. 1, § 611.

24. Ibid., § 603.

25. Ibid., § 602. Cf. Donal O'Connor, "St. Thomas's Commentary on Romans," *Irish Theological Quarterly* 34 (1967): 329–43, at 340–41; Leo Elders, S.V.D., "Le Saint Esprit et la *lex nova* dans les commentaries bibliques de saint Thomas d'Aquin," in *Credo in Spiritum Sanctum*, ed. José Saraiva Martins (Vatican City: Libreria Editrice Vaticana, 1983), 1195–1205; Edward Kaczynsky, O.P., "'Lex Spiritus' in S. Paolo e la sua interpretazione in S. Tommaso," in *Credo in Spiritum Sanctum*, 1207–22.

indwelling Holy Spirit accomplishes this purpose of law far more profoundly than any written law, even the divinely revealed Mosaic law. The "law of the Spirit" manifests itself concretely: "This faith teaches what is to be done: 'His anointing teaches you about everything' (1 Jn 2:27) and inclines the affections to act: 'The love of Christ controls us' (2 Cor 5:14)."[26] Aquinas compares "the Spirit of life" (Rom 8:2) with natural life: "just as the natural spirit makes the life of nature, so the divine Spirit makes the life of grace: 'It is the Spirit that gives life' (Jn 4:63); 'The Spirit of life was in the wheels' (Ezek 1:2)."[27]

The Body of Christ and Adoptive Sonship

Aquinas never separates the Holy Spirit from the Son: as Paul says, the Holy Spirit is "the Spirit of life in Christ Jesus" (Rom 8:2). Because the Holy Spirit is the Spirit of the Father and the Son, we receive the incarnate Son's Spirit as members of his Body. Aquinas states, "For just as the natural spirit does not reach a member not connected to the head, so the Holy Spirit does not reach a man not joined to Christ, the head: 'By this we know that he abides in us, by the Spirit which he has given us' (1 Jn 3:24)."[28] Christ's headship in the Body of Christ would not be salvific for us, however, unless Christ "in the likeness of sinful flesh" had "condemned sin in the flesh," thereby fulfilling for us (and enabling us to fulfill in Christ) "the just requirement of the law" (Rom 8:3–4).

How does Aquinas understand Paul's statement that God has sent "his own Son ... in the likeness of sinful flesh" (Rom 8:3)?[29] He emphasizes that God sends "his own co-substantial and co-eternal Son."[30] The divine Son now exists "in a way in which he did not exist in the world, i.e., visibly by means of the flesh he assumed."[31] Why should the Son of God take on flesh? For Aquinas—interpreting Paul—the answer is twofold: to take away man's sinful alienation from God by his human suffering, and to perfect us by uniting us to the Trinitarian life. "Sinful flesh" is flesh that can suffer; before original

26. Aquinas, *Super epistolam B. Pauli ad Romanos*, ch. 8, lect. 1, § 603.
27. Ibid., § 605.   28. Ibid.
29. Cf. Vincent P. Branick's "The Sinful Flesh of the Son of God (Rom 8:3): A Key Image of Pauline Theology," *Catholic Biblical Quarterly* 47, no. 2 (1985): 246–62, which argues that for Paul "the earthly Jesus did not appear as the paradigm of human virtue. He appeared as a sinner" (262). For the opposite interpretation, shared by Aquinas, see Gordon D. Fee, *Pauline Christology: An Exegetical-Theological Study* (Peabody, Mass.: Hendrickson, 2007), 247. Brendan Byrne, S.J., thinks that Paul means that "all the weakness, temptation and proneness to sin that the biblical tradition characterizes as 'flesh' Christ felt and suffered in his own person, while remaining personally sinless (2 Cor 5:21)" (Byrne, *Romans* [Collegeville, Minn.: Liturgical Press, 1996], 236). Fee points out, "Had Paul intended a more complete identification with us in our sinfulness itself, he could easily have said simply 'in sinful flesh'" (*Pauline Christology*, 247).
30. Aquinas, *Super epistolam B. Pauli ad Romanos*, ch. 8, lect. 1, § 607.
31. Ibid.

sin, God's grace preserved human beings from the material decomposition that is suffering and death: "For the wages of sin is death" (Rom 6:23). Christ Jesus, "in the likeness of sinful flesh," suffers and dies without owing the debt that original sin imposes. With respect to the restoration of the human image of God, therefore, Christ's death heals the wound of sin and reestablishes the relationship of justice between humans and God. Aquinas presents the power of Christ's Cross both in terms of satisfaction for sins and in terms of the devil losing his power over man.[32]

Aquinas emphasizes that "those who are in Christ Jesus" (Rom 8:1) attain the goal of the Mosaic law through the power of Christ's Cross. In order to make this point clear, he quotes Romans 9:30, "The Gentiles who did not pursue righteousness have attained the righteousness which is through faith," and 2 Corinthians 5:21, "For our sake he made him to be sin who knew no sin, so that in him we might become the righteousness of God."[33] In these passages, Aquinas points out, Paul is referring to the holiness that the Mosaic law promised, in other words "the just requirement of the law" (Rom 8:4). This holiness consists in our sharing in the life of the Trinity by living "according to the Spirit" (Rom 8:4). Aquinas observes that setting one's mind on the Spirit (Rom 8:6) is "the cause of grace and glory: 'He who sows in the Spirit will from the Spirit reap eternal life' (Gal 6:8)."[34] As Paul tells the Church in Rome, "But you are not in the flesh, you are in the Spirit, if the Spirit of God really dwells in you" (Rom 8:9). Drawing upon 1 Corinthians, Aquinas interprets this spiritual life in the strong sense of Trinitarian indwelling: "You are God's temple, and God's Spirit dwells in you" (1 Cor 3:16).[35]

With Paul, Aquinas goes on to emphasize that the indwelling of God's Spirit makes us adoptive sons of the Father: "For all who are led by the Spirit of God are sons of God" (Rom 8:14). Our sharing in the Trinitarian life as adoptive sons becomes manifest through our charity and filial fear, the interior markers of what Paul calls "the spirit of sonship" (Rom 8:15).[36] Commenting on Paul's affirmation that "the Spirit himself [is] bearing witness with our spirit that we are children of God" (Rom 8:16), Aquinas states that the Holy Spirit "bears this testimony not with external words that reach men's ears ... but through the effect of filial love He produces in us."[37] Charity is a gift of God, not something that we can give to ourselves.

In describing our adoptive sonship in Christ and his Spirit, Aquinas does not neglect the significance of Christ's Resurrection. Following Paul, he turns to the Resurrection in commenting on Romans 8:11, "If the Spirit of him who

32. See ibid., § 609.
34. Ibid., § 618.
36. See ibid., lect. 3, §§ 638, 643.
33. Ibid., § 610.
35. Ibid., lect. 2, § 626.
37. Ibid., § 645.

raised Jesus from the dead dwells in you, he who raised Christ Jesus from the dead will give life to your mortal bodies also through his Spirit who dwells in you."[38] The perfection of the human image of God requires the resurrection of the body. Arguing that Paul envisions a distinction between "mortal" and "dead" bodies, Aquinas specifies that through his Spirit God raises us not merely from death, but also from the "mortal" condition, from the very possibility of suffering and death.[39] Those risen bodies that are transformed by the Spirit of God will no longer be susceptible to suffering. This glorious sharing in the Trinitarian life, however, does not apply to those who die in mortal sin. As Aquinas points out, "the ones whose bodies were not temples of the Spirit will also rise, although their bodies will be able to suffer."[40]

Suffering and Glorification

Regarding Paul's statement that human beings are "heirs of God and fellow heirs with Christ, provided we suffer with him in order that we may also be glorified with him" (Rom 8:17), Aquinas asks what it means to be an heir of God. On the basis of inheritance at the human level, attested in the relationship of Abraham to Isaac (Gn 25:15), Aquinas reasons that "one's heir is a person who receives or gets his chief goods and not some small gifts."[41] What are God's "chief goods"? Since God is perfectly simple, his Good is himself. Aquinas thus concludes that "the children of God obtain God himself as their inheritance: 'The Lord is my chosen portion' (Ps 16:5)."[42] Unlike humans, who pass on their goods after their death, God does not lose his goods in sharing them, because the divine Good is spiritual and therefore can be participated by many.

But why would it be necessary for us to suffer with Christ in order to share in God's inheritance? The answer, says Aquinas, is that we receive this inheritance by sharing in Christ's: "just as he is the chief Son with whom we share sonship, so he is the chief heir, to whom we are united in the inheritance: 'This is the heir' (Mt 21:38)."[43] Even so, why can we not bypass the suffering of the Cross and, since we are already sharing in the Trinitarian life, move directly to the glory of the risen life that is our inheritance? Aquinas argues that at stake is our conformity to the heir through whom, and only through whom, we share in the inheritance.

Is the inheritance worth the cost of enduring our present sufferings on earth? Paul emphatically replies yes: "I consider that the sufferings of this

---

38. Cf. John G. Gibbs, *Creation and Redemption: A Study in Pauline Theology* (Leiden: E. J. Brill, 1971), 35–39.

39. Aquinas, *Super epistolam B. Pauli ad Romanos*, ch. 8, lect. 2, § 630.

40. Ibid.   41. Ibid., lect. 3, § 647.

42. Ibid.   43. Ibid., § 649.

present time are not worth comparing with the glory that is to be revealed to us" (Rom 8:18). Commenting on this verse, Aquinas offers four reasons for the surpassing value of the glory that God wills to give us: its eternity, its dignity, its manifestation at the final judgment, and its truth. In each case he contrasts temporal glory with the glory that is to come: the former is short-lived, of little value, known to few, and based solely on outward appearances, whereas the latter is unending, supremely valuable, eventually known to all, and based firmly upon inward realities. Furthermore, Aquinas points out that our sufferings can be meritorious if lived out in union with Christ, so that we can hope for eternal life as a reward.

From within this framework of grace, our human nature undergoes transformation through our sufferings. Aquinas states that "in the unrighteous this nature is not yet sanctified, but is as though without form. In the righteous it is partially formed now with grace, but it is still, as it were, without form and awaits the final form which comes through glory."[44] The life of grace gives a new "form" to human nature, by enabling us to enjoy in charity an intellectual communion in the divine life so profound as to be called "vision." Not only humans will be transformed. In Paul's words, "the creation waits with eager longing for the revealing of the sons of God" (Rom 8:19), by which Aquinas understands that God ordains all creation to a new glorious "form." For the present, all creatures, including humans, endure a "bondage to decay" (Rom 8:21), but in the new creation that God is bringing about, all creatures will share, according to diverse modes, in "the glorious liberty of the children of God" (Rom 8:21).[45]

Diversity and Mission

Will all "the children of God," in the final consummation, share equally in the Trinitarian life? In Aquinas's view, Paul does not intend to depict a perfectly egalitarian consummation. He interprets Paul's remark that he has "the first fruits of the Spirit" (Rom 8:23) to be an indication that "the apostles had the Holy Spirit before others and more abundantly than others."[46] What does

44. Ibid., lect. 4, § 659.
45. See also Jan Lambrecht, S.J., "The Groaning Creation: A Study of Rom 8:18–30," *Louvain Studies* 15, no. 1 (1990): 3–18, which notes that for Paul, in some fashion, "the world will share in the glory of the children of God" (14). He rejects, as antithetical to Paul, the notion that the cosmos has its value apart from humanity. He also argues that the doctrine of evolution has shown that material decay, including human disease and death, "would exist regardless of the presence or absence of sin" (15). For a similar view that human suffering cannot all be linked with actual or original sin, see J. Christiaan Beker, "Suffering and Triumph in Paul's Letter to the Romans," *Horizons in Biblical Theology* 7, no. 2 (1985): 105–19, at 113. Beker's description of "a crucial and mysterious 'dark residue' of evil and death in God's created order" (113) is difficult to distinguish from Gnostic dualism.
46. Aquinas, *Super epistolam B. Pauli ad Romanos*, ch. 8, lect. 5, § 676.

it mean to have the Holy Spirit "more abundantly than others"? In this regard, Aquinas emphasizes not knowledge but love; as he remarks, "it is plain that one who loves God more will enjoy him more. Hence, the Lord promises that blessed vision to those who love: 'He who loves me will be loved by my Father and I will love him and manifest myself to him' (Jn 14:21)."[47] Why should one suppose, however, that the apostles had greater charity than that possessed by later Christian saints and martyrs? Aquinas thinks that the answer is that the "first fruits of the Spirit," while in a certain sense present in all generations, are more abundantly present in the apostolic generation, because of the magnitude of their task of spreading the faith, building up the Church, and writing the inspired texts of the New Testament. The success of such labors depended on extraordinary charity, without which the faith could not have been successfully spread nor the inspired writings adequately composed.

Even so, later Christians have also undertaken great labors, and why should God not equally give the grace of the Holy Spirit to them? Aquinas has in view not only Romans 1:5, where Paul observes that he has specially "received grace and apostleship to bring about the obedience of faith for the sake of his name among all the nations," but also Ephesians 4, where Paul offers an account of God's gifting in the Church: "But grace was given to each of us according to the measure of Christ's gift.... And his gifts were that some should be apostles, some prophets, some evangelists, some pastors and teachers, for the equipment of the saints, for the work of ministry, for building up the body of Christ" (Eph 4:7,11–12). Applying to Romans 8:23 Paul's understanding of his apostolic grace, Aquinas observes that "a man's charity is not derived from himself, but from God's grace, which is given to each 'according to Christ's gift' (Eph 4:7). Now he gives to each the grace proportionate to his calling."[48]

Does Aquinas then believe that the apostles receive the grace of the Holy Spirit more abundantly than anyone else? No, because Christ Jesus, in his humanity, receives the grace of the Holy Spirit most fully due to his mission. Similarly the mission of the Virgin Mary, namely to be the mother of the Redeemer, constitutes a greater mission than that of the apostles, for which reason she receives the grace of the Holy Spirit more fully than do the apostles. The grace that the apostles receive "according to the measure of Christ's gift" (Eph 4:7) enables them to receive and deliver to others "the things that pertain to salvation" and thereby to be founders of the Church. In this regard

47. Ibid., § 677.

48. Ibid., § 678. For discussion of this text, and of Aquinas's overall view of Paul, see Thomas F. Ryan, "The Love of Learning and the Desire for God in Thomas Aquinas's *Commentary on Romans*," in *Medieval Readings of Romans*, ed. William S. Campbell, Peter S. Hawkins, and Brenda Deen Schildgen (New York: T&T Clark International, 2007), 101–14.

Aquinas quotes Revelation 21:14, "The wall of the city had twelve foundations and on them the twelve names of the twelve apostles of the Lamb."[49] The apostles can undertake this mission, Aquinas suggests, only because in a special way they possess the "first fruits of the Spirit."

The fact that the "children of God" share in differing degrees in the grace of the Holy Spirit, so that some receive greater charity than others and therefore are prepared more perfectly for the consummation that is the vision of God, follows from the need for particular missions (Christ, Mary, the apostles, and so forth) that uniquely advance the mediation of the grace of the Holy Spirit in accord with God's election. Because God keeps his covenantal oath, he loves his people and chooses them for his salvific purposes, just as Paul is "called to be an apostle, set apart for the gospel of God which he promised beforehand through his prophets in the holy Scriptures" (Rom 1:1–2).

The Holy Spirit's Intercession

Paul's ministry takes place within the context of sin, suffering, and the creation's "bondage to decay" (Rom 8:21). In this regard Aquinas emphasizes that Paul's statement that believers "groan inwardly" (Rom 8:23) does not pertain primarily to a wish to escape physical suffering. Rather, the groaning proceeds "inwardly" because, in Aquinas's words, "it is concerned with internal goods,"[50] namely our full sharing in the Trinitarian life, our "adoption as sons, the redemption of our bodies" (Rom 8:23). The experience of "the distress caused by the postponement of something desired with great longing"[51] fuels our hope for its arrival. Because this hope is infused by the Holy Spirit, we are able to wait for the object of our hope "with patience" (Rom 8:25). With regard to our waiting, Paul states that "the Spirit helps us in our weakness; for we do not know how to pray as we ought, but the Spirit himself intercedes for us with sighs too deep for words" (Rom 8:26). This "weakness" might seem to describe primarily the weakness of the flesh, and Aquinas grants that we wait eagerly for the time when "our mortal bodies will be vivified by the Holy Spirit, when our weakness shall be removed from us."[52] Aquinas argues, however, that the "weakness" is primarily a spiritual one, rooted in the fact that "we do not know how to pray as we ought" (Rom 8:26). Our difficulty, says Aquinas, is that we do not know what is spiritually good for us: we may desire wealth that turns out to be spiritually deadly, we may seek "the removal of a thorn of the flesh" that God has given us so as to keep us humble, we may misappre-

---

49. Aquinas, *Super epistolam B. Pauli ad Romanos*, ch. 8, lect. 5, § 678.
50. Ibid., § 679.   51. Ibid.
52. Ibid., § 687.

hend our motives, and so forth.[53] The Holy Spirit therefore "intercedes" (Rom 8:26) for us so that we might accomplish the mission that God has given us.

But is it proper to say that the Holy Spirit, who is God, intercedes with God? Does God intercede with God? Given the divine unity, this would not make sense. Nor could the Holy Spirit emit "sighs too deep for words" (Rom 8:26) unless he were suffering, which would mean that he experiences in himself some lack and in this way is also "subjected to futility" (Rom 8:20). Only a divine Holy Spirit, lacking nothing, could bring about "the glorious liberty of the children of God." Aquinas therefore suggests that Paul intends to describe the Spirit's activity of "directing and inciting our heart"[54] so that our heart longs for heavenly realities. In short, the Holy Spirit "intercedes for the saints according to the will of God" (Rom 8:27) by uniting believers' wills to God's will. Thanks to the assistance of the Holy Spirit, the prayers of believers are no longer weak and misdirected, but rather aim at the heavenly good that believers hope to attain.

Aquinas on Romans 8:28–39

Our study of Aquinas's commentary on Romans 8:1–27 reveals the context for Aquinas's citation of Romans 8:30 in *Summa theologiae* I, question 23: namely, a rich portrait of human transformation through the missions of the Son and the Holy Spirit. This context makes clear that predestination is about God's eternal plan of deification.

Can the divine missions, however, be frustrated? Romans 8:28–39 takes up this issue. Paul argues that God will accomplish what he eternally purposes: "in everything God works for good with those who love him, who are called according to his purpose" (Rom 8:28). As should already be clear, "those who love him" (Rom 8:28) are "the saints" (Rom 8:27), that is, believers who are being sanctified through love. In ordaining from eternity "the good of the universe," Aquinas states, God has in view first and foremost the saints: "the most excellent parts of the universe are God's saints to each of whom applies the word of Matthew [25:23]: 'He will set him over all his goods.'"[55]

Although God neither wills evil nor requires evil in order to accomplish his purposes, he uses the evils that he permits in the world to advance the salvation of the saints, and thereby to bring about the good for which he creates the universe.[56] In this fashion "God works for good with those who love him,"

53. See ibid., § 690.   54. Ibid., § 693.
55. Ibid., lect. 6, § 697.
56. See Michał Paluch, O.P., "'God Permits the Evil for the Good': Two Different Approaches to the History of Salvation in Aquinas and Bonaventure," *Angelicum* 80, no. 2 (2003): 327–36. Paluch

by exercising particular care, through the grace of the Holy Spirit, to ensure that the troubles of "those who love him" ultimately serve the good of their sanctification. As Aquinas notes, "This is obvious in regard to the penal evils which they suffer.... Hence it says in 1 Peter [3:14]: 'If you suffer for righteousness' sake, you will be blessed.'"[57] According to Aquinas, the Holy Spirit turns to good use even the sins of those who love God. Through their sins the Holy Spirit humbles them, and once they have repented they depend more firmly upon God for salvation, rather than trusting proudly in their own strength.[58]

Why is God so merciful to his saints, working out their salvation even despite their sins? Paul begins Romans 8 with a proclamation of mercy: "There is therefore now no condemnation for those who are in Christ Jesus" (Rom 8:1), who are "those who live according to the Spirit" of Christ (Rom 8:5). Likewise, Romans 8 ends with an emphatic affirmation of God's mercy: "For I am sure that neither death, nor life, nor angels, nor principalities, nor things present, nor things to come, nor powers, nor height, nor depth, nor anything else in all creation, will be able to separate us from the love of God in Christ Jesus our Lord" (Rom 8:39). But why are God's saints privileged in this way? Throughout Romans, Paul rules out the notion that salvation derives from human beings: "Then what becomes of our boasting? It is excluded" (Rom 3:27). Salvation is God's "free gift of righteousness" (Rom 5:17), and this free gift comes "through Jesus Christ our Lord" (Rom 5:21).

Romans 8:28 teaches that "those who love" God are those who "are called according to his purpose." In this regard Aquinas notes that God's "purpose" is to lead some human beings to share in the Trinitarian life. To accomplish this purpose of divine adoption, God calls some by sanctifying them. God's "purpose" is his predestining plan, and his "call" is the election of his "saints," namely those whom the Holy Spirit sanctifies and provides with a mission of charity in the Church.

Foreknowledge and Predestination

Aquinas is aware of interpretations of Romans 8:29 that separate "foreknew" and "predestined" so as to argue that the latter refers solely to God's work in time. But he holds that both foreknowledge and predestination are

---

cites Richard Schenk, O.P., *Die Gnade vollendeter Endlichkeit: Zur transzendentaltheologischer Auslegung der thomanischen Anthropologie* (Freiburg: Herder, 1989), 286–442. Comparing Bonaventure and Aquinas, Paluch observes that "for Bonaventure, it is much easier to say that good brought forth out of evil is 'greater' than the good that was lost" (329). Aquinas strongly emphasizes that God does not need evil in order to accomplish good, although God brings forth good out of evil.

57. Aquinas, *Super epistolam B. Pauli ad Romanos*, ch. 8, lect. 6, § 697.

58. See ibid., § 698.

eternal, differing only conceptually: "foreknowledge implies only the knowledge of future things, whereas predestination implies causality in regard to them."[59] This conceptual distinction has value for understanding the difference between God's permission and his predestination; he can foreknow many things that he has not predestined, and so predestination does not apply to sins. Aquinas remarks that "some say that foreknowledge of good and of evil merits is the reason for predestination and reprobation, in the sense that God predestines certain ones, because he foresees that they will act well and believe in Christ."[60] But to reach this conclusion, Aquinas points out, one would have to rewrite Romans 8:29 as "Those whom he foreknew to be conformed to the image of his Son, he also predestined." When people "act well and believe in Christ," Aquinas notes, they do so because they "are led by the Spirit of God" (Rom 8:14). It follows that "predestination" has to do with *all* the effects of grace in human life, and cannot refer solely to the final reward of human faith and charity. Paul's teachings about the Holy Spirit's actions in the lives of "those who are in Christ Jesus" (Rom 8:1) would be overturned were one to claim that our good works, foreknown by God, bring about our "predestination."

As Aquinas shows, the view that "predestination" pertains solely to the final reward (of foreseen merits) would mean both "that grace is given because of our merits, and that the source of our good works is from us and their consummation from God."[61] Aquinas thus opposes this position not simply because of its Pelagianism, but because of its crimped view of the Trinity's work, from eternity, for our salvation. Predestination includes the whole path by which humans reach the consummation of glory.

Just as predestination specifies God's foreknowledge, so also being "conformed to the image of his Son" (Rom 8:29) specifies God's predestination. As we have seen, predestination entails adopting human persons "into the sonship of God"[62] by the grace of the Holy Spirit. What does such conformity, or adoptive sonship, mean for the human person? Aquinas identifies two aspects

59. Ibid., § 702.

60. Ibid., § 703. For discussion of §§ 703–6, see Jean-Pierre Torrell, O.P., *Saint Thomas Aquinas*, vol. 2: *Spiritual Master*, trans. Robert Royal (Washington, D.C.: The Catholic University of America Press, 2003), 143–44. For Aquinas on reprobation see Paluch, *La profondeur de l'amour divin*, 205–6. Paluch notes that Aquinas's *Commentary on the Sentences* adopts "a conception of reprobation that is near to the conception *post praevisa demerita*" (205), whereas "the texts of the *Summa Theologiae* suggest the 'simultaneity' of the divine decision and of the choice of the free will" (206).

61. Aquinas, *Super epistolam B. Pauli ad Romanos*, ch. 8, lect. 6, § 703. See Catalina Bermudez, "Predestinazione, grazia e libertà nei commenti di san Tommaso alle lettere di san Paolo," *Annales theologici* 4, no. 2 (1990): 399–421, at 406–7.

62. Aquinas, *Super epistolam B. Pauli ad Romanos*, ch. 8, lect. 6, § 704.

of the perfected image of God: sharing the Son's inheritance, and sharing his splendor. Both the Son's inheritance and his splendor are the divine glory, and so being "conformed to the image of his Son" means deification. We become like the divine Image (the Son) by grace, something that is possible because we are created in the image of God. Along these lines, Aquinas explains Paul's statement that God willed to make his incarnate Son "the first-born among many brethren" (Rom 8:29). By our human nature, we receive a participation in God's goodness; by the grace of the Holy Spirit, we participate in the sonship of the Son (insofar as we are being deified). Aquinas states, "Therefore, Christ has us as brothers, both because he communicated to us a likeness of his sonship and because he assumed the likeness of our nature, as it says in Hebrews [2:17]: 'He had to be made like his brethren in every respect.'"[63]

All humans, however, bear the image of God. Should not God then predestine *all* humans "to be conformed to the image of his Son" (Rom 8:29)? In other words, can we accept, as an accurate interpretation of Paul, Aquinas's conceptual distinction between foreknowledge and predestination? On the basis of his view that God's knowledge encompasses everything whereas God's predestination includes only the effects of the grace of the Holy Spirit, Aquinas argues that Paul "says, 'those whom he foreknew he also predestined' not because he predestines all the foreknown, but because he could not predestine them, unless he foreknew them."[64] But Romans 8:29 seems to connect those whom God "foreknew" with "those who love him" (Rom 8:28). If so, "foreknew" and "predestined" would be synonyms. If they are synonyms, then since God foreknows everyone, would not everyone be predestined? Or does Paul use both "foreknew" and "predestined" to refer simply to "all who are led by the Spirit of God" (Rom 8:14)?

Paul suggests that God "foreknew" and "predestined" only "those who love him" (Rom 8:28), namely those who are "in Christ Jesus" (Rom 8:1) and "live according to the Spirit" (Rom 8:5).[65] As we have seen, not all humans participate in the Son and Spirit in this way: "For the mind that is set on the flesh is hostile to God; it does not submit to God's law, indeed it cannot; and those who are in the flesh cannot please God.... Any one who does not have the Spirit of Christ does not belong to him" (Rom 8:7–9). Paul knows that some minds are indeed "set on the flesh." In order not to be "set on the flesh," human minds and hearts need to be "called," that is, to be converted.

According to Aquinas, therefore, "predestined" refers to God's eternal plan for uniting some humans to himself in time, while "called" indicates the man-

---

63. Ibid., § 706.   64. Ibid., § 705.
65. For discussion of Aquinas's mode of interpreting Paul's argument in Romans 8:5–6, see O'Connor, "St Thomas's Commentary on Romans," 333–34.

ner in which humans enter into this union. For this reason Aquinas speaks of a twofold call: the external preaching of the Gospel (including Christ's own preaching), and the internal "impulse of the mind whereby a man's heart is moved by God to assent to the things of faith or of virtue."[66] Without this internal call—predestined "from eternity" among "those things which are to be done in time by the grace of God"[67]—we could not turn our hearts, weighed down by sin, to God. In this regard Aquinas quotes two supportive biblical texts, "No one can come to me unless the Father who sent me draws him" (Jn 6:44) and "Turn us to thyself, O Lord, that we may be turned" (Lam 5:21). Since predestination involves not only conversion but also all steps along the path of deification, Aquinas notes that those "who are called according to his purpose" (Rom 8:28) assent to God's call, so that they are "justified" and "glorified" (Rom 8:30) unto eternal life.

But do all those who assent to God's call receive glorification? Is it impossible to say no to God in this life, once one has said yes? Predestination, Aquinas points out again, pertains to the whole life of the human being, rather than pertaining solely to an initial grace or to a final reward. The "predestined" are those whom God, from eternity, wills to draw into union with himself by the infusion of grace that causes "growth in virtue and grace" and ultimately "exaltation to glory."[68] If the predestination of Christ's Body could be frustrated in time, then one could no longer say with Paul that "in everything God works for good with those who love him, who are called according to his purpose" (Rom 8:28). Indeed, Paul makes radical claims about the efficacy of God's love: "If God is for us, who is against us? He who did not spare his own Son but gave him up for us all, will he not also give us all things with him? Who shall bring any charge against God's elect? It is God who justifies; who is to condemn?" (Rom 8:31–34).[69] Without overthrowing our freedom, God's love accomplishes what God eternally wills to do "for us."

---

66. Aquinas, *Super epistolam B. Pauli ad Romanos*, ch. 8, lect. 6, § 707. See Bermudez, "Predestinazione, grazia e libertà nei commenti di san Tommaso alle lettere di san Paolo," 407.

67. *ST* III, q. 24, a. 1.

68. Aquinas, *Super epistolam B. Pauli ad Romanos*, ch. 8, lect. 6, § 709.

69. In Beker's view, Paul proclaims not only the ultimate triumph of God over the powers of evil, but also universal salvation and the impossibility of the soul's continued existence until the final consummation of all things: see Beker, "Suffering and Triumph in Paul's Letter to the Romans," 118. Beker here goes well beyond Paul's text; more restrained is Byrne's comment on Romans 11:32: "Paul does not have primarily in view all human beings taken in an individual sense; the sense is communal: 'all—that is, Jews as well as Gentiles'" (Byrne, *Romans*, 353). For agreement with Byrne, see G. R. Beasley-Murray, "The Righteousness of God in the History of Israel and the Nations: Romans 9–11," *Review and Expositor* 73, no. 4 (1976): 437–50, at 450. See also Jeremy Cohen, "The Mystery of Israel's Salvation: Romans 11:25–26 in Patristic and Medieval Exegesis," *Harvard Theological Review* 98 (2005): 247–81.

The Unity of Those Who Are in Christ Jesus

For Paul, Aquinas emphasizes, predestination is not an abstract doctrine about an abstract divine plan. Rather, the "predestined" are those who participate fully in the temporal missions of the Son and the Holy Spirit; predestination is the plan of Trinitarian gifting, by which we are configured in charity to Christ.[70] After observing that "those whom he foreknew he also predestined to be conformed to the image of his Son, in order that he might be the first-born among many brethren" (Rom 8:29), Paul asks, "What then shall we say to this?" (Rom 8:31). Aquinas comments that Paul means for us to share in his "amazement" regarding the "great blessings" that God bestows and that no creature can nullify.[71] By far the greatest such blessing is Christ Jesus, whom God gave up to death "for us all" (Rom 8:32). Aquinas reminds us that Christ Jesus does not stand outside the order of predestination: rather, as the Son of God he predestines, and as man he is predestined and is the cause of our predestination.

For this reason his Paschal mystery "for us" cannot be separated from its fruits. Noting that "in the Son of God all things exist in their primordial and pre-operative cause: 'He is before all things and in him all things hold together' (Col 1:17)," Aquinas links this Christological ontology with Paul's soteriological reflection on God the Father: "He who did not spare his own Son, but gave him up for us all, will he not also give us all things with him?" (Rom 8:32).[72] As Aquinas shows, these "all things" are the graces that flow in time from God's eternal salvific causality. Paul is primarily referring, Aquinas says, to "the divine persons to enjoy" and "rational spirits to live with"[73]—although in some way nothing is left out of "all things," since "in everything God works for good with those who love him" (Rom 8:28).

Thus the eternal action according to which God "foreknew," "predestined," "called," "justified," and "glorified" brings about the unity of "those

---

70. Erich Dinkler comments, "The essential connection of chapters 9–11 with 8:28 ff. makes evident that God's *election* comes to us as grace *in and through Christ Jesus*, that God's election and predestination are Christological-soteriological categories, concrete in divine grace and in human faith.... And when we look to the connection with 12:1, 2, we become aware that election includes free decision and individual responsibility." Dinkler, "The Historical and Eschatological Israel in Romans Chapters 9–11: A Contribution to the Problem of Pre-Destination and Individual Responsibility," *Journal of Religion* 36 (1956): 109–27, at 124.

71. Aquinas, *Super epistolam B. Pauli ad Romanos*, ch. 8, lect. 6, § 711.

72. Ibid., § 714. For Paul's allusion to the near-sacrifice of Isaac in Genesis 22, see Nils Alstrup Dahl, "The Atonement—An Adequate Reward for the Akedah? (Ro 8:32)," in *Neotestamentica et Semitica: Studies in Honor of Matthew Black*, ed. E. Earle Ellis and Max Wilcox (Edinburgh: T&T Clark, 1969), 15–29.

73. Aquinas, *Super epistolam B. Pauli ad Romanos*, ch. 8, lect. 6, § 714.

who are in Christ Jesus" (Rom 8:1). Affirming that "when he [Jesus] was given up for us, all things were given to us," Aquinas suggests that the predestination described in Romans 8 can be summed up by 1 Corinthians 3:22–23: "all are yours; and you are Christ's; and Christ is God's."[74] In this vein he emphasizes that Paul has in view "divine election"[75] in history, an election according to which Christ Jesus bears our punishment, takes away our sin, and "intercedes for us" (Rom 8:34). Now that we have been freed from guilt by such a powerful advocate, our election rests upon the most secure ground. Aquinas emphasizes that "God bestows great benefits on his holy ones, and when we consider them, such love of Christ burns in our hearts that nothing can quench it: 'Many waters cannot quench love' (Song of Songs 8:7)."[76]

This does not mean that the election of God's holy ones in Christ grants them worldly peace; on the contrary, Paul quotes Psalm 44:22, "for thy sake we are slain all the day long, and accounted as sheep for the slaughter" (cf. Rom 8:36). If history remains a terrain of suffering for God's holy people, how then is election secure? Aquinas replies that "we do not succeed by our own strength but through Christ's help; hence he [Paul] adds: 'through him who loved us' [Rom 8:37], i.e., on account of his help or on account of the affection we have for him; 'not as though we first loved him, but because he first loved us' (1 Jn 4:19)."[77]

Conclusion

Even more than *Summa theologiae* I, question 23, Aquinas's commentary on Romans 8 makes clear that were one to suppose that "predestination" means merely an aloof divine decision to save some individual human beings, one would have profoundly misunderstood the doctrine. As Aquinas recognizes, for Paul the God who "foreknew" and "predestined" is none other than the Son and Holy Spirit whose temporal missions lead us to the Father. In and through these divine missions, with their manifold temporal effects, we find our mission of faith, hope, and charity. As Paul urges the Church in Rome, "For by the grace given to me I bid every one among you not to think of himself more highly than he ought to think, but to think with sober judgment, each according to the measure of faith which God has assigned him" (Rom 12:3). God assigns us our "measure of faith" so that in the people of God "our boasting ... is excluded" (Rom 3:27); "otherwise," as Paul says, "grace would not be grace" (Rom 11:6).

74. Ibid.
76. Ibid., § 722.

75. Ibid., lect. 7, § 716.
77. Ibid., § 725.

We receive salvation as "one body in Christ" (Rom 12:5) because from eternity, God "foreknew" and "predestined" the accomplishment in Christ's Body of "the free gift of God" that is "eternal life in Christ Jesus our Lord" (Rom 6:23). The many graced individuals who comprise this "one body"— Paul greets by name Phoebe, Prisca, Aquila, Epaenetus, Mary, Adronicus, and many others (Rom 16)—receive their unity from the Spirit of Jesus Christ: "If the Spirit of him who raised Jesus from the dead dwells in you, he who raised Christ Jesus from the dead will give life to your mortal bodies also through his Spirit who dwells in you" (Rom 8:11). The activity of the Son and Spirit in those whom God "foreknew" and "predestined" accomplishes our salvation by giving us the life of faith and charity in the Body of Christ. It is for this reason that Paul rejoices: "If God is for us, who is against us? He who did not spare his own Son but gave him up for us all, will he not also give us all things with him? Who shall bring any charge against God's elect? It is God who justifies; who is to condemn?" (Rom 8:31–34).

Does Paul have a doctrine of "predestination"? In Aquinas's sense of the word, I hope to have shown, Paul certainly does.[78] As a Christological and pneumatological reality, predestination consists in our being taken up into the missions of the Son and Spirit. But can this doctrine be affirmed by Christians if it implies that some individuals do not receive the gift of salvation? Why is it that Paul receives "the Spirit of sonship" (Rom 8:15), while God permits others to reject his Spirit and instead remain in their sins? Commenting on Romans 11:33–36, Aquinas notes that contemplating the judgments of God does not provide Paul with the key to unlock the mystery of salvation and sin. Rather, Paul finds himself drawn further into theological humility: "Above the Apostle endeavored to assign a reason for the divine judgments, by which Gentiles and Jews obtain mercy after unbelief; now he recognizes his inadequacy for such an investigation and exclaims his admiration of the divine excellence."[79] We find ourselves in the same position.

78. Cf. Lee H. Yearley, "St. Thomas Aquinas on Providence and Predestination," *Anglican Theological Review* 49, no. 4 (1967): 420–22. G. B. Caird argues that not only predestination, but also salvation by our free response to grace and universal salvation are defended by Paul in Romans 9–11. In Caird's view, Paul's position requires that we affirm both predestination by grace and the necessity of human free response for salvation; and, while not becoming universalists, we cannot allow ourselves "to set limits to the scope of God's love or to blur the vision of His ultimate victory" (Caird, "Predestination—Romans ix.–xi.," *Expository Times* 68, no. 11 [1956–57]: 324–27, at 327). Caird's position is much closer to Aquinas's than Caird seems to think.

79. Aquinas, *Super epistolam B. Pauli ad Romanos*, ch. 11, lect. 5, § 933. Cf. Dinkler, "The Historical and the Eschatological Israel in Romans Chapters 9–11," 125, as well as my *Predestination: Biblical and Theological Paths* (Oxford: Oxford University Press, 2011).

Bruce D. Marshall

12 *Beatus vir*

Aquinas, Romans 4, and the Role of
"Reckoning" in Justification

Transformation and Imputation

Since the sixteenth century it has often seemed that the theological reading
of Scripture yields two quite different ways of thinking about the justification
of the sinner. One centers on holiness, the other on forgiveness; one on God's
interior work, the other on his exterior word; one on love, the other on faith;
one is Catholic, the other Protestant. These two different ways of looking at
justification go by various names. The one focusing on holiness is often called
an "ontological" account of justification, the one focusing on forgiveness a
"forensic" or "juridical" account. It might be more helpful to call the former
a "transformational" theology of justification, and the latter a "dispositional" theology. The one centers on God's loving transformation of sinners into
saints, the other on God's merciful disposition to forgive sinners who daily
prove that they are not saints.

Both views of justification can and do appeal to the teaching of St. Paul,
especially that of the letter to the Romans. Each, moreover, is clearly aware
that Paul's teaching contains both "transformational" and "dispositional" elements. From the time of the Reformation, however, each view has tended to
play one element off against the other.

So the Council of Trent, for example, defines the formal cause of justification as the righteousness or justice of God *(iustitia Dei)*. "Formal cause" here
means whatever quality or characteristic makes it possible correctly to attribute to a person the righteousness sufficient for salvation. This is not, Trent
observes, the *iustitia* by which God himself is formally just, that is, the divine
attribute of justice that makes God just and is the supreme measure of all justice. This is unique to God, an aspect of the divine nature, and so can never be

possessed by a creature. The formal cause of our justification is that *iustitia* by which God makes *us* just or righteous, the justice he gives us rather than the justice he himself has and is.[1]

So far the two views are on the same page, but Trent immediately goes on to say that having received the gift of this righteousness from God, "we not only are reckoned to be just, but truly are just, and are rightly described as such."[2] Consequently, as the relevant canon later insists, any claim that human beings are justified "by the imputation of Christ's righteousness alone, or by the forgiveness *(remissione)* of sins alone ... or that the grace by which we are justified is merely the favor of God," must be rejected as against the Catholic faith. God's imputation, forgiveness, and favorable disposition toward us are not enough for justification. They have their place, but there is no justification of the ungodly "without the grace and love which have been poured into our hearts by the Holy Spirit, and inhere therein"—an invocation of Romans 5:5, one of the favorite Pauline texts in transformational theologies of justification.[3] Trent evidently grants that justification must include dispositional or juridical elements, but it does so mainly by insisting that these are not *sufficient* for justification. What positive role this part of the Apostle's teaching on justification might play is not explicitly discussed. It is, in other words, left open or undecided, a subject for further theological reflection, of which there has been much.

By contrast, Romans 4 belongs among the favorite texts of dispositional or forensic ways of thinking about justification, with its extended treatment of the faith of Abraham, prompted by Genesis 15:6. Faith was "reckoned to him as righteousness" (4:3, 9, 22) without any works, entitling us to believe that we, like Abraham, will be counted righteous before God not as the reward due our works, but by faith in him who justifies the ungodly (cf. 4:5, 23–24). Thus the Augsburg Confession teaches that we are not justified "by our own

1. Session VI, Decree on Justification, ch. 7: "Demum unica formalis causa est iustitia Dei, non qua ipse iustus est, sed qua nos iustos facit." *Enchiridion symbolorum definitionum et declarationum de rebus fidei et morum*, ed. Heinrich Denzinger and Peter Hünermann, 40th ed. (Freiburg: Herder, 2005), 1529 (hereafter DH). This thought stems from Augustine, and had also been invoked regularly by the Protestant reformers: "Dicitur etiam iustitia dei non solum illa qua ipse iustus est sed quam dat homini cum iustificat impium." *De trinitate* XIV.xii.15, ed. W. J. Mountain and Fr. Glorie, Corpus Christianorum Series Latina 50A (Turnhout: Brepols, 1968), 443.15–17.

2. "Non modo reputamur, sed vere iusti nominamur et sumus" (DH 1529).

3. Canon 11: "Si quis dixerit, homines iustificari vel sola imputatione iustitiae Christi, vel sola peccatorum remissione, exclusa gratia et caritate, quae in cordibus eorum per Spiritum Sanctum diffundatur atque illis inhaereat, aut etiam gratiam, qua iustificamur, esse tantum favorem Dei: anathema sit" (DH 1561). Cf. ch. 7: "[I]ustificatio ipsa ... non est sola peccatorum remissio, sed et sanctificatio et renovatio interioris hominis per voluntariam susceptionem gratiae" (DH 1528).

merit, work, and satisfaction." Instead by faith in Christ "our sins are forgiven for his sake, and justice and eternal life are given to us. For God will count and reckon this faith as justice in his sight, as St. Paul teaches in Rom 3–4."[4] The Augsburg Confession seems to teach that God's reckoning or imputation of righteousness to us through faith *is* sufficient for justification. In its article on justification Paul's teaching on the interior transformation of the sinner by the grace of the indwelling Holy Spirit is passed over in silence. What positive role this element in Paul might play in the justification of the ungodly is thus left as an open question, a subject for further theological debate, of which there has been much.

Since the sixteenth century friend and foe alike have usually taken St. Thomas as the most important and convincing advocate of a transformational understanding of justification. He is thus more or less automatically aligned with one side of the post-Reformation debate about how to understand St. Paul's teaching on justification. Thomas is the Catholic theologian who knows surpassingly well how to articulate the thoroughgoing necessity and efficacy of God's grace for justification and salvation, but who falls short (as his foes, at least, maintain) of doing similar justice to the dispositional element in Paul, especially in Romans and Galatians—to God's mercy in accounting us righteous through faith in Christ, despite our sins.

Thomas, of course, wrote well before the transformational and dispositional themes in Paul's teaching on justification came to be played off against one another, and their apparent opposition virtually institutionalized. It is worth asking, therefore, what he makes of Paul's language about faith being "reckoned" as righteousness, and of the believer's sins being "covered" rather than "imputed" (cf. Rom 4:7–8). Does he really overlook the dispositional or juridical side of Paul's teaching? If not, does he see a conflict between interior transformation and external imputation—or does each have its own proper role in a coherent theology of justification? The *Lectura* on Romans 4 is obviously a good place to start.

4. *Confessio Augustana* IV (G): "[W]ir Vergebung der Sunde und Gerechtigkeit vor Gott nicht erlangen mogen durch unser Verdienst, Werk und Genugtun, sonder ... umb Christus willen durch den Glauben, so wir glauben, daß Christus fur uns gelitten habe und daß uns umb seinen willen die Sunde vergeben [Latin: *remitti*], Gerechtigkeit und ewiges Leben geschenkt wird. Dann diesen Glauben will Gott fur Gerechtigkeit vor ihme halten und zurechnen [Lat.: *imputat*], wie Sant Paul sagt tun Romern am 3. und 4." *Die Bekenntnisschriften der evangelisch-lutherischen Kirche*, 8th ed. (Göttingen: Vandenhoeck & Ruprecht, 1979), 56.

"Reckoning" as God's Recognition of Justice

As Thomas reads Paul, the opening verses of Romans 4 aim to show that Abraham does have glory before God, but not in the way we might expect. Abraham has what leads to glory, that is, to fully glorifying union with God, namely justice or righteousness. This requires that he be justified by faith, and not by the works of the law, since no act of which human beings are capable by their natural powers can generate that interior "justice which has glory in the eyes of God."[5] For just this reason, on Aquinas's reading, St. Paul insists (cf. Rom 4:2) that the justice Abraham had from works of the law may have brought glory before men, who see only the outward deed, but it brought none before God, who sees within.[6] When Paul initially says that "Abraham believed God and it was reckoned to him as justice" (4:3), therefore, it means that God "regarded it as justice that [Abraham] believed," and in this way, rather than by the works of the law, Abraham "had glory before God."[7]

Here, God's reckoning that Abraham is just *(est ei reputatum)* is not a counterfactual judgment on God's part, a covering or ignoring of Abraham's sin. It is, rather, God's perception or recognition of the sober truth about Abraham. Faith, as St. Thomas likes to say, is "the first motion of the mind

---

5. "Iustitia quae habet gloriam apud Deum, ordinatur ad bonum divinum, scilicet futurae gloriae, quae facultatem humanam excedit." *Super epistolam ad Romanos Lectura*, in *S. Thomae Aquinatis Super Epistolas S. Pauli Lectura*, ed. Raphaelis Cai, O.P., vol. 1, 8th ed. (Rome: Marietti, 1953), 1:5–230, *In ad Rom.* 4, lect. 1 (§ 325). (All citations of Aquinas's commentaries on Paul are from this two-volume Marietti edition.)

6. *In ad Rom.* 4, lect. 1 (§ 324), commenting on Rom. 4:2: "Quaesitum est quid Abraham invenit secundum carnalem circumcisionem, et manifestum est quod hoc non invenit ut iustificatus sit 'ex operibus legis,' ita scilicet quod eius iustitia in operibus legis consistat; 'habet quidem gloriam,' scilicet apud homines, qui exteriora facta vident, 'sed non apud Deum' qui videt in occulto" (the Latin text used by Aquinas has "works *of the law*" in Rom. 4:2, though the Vulgate simply says "ex operibus").

Aquinas's argument here (nos. 324–25 of the Romans *Lectura*) might be taken to suggest that the law of Moses (or the "old law," as Aquinas generally puts it) did not require supernatural grace to be obeyed. Rather, since Aquinas correlates it with a justice that does not "exceed human capability" *(facultatem humanam excedit)*, the old law apparently could be observed by our natural powers. Thomas's concern, though, is to insist that the justice that counts before God must be given by God, and cannot be caused by human acts apart from the grace of justification. "Et ideo opera hominis non sunt proportionata ad huius iustitiae habitum causandum, sed oportet prius iustificari interius cor hominis a Deo, ut opera faciat proportionata divinae gloriae" (*In ad Rom.* 4, lect. 1 [§ 325]). The effect is to emphasize, rather than undermine, the need for grace to keep the law. The law can genuinely be kept only by the person who is just before God, and only those are just before God whom God himself justifies. On this see also *Summa Theologiae* I-II, q. 100, a. 12, co. (in part a commentary on Rom. 4:2) and q. 109, a. 4, co.

7. "Et sic patet quod apud Deum, a quo est ei reputatum ad iustitiam quod credidit, gloriam habet." *In ad Rom.* 4, 1 (§ 327).

into God."[8] By it we subject that which is most noble in us, our mind, to God. The justice Paul finds in Abraham's faith consists in precisely this willing submission of the mind to what God teaches.

Justice, after all, is essentially rendering what is due. Every creature owes all that it is and has to God. The creature's justice consists, therefore, in "rendering" all that it is and has to God. This the creature does by being fully conformed—subject—to God's intention for it, which depends on the sort of creature it is. The highest gift God has given human nature is the mind. Our supreme justice therefore consists in the complete subjection of our mind to God. This happens by faith, which believes what God tells us.[9] Since God's intention for us is eternal felicity in union with him, the faith that initiates our conformity to God is, as Aquinas says elsewhere, the real beginning *(inchoatio)* of eternal life—perfect conformity—in us.[10] So when God looks upon believing Abraham he first of all sees not sin that needs to be covered, but real justice, that interior renewal of the heart by which the believer can do what he could never do on his own: bring forth "works proportioned to divine glory."[11]

Of course in seeing this justice in Abraham God simply looks upon what he himself has caused. We certainly do not merit justice by faith, rather "belief itself is the first act of justice which God works in us."[12] But so far God's

8. "Primus motus mentis in Deum est per fidem," citing Heb 11:6. Aquinas continues: "Unde et ipsa fides quasi prima pars iustitiae est nobis a Deo." *In ad Rom.* 3, lect. 3 (§ 302).

9. So Aquinas argues in his exegesis of Gal 3:6, where, as in Rom 4, Paul introduces Gen 15:6 in support of the point that Abraham was just or righteous by faith rather than by the works of the law. "Summa iustitia est reddere Deo quod suum est.... Dei autem est quidquid est in homine, et intellectus et voluntas et ipsum corpus; sed tamen quodam ordine, quia inferiora ordinantur ad superiora, et exteriora ad interiora, scilicet ad bonum animae; supremum autem in homine est mens. Et ideo primum in iustitia hominis est, quod mens hominis Deo subdatur, et hoc fit per fidem. II Cor 10:3: 'in captivitatem redigentes omnem intellectum in obsequium Christi.'" *Super epistolam B. Pauli ad Galatas lectura* 3, lect. 3 (§ 130).

10. "Si quis ergo in formam definitionis huiusmodi verba [Heb 11:1] reducere velit, potest dicere quod fides est habitus mentis, qua inchoatur vita aeterna in nobis, faciens intellectum assentire non apparentibus." *Summa theologiae (ST)* II-II, q. 4, a. 1, co.

11. *In ad Rom.* 4, lect. 1 (§ 325): "Oportet prius iustificari interius cor hominis a Deo, ut opera faciat proportionata divinae gloriae." Cf. *Super epistolam B. Pauli ad Titum lectura* 3, lect. 1 (§ 94): "Idem autem est iustificati et quod prius dixerat regenerati. In iustificatione impii sunt duo termini, scilicet a quo, qui est remissio culpae, et haec est renovatio, et ad quem, qui est infusio gratiae, et hoc ad regenerationem pertinet. Dicit ergo: ideo verbum caro factum est, ut iustificati, id est renovati per gratiam, quia iustificatio non fit sine gratia." These two aspects of justification, leaving the terminus a quo *(renovatio)* and attaining the terminus ad quem *(regeneratio)* are also related as putting off our old corrupt nature and receiving a new one, by participation in the divine nature. "Sciendum est, quod homo indigebat duobus in statu perditionis, quae consecutus est per Christum, scilicet participatione divinae naturae, et depositione vetustatis" (§ 92).

12. Faith "will be counted" *(computabitur)* as righteousness (cf. Rom 4:5), on Thomas's reading of Rom 4, "non quidem ita quod per fidem iustitiam mereatur, sed quia ipsum credere est primus actus iustitiae quam Deus in eo operatur." *In ad Rom.* 4, lect. 1 (§ 331).

reckoning or "reputation" of faith as righteousness seems to play a minor, even redundant, role in Thomas's understanding of Abraham's justification, and so also of ours. Obviously God regards Abraham as just, because he is, and God knows this better than anybody. So understood, "reckoning" involves no voluntary or dispositional element on God's part at all. It simply notes the fact that here, as always, God sees things just as they are.

Aquinas's Terminology

"Reckoning," "imputation," and kindred concepts do, however, play a more significant role in Thomas's theology of justification than has so far come to light. For Thomas justification is properly identified as the remission of sins *(remissio peccatorum)*.[13] To remit sin or guilt, Thomas stresses in the *De malo*, "is nothing other than not to impute sin," or not to reckon it to the sinner. This Aquinas takes to be the clear teaching of Scripture, citing the very passage from the Psalter on which Paul dwells in Romans 4. "Blessed is the man to whom the Lord does not impute sin," says the Psalmist, which Aquinas interprets as a clarifying explanation of the preceding phrase, "Blessed are those whose iniquities are remitted" (Ps 31[32]:1).[14] Given this equation of "remission" with the non-imputation or non-reckoning of sins, it seems quite in order to render

13. Justification is a movement, a transition from a state of sin to a state of justice, and as such is most properly identified by the point at which the movement aims, namely the removal of sin and guilt. See *ST* I-II, q. 113, a. 1, co.; a. 6, co. & ad 1.

This may seem to create a conflict with Thomas's interpretation of Tit. 3, (above, note 11), but the contradiction is only apparent. Thomas observes that we can speak of justification as beginning with the remission of sins, and ending with the infusion of grace (thus *In ad Tit.* 3, lect. 1 [§ 94]), and, conversely, as beginning with the infusion of grace, and ending with the remission of sins (thus I-II, q. 113, a. 1, co.). Both are true, depending on whether one considers justification from the point of view of the justified sinner *(ex parte mobilis*, as Thomas says), in which case the remission of sins is the *terminus a quo* of justification and the infusion of grace its *terminus ad quem*, or from the point of view of God who justifies the sinner *(ex parte agentis)*, in which case the infusion of grace is the *terminus a quo*, and the remission of sins the *terminus ad quem*. See I-II, q. 113, a. 8, ad 1: "Recessus a termino et accessus ad terminum dupliciter considerari possunt. Uno modo, ex parte mobilis. Et sic naturaliter recessus a termino praecedit accessum ad terminum, prius enim est in subiecto mobili oppositum quod abiicitur, et postmodum est id quod per motum assequitur mobile. Sed ex parte agentis, est e converso. Agens enim per formam quae in eo praeexistit, agit ad removendum contrarium, sicut sol per suam lucem agit ad removendum tenebras...Et quia infusio gratiae et remissio culpae dicuntur ex parte Dei iustificantis, ideo ordine naturae prior est gratiae infusio quam culpae remissio. Sed si sumantur ea quae sunt ex parte hominis iustificati, est e converso, nam prius est naturae ordine liberatio a culpa, quam consecutio gratiae iustificantis."

14. *Quaestiones disputatae de malo* 7, a. 11, co.: "Oportet preintelligere quid sit peccatum remitti; quod nichil est aliud quam peccatum non imputari: unde in Psalmo [31:1-2] cum praemisisset: 'Beati quorum remisse sunt iniquitates' quasi exponens subdit 'beatus vir cui non imputavit dominus peccatum'" (Leonine ed., 23:186.172-77).

remissio as "forgiveness," God's willingness not to hold our sins against us.

In order to understand what Aquinas is getting at here, we need some terminological clarifications. Thomas has a complex concept of sin *(peccatum)*, but at its heart is *culpa*—fault or guilt. He often, in fact, uses *culpa* and *peccatum* interchangeably, allowing the chief part of sin to stand for the whole.[15] He can also distinguish, however, not only sin from guilt, but both from evil *(malum)*, finding in each notion a different nuance of human acts and dispositions. Aquinas talks this way, distinguishing these basic terms in some contexts and using them interchangeably in others, because in agents with will, as he sees it, sin, guilt, and evil (that is, evil committed, as distinguished from evil suffered) are coextensive. Any free act is either good, right, and praiseworthy, or evil, sinful, and blameworthy.[16] A genuinely voluntary act must have one or the other of these two mutually exclusive sets of characteristics, and if it has any one characteristic in either set, it has the other two. One and the same evil act, in other words, is both sinful and blameworthy (the agent's fault), but in different respects (or, as Thomas puts it, under different *rationes*). The act is sin *(peccatum)* in that it deviates from the proper aim of free action, namely the enjoyment of God as the supreme good of the creature, it is fault or guilt *(culpa)* in that this deviation originates in the volition of the agent, and it is evil *(malum)* in that it harms the agent, opening up a self-inflicted wound that diminishes the intrinsic goodness of the agent. The same goes, with the values reversed, for a good act.[17]

That to which we properly attribute guilt or fault, the subject of *culpa*, is always the action of a voluntary agent. "Guilt is the evil of the action itself," Thomas stresses, as distinguished from punishment or penalty *(poena)*, which "is the evil of the agent," who suffers the loss of desired goods as a consequence of his culpable actions (see below).[18] *Culpa* is a fact, an objective state of affairs about a voluntary action, namely its disorder or defect as measured by divine

15. Thus, for example, *ST* I-II, q. 113, a. 6, s.c. & co., where "remissio peccatorum" (s.c.) is clearly equivalent to "remissio culpae" (co.).

16. "Bonum vel malum in solis actibus voluntariis constituit rationem laudis vel culpae; in quibus idem est malum, peccatum et culpa." *ST* I-II, 21, 2, co.

17. "Sic igitur patet quod actus bonus vel malus habet rationem laudabilis vel culpabilis, secundum quod est in potestate voluntatis; rationem vero rectitudinis et peccati, secundum ordinem ad finem." *ST* I-II, q. 21, a. 3, co.

18. *De malo* 1, a. 4, co.: "Culpa est malum ipsius actionis, pena autem est malum agentis ... ex malo actionis quod est culpa, sequitur malum agentis quod est pena" (Leonine ed., 23:20.173–74, 179–80). Cf. ad 7: "Malum autem culpe formaliter [that is, by definition] est priuatio modi, speciei et ordinis in ipso actu uoluntatis" (Leonine ed., 21.254–56). See also *ST* I, q. 48, a. 5, co. & ad 4; a. 6, co. As Thomas observes in these passages, an existent actually has a twofold "act," namely its form (the "first act") and the operation it undertakes as the perfection of that form (the "second act"). *Culpa* belongs to the second act *(operatio)*, *poena* to the first.

law.[19] More precisely, guilt for Thomas is the failure of a free act to fit with the agent's highest good, which in the case of creatures with will is the total subjection to their volition to the will of God. "Properly speaking the evil of guilt is opposed to the uncreated good itself, for it is contrary to the fulfillment of the divine will."[20] Guilt is not, therefore, to be equated or confused with any of the subjective dispositions or attitudes that ought to attend it, but often do not, such as sorrow, remorse, or contrition.

There is, to be sure, also a kind of sin for which we are genuinely culpable, even though it is not our own act as discrete individuals, but rather a disordered disposition of our human nature as such: original sin. This complicates the idea that *culpa* is attributable only to voluntary acts, but does not, as Thomas sees it, contradict that axiom. We are not, with respect to our human nature, simply discrete individuals, as though the coming into being of each of us was the origin of a new species. We receive our humanity from others who already have it, and so our humanity makes us first of all members of a body stemming from the first human being—Adam—and only as such discrete agents. By making us members of a body derived from Adam, our humanity makes us participants in Adam's voluntary act of sin, in roughly the way the hand participates in a violent deed originating in the soul, and so can, with the human organism as a whole, be held guilty for it.[21] Much, of course, might be said about this, but for present purposes we only need to observe that St. Thomas does not think original sin is, in the end, an exception to the rule that *culpa* is always voluntary.[22]

The concept of "imputation" or "reckoning"—*imputare* or *reputare*—has its home, on Thomas's account, in the attribution of praise *(laudatio)* or blame *(culpa)* to voluntary agents and their acts.[23] When we praise or blame a person

19. On the role of the eternal law here—namely God himself, considered as the ultimate measure or rule of all action, see *ST* I-II, q. 19, a. 4, co.; q. 21, a. 1, co.

20. *ST* I, q. 48, a. 6, co.: "Malum vero culpae opponitur proprie ipsi bono increato, contrariatur enim impletioni divinae voluntatis, et divino amori quo bonum divinum in seipso amatur." See also *ST* I-II, q. 19, a. 9, co.: "Requiritur ergo ad bonitatem humanae voluntatis, quod ordinetur ad summum bonum, quod est Deus... ad hoc quod voluntas hominis sit bona, requiritur quod conformetur voluntati divinae."

21. Original sin, "cum sit peccatum naturae, est quaedam inordinata dispositio ipsius naturae, quae habet rationem culpae inquantum derivatur ex primo parente" (*ST* I-II, q. 82, a. 1, ad 2), since "multi homines ex Adam derivati, sunt tanquam multa membra unius corporis" (*ST* I-II, q. 81, a. 1, co.).

22. Regarding St. Thomas on original sin, see Mark Johnson, "Augustine and Aquinas on Original Sin: Doctrine, Authority, and Pedagogy," in *Aquinas the Augustinian*, ed. Michael Dauphinais, Barry David, and Matthew Levering (Washington, D.C.: The Catholic University of America Press, 2007), 145–58.

23. Though for Thomas, as in ordinary usage, to "impute" an action to a person generally has a negative connotation. In what follows I analyze Thomas's account of *imputare*; he has, so far as I am aware, no similarly precise account of *reputare*. When applied to human beings, to "reckon" or

for the good or evil quality of his action, we "impute" the action to him, and thereby impute its moral quality as well. "To be praised or to be blamed simply means that the goodness or evil of his action is imputed to someone." In order for an action to be imputed to an agent, two conditions must be met: (1) the agent has to bring about the action, actually and not just possibly cause it, and (2) the action has to be voluntary, that is, subject to the mastery or "domin-ion," the freedom, of the agent. "An act is imputed to an agent when it is in her power, in such a way that she is the master of her act. This happens in all voluntary acts."[24]

So understood, "imputation" obviously has a direct connection with re-sponsibility. To impute an action to a person is to hold that person, as agent, responsible for the action. Imputability, we could say, is a feature of actions with respect to agents, while responsibility is the correlative feature of agents with respect to actions.[25] To hold a person responsible for an action is, in turn, to hold him liable for the consequences of his action, whether those conse-quences be natural, social, or legal. If one person strikes another in a way that involves fault or guilt (say, because she loses her temper at a public debate about health care reform), we link the fault to the person by imputing the ac-tion to her. In so doing we hold the person responsible for the act, and thereby we also hold her responsible or liable for various results of the act: the natural

---

"repute" often has the sense of holding an opinion that is quite possibly mistaken. But in theolo-gical contexts it seems to be synonymous with "to impute," since God makes no mistaken recko-nings, any more than he makes mistaken imputations.

24. Both quotations from *ST* I-II, q. 21, a. 2, co.: "Ex hoc enim dicitur aliquis actus culpabilis vel laudabilis, quod imputatur agenti, nihil enim est aliud laudari vel culpari, quam imputari alicui malitiam vel bonitatem sui actus. Tunc autem actus imputatur agenti, quando est in potestate ip-sius, ita quod habeat dominium sui actus. Hoc autem est in omnibus actibus voluntariis, quia per voluntatem homo dominium sui actus habet." Cf. *ST* I, q. 48, a. 5, co.: "Hoc enim imputatur alicui in culpam, cum deficit a perfecta actione, cuius dominus est secundum voluntatem."

J. M. Ramirez, O.P., among the most thorough and penetrating modern commentators on the *secunda pars*, is right, I think, to see in Thomas's compact formula at *ST* I-II, q. 21, a. 2, co. *(actus imputatur agenti, quando est in potestate ipsius, ita quod habeat dominium sui actus)* two dis-tinct conditions for imputation. "Patet autem quod ad imputabilitatem moralem alicuius actus, duae conditiones cumulative requiruntur: a) quod ille cui imputatur actus fuerit *vera causa vel auctor eius;* b) quod insuper fuerit verus *dominus* eius, quatenus poterat actum illum ponere vel non ponere, aut ponere hunc aut illum actum." Natural agents, such as fire or light, meet condition (a) but not condition (b); for just this reason, while we recognize them as agents or causes, we do not *impute* their action or efficacy to them. Jacobus M. Ramirez, O.P., *De actibus humanis: In I-II Summae theologiae Divi Thomae expositio (QQ. VI–XXI)*, vol. 4 of *Edición de las Obras Completas de Santiago Ramirez, O.P.*, ed. Victorino Rodriguez, O.P. (Madrid: Instituto de Filosofia «Luis Vives», 1972), 588–89 (§ 766).

25. I owe this helpful point to Ramirez: "Imputabilitas et responsabilitas sunt ad invicem cor-relativae, ita quidem ut imputabilitas immediate afficiat actum per ordinem ad agentem, dum re-sponsabilitas afficit immediate agentem per ordinem ad actum." *De actibus humanis*, §765 (*Obras Completas*, 4:588).

consequence of damage to another person's eye when struck by her fist, the social consequence of having her picture on the Internet committing an assault, the legal consequence of a fine and community service.

"Non-Imputation" and God's Disposition to Justify Sinners

These terminological clarifications in hand, we can return to the point that prompted them: St. Thomas's equation of the forgiveness or remission of sins with their "non-imputation" by God. In making this equation, Aquinas follows quite closely Scripture's way of speaking about sin and forgiveness, specifically in Romans 4 and Psalm 31 [32]. But given Thomas's own understanding of imputation, it is not immediately clear how God could ever fail to impute or reckon our sins to us. An action is imputable to a particular agent just in case the action is voluntary and that agent brings about or causes it. We human beings can be mistaken on both counts, and so sometimes wrongly impute actions to agents. But God cannot be mistaken, and so, presumably, imputes precisely those actions that are really imputable, and always attributes them to the correct agent. Moreover, a human act is sin just in case the agent, by doing it, deviates from the true end of human life, namely the enjoyment of God, and this act makes the agent guilty or culpable, since by it the agent freely fails to conform to the will of God. God can no more be mistaken about the moral worth of our acts than about our responsibility for them. How then is it possible for God not to impute our sin and guilt to us—to forgive us?

Here it helps to remember that the imputation of actions and their moral qualities to agents is not an end in itself. We do not ordinarily impute actions to agents simply for the sake of correctly linking the one to the other. Rather we ascribe responsibility for particular actions to particular persons for a distinctive moral purpose, namely to establish the justice of our own response to those actions. The aim of imputation, in other words, is to hold people responsible for their actions by applying the legitimate natural, social, or legal consequences of the act to the agent.

So it is with divine imputation. If God imputes our action to us, his aim is not simply to establish that we did the deed, but to bring the just consequences of the deed to bear on us. In the nature of things—given who God is and what he has made us to be—culpable acts issue in three kinds of damage to the agent, three just consequences that remain even after the sinful act itself has receded wholly into the past.[26]

---

26. The following quick summary suggests many questions I cannot go into here. Scholastic theology worried about how the consequences of sin could remain even after the culpable act and the

First of all, the sinner suffers the degradation, though not the complete destruction, of his natural good, the order and harmony that belongs to him by nature as God's creature. He is, furthermore, stained by sin. Following Peter Lombard and the tradition of commentary on *Sentences* IV, d. 18, Thomas takes the biblical language of "stain" *(macula)* as a metaphor for two states of affairs.[27] It stands for the ugliness that befalls a creature who by *culpa* gives up his likeness to God, thereby ruining his capacity to reflect God's own beauty, and for the distance from God that darkens what reflection of God's light still remains. Finally the sinner incurs, by his culpable act, a debt or liability to punishment *(reatus ad poenam)*. "Penalty" or "punishment" *(poena)* for Thomas is not an arbitrary verdict on God's part, but the natural resistance of the good and the just to that which opposes goodness and justice. None of these three sorts of damage can be repaired by us. We have the power to wound ourselves mortally, but not to heal the damage we have caused.[28]

For God to "impute" our sin to us, therefore, is for him not only to recognize that we have committed evil acts, but to hold us responsible for the damage our culpable deeds have caused. This he does simply by justly allowing the damage we have inflicted upon ourselves to stand. Unrepaired, the disorder and ugliness brought about by sin bar the way to blessedness and salvation, not only morally, but ontologically—thus damaged, we are literally not "fit" for eternal life, not shaped in a way compatible with life in God and union with God. So long as God allows this damage to stand—so long as he imputes our sin to us—he thereby imposes the final *poena* for our *culpa*, justly depriving us of eternal life. "Sin is imputed to a person insofar as it prevents him from attaining his ultimate end, which is eternal blessedness. Sin bars a per-

---

will to commit it—the cause of the damage—were past, and so no longer existed to produce their effects. See, e.g., *ST* I-II, q. 86, a. 2 (on *macula*); q. 87, a. 6 (on *reatus poenae*). For the sake of brevity I also prescind here from the distinction between mortal and venial sin. For Thomas the three basic consequences of sin as here described apply to original and mortal sin, but only in a qualified way to venial sin (see, e.g., *ST* I-II, q. 89, a. 1: venial sin does dim the reflection of God's light by us, but it brings about no abiding stain on the soul).

27. See *Magistri Petri Lombardi Sententiae in IV Libris Distinctae*, bk. IV, d. 18, c. 8 (3–4), 3rd ed. (Grottaferrata: Editiones Collegii S. Bonaventurae Ad Claras Aquas, 1981), 2:364.13–27. For Thomas on *macula animae* as a metaphor, and what the metaphor means, see *ST* I-II, q. 86, a. 1, co.

28. *ST* I-II, q. 109, a. 7, co. offers a useful summary of Thomas's view on the threefold damage wrought by sin: "Incurrit autem homo triplex detrimentum peccando, ut ex supradictis patet, scilicet maculam, corruptionem naturalis boni, et reatum poenae. Maculam quidem incurrit, inquantum privatur decore gratiae ex deformitate peccati. Bonum autem naturae corrumpitur, inquantum natura hominis deordinatur voluntate hominis Deo non subiecta, hoc enim ordine sublato, consequens est ut tota natura hominis peccantis inordinata remaneat. Reatus vero poenae est per quem homo peccando mortaliter meretur damnationem aeternam. Manifestum est autem de singulis horum trium, quod non possunt reparari nisi per Deum."

son from this end both by reason of its guilt and by reason of its liability to punishment."[29]

Conversely, for God to forgive our sins or *not* to impute them is for him to keep the damage they have caused from standing, thereby mercifully sparing us from the dreadful penalty for which they are liable. God's refusal to impute our sins to us isn't a failure to recognize that our acts have been evil, or a pretense that we have not really done the deeds. It is, instead, a generous repair of the damage they have done, and with that a genuine removal of the ultimate liability to punishment that they incur.

For St. Thomas, then, when God forgives or "remits" our sins, he refuses to ascribe or impute them to us *ad poenam*—for the purpose of punishing us for them. This is the precise meaning of both St. Paul and the Psalmist when they say (Rom 4:7 and Ps 31[32]:2) that the one to whom God does not impute sin is blessed. The final consequence of sin, Thomas recalls, is "liability to punishment, and it is with reference to this that [Paul] says 'Blessed is the man to whom to Lord does not impute sin'—that is, in order to punish it."[30] Similarly when David prays, "Blot out my iniquity" (Ps 50[51]:1), he is begging God, "Do not impute iniquity to me for the purpose of punishment."[31] Other scriptural

29. See *De malo* 7, a. 11, co.: "Imputatur autem peccatum alicui in quantum per ipsum impeditur homo a consequutione ultimi finis qui est beatitudo eterna, a qua impeditur homo per peccatum et ratione culpe et ratione reatus pene." Thomas continues: "Ratione quidem culpe, quia cum beatitudo eterna sit perfectum <bonum> hominis, non compatitur secum aliquam bonitatis minorationem; ex hoc autem ipso quod aliquis actum peccati commisit, incurrit quandam boni minorationem, in quantum scilicet factus est uituperabilis et indecentiam quandam habens ad tantum bonum. Ex hoc uero quod reus est pene etiam impeditur a beatitudine perfecta, que omnem dolorem et penam excludit: 'Fugiet enim ibi dolor et gemitus,' ut dicitur Ys. XXXV[:10]" (Leonine ed., 23:186.177–187.191). On created grace as the "shape" or imprint that conforms us to the divine persons, and so removes the "unsuitability" *(indecentiam)* of our "having so great a good," see Bruce D. Marshall, *"Ex Occidente Lux?* Aquinas and Eastern Orthodox Theology," in *Modern Theology* 20, no. 1 (2004): 23–50, especially 28–30. Also published in *Aquinas in Dialogue: Thomas for the Twenty-First Century,* ed. J. Fodor and F. C. Bauerschmidt (Oxford: Blackwell, 2004), 19–46, esp. 24–26.

30. *In ad Rom.* 4, lect. 1 (§ 338): "Tertio vero est reatus poenae et quantum ad hoc dicit 'beatus vir cui non imputavit Dominus peccatum,' scilicet ad poenam." This way of taking *non imputavit* is an established gloss on Ps 31:1–2, as Aquinas elsewhere observes (see below, note 33), as well as on Rom 4:7. See, e.g., Peter Lombard's gloss on the Psalms, PL 191, 318C, which attributes this reading to Alcuin, and the Lombard's *Collectanea* on the letters of Paul, PL 191, 1369D.

31. *In Psalmos Davidis expositio* 50, § 1: "Et hoc est quod dicit, 'dele iniquitatem meam,' idest non imputes mihi iniquitatem ad poenam. Is. 43:[25] 'Ego sum qui deleo iniquitates vestras'" (Parma ed., 14:345a–b); *In Psalmos* 50, § 6: 'Et omnes iniquitates meas dele'; quasi dicat: scio quod malum coram te feci: et ideo rogo ut avertas faciem tuam a peccatis meis, idest non consideres peccata mea ad puniendum: Ezech. 18[:22]: 'omnium iniquitatum eius non recordabor'" (348a).

Thomas's just-quoted course on the Psalms, left unfinished at his death and in all likelihood his last exegetical work, has drawn relatively little scholarly attention. But see Martin Morard, "À propos du *Commentaire des Psaumes* de saint Thomas d'Aquin," *Revue thomiste* 96 (1996): 653–70.

locutions have the same sense. When God is said (or entreated) to "hide his face" from our sins, "not to see" them, to "cover" them, to "remember" them no more, and so forth, the meaning is not that God literally has no knowledge of our sins, but that in mercy he refuses to impose their merited consequences on us.

At the resurrection of the dead, in fact, all our sins will be known not only to God (as they already are), but to us and to the rest of risen humanity. This will be an occasion for consternation and shame, however, only to the extent that we have tried to hide our sins, rather than repent of and confess them. For the saints (that is, the justified) the final exposure of their sins will be a time to rejoice in God, since their sins will lie open as forgiven—not imputed—in God's unfathomable mercy. "That the sins of the saints are revealed will not be a cause of embarrassment or shame for them, any more than it was for Mary Magdalene when her sins were read out publicly in Church.... The sins of the just will become known not as sins, but as forgiven. From this comes not misery, but glory."[32] When God is said to "wipe away" (literally "delete," in Aquinas's Latin) or "cover" the sins of the saints, the point is not that he or we ever lose track of them, but that they become, in the end, only a reason to glorify God for his goodness to us. "Sins are said to be 'deleted' in that God does not look upon them so as to punish them."[33]

Understood in this way, the concept of the remission or non-imputation of sin seems to answer an obvious question posed by our initial notion of being "reputed righteous," which was simply God's inevitable recognition of the justice he himself has caused in the creature (see the second section, above). Why does God cause this justice in the first place, the justice that actually heals the wound of sin, repairing sin's interior damage and leaving nothing in

---

32. "Quod peccata sanctorum revelantur, non poterit eis esse in erubescentiam vel verecundiam, sicut nec Mariae Magdalenae est in confusionem quod peccata sua in Ecclesia publice recitantur; quia verecundia est timor ingloriationis, ut dicit Damascenus, qui in beatis esse non poterit. Sed talis publicatio erit eis ad magnam gloriam propter poenitentiam quam fecerunt, sicut et confessor approbat eum qui magna scelera fortiter confitetur.... Peccata iustorum non venient in notitiam ut peccata, sed ut dimissa; sic enim considerationi cuiuslibet occurrent. Unde ex hoc non sequitur confusio, sed gloria." *Scriptum super IV Sententiarum Petri Lombardi* d. 43, q. 1, a. 5, qla. 2, ad 3; d. 43, expos. textus (Parma ed., 7/2:1069b, 1070b). Cf. III, q. 84, a. 9, co.: "Post hanc vitam autem sancti non sunt susceptivi doloris; unde displicebunt eis peccata praeterita sine omni tristitia, secundum illud Is. 65[:16], 'Oblivioni traditae sunt angustiae priores.'"

33. "Dicuntur autem peccata esse deleta, quia Deus non videt ea ad puniendum" (*In IV Sent.* d. 43, q. 1, a. 5, qla. 2, ad 3 [Parma ed., 7/2:1069b]). The biblical concept of "covering" can also be taken this way: our sins "dicuntur autem tegi, inquantum Deus ea non videt ad puniendum, sicut exponit Glossa super illud Psal. 31[:1]: beati quorum remissae sunt iniquitates" (*In IV Sent* d. 43, expos. textus [Parma ed., 1070b]). Similarly *In ad Rom.* 4, lect. 1 (§ 336): "Dicuntur autem peccata tegi divino conspectui, inquantum non inspicit ad ea punienda." There is more, however, to the notion of "covering"; see below.

us that merits the punishment of final separation from God? This doesn't just happen, but is a deliberate divine action, and so presupposes a specific intention and disposition on God's part. Essential to that disposition, it seems, is the non-imputation or non-reckoning of sins or faults. God forbears to count our sins against us, by imposing the penalty their guilt deserves, and instead restores the harmony and beauty of the creature by the utterly undeserved gift of sanctifying grace. The gift requires the forbearance. God holds in check his right to punish the outrages we have committed against him, and instead treats us with patience and mercy. All sin, Aquinas observes in comment on Romans 4:7, is an offense against God, and God handles this offense by refusing to hold it against the offender, "just as a man is said to let go of—remit—an offense done to him."[34]

There clearly is, then, a dispositional element in God's justification of the ungodly, and not only a causal and transformational element. God's favorable disposition naturally motivates the action by which he causes sinners to become righteous. Still, I think we ought to be cautious about simply equating God's disposition to justify sinners with his refusal to reckon or impute our sins to us. Aquinas is pretty clear, in fact, that this forensic aspect of justification is only the needed negative corollary of a more basic attitude: God's spontaneous love for those lost in the far country of sin.

Thus in *Summa theologiae* I-II, q. 113, a. 2, for example, Aquinas asks whether a transforming infusion of grace is necessary for the justification of the ungodly, in addition to the forgiveness *(remissio)* of sins. Just to ask the question indicates that neither justification nor the remission of sin can be reduced to or equated with the infusion of grace.[35] But when an objector sug-

34. *In ad Rom.* 4, lect. 1 (§ 338): "Sunt enim in peccato tria, quorum unum est offensa Dei, et quantum ad hoc dicit 'beati quorum remissae sunt iniquitates,' secundum quod homo dicitur remittere offensam sibi factam. Is. 40:2: 'dimissa est iniquitas illius.'" Cf. *In IV Sent.* d. 18, q. 1, a. 2. qla. 2, sol. (§58), in answer to the question whether the stain of sin can be forgiven *(remitti)*: "Secundum hoc quod se ad nos sua benignitate convertit, dicitur peccatum nostrum remittere: sicut nos offensam alicui remittimus, cum ad eum propter offensam praeteritam ulterius malevolentiam non servamus...et propter hoc etiam Deus remittendo peccatum dicitur ipsum tegere, quasi non aspiciens ad praeteritum peccatum, ut ratione eius gratiam nobis deneget" *S. Thomae Aquinatis Scriptum super Sententiis*, ed. M. F. Moos (Paris: Lethielleux, 1947), 4:937–38.

35. The infusion of grace and the forgiveness of sins are distinct, more precisely, in the most basic possible way: we count them as two rather than as one. As St. Thomas puts it, they must be "connumerated." "Posset enim esse infusio gratiae sine hoc quod culpa remitteretur, sicut in statu innocentiae fuit, et in Christo homine quantum ad primum instans suae conceptionis; et ideo infusio gratiae non includit culpae remissionem. Unde cum ad iustificationem impii, de qua loquimur, sit necessaria culpae remissio, oportet quod connumeretur gratiae infusioni" *(In IV Sent.* d. 17, q. 1, a. 3, qla. 5, sol. [§§ 113–14; Moos ed., 843]; cf. *Quaestiones disputatae de veritate* 28, a. 6, s.c. 1 [Leonine ed., 22/3:837.34–36]). While brought about by one and the same divine action, *infusio*

gests—invoking, as one would expect, Psalm 31(32):2—that God's *reputatio*, his refusal to reckon our sins against us, ought to be enough for justification, Thomas demurs. That God does not count our sins against us stems from God's love for us, and not the other way around.[36] Unlike ours, God's love is causal and creative. God's love creates goodness and value in God's beloved, rather than being elicited by goodness already there.[37] As the negative corollary or "flip side" of God's saving love for sinners, God's will not to reckon our sins to us must also be causal and transformatory, if in an indirect way. So understood, "non-imputation" cannot be wholly forensic. Since it presupposes that love which by nature creates value in what it loves, rather than attributing a value it fails to impart, God's refusal to impute sins must share in the production of love's effect. In this case, the effect is sanctifying grace, the interior transformation that makes us acceptable to God.[38] Seen as the effect of "non-imputation," the grace that transforms us and makes us new creatures in Christ *frees* us from being worthy of eternal punishment. Seen directly, as the effect of God's love, this same grace *makes* us worthy of eternal life.[39]

We can see, then, that for Aquinas justification involves a genuinely forensic disposition on God's part, but so far no purely forensic one. In particular there seems to be no counterfactual aspect to justification. Out of love, God declines to count our sin against us, so that he can get on with the business of removing it, of making us new creatures in Christ. He forgives us, it appears,

---

and *remissio* are irreducibly distinct effects of that action: "Et sic differunt, secundum differentiam culpae quae tollitur, et gratiae quae infunditur" (*ST* I-II, q. 113, a. 6, ad 2).

In the polemical context of the post-Reformation West, Catholic theology has often overlooked this important point, and treated the forgiveness of sins as a more or less disposable synonym for the infusion of grace. Thus, *inter alia*, the comment on *ST* III, q. 88, a. 1, ad 4 (see below, note 49) in the Blackfriars edition of the *Summa theologiae*: "This is far from Luther's doctrine of grace cloaking man's sinful condition. Grace interiorly transforms him; this *is* forgiveness" (my emphasis; *Summa theologiae*, vol. 60, *Penance*, trans. and ed. Reginald Masterson, O.P., and T. C. O'Brien, O.P. [New York: McGraw-Hill, 1966], 122, n. g).

36. "Quod enim alicui non imputetur peccatum a Deo, ex divina dilectione procedit." *ST* I-II, q. 113, a. 2, ad 2.

37. "Amor Dei est infundens et creans bonitatem in rebus." *ST* I, q. 20, a. 2, c.

38. *ST* I-II, q. 113, a. 2, obj. 2: "Remissio culpae consistit in reputatione divina; secundum illud Psalmi 31[:2], 'beatus vir cui non imputavit dominus peccatum.' Sed infusio gratiae ponit etiam aliquid in nobis, ut supra habitum est. Ergo infusio gratiae non requiritur ad remissionem culpae." Ad 2: "Sicut dilectio Dei non solum consistit in actu voluntatis divinae, sed etiam importat quendam gratiae effectum, ut supra dictum est [110, 1, c]; ita etiam et hoc quod est Deum non imputare peccatum homini, importat quendam effectum in ipso cuius peccatum non imputatur."

39. See *De veritate* 28, a. 2, ad 6, which faces the same objection stemming from Ps. 31(32):2. "Sicut dilectio Dei qua nos diligit, consequenter aliquem effectum in nobis relinquit, scilicet gratiam per quam digni reddimur vita aeterna ad quam nos dirigit, ita hoc ipsum quod est Deum non imputare nobis nostra delicta, ex consequenti relinquit in nobis aliquid per quod a reatu praedicto digni sumus absolvi; et hoc est gratia" (Leonine ed., 22/3:823.240–47).

not in spite of what we have done, but on account of what he will make of us. So far, at least, there is no suggestion that God's love for us prompts him simply to overlook our sin, or treat it as though it had not happened.

"Non-Imputation" as Covering Sin

Aquinas's account of justification is usually assumed to stop here, at least when it comes to forensic dispositions such as reckoning or non-imputation. And well it should, a lot of Catholic theologians are likely to say. There is no good use for any stronger forensic notion. If we try to press Scripture's forensic language further than Thomas has already done, we turn justification into a legal fiction, even a kind of self-deception on God's part. Catholic theology has to be on guard against any suggestion that in justifying the ungodly, God somehow pulls the wool over his own eyes, concealing the ugly truth about us from himself rather than doing anything about it.

If we read only the questions on grace in the *Summa theologiae*, we might in fact get the impression that St. Thomas has nothing further to say on the matter. And this would leave us at something of a loss about how to cope with an objection that comes from more stringently dispositional theologies of justification. As we have already recalled, the Psalms speak not only of God remitting sin and not imputing sin to us, which Aquinas can treat in an incipiently causal way, but of God "covering" sin (Ps 31[32]:1) and hiding his face from it (Ps 50:11 [51:9]). Scriptural locutions of this kind receive added weight from Paul's invocation of Psalm 31(32):1 in order to clarify the paradigmatic character of Abraham's faith: "Blessed are those whose sins are covered" (Rom 4:7). It surely counts against Aquinas's theology of justification if he cannot do justice to these biblical modes of speech. More precisely: he seems to treat these locutions as though they simply mean that God chooses to look at sin in a particular way, or for a particular purpose (to remove it rather than to punish it). But this forces Scripture into the mold of a transformational theology of justification. Surely the more natural sense of these passages, so the objection goes, is not that God looks on our sin in one way rather than another, but that he does not to look on it at all.

When we turn to Thomas's commentaries on the pertinent biblical passages, though, we find that he faces this exegetical problem directly. Sin offends God and damages the creature, adding to the offense. In justifying sinners, as we have seen, God forbears to act on the offense against him, which would mean withholding grace from us (justly, to be sure). And he graciously repairs sin's damage, removing the self-incurred penalty of sin by making us once again suited for intimacy with him. But sin involves even more than an offense to God and a debt or liability for punishment. There is also, in all sin, a particular disordered act. This is *culpa* in the strict sense. Here "guilt" or "fault" is not, as sometimes in Aquinas, a broad synonym for "sin" as a whole, but refers to each free act by which we refuse submission and conformity to God. It is this act that, each time, introduces deformity into the will and "stain" into the soul. God can and does correct the deformity, remove the stain, and thereby eliminate our liability to punishment. But *that* I have committed this disordered act can never be changed, even by divine power. It can only be covered, as the Psalmist says, treated, by divine mercy, as though it had not happened. Saint Thomas comments: "Another [element of sin—besides offense and debt] is the guilty disordered act itself. Once this has been perpetrated, there is no way it can be undone. Instead it is covered by the hand of God's mercy, and treated as though it had not been done."[40]

Thomas spells this out more precisely in his late commentary on the Psalm text cited by Paul in Romans 4:7: "Blessed are those whose sins are covered" (Ps 31[32]:1). Though he speaks of "stain" *(macula)* instead of "guilt" *(culpa)*, Thomas introduces here basically the same threefold distinction with regard to sin that he proposes in the Romans *Lectura*.[41] Sin involves an offense to God, a deformity or stain on the person of the sinner, and a liability to punishment. And Thomas (again) correlates each of these with one of the verbs of Ps 31(32):1–2: offense is "remitted" or forborne, stain is "covered," the debt of punishment is "not imputed." Sins are stains on the soul, and as such are foul and revolting. Something needs to be done, so that the eye of anyone looking on such ugliness will not be offended. What God does, in fact, is "cover the wickedness of sin," as the Psalm teaches. "But how?"

40. *In ad Rom.* 4, lect. 1 (§ 338): "Aliud autem est ipse actus inordinatus culpae, qui non potest non fuisse factus ex quo semel perpetratus est, sed tegitur manu misericordiae divinae, ut quasi pro non facto habeatur."

Here, at least, the proximity of Luther's understanding of justification to the teaching of St. Thomas cannot escape notice. Luther, to be sure, can say things like, "God actually dissembles with our sins, treating them as though they were not sins" (*In epistolam S. Pauli ad Galatas Commentarius*, commenting on Gal 3:6: "Verum haec peccata dissimulat Deus suntque apud eum, quasi non essent peccata." D. *Martin Luthers Werke, Kritische Gesamtausgabe* [Weimar: Hermann Böhlaus Nachfolger, 1883–], 40/I:367.17–18. Cf. *Luther's Works*, vol. 26 [St. Louis, Mo.: Concordia, 1963], 232, which softens "verum ... dissimulat" to "overlooks"). Such statements may seem to make Luther the veritable Platonic form of a theologian who thinks of justification as a matter of God pulling the wool over his own eyes. But even *dissimulat* seems, in context, like a rhetorically flamboyant expression of the idea that follows, namely that God treats our sins—in a way, *quasi*—as though they were not sins. And this is essentially what Thomas says in the Romans *Lectura*. God does not impute our sin to us, but instead treats it—in a way—as though it had not been done: *quasi pro non facto habeatur*. Conversely, there are clearly transformational elements in Luther's theology of justification, as Michael Waldstein's chapter 15 in this volume helpfully shows. See also my essay, "Justification as Declaration and Deification," *International Journal of Systematic Theology* 4, no. 1 (2002): 3–28.

41. At § 338; see the previous note, together with notes 30 and 34.

In order to answer this question adequately, Aquinas says in reply, we need to understand that from the sinful act results a twofold stain: "In peccato enim duplex est deformitas." On the one hand there is *macula* in the strict sense, the deformity of soul and distance from God brought about when the disordered act casts away sanctifying grace. This, Aquinas says (as we would expect), "is not covered, but is totally removed, because grace is given [to the sinner]." On the other hand, "there is the stain of the past act of sin." And this, Aquinas says (as he had in the *Lectura* on Romans), "is not taken away, because it is not given to the sinner that he did not commit the act. The gift rather is that its guilt is not imputed—reckoned—to him. Instead it is covered."[42] In just this twofold way, God not only cleanses our souls, but covers our sinful acts. For God to forgive sins is not only for him to be undeterred by the foulness of what he intends to change, but for him to overlook—to cover—what cannot be changed.[43]

Here, as Thomas is clearly aware, we run up against a metaphysical rock

42. All quotations in the last two paragraphs are from *In Psalmos* 31, § 1: "Peccata sunt maculae animae: Hier. 2[:36]: 'quam vilis facta es' etc. Quando quis habet in se turpe, et illud tegitur, tunc oculos intuentis turpitudo non offendit. Deus autem tegit turpitudinem peccatorum: sed quomodo? Totaliter, scilicet abluendo animam. In peccato enim duplex est deformitas. Una scilicet ex privatione gratiae qua privatur peccator: et haec totaliter tollitur, et non tegitur, quia datur ei gratia. Alia macula est ex actu peccati praeterito: et haec non deletur, quia non datur ei quod non fecerit, sed quod non imputetur ei ad culpam: et haec tegitur" (Parma ed., 14:257a). See also book 4 of the *Scriptum:* "Peccatum autem quod erat obstaculum interpositum [=macula obscuritatis], prohibens gratiae claritatem, non potest removeri ut factum non sit, sed ut effectum avertendi Deum a nobis non habeat, qui propter aversionem qua ab eo aversi propter peccatum fuimus, a nobis aversus manebat" (*In IV Sent.* d. 18, q. 1, a. 2. qla. 2, sol. [§ 58; Moos ed., 937]; cf. above, note 34).

43. For much the same idea, viz., that God "turns his face" from or declines "to remember" our culpable acts, which cannot, as such, be undone, see *In Psalmos* 50, § 6: "Peccatum enim removetur non hoc modo quod peccatum non fuerit; sed quod non imputetur ei peccatum commissum ad poenam, secundum illud Ps. 31[:2]: 'beatus vir' . . . ideo [David] petit ut non consideret peccatum eius, sed sit immemor eius; et ideo dicit, 'averte faciem tuam a peccatis meis'" (Parma ed., 14:348a).

Aquinas offers a striking twist on the same idea at *Super epistolam B. Pauli ad Colossenses lectura* 2, lect. 3 (§ 113). On the cross Christ has cancelled the "bond of indebtedness" against us (Col 2:14; the Vulgate simply borrows the Greek word *chirographum*), "quia non remittit sic ut faciat quod non peccaveris, sed quia non est in memoria Dei ad puniendum, nec in Daemonis memoria ad accusandum, nec in te ad contristandum. Ps. 31:1: 'beati quorum remissae sunt iniquitates, et quorum tecta sunt peccata,' etc." How, Aquinas goes on to ask, does Christ do this? "'In cruce' . . . ideo simul cum morte Christi, hoc chirographum est destructum . . . id est sustulit de rerum natura" (§ 115). Here Aquinas expresses the idea that God no longer remembers our past acts of sin in terms closely reminiscent of patristic theologies of the cross, prompted, as they were, by Col 2:14. The sins of humanity have created a debt we cannot repay, and we all stand under a "bond of indebtedness" that makes us liable to accusation from the devil, punishment from God, and sorrow for what we have brought upon ourselves. But on the cross Christ has torn up this bond

that cannot be moved. Even God cannot change the past—not because he lacks the power to do it, but because it cannot be done. The notion of changing the past implies a contradiction. It can no more be brought about, Thomas argues, that Socrates did not sit at a particular time when he did sit than it can be brought about that Socrates, sitting here and now, does not sit here and now. The logic of the past tense of the verb is the same as that of the present tense.[44] God can and does heal all the ontological damage caused by our disordered sinful acts, leaving nothing in us that merits penalty and blocks our union with him. But it will forever be true that we once committed the acts themselves. Yearning to make it otherwise is not true penitence, but folly. The true penitent has sorrow over what cannot be changed, not the empty hope of erasing the past.[45]

Yet Scripture teaches that the one whose sin God covers is blessed. We are not left to sorrow forever over what cannot be changed, even by God. Once covered by the merciful hand of God, our sins cannot be uncovered. Their guilt cannot, now or ever, be reckoned to us. If we are now to recall the forgiven sins of our past as they actually are, we must look on them as God does. And God sees them only as covered. Should they now drive us to fear or despair, we effectively try to uncover them, to look on them as even God refuses

---

that stood against us—"wholly withdrawn it from reality," in Thomas's phrase *(sustulit de rerum natura)*—and so has wiped out our debt entirely.

The *chirographum* that Christ destroys on the cross is, more precisely, a handwritten device for *remembering* debt before the law (*In III Sent.* d. 19, expos. textus [§ 118]: "Chirographum dicitur a *chiros*, quod est manus, et *grapha*, quod est scriptura; quasi scriptura manualis, quae memoriam debitorum facit et obligationem ad solvendum" [Moos ed., 3:605]). So because of what Christ has done, God no longer "remembers" our sins—no longer looks on them as a debt demanding payment (to be exacted by the punishment of eternal death)—the devil's accusations are now empty, and we are freed from sorrow over our past. Thus Aquinas interprets the loan word *chirographum* in Col 2:14 in just the sense it had in early Christianity, namely as a legal writ that constituted proof of debt, and was torn up *(scindebatur)* when the debt was either repaid or forgiven: "Consuetudo enim erat quod solvens omnia ad quae quis tenebatur, scindebatur chirographum. Homo autem erat in peccato, sed Christus solvit pro bonis patiendo. Ps. 68:5 (69:4): 'quae non rapui, tunc ex[s]olvebam.' Et ideo simul cum morte Christi, hoc chirographum est destructum" (*In ad Col.* 2, lect. 3 [§ 115]). On all this see Gary A. Anderson's compelling study of sin as debt in scripture, rabbinic Judaism, and early Christianity: *Sin: A History* (New Haven: Yale University Press, 2009), esp. 111–32.

44. As Aquinas points out when the question whether God can change the past comes up in the *Summa theologiae*'s treatment of divine power: "Sub omnipotentia Dei non cadit aliquid quod contradictionem implicat. Praeterita autem non fuisse, contradictionem implicat. Sicut enim contradictionem implicat dicere quod Socrates sedet et non sedet, ita, quod sederit et non sederit.... Unde praeterita non fuisse, non subiacet divinae potentiae" (I, q. 25, a. 4, co.).

45. See III, q. 85, a. 1, ad 3: "Dolere de eo quod prius factum est cum hac intentione conandi ad hoc quod factum non fuerit, esset stultum. Hoc autem non intendit poenitens, sed dolor eius est displicentia seu reprobatio facti praeteriti cum intentione removendi sequelam ipsius, scilicet offensam Dei et reatum poenae. Et hoc non est stultum."

to look. By covering our culpable acts, God turns the memory of them from a reason for despair to a further opportunity for gratitude. In the end, when the secret thoughts of all our hearts are laid bare before him with whom we have to do, "the sins of the just will become known not as sins, but as forgiven. From this comes not misery, but glory."[46]

Among the standard questions of scholastic theology was whether sins, once forgiven, could return. The sense of the question was not whether a particular *kind* of sin can recur when previous acts of that kind have been forgiven. Obviously it can. The issue, rather, was whether particular sinful *acts*, once forgiven, can ever again be held against us by God. For Thomas this question becomes an opportunity to underline the way in which the sacrament of penance offers, here and now, a share in the eschatological consolation of the saints. An objector claims that sins once forgiven can in fact return to accuse us, and he cites in his favor precisely Paul's appeal to Psalm 31(32):1. According to the Apostle grace covers past sins. But grace can be lost through subsequent grave sin. Mortal sin not only casts away grace here and now, but in the process removes the divine covering from our past sins. "The sins which had been committed before," the objector concludes, "return uncovered."[47]

But this cannot be, Aquinas replies. It amounts to nothing less than a denial of the faithfulness of God and the reliability of his promises. Saint Paul teaches that God never takes back a gift once given: "The gifts and the calling of God are without repentance" (Rom 11:29). Sins once covered are covered forever, even if the forgiven sinner later commits the same kind of sin again. To suppose otherwise is to think that God might repent of his forgiveness, or any other gift, and withdraw it from us.[48] Grace can be lost, but what the grace

---

46. See above, note 32.

47. *ST* III, q. 88, a. 1, obj. 4: "Praeterea, peccata praeterita per gratiam teguntur, ut patet per apostolum, Rom. 4[:7], inducentem illud Psalmi [31:1], 'beati quorum remissae sunt iniquitates et quorum tecta sunt peccata.' Sed per peccatum mortale sequens gratia tollitur. Ergo peccata quae fuerant prius commissa, remanent detecta. Et ita videtur quod redeant."

48. *ST* III, q. 88, a. 1, s.c.: "Apostolus dicit, Rom. 11[:29], 'sine poenitentia sunt dona Dei, et vocatio.' Sed peccata poenitentis sunt remissa per donum Dei. Ergo per peccatum sequens non redeunt dimissa peccata, quasi Deus de dono remissionis poeniteat." Cf. *Super epistolam B. Pauli ad Hebraeos lectura* 8, lect. 3 (§ 411): "Rom. 11:29: 'Sine poenitentia enim sunt dona et vocatio Dei,' etc., id est, Deus non poenitet, quod hic peccata remiserit, quasi iterum puniendo."

Rom 11:29 has other vital applications for Thomas, in particular regarding God's faithfulness to the Jewish people, Israel according to the flesh. Aquinas regards it as the plain teaching of Paul that the Jews have not, even by their hostility *(inimicitia)* to the Gospel, forfeited the salvation promised to their forefathers. "Posset enim aliquis obviando dicere quod Iudaei, et si olim fuerint charissimi propter patres, tamen inimicitia, quam contra Evangelium exercent, prohibet ne in futurum salventur. Sed hoc Apostolus falsum esse asserit ... quasi dicat: quod Deus aliquid aliquibus donet vel aliquos vocet, hoc est 'sine poenitentia,' quia de hoc Deum non poenitet." *In ad Rom* 11, lect. 4 (§ 924). On this topic see Bruce D. Marshall, *"Quasi in Figura:* A Brief Reflection

of God has once accomplished can never be changed. The sorrowing penitent need never fear that sins forgiven in a good confession will later be "uncovered" and held against him. Now and forever they are seen by God, and so should be seen by us, only as forgiven. Thomas concludes: "The stain of sin and the debt of eternal punishment grace simply removes. But it covers past acts of sin, so that God does not, because of them, deprive a person of grace and exact the debt of eternal punishment. And what grace once does remains forever."[49]

Beatus Vir

In St. Thomas's understanding of justification, then, there is not only a causal and transformational element, nor only a forensic disposition ordered to a transformational act, but also the element of a purely forensic disposition. To be sure, there is much more to Aquinas's theology of justification than this. In particular, St. Thomas sees in the passion of Christ more than the root from which springs the sacramental communication of interior transforming grace, important as that is. Christ's passion and cross are equally the root of God's disposition to cover our sins, and not impute them to us. God reconciles the world to himself, as St. Paul teaches, in Christ, and this happens when God "does not reckon their sins to them" (2 Cor 5:19, Vulg.: *non reputans illis delicta ipsorum*). Thomas comments: "That is, he does not remember the sins of those for whom Christ has made full satisfaction, whether actual or original, for the sake of punishing them. In this sense God is said to have reconciled us to himself, in that he does not impute our sins to us. Ps 31[32]:2: 'Blessed is the man to whom the Lord does not impute his sin.'"[50] Our justification therefore stems ultimately from the love the Father has for his Son, who in fulfillment of ancient cultic figures offered himself up as the bloody propitiation for our sins, an offering "applied to us," as Thomas observes, "by faith" (cf. Rom 3:25).[51] Justification for St. Thomas thus has an irreducibly Christological and

---

on Jewish Election, after Thomas Aquinas" and "Postscript and Prospect," in *Nova et Vetera* (English) 7, no. 2 (2009): 477–84, 523–28.

49. *ST* III, q. 88, a. 1, ad 4: "Dicendum quod gratia simpliciter tollit maculam et reatum poenae aeternae, tegit autem actus peccati praeteritos, ne scilicet propter eos Deus hominem gratia privet et reum habeat poenae aeternae. Et quod gratia semel facit, perpetuo manet."

50. *Super II Epistolam B. Pauli ad Corinthios lectura* 5, lect. 5 (§ 198): "Et hoc non reputans illis delicta ipsorum, id est non habens in memoria illorum delicta, tam actualia quam originalia, ad puniendum, pro quibus Christus plene satisfecit. Et secundum hoc dicitur nos reconciliasse sibi, inquantum non imputat delicta nostra nobis. Ps. 31:2: 'Beatus vir cui non imputavit Dominus peccatum.'"

51. The quoted phrase is from *In ad Rom.* 3, lect. 3 (§ 309): "Haec autem mors Christi nobis applicatur per fidem, qua credimus per suam mortem mundum redemisse." It follows this exegesis of Rom 3:25: "Et sic, dum satisfaciendo, [Christus] nos redimit a noxa peccati, Deum peccatis

Trinitarian shape, which is essential for understanding in an adequate way how (that is, with what justice) God can fail to impute our sins to us. But this is a matter for another time.

Aquinas cannot, in any case, be summoned as chief witness for a transformational theology of justification, in opposition to a dispositional and forensic one. For him the two evidently are not opposites. While justification cannot, as a whole, be purely dispositional or forensic, there must be a purely forensic moment in justification. When God declines to reckon or impute our sins to us, he does more than forgo his undoubted right to punish us for our sin and corruption rather than change us for the better, important as that is. He overlooks what is odious to him, but which he cannot change, namely our past sinful acts themselves. He covers them, conceals them from his sight, and treats them as though they were not. He remembers our sins no more, as Scripture often consoles us by teaching. This too belongs among the blessings of those who share the faith of Abraham, who are blessed because the Lord remits their sin, and does not reckon it against them.

---

nostris propitium facit, quod petebat Psalmista [78(79):9] dicens: 'propitius esto peccatis nostris': et ideo dicit eum 'propitiatorem.' I Io. 2:2: 'propitiatio.' In cuius figura, Ex. 25:17, mandatur quod fiat propitiatorium, id est quod Christus ponatur super arcam, id est, Ecclesiam" (§ 308). For the link, by way of Rom 3:25, between the forgiveness of sins by faith in Christ and the sacramental mediation of the efficacy of his passion, see *ST* III, q. 62, a. 5, ad 2: "Per fidem Christus habitat in nobis, ut dicitur Ephes. 3[:17]. Et ideo virtus Christi copulatur nobis per fidem. Virtus autem remissiva peccatorum speciali quodam modo pertinet ad passionem ipsius. Et ideo per fidem passionis eius specialiter homines liberantur a peccatis, secundum illud Rom. 3[:25], 'quem proposuit Deus propitiatorem per fidem in sanguine eius.' Et ideo virtus sacramentorum, quae ordinatur ad tollendum peccata, praecipue est ex fide passionis Christi."

Charles Raith II

༄

13   Portraits of Paul

Aquinas and Calvin on Romans 7:14–25

In 1541 Gasparo Contarini, appointed papal legate of the Roman Catholic Church, gathered together at the Diet of Regensburg theologians representing both Catholic and Protestant positions in order to discuss, among other things, the doctrine of justification. Anthony N. S. Lane, while analyzing article 5 of the Regensburg Colloquy, makes the point on numerous occasions that the crux of the issue concerned the basis of one's acceptance before God: is it due to imputed righteousness alone or also due to inherent righteousness?[1] Answering this question hinges in large part on how one understands the transformation that occurs through God's sanctifying work on the believer. As Lane notes, "The reason why the Reformers insisted on imputed righteousness was that both our own inherent righteousness and the righteousness of our works remain imperfect and it is not on that basis that we can stand before God."[2] A key location for exploring how John Calvin and Thomas Aquinas envision the Spirit's transforming work in the believer (i.e., inherent righteousness) and the good works that follow is Romans 7:14–25.[3] Since both

1. Anthony N. S. Lane, "Twofold Righteousness: A Key to the Doctrine of Justification? Reflections on Article 5 of the Regensburg Colloquy (1541)," in *Justification: What's at Stake in the Current Debates?* ed. Mark Husbands and Daniel J. Trier (Downers Grove, Ill.: InterVarsity Press, 2005), 215; idem., *Justification by Faith in Protestant-Catholic Dialogue: An Evangelical Assessment* (London: T&T Clark, 2002), 158–67.
    2. Lane, "Twofold Righteousness," 217.
    3. Romans 7:14–25 was in fact a central location for Reformers' confrontation with the Roman Church; see J. I. Packer, "The 'Wretched Man' Revisited: Another Look at Romans 7:14–25," in *Romans and the People of God*, ed. Sven K. Soderlund and N. T. Wright (Grand Rapids, Mich.: Eerdmans, 2002), 71–72. According to Packer, many of the Reformers used Rom 7:14–25 to show that "there is sin in the best Christians' best works." James Dunn has observed that Rom 7:14–25 "will in large measure determine our understanding of Paul's theology as a whole, particularly his anthropology and soteriology" ("Romans 7:14–25 in the Theology of Paul," *Theologische Zeitschrift* 31, no. 5 [1975]: 257).

Aquinas and Calvin provide an interpretation of the *ego* of 7:14 as the graced Apostle Paul,[4] their commentaries on the struggle presented in 7:14–25 provides a resource for understanding how they envision the Christian moral life, in terms of both the effects of sin and the restoring work of grace on human nature.[5] I will first analyze Aquinas's and Calvin's description of the Apostle Paul's "flesh" and "spirit" in 7:14–25, paying particular attention to the negative effects of sin and healing effects of grace. I will then unfold the portraits of Paul's moral life that emerge from their commentaries on 7:14–25 in light of their judgments regarding "flesh" and "spirit." Last, I will draw out some implications of their interpretations that highlight similarities and differences particularly surrounding their anthropological and soteriological judgments.

4. I will leave aside for now contemporary arguments—and the validity of those arguments—against interpreting the *ego* of 7:14 as portraying human experience, whether Christian or otherwise. See, for example, N. T. Wright, who believes his own interpretive framework renders the notion of the "Christian struggle" in Rom 7:14–25 "beside the point" (*The New Interpreter's Bible*, vol. 10, *The Letter to the Romans* [Nashville: Abingdon Press, 2002], 552). Mark Reasoner is even more insistent on the rejection, claiming, "The various appeals to human experience that have haunted the exegesis of this locus since Augustine must be resisted as far as is possible" (*Romans in Full Circle: A History of Interpretation* [Louisville, Ky.: Westminster/John Knox Press, 2005], 82).

5. Both Aquinas and Calvin explicitly appropriate Augustine's take on the *ego* of Rom 7:14–25, although they do so in different ways. Calvin appropriates Augustine's interpretive change from pre-converted Paul to converted Paul as a signal to wholly reject a reading of Rom 7:14–25 in terms of the non-Christian (*Commentarius in Epistilorum Pauli ad Romanos*, ed. T. H. L. Parker, [Leiden: Brill, 1981], 149.33–38; citations include page and line numbers). Aquinas, however, merely references Augustine's change of position (§ 558) and proceeds as if the two options are equally worthy of attention (section numbers taken from Aquinas, *Super epistolam ad Romanos*, in vol. 1 of Thomas Aquinas, *Super Epistolas Sancti Pauli*, ed. Raphaelis Cai, 8th ed. [Rome: Marietti, 1953]). These different appropriations reflect different emphases of the interpreters. Calvin acknowledges that Paul argues for the goodness of the law in Rom 7, but more is at stake for Calvin in terms of the state of the *ego* in v.14. Romans 7:14–25 provides Calvin the opportunity to set forth a description of the regenerate Christian in the face of his opponents on issues such as justification, law and grace, and (especially) merit. Thus there can be no ambiguity regarding the status of the *ego*. Thomas, however, sees the principal point to be a demonstration of the goodness of the Law and places both *egos* in the service of demonstrating this principle. To be sure, as the commentary unfolds Aquinas feels forced by the text to conclude that the text is understood "better" *(melior)* (§§ 558, 570) if the *ego* is the Apostle Paul in a state of grace, but either state suffices to support the principal point of highlighting the Law's goodness. Reasoner therefore overstates the case when he claims that Aquinas is "focused" on indentifying whom the *ego* is in Rom 7:7–25 (*Romans in Full Circle*, 74). Aquinas is focused instead on upholding the goodness of the Law (§§ 532, 556). For a discussion regarding Calvin's choice of the regenerated Paul, see R. Ward Holder, "Calvin's Hermeneutic and Tradition: An Augustinian Reception of Romans 7," in *Reformation Readings of Romans*, ed. Kathy Ehrensperger and R. Ward Holder (New York: T&T Clark, 2008), 98–199; David Steinmetz, *Calvin in Context* (Oxford: Oxford University Press, 1995), 111.

"Flesh" and "Spirit" in Romans 7:14–25

Aquinas

Paul describes his "flesh" in Romans 7:14–25 as the part of himself where "nothing good dwells" (7:18) and which serves the "law of sin" and is in conflict with the "mind" and its service to the "law of God" (7:25). For Aquinas, Paul's pejorative claims about his flesh are essentially descriptions of the *fomes peccati* ("inclination of sin"). According to Aquinas, the *fomes*, which is the punishment *(poena)* resulting from the sin of the first parent (§§ 561, 587),[6] dwells in one's lower powers of the sensitive appetite and gives rise to disordered "desires" *(concupiscentiae)*.[7] These desires precede the judgment of the intellect (§ 563) and, because they are disordered, incline a person to that which is contrary to the good (§§ 563, 573, 587) and thus contrary to the Law.[8] When Paul states in 7:18, "sin dwells in my flesh," "sin" is understood as the *fomes*, and "flesh" as the sensitive powers (§§ 573, 555).[9]

On the other hand, there is the "spirit" or "mind" *(mens)*, which is in opposition to the flesh. Aquinas interprets these two terms as referring to Paul's reason. When Paul states in 7:14, "*I* am carnal," the "I" for Aquinas stands for reason, which is the "chief thing in man" *(principale in homine)* or "more important" part of man (§§ 559, 585).[10] Aquinas claims that a person *is* according to his or her reason *(homo est id quod est secundum rationem)*, so that Paul can

---

6. Aquinas attributes a twofold cause to the *fomes* in relation to it being a punishment for sin. The first cause is sin itself, which is indicated above; the second cause is God, who imposed the punishment of the *fomes* on "sinful man" (§ 587). This punishment is termed a "law" in 7:23, according to Aquinas, because "it was introduced by the law of divine justice, just as the sentence of a just judge has the force of law" (ibid.).

7. The adjective "disordered" indicates that for Aquinas concupiscence is per se part of the human composition but negatively affected by the "sin of the first parent" (*Summa theologiae* [*ST*] I-II, q. 85, a. 3). For Calvin, however, original sin *creates* the presence of concupiscence (see his *Institutio Christianae Religionis* 2.1.8–9 [CCEL online: http://www.ccel.org]; abbreviated *Inst.* throughout the essay. As a guide for the English, I consult the Ford Lewis Battles translation in *The Library of Christian Classics*, vol. 20 [Louisville, Ky.: Westminster/John Knox Press, 1960]).

8. It is these same interpretive moves, argues Steinmetz, that is, the distinction between lower and higher faculties, the emphasis on concupiscence as punishment for sin rather than sinful, and the distinction between perfection in this life and the life to come (see below), that enabled sixteenth-century Catholic commentators to read Rom 7:14–25 as the graced person "without falling into self-contradiction on the one hand or Lutheranism on the other" (*Calvin in Context*, 304).

9. Aquinas does grant when interpreting 7:23, "I see a law in my members," that the *fomes* in a way "spread over [*diffusive*] all members which play a role [*diserviunt*] for concupiscent desire in sinning" (§ 588); see *ST* I-II, q. 90, a. 1, ad. 1.

10. Reason also corresponds to the "inner man" of 7:22 (§ 585). Aquinas clarifies that he is not speaking in the Platonic way of a human being as merely a soul using a body, or in Tertullian's way of the soul being fashioned according to man's figure (§ 585); *ST* I, q. 75, a. 4.

say in 7:17, "it is no longer I that do it but sin which dwells in me," since his reason, as we shall see, does not consent to the *fomes* (§ 570).[11]

Given that the Paul of 7:14–25 is the graced Paul, how does Aquinas understand the effects of grace in relation to the flesh and spirit? Aquinas claims that the justifying grace of Christ resides not in the flesh (where concupiscence resides, namely in the sensible appetites) but in the mind, in one's rational capacity (§ 573).[12] It is critical for Aquinas that Paul states in 7:18a that no good dwells "in the flesh," for the good of grace *does* dwell in the mind *(mens)* (§ 574). For Aquinas, the healing of the mind by grace enables a person to judge not only the good in general, which is possible for the person not in grace—although this judgment may not result in a good deed—but also to judge and will the *particular* good.[13] As Aquinas states, the healed mind allows for "a complete act of willing which lasts through the act of choosing a particular deed" (§ 565).[14] On this account, the flesh still gives rise to inclinations that are contrary to reason, since grace does not heal the flesh, and thus Paul can state in 7:23 that he is still "captive" to the law of sin in the members (i.e., movements of concupiscence [*motus concupiscentia*]) (§ 588). But reason is healed to know what the good is and enabled so as not to submit itself to the inordinate desires.[15] Commenting on the phrase "Wretched man that I am"

---

11. Aquinas further explains the relationship between reason and the *fomes* in *ST* I-II, q. 91, a. 6.

12. Aquinas derives this point from Rom 8:10, "If Christ is in us, the body is indeed dead because of sin, but the spirit lives because of justice" (§§ 573, 629). If grace resided in the flesh as well, one would not only will the good with mind but also accomplish the very good they will without the hindrance of concupiscence (§ 580). In actuality, however, a person in grace is unable to do the good so as to exclude concupiscence entirely; see *ST* I-II, q. 109, a. 8.

13. The person not in grace may have a correct judgment about the good in general, but "a bad habit or a perverse passion" results in the will going astray, so that in a particular case, that person does not judge rightly about the good (§ 565; see *ST* II-II, q. 77, a. 2). The same is true with avoiding evil: an ungraced person can have a general hatred of evil, but this general hatred is "frustrated in a particular choice by the inclination of a habit or passion" (§ 566). This is not to say that the ungraced person can *never* will a particular good proportionate to their nature, as Aquinas affirms in *ST* I-II, q. 109, a. 2, recalling things like "building dwellings, plating vineyards, and the like." Rather the ungraced person, who is unable, so it seems, to cultivate natural *virtue* apart from grace, does not pursue the proportionate natural good "so as to fall short in nothing." And without the natural virtues, the ungraced person lacks the regularity, reliability, and totality in willing the particular good; see *ST* I-II, q. 65, a. 2; q. 109, aa. 2, 8; Michael Sherwin, O. P., *By Knowledge and By Love: Charity and Knowledge in the Moral Theology of St. Thomas Aquinas* (Washington, D.C.: The Catholic University Press, 2005), 124. I want to thank Richard Meloche for numerous discussions and debates regarding Aquinas and the ability (or inability) for cultivating natural virtue apart from grace.

14. For more on human action in Aquinas, see Joseph Pilsner, *The Specification of Human Actions in St Thomas Aquinas* (Oxford: Oxford University Press, 2006).

15. For a further explanation of the relationship between the rational and sensible powers described in terms of "political" and "despotic" rule, see *ST* I, q. 81, a. 3; I-II, q. 17, a. 7; q. 109, a. 9. It is essential for Aquinas that the sensitive appetites, in which the *fomes* dwell, have a certain

(7:25), Aquinas states that wretchedness dwells in man "either in flesh only, as in the just man, or also in the mind, as in the sinner" (§ 590). The soteriological effects of justifying grace leave the graced person in a "war" in which reason puts up a resistance—a successful resistance—to the disordered concupiscence of the flesh (§ 588).[16]

Calvin

Calvin is less focused on the particular faculties of human nature (e.g., intellect, will, passions) and instead subsumes all the faculties under the one description of "flesh" when speaking of the unregenerate, "flesh" and "spirit" when speaking of the regenerate. Calvin states that "flesh" *(carnis)* in 7:14 and 7:18, and its synonym "members" in 7:23, entails "all the endowments of human nature [*omnes hominae naturae dotes*], and everything that is in man [*omnino quicquid in homine est*], except the sanctification of the Spirit" (151.101–3). Calvin calls the "flesh" the "natural character" *(ingenium)* of a person at birth (147.56), or more pointedly one's "nature" (151.7).[17] To be sure, God endowed human beings with a spiritual soul that enabled humans to surpass the brute animals, yet by departing from the "law of his creation," humans have become "carnal and earthly." Although mankind still surpasses brute animals, the soul deprived of its spiritual excellence has degenerated and thus is rightly likened to the body in 7:24, "the body of death."[18]

---

independence from the intellectual appetites. This independence, as we shall see, allows Aquinas to dismiss the actual rise of disordered concupiscence as sin per se.

16. It is helpful to note Aquinas's comments on Rom 7:8, "Through the commandment, sin worked in me all concupiscence [*omnem concupiscentiam*]." Aquinas explains that with the coming of Christ's grace, the effects of original sin remain in terms of the *fomes peccati* or "habitual concupiscence" *(concupiscentia habitual)*, which works all actual concupiscence in a person. Aquinas differentiates the actual concupiscence both in terms of kinds of concupiscence (e.g., the covetousness in stealing, the covetousness in adultery, etc.) and in terms of the degrees *(gradus)* of concupiscence, which are thought *(cogitatio)*, pleasure *(delectatio)*, consent *(consensus)*, and deed *(opus)* (§ 542). The healing work of grace as depicted in Rom 7:14–25 prevents the degrees of concupiscence from reaching the stage of consent, which would result in reason giving itself over to the thoughts and pleasures of concupiscence.

17. Calvin is clear to distinguish between nature as created by God and nature as the derangement caused by sin. Calvin explains, "We call it 'natural' in order that no man may think that anyone obtains it through bad conduct, since it holds all men fast by hereditary right" (*Inst.* 2.1.11; see *The Bondage and Liberation of the Will: A Defense of the Orthodox Doctrine of Human Choice against Pighius*, ed. A. N. S. Lane and trans. G. I. Davies [Grand Rapids: Baker Books, 1996], 40; abbreviated *BLW* throughout. One finds this distinction in Augustine's *On Free Choice of the Will*: "We also use 'human nature' in two senses. In the strict sense, we mean the nature with which human beings were first created, a nature blameless after its kind. But we can also mean the nature of those of us who are born under the penalty of that [original] sin: mortal, ignorant, and enslaved to the flesh" (trans. Thomas Williams [Indianapolis, Ind.: Hackett Publishing, 1993], 108).

18. Commenting on "mortal body" in Rom 6:12, Calvin states that in the present "degenerate

On the other side is the "spirit," which is the renewed part of the corrupt nature, the newness that is a gift of the Holy Spirit and thus called "spirit" (147.59). It is the part of the soul "purified from evil" and "refashioned" so that the image of God shines through (151.3–5). The regenerated person is thus divided, "in a way a two-fold creature" *(quodammodo duplex est)*, in that part of his mind, affections, and heart are renewed while part is not.[19] According to Calvin, the renewed part is called the "mind" in 7:25, "I serve the law of God with my mind," which, Calvin explains, is not a reference to the "rational part of the soul honored by philosophers" but that part "illuminated" *(illustrare)* by the Spirit of God, in order that it might understand and will rightly *(recte sapiat et velit)* (155.39). This spiritually regenerated part of the soul corresponds to the "inward man" of 7:22[20] and is called inward *par excellence*, because it possesses the heart and "hidden affections" *(reconditos affectus)* (153.73–75). It is contrasted with the "appetites of the flesh" *(appetitus carnis)*, which wander "as it were outside of man" *(quasi extra hominem)* (153.74–75).

A key aspect to Calvin's anthropology and soteriology in Romans 7:14–25 is his emphasis on the *affectus*. The sanctification of the Spirit produces "affections" that lead one to obedience to God. The phrases "want" and "do not want" in 7:15 correspond to these affections, and the phrase "law of the mind" in 7:23 is "an affection rightly ordered" *(affectum rite compositum)* (153.79). Like Aquinas's *fomes*, these affections arise prior to the intellect, although Calvin speaks of them not in terms of "lower" but rather "deeper."[21] The most

---

state" the soul is "fixed to earth, and so enslaved to our bodies" that the soul has "fallen from its proper excellence"; human beings are indeed "corporeal," because they have been deprived of heavenly grace *(privatus coelesti gratia)*, and are merely a "kind of false shadow or image" *(fallax tantum umbra vel imago)* (128.83). Our spiritual newness by the Holy Spirit is "divine" and restores the image of God in us; for more on Calvin's doctrine of the soul, see Irene Backus, *Historical Method and Confessional Identity in the Era of the Reformation (1378–1615)* (Leiden: Brill, 2003), 86–101; Paul Helm, *John Calvin's Ideas* (Oxford: Oxford University Press, 2006), 157–83.

19. One of the critiques of Catholic polemicist Albert Pighius (1490–1542) against Calvin, at least as Calvin tells it, was Calvin's division of the believer's soul into two parts. Calvin argues from the seventh chapter of Romans, however, where Paul "bemoans the common bondage of the faithful in his own person," that Paul's teaching on the contrary desires of the will, combined with Paul's teaching on the "old man" and our need to renew the heart and mind into the image of God, demonstrate that in Paul, there is will against will, desire against desire, and mind against mind, so that Paul is a divided man *(BWL,* 179–80).

20. Calvin recognizes the phrase "inward man" of 2 Cor 4:16, but claims the phrase is used differently in Rom 7. The context of Rom 7 "requires" a different interpretation (153.71–75).

21. To be sure, Aquinas draws attention to the role of the affections proper, as well. Just to give one example, Aquinas states in his commentary on Galatians that to "walk by the Spirit" is for the Holy Spirit to "stir up" *(instigare)* and "incline" *(inclinare)* the affection for right willing (Marietti ed., vol. 1 [1959], § 308). It is to say that Calvin places upon them an emphasis, especially in relation to reason, that goes beyond that of Aquinas.

pronounced dichotomy within the regenerated person for Calvin, then, is the "disagreement by the flesh from the affection of the spirit" *(dissentiat a sua carne, spirituali affectu)* (150.79).

With their perspectives on "flesh," "spirit," and the healing work of grace in place, we now turn to consider the portraits of Paul conveyed by Aquinas and Calvin.

Portraits of Paul Painted from Romans 7:14–25

Aquinas

When Paul states in 7:14, "I am carnal, sold under sin," Aquinas claims that Paul's reason (the "I") is carnal by being "under attack from the flesh" (§ 560). He is "sold under sin" in that the *fomes* exist in his flesh and create a "rebellion" of his desires against his reason (§ 561). Similarly, when Paul says in 7:25b, "with my flesh, *I* serve the law of sin," Aquinas claims that Paul "serves" sin inasmuch as his flesh is moved to concupiscent desire *(movetur concupiscendum)* against his reason (§ 594). But the key is that these disordered desires do not come to fruition in an actual act of sin. When Paul states in 7:15, "For what I do, I do not understand," the "doing" for Aquinas is interpreted as Paul's "desiring," in that Paul desires *(concupiscentia)* evil through a passion in the sensitive appetite (§ 563).[22] But this desire, which precedes reason, is subsequently impeded by reason.

It is significant for Aquinas that Paul states at 7:15 "I do not understand" *(non intelligo)* rather than "I understand it is not to be done" *(intelligo non esse faciendum)*, since the later conveys that a deed is performed, while the former merely reflects the anthropological principle that desire arises prior to reason's judgment but, because of grace, is subsequently impeded by reason. It would require Paul "performing a deed or consenting with the mind" *(exequendo in opere vel consentiente mente)* for Paul to commit a sin (§ 563). In what way, then, does Paul in 7:15b "not do the good I want" *(non ago hoc bonum, quod volo agere)*? The good Paul wants is to "preserve his mind from wicked desires," but since even in the performance of a good act there are still disorderly movements of desire that arise from the sensitive appetites, Paul claims to be unable to accomplish this good (§ 565). This is in fact the reason for Paul's exclamation in 7:25a, "Who will deliver me from this body of death?" Paul longs for the resurrection, through which the *fomes peccati* will be completely eradicated (§ 592).

---

22. Commenting on 7:15b, Aquinas states, "'I do' refers to an incomplete action which has gone no further than the sense appetite and has not reached the stage of consent" (§ 565).

In light of what is to come in Calvin's exposition, we ask: is there *any* sin Paul admits to committing in Romans 7:14–25? According to Aquinas, there is. Paul commits a "sin of omission." Although Paul does not commit a sinful deed through the mind's consent to the *fomes*, Paul does sin by not *preventing* the influence of these "perverse desires" *(pravae concupiscentiae)* on his mind. When introducing 7:15b, Aquinas states, "In regard to the omission of the good [i.e., the sin of omission (§ 564)] therefore, Paul says, 'For I do not do the good I want'" (§ 565). The rise of perverse concupiscence per se does not constitute a sin, but it is Paul's failure to prevent the rise of the desires that renders Paul sinful insofar as he falls short of doing the good of preventing these desires.[23] Yet again, by not consenting to these desires with the mind, Paul speaks truthfully in 7:17 and 7:20: "it is no longer I [namely, reason] that do it but sin which dwells in me" (§ 569).[24] There are therefore no sins of commission. In fact, the *fomes* do not prevent Paul from doing truly good deeds. When Paul states in 7:18b, "I can will what is right," Aquinas claims that by grace Paul can fully will and, Aquinas adds, actually perform "some good" *(aliquid boni facio)* by resisting concupiscence and acting against it. When Paul immediately adds, "But I cannot do it," Aquinas interprets this to mean he "cannot do" this good "so as to exclude concupiscence altogether" (§ 580), as Aquinas previously argued (see § 565).[25] Paul, then, remains bound to his disordered desires in the sensitive appetite, although through his healed reason he can resist consenting to these desires and is furthermore enabled to actually perform the good.

It is helpful for understanding Aquinas's Pauline portrait to highlight why Aquinas favors the *ego* in a state of grace over the non-Christian *ego*. Two verses are of particular importance. The first is 7:17, "it is no longer I that do it, but sin which dwells [*habitat*] in me." For Aquinas, one of the central differences between someone who is ungraced and someone who is graced is whether or not one's reason consents *(consentire)* to the desires of the flesh *(fomes*

---

23. See *ST* I-II, q. 74, a. 2, 3, where Aquinas explains that all the powers that the will can move or restrain in their acts are the subjects of sin, which includes the sensitive appetite, since it is naturally inclined to be moved by the will. Yet, the rise of disordered concupiscence, since it does not occur from the deliberation of reason, is called a "venial sin," which, Aquinas explains, are sins not in the proper sense but rather "something imperfect in the genus of sin" *(quiddam imperfectum in genere peccat).*

24. As Aquinas explains in *ST* I-II, q. 10, a. 3, when both the reason and will remain "free" (i.e., "not entirely engrossed by the passion"), "there is no movement of the will in that man, and the passion alone holds its sway; or if there be a movement of the will, it does not necessarily follow the passion."

25. See *ST* I-II, q. 10, a. 3, ad 1, where Aquinas states, "Although the will cannot prevent the movement of concupiscence from arising ... it is in the power of the will not to will to desire, or not to consent to concupiscence."

peccati). Although sinful desires may rise within the person in a state of grace, that person's reason, having been healed and assisted by grace, will not consent to those desires. Aquinas thus claims at 7:17 that if the "I" (i.e., reason) is no longer the agent of the sinful act, then the "I" "cannot be properly understood of a man in sin" (§ 570). For the ungraced person, reason consents to sin and therefore that person commits it.[26] Although Aquinas is still willing to give an interpretation of 7:17 in terms of the ungraced person—doing so by an appeal to an action's "principal agent acting in virtue of its proper characteristics," which refers to the flesh and not reason—Aquinas admits up front that this interpretation is "forced" (§ 571).

The second verse is 7:18a, "For I know that good does not dwell in me, that is, in my flesh." The qualifier, "that is, in my flesh," is a critical insertion for understanding the indwelling of the good. According to Aquinas, grace, which is the "good" of 7:18a, dwells in the rational part of a person and not in the lower parts, where corrupt concupiscence is found (i.e., the flesh). Paul's assertion that "good" dwells in him means he has received Christ's grace in his mind (§ 573) but not "in my flesh." This qualifier would be superfluous, claims Aquinas, if Paul had been speaking in terms of the ungraced person, since "in a sinner the good of grace does not dwell either in regard to the flesh or the mind" (§ 576). Again, Aquinas offers a "forced" explanation for the ungraced person, namely that in the ungraced man, the good of grace dwells neither in the flesh nor in the mind (§ 576), but this forced interpretation is even less robust than the previous one.

Calvin

When Paul claims in 7:14, "I am carnal, sold into sin," Calvin explains that Paul is speaking of his "nature" and thus demonstrates that all his parts—his mind, heart, and all his actions—are inclined toward sin, being driven by sin, although not in terms of compulsion but by his own free will (147.74–76).[27] Paul in 7:15a "does what he knows not" in that he does not acknowledge his imperfect works as his own *(non agnoscere ut sua)* because of his regeneration; instead, he hates them with the affection wrought in him by the Spirit (149.39–40). Calvin acknowledges that this is not to say that Paul is always

26. Aquinas is guided by Augustine on this point, quoting Augustine from a gloss in Lombard's *Collectanea* (col. 1429): "Greatly deceived is the man who has consented to the desires of the flesh and decides to do what they desire and then thinks he can say to himself: 'It is not I doing this'" (§ 570).

27. Calvin is clear that he has no place for coercion, compulsion, or force as it pertains to human choice; see *BLW*, 204; *Inst.* 2.3.5, 2.4.1, 2.5.1. But Calvin also wants to maintain that apart from grace, human beings cannot choose what is good in the sight of God. The complexities of this argument, particularly Calvin's use of Aristotle in differentiating necessity from coercion, take us beyond the scope of this chapter.

incapable of doing good altogether, since by stating in 7:17, "it is no more I that do it but sin which dwells in me," Paul denies that he is "wholly possessed by sin" *(totum a peccato occupari)* and "exempts himself from bondage to it" *(ab eius servitute se eximit)* (150.84–85). But when he says in 7:15b that he "does what he does not will," Paul shows that he is unable to pursue the good with "due alacrity" *(decet alacritate)* and "right exertion" *(iusta strenuitate),* and thus fails in doing the good he wished by "stumbling through the weakness of the flesh" (149.55–150.57). Because of the regeneration of the Spirit, Paul can say in 7:19 that "to will is present," which Calvin interprets as the "readiness of faith," or in 7:22, "I delight in the law of God," since Paul is "judging and esti-mating" himself by the regenerated part of his soul (153.59–60). This readiness or delight is formed in Paul by the Spirit and enables Paul to "consent to the law seriously and with most eager desire of his heart" *(serio quoque et promp-tissimo pectoris desiderio consentit)* (150.75–76). Yet by immediately claiming in 7:19b, "but to do that which is good is not [present]," Paul acknowledges that he regards no work that he does as being free from "fault," so that even Paul's "best work" is "always corrupted by some mark of sin [*macula*], so that no re-ward [*merces*] can be hoped for, except insofar as God pardons [*ignoscit*] them" (151.23–25).[28]

This leads to Paul's "anxious cry of distress" in 7:24, "Who shall deliver me out of this body of death?" Paul demonstrates that "even the most perfect are subject to misery" (154.9–10), since when they "examine themselves thor-oughly, they find nothing in their own nature but wretchedness" (154.10–11). This should not lead to despair or murmuring against God, however, as Paul shows by immediately stating in 7:25a, "I thank God through Jesus Christ our Lord" *(Gratias ago Deo, per Iesum Christum Dominum nostrum).*[29] Even as

---

28. Commenting on Rom 3:22, Calvin states that although works are *considered* just before God upon one's being in Christ through faith, the works are still imperfect in themselves. Rather, they are purified through the blood of Christ, so that "God rewards our works as perfect, because their defects are covered by free pardon" *(opera nostra, ceu perfecta, remuneratur Deus, quia defectus gratuita venia tegitur)* (71.51–52). The gratuitous justification received through faith puts God in a propitious relationship toward that individual. In this relationship God enables his or her works to be reward-worthy by "covering" the work's defilement with the purity of Christ; the works them-selves must be justified, pardoned of their imperfection and impurity (*Canons and Decrees of the Council of Trent, with an Antidote,* in *Selected Works of John Calvin: Tracts and Letters,* edited and trans. Henry Beveridge and Jules Connet [Grand Rapids, Mich.: Baker Book House, 1983], 3:145; abbreviated *Antidote* throughout). In sum, "Since only works uninfected with defilement [*sordibus*] are counted just, it is quite evident that no human work whatever can please God, except through a favor [*indulgentia*] of this kind" (84.74–76); see *Inst.* 3.14.9; see also John H. Leith, *John Calvin's Doctrine of the Christian Life* (Louisville, Ky.: Westminster John Knox Press, 1989), 95–106.

29. Compare with Aquinas's text: *Gratia Dei per Iesum Christum Dominum nostrum.* While Calvin's Paul is "giving thanks" *(gratias ago)* in 7:25, Aquinas's Paul is highlighting the work of God's grace *(gratia Dei).*

Paul examines his defects, he does not forget what he has received and thus "rests in the grace of God" (155.28). All is summarized for Calvin in 7:25b, "I with the mind serve the law of God, but with the flesh the law of sin." Paul teaches that on account of the ongoing remaining flesh, believers "never reach the goal of righteousness" and are always "defiled with much corruption." Yet because of the sanctification of the Spirit, they are also able to "understand and will aright" and thus serve the law of God with an "earnest desire of the heart" (155.35–42).

Implications of the Portrait

David Steinmetz rightly points out that we must not oversimplify interpretations of Romans 7 by neatly categorizing them as either Catholic portraits of Paul or Reformed portraits.[30] The issues are far too complex and the judgments too intertwined for such categorization, as we shall see. At the same time, we find that Aquinas's and Calvin's conceptions of the "Christian struggle" as conveyed in 7:14–25 embody judgments important to the distinction between Catholic and Reformed traditions. In this section, we will focus on the topics of the nature of sin, the notion of perfection, merit, and Paul's apostolicity.

Nature of Sin

Aquinas focuses on the dynamic relationship between the mind and the *fomes:* although the *fomes* gives rise to disordered desires that lead the believer away from the good, the mind, having been healed by the grace of Christ, is able to put up a successful resistance to the *fomes* and instead choose the good. Calvin, on the other hand, is broader in his description, situating the struggle between the whole of the individual as "natural" and the whole of the individual as "taken over" by the Spirit, that is, sanctified. The believer is "as it were a two-fold man." Aquinas and Calvin agree that Paul is justified by faith through grace in Christ, and Christ's justification effects healing in Paul that disposes him toward love and obedience to God.[31] As noted above, Calvin grants that one can "understand and will aright" on account of grace, and that the Spirit creates "holy affections" that enable one to resist the flesh. Calvin also stresses that Paul is not denying that he does good; his issue is

30. Steinmetz, *Calvin in Context*, 110–121.

31. My concern in this section is not their respective doctrines of justification, and therefore I will not go into detail regarding the similarities and differences of that particular doctrine (e.g., imputation, infusion, forensic, etc.). My concern is to analyze the picture of Paul's moral life in light of the effects of grace on the justified believer.

with the effects of the flesh on Paul's ability to do the *perfect* good.[32] Aquinas, too, addresses Paul's ability to do the perfect good, and like Calvin he denies a certain perfection of Paul.[33] Aquinas and Calvin agree that Paul remains a sinner, and full healing does not occur until after death. As Aquinas demonstrates, as long as Paul remains in the flesh he remains a sinner in his struggle with his disordered desires. It is impossible to rid oneself entirely of the *fomes* in this life. Aquinas goes on to affirm, however, that Paul performs truly good works that are meritorious, and that although Paul sins he remains justified on account of his intrinsic or transformative justice. Calvin, on the other hand, denies the meritorious nature of Paul's works, as well as the notion that Paul has been transformed to the extent of having his justice as the grounds for justification. Given the agreements between Aquinas and Calvin above, how to they come to such different judgments? One of the keys pertains to their judgment regarding the nature of Paul's sin.[34]

For Aquinas, grace has brought healing to Paul's reason and to such an extent that Paul does not consent to the sinful desires of concupiscence. Aquinas locates the meritoriousness of the act in the movement of the mind, whatever may be the disordered movement of the sense appetites. Even with the presence of concupiscence, Paul is able to perform a truly good act. To be sure, with the rise of concupiscence Paul commits the *venial* sin of omission by failing to prevent the rise of these desires. But it is important that the sin is only venial, as can be seen from *Summa theologiae (ST)* I-II, q. 74, a. 4, where Aquinas asks whether sin (generally speaking) is compatible with virtue. Aquinas argues that sin is in fact compatible with virtue, and thus one can both be justified (i.e., possess the virtues of faith, hope, and love) and commit sin. A justified person can retain his or her charity while still committing sin. But this is where the distinction between mortal and venial sin is crucial. The sin compatible with charity is venial sin, not mortal sin. Mortal sin puts one in a state of damnation. Mortal sin is contrary to charity; if charity is extinguished by one act of mortal sin,[35] the other virtues disappear as virtues.

---

32. On this point, see Richard Muller, "'Scimus Enim Quod Lex Spiritualis Est': Melanchthon and Calvin on the Interpretation of Romans 7:14–23," in *Philip Melanchthon (1497–1560) and the Commentary*, ed. Timothy J. Wengert and M. Patrick Graham (Sheffield: Sheffield Academic Press, 1997), 234–35.

33. See below for more on perfection.

34. The other key is their understanding of perfection, which I address below.

35. In *ST* I-II, q. 87, a. 3, Thomas expounds upon his reason for rooting eternal punishment in an act against charity. Charity is the principle by which a person adheres to the last end of the divine order, that end being God. Aquinas then asserts that if the principle by which a person takes part in a particular order is destroyed, there is a debt of punishment corresponding to the disturbance of the order. Mortal sin destroys the principle of charity in the divine order and thus

Venial sin, however, is not contrary to charity, and thus venial sin does not banish charity.[36] Aquinas can thus affirm that Christians can still commit venial sins, as is the case with Paul, and remain in a justified state before God on account of their intrinsic justice.[37]

Calvin, on the other hand, makes two moves that differ from Aquinas as pertains to the nature of Paul's sin. First, although Calvin maintains that Paul's healing is partial, even if ever-increasing, so that there still remains Paul's sinful *affectus* that arise prior to the judgment of the intellect, as is the case of disordered concupiscence for Aquinas, Calvin claims that the presence of the sinful *affectus* is per se sin, which is not the case for Aquinas.[38] For Calvin, disordered or depraved affections are sinful "however much we may withhold consent" (142.4–6), and he explicitly argues against the "Papists" who "fiercely maintain that [concupiscence] in the regenerate is not sin" (142.12).[39]

---

incurs the corresponding debt of eternal punishment, which is the proportionate punishment to the severity of destroying charity. Venial sin does not do this, since a person may be too much or too little intent on a particular thing in the order but he or she does not have preference for these things above the last end (*ST* I-II, q. 87, a. 5).

36. In *ST* I-II, q. 77, a. 8, Thomas gives three ways in which a sin may be considered venial. First, from its cause *(ex causa)*, that is, if the sin has a cause that should receive pardon *(venia)* (e.g., ignorance, weakness); second, from its issue *(ex eventu)*, that is, all sins become venial through repentance (i.e., they receive pardon [*venia*]); third, from its genre *(ex genere)* (e.g., an idle word). It is possible, however, that if a venial sin is committed regularly, it can destroy charity by forming a contrary vice.

37. From this account, it becomes clearer what the effects would be if one rejected the venial/mortal distinction and instead maintained that all sins are mortal. On Aquinas's account, one would be unable to stand in a state of justification in this life. But this is untenable, since people are justified and reach salvation. Therefore, the justice by which one stands at peace with God must be something "alien" to that person, something that is imputed to a person in such a way that our (mortal) sins do not render it void. This is exactly the move that Calvin makes.

38. In his commentary on Rom 8:1, Aquinas engages the thought of "some" (Aquinas may be thinking of Anselm [see *ST* I-II, q. 89, a. 5]) who hold that the movements of concupiscence are damnable in unbelievers, although not in believers by virtue of being "in Christ Jesus." But according to Aquinas, these movements are not damnable in unbelievers either, since the desire has not reached the consent of reason, which is a requirement of a damnable sin (i.e., a mortal sin) (see *ST* I-II, q. 79, a. 4). Therefore, the movements of concupiscence are damnable for neither unbelievers nor believers (§§ 597–98; see *ST* I-II, q. 89, a. 5).

39. Barbara Pitkin argues that one of the "most significant" departures of the Reformers from the dominant consensus on sin was Luther's claim, followed by Calvin, that postbaptismal concupiscence was sin. Pitkin states, "Though Luther appealed to Augustine to support his view that the concupiscence that remains after baptism is still sin, Augustine's own position is more likely that postbaptismal concupiscence is *vitium* but not sin" ("Nothing but Concupiscence: Calvin's Understanding of Sin and the *Via Augustini*," *Calvin Theological Journal* 34, no. 2 [1999]: 367). Christopher Allen argues, however, that Trent departed from earlier Catholic teaching by denying sin in the justified ("The Pastoral and Political Implications of Trent on Justification: A Response to the ARCIC Agreed Statement *Salvation and the Church*," *Churchman* 103 [1989]: 15–31; cited in Lane, *Justification by Faith*, 170). Steinmetz comments that the issue that sixteenth-century

Commenting in his *Antidote* to the Council of Trent, Calvin points to
7:14–25 as a demonstration that "sin" does not stand merely for the cause or
punishment of sin, since Paul calls it a "law" and "evil." Instead, Paul is demonstrating that "repugnance to the law of God is truly sin," and therefore concupiscence "of its own nature is sin."[40] In his commentary on 7:7, where Paul
references the commandment, "Thou shall not covet," Calvin makes the object of the commandment not an action but the covetous desires themselves.[41]

Catholic commentators had with the "heretics," "especially Lutheran heretics," is, "they regard any
stirring of concupiscence as sinful in itself apart from the will's consent" (*Calvin in Context*, 305). I
note that there is one weakness in the accounts of Pitkin and Steinmetz: though some theologians
at the time of the Reformation regarded concupiscence as altogether unsinful, Pitkin and Steinmetz do not sufficiently engage the controversy surrounding concupiscence in regard to its status
as mortal or venial. Calvin approvingly acknowledges that there are those who hold to be sin "desire without deliberate consent." The problem, however, is that they call it venial and they limit sin
proper (i.e., mortal) to a *direct* transgression of the Tenth Commandment. Calvin sought to uni-
versalize the sin of concupiscence by rooting it in something prior to the deliberate act, that is, in
the powers of the soul itself (*Inst.* 2.8.58), as well as to establish this sin as a mortal sin (*Inst.* 2.8.59).
    40. Calvin, *Antidotes*, 87. Calvin's cites numerous passages from Augustine, but the most
prominent one is taken from Augustine's fifth book against Julian, which, according to Calvin,
demonstrates that Augustine held "the concupiscence of the flesh, which the Good Spirit resists,
is also sin, because there is disobedience in it against the dominion of the mind, and the punishment of sin because inflicted on the demerits of the disobedient, and the cause of sin from defect
of will or corruption of nature" (88). Calvin is a little less certain about Augustine's position in
Inst. 3.3.10, however, agreeing that Augustine at times seems to deny that remaining concupiscence
is sin: "There is this difference apparently between Augustine and us, that while he admits that
believers, so long as they are in the body, are so liable to concupiscence that they cannot but feel it,
he does not venture to give this disease the name of sin. He is contented with giving it the name
of infirmity, and says, that it only becomes sin when either external act or consent is added to
conception or apprehension; that is, when the will yields to the first desire." But Calvin also acknowledges, "Augustine himself does not always refrain from using the name sin." For Aquinas,
such tension in Augustine's language contributes to the need to distinguish between types of sin
such as mortal and venial.
    41. For Calvin, Augustine is right, if rightly understood, in claiming that the whole law is
included in this commandment, since this commandment straightforwardly condemns the concupiscence (the "hidden disease") from which stem the evil actions addressed by the other commandments; since there is a "great difference between a deliberate purpose and the appetites by
which we are provoked" (*multum inter deliberatam voluntatem interest, et appetites quibus titil-
lamur* [142.103–4]), this last commandment clearly demonstrates that even the "appetites" and
"corrupt lusts" (*vitiosa cupiditas*) that move to evil are condemned, "however much we withhold
our consent" (*utcunque non accedat consensus* [142.105–6]). Aquinas, too, refers to Augustine in
agreement, but according to Aquinas, Augustine's point is that concupiscence is a "general sin"
in that it is "common" to all sins. By "general sin," Aquinas makes clear it is not a generality of
genus or species, but a generality of causality, since "the root and cause of every sin is some *special
concupiscence*" (§ 538; italics added). In an analogous manner, then, as a common cause of sin, concupiscence generally speaking is called a "general sin." At the same time, Aquinas's phrase, "special concupiscence," is essential for understanding Paul's use of the commandment, "Thou shalt
not covet." This commandment addresses a particular manifestation of a special concupiscence,
since the entire phrase states, "Thou shalt not covet your neighbor's property." For Aquinas, this

For Calvin, the commandments go deeper (or "higher") in their requirements for uprightness than can be found in either civic laws or in the philosophy. Although civic laws punish "intention" *(consilia)* and philosophers "with greater refinement" locate vice and virtue in the "mind" *(animus)*, God penetrates deeper into one's nature and declares concupiscence, which is "more concealed than the will," to be sin.[42] For Calvin, then, Romans 7 ends the controversy of being able to truly keep the commandments of the law on account of the ongoing presence of disordered desires.[43]

Second, Calvin rejects the distinction between venial and mortal sin, so that all sin is mortal sin, and thus all of Paul's works by being tainted by these *affectus* are mortally sinful before the judgment of God and deserve shame and death rather than reward.[44] Although Calvin admits in his *Institutes* that the stain on the works of the saints is "slight," Paul continues to commit mortal sin by breaking the Tenth Commandment, "You shall not covet."[45] In light of the Tenth Commandment, Calvin addresses those who teach that venial sin is "desire without deliberate assent, which does not long remain in the heart."[46] Calvin refutes the notion that this desire does not break the Tenth Commandment. For Calvin, the desire itself would not surface did not the individual "lack those things required in the law." Since the command is to love God with the whole heart, mind, and soul, "unless all the powers of the soul are intent on loving God, we have already abandoned obedience to the law."[47]

---

commandment, then, addresses the concupiscence of "avarice." The commandment is therefore not straightforwardly condemning concupiscence per se as a sin, but rather the commandment addresses a particular kind of corrupt concupiscence (§ 537), which can be applied to all particular forms of concupiscence, and condemns the act (the sin proper) stemming from that particular concupiscence.

42. In *Inst.* 2.8.49 Calvin, while commenting on the Tenth Commandment, distinguishes between "intention" *(consilium)* and "coveting" *(concupiscentia)*, the former being the "deliberate consent of will where lust subjects the heart [*deliberata voluntatis consensio, ubi animum libido subiugavit*]," while the latter, which is that which is prohibited by the Tenth Commandment, can exist without such deliberation or consent of the mind.

43. Calvin, *Antidote*, 134.

44. Calvin explicitly rejects the distinction between mortal and venial sin at *Inst.* 2.8.58–59, claiming that all sin "is a violation of the law, upon which God's judgment is pronounced without exception." It is quite surprising that in A. N. S. Lane's otherwise excellent work *Justification by Faith in Catholic-Protestant Dialogue* that, when addressing the topic of "Does Sin Remain in the Christian" (167–76), Lane says nothing about the mortal-venial distinction, which is crucial for understanding the Catholic position on remaining sin in the justified.

45. Calvin engages the notion of "venial sin" and its connection to concupiscence at *Inst.* 2.8.58, and he argues that although the doctrine of venial sin maintains that the rise of concupiscent desire is a break of the Tenth Commandment, it does not see the rise itself as a consequence of lacking those things required by the Law.

46. *Inst.* 2.8.58.

47. Ibid.

The comfort for the believer, however, is that although of its own nature con-cupiscence is mortal sin, for the justified "it is not imputed and the guilt is abolished by the grace of Christ."[48]

Perfection

Underlying Aquinas's and Calvin's portraits is also a different understand-ing of perfection. For Calvin, obedience to the law consists in obedience that flows from "perfect love," so that "in the judgment of God nothing is genuine and good, save what flows from perfect love to Him."[49] If a person has perfect love for God, however, Calvin believes, there would not arise the disordered desires of the flesh, nor would there arise any thoughts at all contrary to love.[50] Perfect love consists in the whole of one's being fully participating in obedience to God without the presence of any perverse desire. Calvin claims in *Inst.* 2.8.50 that he learned from Augustine, "God commands a strong and ardent love, which is not to be impeded by any portion, however minute, of concupiscence." The very presence of disordered desires thus demonstrates an individual's im-perfect love and therefore the corresponding imperfect obedience in keeping God's commandments.[51] In *Inst.* 2.7.5, Calvin again notes Augustine, this time on imperfection of our love for God in this life, and states, "The law cannot be fulfilled in this life of the flesh, if we observe the weakness of our own nature." Calvin concludes on perfection: "We never attain to [the perfection of char-ity] unless we fulfill all the parts of charity; and will thence infer, that as all are most remote from such fulfillment, the hope of perfection is excluded."[52] Disordered desires are not removed in this life, and therefore it is impossible for any person in this life to obey the law with perfect charity. Since no work of the believer is perfect, no work of the believer is meritorious, but rather the work must be first "justified" before God receives it and grants rewards for it. This occurs for believers due to being united to Christ through faith.

Aquinas, however, also admits, like Calvin, that Paul does not have a form of perfect love for God that will occur only in beatitude. He also admits that

48. Calvin, *Antidote*, 87. Calvin agrees with Trent that God hates nothing in the justified, but only because "God pardons what he might justly hate" (86).

49. Ibid., 130, 156–58. At *Inst.* 2.8.51, Calvin claims that "nothing more is required" for perfec-tion than obedience to the Ten Commandments through charity.

50. See *Inst.* 2.8.50: "Were your mind wholly imbued with charity, no portion of it would re-main for the entrance of such thoughts [that are hurtful to your brother]. Insofar, therefore, as the mind is devoid of charity, it must be under the influence of concupiscence."

51. Calvin, *Antidote*, 160–61. Because Calvin believes that Trent interprets concupiscence as "a mere whetstone to sharpen virtue" (87), Calvin derides the Fathers of Trent for making "the foulest lust praiseworthy trials of virtue" (161).

52. *Inst.* 3.18.8.

there are disordered desires in Paul that will be removed only through the resurrection. But Aquinas still maintains that Paul commits condignly meritorious works and thus truly fulfills the law. How can Aquinas hold this position? One reason pertains to Aquinas's understanding of virtue, and the other to Aquinas's anthropology. Aquinas can affirm that charity, as a virtue, truly exists in Paul, as well as faith, while maintaining that Paul will have perfect charity and the clearest intellectual vision of God only in beatitude.[53] Aquinas distinguishes between the possession of and participation in the gift of charity in such a way that a person is able to possess charity and perform a charitable act that fulfills the law and corresponds to a human's supernatural end without necessitating that a person has the most intense participation in the virtue of charity.[54] When God infuses charity into the soul, the individual obtains a perfection in charity that consists not in loving God as much as is humanly possible but rather in removing all obstacles contrary to the love of God.[55] This manifests itself in joyful obedience to the law of love and avoidance of sin and concupiscence. Individuals can possess love for God by possessing the virtue of charity, while also declaring that they do not love God to the extent that hope to in the future. In *ST* I-II, q. 67, a. 6, Aquinas, while agreeing that "the charity of the wayfarer cannot attain to the perfection of the charity of heaven," roots the less perfect nature of wayfarer charity not in the virtue of charity itself, as if the charity of the wayfarer were of a different kind than the charity of heaven ("Charity is not done away by the perfection of glory but remains identically the same"), but rather in the cause of char-

---

53. One of the best contemporary accounts of Aquinas's teaching on perfection, from which my analysis draws substantially, is Edgardo A. Colón-Emeric, *Wesley, Aquinas, and Christian Perfection: An Ecumenical Dialogue* (Waco, Tex.: Baylor University Press, 2009). Most pertinent to my analysis is chapter 4, "Aquinas on the Way to Christian Perfection."

54. Aquinas looks at fulfilling the commandments of the law in two ways: in terms of the *substance* of the work, and in terms of the *mode*. For example, a person can give money to the poor (i.e., the substance of the work) seeking to gain the praise of his friends (i.e., the mode); or a person can give money to the poor (i.e., the substance) out of love for God (i.e., the mode). The right mode for obedience is charity for God. It is noteworthy that Aquinas removes the mode of keeping the law from the punishment of the law (*ST* I-II, q. 100, a. 9). Thus, individuals avoid punishment because they fulfilled its substance, even if from the wrong principle (*ST* I-II, q. 100, a. 10). To be sure, such an act would still not be considered a meritoriously just act before God, since such acts require God's grace and are performed in charity (*ST* I-II, q. 100, a. 12).

55. Colón-Emeric, *Wesley, Aquinas, and Christian Perfection*, 109. Colón-Emeric makes three distinctions regarding perfect charity. Considered on the part of the beloved, perfect charity consists in loving God as much as God is lovable, which no creature can do in this life or in the next. Considered on the part of the lover, perfect charity can be considered in two ways. The first sense consists of the lover loving as much as is humanly possible, thus loving God at all times in every act. This occurs only in glory. The second sense consists in removing obstacles contrary to the love of God. This is the perfection of charity possible in the present life.

ity, which is one's knowledge of God, so that as that knowledge becomes perfect in heaven, so does one's charity reach the highest perfection.[56] Because of the different degrees of perfection of charity, Aquinas can agree with Calvin that Paul's works are not done out of perfect charity, if by this Calvin means the highest perfection of knowledge and charity that occurs in heaven. The fact that Paul commits the venial sin of omission for failing to avoid the rise of the disordered desires demonstrates that Paul has a greater perfection yet to attain.[57] And even in the present life, a person who possesses the virtue of charity can participate in this virtue in a greater or lesser way.[58] Aquinas can affirm that the same work can be done out of more or less charity, so that the same condignly meritorious work could be performed with even greater love. Nevertheless, these admissions do not detract from the fact that works of the believer are done out of charity, however intense it may be, and therefore truly fulfill the law, because faith and love are truly present within the believer due to God's grace, even if not present in their highest intensity.[59]

What about the presence of the disordered desires? Why for Aquinas do they not render all works as "tainted" and therefore unable to truly fulfill the law? The answer is due in part to Aquinas's understanding of the relationship between human reason and the carnal appetites from which stem the disordered desires. Aquinas, drawing from Aristotle, likens the relationship between reason and the carnal appetites in political terms, describing the rule of reason over the carnal appetites as a "royal and political sovereignty" rather than a "despotic sovereignty."[60] What this means for Aquinas is that the carnal appetites, although ruled by reason, have a certain independence from reason and therefore can act without the command of reason and at times counter to the command of reason.[61] With the coming of grace, the virtues of

56. On the relationship between knowledge and love in Aquinas, see Sherwin, *By Knowledge and By Love.*

57. See *ST* II-II, q. 24, a. 8, ad 2.

58. Aquinas's use of virtue ethics undergirds his vision for the whole of justification as both complete and progressive. Justification is fully given at one's initial justification, that is, the individual is truly made just through grace and declared at peace with God. Nevertheless, the individual is able to increase in his or her participation in the virtues of faith, hope, and love, and therefore increase in justification inasmuch as the individual participates more deeply in the virtues of faith, hope, and love as those virtues intensify within the believer.

59. It must be kept in mind that Aquinas's claim that individuals can possess perfect charity as wayfarers is not the equivalent of claiming wayfarers have perfect conformity to Christ: "The adoption as sons of God is through a certain conformity of the image of the nature son of God. Now this takes place in two ways: first, by the grace of the wayfarer, which is imperfect conformity; secondly, by glory, which is perfection conformity" (*ST* III, q. 45, a. 1). Possessing a form of perfect charity as a wayfarer still leaves the wayfarer imperfectly conformed to Christ.

60. *ST* I-II, q. 9, a. 2, ad. 3; I-II, q. 17, a. 7.

61. Calvin does not seem to have a place for this sort of "political" relationship between the

faith and charity now reside in the rational part of the human—the intellect and will—from which come works that fulfill the law; but the carnal appetites have yet to be healed.[62] The result is a dynamic in which carnal desires arise that do not stem from reason's command and are contrary to reason's command but are subsequently checked by reason from reaching the place of consent. The graced individual can therefore avoid mortal sin by not consenting to the desires and instead fulfill the commandments of the law through charity while struggling with the carnal desires and even committing venial sin. But as noted above, the habit of charity and venial sins are able to coexist.[63]

It seems that from Aquinas's perspective, Calvin correctly points to the lack of love that humans have for God in this wayfarer life; believers do not love God as much as is humanly possible. He is correct to note the presence of the flesh as a sign of not having a most perfect love of God and the dimness of one's present vision of God as hindering Christians from this most perfect love. Believers do not presently fulfill the law of love in the highest way and must await glory to do so. But for Aquinas, Calvin uses heavenly standards to judge the wayfarer life, so that he does not provide enough room for the presence of disordered desires as compatible with a form of charity that fulfills the law. Calvin judges the works of believers through the paradigm of the highest

---

disordered desires and reason; see Margaret Miles, "Theology, Anthropology, and the Human Body in Calvin's *Institutes of the Christian Religion*," *Harvard Theological Review* 74, no. 3 (1981): 310.

62. *ST* I-II, q. 109, a. 8.

63. *ST* II-II, q. 24, a. 8. It is interesting to note that both Aquinas and Calvin employ Augustine to arrive at different conclusions regarding the perfection of charity. Aquinas uses Augustine as his authoritative text for *ST* II-II, q. 24, a. 8, to argue *for* the presence of perfect charity in this life and therefore the ability to fulfill the law even with the presence of remaining "flesh," while Calvin uses Augustine in *Inst.* 2.7.5 and *Inst.* 2.8.50 to argue *against* the presence of perfect charity in this life and therefore the inability to fulfill the law due to the presence of remaining "flesh." Aquinas does recognize in *ST* II-II, q. 24, a. 8 that Augustine at times sounds contrary to his position, quoting Augustine as saying, "Whatever kindles charity quenches cupidity, but where charity is perfect, cupidity is done away altogether," which sounds strikingly similar to the point Calvin makes regarding perfect charity. Aquinas, however, once again employs the crucial distinction between venial and mortal sins in order to claim that in the term "cupidity" Augustine is addressing venial sins, which are, again, compatible with the habit of charity, so that from Aquinas's perspective although Augustine is right as it pertains to the perfection of charity in glory, where all cupidity will be removed, his comment does not detract from claiming a certain perfection of charity in the wayfarer that fulfills the law, as mentioned above. When Calvin cites Augustine against perfect charity, stating, "Love so follows knowledge that no one can love God perfectly who does not first fully know his goodness. While we wander upon the earth, 'we see in a mirror dimly.' Therefore, it follows that our love is imperfect" (*Inst.* 2.7.5), from which Calvin concludes, "It is impossible, then, in this flesh to fulfill the law, if we observe the weakness of our nature," Aquinas would understand Augustine's statement as addressing the perfection of charity that corresponds to loving God as much as is humanly possible, which occurs only in glory, where God is beheld "face to face." But for Aquinas, this does not negate the presence of charity in this life that enables a fulfillment of the law corresponding to the wayfarer perfection.

perfection of love that is possible only in glory, while for Aquinas there is a form of love for God possible in this present life that does fulfill the law, albeit not in the most perfect way. By being moved by God through these virtues instilled in the believer by grace, the believer is able to perform condignly meritorious works that truly fulfill the law even while struggling with the flesh and hoping for greater love in the future.

Merit

The portraits of Aquinas and Calvin also have implications for a doctrine of merit. Calvin is well aware that his portrait of Paul in Romans 7:14–25, particularly his claim that even Paul's best works are accepted by God only by being first pardoned of their sin in Christ (151.23–25),[64] undermines the doctrine of merit being taught by his opponents, who assert, according to Calvin, "A man once for all reconciled to God through faith in Christ may be reckoned righteous before God by good works and be accepted by the merit of them."[65] For Calvin, as he makes clear throughout his Romans commentary, the works of even the saintliest of saints are always tainted and therefore cannot be considered meritorious. "The spots and blemishes of the works (of the justified) are covered by the purity of Christ, lest they should come into judgment, and being unpolluted by any defilements, thereby considered righteous. It is quite clear that apart from such forbearances no human work at all can please God" (85.73–76).

For Aquinas, however, Paul's good works that occur through the supernaturally infused gift of charity truly fulfill the Law and in such a way as to be condignly meritorious. The presence of disordered concupiscence does not de facto negate the condignly meritorious nature of a good work; Paul is able

---

64. Calvin makes a similar argument in his commentary on Romans 4, where he states, "The spots and blemishes of the works (of the justified) are covered by the purity of Christ, lest they should come into judgment, and being unpolluted by any defilements, thereby considered righteous. It is quite clear that apart from such forbearances no human work at all can please God" (85.73–76). These observations support Packer's claim that the Reformers used Rom 7:14–25 to show that "there is sin in the best Christians' best works" ("The 'Wretched Man' Revisited," 71). Richard Muller, in his introduction to Dewey J. Hoitenga Jr., *John Calvin and the Will: A Critique and Corrective* (Grand Rapids, Mich.: Baker Book House, 1997), 8, reminds those who study Calvin's understanding of the will to keep in mind "the context of debate in which Calvin lived and worked and his assumption of the non-meritorious nature of any and all goods works."

65. *Inst.* 3.14.11. For an extended comparison of Aquinas and Calvin on merit, see Charles Raith II, "Calvin's Critique of Merit, and Why Aquinas (Mostly) Agrees," *Pro Ecclesia* 20 (2011): 135–66, where it is argued that Calvin's three main objections against his opponent's teaching on merit—(a) it being conveyed as a grounds alongside of faith for salvation, (b) the act being understood within a competitive causal schema, and (c) the act being granted a worth corresponding to the reward—largely miss Aquinas as a target.

to possess charity without charity existing as it will in the future state of highest perfection (i.e., beatitude). The good work performed in Paul's imperfect state does not necessitate the claim that the good work is "tainted," but rather Paul looks forward to the day that his obedience will be unhindered, that is, without the presence of the *fomes*.[66] The fact that Paul is not yet perfected but performs a meritorious work reveals that for Aquinas a condignly meritorious work is not the equivalent of a work done in the state of perfection. The same work considered condignly meritorious could be done out of greater charity, in greater faith, and with greater hope; the work's condignity refers not to a work of highest perfection but to the fact that it truly fulfills the substance of God's command through the principle that corresponds to one's supernatural end, that is, grace.

Paul's Apostolicity

The fact that the *ego* of 7:14 is understood as the *Apostle* Paul colors Aquinas's and Calvin's interpretation on account of their approaches to Paul's apostolicity. For Aquinas, Paul's apostolicity significantly distinguishes Paul from the common lot of Christian believers, not merely in terms of authority but also in terms of moral exemplarity. The apostles, according to Aquinas, "have the first fruits of the Spirit," and had the Holy Spirit "before others and more abundantly than others" (§ 676). They are "greater than all other saints," whether it is in "virginity or learning or martyrdom," since "they have the spirit more fully" and have been given grace more abundantly than all else, with the exception of Christ and Mary (§ 678).[67] Aquinas's prologue to his lectures on Romans paints a picture of Paul as the "chosen vessel of God." Picking up on the term *vessel*, Aquinas gives an illustrious presentation of the Apostle: he is a "golden vessel" on account of his remarkable wisdom and "contains" Christ in both his intellect and his affections; his "use" was to carry forth the name of Christ both in words and in body, and his "usefulness" was the result of being free of sin and error (§§ 1–10). This is the Paul that Aquinas brings to his exposition of the *ego* of 7:14–21.

Calvin, on the other hand, shows no indication of bringing this sort of apostolic uniqueness into his interpretation of 7:14–25. In fact, we find Calvin's

---

66. For a more thorough discussion of Aquinas's doctrine of merit, see Joseph Wawrykow, *God's Grace and Human Action: "Merit" in the Theology of Thomas Aquinas* (Notre Dame, Ind.: University of Notre Dame Press, 1995); Michael Root, "Aquinas, Merit, and Reformation Theology after the *Joint Declaration on the Doctrine of Justification," Modern Theology* 20, no. 1 (2004): 5–22.

67. See Thomas F. Ryan, "The Love of Learning and the Desire for God in Thomas Aquinas's *Commentary on Romans*," in *Medieval Readings of Romans*, ed. William S. Campbell, Peter S. Hawkins, and Brenda Deen Schildgen (New York: T&T Clark, 2007), 107.

depiction of Paul in 7:14–25 more readily applicable to the Christian experience of the common lot of the faithful. As Richard Muller observes, "Calvin nowhere denies that Paul speaks in the first person with a view toward using his own experience as an example, but Calvin also evidences no interest in arguing the case for an autobiographical passage."[68] Calvin's account of the *ego* of 7:14–25 clearly has the Apostle Paul in mind, but Calvin's Paul is more reflective of the everyday Christian believer in the battle of flesh and spirit.

Although these stances partially reflect the social circumstances of the interpreters, in that Aquinas as a scholastic Dominican friar leads to a portrait that conveys Paul as an example of the *vita apostolica*,[69] while Calvin as a pastor of the church in Geneva leads to a portrait more like the everyday congregate in his church, these positions toward the Apostle reflect broader interpretive trends in Aquinas's and Calvin's interpretation of Romans. In short, Calvin tends to generalize the human lot where Aquinas likes to particularize; or said another way, where Aquinas sets forth a hierarchy of humanity, Calvin asserts a democracy.[70] To give but three examples outside 7:14–25, Aquinas claims when interpreting 1:20, "For the invisible things of God from the creation of the world are clearly seen ... so they are without excuse," that the particular subject of this verse (the "they") is the "wise men among the Gentiles"

---

68. "'Scimus Enim Quod Lex Spiritualis Est'," 230. This observation supports C. E. B. Cranfield, *A Critical and Exegetical Commentary on the Epistle to the Romans*, 2 vols. (Edinburgh: T&T Clark, 1975–79), who argues that Calvin emphasizes the aspect of "general Christian experience" over an autobiographical portrait of Paul's mature Christian experience (1:344–45).

69. Ryan connects Aquinas's emphasis on the *apostolic* uniqueness of Paul to Aquinas's own position as a Dominican friar. He observes that Paul provided Aquinas with a model for the *vita apostolica* in the Dominican Order ("Love of Learning," 109).

70. In his comparison of Aquinas and Calvin on the doctrine of implicit faith, Arvin Vos makes this telling statement: "In the matter of the position one has in church and society, Aquinas is affirming degrees of responsibility tied to the conditions found in a hierarchically ordered society. The higher one's position, the more perfect his knowledge of matter of faith must be. Calvin makes no mention of such a distinction. He would not have anyone be satisfied with a faith that is only implicit" (*Aquinas, Calvin, and Contemporary Protestant Thought: A Critique of Protestant Views on the Thought of Thomas Aquinas* [Washington, D.C.: Christian University Press, 1985], 25); cf. Russell Dykstra, "A Comparison of Exegesis: John Calvin and Thomas Aquinas (3)," *Protestant Reformed Theological Journal* 35 [2002]: 15–16, who makes a similar observation using Aquinas's and Calvin's commentaries on Ephesians 1:14 regarding the contrast between Aquinas's particularizing and Calvin's universalizing. See also David Steinmetz, "The Scholastic Calvin," in *Protestant Scholasticism: Essays in Reassessment*, ed. Carl R. Trueman and R. Scott Clark (Carlisle, UK: Paternoster Press, 1999), 29, who notes that with Calvin came the general move away from theology being understood for the university elite alone, as with medieval Scholasticism, to theology for the whole church, which Calvin understood as both mother and school. This shift required that Calvin see all Christians, "no matter how limited their capacity," as having a theological task. Steinmetz concludes, "Calvin's reconception of theology as a school theology for the church represents a democratization and expansion of the scholastic ideal" (30).

who knew the truth about God (§ 113); since for Aquinas the knowledge of which Paul speaks is second-order knowledge,[71] and this sort of knowledge is obtained only by a few "and that after a long time, and with the admixture of many errors" (*ST* I, q. 1, a. 1; *Summa contra Gentiles* I.4), Paul is speaking particularly of the wise Gentiles. Calvin's interpretation, however, rejects this particularization and claims, "It was not particular to philosophers to think that they were wise in the knowledge of God, but it was equally common to all nations and classes of men" (31.96–98). For Calvin the knowledge of which Paul speaks is "innate [*ingentia*], and comes forth [*prodit*] with us, so to speak, from the womb" (31.101–102); there is, then, no *ratio* for particularizing the subject of the verse. Second, when Paul states at 8:23, "We have the first-fruits of the Spirit," Aquinas takes this verse as indicating that the apostles had the Holy Spirit "before others and more abundantly than others" (§ 676), while Calvin rejects any reference to a "rare and notable excellence" of the Spirit (176.76) and claims the verse refers to "all believers who are sprinkled in this world with even a little drop of the Spirit" (176.79). Lastly, Aquinas claims, commenting on 8:28–30, that Paul's knowledge of his own predestination is particular to the Apostle; it is the result of a special revelation that he received from God (§ 734). Calvin, however, rejects this particularization and claims that this knowledge is available to all those who are predestined (187.24–27; 191.70–74); if it were particular to Paul through a special revelation, the doctrine would be not only "lacking warmth" but "completely lifeless" (187.27–28). We find, then, that Aquinas's disposition to envision humanity in particularized and hierarchical terms[72] contrasted with Calvin's general democratizing of those hierarchical distinctions influence their interpretive judgments of Romans in general and their portraits of Paul in particular, given that the *ego* is the *Apostle* Paul.

Conclusion

In sum, Aquinas's Paul still struggles with the rise of disordered concupiscence, which resides in the lower powers of the sensible appetite, but on account of the healing work of grace on Paul's reason, which is itself in harmony with the Law, he resists succumbing to these temptations. Paul can perform a

---

71. See Aquinas's use of Romans 1:20 as the *sed contra* in the article on the ability to demonstrate God's existence (*ST* I, q. 2, a. 2).

72. It is telling of Aquinas's perspective that when addressing the various ecclesial "states" (*status*) he draws attention to the episcopal and religious states as states of perfection and does not even consider the state of the laity (*ST* II-II, q. 184, a. 4); Colón-Emeric, *Aquinas on the Way to Perfection*, 101.

truly good work—a condignly meritorious work—although still committing the venial sin of omission for failing to prevent the rise of these disordered desires. Aquinas's portrait of Paul as apostle provides an example to which Aquinas believes all Christians should strive, especially those who follow the *vita apostolica*. Calvin's Paul is likewise in the Christian struggle, although he is partially healed in all his parts and partially not. Due to his incomplete regeneration, even his best work is tainted by sin and thus can be acceptable to God only if it is first purified through Christ. Since Calvin rejects the venial/mortal distinction of sin, Paul's sin is worthy of the punishment of death, but thanks to being united to Christ in faith he is forgiven of this punishment and even receives rewards for his imperfect works. Calvin's portrait of Paul as apostle provides insight into his vision of the common struggle of each justified believer. When taken together, the portraits of Paul as exemplar and Paul as the common Christian present a robust picture of the Christian pilgrimage from inception to maturity. Particular parts of the portraits are difficult to reconcile, however, particularly regarding the nature of sin and the notion of perfection. But it is not always a case of either/or. Aquinas and Calvin each contribute unique insights into understanding the Christian struggle, and they agree that the struggle itself is a testimony to a gracious God, who has enlivened an otherwise dead spirit, enabling the Christian to partake in a lifelong journey of resisting the flesh and cultivating the spirit—activities that will be brought to their consummation in resurrection glory.

Geoffrey Wainwright

☙

14   Rendering God's Glory
St. Paul and St. Thomas on Worship

My plan is to highlight in St. Paul's Letter to the Romans—and therefore, of course, in St. Thomas's lectures on the epistle—those passages that have a particular bearing on worship, and to do so in the sequence adopted by the Apostle and followed by his commentator.

Romans 1:20(b)–25 (Thomas, cap. 1, lect. 7, §§ 123–45)

Here we find fundamental theology and anthropology formulated in terms of worship, whereby the truth of God is positively declared and human-kind is shown in its divine calling and (failed) obligation.

God is properly worshiped both for what *he is in himself* and for what *he does as creator.*

Simply as God, God is "glorious" (§ 134): this glory "is nothing less than the brilliance *(claritas)* of the divine nature, for 'he dwells in unapproachable light' (1 Tm 6:16)." The "glory with which God is himself glorious" *(gloria quâ Deus in se gloriosus est)* is "incomprehensible and infinite." Moreover, God alone is "immortal" (cf. again 1 Tm 6:16), being "altogether unchangeable, for every change is a form of ceasing to be" *(omnis enim mutatio quaedam cor-ruptio est);* and "his nature is sublime" (Ps 48:1: "Great is the Lord"). To God as such belong "glory and honor" (cf. 1 Tm 1:17). Correspondingly, there is a "glory with which man glorifies God when he shows him worship" *(gloria quâ homo Deum glorificat, ei cultum latriae exhibendo).* Thus it may be said that

In this chapter the Latin text and the numbering of the paragraphs correspond to *Sancti Thomae Aquinatis super Epistolas Sancti Pauli lectura*, ed. Raphaelis Cai, O.P., 8th ed. (Rome: Marietti, 1953), 1:1–230. A French translation of the lectures, with detailed cross-references to other works by St. Thomas, is found in *Thomas d'Aquin: Commentaire de l'Épître aux Romains*, ed. and trans. Jean-Éric Stroobant de Saint-Éloi, O.S.B. (Paris: Éditions du Cerf, 1999).

glory is also "rendered" to God by the worship that recognizes him for what he *is*, namely, "eminent above all things" (§ 127).

Then honor is also due to God as the *creator*: "the source of existence for all things" *(principium essendi omnibus per creationem)* (§ 142), and the "cause of everything good" *(omnium bonorum causa)* (§ 127). And particularly for his benefactions, God is owed "thanksgiving" *(gratiarum actio):* "Give thanks to him in all circumstances" (1 Thes 5:18).

As a creature, and indeed one to whom good has been shown, *man* is called and obliged to worship God the creator and benefactor. The verb *debere* occurs frequently in these contexts: "Men owed Him worship: inwardly the worship of a pious love ('If anyone is a worshiper of God and does his will, him he hears' [John 9:31]); outwardly, the service of latria ('The Lord, your God, shall you adore and him alone shall you serve' [Deut. 6:13])."[1] To "bless God" *(benedicere Deum)* is "to recognize his goodness with our heart and confess it with our mouth" *(eius bonitatem corde recogniscimus et ore confitemur)* (§ 144): "When you bless God, exalt him with all your strength" (Ecclus 43:30). The "cultus latriae" consists chiefly "in sacrifices and the oblation, through which man professes God to be the author of all good things" *(in sacrificiis et oblatione consistit, per quam homo profitetur omnium bonorum Deum esse auctorem)* (§ 143). Thus words of praise and cultic actions alike express the worship of the heart and mind.

So far, we have been speaking of the "truth" of things—of God and of man—but this truth has been made to stand out against "the lie" that fallen humankind has chosen to commit in its worship of the creature rather than the creator; and it is the point of Paul's argument at this stage of his epistle to convict mankind of sin. Knowledge of God's power and wisdom has always been available to man's reason from what God has made, which itself—precisely in distinction from its transcendent creator—is not divine, neither the sun and the moon and the stars nor man himself as God's living image. Man's "ignorance" results from his rejection of God in favor of reliance on mortal creatures. Worship is, then, futile and culpably false when it is offered to "objects of wood and stone"—likenesses of man or even of the lower animals. Ultimately, this is self-idolatry: men have "attributed their blessings to their own talent and power" (§ 127); "they put their trust in themselves and not in God, ascribing their blessings not to God but to themselves" (§ 129).[2]

1. "Debetur ei ab homine, interius quidem, cultus secundum pium affectum [Io. IX, 31]; exterius vero, debetur ei servitus latriae, secundum illud Deut. VI, 13" (§ 142).

2. In the second half of chapter 1, Paul is dealing especially with the failings of the Gentiles. In chapters 2 and 3 he will include the people of Israel in the indictment. A propos Romans 2:22 (§§ 234–36), Thomas says that the Apostle "indicates their failings with respect to God": first, "they

At this point it may be noted that I have been using the normal English word "worship" as verb or noun where Thomas uses the Latin verbs *colo* and *servire* and the nouns *cultus* and *latria*. By its etymology, "worship" carries the connotation of "worth" or "value," as does the Latin root *dignus*; and since Thomas will later speak of the *dignitas* of God (notably in his exposition of Romans 11:33–36), "worship"—as the active recognition of God's worth or value—is a proper match to Thomas's thought from the start.[3]

Romans 3:21–26 (Thomas, cap. 3, lect. 3, §§ 299–312)

Man's universally failed obligation to glorify God has been set right by God himself and his action in Christ. "Because all have sinned and cannot of themselves be justified, they need some other cause to make them just" (§ 306). In the mercy of God, this has been supplied by Christ who, himself without sin, underwent in his death the penalty incurred by sin. Men may now be justified through faith in Christ. This faith is "freely" given: it is precisely "gratis" (§ 306): "By the grace of God I am what I am" (1 Cor 15:10), so that the justification itself "redounds to God's glory" *(in gloriam Dei cedit)*, not man's (§ 305, citing Psalm 115:1: "Not unto us, O Lord, not unto us, but unto thy name give glory, for thy mercy and for thy truth's sake," and Psalm 66:2: "Give God the glory"). The faith by which grace is received is itself active in the sense that—thanks to the indwelling Christ (Eph 3:17)—the believer may perform works of love (Gal 5:6; 1 Jn 4:16). Having set out here "the origin of grace," the Apostle at chapter 12 will move on (says his commentator at that

sin against His worship [*contra ipsius cultum*]," for while they may "abhor idols [*idola*], knowing from the Law that they are not to be worshipped [*non esse colenda*]," they nevertheless "commit sacrilege by abusing the things of divine worship [*abutendo his quae pertinent ad divinum cultum*]" (citing Mal 1:12); second, their evil deeds and practices caused the Law, and hence the Name of its Author, to be defamed among the Gentiles (citing Is 52:5 and Ez 36:22).

3. In § 192 Thomas speaks of the "infinite worthiness" (*infinita dignitas*) of God. In his exposition of Romans 1, Thomas makes statements about God's being and nature that depend on his own much fuller teaching elsewhere. Nor does he here touch on the questions posed for the *language* of worship by the "ineffability" of God. In this connection, one may think of St. Augustine in *De doctrina christiana* (I. 6): "Although nothing can be spoken in a way worthy of God, he has sanctioned the homage of the human voice, and chosen that we should derive pleasure from our words in praise of him [*et tamen deus, cum de illo nihil digne dici possit, admisit humanae vocis obsequium et verbis nostris in laude sua gaudere nos voluit*]" (CCSL 32:9–10; PL 34:21). In *Summa theologiae (ST)* II-II, q. 81, a. 7, Thomas writes: "We pay God honor and reverence, not for his sake (because he is himself full of glory to which no creature can add anything), but for our own sake, because by the very fact that we revere and honor God, our mind is subjected to him: wherein its perfection consists." *ST* II-II, q. 91, aa. 1–2 would also be interesting for our purposes: "Of Taking the Divine Name for the Purpose of Invoking it by Means of Praise"—whether by spoken words or by song.

point) to teach "how grace should be used"—and it will so be in the worship of God. Already in his exposition of Romans 3, Thomas can speak again—and indeed a fortiori—of the glory that is "owed" to God by the human creature on account of the very grace by which he has now been redeemed: *per gratiam ipsius, scilicet Dei, cui ex hoc debetur gloria* (§ 306).

In view of the general scope of the present exercise, it must at least be noted that Christ's death is presented in this passage of Romans 3 in terms of a cultic sacrifice, as also in the first part of Romans 8 (a "sin-offering" or "sacrifice for sin"); but there is no room here to enter into the ecumenically controversial question concerning the sacrificial character of the Church's Eucharist; nor does Thomas deal with the matter in his commentary on Romans.

Romans 8:14–32 (Thomas, cap. 8, lect. 3–6, §§ 634–714)

Having expounded the event and meaning of Christ's death in cultic terms, the Apostle—in the middle of Romans 8—sets out its benefits for believers in euchological terms, and in a Trinitarian pattern. The Spirit of God who raised his Son from the dead already "indwells" and "leads" those who, in Christ, are the adoptive "sons of God." In commenting on their Spirit-enabled cry of "Abba, Father," Thomas makes a first reference to the Lord's Prayer: "We confess that we have God as our Father, when we follow the Lord's instruction to pray, 'Our Father, who art in heaven' (Mt 6:9). And since it is suitable not only for the Jews but also for Gentiles to say this, he uses two words to signify 'Father,' namely, 'Abba,' which is Hebrew, and 'Pater,' which can be Latin or Greek." Spoken "not so much with the sound of our voice as with the intention of our heart, an intention so strong that it is called a cry," this expression of appropriate filial fear and love is inspired by the Holy Spirit (§§ 644–45).[4]

---

4. Limitations of space forbid me—despite the "liturgical" focus of this piece—to go into St. Paul's teaching on baptism in Romans 6 and St. Thomas's exposition of it. In the present connection, the key verse would be verse 4: "We were buried therefore with him by baptism into death, so that as Christ was raised from the dead by the glory of the Father, we too might walk in newness of life." The living of the baptized "unto God" (v. 10) is living "to the honor of God and after his likeness" (*viventes Deo, id est, ad honorem vel similitudinem Dei*) (§ 491). To sneak in just a few ritual-theological notes: In § 474 Thomas observes that "there is a threefold immersion in baptism not only to indicate belief in the Trinity but also to represent the three days of Christ's burial. And just as the three days of burial constituted only one burial, so the triple immersion constitutes just one baptism. That is also why solemn baptism is celebrated in the Church on Holy Saturday, when the burial of Christ is commemorated, and on the vigil of Pentecost in honor of the Holy Spirit, from whose power the water of baptism derives its cleansing force: 'Unless one is born of water and the Spirit he cannot enter the kingdom of heaven' (John 3:5)." At Romans 8:1 (§ 596), Thomas alludes to baptism as "the sacrament of faith." At Romans 10:11–12 (§ 832), he explains that "the baptized are anointed on the forehead with chrism in the form of a cross, so that they will not be ashamed

Thomas then takes up from the Apostle the theme of glory. In the face of the sufferings of the present time, the glory implicitly promised with the resurrection in verse 11 must be considered as deferred. There would be conclusions to draw for worship when Thomas speaks about the excellence of the glory—cognitive, corporeal, even cosmic—still to be revealed to, in, and through Christ's fellow heirs, for the redemption of whose bodies the entire creation joins in awaiting as for its own liberation. Christ's "fellow heirs" are to "share in his splendor": "By enlightening the saints with the light of wisdom and grace, he makes them be conformed to himself" (§ 704). This is a glory "quae claritatem quamdam dignitatis insinuat" (§ 654). In this context Thomas again cites Psalm 149:5: "The saints shall exult in glory." Already in explicating Romans 2:7, Thomas wrote thus with regard to the desired threefold reward promised to those who "continue patiently in well-doing" (§ 197):

The first thing is glory, which signifies the splendor of the saints: either intrinsic glory, with which the mind will be filled: "The Lord will fill your soul with brightness" (Isa. 58:11), or external glory, with which their body will shine: "The just shall shine like the sun in the kingdom of their father" (Matt. 13:43). "The saints shall exult in glory" (Ps. 149:5).

The second is honor, through which is signified the dignity of the saints and the reverence paid to them by every creature. For they will be kings and priests: "Thou hast made them a kingdom and priests to our God" (Rev. 5:10), and they will be "numbered among the sons of God" (Wisdom 5:5)....

The third is immortality, because that glory and honor will not pass, as they do in this world: "They [i.e., athletes] do it to receive a perishable wreath, but we an imperishable" (1 Cor. 9:25).

Along those lines, worship might be expounded as the graciously given and faithfully enacted participation in Christ the true Son who himself is, as St. Thomas notes with appeal to Hebrews 1:3, eternally "begotten of the Father as the splendor of His glory" (§704), and who has now become by virtue of his redemptive passion "the first-born of many brethren" destined for glory (§§ 706, 712–14).[5]

---

to confess Christ crucified" (referring back to Rom 1:16). In explicating the somewhat puzzling Romans 11:29 ("The gifts of God are *sine paenitentia*"), Thomas develops—as to "repentance"—the respective meanings of baptism and the sacrament of penance (§§ 927–29).

5. Here the liturgist naturally recalls the sacramental concreteness and transformative grace of the Eucharist as it is sung in the antiphon of the Corpus Christi office that is attributed to St. Thomas (and echoed by the Council of Trent in its *Decree on the Eucharist*, 2): "O sacrum convivium, in quo Christus sumitur, recolitur memoria passionis eius, mens impletur gratia et futurae gloriae nobis pignus datur." Regarding the final prospect and its anticipation, see Geoffrey Wainwright, *Eucharist and Eschatology* (New York: Oxford University Press, 1981).

Meanwhile the glory's manifestation must be awaited in patience and in hope. In these circumstances, the commentator returns to the "Our Father" when he has to explain why or how, in the act of prayer, "the Spirit helps us in our weakness" (Rom 8:26). This passage (§§ 690–91) may be quoted *in extenso* on account of its euchological interest (with the first, third, fourth, and fifth petitions of the Lord's Prayer being clearly quoted or alluded to).

The Apostle says there are two things we do not know, namely, what we should ask for in prayer and the manner in which we ought to ask. But both seem to be false.

For in the first place we know what we should ask for, because the Lord taught us in Matthew: "Hallowed be thy name, and so on."

The answer is that we can know in a general way what it is suitable to pray for, but we cannot know this in particular. First of all, if we desire to perform a virtuous deed, which is to fulfill God's will on earth as it is in heaven, it can happen that the virtuous deed does not befit this or that person. For example, the quiet of contemplation is not expedient for a person who can press onward usefully in action.... Secondly, a person desires a temporal good to sustain life, which is to seek one's daily bread, but it puts him in danger of death; for many have perished because of riches.... Thirdly a person desires to be freed from a bothersome trial which, nevertheless, is for him a guardian of humility. For example, St. Paul sought the removal of a thorn of the flesh, but it had been given him to keep him from being too elated by the abundance of revelations....

Likewise, it also seems that we know how to pray as we ought, since it says in James (1:7): "let him ask in faith, with no doubting." Here, too, the answer is that we can know in general, but we cannot discern exactly the special motive; for example, whether we are asking from anger or from a zeal for justice.

In interpreting the Spirit's "intercession" for us (§§ 692–94), Thomas wards off any notion that the Holy Spirit may be "a creature and lower than the Father and Son" and takes the Apostle to mean that "the Spirit makes us ask, inasmuch as he causes right desires in us, because to ask is to make desires known. Now right desires arise from the ardor of love, which he produces in us" (citing Rom 5:5: "Now God's love has been poured into our hearts through the Holy Spirit which has been given us"). "And with the Holy Spirit directing and inciting our heart, our desires cannot but be profitable to us.... God searches the hearts and knows, i.e., approves, what is the mind of the Spirit, i.e., what the Spirit makes us desire.... The desires which the Holy Spirit causes in the saints are accepted by God, because the Spirit intercedes for the saints, i.e., makes them ask according to the will of God, i.e., for things pleasing to God."[6]

6. On examining Thomas's commentary at this point in fuller detail than has been possible here, a person raised on the English *Book of Common Prayer* cannot but recall the opening collect of the Order of Holy Communion: "Almighty God, unto whom all hearts be open, all desires

In Thomas's commentary, we may skip to the next of our selected passages, where the Trinitarian pattern of worship and prayer is again brought out.

Romans 11:33–36 (Thomas, cap. 11, lect. 5; §§ 933–52)

Having earlier in the epistle established the universal solidarity of Gentiles with Jews in sin and guilt and the inclusion of both in salvation through Christ, the Apostle in chapters 9–11 again surveys their relationship in the eyes of God and in history, concluding that "God has concluded all in unbelief, that he might have mercy upon all." This conclusion prompts the Apostle to an outburst of praise, which his commentator interprets in Trinitarian fashion:

O the depth of the riches and wisdom and knowledge of God! How incomprehensible are his judgments and how unsearchable his ways! "For who has known the mind of the Lord, or who has been his counsellor?" [Isa. 40:13]. "Or who has given a gift to him that he might be repaid?" [Job 41:11]. For from him and through him and in him are all things. To him be glory unto the ages of ages. Amen.

The Apostle, says Thomas, "exclaims his admiration of the divine excellence" in all the mentioned respects. Particularly interesting for our subject is the commentator's exposition of the three Pauline prepositions—*ex, per,* and *in*—that relate "all things" (except sin) to God. In summary (§ 949):

All things are *from* him, i.e., God as from the first operating power. All things are *through* him, inasmuch as he makes all things through his wisdom. All things are *in* him as kept in his goodness which preserves them [*in bonitate conservante*].

Now these three things, namely, power, wisdom and goodness, are common to the three persons [of the Godhead]. Hence, the statement that "from him and through him and in him are all things" can be applied to each of the three persons. Nevertheless, the power, which involves the notion of principle, is appropriated to the Father, who is the principle of the entire Godhead; wisdom to the Son, who proceeds as Word, which is nothing else than wisdom begotten; goodness is appropriated to the Holy Spirit, who proceeds as love, whose object is goodness.

Therefore, by appropriation we can say: *from him,* namely from the Father, *through him,* namely through the Son, *in him,* namely in the Holy Spirit, are all things.

---

known, and from whom no secrets are hid: Cleanse the thoughts of our hearts by the inspiration of thy Holy Spirit, that we may perfectly love thee, and worthily magnify thy holy Name; through Christ our Lord. Amen." Behind that stood a vesting prayer in the Sarum Missal and, in turn, a prayer found in various sacramentaries already toward the end of the first millennium. At Romans 10:12–13 (§ 834), Thomas remarks that "calling on the name of the Lord" is done by "calling on Him through love and devout worship" (Thomas plays on the Latin "in-vocare": "Est autem invocare, in se vocare per affectum et devotum cultum").

Thus when Thomas moves with Paul to the ascription of worship (both "honor" and "glory"), he envisages the sovereign and all-sufficient Triune God (§ 950):

When he [the Apostle] says, *To him be honor and glory forever*, he allows God's dignity, which consists in the two things previously mentioned. For from the fact that all things are from Him and through Him and in Him, honor and reverence and subjection are owed Him by every creature: "If I am a father, where is my honor?" (Mal. 1:6). But from the fact that He has not received either counsel or gifts from anyone, glory is owed Him; just as on the contrary it is said of man: "If then you received it, why do you boast as though it were not a gift?" (1 Cor. 4:7). And because this is proper to God, it says in Isaiah (42:8): "I am the Lord; my glory I give to no other."[7]

"Unto the ages of ages" is interpreted by Thomas as referring either to the surpassing nature of God's glory or to God's eternity as—"though one and simple in itself"— "containing" all ages (§ 951). And "Amen" means "May it be so" (§ 952).

Romans 12 (Thomas, cap. 12, lect. 1, §§ 953–67)

At the transition from chapter 11 of the epistle to chapter 12, direct doxology passes into evangelically grounded exhortation. Having earlier shown "the origin of grace," says Thomas, the Apostle now "teaches how grace should be used" (§ 953). The "moral instruction" proceeds both individually (ethically) and corporately (ecclesially). It is all placed under a cultic rubric: "I beseech you therefore, brothers [and sisters], by the mercy of God, that you present your bodies as a living sacrifice, holy, pleasing to God, your reasonable service."

"Perfection of life" relates in the first place to "the sanctity by which a man serves God." How one presents oneself to God is a matter of both body and

7. The Trinitarian interpretation of the prepositions in Romans 11:36 was not an innovation on Thomas's part. It is found frequently in Augustine: for example, *De trinitate* I, 12; II, 25; V, 9; VI, 7, and so on; and was taken up, for instance, by Ildefons of Toledo, *Annotationes de cognitione baptismi*, 131 (PL 96:166). Commenting on Romans 1:9 ("I thank my God through Jesus Christ"), Thomas declares that "thanks should be returned to God in the same order in which graces come to us, namely, through Jesus Christ [*eodem enim ordine debet gratiarum actio in Deum recurrere quo gratiae a Deo in nos deveniunt, quod quidem est per Iesum Christum*]" (citing Rom. 5:2 for the "from God" direction). (We may note that St. Augustine, like St. Basil of Caesarea before him, showed that Christ's role in mediation, whether of grace or of prayer, does not imply the Son's subordination or inferiority to the Father.) At Romans 8:34 (§ 720), Thomas states the twofold manner of Christ's heavenly intercession: he "prays for us" (citing Jn 17:20, 24); and he "presents to his Father's gaze the human nature he assumed for us and the mysteries celebrated in it [*interpellat pro nobis humanitatem pro nobis assumptam et mysteria in ea celebrata conspectui paterno repraesentando*]" (citing Heb 9:24).

soul (§ 953). Thomas invokes St. Augustine for the principle that "a visible sacrifice offered outwardly to God is a sign of an invisible sacrifice, whereby one offers himself and all he possesses for God's service" (§ 957).[8]

Now, says Thomas, man possesses three goods (§ 958): first, the soul, "which is presented to God by humble devotion and contrition: 'The sacrifice acceptable to God is a contrite spirit' (Psalm 51:17)"; second, the "external goods, which a man presents to God by giving alms: 'Do not neglect to do good and to share what you have, for such sacrifices are pleasing to God' (Heb 13:16)"; third, "a man has the good which is his own body." This last can be presented to God as a sacrifice in three ways (§ 959): when a man "exposes his body to suffering and death for God's sake" (cf. Eph 5:2; Phil 2:17); when he "weakens his body by fasts and watchings in the service of God" (cf. 1 Cor 9:27); when he "uses his body to perform acts of justice and of divine worship" (cf. Rom 6:19). As presented to God (§§ 960–62), the sacrifice will be "living" (by virtue of the abundant life that Christ vouchsafes to the believer; cf. Gal 2:20; Jn 10:10) and "holy" (made so "by the devotion with which we bind our bodies to the service of God"; cf. Lv 20:7) and "pleasing to God" ("by reason of a right intention"; cf. Ps 56:13). Further to the body: with regard to external acts, says Thomas in developing the notion of "reasonable service" *(rationabile obsequium)*, a "wise discretion" is proper (§ 963), even in the case of martyrdom, for "all things should be done decently and in order" (1 Cor 14:40); and even in lesser cases, "a discreet limit is imposed by the requirements of love"—with appeal being made to Jerome: "Does not rational man lose his dignity, if he chooses to fast and watch at the expense of his bodily health or incur the marks of madness or sadness from singing the Psalms and office?"[9] The "external acts, in which our bodies are presented to God, stand as means to the end" (§ 964).

The just man's internal acts in the intrinsic service of God are those good and just acts by which he "believes, hopes and loves" (§ 964). Here no limit is set: "You shall love the Lord your God with all your heart and with all your mind and with all your might" (Dt 6:4). With that, Thomas moves into a more developed account of how man is to present himself to God as regards the soul (§§ 965–67). This depends on being "renewed in mind," "the sense by which man forms judgments about what is to be done." "When man was created, this sense was sound and vigorous"; by the grace of the Holy Spirit, it has now become possible to "take up again that beauty and elegance which the mind once had"—and thus perceive the will of God, which is sweet ("taste

8. See Augustine, *De civitate Dei* X, 5 and 19 (CCSL 47:277 and 293; PL 41:282 and 297).
9. St. Thomas seems to be citing Gratian's *Decretum*, III. 5. 24 (PL 187:1862), which echoes a passage in Jerome's *Regula monachorum*, 14 (PL 30:369).

and see") and pleasant ("rejoicing the heart"): that is our "sanctification," and nothing less than our "perfection," "uniting us, as it were, with the end" *(quasi coniungens nos fini)* (§ 967).

The consequences for ecclesial behavior are then set forth by the Apostle and his commentator.

Romans 15:5–13 (Thomas, cap. 15, lect. 1, §§ 1142–62)

After dealing in chapter 14 with behavioral and attitudinal controversies in the Roman Church that may have had to do with the varied Jewish or Gentile origins of its members, Paul in chapter 15 pleads for their resolution for the sake—quite concretely—of the community's liturgy: "May the God of patience and consolation (or encouragement) grant you to be of one mind with one another, in accord with Christ Jesus, that with one mind and with one mouth you may glorify the God and Father of our Lord Jesus Christ" (vv. 5–6). "One confession of the voice comes from unity of faith" (cf. 1 Cor 1:10), says Thomas, and it "glorifies the God—Creator of all things—and Father of Jesus Christ, through whom he has adopted us as his sons" (§ 1149). Mutual welcome is in order, because "Christ welcomed you who are assembled in the unity of faith composed of Jews and Gentiles" *(Christus vos suscepit, qui estis congregati in unitate fidei ex Iudaeis et gentibus)* (§ 1154). By the truth and mercy of God, both are now to sing the "new song" of God's praise under the unique rule of Christ (vv. 7–12).

Trespassing into Thomas's second lecture on chapter 15 (§§ 1163–77), we note his attention to the Apostle's use of the language of worship about his own evangelistic activity.[10] To be "a minister of Christ Jesus to the Gentiles" is "to serve God in the conversion of the Gentiles." The purpose of the grace

10. In expounding Romans 1:9 ("For God is my witness, whom I serve in my spirit in the gospel of his Son"), Thomas had spoken of the Apostle's evangelical service as the worship *(latriae cultus)* of the one God who is to be worshipped (citing Dt 6:13), and of the manner of that service thus: "Not only in outward bodily service, but especially within, according to the spirit" (citing Jn 4:24). In the same Pauline context, Thomas offers three modes of "prayer without ceasing" (citing also 1 Thes 5:7 and Lk 18:1): first, "as to the act of prayer itself, one is praying always or without ceasing, if he prays at the appointed times and hours" (cf. Acts 3:1); second, "as to the purpose of prayer, which is that our mind rise up to God, a man prays as long as he directs his entire life to God ('Whether you eat or drink, or whatever you do, do all to the glory of God' (1 Cor 10:31)"; third, as giving cause for prayer, as "when a person's actions towards others cause them to pray for him, so that he himself seems to be praying, as in the case of those who give alms to the poor who then pray for them" (citing Ecclus 29:12). As to "Be constant in prayer" at Romans 12:12 (§ 992), Thomas comments: "By prayer, consideration is aroused in us and fervor kindled, we are stimulated to serve God, the joy of hope is increased in us, and we gain help in tribulation" (citing, for this last, Ps 120:1).

given to Paul is "that the offering of the Gentiles may be made, i.e., the nations converted by [his] ministry, in which he offered, as it were, a sacrifice and oblation to God, as it says in Philippians [2:17]: 'Even if I am poured as a libation upon the sacrificial offering of your faith, I am glad and rejoice with you all.'" The Apostle "gives glory to God for the fruit he has produced"—a glory in which he rejoices not chiefly on his own account but because of Christ's work in him (cf. Is 27:12; Jn 15:5) and the power of the Holy Spirit operative in his words and deeds among those who hear and see him (cf. Heb 2:4; 1 Cor 6:11); and this glory he refers to the Father: "Not to us, O Lord, not to us, but to thy name give glory" (Ps 115:1). And all this is reflected in the prayers that the Apostle solicits for himself from the Church in Rome in the final verses of chapter 15 (treated in Thomas's third lecture on the chapter; §§ 1178–92).

The sixteenth and last chapter of the epistle will then be largely devoted to personal greetings for Christians in and around the Roman Church, offered indeed from "all the churches" that are "assembled in the name and faith of Christ," because, as Thomas explicates (§ 1212), "all wish your salvation and pray for you: 'Pray for one another, that you may be saved' (Jas 5:16)." Meantime the Roman Christians are to "greet one another with a holy kiss."[11]

Romans 16:25–27 (Thomas, cap. 16, lect. 2, §§ 1223–29)

With the *textus receptus*, Thomas of course takes the (grammatically awkward!) concluding doxology of Romans 16:25–27 as coming from the Apostle.

The address of the "thanksgiving" *(gratiarum actio)* is to "Him who is able to strengthen you" in the faith of the Gospel, that is to say, the Trinity. Again, "the only wise God" is the Trinity, for "the perfection of the whole Trinity is the same," inasmuch as mutual knowledge obtains among all three persons. That knowledge here embraces the long-hidden mystery that has now been revealed, whether that refers to the Incarnation itself or to Paul's preaching of the Gospel among the Gentiles and their conversion. To Jesus Christ, who while on earth himself glorified the Father (cf. Jn 17:4) and now mediates the worship of the Church, is ascribed both "honor and glory"—honor "through the reverence paid by every creature" (citing Phil 2:10: "At the name of Jesus every knee shall bend"), and glory "in regard to the full godhead" (citing Phil 2:11: "And every tongue confess that Jesus Christ is Lord in the glory of God

11. Just one last ritual note: Commenting on Romans 16:16, Thomas distinguishes the "holy kiss" from both a sensual one (cf. Prv 7:13) and a deceitful one (cf. Prv 27:6): "The holy kiss is given as a sign of the Blessed Trinity: 'O that he would kiss me with the kiss of his mouth' (Song 1:2). From this the custom arose in the Church whereby the faithful give one another the kiss of peace during the solemnities of the Mass" (§ 1211).

the Father"), and this "not for a time, but for evermore" (citing Heb 13:8: "Jesus Christ is the same yesterday and today and for ever").[12]

In this exercise, while highlighting the incidences of the epistle for worship and prayer, I have treated dogmatic and ethical topics in the systematically satisfactory sequence in which they occur in the Pauline original and its commentary by Thomas; and the scriptural and traditional correspondence thereby found between the *lex orandi* and the *lex credendi* together with their issuance in the *lex vivendi* confirms that the "praise of God" is to be located in "worship, doctrine, and life"—as readers of my book *Doxology* already knew.[13]

In fine: datur a Sacra Scriptura bene explicata ut leges orandi vel credendi invicem sibi respondeant et ad legem vivendi concurrant. Hoc autem iam sciebant lectores libri mei "Doxologia: cultu et doctrina atque vita laudandus est Deus."

12. It may be remembered that St. Athanasius, in his *Contra gentes* and *De Incarnatione Verbi*, weaves the contrasting threads of true worship versus idolatry throughout his telling of the tale of creation, fall, and redemption, until he can conclude, in the light of the spread of the Gospel in his own day, that "Christ alone is worshiped by all as one and everywhere the same; and what the weakness of the idols was unable to effect—to persuade, namely, even those living nearby—this Christ has done, who has persuaded not only those nearby but the entire world, to worship one and the same Lord, and through him God his Father" (*De Incarnatione Verbi*, 46). And St. Athanasius ends that treatise with the eschatological prospect and a present Trinitarian doxology, referring to "what has been reserved for the saints in the kingdom of heaven, 'which eye has not seen, nor ear heard, nor the heart of man conceived' [1 Cor 2:9], all the things which have been prepared for those who live in virtue and love God and the Father, in Jesus Christ our Lord, through whom and with whom, to the Father with the Son himself in the Holy Spirit, be honor and power, and glory, for ever and ever, Amen" (ibid., 57).

13. Geoffrey Wainwright, *Doxology: The Praise of God in Worship, Doctrine and Life: A Systematic Theology* (New York: Oxford University Press, 1980; 10th impression 2006).

Michael Waldstein

❧

15 The Trinitarian, Spousal, and Ecclesial Logic of Justification

The Breakthrough of the Reformation

In a justly famous passage, Martin Luther writes,

I had indeed been captivated with an extraordinary ardor for understanding Paul in the Epistle to the Romans. But up till then ... a single word in Chapter 1:17, "In it the righteousness of God is revealed," ... stood in my way. For I hated that word "righteousness of God," which, according to the use and custom *of all the teachers*, I had been taught to understand *philosophically* regarding the formal or active righteousness, as they called it, with which God *is righteous and punishes* the unrighteous sinner.

Though I lived as a monk without reproach, I felt that I was a sinner before God with an extremely disturbed conscience. I could not believe that he was placated by my satisfaction. *I did not love*, yes, I hated the righteous God who punishes sinners, and secretly, if not blasphemously, certainly murmuring greatly, I was angry with God, and said, "As if, indeed, it is not enough, that miserable sinners, eternally lost through original sin, are crushed by every kind of calamity by the law of the Decalogue, without having God add pain to pain by the gospel and also by the gospel threatening us with his righteousness and wrath!" Thus I raged with a fierce and troubled conscience. Nevertheless, I beat importunately upon Paul at that place, most ardently desiring to know what St. Paul wanted.

At last, by the mercy of God, meditating day and night, I gave heed to the context of the words, namely, "In it the righteousness of God is revealed, as it is written, 'He who through faith is righteous shall live.'" There I began to understand that the righteousness of God is that by which the righteous lives by a gift of God, namely by faith. And this is the meaning: the righteousness of God is revealed by the gospel, namely, the passive righteousness with which merciful God justifies us by faith, as it is written, "He who through faith is righteous shall live." Here I felt that I was altogether *born again* and had *entered paradise* itself through open gates. There a totally other face of the entire Scripture showed itself to me.... And I *extolled my sweetest word with a love* as great as the hatred with which I had before hated the word "righteousness of God." Thus that place in Paul was for me truly *the gate to paradise.*[1]

This passage is sometimes quoted as expressing the key breakthrough of the Reformation against the distortions of the Gospel in Catholic theology before Luther.

As an aside, it is curious that Luther says about his former life, "I lived as a monk without reproach," and at the same time confesses, "I did not love, yes, I hated the righteous God who punishes sinners, and secretly, if not blasphemously, certainly murmuring greatly, I was angry with God." By what measure did he judge his life as a monk to be "without reproach"? The love of God and neighbor is the true measure, and he himself reproaches himself for his hatred of God.

Partly by contrast with this hatred, one can see in the text just quoted that the new understanding of Romans 1:17 that came to define Luther's faith also involves love. "I extolled my sweetest word with a love as great as the hatred with which I had before hated the word 'righteousness of God.'"

Immediately after the passage just quoted Luther continues by pointing out that after his discovery of the meaning of Romans 1:17, he found a similar understanding of God's righteousness in St. Augustine: "Later I read Augustine's *The Spirit and the Letter*, where ... I found that he, too, interpreted God's righteousness in a similar way, as the righteousness with which God clothes us when he justifies us. Although this was heretofore said imperfectly and he did not explain all things concerning imputation clearly, it nevertheless was pleasing that God's righteousness with which we are justified was taught."[2] Had Luther read St. Thomas's *Lectures on Romans*, he would have been pleased that God's righteousness was taught even by the greatest master among the Scholastics.

Iustitia Dei can be understood in two ways:

In one way it can refer to the justice by which God is just: "The Lord is just and has loved justice" (Ps 11:7). Taken this way, the sense is that *the justice of God*, by which he is just in keeping his promises, *is revealed in him* [*in eo*], namely, in the man who believes the Gospel, because he believes that God has fulfilled what he promised about sending Christ. And this is *from faith*, namely, [the faith] of God who promised: "The Lord is faithful in all his words" (Ps 145:13); *to faith*, namely of the man who believes.

Or it can refer to the justice of God by which God makes men just. For the justice

1. Martin Luther, "Introduction to the Complete Edition of His Latin Works," in *Career of the Reformer IV*, ed. Lewis William Spitz (Philadelphia: Fortress Press, 1960), 336–37, emphasis added.
2. Ibid., 337.

of men is that by which men presume to make themselves just by their own efforts: *Not knowing the justice of God and seeking to establish their own justice, they did not submit to the justice of God* (Rom 10:3). This justice [of God] is revealed in the gospel inasmuch as men are justified by faith in the gospel in every age.[3]

St. Thomas offers two readings of *iustitia Dei*. He does not choose between them, nor does he invite his readers to choose, but in accord with his thesis that there can be several true senses of the letter in Scripture,[4] he proposes both readings as equally legitimate.

The point of departure of his first reading is the justice of God understood as God's *fides*, God's faithfulness to his own promises. "From faith to faith" means "from God's faith to the believer's faith." It is curious that in his first reading St. Thomas understands the antecedent of ἐν αὐτῷ *(in eo)* in 1:17 to be the believer rather than, as he himself understands the phrase in his second reading, the Gospel. God's faithfulness to his promises is revealed *in the believer*. Of course, to say that the faithfulness of God is *revealed in the Gospel* is precisely to say that according to the Gospel this faithfulness is at work and is thus *revealed in the believer*, namely, by the gift of faith.

For St. Thomas, *iustitia Dei* is not the *philosophical* doctrine all of Luther's teachers taught him, namely, distributive justice expressed by punishment, but the properly theological doctrine of God's *fides*, his faithfulness to his promises.

St. Thomas's first reading of 1:17 resembles the reading offered by a proponent of "New Perspectives on Paul," N. T. Wright. After laying out in tabular form all the possibilities and proposals for the meaning of δικαιοσύνη θεοῦ, Wright chooses the following:

The gospel, he says, reveals or unveils God's own *righteousness*, which operates through *the faithfulness of Jesus Christ* for the benefit of all those who in turn are faithful ("from faith for faith"). In other words, when Paul announces that Jesus Christ is Lord, the Lord of the world, he is in that very act and announcement unveiling before the world the great news that the one God of all the world has been *true to his word*, has dealt decisively with the evil that has invaded his creation, and is now restoring justice, peace, and truth. This is the fundamental thing that Paul wants the Roman church, and indeed the whole world, to grasp.[5]

3. St. Thomas, *Super epistolam ad Romanos Lectura* [henceforth *In ad Rom.*] in *Super Epistolas S. Pauli Lectura*, vol. 1, ed. Raphaelis Cai, 8th ed. (Rome: Marietti, 1953), § 102.

4. Cf. St. Thomas, *ST* I, q. 1, a. 10, co. An even clearer statement of the same thesis is found in Thomas Aquinas, *Lectura Romana in Primum Sententiarum Petri Lombardi*, ed. Leonard Boyle and John Boyle (Toronto: Pontifical Institute of Medieval Studies, 2006), prol., d. 4, q. 1, ad 3, p. 79.

5. N. T. Wright, *What Saint Paul Really Said: Was Paul of Tarsus the Real Founder of Christianity?* (Grand Rapids, Mich.: Eerdmans, 1997), 109, emphasis added.

The essential point shared by St. Thomas's first reading and Wright's reading is that the justice or righteousness of God consists in God's *faithfulness to his promises* (St. Thomas), in his being *true to his words* (Wright). Both also read "from faith to faith" as grounding our faith in God's faith.

In his second reading, St. Thomas interprets the genitive in *iustitia Dei*, "justice of God," as a genitive of origin.[6] *Iustitia Dei* is a justice that comes from God and is given to the sinner through the gift of faith. This reading is very close to Luther. Here, once again, is Luther: "The righteousness of God is that by which the righteous lives by a gift of God, namely by faith. And this is the meaning: the righteousness of God is revealed by the gospel, namely, the passive righteousness with which merciful God justifies us by faith."[7] Another important proponent of the "New Perspectives on Paul," James Dunn, seems to bring the interpretation of Romans 1:17 full circle back to St. Thomas. Protesting against "either-or exegesis," he takes the genitive in δικαιοσύνη θεοῦ to be both subjective in the sense of God's covenant faithfulness (N. T. Wright and St. Thomas's first reading) and a genitive of origin (Luther and St. Thomas's second reading). He also takes the verb δικαιόω (justify) to signify both "declare righteous" and "make righteous."[8] The link between these two had already been powerfully expressed by the early Hans Küng in his dialogue with Karl Barth:

Unlike the word of man, the word of God does what it signifies. God said, "Let there be light" and there was light. He said, "Be clean" and it was clean. God commands the demons, and they get out. He speaks harshly to the wind and the waves, and there is a deep calm. He says, "This is my body." And it is His body. He says, "Stand up." And the dead man rises. The sinner's justification is exactly like this. God pronounces the verdict, "You are just." And the sinner is just, really and truly, outwardly and inwardly, wholly and completely. His sins are forgiven, and man is just in the heart. The voice of God never gets lost in the void.[9]

In chapter 12 in this volume, Bruce Marshall showed, conversely, that reckoning plays a key role in St. Thomas: the sinful act itself cannot be canceled, but God covers it and does not impute it to the one who performed it.

Can we, therefore, pack our ecumenical bags with the conclusion that Luther and St. Thomas agree and travel home in peace?

6. A clear example of a genitive of origin is found in Luke 3:6, "All flesh shall see the salvation of our God [τὸ σωτήριον τοῦ θεοῦ]."

7. Luther, "Introduction to the Complete Edition of His Latin Works," 337.

8. See James D. G. Dunn, *The Theology of Paul the Apostle* (Grand Rapids, Mich.: Eerdmans, 1998), 341–344, in particular, 344.

9. Hans Küng, *Justification: The Doctrine of Karl Barth and a Catholic Reflection / with a Letter from Karl Barth*, translation from the 4th German ed. by Thomas Collins, Edmund E. Tolk, and David Grandskou (London: Thomas Nelson, 1964), 313.

The Spousal Logic of Justification

Luther expresses the spousal logic of justification in a powerful passage of his pamphlet "On the Freedom of the Christian":

The third incomparable benefit of faith is that it unites the soul with Christ as a bride is united with her bridegroom. By this mystery, as the Apostle teaches, Christ and the soul become one flesh [Eph 5:31–32]. And if they are one flesh and there is between them *a true marriage*—indeed the most perfect of all marriages, since human marriages are but poor examples of *this one true marriage*—it follows that everything they have they hold in common, the good as well as the evil. Accordingly the believing soul can boast of and glory in whatever Christ has as though it were its own [*tamquam suis*], and whatever the soul has Christ claims as though it were his own. Let us compare these and we shall see inestimable benefits. Christ is full of grace, life, and salvation. The soul is full of sins, death, and damnation. Now let faith come between them and sins, death, and damnation will be Christ's, while grace, life, and salvation will be the soul's; for if Christ is a bridegroom, he must take upon himself the things which are his bride's and bestow upon her the things that are his. If he gives her his body and very self, how shall he not give her all that is his? And if he takes the body of the bride, how shall he not take all that is hers?

... By *the wedding ring of faith* he shares in the sins, death, and pains of hell which are his bride's. As a matter of fact, he makes them his own and acts as if they were his own and as if he himself had sinned; he suffered, died, and descended into hell that he might overcome them all.... Thus the believing soul by means of the pledge of its faith is free in Christ, its bridegroom, free from all sins, secure against death and hell, and is endowed with the eternal righteousness, life, and salvation of Christ its bridegroom. So he takes to himself a glorious bride, "without spot or wrinkle, cleansing her by the washing of water with the word" [cf. Eph 5:26–27] of life, that is, by faith in the Word of life, righteousness, and salvation. In this way he marries her in faith, steadfast love, and in mercies, righteousness, and justice, as Hosea 2:19–20 says.

Who then can fully appreciate what this royal marriage means? Who can understand the riches of the glory of this grace? Here this rich and divine bridegroom Christ marries this poor, wicked girl, redeems her from all her evil, and adorns her with all his goodness. Her sins cannot now destroy her, since they are laid upon Christ and swallowed up by him. And she has that righteousness in Christ, her husband, of which she may boast as of her own and which she can confidently display alongside her sins in the face of death and hell and say, "If I have sinned, yet my Christ, in whom I believe, has not sinned, and all his is mine and all mine is his," as the bride in the Song of Solomon 2:16 says, *"My beloved is mine and I am his."*[10]

---

10. Luther, "On the Freedom of the Christian," in *Career of the Reformer I*, ed. Harold J. Grimm, trans. W. A. Lambert (Philadelphia: Fortress Press, 1957), 351–52, emphasis added.

This spousal vision of justification does not seem to be a marginal part of Luther's teaching. It is, of course, profoundly biblical, from Hosea to the bridegroom of John 3:29 to wedding of the Lamb in the book of revelation. It shows that the almost mechanical opposition between eros and agape attempted by Anders Nygren is artificial.[11] Already philological grounds ought to warn us against it. After David's son Amnon rapes his half-sister Tamar, we are told, the hatred he felt for her was "greater than the lust he had felt for her" (New Revised Standard Version; ὑπὲρ τὴν ἀγάπην ἣν ἠγάπησεν αὐτήν: greater than the agape with which he agapized her) (2 Sm 13:15). Steeped as he was in the Septuagint, St. Paul would not have found this erotic use of ἀγάπη surprising.

The principal point to be taken from this marvelous text of Luther is that *spousal love* is an *essential dimension of faith* as Luther understands it.

In this respect Luther stands in deep continuity with St. Thomas. In a list of four benefits of faith, St. Thomas gives first place to marital union with Christ: "Faith produces four goods. The first is that by faith the soul is joined to God, for by faith the Christian soul contracts a certain marriage, as it were, with God. 'I will take you for my wife in faith' (Hos 2:20)."[12] Faith, St. Thomas argues elsewhere, is the foundation of all spiritual goods, because it brings us into spousal union with Christ:

Faith is the foundation of all spiritual goods, according to the words of the Apostle, "Faith is the substance (that is, the foundation) of things to be hoped for" (Heb 11:1). Faith is also that by which the soul is given life through grace, according to the words of the Apostle, "The life I live now in the flesh I life in the faith of the Son of God" (Gal 2:20); and Habacuc, "The just shall live on account of his faith" (Hab 2:4). It is that through which the soul is cleansed of sin. "They purify their hearts through faith" (Acts 15:9). It is that by which the soul is adorned with justice. The justice of God, however, is by the faith of Jesus Christ. It is that through which the soul is united in marriage to God, "I will take you for my wife in faith" (Hos 2:20).[13]

The Ecclesial Logic of Justification

One might find Luther's spousal text in "On the Freedom of the Christian" excessively individualistic. He does not make clear that the bride in Hosea and Paul is not the individual person, but the people of Israel and the Church. "This wedding was publicly celebrated when he joined *the Church* to

---

11. See Anders Nygren, *Agape and Eros* (Philadelphia: Westminster Press, 1953).
12. St. Thomas, *In Symbolum Apostolorum*, prologue.
13. St. Thomas, *Super Decretales*, § 1.

himself by faith, "I will take you for my wife in faith" (Hos 2:20)."[14] In defense of Luther, one can point out that in another important spousal text he does bring out the ecclesial logic of justification. Commenting on the verse in the wedding Psalm, "At your right hand stands the queen, arrayed in gold" (Ps 45:10), he writes,

> He calls the bride "the queen," His spouse. She stands as though all in gold. *This bride is the church* and the entire body, particularly that which was taken over from the synagogue. Paul and the other Apostles converted many cities and peoples, among whom there were also princes and kings. Thus Sergius was converted (Acts 13:7 ff.). But the bride is one, gathered from all these members of kings and princes, the weak and the poor, virgins and married people—and from all of these is formed *one bride, the church*. This is common usage, that Christ is called the bridegroom and the church, the bride, as in Eph. 5:23 ff. and other passages. He calls her through Holy Baptism and the Word of the Gospel, and adorns and clothes her with mercy, grace, and the remission of sins. That is what he means when he says, "She stands at your right hand." It is a magnificent compliment, and it is also appropriate that no one be nearer the bridegroom than the bride herself. But the principal thing is that *the church has everything that is Christ's* and that two bodies have become one, so that what belongs to the church is Christ's and in the same way what belongs to Christ is the church's.
>
> These things are greater than human speech can present or our heart comprehend. Still it is represented faintly in marriage, where the supreme love of the bridegroom is for the bride, one faith, one body, and one mind. Between Christ and the church the relation is real, whereas in physical marriage we find only images and representations of this spiritual marriage, where Christ is the bridegroom and everything He has He gives to the church....
>
> ... I know, too, that [Christ] has been appointed the Bridegroom and has conveyed to His bride, the church, all that He has. *I am a part of His church.* For I have sure signs and pledges, namely, Baptism, the Gospel, the Eucharist, that witness to the fact that *I am a member of Christ.*[15]

Luther is thus clearly aware of the ecclesial character of justification. It is as a member of the body of Christ that the individual person is justified. Once again, this text has the ring of a fundamental theological principle. Here one hears the true Luther, the Luther of the biblical understanding of love.

---

14. St. Thomas, *Super Evangelium S. Ioannis Lectura*, ed. Raphaelis Cai, 5th ed. (Rome: Marietti, 1952), § 338.

15. Luther, *Selected Psalms I*, ed. Jaroslav Pelikan (St. Louis, Mo.: Concordia, 1955), 259ff.

Luther's Rejection of the Doctrine of
Faith Formed by Love

Luther's spousal texts quoted above indicate that he sees justification as involving both faith and love. It seems, therefore, that he would agree with the following thesis of St. Thomas:

Just as the body lives its natural life through the soul, so the soul lives the life of grace through God. First of all, God dwells in the soul through faith: "That Christ may dwell in your hearts through faith" (Eph 3:17); but this indwelling is not perfect, unless faith is formed by love, which by the bond of perfection unites us to God, as Col 3:14 says. Consequently, the phrase, lives by faith, must be understood of formed faith.[16]

Despite his clear affirmation of the spousal logic of justification, Luther most emphatically denies this doctrine of formed faith:

Do not let yourself be swayed here by the wicked gloss of the sophists, who say that faith justifies only when love … [is] added to it. With this pernicious gloss they have darkened and distorted some of the finest texts.… If faith does not justify without love, then faith is vain and useless, and love alone justifies; or unless faith is formed and adorned by love, it is nothing.

… This gloss is to be avoided as *a hellish poison*, and we must conclude with Paul: By faith alone, not by faith formed by love, are we justified. We must not attribute the power of justifying to a "form" that makes a man pleasing to God; we must attribute it to faith, which *takes hold of Christ* the Savior Himself *and possesses Him* in the heart. This faith justifies *without love and before love*.[17]

If the doctrine of formed faith is such a hellish poison, what should one say about the spousal union brought about by faith? Is it a spousal union without spousal love? Luther's answer is astonishing:

When we are involved in a discussion of justification, there is no room for speaking about the Law. The question is what Christ is and what blessing He has brought us. Christ is not the Law; He is not my work or that of the Law; *He is not my love* or that of the Law; He is … the Redeemer of those who are under the Law. By faith we are in Him, and He is in us (John 6:56). This Bridegroom, Christ, must be *alone with His bride in His private chamber*, and all the family and household must be *shunted away*. But later on, when the Bridegroom opens the door and comes out, then let the servants return to take care of them and serve them food and drink. *Then let* works and *love begin*.[18]

16. St. Thomas, *In ad Rom.*, § 108.

17. Luther, *Lectures on Galatians 1535: Chapters 1–4*, ed. Walter A. Hansen (St. Louis, Mo.: Concordia, 1963), 136, emphasis added.

18. Ibid., 137, emphasis added.

The image is devastatingly clear. In the chamber, where the spousal union be-tween God and the Church takes place, only faith is allowed. Love is shunted away and must wait outside the door until the union is completed. Only then is love allowed to enter to serve the married pair. What takes place in the inti-macy of the bridal chamber is not love. This is not the same Luther that speaks through the spousal texts quoted above. It is the angry Luther, who needs to cut off the Papists at the root. It is, perhaps, also the Luther who received a Nominalist philosophical formation.

Could there be a more radical denial of the spousal logic of justification? Is love not present at least in the bridegroom, who takes the body of his bride and gives himself to her? And does this love of the redeemer not shape the response of the bride who lets her body be taken and who takes his body? Can she re-ceive his gift of self and give herself—without love? Can love be shunted away?

Luther's Argument against Formed Faith

Let us examine one of Luther's arguments against the doctrine of justifica-tion by formed faith. It is an argument by *reductio ad absurdum.* "If faith does not justify without love, then faith is vain and useless, and love alone justifies; or unless faith is formed and adorned by love, it is nothing."

Does St. Thomas hold what Luther sees as the inevitable absurd con-sequence of the doctrine of formed faith? What exactly does it mean for St. Thomas that *faith* justifies, *faith rather than love,* a formed faith, granted, but nevertheless *faith?* Saint Thomas argues that in the justification of the sin-ner, faith is the first effect of grace. It, without any preceding works, is the entrance door opened by God to all other blessings.

God's justice is said to exist through faith in Christ Jesus, not as though by faith we merit being justified, as if faith exists from ourselves and through it we merit God's justice, as the Pelagians assert; but because in the very justification, by which we are made just by God, *the first motion of the mind toward God is through faith:* "Whoever would draw near to God must believe" (Heb 11:6). Hence faith, as *the first part of jus-tice,* is given to us by God: "By grace you have been saved through faith; and this is not your own doing; for it is the gift of God" (Eph 2:8).

But this faith, out of which justice exists, is not the unformed faith about which James 2:26 says, "Faith without works is dead," but it is faith formed by love, about which Gal 5:6 says, "For in Christ Jesus neither circumcision nor uncircumcision is of any avail, but faith [working through love]," through which Christ dwells in us; "that Christ may dwell in your hearts through faith" (Eph 3:17), which does not happen without love: *"He who abides in love abides in God and God in him"* (1 John 4:16).[19]

---

19. Ibid., § 302, emphasis added.

It is thus clear that St. Thomas would not agree with a construal of his position that removes faith from its first place in the justification of the sinner and gives that first place to love instead.

One reason why faith is first (and here St. Thomas seems once again to be quite close to Luther) is that *faith, precisely as faith,* takes the objective redemption achieved by Christ, *assents* to it, and *applies* it to the believer.

[The Apostle] indicates *how the effect of redemption reached us,* when he says, *by faith* in his blood, i.e., faith concerning his blood poured out for us. For in order to satisfy for us, it was fitting that he undergo the penalty of death for us, a penalty man had incurred by sin, as indicated in Genesis 2:17, "In the day that you eat of it you shall die." Hence 1 Peter 3:18 states, "For Christ also died for sins once for all." This death of Christ *is applied* to us *through faith,* by which we believe that the world has been redeemed by His death: "I live by faith in the Son of God, who loved me and gave himself for me" (Gal 2:20). For even among men payment made by one man does not benefit another, unless [that other] *ratifies* it.[20]

Faith, *precisely as faith, assents* to the objective blessings of Christ, *ratifies* them, and thereby *applies* them to the sinner. It receives Christ's spousal gift of himself in a spousal manner, that is, with spousal love that qualifies faith as a spousal faith. Nevertheless, the primacy of faith in justification remains.

Saint Thomas's understanding of faith as *applying* Christ's saving passion to the sinner is in some respects close to Luther's.

What the scholastics have taught about justifying faith "formed by love" is an empty dream. For the faith that *takes hold of Christ,* the Son of God, and is adorned by Him is the faith that justifies, not a faith that includes love. For if faith is to be sure and firm, it *must take hold of nothing but Christ alone;* and in the agony and terror of conscience it has nothing else to lean on than this pearl of great value (Matt. 13:45–46). Therefore whoever *takes hold of Christ* by faith, no matter how terrified by the Law and oppressed by the burden of his sins he may be, has the right to boast that he is righteous. How has he this right? By that jewel, Christ, *whom he possesses by faith.* Our opponents fail to understand this. Therefore they reject Christ, this jewel; and *in His place they put their love,* which they say is a jewel. But if they do not know what faith is, it is impossible for them to have faith, much less to teach it to others. And as for what they claim to have, this is nothing but a dream, an opinion, and natural reason, but not faith.[21]

Luther charges that his opponents "reject Christ, this jewel; and *in His place they put their love,* which they say is a jewel." A moral act flowing from human free will displaces the gift that is Christ himself.

---

20. Ibid., § 309, emphasis added.
21. Luther, *Lectures on Galatians,* 88.

If love is the form of faith, then I am immediately obliged to say that love is the most important and the largest part in the Christian religion. And thus I lose Christ, His blood, His wounds, and all His blessings; and *I cling to love*, so that I love, and *I come to a moral kind of "doing,"* just as the pope, a heathen philosopher, and the Turk do.[22]

For Luther, the most precious thing about faith is not that it is a perfection of the believer, but that it grasps Christ, just as in spousal union, the most important thing is not the disposition and change in one's own heart and body, but reaching the beloved, taking hold of the beloved. Is this logic not preeminently found in spousal love? Does not the primary meaning of spousal love lie precisely in taking hold of the beloved? I think the Luther of the spousal texts would unhesitatingly respond, yes.

The question of merit can be fruitfully approached from here as well. Both love and merit found their way back into Lutheran doctrine already in the first generation. In fact, St. Thomas explains merit in terms that make perfect sense within the spousal logic of justification.

The amount of one's merit depends principally and in respect to essential reward on charity. For the essential reward consists in the joy one has in God. But it is plain that one who loves God more will enjoy Him more. Hence, the Lord promises that blessed vision to those who love: "He who loves me will be loved by my Father and I will love him and manifest myself to him" (John 14:21).[23]

Noncompetitive Causality

In arguing against formed faith Luther seems to have the suspicion that the Papists understand love as an act that flows from human free will *rather than* from Christ's redeeming passion. Boasting is the necessary consequence. The Papists boast in their own act of love rather than in Christ, their bridegroom.

On the contrary, St. Thomas understands love as one of the gifts given by Christ when he justifies the sinner. At the same time, he sees it as an act for which we are fully responsible.

An action is attributed more to the principal agent than to the secondary, as when we say that the hammer does not make the box but the carpenter by using the hammer. But man's will is moved to good by God, as it says above: "All who are led by the Spirit of God are sons of God" (Rom 8:14); therefore, an inward action of man is not to be attributed principally to man but to God: "It is God who of his good pleasure works in you both the will and the performance" (Phil 2:13).

22. Ibid., 268, emphasis added.
23. St. Thomas, *In ad Rom.*, § 677.

But if willing does not depend on the man willing or exertion on the man exerting himself, but on God moving man to this, it seems that man is not master of his own action, which pertains to freedom of will.

But the answer is that God moves all things, but in diverse ways, inasmuch as each is moved in a manner befitting its nature. And so man is moved by God to will [inwardly] and to perform outwardly in a manner consistent with free will. Therefore, willing and performing depends on man as freely acting; but on God and not on man, as initial mover.[24]

What I want to draw attention to in this text is the noncompetitive relation between divine and human causality. Love depends on the human person freely acting, and at the same time, without any competition, it depends primarily and comprehensively on God moving the will.

To a thinker trained in Nominalist metaphysics, this noncompetitive relation between causes will seem impossible and contradictory. As a first step, therefore, what is needed to respond to the anti-Papist Luther from the Thomistic point of view is a metaphysical argument. Here is at least a thumbnail sketch of such an argument. God is *not a being*, one among other beings, *outside* all other beings just as each is outside all the others. God is rather *ipsum esse*, "being itself." As *ipsum esse* he is, in St. Augustine's famous phrase, *interior intimo meo*, "more interior than my innermost."[25] In contrast to the causality of particular beings, which competes against the causality of the beings they act upon (as in the case of a marionette that is pulled by strings attached to it rather than moving itself from within), God's causality is *creative*. To the degree, therefore, in which God acts and causes, he creates, he sets the creature into *its own being and activity from within* rather than overwhelming it from without, canceling its own activity and threatening its being. A dim echo of this noncompetitive relation is found in spousal love. The impact of the two lovers on each other does not reduce the life and activity that is in each but increases it: "man can only find himself in a sincere gift of self" (*Gaudium et spes* 24:3). Once again, it seems to me that the Luther of the spousal texts would agree.

The Trinitarian Logic of Justification

The same truth can be observed on a deeper level in the grace of adoption, which St. Thomas sees as the very heart of justification in accord with Romans 8:14–15 and Galatians 4:6. In his comments on Romans 5:5, "God's love has

---

24. Ibid., § 777.
25. St. Augustine, *Confessions*, book 3, ch. 6, § 11.

been poured into our hearts through the Holy Spirit that has been given to us," he says. "To receive the gift of the Holy Spirit, who is the love of the Father and the Son, is to be brought to participate in the Love who is the Holy Spirit, and by this participation we are made lovers of God."[26]

This love is a specifically filial love. "God has sent the Spirit of his Son into our hearts, crying, Abba! Father!" (Gal 4:6). St. Thomas comments,

[Regeneration] comes about through a spiritual seed that is transmitted into the place of spiritual generation, namely, into the human mind or heart, because through the renewal of the mind we are generated so as to become sons of God. The spiritual seed is the grace of the Holy Spirit: "The one who is generated from God does not sin, because generation from God protects him, etc." (1 John 5:18). And this seed contains in its power the whole perfection of blessedness. This is why it is called "pledge" or "arrha" of blessedness (Eph 1:14). "A new spirit I will put within you" (Ezek 36:26) that cries out, that is, makes [us] cry out, "Abba, Father," not by volume of sound, but by greatness and fervor of affection. For, we cry, "Abba, Father," when through affection we are inflamed to the desire of God by the heat of the Holy Spirit. "We have not received a spirit of slavery, etc." (Rom 8:15).[27]

Saint Thomas brings out the Trinitarian logic of the doctrine of justification. How does this Trinitarian logic help us to grasp the noncompetitive relation between the action of the Spirit and the act of human love in the justification of the sinner?

"As the Father has Life in himself, he has given to the Son also to have Life in himself" (John 5:26). Saint Thomas comments,

He shows the equality of the Son to the Father when he says, as the Father has Life in himself; and he shows their distinction when he says, he has given to the Son. For the Father and the Son are equal in Life; but they are distinct, because the Father gives, and the Son receives. However, we should not understand this to mean that the Son receives life from the Father as if the Son first existed without having life ... because in the Son there is nothing that exists prior to the reception of life. For as Hilary says: "the Son has nothing except [as] born [*filius nihil habet nisi natum*]," i.e., nothing but what he receives through his birth. And since the Father is Life itself, the meaning of, "he has given to the Son to have Life in himself," is that the Father produced the Son [as] Life.[28]

In the Trinity, the Son's complete dependence on the Father and his full equality with the Father in having Life in himself do not exclude each other.

---

26. St. Thomas, *In ad Rom.*, § 392.

27. St. Thomas, *Super epistolam ad Galatas Lectura*, in *Super Epistolas S. Pauli Lectura*, vol. 1, ed. Raphaelis Cai (Rome: Marietti, 1953), § 214–15.

28. St. Thomas, *Super Ioann.*, § 782.

In this respect, the logic of the begetting of the Son in the Trinity is the ultimate root of the logic of creation and of justification by the grace of adoption. It is also the ultimate root of the spousal relation between Christ and the Church. Of course, an infinite gulf separates creation and redemption from the processions of the persons in the Trinity. Still the former are shaped according to the pattern of the latter.[29]

Trinitarian reflection is not as unfolded in Luther as it is in St. Thomas. Still, it does not seem likely that the Luther of the spousal texts would object to the Trinitarian logic of justification, because it is as thoroughly biblical as the spousal logic. Greater emphasis on this Trinitarian logic would perhaps allow him not to betray his key intuition, in agreement with St. Thomas, that justification essentially involves spousal love.

29. For a parallel argument that focuses on the Trinity and creation, see Gilles Emery, *La Trinité créatrice: Trinité et création dans les commentaires aux Sentences de Thomas d'Aquin et de ses précurseurs Albert le Grand et Bonaventure* (Paris: J. Vrin, 1995).

Robert Louis Wilken

~

16   Origen, Augustine, and Thomas

Interpreters of the Letter to the Romans

Every commentator on the letter of Paul to the Romans seeks to discover a
central theme that holds everything in the book together. But the best and
most profound interpreters know that the epistle is so rich, its arguments so
varied, its range of topics so grand, that the most substantive writing of the
Apostle cannot be brought easily under a single rubric. Already in the third
century, Origen of Alexandria, the first to write a verse by verse commentary
on Romans, realized this. And in a characteristically perceptive passage in his
commentary he compares what he calls Paul's "apostolic discourse" to the palace of a great king.

In this palace the Apostle is being led about by a mighty king in the royal
treasuries and apartments. The rooms have different entrances, all unmarked,
and he discovers that he enters through one door, yet leaves from another. And
the things he is shown are never disclosed to him at once nor fully, because
the door is never opened wide. And when the faithful steward, that is, Paul,
brings others to the palace he wisely recognizes that he too should give only
intimations rather than detailed accounts of what he has seen. It is not that
things are concealed, for they are shown, but by the way they are presented the
layout of the palace and its adornments remain a mystery.[1]

In his study of the Letter to the Romans written in the last decade of his
life, Origen, whose native language was the same as that of the Apostle, and
who was writing in Caesarea in the Holy Land, knew that no matter how
much learning, intelligence, spiritual discernment one brings to the epistle, in
the end all one can do is describe what one has seen, never grasping the whole.

1. Origen, *Commentary on Romans (CRm)* 5.1.9. *Commentarii in Epistulam ad Romanos*, ed.
Theresia Heither, O.S.B. (Freiburg in Breisgau: Herder, 1990–96), trans. Thomas Scheck as *Origen
Commentary on the Epistle to the Romans* (Washington, D.C.: The Catholic University of America
Press, 2001–2).

Like Origen's Commentary on Romans, St. Thomas's *Lectures on the Epistle of St. Paul to the Romans* is a chapter by chapter and verse by verse exposition of the entire epistle, written toward the end of his life.[2] Thomas had left Paris in the spring of 1272 to return to Italy and organize a *studium generale* of theology in Naples. In planning his lectures he had decided to focus on the letters of St. Paul, particularly the Epistle to the Romans. This was not the first time he had lectured on St. Paul. He had already taken up Paul's letters more than a decade earlier in Orvieto, and now he returned to the writings of the Apostle. It is not clear how these two series of lectures relate to each other, but it seems that the early chapters of the present text of the commentary are a revision of what he had written earlier.[3]

Scholars are fairly confident that Thomas lectured on the Epistle to the Romans in Naples before he died because of a dream that is reported by Torromeo, one of his biographers. It was said that one day when Thomas was seated in his chair commenting on the epistle, the Apostle himself walked into the room. Thomas asked St. Paul whether he was expounding the text according to what the Apostle had intended. Saint Paul said that Thomas was explaining his words insofar as they could be understood in this life, but a time would come when he could understand them fully. Then the Apostle grabbed Thomas's cape, dragged him out of the room, and took him away. Three days later news of Thomas's death reached Naples.

In commenting on this story the modern biographer of Thomas, Jean-Pierre Torrell, says that it shows that in the hagiographical tradition there is a memory of Thomas lecturing on St. Paul in Naples at the end of his life. And in terms of a historical account of the life of St. Thomas that seems reasonable. However, in reading through the account, I was struck more by the content of St. Paul's comment, that in this life even a theologian as great as St. Thomas Aquinas would not be able to comprehend the fullness of the truth found in Paul's epistles.

Origen's metaphor of "apostolic discourse" as a palace of many rooms whose interior is disclosed only in bits and pieces is useful to introduce Thomas's commentary. As one moves through the text the range of topics mounts, and one has a sense that the whole is never visible. The reader is at a loss how to relate, let us say, the discussion of the natural knowledge of God in chapter 1, the justice of God in 3, Abraham's faith in 4, the sin of Adam in 5, "sin dwells

2. *Super Epistolas S. Pauli Lectura*, ed. R. Raphaelis Cai, O.P. (Rome: Marietti, 1953).

3. On the date of the lectures on Romans see Jean-Pierre Torrell, O.P., *Saint Thomas Aquinas*, vol. 1, *The Person and His Work*, trans. Robert Royal (Washington, D.C.: The Catholic University of America Press, 1996), 250–57; also Thomas Domanyi, *Der Römerbriefkommentar des Thomas von Aquin: Ein Beitrag zur Untersuchung seiner Auslegungsmethoden*. (Bern: Peter Lang, 1979).

within me" (7:17) in chapter 7, election and the relation of Christianity to Judaism in chapter 9, and political authority in 13. Which is say that Thomas wrote a genuine commentary, not an essay on Pauline themes filtered through the theological and philosophical debates of the thirteenth century.

The words of St. Paul stand at the center of Thomas's exposition and the interpretation is informed and controlled by the skillful citation of apt passages from elsewhere in the Scripture. Though Thomas is interpreting St. Paul, the horizon of his commentary is the Bible as a whole. For Thomas Scripture interprets Scripture, and one of the pleasures in reading the commentary is discovering which biblical texts he calls on to interpret the passage before him.

For example, here is a delightful instance from the very end of the commentary. After naming a number of people he wished to greet in Rome, Paul says "greet one another with a holy kiss." Thomas comments that Paul uses the expression "holy kiss" to distinguish this kiss from a sensual kiss such as the kiss of the harlot mentioned in Proverbs: "seizing the young man she kisses him" (Prv 7:13), or from a deceitful kiss, about which Proverbs says: "Better are the wounds of a friend than the deceitful kisses of an enemy" (Prv 27:6). The "holy kiss," says Thomas, is a sign of the Blessed Trinity, as in the Song of Songs, "O that he would kiss me with the kiss of his mouth" (Sg 1:2). And it was this kiss, he adds, that led to the custom of the faithful sharing a kiss of peace during the "solemnities of the Mass" *(missarum solemnia)*.[4]

Or take another passage I found particularly illuminating, Romans 5:1–2, "Being justified therefore by faith, let us have peace with God, through our Lord Jesus Christ, through whom also we have access through faith to this grace in which we stand." I have always wondered why St. Paul uses the term "stand" in this passage: the "grace in which we stand." Thomas explains that it is because he is speaking about the "state of grace" *(statum gratiae)*, that is, grace as a condition in which one lives, a disposition that allows the soul to have fellowship with God, not an external force that works on the believer. Through grace, he writes, we not only rise from sins *(non solum resurreximus a peccatis)*, but "we stand firm and erect [*stamus, fixi et erecti*] with our affections fixed on heavenly things." To support his interpretation, and to explain St. Paul's use of the term "stand," he cites Psalm 120(121):2: "our feet were standing" *(stantes)* in Jerusalem. Note that in the psalm "stand" is used in the present tense, indicating, in Thomas's view, that Paul is referring to an ongoing disposition, not a momentary visitation of divine goodness. He also cites Psalm 19(20):8, "We have risen and stand upright" *(nos autem surreximus et erecti sumus)* and uses the term "upright" *(erecti)* from the psalm to illustrate

---

4. *In ad Rom.* 16, lect. 1, § 1211.

what is meant by "stand," namely that the primary consequence of grace is faith.[5]

This marshalling of words and images from elsewhere in the Bible is not a form of proof-texting. In many cases the text cited does not have any obvious relation to the passage under discussion. Something deeper is at work. The citation of other biblical texts gives Thomas a vocabulary drawn from the Scriptures to interpret and present the teaching of the Scriptures. That is, though he will use technical theological language when necessary, more often in the commentary his thinking is done in the language of the Bible, and the interpretation is freighted with meanings associated with biblical history. "Standing" in the psalm is not simply a matter of being erect; the psalm says "our feet were standing in Jerusalem," invoking the holy city where God is present. Instead of translating the words of the Bible into another language, for example one that is more strictly theological, he interprets the text by rendering what is in one part of the Bible with words and images found elsewhere.

Thomas is not of course unique in using Scripture to interpret Scripture. This way of interpreting the Bible was developed in the early church and was practiced by all the Church Fathers. For example, Augustine's homilies on the psalms and in other sermons usually begin with the citation of an appropriate passage from elsewhere in the Scripture that allows the hearer to enter more deeply into the passage that has been read. As a commentator Thomas stands solidly within the classical tradition of Christian biblical interpretation. This is not insignificant, for in other writings it is evident that his way of doing theology is quite different from that of the Church Fathers. But as an exegete he belongs in the company of Jerome, Ambrose, Augustine, Gregory of Nyssa, or Cyril of Alexandria. Theology is *sacra pagina*, and theology and scriptural interpretation are one.

In the passage before us in Romans 5, "the grace in which we stand," Thomas is dealing with an explicitly theological topic. But he uses the same technique to illuminate other aspects of the epistle, for example Paul's affections. At the beginning of chapter 9 St. Paul expresses his sadness that his own people, the Jews, have not embraced Christ. "I am speaking the truth in Christ, and I am not lying, my conscience bears me witness in the Holy Spirit, that I have great *sorrow* and unceasing anguish in my heart" (9:1–2).

Thomas is moved by Paul's feelings for his people and proceeds to examine closely his use of the term "sorrow." First he quotes Lamentations to highlight the magnitude of what St. Paul is speaking about, "Vast as the sea is your ruin" (Lam 2:13). Then he poses an objection by citing a passage from Sirach that

5. *In ad Rom.* 5, lect. 1, § 383.

seems to conflict with Paul's sentiment, "Give not up your soul to *sadness*" (Sir 30:22). But, says Thomas, this sentiment, that sadness is inappropriate in a wise man, is a Stoic doctrine. It is not the teaching of the Bible. For even the Lord was saddened by his approaching death. "My soul is sorrowful even to death" (Mt 26:38). Further, since we are to love our neighbor as ourselves, it is right to grieve with a neighbor. For in 2 Corinthians Paul says, "I fear that I may have to mourn over many of those who sinned" (2 Cor 12:2).

There is, then, says Thomas a "godly sadness" that springs from divine love, as Paul says, "For godly grief produces repentance and leads to salvation" (2 Cor 7:10). This is the sadness Paul was speaking about. And to drive home the point he notes that Paul says his "anguish" was "unceasing," explaining the participle "unceasing" by citing the prophet Jeremiah: "That I might weep *day and night* for the slain of my people" (9:1). Finally he emphasizes that Paul's "sorrow" was genuine, "not superficial but rooted in the heart," as in Lamentations, "My eyes are spent in weeping.... My *heart* is poured out in grief" (Lam 2:11).[6] Thomas's commentary is a book to be read slowly with one's Bible at hand, to ponder not only the verse he is commenting on but also the wide range of texts from all over the Scripture he puts before the reader.

From the way Thomas moves through the exposition of the term "sorrow" in Romans 9 it is evident that that there are similarities to the *quaestio* method used in the *Summa*. He discusses the issue at hand by first raising objections, then responding to them. But the commentary does not read like an article in the *Summa*.[7] Thomas's attention remains fixed on the actual words of St. Paul, and the aim of the exposition is to explain why Paul uses the words he does and what they mean within the context of the Bible as a whole. In this case, by focusing on the term "sorrow" he adds an affective dimension to his discussion of the Jews in Romans 9 and, one might add, to Christian attitudes toward the Jews.

These three examples show that Thomas took great delight in thinking with the Bible and expressing his ideas in the language of the Bible. His deep knowledge of the Scriptures allows him to marshal illuminating passages almost at will. A concordance to the Bible was completed in 1230 under the direction of Hugo de Saint-Cher, a Dominican with the help of his fellow Dominicans, and it is possible Thomas had access to it. But Hugh of Cher's concordance did not include quotations; it was simply an index to passages where a word occurred. Though it would have helped Thomas locate some passages,

6. *In ad Rom.* 9, lect. 1, § 738.
7. There are exceptions of course. The commentary on Romans 5:12 is a small theological essay. On Thomas's interpretation of this passage in relation to other medieval commentators, see Domanyi, *Der Römerbriefkommentar des Thomas von Aquin*, 231–66.

it is unlikely he could have found many of the texts he draws on simply by consulting an index of biblical words.

Of course Thomas had at his disposal earlier commentaries on Romans as well as other writings of the fathers in which Romans is cited frequently. In some cases it is evident that his way of handling a particular text was suggested by other writers, often St. Augustine.[8] Take for example his commentary on the opening verse of Romans 12.

"I beseech you therefore, brothers, by the mercy of God, that you present you bodies as a living sacrifice, holy, pleasing to God, your reasonable service" *(rationabile obsequium)* (12:1). To explain the phrase "present your bodies as a living sacrifice" Thomas directs the reader to Augustine's *City of God*, book 10. There Augustine cites Romans 12:1 to show that the body can be a sacrifice. Thomas also cites two other passages that Augustine uses in this section of the *City of God*, Psalm 51:18, "the sacrifice acceptable to God is a contrite spirit," and Hebrews 13:16, "Do not neglect to do good and to share what you have, for such sacrifices are pleasing to God."[9]

The first, Psalm 51, Thomas takes to refer to the "soul," that is, to something interior, because of the term "spirit" in "broken spirit" *(spiritus contribulatus)*, and the second, "share what you have," to something external, for example, the giving of alms.[10] An attentive reader will know that with the mention of "interior" and "exterior" aspects of sacrifice Thomas is working his way to say something about the nature of human acts.[11]

Once he has explained what is meant by sacrifice in Romans Thomas comments on each of the four words or phrases that qualify the term "sacrifice" in the passage, "living, holy, pleasing to God, your reasonable service" by citing

---

8. Augustine did not write a complete commentary on Romans. An early work, *Propositions from the Epistle to the Romans (Expositio quarundam propositionum ex epistola ad Romanos)*, is a short set of responses Augustine gave to fellow clergy who had questions about the epistle. Another early work, the *Unfinished Commentary (Epistolae ad Romanos Inchoata Expositio)* deals only with the opening verses. See *Augustine on Romans: Propositions from the Epistle to the Romans; Unfinished Commentary on the Epistle to the Romans*, trans. Paula F. Landes, Society of Biblical Literature Texts and Translations 23: Early Christian Literature Series 6 (Chico, Calif.: Scholars Press, 1982). The essay "To Simplicianus" deals with Rom 7:7–25 and 9:10–29 and represents a shift in Augustine's thinking. Besides these writings his interpretation of Romans can be gleaned from his other works in which he cites the epistle.

9. *City of God*, 10.5-6.

10. *In ad Rom.* 9, lect. 1, § 958.

11. Thomas also mentions a third feature of sacrifice, temperance. Augustine had mentioned "temperance" (*City of God*, 10.6), but Thomas makes this concrete by specifying forms of "temperance," namely "fasts" and "vigils," as a way of serving God. And again he comes up with an inspired choice of a text to support his exegesis, Paul's words: "I pommel my body and subdue it" (1 Cor 9:27).

four passages from the Old Testament. Three come from Leviticus, for example, "The priest shall burn them all on the altar as a burnt offering, a pleasing odors to the Lord" (Lv 1:9).[12] But then he steps back from the text before him to reflect more generally on the nature of human acts by which we serve God. In other words "sacrifice" becomes the model for moral acts. "Justice," he says, consists chiefly in internal acts, for example, believing hoping, loving, for in Luke we read: "The kingdom of God is within you" (Lk 17:21) But external acts are also necessary "as a means to the end." This is why St. Paul says that our "bodies" are a sacrifice to God.[13]

As this passage makes clear, Thomas thought his task as commentator was not simply to analyze and explain what the words of the epistle signify. The goal of interpretation is not primarily to expound what Paul thinks, but to address the *res*, the subject matter that is presented by the text. The words of the Scripture are signs given to the Church to enter more fully into the mystery of God present in history and in human life. So his discussion of sacrifice leads him to offer, if only sketchily, an account of the nature of human acts in service of God.

With the exposition of Romans 12:1 in mind, one will read q. 91, a. 4, in the *prima secundae* with fresh eyes. There, in discussing divine law, Thomas shows that human beings are directed to perform acts in view of their "last end." If our actions were directed only to ends appropriate to their natural faculties, there would be need of nothing other than the natural or human law. For human beings are able to judge only exterior acts, not interior movements. But for the "perfection of virtue" it is necessary for man to "conduct himself aright in both kinds of acts," that is, interior as well as exterior. In other words, virtuous acts are like the offering of the body as a sacrifice.

Thomas does not mention sacrifice in this article, but it hovers in the background and in q. 85, a. 3, of the *secunda secundae*, "whether the offering of sacrifice is a special act of virtue," he brings together acts of virtue and sacrifice. There he does cite Romans 12:1, and presents the nature of sacrifice in exactly the same terms as in the commentary. Sacrifice can be viewed from three perspectives, as a good of the soul that is offered to God inwardly by prayer, devotion, and other "interior acts." This is the principal sacrifice. The second has to do with the body, for example, offering the body in martyrdom or in abstinence. The third has to do with external things, for example, giving of our possessions.

Sacrifice, because it has an internal and an external aspect, serves as a

---

12. Also Mal 1:14, Lv 22:3, Lv 20:7.
13. *In ad Rom*, 9, lect 1, § 964.

model for moral acts in general. An acceptable sacrifice, one that is our "reasonable service" (Rom 12:1), must have an interior disposition, that is, humble devotion, for the psalmist says "the sacrifice acceptable to God is a contrite *spirit*"; at the same time sacrifice has an external dimension because Paul says that it is our bodies that we offer to God. Hence the just man, says Thomas, relates to God by internal and external acts, that is, acts that are directed to a final end, that is, to God, as well as to natural ends.[14]

In the case of Romans 12 one can see a fairly direct line between the commentary and his discussion of the nature of human acts in the *Summa*. In other cases the commentary moves in a direction different from what one finds in the *Summa*. A good example is the discussion of Romans 2:13–17, the famous passage that is often cited as support for a doctrine of natural law. Few texts from St. Paul have been so controversial in the history of Pauline exegesis up to the present day.

The earliest Christian commentator on this passage, Origen of Alexandria, interprets the text as referring to a natural law. He observes that Paul uses the term *nomos* in Romans to refer to different kinds of law, for example, to Mosaic law, to other parts of the Old Testament, to natural law, to the law of cities. In Romans 2 when Paul speaks of the Gentiles doing the things of the law he does not mean the Gentiles are observing the law with respect to the Sabbath or new moon celebrations. "It is not *that* law which is written in the hearts of the Gentiles. He has in mind what they are able to perceive by nature [*sentire naturaliter*], for example that they should not commit murder nor adultery, nor steal, nor speak falsely, and should honor their father and mother, and the like." To which he adds "perhaps also written in the hearts of the Gentiles is the one God is Creator of all things."[15]

In his early writings Augustine cites or alludes to Romans 2 to establish that there is a universal moral law that is different from the Mosaic Law.[16] In later works, however, after he had studied Romans more carefully, and been faced with Pelagius's teaching, he strives to give Romans 2 an interpretation that rules out the possibility one can follow the moral law without the infusion of grace. A key passage is found in his work, *On the Spirit and the Letter.*

14. In discussing the relation between Thomas's commentaries and the *Summa*, John Boyle makes the interesting suggestion that instead of viewing the commentaries as an aid to understanding the *Summa* one might consider the *Summa* as a "guide to understanding Scripture." See his "St. Thomas and Sacred Scripture," *Pro Ecclesia* 4, no. 1 (1995): 103.

15. *CRm* 2.9 (Heither, 1:228).

16. *Against Faustus* 19.2. See Simon J. Gathercole, "A Conversion of Augustine: From Natural Law to Restored Nature in Romans 2:13–16," in *Engaging Augustine on Romans*, ed. Daniel Patte and Eugene Teselle (Harrisburg, Pa.: Trinity Press International, 2002), 147–172.

After setting forth his critique of Pelagius and stating his own positive statement, that it is through the gift of the Spirit who enkindles love that we are able to "cleave to God," Augustine says that Romans 2:14ff. poses a difficulty. For Paul says: "When the Gentiles which have not the law, do by nature the things contained in the law, these, not having the law, are a law unto themselves; which show the work of the law written in their hearts." Here Paul's language seems to "obscure the difference between the new covenant in which the Lord promised to write his law in the hearts of his people"[17] and a natural law written on the hearts of nonbelievers. If the Gentiles are said to have the law written on their hearts, how do they differ from the "faithful of the new covenant" of whom it is said that they would have the law written on their hearts?[18]

To solve this exegetical dilemma Augustine proposes an original solution. In Romans 2 Paul is speaking about Gentile Christians, not Gentile unbelievers. "It is possible," he writes, "that Gentiles of whom the apostle speaks as having the law written in their hearts are those of the new covenant." Then he proceeds to support his interpretation by citing Romans 1:16, that the gospel is "the power of God to salvation to everyone that believes, to the Jew first and also to the Greek," observing that the term "gentiles" in Romans 2:14 means Greeks, as in the phrase "to the Jew first and also to the Greek." And so, concludes Augustine, when Paul speaks of Gentiles who "have the works of the law written in their hearts" he has in mind "those who believe in Christ, because they come to the faith without having received the law beforehand as the Jews."[19] In other words Romans 2:13–16 does not support a doctrine of natural law.

Thomas discusses Romans 2:14 in the well-known passage in q. 91, a. 2, of the *prima secundae*, "whether there is a natural law." In the *sed contra* he cites the text accompanied by a gloss: "Although they have no written law, yet they have the natural law whereby each one knows, and is conscious of what is good and what is evil." Romans 2:14 is offered as the primary biblical support for his teaching on natural law.

The commentary on Romans, however, takes a different approach to Romans 2.[20] There the discussion centers on why the observance of the Jewish law does not "suffice for salvation." In other words in the commentary the "natural law" passage is read within the context of chapters 1 and 2. Hence Thomas notes that the term "by nature" *(naturaliter)* causes some difficulty,

17. Augustine is thinking of Jeremiah 31:33.
18. *Spirit and Letter* 43.26
19. Ibid. 25.42–27.48.
20. For a discussion of Thomas's interpretation of another passage on "natural law," Roman 1:20, in the commentary and in the *Summa*, see Eugene F. Rogers Jr., "The Narrative of Natural Law in Aquinas's Commentary on Romans 1," *Theological Studies* 59, no. 2 (1998) 254–76.

and he joins hands with Augustine. The difficulty with the *naturaliter* is that it gives support to the Pelagians, who taught that one could observe the law by one's "natural powers." But that cannot be Paul's meaning. Therefore, the phrase "by nature" must mean "nature reformed by grace. Paul is speaking of Gentiles converted to the faith, who began to observe the moral precepts of the law by the help of Christ's grace."[21]

But then he adds another possibility. *Naturaliter* can mean "that the natural law shows them what should be done [*quid sit agendum*]." And in support of this interpretation he cites Psalm 4:6. "There are many who say, 'Who shows us good things? The light of thy countenance, O Lord, is signed on us,'" that is, the light of natural reason given by the image of God is imprinted on us. But then he adds a qualifier: even though Paul speaks about a natural law, he does not eliminate the need for grace, just as the knowledge of sin through the law (Rom 3:20) does not exclude the necessity for "grace to move the affections."[22]

Two points: First, Thomas's exposition in the commentary allows for the interpretation that he gives in the *Summa*, that *naturaliter* can refer to the natural law. But the controlling interpretation in the commentary takes Romans 2 in light of the opening chapters of the epistle as worked out by Augustine in the Pelagian controversy. *Naturaliter* (by nature) means nature reformed by grace.

In his commentary on Romans Thomas is working within a tradition of interpretation forged by St. Augustine during the Pelagian controversy. This is evident in how he explains the central theme of the epistle. All of the epistles of St. Paul, he writes, deal with the grace of Christ, for Paul's entire teaching has to do with the grace of Christ. Among the epistles, Romans, says Thomas, sets forth the grace of Christ "as it is in itself." To which he adds the charming suggestion that the two epistles to the Corinthians deal with grace as it exists in the sacraments of the Church, the first on the nature of the sacraments, the second on the dignity of the minister. Galatians then treats superfluous sacraments, Jewish rites, to which certain persons wished to join the new sacraments.

Thomas's phrase the grace of Christ "as it is in itself" is noteworthy, for it confirms the Augustinian influence on his exegesis of Romans.[23] Although Thomas had read Origen, it is Augustine he follows. This is evident in the way Origen and Augustine explain the purpose of the epistle. The Epistle to the Romans, says Origen, deals with the "Law of Moses, the calling of the Gen-

---

21. *In ad Rom.* 2, lect. 3, § 216.

22. Ibid. Psalm 4:6 is cited in the *Summa theologiae* I, q. 84, a. 5, on whether the intellectual soul knows material things in the eternal types.

23. *In ad Rom.*, prologue, § 12.

tiles, Israel according to the flesh and Israel which is not according to the flesh, the circumcision of the flesh and of the heart, the spiritual law and the law of the letter." Origen identifies the "law" spoken of in the epistle as the "law of Moses" and then proceeds to mention things that have to do with the observance of the Law among the Jews, what he calls the "law of the letter" to contrast it with the "spiritual law."[24] Accordingly, for Origen the polarity in the epistle is not between grace and works, but between a righteousness according to the letter of the law, that is, observing the Jewish Law, and a righteousness based on the spiritual law.[25]

Note how differently Augustine puts things: "Above all else, one should understand that this letter addresses questions of the works of the law and of grace."[26] Like Origen, Augustine sets up a dialectic between works of the law and works of grace, but for him the term "law" signifies something more general and is not linked specifically to the Mosaic Law, that is, to observance. Elsewhere he says that the Epistle to the Romans shows that it is not through God's "gift of the law" that we are able to do "works of justice," but through "divine aid."[27] Here too there is no mention of the Jewish law, and the phrase "gift of the law" has the Pelagian sense of the "gift of the commandments that teach the right way of life."[28]

Elsewhere Augustine says that the term "law" in Paul should not be taken in the sense "only of those *sacramenta* [i.e., ritual acts] that were given to them [the Jews] as figures of the promise, but also of the works in whose performance is the life of righteousness."[29] Significantly he illustrates his point by reference to the Decalogue. That is, for Augustine not only is "law" understood in the more general sense of moral law, but the term "works" now refers to actions that human beings do in hope of gaining favor with God.

For Origen chapters 9–11 on the Jews and the Christ are the climax of the epistle, whereas for Augustine they were a tract on the logic of grace that leads inevitably to election.[30] So, when Thomas says at the beginning of the

---

24. *CRm*, preface (Heither, 1:70; Scheck, 1:57)

25. "Israel was observing the law of justice according to the letter" and had not attained the law of the Spirit. "We have thoroughly discussed faith in Christ and the works of the law at the beginning of this letter; and therefore, so that we do not repeat the same things, we shall expound the present passage by using a few statements of the Apostle himself." *CRm* 7.19.7 (Heither, 4:182–84; Scheck, 2:129).

26. *Expositio quarundam propositionum*, pref.

27. *Spirit and Letter* 12.20.

28. Ibid. 2.5

29. Ibid. 23.14.

30. On the interpretation of Romans 9–11 in the early Church see Peter Gorday, *Principles of Patristic Exegesis: Romans 9–11 in Origen, John Chrysostom, and Augustine* (New York: Edwin Mellen Press, 1983).

commentary that the central theme is grace "as it is in itself," he is speaking the language of Augustine. At key points this is evident. In chapter 3 at the words "no human being will be justified in [God's] sight by works of the law" (Rom 3:20), Thomas says that Paul is not only speaking about ritual acts, for example circumcision. He has in mind also "moral precepts" and teaches that "not by any works of the law, even those commanded by the moral precepts, is man justified," for he states, "But if it is by grace it is no longer on the basis of works" (Rom 11:6). In other words "works" is used in the sense of all works that are thought to justify.[31]

Thomas says that in the passage in chapter 3 "*now* the justice of God is made manifest without the law" (Rom 3:21), the "now" refers to the "time of grace," recalling Augustine's four stages, *ante legem* (prior to the law), *sub legem* (under the law), *sub gratia* (under grace), and *in pace* (in peace).[32] Accordingly he understands Paul's words to be a refutation of the Pelagians. "God's justice is said to exist through faith in Christ Jesus, not as though by faith we merit being justified, as if faith exists from ourselves and through it we merit God's justice, as the Pelagians assert; but because in that justification, by which we are made just by God, the first movement of the mind toward God is through faith." "Hence," he continues, "faith itself as the first part of justice is given by God; 'By grace you have been saved through faith; and this is not your own doing; for it is the gift of God'" (Eph 2:8).[33]

If one turns back to Origen's commentary, he too cites the same passage from Ephesians 2 when expounding Romans 11:6, "no longer on the basis of works; otherwise grace would no longer be grace." But Origen interprets works of the law as circumcision, sacrifices, observance of the Sabbath and festivals, and these, he explains, are the works that St. Paul is speaking of when he writes, "not on the basis of works; otherwise, grace would no longer be grace" (Eph 2:8).[34] At Romans 11:6, Thomas, however, cites, the letter to Titus: "He saved us, not because of deeds done by us in justice, but in virtue of his own mercy" (Ti 3:5). In other words Thomas understands Paul to be as speaking about works in general, not the specific works having to do with Jewish observance of the Law. "If grace is given in virtue of works, grace would no longer be grace, for it is given freely: 'Justified freely by his grace'" (Rom 3:24).[35]

---

31. *In ad Rom.* 3, lect. 2, § 297. Other passages: "not deeds done by us but in virtue of his mercy" (§ 372); "not because of works but through grace" (§ 373); God's choice "not from works but from grace" (§ 377); mention of Pelagians, grace, and merits (§ 379); "justice through faith not that of works" (§ 401).

32. *Expositio quarundam propositionum*, 13–18.

33. *In ad Rom.* 3, lect. 3, § 302.

34. *CRm* 8.8.6 (Heither, 4:248; Scheck 2:159).

35. *In ad Rom.* 11, lect. 1, § 871. For discussion of these themes in the interpretation of Romans

Here then are two different ways of interpreting Romans, the one reading it in the context of the relation of Christians to Jews, the other in light of the understanding of grace and works developed in Western Christianity after the Pelagian controversy. Each in its own way deepens our understanding of the letter. By citing Titus 3:5 Thomas gains a foothold within the New Testament to support the Augustinian understanding of grace and works. Origen, however, does not see it that way. He cites Titus 3:5 twice in the commentary and each times takes "works" to refer to the Law of Moses.[36]

One should not, however, conclude that in the commentary Thomas ignores what Paul says about the Jews. In his exposition of Romans 9–11 he has given much thought to the place of the Jews in the divine economy.[37] I have already noted his exposition of the term "sorrow" in Romans 9:2, but he also discusses the privileges of the Jews in 9:4–5 (covenants, law, patriarchs, et al.) under the rubric "the greatness of the Jewish race." And here too he betrays the influence of Augustine.

Augustine had said that the "Jews serve us as our *capsarii*, for they carry our books for us."[38] The term refers to slaves who carried the satchel *(capsa)* that held the books of boys going to their lessons. At 9:12, "the elder will serve the younger," Thomas uses precisely the same term with respect to the Jews. The Jews are our *capsarii*, those who "guard the books from which the truths of our faith are drawn."[39] Elsewhere he also cites Psalm 59:12, "do not slay my people," the text that was the basis of Augustine's witness doctrine.[40] But that is a topic for another day. I wish only to say that if one reads Paul's letter to the Romans deeply enough, as Origen, Augustine, and Thomas did, not only grace but also the Jewish people will figure large in one's thinking.

In reading Thomas's commentary one does not have to choose between different interpretations of a passage. Thomas will often offer two interpretations, explaining why each one is possible and fitting. A good example occurs at Romans 5:5. "The love of God is poured out in our hearts, through the Holy Spirit who is given us." The question here is whether "love of God" refers to the love God has for us (subjective genitive) or to our love for God (objective genitive).

see Thomas P. Scheck, *Origen and the History of Justification* (Notre Dame, Ind.: University of Notre Dame Press, 2008).

36. *CRm* 3:5.

37. On this topic see Steven C. Boguslawski, O.P., *Thomas Aquinas on the Jews* (Mahwah, N.J.: Paulist Press, 2008).

38. *Enarrationes in Psalmos* 40.14 (PL 36:463).

39. § 761.

40. § 439. On Augustine's use of Psalm 59:12 with respect to the Jews, see Paula Fredriksen, *Augustine and the Jews: A Christian Defense of Jews and Judaism* (New York: Doubleday, 2008), 276.

Romans 5:5 was one of St. Augustine's favorite biblical passages, and he always took it to mean our love for God. Modern commentators take the passage to mean God's love for us.[41] Thomas presents both interpretations and supports each by other biblical texts.[42]

To confirm the first, God's love for us, he cites Jeremiah, "He loved you with an everlasting love" (31:3), and for the second, our love for God, Romans 8: "I am sure that nothing in all creation will be able to separate us from the love of God" (8:39). Both loves, says Thomas, are poured into our hearts by the Holy Spirit.

Then he adds: "For the Holy Spirit, who is the love of the Father and of the Son, is given to us that we might participate in the Love who is the Holy Spirit, and by this participation we are made lovers of God. That we love him is a sign that he loves us." In support he cites Proverbs: "I love those who love me" (Prv 8:17) on the one side and 1 John on the other: "Not that we loved God but that he first loved us" (4:10).

In the end, though scrupulously presenting each interpretation with supporting texts, he seems to favor the Augustinian view that the love spoken of here is our love for God. For he ends by saying that the love poured into our hearts "leads to the perfecting of all the moral habits and acts of the soul."

But even though he leans toward the Augustinian interpretation, Thomas allows the reader to make the choice. As a commentator he did not think it was his task to persuade others to accept his interpretation. His aim was to his lead students of St. Paul more deeply into the Word of God, to show how specific words and images can be read in the context of the Bible as a whole and of Christian teaching. By practicing this kind of exegesis he deepens in us the love of the one God, Father, Son, and Holy Spirit, revealed in the sacred Scriptures. Like Origen, he knew that in the Letter to the Romans one never sees things fully. For God dazzles us with an excess of truth.

41. See, for example, Joseph Fitzmeyer, *Romans: A New Translation with Introduction and Commentary* (New York: Doubleday, 1993), 398.
42. § 392.

Bibliography

Adams, Edward. "Abraham's Faith and Gentile Disobedience: Textual Links between Romans 1 and 4." *Journal for the Study of the New Testament* 65 (1997): 47–66.

Aillet, Marc. *Lire la Bible avec saint Thomas.* Fribourg: Editions Universitaires, 1993.

Alexander of Hales. *Summa theologica seu sic ab origine dicta "Summa Fratris Alexandri."* Studio et cura Patres Collegii S. Bonaventurae. 5 vols. Quaracchi: Editiones Collegii S. Bonaventurae ad Claras Aquas, 1924–1948.

Allen, Christopher. "The Pastoral and Political Implications of Trent on Justification: A Response to the ARCIC Agreed Statement *Salvation and the Church.*" *Churchman* 103 (1989): 15–31.

Anderson, Gary A. *Sin: A History.* New Haven, Conn.: Yale University Press, 2009.

Aristotle. *The Ethics of Aristotle: The Nicomachean Ethics.* Translated by J. A. K. Thomson. Penguin Classics. London: Penguin, 1953.

Athanasius. *De Incarnatione Verbi.* Patrologia Graeca, edited by J.-P. Migne, 25. Paris, 1884.

Augustine. *Augustine on Romans: Propositions from the Epistle to the Romans; Unfinished Commentary on the Epistle to the Romans.* Translated by Paula F. Landes. Society of Biblical Literature Texts and Translations 23: Early Christian Literature Series 6. Chico, Calif.: Scholars Press, 1982.

———. *The City of God.* Translated by Marcus Dods. New York: Modern Library, 1994.

———. *Confessionum.* Patrologia Latina, edited by J.-P. Migne, 32. Paris, 1845.

———. *Contra duas epistulas pelagianorum.* Patrologia Latina, edited by J.-P. Migne, 44. Paris, 1845.

———. *Contra duas epistulas pelagianorum.* In *Premières polémiques contre Julien.* Bibliothèque Augustinienne 23. Paris: Desclée de Brouwer, 1974.

———. *Contra faustum manichaeum.* Patrologia Latina, edited by J.-P. Migne, 42. Paris, 1845.

———. *De civitate Dei.* Patrologia Latina, edited by J.-P. Migne, 41. Paris, 1845.

———. *De civitate Dei.* Corpus Christianorum Series Latina 47–48. Turnholt: Brepols, 1955.

———. *De civitate Dei.* Translated by Marcus Dods. New York: Modern Library, 1994.

———. *De doctrina christiana.* Edited by Joseph Martin. Corpus Christianorum Series Latina 32. Turnholt: Brepols, 1962.

———. *De doctrina christiana.* Patrologia Latina, edited by J.-P. Migne, 34. Paris, 1845.

———. *De duabus animabus contra manichaeos.* Patrologia Latina, edited by J.-P. Migne, 42. Paris, 1845.

303

———. *De duabus animabus*. In *Six traités anti-manichéens*. Bibliothèque Augustinienne 17. Paris: Desclée de Brouwer, 1961.

———. *De Genesi ad litteram*. Patrologia Latina, edited by J.-P. Migne, 34. Paris, 1845.

———. *De Genesi ad litteram*. Vol. 2. Bibliothèque Augustinienne 49. Paris: Desclée de Brouwer, 1972.

———. *De magistro*. Patrologia Latina, edited by J.-P. Migne, 32. Paris, 1845.

———. *De magistro*. Corpus Christianorum Series Latina 29. Turnhout: Brepols, 1970.

———. *De mendacio*. Edited by Joseph Zycha. Corpus Scriptorum Ecclesiasticorum Latinorum 41. Vienna: F. Tempsky, 1900.

———. *De moribus ecclesiae catholicae et de moribus manichaeorum*. Patrologia Latina, edited by J.-P. Migne, 32. Paris, 1845.

———. *De moribus ecclesiae catholicae et de moribus manichaeorum*. In *Problèmes moraux*. Bibliothèque Augustinienne 2. Paris: Desclée de Brouwer, 1948.

———. *De nuptiis et concupiscentia*. Patrologia Latina, edited by J.-P. Migne, 44. Paris, 1845.

———. *De nuptiis et concupiscentia*. In *Premières polémiques contre Julien*. Bibliothèque Augustinienne 23. Paris: Desclée de Brouwer, 1974.

———. *De perfectione iustitiae hominis*. Patrologia Latina, edited by J.-P. Migne, 44. Paris, 1845.

———. *De perfectione iustitiae hominis*. In *La crise pélagienne*. Vol. 1. Bibliothèque Augustinienne 21. Paris: Desclée de Brouwer, 1966.

———. *De spiritu et littera*. Patrologia Latina, edited by J.-P. Migne, 44. Paris, 1845.

———. *De Trinitate*. Edited by W. J. Mountain and Fr. Glorie. Corpus Christianorum Series Latina 50 and 50A. Turnholt: Brepols, 1968.

———. *Enarrationes in Psalmos*. Patrologia Latina, edited by J.-P. Migne, 36–37. Paris, 1845.

———. *Enchiridion*. Patrologia Latina, edited by J.-P. Migne, 40. Paris, 1845.

———. *Œuvres de Saint Augustin: mélanges doctrinaux*. Bibliothèque Augustinienne 10. Paris: Desclée de Brouwer, 1952.

———. *Expositio quarundam propositionum ex Epistola ad Romanos*. Patrologia Latina, edited by J.-P. Migne, 35. Paris, 1845.

———. *Mélanges doctrinaux*. Bibliothèque Augustinienne 10. Paris: Desclée de Brouwer, 1952.

———. *On Free Choice of the Will*. Translated by Thomas Williams. Indianapolis, Ind.: Hackett Publishing, 1993.

———. *Rectractationum*. Translated by A. Mutzenbecher. Corpus Christianorum Series Latina 57. Turnholt: Brepols, 1984.

———. *Soliloquia*. In *Dialogues philosophiques*, vol. 1. Bibliothèque Augustinienne 5. Paris: Desclée de Brouwer, 1948.

———. *Soliloquiorum*. Patrologia Latina, edited by J.-P. Migne, 32. Paris, 1845.

Avemarie, Friedrich. *Tora und Leben: Untersuchungen zur Heilsbedeutung der Tora in der frühen rabbinischen Literatur*. Texte und Studien zum antiken Judentum 55. Tübingen: Mohr Siebeck, 1996.

Backus, Irene. *Historical Method and Confessional Identity in the Era of the Reformation (1378–1615)*. Studies in Medieval and Reformation Thought. Leiden: Brill, 2003.

Baglow, Christopher. *"Modus et Forma": A New Approach to the Exegesis of Saint*

Thomas Aquinas with an Application to the Lectura super Epistolam ad Ephesios. Analecta Biblica 149. Rome: Editrice Pontifio Istituto Biblico, 2002.

Barreda, Jesús Ángel. "Ideología y pastoral misionera en el 'De unico vocationis modo.'" *Studium* 21 (1981): 186–354.

———. "Primera anunciación y bautismo en Bartolomé de Las Casas." *Ciencia Tomista* 116 (1989): 291–316.

Barth, Karl. *Church Dogmatics.* Vol. 1, bk. 2, *The Doctrine of the Word of God.* Edited by G. W. Bromiley and T. F. Torrance. Translated by G. T. Thomson and Harold Knight. London: T&T Clark, 2004.

———. *Die kirchliche Dogmatik.* Vol. 1, bk. 2, *Die Lehre vom Wort Gottes: Prolegomena zur kirchlichen Dogmatik.* Zollikon: Evangelischer Verlag, 1938.

———. *Der Römerbrief.* 2nd ed. Munich: Kaiser, 1922.

Basta, Pasquale. *Abramo in Romani 4: L'analogia dell'agire divino nella ricerca esegetica di Paolo.* Analecta Biblica 168. Rome: Pontificio Istituto Biblico, 2007.

Bataillon, Marcel. *Estudios sobre Bartolomé de las Casas.* Barcelona: Ediciones Península, 1976.

Beale, G. K. and D. A. Carson, eds. *Commentary on the New Testament Use of the Old Testament.* Grand Rapids, Mich.: Baker Academic, 2007.

Beasley-Murray, G. R. "The Righteousness of God in the History of Israel and the Nations: Romans 9–11." *Review and Expositor* 73, no. 4 (1976): 437–50.

Beker, J. Christiaan. "Suffering and Triumph in Paul's Letter to the Romans." *Horizons in Biblical Theology* 7, no. 2 (1985): 105–19.

Benedict XVI. *Saint Paul.* Translated by *L'Osservatore Romano.* San Francisco: Ignatius Press, 2009.

Berceville, Gilles, and Eun-Sil Son, "Exégèse biblique, théologique et philosophique chez Thomas d'Aquin et Martin Luther commentateurs de Romains 7, 14–25." *Recherches de Science Religieuse* 91, no. 3 (2003): 373–95.

Bermudez, Catalina. "Predestinazione, grazia e libertà nei commenti di san Tommaso alle lettere di san Paolo." *Annales Theologici* 4, no. 2 (1990): 399–421.

Blankenhorn, Bernhard. "The Place of Romans 6 in Aquinas's Doctrine of Sacramental Causality: A Balance of History and Metaphysics." In *Ressourcement Thomism: Sacred Doctrine, the Sacraments, and the Moral Life,* edited by Reinhard Hütter and Matthew Levering, 136–49. Washington, D.C.: The Catholic University of America Press, 2010.

Bockmuehl, Markus. "Abraham's Faith in Hebrews 11." In *The Epistle to the Hebrews and Christian Theology,* edited by Richard J. Bauckham et al., 364–73. Grand Rapids, Mich.: Eerdmans, 2009.

Boersma, Hans. *Nouvelle Théologie and Sacramental Ontology: A Return to Mystery.* Oxford: Oxford University Press, 2009.

Boguslawski, Steven C. *Thomas Aquinas on the Jews: Insights into his Commentary on Romans 9–11.* Mahwah, N.J.: Paulist Press, 2008.

Bouillard, Henri. *Conversion et grâce chez S. Thomas d'Aquin.* Paris: Aubier, 1941.

Boyle, John F. "Authorial Intention and the *Divisio Textus.*" In *Reading John with St. Thomas Aquinas: Theological Exegesis and Speculative Theology,* edited by Michael Dauphinais and Matthew Levering, 3–8. Washington, D.C.: The Catholic University of America Press, 2005.

————. "St. Thomas and Sacred Scripture." *Pro Ecclesia* 4, no. 1 (1995): 92–104.

————. "The Theological Character of the Scholastic 'Division of the Text' with Particular Reference to the Commentaries of St. Thomas Aquinas." In *With Reverence for the Word: Medieval Scriptural Exegesis in Judaism, Christianity and Islam*, edited by Jane McAuliffe, Barry Walfish, and Joseph Goering, 276–83. Oxford: Oxford University Press, 2003.

Branick, Vincent P. "The Sinful Flesh of the Son of God (Rom 8:3): A Key Image of Pauline Theology." *Catholic Biblical Quarterly* 47, no. 2 (1985): 246–62.

Bunnenberg, Johannes. *Lebendige Treue zum Ursprung: Das Traditionsverständnis Yves Congars*. Walberger Studien 14. Mainz: Grünewald, 1989.

Burnell, Peter. "Concupiscence." In *Augustine through the Ages: An Encyclopedia*, edited by Allan D. Fitzgerald, 224–27. Grand Rapids, Mich.: Eerdmans, 1999.

Byrne, Brendan. *Romans*. Sacra Pagina 6. Collegeville, Minn.: Liturgical Press, 1996.

Cahalan, John C. "Natural Obligation: How Rationally Known Truth Determines Ethical Good and Evil." *Thomist* 66, no. 1 (2002): 101–32.

Caird, G. B. "Predestination—Romans ix.–xi.," *Expository Times* 68, no. 11 (1957): 324–27.

Calvin, John. *The Bondage and Liberation of the Will: A Defense of the Orthodox Doctrine of Human Choice against Pighius*. Edited by A. N. S. Lane. Translated by G. I. Davies. Texts and Studies in Reformation and Post-Reformation Thought 2. Grand Rapids, Mich.: Baker Books, 1996.

————. *Calvin: Institutes of the Christian Religion*. Vol. 1. Library of Christian Classics 20. Louisville, Ky.: Westminster/John Knox Press, 1960.

————. *Canons and Decrees of the Council of Trent, with an Antidote*. In *Selected Works of John Calvin: Tracts and Letters*. Vol. 3, *Tracts, Part 3*. Edited and translated by Henry Beveridge and Jules Connet. Grand Rapids, Mich.: Baker Book House, 1983.

————. *Commentarius in Epistilorum Pauli ad Romanos*. Edited by T. H. L. Parker. Leiden: Brill, 1981.

————. *Institutio Christianae Religionis*. Vol. 1, *Pars Prior*. Berlin: Gustavum Eichler, 1834. http://www.ccel.org/ccel/calvin/institutio1.toc.html.

Campbell, Douglas A. *The Deliverance of God: An Apocalyptic Rereading of Justification in Paul*. Grand Rapids, Mich.: Eerdmans, 2009.

————. "Romans 1:17: A *Crux Interpretum* for the *Pistis Christou* Debate." *Journal of Biblical Literature* 113, no. 2 (1994): 265–85.

Campbell, William S., Peter S. Hawkins, and Brenda Deen Schildgen, eds. *Medieval Readings of Romans*. New York: T&T Clark International, 2007.

Cantalamessa, Raniero. Lenten Sermon to the Pontifical Household, February 29, 2008. Translated by Joseph G. Trabbic. http://www.cantalamessa.org/en/prediche View.php?id=238.

Capéran, Louis. *Le problème du salut des infidèles*. Toulouse: Grand Séminaire, 1934.

Castillo Mattasoglio, Carlos. *Libres para creer: la conversión según Bartolomé de las Casas en la Historia de las Indias*. Lima: Fondo Editorial de las Pontificia Universidad Católica del Perú, 1993.

Cerfaux, Lucien. *La théologie de l'Église suivant saint Paul*. Unam Sanctam 10. Paris: Cerf, 1942.

Cessario, Romanus. *The Godly Image: Christ and Salvation from Anselm to Aquinas.* Petersham, Mass.: St. Bede's Publishing, 1990.

Chenu, Marie-Dominique. *Aquinas and His Role in Theology.* Translated by Paul Philibert. Collegeville, Minn.: Liturgical Press, 2002.

Childs, Brevard S. *The Church's Guide for Reading Paul: The Canonical Shaping of the Pauline Corpus.* Grand Rapids, Mich.: Eerdmans, 2008.

————. *The Struggle to Understand Isaiah as Christian Scripture.* Grand Rapids, Mich.: Eerdmans, 2004.

Chrysostom, John. *Homilies on Romans.* In *A Select Library of Nicene and Post-Nicene Fathers of the Christian Church.* First Series. Vol. 11, *Chrysostom: Homilies on the Acts of the Apostles and the Epistle to the Romans.* Edited by Philip Schaff and Henry Wace, 335–564. Grand Rapids, Mich.: Eerdmans, 1978.

Clement [pseud.]. "Recognitions of Clement." In *Ante-Nicene Fathers.* Vol. 8, *The Twelve Patriarchs, Excerpts and Epistles, The Clementina, Apocrypha, Decretals, Memoirs of Edessa and Syriac Documents, Remains of the First Ages,* edited by Alexander Roberts and James Donaldson, 75–211. Christian Literature Publishing, 1886; reprint, Peabody, Mass.: Hendrickson Publishers, 1999.

Cohen, Jeremy. *The Friars and the Jews: The Evolution of Medieval Anti-Judaism.* Ithaca, N.Y.: Cornell University Press, 1984.

————. *Living Letters of the Law: Ideas of the Jew in Medieval Christianity.* Berkeley: University of California Press, 1999.

————. "The Mystery of Israel's Salvation: Romans 11:25–26 in Patristic and Medieval Exegesis." *Harvard Theological Review* 98 (2005): 247–81.

Colón-Emeric, Edgardo A. *Wesley, Aquinas, and Christian Perfection: An Ecumenical Dialogue.* Waco, Tex.: Baylor University Press, 2009.

Congar, Yves M.-J. "The Church: The People of God." In *Concilium: Theology in the Age of Renewal.* Vol. 1, *The Church and Mankind,* 11–37. Glen Rock, N.J.: Paulist Press, 1965.

————. "'Ecclesia' et 'populus (fidelis)' dans l'ecclésiologie de S. Thomas." In *St. Thomas Aquinas 1274–1974: Commemorative Studies.* Vol. 1. Edited by Armand A. Maurer et al., 159–73. Toronto, Ont.: Pontifical Institute of Mediaeval Studies, 1974. Reprinted in *Thomas d'Aquin: sa vision de théologie et de l'Eglise.* London: Variorum, 1984.

————. *Fifty Years of Catholic Theology: Conversation with Yves Congar.* Edited by Bernard Lauret. Philadelphia: Fortress, 1988.

————. *I Believe in the Holy Spirit.* Vol. 3, *The River of the Water of Life (Rev 22:1) Flows in the East and in the West.* Translated by David Smith. New York: Seabury Press, 1983.

————. "The Idea of the Church in St. Thomas Aquinas." *Thomist* 1, no. 3 (1939): 331–59.

————. *Lay People in the Church: A Study for a Theology of the Laity.* Rev. ed. Translated by Donald Attwater. London: Chapman, 1965; reprint, Westminster, Md.: Christian Classics, 1985.

————. *L'Église: De saint Augustin à l'époque modern.* Histoire des dogmes 3. Paris: Cerf, 1970.

————. *Power and Poverty in the Church.* Translated by Jennifer Nicholson. London: Chapman, 1965.

———. "St. Thomas Aquinas and the Spirit of Ecumenism." *New Blackfriars* 55, no. 648 (1974): 196–209.

———. *This Church That I Love.* Translated by Lucien Delafuente. Denville, N.J.: Dimension, 1969.

———. "Traditio thomistica in materia ecclesiologica." *Angelicum* 43, no. 3–4 (1966): 405–28. Reprinted in *Thomas d'Aquin: sa vision de théologie et de l'Eglise.* London: Variorum, 1984.

———. *Tradition and Traditions: The Biblical, Historical, and Theological Evidence for Catholic Teaching on Tradition.* Translated by Michael Naseby and Thomas Rainborough. London: Burns and Oates, 1966; reprint, San Diego, Calif.: Basilica; Needham Heights, Mass.: Simon and Schuster, 1998.

———. *Un Peuple messianique: l'Église, sacrement du salut; Salut et liberation.* Paris: Cerf, 1975.

Cranfield, C. E. B. *A Critical and Exegetical Commentary on the Epistle to the Romans.* 2 vols. Edinburgh: T&T Clark, 1975–79.

Cueppens, Franziscus. "Quod S. Thomas de multiplici sensu litterali in s. Scriptura senserit?" *Divus Thomas* 33 (1930): 164–73.

Dahl, Nils Alstrup. "The Atonement—An Adequate Reward for the Akedah? (Ro 8:32)." In *Neotestamentica et Semitica: Studies in Honor of Matthew Black*, edited by E. Earle Ellis and Max Wilcox, 15–29. Edinburgh: T&T Clark, 1969.

Daniélou, Jean. *God and the Ways of Knowing.* Translated by Walter Roberts. Cleveland, Ohio: Meridian Books, 1957.

Dauphinais, Michael, and Matthew Levering, eds. *Reading John with St. Thomas Aquinas: Theological Exegesis and Speculative Theology.* Washington, D.C.: The Catholic University of America Press, 2005.

Davidson, Richard. *Typology in Scripture.* Berrien Springs, Mich.: Andrews University Press, 1981.

Davis, Ellen F., and Richard B. Hays, eds. *The Art of Reading Scripture.* Grand Rapids, Mich.: Eerdmans, 2003.

Denzinger, Heinrich, and Peter Hünermann, eds. *Enchiridion symbolorum definitionum et declarationum de rebus fidei et morum.* 40th ed. Freiburg: Herder, 2005.

Die Bekenntnisschriften der evangelisch-lutherischen Kirche. 8th ed. Göttingen: Vandenhoeck und Ruprecht, 1979.

Dinkler, Erich. "The Historical and Eschatological Israel in Romans Chapters 9–11." *Journal of Religion* 36 (1956): 109–27.

DiNoia, J. A., and Bernard Mulcahey. "The Authority of Scripture in Sacramental Theology: Some Methodological Observations." *Pro Ecclesia* 10, no. 3 (2001): 329–45.

Domanyi, Thomas. *Der Römerbriefkommentar des Thomas von Aquin: Ein Beitrag zur Untersuchung seiner Auslegungsmethoden.* Basler und Berner Studien zur historischen und systematischen Theologie 39. Bern: Peter Lang, 1979.

Duffy, Stephen J. "Anthropology." In *Augustine through the Ages: An Encyclopedia*, edited by Allan D. Fitzgerald, 24–31. Grand Rapids, Mich.: Eerdmans, 1999.

Dunn, James D. G. *Jesus, Paul, and the Law: Studies in Mark and Galatians.* Louisville, Ky.: Westminster/John Knox, 1990.

———. *The New Perspective on Paul.* Rev. ed. Grand Rapids: Eerdmans, 2008.

———. "Once More, PISTIS CHRISTOU." In *Pauline Theology*. Vol. 4, *Looking Back, Pressing On*, edited by E. E. Johnson and D. M. Hay, 61–81. Atlanta: Scholars, 1997.

———. *Romans*. 2 vols. Word Biblical Commentary 38. Dallas: Word Books, 1988.

———. "Romans 7:14–25 in the Theology of Paul." *Theologische Zeitschrift* 31, no. 5 (1975): 257–73.

———. *The Theology of Paul the Apostle*. Grand Rapids, Mich.: Eerdmans, 1998.

———. *Unity and Diversity in the New Testament: An Inquiry into the Character of Earliest Christianity*. 2nd ed. Philadelphia: Trinity Press International, 1990.

Dykstra, Russell. "A Comparison of Exegesis: John Calvin and Thomas Aquinas (3)." *Protestant Reformed Theological Journal* 35, no. 2 (2002): 10–22.

Elders, Leo. "Le Saint Esprit et la *lex nova* dans les commentaries bibliques de saint Thomas d'Aquin." In *Credo in Spiritum Sanctum*. Vol. 1, edited by José Saraiva Martins, 1195–1205. Teologia e Filosofia 6. Vatican City: Libreria Editrice Vaticana, 1983.

Emery, Gilles. "The Holy Spirit." In *The Cambridge Companion to the Summa Theologiae*, edited by Philip McCosker and Denys Turner. Cambridge: Cambridge University Press, forthcoming.

———. *La Trinité créatrice: Trinité et création dans les commentaires aux Sentences de Thomas d'Aquin et de ses précurseurs Albert le Grand et Bonaventure*. Paris: J. Vrin, 1995.

———. "*Theologia* and *Dispensatio*: The Centrality of the Divine Missions in St. Thomas's Trinitarian Theology." *Thomist* 74 (2010): 515–61.

———. *The Trinitarian Theology of Saint Thomas Aquinas*. Oxford: Oxford University Press, 2007.

———. *The Trinity: An Introduction to Catholic Doctrine on the Triune God*. Translated by Matthew Levering. Washington, D.C.: The Catholic University of America Press, 2011.

Fabro, Cornelius. "Le *Liber de bona fortuna* de l'*Éthique à Eudème* d'Aristote et la dialectique de la divine Providence chez saint Thomas." *Revue Thomiste* 88, no. 4 (1988): 556–72.

Fant, Clyde E., Jr., and William M. Pinson Jr., eds. *Twenty Centuries of Great Preaching: An Encyclopedia of Preaching*. Waco, Tex.: Word Books, 1971.

Farkasfalvy, Denis. "Inspiration and Interpretation." In *Vatican II: Renewal within Tradition*, edited by Matthew L. Lamb and Matthew Levering, 77–100. New York: Oxford University Press, 2008.

Fee, Gordon D. *Pauline Christology: An Exegetical-Theological Study*. Peabody, Mass.: Hendrickson, 2007.

Fitzgerald, Allan D. "Body." In *Augustine through the Ages: An Encyclopedia*, edited by Allan D. Fitzgerald, 105–7. Grand Rapids, Mich.: Eerdmans, 1999.

Fitzmyer, Joseph A. "Problems of the Literal and Spiritual Senses of Scripture." *Louvain Studies* 20, no. 2–3 (1995): 134–46.

———. *Romans: A New Translation with Introduction and Commentary*. Anchor Bible 33. New York: Doubleday, 1993.

Fredriksen, Paula. *Augustine and the Jews: A Christian Defense of Jews and Judaism*. New York: Doubleday, 2008.

———. "Beyond the Body/Soul Dichotomy: Augustine on Paul against the Manichees and the Pelagians." *Recherches Augustiniennes* 23 (1988): 87–114.

———. "Paul." In *Augustine through the Ages: An Encyclopedia*, edited by Allan D. Fitzgerald, 621–25. Grand Rapids, Mich.: Eerdmans, 1999.

Frei, Hans. *The Eclipse of Biblical Narrative: A Study in Eighteenth and Nineteenth Century Hermeneutics.* New Haven, Conn.: Yale University Press, 1974.

Gaca, Kathy L. "Paul's Uncommon Declaration in Romans 1:18–32 and Its Problematic Legacy for Pagan and Christian Relations." In *Early Patristic Readings of Romans*, edited by Kathy L. Gaca and L. L. Welborn, 1–33. Romans through History and Cultures Series. New York: T&T Clark, 2005.

Gallagher, Conan. "Concupiscence." *Thomist* 30, no. 3 (1966): 228–59.

García Martínez, Florentino, and Eibert J. C. Tigchelaar, eds. *The Dead Sea Scrolls Study Edition.* Vol. 1, 1QI–4Q273. Leiden: Brill, 1997.

Garrigou-Lagrange, Réginald. *The One God: A Commentary on the First Part of St. Thomas' Theological Summa.* Translated by Dom Bede Rose. St. Louis, Mo.: Herder, 1954.

———. *Predestination.* Translated by Dom Bede Rose. Rockford, Ill.: Tan Books, 1998.

Gathercole, Simon J. "A Conversion of Augustine: From Natural Law to Restored Nature in Romans 2:13–16." In *Engaging Augustine on Romans*, edited by Daniel Patte and Eugene Teselle, 147–72. Harrisburg, Pa.: Trinity Press International, 2002.

Gibbs, John G. *Creation and Redemption: A Study in Pauline Theology.* Leiden: Brill, 1971.

Giussani, Luigi. *The Religious Sense.* Translated by John Zucchi. San Francisco: Ignatius Press, 1990.

Gooch, Paul W. "Sovereignty and Freedom: Some Pauline Compatibilisms." *Scottish Journal of Theology* 40, no. 4 (1987): 531–42.

Goodspeed, Edgar J. "Some Greek Notes." *Journal of Biblical Literature* 73, no. 2 (1954): 84–92.

Gorday, Peter. *Principles of Patristic Exegesis: Romans 9–11 in Origen, John Chrysostom, and Augustine.* New York: Edwin Mellen Press, 1983.

Gorman, Michael J. *Cruciformity: Paul's Narrative Spirituality of the Cross.* Grand Rapids, Mich.: Eerdmans, 2001.

———. *Inhabiting the Cruciform God: Kenosis, Justification, and Theosis in Paul's Narrative Soteriology.* Grand Rapids, Mich.: Eerdmans, 2009.

Gratian. *Decretum.* Patrologia Latina, edited by J.-P. Migne, 187. Paris, 1855.

Greenman, Jeffrey P., and Timothy Larsen, eds. *Reading Romans through the Centuries: From the Early Church to Karl Barth.* Grand Rapids, Mich.: Brazos Press, 2005.

Grelot, Pierre. "Le retribution individuelle: Dossier biblique." *Revue Thomiste* 107, no. 2 (2007): 179–220.

Gutiérrez, Gustavo. *Las Casas: In Search of the Poor of Jesus Christ.* Maryknoll, N.Y.: Orbis Books, 1993.

Hahn, Scott W. *Covenant and Communion: The Biblical Theology of Pope Benedict XVI.* Grand Rapids, Mich.: Brazos, 2009.

———. *Kinship by Covenant: A Canonical Approach to the Fulfillment of God's Saving*

Promises. Anchor Yale Bible Reference Library. New Haven, Conn.: Yale University Press, 2009.

———. "Worship in the Word: Toward a Liturgical Hermeneutic." *Letter and Spirit: A Journal of Catholic Biblical Theology* 1 (2005): 101–36.

Hall, Pamela. *Narrative and the Natural Law*. Notre Dame, Ind.: University of Notre Dame Press, 1994.

Hanke, Lewis. *All Mankind Is One: A Study of the Disputation between Bartolomé de Las Casas and Juan Ginés de Sepúlveda in 1550 on the Intellectual and Religious Capacity of the American Indians*. DeKalb: Northern Illinois University Press, 1974.

Hays, Richard B. *Echoes of Scripture in the Letters of Paul*. New Haven, Conn.: Yale University Press, 1989.

———. *The Faith of Jesus Christ: The Narrative Substructure of Galatians 3:1–4:11*. 2nd ed. Grand Rapids, Mich.: Eerdmans, 2002.

Healy, Nicholas M. "Ecclesiology and Communion." *Perspectives in Religious Studies* 31, no. 3 (2004): 273–90.

Helm, Paul. *John Calvin's Ideas*. Oxford: Oxford University Press, 2006.

Holder, R. Ward. "Calvin's Hermeneutic and Tradition: An Augustinian Reception of Romans 7." In *Reformation Readings of Romans*, edited by Kathy Ehrensperger and R. Ward Holder, 98–199. New York: T&T Clark, 2008.

Hood, John Y. B. *Aquinas and the Jews*. Philadelphia: University of Pennsylvania Press, 1995.

Hübner, Hans. *Law in Paul's Thought: A Contribution to the Development of Pauline Theology*. Studies of the New Testament and Its World. Edinburgh: T&T Clark, 1984.

Hunt, Anne. *What Are They Saying about the Trinity?* New York: Paulist Press, 1998.

Ildefons of Toledo. *Annotationes de cognitione baptismi*. Patrologia Latina, edited by J.-P. Migne, 96. Paris, 1851.

Ishamel ben Elisha. *Mechilta D'Rabbi Ismael*. Edited by H. S. Horovitz and I. A. Rabin. Jersualem: Bamberger and Wahrman, 1960.

Jerome. *Regula monachorum*. Patrologia Latina, edited by J.-P. Migne, 30. Paris, 1846.

Jewett, Robert. *Romans: A Commentary*. Hermeneia. Minneapolis, Minn.: Fortress Press, 2006.

Johnson, Luke Timothy. "Romans 3:21–26 and the Faith of Jesus." *Catholic Biblical Quarterly* 44, no. 1 (1982): 77–90.

Johnson, Mark F. "Another Look at the Plurality of the Literal Sense." *Medieval Philosophy and Theology* 2 (1992): 117–41.

———. "Augustine and Aquinas on Original Sin: Doctrine, Authority, and Pedagogy." In *Aquinas the Augustinian*, edited by Michael Dauphinais, Barry David, and Matthew Levering, 145–58. Washington, D.C.: The Catholic University of America Press, 2007.

Kaczynsky, Edward. "'Lex Spiritus' in S. Paolo e la sua interpretazione in S. Tommaso." In *Credo in Spiritum Sanctum*, edited by José Saraiva Martins, 1207–22. Vatican City: Libreria Editrice Vaticana, 1983.

Kantorowicz, Ernst H. *The King's Two Bodies: A Study in Mediaeval Political Theology*. 2nd ed. Princeton, N.J.: Princeton University Press, 1997.

Käsemann, Ernst. *Commentary on Romans*. London: SCM Press, 1980.

Keating, Daniel A. *Deification and Grace*. Naples, Fla.: Sapientia, 2007.

———. "Justification, Sanctification, and Divinization in Thomas Aquinas." In *Aquinas on Doctrine: A Critical Introduction*, edited by Thomas G. Weinandy, Daniel A. Keating, and John P. Yocum, 139–58. New York: T&T Clark International, 2004.

Keaty, Anthony. "The Holy Spirit Proceeding as Mutual Love." *Angelicum* 77, no. 4 (2000): 533–57.

Kennedy, Robert G. "Thomas Aquinas and the Literal Sense of Scripture." PhD diss., University of Notre Dame, 1985.

Kerr, Fergus. "Yves Congar: From Suspicion to Acclamation." *Louvain Studies* 29, nos. 3–4 (2004): 273–87.

Kim, Seyoon. *The Origin of Paul's Gospel*. Wissenschaftliche Untersuchungen zum Neuen Testament 2:4. Tübingen: Mohr-Siebeck, 1984.

Koster, Mannes Dominikus. *Ekklesiologie im Werden*. Paderborn: Bonifacius, 1940.

Kovacs, Judith, and Christopher Rowland. *Revelation: The Apocalypse of Jesus Christ*. Oxford: Blackwell, 2004.

Kuffel, Thomas. "St. Thomas's Method of Biblical Exegesis." *Living Tradition* 38 (1991): 1–12.

Küng, Hans. *Justification: The Doctrine of Karl Barth and a Catholic Reflection*. Translation from the 4th German ed. by Thomas Collins, Edmund E. Tolk, and David Grandskou. London: Thomas Nelson, 1964.

Lagrange, M. J. *Saint Paul: Epitre aux Romains*. Paris: J. Gabalda, 1950.

Lambrecht, Jan. "The Groaning Creation: A Study of Rom 8:18–30." *Louvain Studies* 15, no. 1 (1990): 3–18.

Lane, Anthony N. S. *Justification by Faith in Protestant-Catholic Dialogue: An Evangelical Assessment*. London: T&T Clark, 2002.

———. "Twofold Righteousness: A Key to the Doctrine of Justification? Reflections on Article 5 of the Regensburg Colloquy (1541)." In *Justification: What's at Stake in the Current Debates?* edited by Mark Husbands and Daniel J. Trier, 205–25. Downers Grove, Ill.: InterVarsity Press, 2005.

Larcher, Chrysostome. *Etudes sur le Livre de la Sagesse*. Paris: Lecoffre, 1969.

Las Casas, Bartolomé. *Apologética historia Sumaria*. Vols. 1 and 2. Edited by Edmundo O'Gorman. Mexico City: Instituto de Investigaciones Históricas de la Universidad Nacional Autónoma de México, 1967.

———. "Carta a los dominicos de Chiapa y Guatemala." In *Obras Completas*. Vol. 13, *Cartas y Memoriales*. Madrid: Alianza Editorial, 1995.

———. *Del único modo de traer a todos los pueblos a la verdadera religion*. Edited by Agustín Millares Castro. Pánuco, Mexico: Fondo de Cultura Económica, 1942.

———. *Obras Completas*. Vol. 2, *De unico vocationis modo*. Madrid: Alianza Editorial, 1990.

———. *Obras Completas*. Vol. 3, *Historia de las Indias*. Madrid: Editorial Alianza, 1994.

———. *Obras Completas*. Vol. 9, *Apología*. Madrid: Editorial Alianza, 1988.

La Soujeole, Benoît-Dominique de. "Le mystère de la prédication." *Revue Thomiste* 107, no. 3 (2007): 355–74.

Leith, John H. *John Calvin's Doctrine of the Christian Life*. Louisville, Ky.: Westminster/John Knox Press, 1989.

Levering, Matthew. *Biblical Natural Law: A Theocentric and Teleological Approach.*
Oxford: Oxford University Press, 2008.

———. *Christ's Fulfillment of Torah and Temple: Salvation according to Thomas Aquinas.* Notre Dame, Ind.: University of Notre Dame Press, 2002.

———. *Participatory Biblical Exegesis: Toward a Theology of Biblical Interpretation.*
Notre Dame, Ind.: University of Notre Dame Press, 2008.

———. *Predestination: Biblical and Theological Paths.* Oxford: Oxford University
Press, 2011.

Lischer, Richard, ed. *The Company of Preachers: Wisdom on Preaching: Augustine to
the Present.* Grand Rapids, Mich.: Eerdmans, 2002.

Lonergan, Bernard. *Collected Works of Bernard Lonergan.* Vol. 1, *Grace and Freedom:
Operative Grace in the Thought of St. Thomas Aquinas.* Toronto: University of Toronto Press, 1988.

Lubac, Henri de. *Catholicism: Christ and the Common Destiny of Man.* Translated by
Lancelot C. Sheppard and Elizabeth Englund. San Francisco: Ignatius, 1988.

———. "The Conditions of Ontological Affirmation." In *Theological Fragments.*
Translated by Rebecca Howell Balinski, 377–92. San Francisco: Ignatius Press,
1989.

———. *Corpus Mysticum: The Eucharist and the Church in the Middle Ages: Historical Survey.* Translated by Gemma Simmonds with Richard Price and Christopher
Stephens. Edited by Laurence Paul Hemming and Susan Frank Parsons. London:
SCM, 2006.

———. *Corpus mysticum: l'Eucharistie et l'Église au moyen age: Étude historique.*
Théologie 3. Paris: Aubier, 1944.

———. *History and Spirit: The Understanding of Scripture according to Origen.* Translated by Anne Englund Nash and Juvenal Merriell. San Francisco: Ignatius Press,
2007.

———. *Medieval Exegesis: The Four Senses of Scripture.* Vols. 1–3. Translated by Mark
Sebanc (vol. 1) and E. M. Macierowski (vols. 2 and 3). Ressourcement. Grand Rapids, Mich.: Eerdmans, 1998–2000.

———. *Scripture in the Tradition.* Translated by Luke O'Neill. New York: Herder and
Herder, 2000.

———. *The Splendor of the Church.* Translated by Michael Mason. New York: Sheed
and Ward, 1956; reprint, San Francisco: Ignatius, 1999.

Luther, Martin. *In epistolam S. Pauli ad Galatas Commentarius ex praelectione D.
Martini Lutheri collectus.* In *D. Martin Luthers Werke: Kritische Gesamtausgabe.*
Vol. 40, part 1. Weimar: Hermann Böhlaus Nachfolger, 1911.

———. *Career of the Reformer I.* Edited by Harold J. Grimm, translated by W. A.
Lambert. Vol. 31 of *Luther's Works.* Philadelphia: Fortress Press, 1957.

———. *Career of the Reformer IV.* Edited by Lewis William Spitz. Vol. 34 of *Luther's
Works.* Philadelphia: Fortress Press, 1960.

———. *Lectures on Galatians 1535: Chapters 1–4.* Edited by Walter A. Hansen. Vol. 26
of *Luther's Works.* St. Louis, Mo.: Concordia, 1963.

———. *Luther's Works.* General editors Jaroslav Pelikan (vols. 1–30) and Helmut T.
Lehmann (vols. 31–55). St. Louis, Mo.: Concordia; Philadelphia: Fortress Press;
1955–86.

——. *Selected Psalms I.* Edited by Jaroslav Pelikan. Vol. 12 of *Luther's Works.* St. Louis, Mo.: Concordia, 1955.

MacIntyre, Alasdair. "Moral Philosophy: What Next?" In *Revisions: Changing Perspectives in Moral Philosophy*, edited by Stanley Hauerwas and Alasdair MacIntyre, 1–15. Notre Dame, Ind.: University of Notre Dame Press, 1983.

——. *Three Rival Versions of Moral Enquiry: Encyclopaedia, Genealogy and Tradition.* Notre Dame, Ind.: University of Notre Dame Press, 1990.

——. *Whose Justice? Which Rationality?* London: Duckworth, 1988.

Margerie, Bertrand de. "Mort sacrificielle du Christ et peine de mort chez saint Thomas d'Aquin, commentateur de saint Paul." *Revue Thomiste* 83, no. 3 (1983): 394–417.

Maritain, Jacques. "On Knowledge through Connaturality." In *Natural Law: Reflections on Theory and Practice*, edited by William Sweet, 13–24. South Bend, Ind.: Saint Augustine's Press, 2001.

Marshall, Bruce D. "*Ex Occidente Lux*? Aquinas and Eastern Orthodox Theology." *Modern Theology* 20, no. 1 (2004): 23–50. Reprinted in *Aquinas in Dialogue: Thomas for the Twenty-First Century*, edited by J. Fodor and F. C. Bauerschmidt, 19–46. Oxford: Blackwell, 2004.

——. "Justification as Declaration and Deification." *International Journal of Systematic Theology* 4, no. 1 (2002): 3–28.

——. "Postscript and Prospect." *Nova et Vetera* (English) 7, no. 2 (2009): 523–28.

——. "*Quasi in Figura*: A Brief Reflection on Jewish Election, after Thomas Aquinas." *Nova et Vetera* (English) 7, no. 2 (2009): 477–84.

Martin, Dale B. *The Corinthian Body.* New Haven, Conn.: Yale University Press, 1995.

Martin, Francis. *Sacred Scripture: The Disclosure of the Word.* Naples, Fla.: Sapientia Press, 2006.

Martin, Thomas F. "*Miser ego homo*": *Augustine, Paul and the Rhetorical Moment.* Ann Arbor, Mich.: University Microfilms, 1995.

McGrath, Alister. *Iustitia Dei: A History of the Christian Doctrine of Justification.* 2nd ed. Cambridge: Cambridge University Press, 1998.

Melina, Livio. *Sharing in Christ's Virtues: For a Renewal of Moral Theology in Light of Veritatis Splendor.* Translated by William E. May. Washington, D.C.: The Catholic University of America Press, 2001.

Merton, Thomas. *The Ascent to Truth.* London: Hollis and Carter, 1951.

Miles, Margaret. "Theology, Anthropology, and the Human Body in Calvin's *Institutes of the Christian Religion*." *Harvard Theological Review* 74, no. 3 (1981): 303–23.

Milhou, Alain. "Las Casas: Prophétisme et millénarisme." *Études*, March 1992, 393–404.

Min, Anselm K. *Paths to the Triune God: An Encounter between Aquinas and Recent Theologies.* Notre Dame, Ind.: University of Notre Dame Press, 2005.

Montague, George T. *The Living Thought of St. Paul: An Introduction to Pauline Theology through Intensive Study of Key Texts.* Milwaukee: Bruce Publishing, 1966.

——. *Understanding the Bible: A Basic Introduction to Biblical Interpretation.* Rev. ed. Mahwah, N.J.: Paulist Press, 2007.

Moo, Douglas J. *The Epistle to the Romans.* New International Commentary on the New Testament. Grand Rapids, Mich.: Eerdmans, 1996.

———. *Romans 1–8.* Wycliffe Exegetical Commentary. Chicago: Moody Press, 1991.

Morard, Martin. "À propos du *Commentaire des Psaumes* de saint Thomas d'Aquin." *Revue Thomiste* 96, no. 4 (1996): 653–70.

Moreno, Anthony. "The Nature of St. Thomas's Knowledge *per Connaturalitatem.*" *Angelicum* 47, no. 1 (1970): 44–62.

Muller, Richard. "Introduction." In *John Calvin and the Will: A Critique and Corrective*, by Dewey J. Hoitenga Jr. Grand Rapids, Mich.: Baker Book House, 1997.

———. "'Scimus Enim Quod Lex Spiritualis Est': Melanchthon and Calvin on the Interpretation of Romans 7:14–23." In *Philip Melanchthon (1497–1560) and the Commentary*, edited by Timothy J. Wengert and M. Patrick Graham, 216–37. Sheffield: Sheffield Academic Press, 1997.

Murdoch, Iris. *Reality and the Good.* London: Routledge, 1970.

Nicolas, Jean-Hervé. "La volonté salvifique de Dieu contrariée par le péché." *Revue Thomiste* 92, no. 2 (1992): 177–96.

Nichols, Aidan. *Discovering Aquinas: An Introduction to His Life, Work, and Influence.* Grand Rapids, Mich.: Eerdmans, 2002.

Novak, David. *Talking with Christians: Musings of a Jewish Theologian.* Grand Rapids, Mich.: Eerdmans, 2005.

Nygren, Anders. *Agape and Eros.* Philadelphia, Pa.: Westminster Press, 1953.

O'Connor, Donal. "St. Thomas's Commentary on Romans." *Irish Theological Quarterly* 34 (1967): 329–43.

Old, Hughes Oliphant. *The Reading and Preaching of the Scriptures in the Worship of the Christian Church: The Medieval Church.* Grand Rapids, Mich.: Eerdmans, 1999.

Oliva, Adriano. *Les débuts de l'enseignement de Thomas d'Aquin et sa conception de la sacra doctrina.* Paris: J. Vrin, 2006.

O'Meara, Thomas F. *Thomas Aquinas: Theologian.* Notre Dame, Ind.: University of Notre Dame Press, 1997.

Origen. *Commentarii in Epistulam ad Romanos/ Römerbriefkommentar.* 6 vols. Edited by Theresia Heither. Fontes Christiani 2 (1–6). Freiburg im Breisgau: Herder, 1990–96.

———. *Commentary on the Epistle to the Romans.* Translated by Thomas P. Scheck in *The Fathers of the Church*, vols. 103–4. Washington, D.C.: The Catholic University of America Press, 2001–2.

———. *Contra Celsum.* Patrologia Graeca, edited by J.-P. Migne, 11. Paris, [1857].

Packer, J. I. "The 'Wretched Man' Revisited: Another Look at Romans 7:14–25." In *Romans and the People of God*, edited by Sven K. Soderlund and N. T. Wright, 70–81. Grand Rapids, Mich.: Eerdmans, 2002.

Paluch, Michał. "'God Permits the Evil for the Good': Two Different Approaches to the History of Salvation in Aquinas and Bonaventure." *Angelicum* 80, no. 2 (2003): 327–36.

———. *La profondeur de l'amour divin: evolution de la doctrine de la prédestination dans l'oeuvre de saint Thomas d'Aquin.* Paris: J. Vrin, 2004.

Pérez Fernández, Isacio. "De Las Casas a Marx." *Studium* 17, no. 2 (1977): 345–64.

———. "El perfil profético del padre Las Casas." *Studium* 15, no. 2 (1975): 281–359.

———. "El protector de los indios y profeta de los españoles." *Studium* 14, no. 3 (1974): 543–65.

———. "La doctrina de Santo Tomás en la mente y en la acción del Padre Las Casas." *Studium* 27, no. 2 (1987): 269–95.

Pesch, Otto Hermann. *Thomas von Aquin. Grenze und Grösse mittelalterlicher Theologie.* Mainz: Matthias-Grünewald-Verlag, 1988.

Peter Lombard. *Collectanea.* Patrologia Latina, edited by J.-P. Migne, 191–92. Paris, 1854–55.

———. *Commentarium in Psalmos.* Patrologia Latina, edited by J.-P. Migne, 191. Paris, 1854.

———. *Magistri Petri Lombardi Sententiae in IV Libris Distinctae.* 3rd ed. 2 vols. Grottaferrata: Editiones Collegii S. Bonaventurae Ad Claras Aquas, 1971–81.

Pieper, Josef. *Four Cardinal Virtues.* Translated by Richard Winston et al. Notre Dame, Ind.: University of Notre Dame Press, 1966.

———. *Living the Truth: The Truth of All Things and Reality and the Good.* Translated by Lothar Krauth and Stella Lange. San Francisco: Ignatius Press, 1989.

———. "The Rights of Others." In *Problems of Modern Faith: Essays and Addresses.* Translated by Jan van Heurck, 203–18. Chicago: Franciscan Herald Press, 1985.

Pilsner, Joseph. *The Specification of Human Actions in St Thomas Aquinas.* Oxford: Oxford University Press, 2006.

Pinckaers, Servais. *The Sources of Christian Ethics.* Translated by Mary Thomas Noble. Washington, D.C.: The Catholic University of America Press, 1995.

Pitkin, Barbara. "Nothing but Concupiscence: Calvin's Understanding of Sin and the *Via Augustini.*" *Calvin Theological Journal* 34, no. 2 (1999): 347–69.

Plotinus. *Enneads.* Translated by A. H. Armstrong. Loeb Classical Library. Cambridge, Mass.: Harvard University Press, 1966.

Pontifical Biblical Commission. *The Jewish People and Their Sacred Scriptures in the Christian Bible.* Vatican Documents. Vatican City: Libreria Editrice Vaticano, 2002.

Potterie, Ignace de la. "Interpretation of Holy Scripture in the Spirit in Which It Was Written." In *Vatican II: Assessment and Perspectives I,* edited by René Latourelle, 220–66. New York: Paulist Press, 1988.

Principe, Walter. "Affectivity and the Heart in Thomas Aquinas's Spirituality." In *Spiritualities of the Heart,* edited by Annice Callahan, 45–63. New York: Paulist Press, 1990.

Raith, Charles, II. "Calvin's Critique of Merit, and Why Aquinas (Mostly) Agrees." *Pro Ecclesia* 20 (2011): 135–66.

Ramirez, Jacobus M. *Edicion de las Obras Completas de Santiago Ramirez, O.P.,* edited by Victorino Rodriguez. Vol. 4, *De actibus humanis: In I-II Summae theologiae Divi Thomae expositio (QQ. VI–XXI).* Madrid: Instituto de Filosofia «Luis Vives», 1972.

Reasoner, Mark. *Romans in Full Circle: A History of Interpretation.* Louisville, Ky.: Westminster/John Knox Press, 2005.

Rikhof, Herwi. "Thomas on the Church: Reflections on a Sermon." In *Aquinas on Doctrine: A Critical Introduction,* edited by Thomas G. Weinandy, Daniel A. Keating, and John P. Yocum, 199–223. London: T&T Clark, 2004.

Rist, John M. "Augustine, Aristotelianism and Aquinas: Three Varieties of Philosophical Adaption." In *Aquinas the Augustinian,* edited by Michael Dauphinais,

Barry David, and Matthew Levering. Washington, D.C.: The Catholic University of America Press, 2007.

Rivera, Luis N. *A Violent Evangelism: The Political and Religious Conquest of the Americas*. Louisville, Ky.: Westminster/John Knox Press, 1992.

Roberts, Alexander, and James Donaldson, eds. *Ante-Nicene Fathers*. Vol. 8. Peabody, Mass.: Hendrickson, 1999.

Rock, Augustine. *The Theological Concept of Preaching according to St. Thomas Aquinas*. Dubuque, Iowa: Wm. C. Brown, 1958.

Rogers, Eugene F. "The Narrative of Natural Law in Aquinas's Commentary on Romans 1." *Theological Studies* 59, no. 2 (1998) 254–76.

Root, Michael. "Aquinas, Merit, and Reformation Theology after the *Joint Declaration on the Doctrine of Justification*." *Modern Theology* 20, no. 1 (2004): 5–22.

Rousselot, Pierre. *The Intellectualism of Saint Thomas*. Translated by James E. O'Mahony. London: Sheed and Ward, 1935.

Ruiz Maldonado, Enrique. "Tomás de Aquino, Bartolomé de las Casas y la controversia en las indias." *Studium* 14, no. 3 (1974): 519–42.

Ryan, Thomas F. "The Love of Learning and the Desire for God in Thomas Aquinas's *Commentary on Romans*." In *Medieval Readings of Romans*, edited by William S. Campbell, Peter S. Hawkins, and Brenda Deen Schildgen, 101–14. New York: T&T Clark International, 2007.

Sabra, George. *Thomas Aquinas' Vision of the Church: Fundamentals of an Ecumenical Ecclesiology*. Tübinger theologische Studien 27. Mainz: Matthias-Grünewald, 1987.

Santos Hernández, Ángel. *Salvación y paganismo: el problema teológico de la salvación de los infieles*. Santander, Spain: Editorial Sal Terrae, 1960.

Scheck, Thomas P. *Origen and the History of Justification*. Notre Dame, Ind.: University of Notre Dame Press, 2008.

Schenk, Richard. *Die Gnade vollendeter Endlichkeit: Zur transzendentaltheologischer Auslegung der thomanischen Anthropologie*. Freiburger theologische Studien. Freiburg: Herder, 1989.

Schlatter, Adolf. *Gottes Gerechtigkeit: Ein Kommentar zum Römerbrief.* 5th ed. Stuttgart: Calwer Verlag, 1975.

Schliesser, Benjamin. *Abraham's Faith in Romans 4: Paul's Concept of Faith in Light of the History of Reception of Genesis 15:6*. Wissenschaftliche Untersuchungen zum Neuen Testament 2:224. Tübingen: Mohr Siebeck, 2007.

Schreiner, Thomas J. *Paul: Apostle of God's Glory in Christ: A Pauline Theology*. Downers Grove, Ill.: InterVarsity Press, 2001.

Sepúlveda, Juan Ginés de. *Obras Completas*. Vol. 3, *Democrates Secundus*, edited by A. Moreno Hernández, translated by Ángel Losada. Salamanca, Spain: Exmo. Ayuntamiento de Pozoblanco, 1997.

Sherwin, Michael. *By Knowledge and by Love: Charity and Knowledge in the Moral Theology of St. Thomas Aquinas*. Washington, D.C.: The Catholic University of America Press, 2005.

Smalley, Beryl. *The Study of the Bible in the Middle Ages*. Notre Dame, Ind.: University of Notre Dame Press, 1965.

Steinmetz, David. *Calvin in Context*. Oxford: Oxford University Press, 1995.

———. "The Scholastic Calvin." In *Protestant Scholasticism: Essays in Reassessment*, edited by Carl R. Trueman and R. Scott Clark, 16–30. Carlisle, UK: Paternoster Press, 1999.

Stendahl, Krister. "The Apostle Paul and the Introspective Conscience of the West." In *Paul among Jews and Gentiles*, 80–92. Philadelphia: Fortress Press, 1976.

Stiltner, Brian. "Who Can Understand Abraham? The Relation of God and Morality in Kierkegaard and Aquinas." *Journal of Religious Ethics* 21, no. 2 (1993): 221–45.

Stowers, Stanley. "What Is 'Pauline Participation in Christ'?" In *Redefining First-Century Jewish and Christian Identities: Essays in Honor of Ed Parish Sanders*, edited by Fabian E. Udoh et al., 352–71. South Bend, Ind.: University of Notre Dame Press, 2008.

Stump, Eleonore. *Aquinas*. London: Routledge, 2005.

———. "The God of Abraham, Saadia and Aquinas." In *Referring to God: Jewish and Christian Philosophical and Theological Perspectives*, edited by Paul Helm, 95–119. New York: St Martin's Press, 2000.

Tábet, Miguel Ángel. "Il senso litterale e il senso spirituale della Sacra Scrittura: Un tentative di chiarimento terminologico e concettuale." *Annales theologici* 9, no. 1 (1995): 3–5.

Thomas Aquinas. *Commentaires de saint Thomas d'Aquin sur tout les épitres de S. Paul*. Translated by Abbé Bralé. 6 vols. Paris: Vivès, 1869–74.

———. *Commentary on Aristotle's Nicomachean Ethics*. Translated by C. I. Litzinger. Aristotelian Commentary Series. Notre Dame, Ind.: Dumb Ox Books, 1993.

———. *Commentum in Quator Libros Sententiarum Magistri Petri Lombardi*. 2 vols. Parma: Petri Fiaccadori, 1856–58.

———. *In Epistolam ad Romanos*. In *Opera Omnia*, vol. 20, edited by S. E. Fretté. Paris, 1876.

———. *In Psalmos Davidis expositio*. In *Opera Omnia*, vol. 14. Parma: Petri Facciadori, 1863.

———. *In Symbolum Apostolorum*. In *Corpus Thomisticum*, edited by E. Alarcón. Pamplona: Universidad de Navarra, 2000–. http://www.corpusthomisticum.org/csv.html.

———. *Lectura Romana in Primum Sententiarum Petri Lombardi*. Edited by Leonard Boyle and John Boyle. Toronto, Ont.: Pontifical Institute of Medieval Studies, 2006.

———. *Lectures on the Letter to the Romans*. Translated by Fabian Larcher. Edited by Jeremy Holmes. Ave Maria, Fla.: Aquinas Center for Theological Renewal. http://www.avemaria.edu/uploads/pagesfiles/4283.pdf.

———. *On the Power of God (Quaestiones Disputatae de Potentia Dei)*. Translated by the English Dominican Fathers. London: Burns, Oates and Washbourne, 1932; reprint, Westminster, Md.: Newman Press, 1952.

———. *Quaestiones de Quolibet*. Opera Omnia 25 A–B. Rome: Commissio Leonina, 1996.

———. *Quaestiones Disputatae de Malo*. Opera Omnia 23. Rome: Commissio Leonina, 1982.

———. *Quaestiones Disputatae de Potentia Dei*. In *Corpus Thomisticum*, edited by E. Alarcón. Pamplona: Universidad de Navarra, 2000–. http://www.corpusthomisticum.org/qdp4.html.

———. *Quaestiones Disputatae de Veritate*. Opera Omnia 22 A–C. Rome: Editori di San Tommaso, 1972–76.

———. *Scriptum super Libros Sententiarum*. Edited by Mandonnet. 2 vols. Paris: Sumptibus P. Lethielleux, 1929.

———. *Scriptum super Sententiis*. Edited by M. F. Moos and P. Mandonnet. 2 vols. Paris: Sumptibus P. Lethielleux, 1929–47.

———. *Summa contra Gentiles*. Opera Omnia 13–15. Rome: Riccardi Garroni, 1918–30.

———. *Summa theologiae*. 4 vols. Ottawa: Commissio Piana, 1953.

———. *Summa theologiae*. Translated by the Fathers of the English Dominican Province. New York: Benziger Bros., 1947; reprint, Christian Classics, 1981.

———. *Summa theologiae*. Vol. 60, *Penance*, translated and edited by Reginald Masterson and T. C. O'Brien. New York: McGraw-Hill, 1966.

———. *Super II Epistolam ad Corinthios lectura*. In *Super Epistolas Sancti Pauli lectura*, vol. 1, edited by Raphaelis Cai. 8th ed. Rome: Marietti, 1953.

———. *Super Decretalem*. Opera Omnia 40E. Rome: Editori di San Tommaso, 1969.

———. *Super Epistolam ad Colossenses lectura*. In *Super Epistolas Sancti Pauli lectura*, vol. 2, edited by Raphaelis Cai. 8th ed. Rome: Marietti, 1953.

———. *Super Epistolam ad Galatas lectura*. In *Super Epistolas Sancti Pauli lectura*, vol. 1, edited by Raphaelis Cai. 8th ed. Rome: Marietti, 1953.

———. *Super Epistolam ad Hebraeos lectura*. In *Super Epistolas Sancti Pauli lectura*, vol. 2, edited by Raphaelis Cai. 8th ed. Rome: Marietti, 1953.

———. *Super Epistolam ad Romanos lectura*. In *Super Epistolas Sancti Pauli lectura*, vol. 1, edited by Raphaelis Cai. 8th ed. Rome: Marietti, 1953.

———. *Super Epistolam ad Titum lectura*. In *Super Epistolas Sancti Pauli lectura*, vol. 2, edited by Raphaelis Cai. 8th ed. Rome: Marietti, 1953.

———. *Super Epistolam B. Pauli ad Romanos lectura*. In *Corpus Thomisticum*, edited by E. Alarcón. Pamplona: Universidad de Navarra, 2000–. http://www.corpusthomisticum.org/cro00.html.

———. *Super Evangelium S. Ioannis lectura*. Edited by Raphaelis Cai. 5th ed. Rome: Marietti, 1952.

———. *Thomas d'Aquin: Commentaire de l'Épître aux Romains*. Edited and translated by Jean-Éric Stroobant de Saint-Éloi. Paris: Cerf, 1999.

———. *The Treatise on the Divine Nature: Summa Theologiae I, 1–13*. Translated, with commentary, by Brian J. Shanley. Indianapolis, Ind.: Hackett Publishing Group, 2006.

Torrell, Jean-Pierre. "'Dieu conduit toutes choses vers leur fin.' Providence et gouvernement divin chez Thomas d'Aquin." In *Ende und Vollendung. Eschatologische Perspektiven im Mittelalter*, edited by J. A. Aertsen and M. Pickavé, 561–94. Berlin: Walter de Gruyter, 2002.

———. "Nature and Grace in Thomas Aquinas." In *Surnaturel: A Controversy at the Heart of Twentieth-Century Thomistic Thought*, edited by Serge-Thomas Bonino, translated by Robert Williams, 155–88. Ave Maria, Fla.: Sapientia Press, 2009.

———. "Note" on *Summa Theologiae* III, q. 56, a. 1. In *Encyclopédie Jésus le Christ chez saint Thomas d'Aquin*, 1224–26. Paris: Cerf, 2008.

———. *Saint Thomas Aquinas*. Vol. 1, *The Person and His Work*, translated by Robert

Royal. Washington, D.C.: The Catholic University of America Press, 1996; rev. ed., 2005.

———. *Saint Thomas Aquinas*. Vol. 2, *Spiritual Master*, translated by Robert Royal. Washington, D.C.: The Catholic University Press of America, 2003.

———. "Saint Thomas et les non-chrétiens." *Revue Thomiste* 106, no. 1 (2006): 17–49.

———. "Yves Congar et l'ecclésiologie de Saint Thomas d'Aquin." *Revue des sciences philosophiques et théologiques* 82, no. 2 (1998): 201–42.

Valkenberg, Wilhelmus. *Words of the Living God: Place and Function of Holy Scripture in the Theology of St. Thomas Aquinas*. Leuven, Belgium: Peeters, 2000.

VanLandingham, Chris. *Judgment and Justification in Early Judaism and the Apostle Paul*. Peabody, Mass.: Hendrickson, 2006.

Vliet, Cornelis Th. M. Van. *Communio sacramentalis: Das Kirchenverständis von Yves Congar – genetisch und systematisch betrachtet*. Mainz: Matthias-Grünewald, 1995.

Vos, Arvin. *Aquinas, Calvin, and Contemporary Protestant Thought: A Critique of Protestant Views on the Thought of Thomas Aquinas*. Washington, D.C.: Christian University Press, 1985.

Wadell, Paul J. *The Primacy of Love: An Introduction to the Ethics of Thomas Aquinas*. New York: Paulist Press, 1992.

Wainwright, Geoffrey. *Doxology: The Praise of God in Worship, Doctrine and Life: A Systematic Theology*. New York: Oxford University Press, 1980.

———. *Eucharist and Eschatology*. New York: Oxford University Press, 1981.

Waldstein, Michael. "On Scripture in the Summa Theologiae." *Aquinas Review* 1, no. 1 (1994): 73–94.

Watson, Francis. *Paul, Judaism and the Gentiles*. Society for New Testament Studies Monograph Series 56. Cambridge: Cambridge University Press, 1986.

———. *Paul, Judaism, and the Gentiles: Beyond the New Perspective*. Rev. ed. Grand Rapids, Mich.: Eerdmans, 2007.

Watson, Nigel M. "Authorial Intention: Suspect Concept for Biblical Scholarship." *Australian Biblical Review* 35 (1987): 6–13.

Wawrykow, Joseph P. "Church." In *The Westminster Handbook to Thomas Aquinas*, 25–28. Louisville, Ky.: Westminster/John Knox Press, 2005.

———. *God's Grace and Human Action: "Merit" in the Theology of Thomas Aquinas*. Notre Dame, Ind.: University of Notre Dame Press, 1995.

Weinandy, Thomas G., Daniel A. Keating, and John P. Yocum, eds. *Aquinas on Scripture: An Introduction to His Biblical Commentaries*. London: T&T Clark International, 2005.

White, Victor. "Thomism and Affective Knowledge." *New Blackfriars* 25, no. 294 (1944): 321–28.

Wielockx, Robert. "Au sujet du commentaire de saint Thomas sur le 'Corpus paulinum'. Critique littéraire." *Doctor Communis*, n.s., 13, no. 1–2 (2009): 150–84.

Wilken, Robert L. "How to Read the Bible." *First Things* 181 (2008): 24–27.

Willimon, William H., and Richard Lischer, eds. *Concise Encyclopedia of Preaching*. Louisville, Ky.: Westminster/John Knox Press, 1995.

Witherington, Ben, III. *Paul's Letter to the Romans: A Socio-Rhetorical Commentary*. Grand Rapids, Mich.: Eerdmans, 2004.

Wood, Susan K. *Spiritual Exegesis and the Church in the Theology of Henri de Lubac.* Grand Rapids, Mich.: Eerdmans, 1998.

Wright, Tom (N. T.). *Justification: God's Plan and Paul's Vision.* London: SPCK, 2009.

———. *The Last Word: Beyond the Bible Wars to a New Understanding of the Authority of Scripture.* San Francisco: HarperSanFrancisco, 2005.

———. *The Letter to the Romans: Introduction, Commentary, and Reflections.* In *The New Interpreter's Bible,* vol. 10. Edited by Leander E. Keck. Nashville, Tenn.: Abingdon Press, 2002.

———. *What Saint Paul Really Said: Was Paul of Tarsus the Real Founder of Christianity?* Grand Rapids, Mich.: Eerdmans, 1997.

Wyschogrod, Michael. "A Jewish Reading of St. Thomas Aquinas on the Old Law." In *Understanding the Scriptures,* edited by Clemens Thoma and Michael Wyschogrod, 125–40. Mahwah, N.J.: Paulist Press, 1987.

Yearley, Lee H. "St. Thomas Aquinas on Providence and Predestination." *Anglican Theological Review* 49, no. 4 (1967): 409–23.

Contributors

Bernhard Blankenhorn, O.P., is a Dominican friar and Catholic priest. He is completing his doctoral thesis on Dionysian mysticism in Albertus Magnus and Thomas Aquinas at the University of Fribourg. He has published articles in *Angelicum,* the *Freiburger Zeitschrift für Philosophie und Theologie,* and *Nova et Vetera.*

Markus Bockmuehl is a fellow of Keble College and professor of biblical and early Christian studies in the University of Oxford. Among his books are *The Epistle to the Philippians; Jewish Law in Gentile Churches;* and *Seeing the Word: Refocusing New Testament Study.* He has recently edited volumes on Messianism (*Redemption and Resistance,* with J. Carleton Paget); on the New Testament and Christian dogmatics (*Scripture's Doctrine and Theology's Bible,* with A. J. Torrance); and on Jewish and Christian eschatology (*Paradise in Antiquity,* with Guy G. Stroumsa).

Hans Boersma holds the J. I. Packer Chair in Theology at Regent College, Vancouver. His books include *Violence, Hospitality and the Cross: Reappropriating the Atonement Tradition; Nouvelle Théologie and Sacramental Ontology: A Return to Mystery;* and *Heavenly Participation: The Weaving of a Sacramental Tapestry.* Together with Matthew Levering, Boersma is co-director of the Center for Catholic-Evangelical Dialogue (CCED). He preaches regularly in his local church, the Immanuel Christian Reformed Church of Langley, British Columbia.

John F. Boyle is professor of theology and Catholic studies at the University of St. Thomas in Minnesota. He has published a number of essays on St. Thomas on Scripture. With Leonard E. Boyle, O.P., he edited the critical edition of St. Thomas's *Lectura romana in primum Sententiarum Petri Lombardi.*

Edgardo Antonio Colón-Emeric is assistant professor of theology and faculty advisor for the Hispanic House of Studies at Duke Divinity School. His research interests include ecumenism and questions emerging from the encounter between Christian theology and Latino culture. Colón-Emeric is the author of *Wesley, Aquinas and Christian Perfection: An Ecumenical Dialogue.*

Holly Taylor Coolman is an assistant professor of theology at Providence College. She completed doctoral work at Duke University in 2006, where her dissertation drew on Aquinas and Calvin to argue for a thoroughly Christological account of the Mosaic Law, and her recent research has continued to explore the Law, the thought of Aquinas, and Christian theologies of the Jewish people.

Adam Cooper is a lecturer in theology at the John Paul II Institute for Marriage and Family in Melbourne, Australia. He holds a PhD from the University of Durham and an STL from the Lateran University. His teaching and research interests lie primarily in patristic theology and the theology of the body. His publications include two books, *The Body in Saint Maximus the Confessor: Holy Flesh, Wholly Deified* and *Life in the Flesh: An Anti-Gnostic Spiritual Philosophy*.

Michael Dauphinais is academic dean and associate professor of theology at Ave Maria University. He is the author with Matthew Levering of *Holy People, Holy Land: A Theological Introduction to the Bible* and *Knowing the Love of Christ: An Introduction to the Theology of St. Thomas Aquinas*. Among his edited books are *Aquinas the Augustinian* (with Barry David and Matthew Levering) and *Reading John with St. Thomas Aquinas* (with Matthew Levering).

Gilles Emery, O.P., is professor of dogmatic theology at the University of Fribourg. He is a member of the International Theological Commission of the Catholic Church. He specializes in Trinitarian theology and in the thought of St. Thomas Aquinas. His most recent book is *The Trinity: An Introduction to Catholic Doctrine on the Triune God*.

Scott W. Hahn holds the Pope Benedict Chair of Biblical Theology at St. Vincent Seminary and is professor of theology and Scripture at Franciscan University of Steubenville. Founder of the St. Paul Center for Biblical Theology, he is the author of over twenty books, including *Kinship by Covenant, Covenant and Communion,* and *The Kingdom of God as Liturgical Empire: A Theological Commentary on 1-2 Chronicles*. Hahn is the editor of *Letter & Spirit: A Journal of Catholic Biblical Theology*.

John A. Kincaid is a graduate of Covenant Theological Seminary and Duke Divinity School, and is currently a doctoral candidate in theology at Ave Maria University, where he is working on the theology of justification in St. Thomas Aquinas in light of the New Perspective on Paul.

Mary Healy teaches Scripture at Sacred Heart Major Seminary in Detroit. She is co-editor of the Catholic Commentary on Sacred Scripture (Baker Academic) and the author of its first volume, *The Gospel of Mark*.

Matthew Levering is professor of theology at the University of Dayton. With Reinhard Hütter, he is co-editor of the quarterly journal *Nova et Vetera*. He is the author most recently of *The Betrayal of Charity: The Sins That Sabotage Divine Love* and *Predestination: Biblical and Theological Paths*. He has recently edited *Ressourcement Thomism* (with Reinhard Hütter) and *The Oxford Handbook of the Trinity* (with Gilles Emery, O.P.).

Bruce Marshall is Lehman Professor of Christian Doctrine in the Perkins School of Theology at Southern Methodist University. He is the author of *Trinity and Truth* and *Christology in Conflict*, and is presently at work on a book on the Trinity, faith, and reason in Aquinas and contemporary Catholic theology. He is a past president of the Academy of Catholic Theology.

Charles Raith II is a lecturer in the Honors College of Baylor University. His articles have appeared in *International Journal of Systematic Theology, Journal of Theological Interpretation*, and *Pro Ecclesia*. His dissertation, "Aquinas and Calvin on Romans: Theological Exegesis and Ecumenical Theology," is an extensive comparative analysis of Aquinas's and Calvin's commentaries on Romans.

Geoffrey Wainwright is the Cushman Professor of Christian Theology at the Divinity School of Duke University. He writes widely in matters of systematic and liturgical theology. For twenty-five years he chaired on the Methodist side the Joint Commission for Dialogue between the World Methodist Council and the Roman Catholic Church.

Michael Waldstein is Max Seckler Professor of Theology at Ave Maria University. He has also taught at the University of Notre Dame, and he served as the founding president of the International Theological Institute in Gaming, Austria. He has recently published a new translation of John Paul II's *Man and Woman He Created Them: A Theology of the Body*.

Robert Louis Wilken is the William R. Kenan, Jr., Professor of the History of Christianity Emeritus at the University of Virginia. His most recent book is *The Spirit of Early Christian Thought: Seeking the Face of God*.

Index

Abraham, xiii, xvii, 2, 40–51, 71, 166–67,
169–70, 204, 217, 219–21, 231, 237, 289;
binding of Isaac, 40; circumcision of, xiii,
42, 46–47, 50, 189; faith of, 39, 45–46,
217, 237; father of justified, 45; hope of,
49; uncircumcised, 42
Acts of the Apostles, ix, 2, 90, 138, 149, 159,
279, 280
Adam, 21n63, 80, 137, 178n30, 223, 289; and
Eve, 8, 30
adoption (adoptive filiation/sonship),
xv, xvii, 65–68, 71, 77–78, 104, 129–31,
144–47, 155, 172n15, 182, 196, 203, 207,
209–10, 255n59, 265, 271, 285, 287; filial
adoption of Israel, 65; moral dimension
of, 145; ontological dimension of, 145;
predestined to, 68, 202–4, 209
affections, xvii, 126, 155, 202, 243, 248, 250,
258, 290, 291, 297; of lovers, 62
Against Julian (Augustine), 15, 251n40
Alexander of Hales, 13, 28, 88, 91, 186n8
apostles, xv, xvii, 65n47, 86–87, 96, 110,
137–38, 140, 205–7, 258, 260, 280
appetite, xviii, 120–21, 251n41; carnal,
255–56; concupiscible, 14, 75, 149n97, 241;
irascible, 75–76; sensitive, 16–20, 22, 25,
28n75, 29, 34–35, 76, 240, 244–45, 249;
unnatural, 29; well-disposed, 121
Aqedah, 166–67
Aristotle, 29, 38, 114, 120, 122, 168, 201, 255
Arius, 133
Augustine, St., xii, xix, 1, 22, 29, 35, 45, 75,
83, 97, 104n9, 110, 120–22, 130n10, 133,
134, 135n31, 136n35, 153n117, 160, 164–65,
169, 170n13, 185n3, 186n11, 199, 217n1,
239nn4–5, 242n17, 246n26, 256n53,
263n3, 269n7, 270, 275, 285, 291, 293,
296, 301; anthropology of, 6, 10–11, 28,
32, 37–38; on concupiscence, 6–9, 13, 17,
250n39, 251nn40–41, 253; dualism of,
6–10; early period, 5–6, 9, 15–16, 18, 295;

on the fall, 7; on grace, 5–7, 9, 11, 17–18,
30n78, 294, 298–300; late period, 7–9,
15, 17–18, 20, 25, 31; Manichees, 6, 9–10,
38; middle period, 6; misinterpretation of
Paul, 37; and Pelagianism, 6–8, 10–11, 297;
on Rom 7:14–25, xvii–xviii, 7; on the will,
7, 10, 18, 30, 36
Averroes, 51

baptism, xiii, 7, 9n27, 11–12, 48, 60, 66–67,
71–73, 93–94, 96, 98–99, 143, 178n30,
189, 250n39, 265n4, 280; as healing, 24; as
slavery to God, 3
Barth, Karl, 47n25, 52–53, 277
Berengar of Tours, 57
Bockmuehl, Markus, xii–xiii, 41n6
body, xvii, 2, 6–9, 11–14, 16, 21–22, 24–25,
27, 125–26, 142–45, 204, 207, 215, 242n18,
270, 281, 293–94; degradation of, 115,
122–23; Paul's, x; as symbol, 12
Boersma, Hans, xi n15, xiii, 53n5, 55n9
Boguslawski, Steven, xi n13, xiv, 44, 104–5,
128n4, 196n1, 198n12, 300n37
Bouillard, Henri, 89
Boyle, John F., xii, xiv, 76n3, 164n3, 165–66,
276n7, 295n14

Cajetan, Thomas de Vio, 85, 94n43
Calvin, John, xvii–xviii, 5, 42, 238–39, 240n7,
242–53, 255–61
Catharism, 21
Cerfaux, Lucien, 64
Chenu, Marie-Dominique, 63
Christ, Jesus: actions of, 139; and apostles,
138; conformity to, 142–45, 255; Cross of,
11, 203–4, 233n43, 236; "head," xv, 58, 60,
69–71, 131–32, 140–41, 198, 202; as Heir,
145; hermeneutical key, 50; humanity
of, 130, 137, 139–40, 161; incarnation/
hypostatic union of, 130; incorporation
into, 70, 72; indwelling, 125, 143, 150,

188–89, 195, 198, 202, 203, 206, 210, 212,
214–21, 231, 236–37, 247–49, 253–59, 261,
264, 267, 271–72, 274–80, 284, 289–91,
296–300; act of, 44, 94; caused by God,
97; in Christ, xiii–xvi, 48, 50, 110, 125,
160, 167, 218, 257, 264, 282, 299; explicit,
88–89; "formed by love," xvii, 281–83;
hermeneutic of, xvi, 194; implicit, xiii,
259n70; justifying, 42, 46, 283; sign of, xii,
47n23; theological virtue, 44, 80
Father, 134–36, 142–47, 157–62, 213; "first
principle," 135
fault (*culpa*), xvii, 72n89, 79–80, 220–26,
229n35, 230n38, 232n40, 233n42
flesh, ix, xii–xiii, 2–4, 6–27, 29–37, 75, 104,
126, 137–38, 142–43, 200–203, 211, 239;
weakness of, 201, 207, 247
flesh/spirit, xii, 2–4, 15, 20, 22–23, 25,
27–32, 36–38; in Augustine, 1, 5, 6, 8–11;
Manichees on, 6
fomes peccati, 12–13, 240, 244
forgiveness, xii, xvii–xviii, 45, 63, 79, 90, 125,
216–17, 225, 229, 235
Fredriksen, Paula, 6

Giussani, Luigi, 114
God: as divine author, xvi, 177–79, 188; as
interior teacher, 23; mercy of, 264, 269,
271, 274, 293; union with man, xvii, 68,
117, 130–31, 212, 219–20, 226, 234
Grace, xii, xviii, 1, 5–6, 9, 11, 16–17, 19–25,
28–31, 34, 37, 40, 43–44, 48–50, 62–63,
69, 75, 79–80, 82, 92, 96–99, 123, 126, 128,
131, 137, 141–46, 148–49, 154, 162, 179, 188,
196–97, 200, 202, 205, 212–15, 217, 231,
235–36, 239, 242–47, 249, 254, 256–58,
260, 264–66, 269, 271, 278–82, 285, 287,
290–91, 295, 298–300; and baptism, 7; of
Christ, 20, 60–61, 68, 72–73, 77–78, 81,
132–33, 138, 140, 155–56, 241, 248, 253, 297;
created, 36, 227n29; evangelical, x, 77–78,
81, 132–33; God's, xix, 86, 90–91, 203, 206,
218, 255; of the Holy Spirit, xiii, xiv–xvii,
125, 138, 152–53, 198, 201, 206–7, 209–11,
270, 286; justifying, 79, 241–42; necessity
of, 91; operative, 18, 125; sanctifying, 35,
68, 125, 130, 140, 229–30, 233
Gregory the Great, St., 157

Hahn, Scott W., xvi, 172n15, 178n29, 180n33
Hays, Richard, 167, 180

history, xi; four states of, 6; salvation, 6, 188,
191
Holy Spirit: Bond of Love, 134; and Christ,
136–44; in the Church, 141, 160; and
economy, 127, 133, 139, 160; as Gift, xv, 135,
139, 150–51, 154, 161; gift of fear, 146; gifts
of, 129, 136, 144, 146–47, 181; guidance of,
147; as healer of the whole person, xii, 24;
human desire and, 156–59; indwelling,
xviii, 23, 125, 143, 150, 154, 202–3, 218, 265;
inspiration of Scriptures, 129, 165;
"instinct of," 147–48, 151; intercession of,
xvii–xviii, 158, 192, 207–8, 267; "law of,"
153–56; and liberty, 129, 136, 208; as life,
140; Love, 134, 136, 150–51, 153, 161, 286,
301; and merit, 152; natural spirit as
analogous to, 141; and the New Law, 109,
129, 155; person of, 133, 151, 161; and prayer,
156–58; preacher as instrument of, 87;
procession of, xv, 134–35, 287; prophecy,
158–59; relation to Son, 142; sent by
Christ, 159n140; spiration, 135, 142; and
theological virtues, xv, 44, 50, 80, 96, 129,
149–54, 214, 249; visible mission of, 138,
140
Hood, John, xiv, 103–5

the "I," xvii, 11, 15–16, 240; knowledge
of good, 4; knowledge of the law, 4;
personified sin of, 4; as reason, 246
idolatry, xvii, 8, 16, 26–27, 191–92, 273n12; as
abandonment of wisdom, 116
ignorance, 115–16, 263; involuntary, 120; as
result of sin, 120
imputation, 126, 216–21, 223–25, 275
intellect, xiv–xv, 19, 20, 24, 27, 35–36, 86–87,
92–95, 97–99, 103, 113–14, 117, 119–27, 135,
154, 159, 168, 240, 242–43, 250, 256, 258
Isidore of Seville, 122

James of Viterbo, 59
Jews, xii–xv, 41–47, 49–50, 66–67, 73, 81–82,
101–12, 132, 138, 155, 166, 172, 188, 194, 215,
265, 268, 271, 291–92, 296, 298; attitudes
against, xiv, 39, 101, 103; relationship with
Gentiles, 3–4, 40, 51, 60, 65, 300
John, Gospel of, 2, 41, 138, 263, 279, 281–82,
284, 286
justice, xvii, 14, 44, 50, 67, 72, 77–79, 82, 133,
146n86, 149n97, 159, 167, 170–71, 199, 203,
216–21, 225–26, 228, 231, 237, 249–50,

usticejustice

passions, xv, xviii, 3, 6–7, 9, 11, 18, 25, 29–31, 120, 139, 190–91, 201, 242

Paul, St.: on "body of Christ," 58, 69, 142, 206, 215; dualist cosmology of, 5, 6, 11, 34, 37; metaphysical/moral dualism, 4, 7, 9–10, 16, 31, 36; moral exhortation of, 3–5, 11, 25, 31, 35, 78; "new perspective" on, xvi, 43, 171, 276–77; "realism" of, 4, 24; "works of the law," 42–43, 219, 296, 298–99

perfection, ix–x, xviii, 9, 77–79, 194, 199, 204, 222, 248–49, 253–58, 261, 269, 271–72, 281, 284, 286, 294

Pieper, Joseph, 113, 123

Pinckaers, Servais, 19

pistis Christou debate, xvii, 166–67, 176–77, 182

Plato, 13, 22; dualism of, 21

Plotinus, 114

pneuma, 2–4, 23–24, 32, 35

preacher, xiv, 62–63, 83–84, 86– 91, 94–100, 188, 190; canonical mission, 87; commissioned, 87; "the good life of," 88

preaching, xiii, xiv, 61–63, 70, 73, 83–100, 136, 138, 187, 190, 212, 272; delayed, 90; exterior word, 86–87, 216; faith and, 95

predestination, ix, xiv, xvi–xvii, 60, 71, 80, 91, 99, 260; of Christ, xvi, 68–69, 212; divine goodness, 198–99, 211; foreknowledge and, 209–11; glorification and, 196, 204–5, 211–12; God's will in, 198–99, 208; image of God and, 203–4, 211; merit and, 199, 205, 210; Paul on, 196–215; and providence, 197; in Rom 8:1–39, 200–214; suffering and, 196, 202–5, 207–8, 214; in *Summa theologiae,* 196–200; temporal missions of Son and Spirit, 196, 213–14

prudence, xv, 6, 122–25, 148–49; chastity and, 123–24; Rousselot and, 123; virtue of, 122

Psalms of Solomon, 41

Raith, Charles, xvii–xviii, 257n65

reason, 9, 13, 20–22, 107, 117–24, 126, 136, 185, 201, 240–46, 249–50, 254–56, 260, 263; carnal, 16–17, 23; natural, 96, 115, 118, 135, 283, 297; operation of, 19; practical, 34, 106

reckoning, 218–19, 221, 223, 231, 277

resurrection, 24, 47, 105, 139, 143, 156, 161, 203–4, 228, 244, 254, 261, 266; of the flesh, 9, 139, 204, 228

righteousness, xvi, 42–46, 49–50, 126, 170–72, 173–75, 178–80, 203, 209, 216–21, 238, 248, 274–78, 298; by faith, 40, 277

Saadya, 51

Sabra, George, 60n27, 63–65

salvation, xvii, 6–7, 44, 47, 53, 61–62, 64, 71, 81, 91, 93–96, 98–99, 102, 104–6, 111, 132–33, 138–39, 141, 160–61, 173, 190, 193, 197–98, 206, 208–10, 215–16, 218, 226, 268, 272, 279, 292, 296

Sarx, 2, 5, 9–11, 21, 24, 33, 35; destroyed by Christ's *pneuma,* 4; sphere of sin, 3–4

Schlatter, Adolf, 46

Scripture: profundity of, xvi, 129; spiritual sense, 183, 187–91; literal sense, xvi, 186–88, 191–93

Second Vatican Council, 53; *Lumen Gentium,* 54, 64–65

Sin: dominion of, 12, 14, 70; forgiveness of, xiii, 45, 90, 125; God's covering of, 231–36, 277; mortal, xiv, xviii, 15, 17–19, 22, 27, 34, 45, 102, 109, 204, 235, 249, 252–53, 256; non-imputation, xvii, 221, 225–36; as opposed to God, 3; personified, 3–4; power of, 12; slavery to, xiii, 3, 80, 82; "sparks of," 12, 15, 17, 19, 22–24, 27–28, 34–35; stain of, 232–33, 236; as uncleanness, 14; venial, xviii, 45, 249–50, 252, 255–56, 261; voluntary nature of, 9; wounds of, 8–9, 30

Socrates, 113, 116, 234

soul, xvii–xviii, 2, 6–9, 12–14, 16–17, 19–22, 27, 30, 37, 47, 63, 79–80, 91, 114, 116, 123, 125, 137, 141–42, 144–45, 148–51, 153–55, 185, 190, 194–95, 212, 223, 232–33, 242–43, 247, 252, 254, 260, 270, 278–79, 281, 290, 292–94, 301; disordered, 8

spirit, xii, 2–9, 14–15, 17, 20–21, 23–26, 35–37, 70–71, 122–23, 140–42, 153, 158, 181, 201–3, 239–44, 258, 261, 270–71, 286, 293, 295; lust of, 7

Stendahl, Krister, 4, 11

stoicism, 8, 124, 292

Stowers, Stanley, 2

Stump, Eleonore, 119, 122

supercessionism, 39

theological (ecclesial) exegesis, xv, xvi, xix, 1, 5, 9–10, 14–16, 22, 24–26, 31–32, 37–38, 43, 45–46, 50, 51, 115, 117, 128–29, 131,